MODERN
REAL ESTATE
DOCUMENTATION

Robert Kratovil J.D.

Member American Bar Association,
Illinois State Bar Association, and
Chicago Bar Association

Prentice-Hall, Inc.

Englewood Cliffs, New Jersey

Prentice-Hall International, Inc., *London*
Prentice-Hall of Australia, Pty., Ltd., *Sydney*
Prentice-Hall of Canada, Ltd., *Toronto*
Prentice-Hall of India Private Ltd., *New Delhi*
Prentice-Hall of Japan, Inc., *Tokyo*

© 1975 *by*

Prentice-Hall, Inc.

Englewood Cliffs, New Jersey

Third Printing. . . . .March, 1978

"This publication is designed to provide accurate and authoritative information in regard to the subject matter covered. It is sold with the understanding that the publisher is not engaged in rendering legal, accounting, or other professional service. If legal advice or other expert assistance is required, the services of a competent professional person should be sought."

—From the Declaration of Principles jointly adopted by a Committee of the American Bar Association and a Committee of Publishers and Associations.

Library of Congress Cataloging in Publication Data
Kratovil, Robert,
    Modern real estate documentation.

    Includes bibliographical references.
    1. Real property--United States. I. Title.
KF570.K695   346'.73'043   74-26628
ISBN 0-13-597302-3

Printed in the United States of America

To Ruth and Tony

Other Books by Robert Kratovil

Real Estate Law

Modern Mortgage Law and Practice

A Word from the Author

In the forty-plus years since I was admitted to the practice of law, all of them spent in the area of real property law, mountains of legal documents have moved across my desk. It has been my rare privilege to work on complex problems with the finest property lawyers in the country, and my debt to them is enormous. As real estate deals have grown more complex, the inevitable differences in philosophy have made their appearance, and a variety of documentation has proliferated. A real property lawyer, like myself, is often in the enviable position of sitting constantly before a smorgasbord of superb legal delicacies, and contributing enthusiastically to the menu. In accordance with the traditions of the legal profession, learning and experience have been shared. No other professional group makes a greater effort to share expertise than the real property bar. I am proud indeed to be numbered among the members of this elite group. I cannot begin to acknowledge my debt to the countless lawyers with whom I have worked and learned. All I can say is that it has been an immensely rewarding experience.

My experience on the Advisory Committee of the Uniform Land Transactions Code Committee encourages me in the belief that in the years to come a Code, introducing a measure of uniformity in land transactions, will make its appearance in the legislatures. That time seems to me to be some years away. Meanwhile, the local and often antiquated rules of real property law peer over our shoulders as we draft, and the need to innovate in the absence of court decisions complicates our task.

To pull together all this learning and this complex and varied law as it applies to a multitude of diverse transactions, is a task of monumental proportions. Nevertheless, I have undertaken it here, knowing full well that among my brethren there will be those who prefer their draftsmanship to mine. I would be the last to quarrel with them.

I cannot conclude without acknowledging the help of my old and valued friend, Abert Marks, of the Chicago Bar. My wife's help in collating, proofreading, and offering encouragement was, as always, beyond price. My son, Tony, also helped in organizing the mountains of papers out of which I culled the contents of this text.

Robert Kratovil

Table of Texts Referred to

Arnold, *Modern Real Estate and Mortgage Forms*
Arnold and Smith, *Real Estate and Mortgage Forms*
Basye, *Clearing Land Titles* (2d ed. 1970) (herein *Basye*)
Friedman, *Leases* (1974)
Gordon's, *Modern Annotated Forms of Agreement* (herein *Gordon's Modern Forms*)
Kratovil, *Modern Mortgage Law and Practice* (herein *Kratovil, Mortgages*)
Kratovil, *Real Estate Law* (6th ed. 1974) (herein *Kratovil, Real Estate Law*)
McMichael, *Leases, Percentage, Short and Long Term* (6th ed. 1974) (herein *McMichael*)
Rabkin and Johnson, *Current Legal Forms with Tax Analysis* (herein *Rabkin*)
Reskin and Sakai, *Modern Real Estate and Mortgage Forms, Condominiums*
Rohan, *Real Estate Financing—Forms* (herein *Rohan*).

The forms contained in this book have been carefully selected in order to cover the situations and problems of the subject matters as completely as possible. They will be useful to lawyers for adaptation to specific situations in connection with which they are to be used. Laymen will find them informative on the contingencies and problems which should be considered, but should consult their own legal counsel before entering into any contract or business arrangements based on these forms. Also, legal requirements often vary from state to state. Local counsel should therefore be consulted before these forms and form paragraphs are used in legal transactions.

Table of Common Forms and Clauses with References to Forms Sources and Discussions (Treatises and Articles)

Advertising agreements
    Gordon's, *Modern Forms*

Affidavits
    Gordon's, *Modern Forms*

Air Rights
    Rohan, § 12.01 *et seq*
    Wright, *The Law of Air Space*

Assignments
    Gordon's, *Modern Forms*
    Rabkin, Vol. II

Broker's Forms
    Gordon's, *Modern Forms*
    Kratovil, *Real Estate Law* (6th Ed. 1974)

Building Contracts
    Gordon's, *Modern Forms*

Collective Bargaining
    Rabkin, Vol. V

Condominium
    Reskin & Sakai, *Modern Real Estate & Mortgage Forms, Condominiums*
    Rabkin, Vol. VIII

Condominium periodicals
    Insurance, 19 Practical Law 13 (Nov. 1973)
    Leasehold Condo, 2 Conn. L. Rev. 37
    Mortgage Financing, 24 Bus. Law 445
    Practical Problems of Operation, 2 Conn L. Rev. 12
    Resort Condo, 2 Conn L. Rev. 50

Construction Contracts periodicals
    19 Practical Law. 37 (May 1973)
    Defaulted jobs
        Representing Architect & Engineer, 8 Forum 481
        Representing the Owner, 8 Forum 493
        Representing the Subcontractor, 8 Forum 473

ABA Real Prop. Prob. & Tr. J. (1964) p. 4 (Lease as a Credit Instrument)
Gordon's, *Modern Forms*
Schwartz, *Lease Drafting in Massachusetts*
Rohan
Rabkin, Vol. X
10 U. Fla. L. Rev. 1 (Mortgage clauses)
McMichael

Leases—Assignments and Subleases
Friedman, *Leases*
Arnold, *Modern Real Estate & Mortgage Forms* Forms Supp. 2.341 to 2.347

Leases—Commercial
PLI Real Estate Law, Practice, Handbook *Commercial Real Estate Leases* (5th
Friedman)

Leases—Damage or Destruction of Premises
Arnold, *Modern Real Estate and Mortgage Forms*, Forms Supp. 2.322 to 2.324,
2.108 to 2.111

Leases—Eminent Domain Clause
Arnold, *Modern Real Estate & Mortgage Forms*, Forms 2.115 to 2.122, Forms
Supp. 2.325 to 2.326.1
3 ABA Real Prop. Prob. & Tr. J. 242

Leases—Escalation Clauses
Arnold, *Modern Real Estate & Mortgage Forms*, Forms Supp. 2.266 to 2.268,
2.273 to 2.280.1, 2.301, 2.24, 2.25

Leases—Ground Leases
California Ground Lease Practice
48 Yale L. J. 1400
10 U. of Miami L. Rev 1
4 ABA Real Prop. Prob. & Tr. J. 437 (1969)

Leases—Insurance Clauses
7 The Forum 130
ABA Real Prop. Prob. & Tr. J. 532 (Winter 1970)

Leases—Net Leases
8 Practical Law 15 (Feb. 1962)

Leases—Office & Warehouse
17 Practical Law 79 (March 1971)

Leases—Negotiating for Landlord
25 U. of Miami L. Rev 361

Leases—Percentage
Arnold, *Modern Real Estate & Mortgage Forms*, Forms Supp. 2.256 to 2.264,
2.12 to 2.15
Percentage Leases, Building Managers Assn. of Chicago

Partnerships & Limited Partnerships
>   Arnold & Smith, *Modern Real Estate & Mortgage Forms*
>   Reskin & Sakai, *Modern Real Estate & Mortgage Forms, Condominium*
>   Rabkin, Vol. I, Vol. VIII

Planned Unit Developments
>   1 Real Est. L. J. 5
>   2 Real Est. L. J. 523
>   1 Environmental Affairs 694
>   55 Mo. L. Rev 27
>   7 ABA Real Prop. Prob. & Tr. J. 61

Pledges
>   Gordon's *Modern Forms* (Collateral Security Agreements)
>   Rabkin, Vol. II

Representations & Covenants
>   Arnold, *Modern Real Estate & Mortgage Forms*, Forms 3.63 to 3.78, Forms
>   Supp. 2.283

Sale of Stock and Business Assets
>   Rabkin, Vol. II

Secured Transactions
>   Rabkin, Vol. II A

Shopping Centers
>   Rohan, § 14.01 *et seq.*
>   Rabkin, Vol. IX
>   Operating Agreements, 7 ABA Real Prop. Prob. & Tr. J. 812

Syndications
>   Rabkin, Vol. VIII

Subordination, Non-disturbance and Attornment Clauses & Agreements
>   Friedman, *Leases*
>   Arnold, *Modern Real Estate & Mortgage Forms*, Forms Supp. 2.348, 2.349,
>   2.350, 2.173 to 2.177, 3.254, 3.155
>   4 ABA Real Prop. Prob. and Tr. J. 466 (1969)

Tenancies in Common
>   Rabkin, Vol. VIII

Trusts—Business Trusts
>   Rabkin, Vol. IA

Trusts—Real Estate Investment Trusts
>   Arnold & Smith, *Modern Real Estate & Mortgage Forms*
>   Rohan, § 2.04, § 11.01 *et seq.*
>   Rabkin, Vol. VIII

Truth in Lending
>   Arnold, *Modern Real Estate & Mortgage Reports*

Table of Forms

CONTENTS

Contents

1

How to Use This Book

§ 1. In general. In an effort to telescope the material presented, separate chapters have been created to contain material that is relevant to all types of documents and transactions: contract of sale, deed, mortgage, lease, etc. For example, if a corporation is executing the document, you must know whether at that time it is in good standing and has not been dissolved. *See* Chapters 5 and 6.

§ 2. Abbreviations. Again, in an effort to conserve space, abbreviations are used. *R* is used to designate a seller, grantor, mortgagor, or assignor. *E* is used to designate a purchaser, grantee, mortgagee, or assignee. *E-1* is used to designate a first mortgagee where a junior mortgage is present. *E-2* is used to designate the junior mortgagee. *L* is a landlord, *T* a tenant. Where there is danger of confusion, as where a paragraph discusses several different transactions, abbreviations are not used.

§ 3. Forms. Obviously reproduction of lengthy forms is impossible in a text of this size. Hence, references are made to sources where such forms can be found. However, the form should be read critically and modified in accordance with the suggestions contained herein. There is no such thing as a good form. A form that is good for a lessor is probably bad for a lessee. And a form should not be used unless the legal effect of each paragraph is understood. The structure of many of our forms developed out of bitter experience. During the depression, for example, mortgagors got together with their tenants and cancelled valuable leases, the mortgagor pocketing a fee for doing so. Out of this experience came the assignment of leases and rents. Kratovil, *Mortgages* § 303.

§ 4. What this text does and does not do. To a very great extent this text is composed of relatively non-technical explanations of modern real estate documents, what they are and why they are used. A very large set of books would be needed to set forth various ground leases and commercial leases. Hence, no attempt is made to include such forms. It is my experience that once a lawyer knows the "why" of a given document or clause, he is capable of translating this into English. If he doesn't know the "why," a trip through the typical form book can be fraught with danger. A clause that is quite satisfactory to a seller can be disastrous to a buyer, for example.

Moreover, the stilted language of the old forms is somewhat out of style today. By this time all lawyers know that the phrase "party of the first part" is hopelessly out of date. The antiquated repetitions such as "remise," "release," "alien," "convey," and "quitclaim," are disappearing.

The courts mean to drive out unconscionable contracts and unconscionable clauses in contracts. This raises a problem to every draftsman. He can stay up nights drafting clauses that protect his client. In the end he must ask himself, "what will the courts do with this?"

The concept of unconscionability has also made many common form clauses, probably much more than 50 percent of them, unenforceable. For this reason alone, all existing forms must be regarded with suspicion. In most states, for example, the typical pro-landlord residential lease is as dead as the dodo.

§ 5. **What you can do about the "new look" in real estate law.** In addition to avoiding the use of loaded, old forms, the lawyer can help the court understand the "why" of a particular form or clause. Not all judges are familiar with the economics behind a given real estate transaction. In a fully "net" lease, there is no harm in stating that

> The economics of this transaction, as bargained for by the parties, are such that the landlord is to receive, as net to him, the rents the tenant has agreed to pay, regardless of what damage or destruction occurs to the improvements, what new laws are enacted placing additional charges on the land, what new laws are enacted restricting the use of the land, or whatever circumstance not described in this lease occur that might make continued occupancy by the tenant unprofitable. The parties, at arm's length, and bargaining on equal terms, have agreed that all such risks are to be "borne by the tenant."

The argument can be made that all we are doing is creating a new form of boiler-plate. It is unlikely that the courts will take this route. The simpler the language, the better you explain the economic realities, the more readiness you will find in the courts to accept your drafting. This is especially true of large-scale transactions, where equality of bargaining power is almost always present. In the small-scale transaction, explanations are useless unless they are rational and convincing, as is explained in Chapter 16. However, even where a consumer-type party is involved, I see no reason why a clause in bold type explaining the economic realities would not help. For example, in the states that still permit forfeiture of installment contracts, great pressure exists to invalidate this clause. Suppose, however, this clause were introduced with an explanation:

> The value of this property and the amount of the buyer's down payment are such that the seller would sustain an economic loss if he were compelled to foreclose this as a mortgage until the buyer has built up an equity. Requirement of foreclosure would remake this transaction into something totally unacceptable to the seller. Accordingly, the parties have agreed that the seller should have the remedy of forfeiture until ___ percent of the purchase price has been received by the seller.

§ 6. **Reading text in full.** It would take countless cross-references to tie together the various portions of this text that deal with the same problem. For this reason, it seems best for the user of this text to read it through, from cover to cover, so that when he encounters a particular problem, memory will jog him into looking in several places, whereupon the index will be of assistance, as will the chapter headings. This has an additional virtue. Many lawyers like to say, "I don't know all the law, but I know where to find it." This is an unsound approach. There are thousands of traps in the law. If you don't sense the presence of a trap, it is unlikely that you will research the problem.

§ 7. Reference material. Some reference material is placed at a chapter's end. Some general sources are:

ALI-ABA Publications (get current list and index future releases on 4 x 6 cards)

Bar journals (local journals)

Continuing Legal Education (local forms will comply with local law)

Dickerson, *The Fundamentals of Legal Drafting* (1965)

The Forum (ABA Negligence Section. Good source on insurance, surety bonds, building construction)

Friedman, *Leases* (PLI 1974) (invaluable)

Kratovil, *Real Estate Law* (6th ed. 1974)

Kratovil, *Modern Mortgage Law and Practice* (1972)

Osborne, *Mortgages* (2nd ed.)

Law Review Digest, Kimball-Clark Pub. Co., Boonton, N.J. 07005 (extracts from leading law review articles and index to other periodical literature).

PLI Publications (get current list and index future releases on 4 x 6 cards)

The Practical Lawyer (ABA)

Real Property, Probate and Trust Journal (ABA)

Real Estate Law Journal (Warren, Gorham & Lamont)

Real Estate Review (Warren, Gorham & Lamont)

FORM BOOKS

Arnold, *Modern Real Estate & Mortgage Forms*

Gordon's Modern Annotated Forms, Revised (herein Gordon's Forms)

Rohan, *Real Estate Financing*

2

Drafting in General

§ 8. General considerations in drafting. Of course there are some rules in drafting that are applicable to all complex legal documents. Since redrafts are the rule rather than the exception, each draft should be dated. Preferably the draft should be placed in a separate file with a suitable caption, *e.g.,* "Draft of April 21, 1975." Where re-drafted sheets are substituted, these should also be dated and inserted in all drafts. Be sure that your correspondence is preserved, for example, a letter stating: "Kindly insert redrafted pages 11, 17 and 18 enclosed, all dated May 21, 1975, in your draft dated April 21, 1975."

Be sure the names of the parties are given correctly and an appropriate abbreviated form given early in the document, *e.g.* "General Harbor and Dock Construction Company of New Jersey" (hereafter called "Dock Company"). Nobody uses "party of the first part" these days.

§ 9. Captions or catch-lines. Captions are used, for example, in a contract of sale of improved property, *e.g.* "Risk of loss in a case of damage to or destruction of improvements prior to closing of deal." Most lawyers include a clause that: "Captions or catch-lines are inserted for convenience only and are not to be considered in construing the paragraphs so entitled."

A table of contents is placed as the first page of the document and is so entitled, using the captions or catch-lines and giving the page where the paragraph first appears.

A table of definitions is included in all substantial documents.

If several men in the firm work on various sections or drafts, the name of the author should be given on the page or section, so that if questions as to meaning or purpose arise, the author can be contacted. It is dangerous to draft out of a document a legitimate element of protection the original author included. He may have known a point of law the re-draftsmen had overlooked.

It is a matter of convenience to divide the document into Articles. For example in a ground lease, "Article IV Construction of Building." All clauses relating to construction of the building are grouped in this article. This eliminates the helter-skelter drafting with related paragraphs scattered in various portions of the document.

Technical language should be avoided where possible. A phrase like "consequential damages" has so many conflicting meanings, all supported by court decisions, that it causes nothing but trouble.

Clauses taken from form books or files of the law firm should never be used unless the draftsman understands their meaning, purpose, and applicability to the document.

§ **10. Research always precedes drafting.** No responsible attorney draws a lease in Massachusetts without first reading from cover to cover Schwartz, *Lease Drafting in Massachusetts*. Every large law firm has a librarian who has a list of such titles available. If the firm is too small to have such a librarian, consult the librarian of the local court or bar library.

In doing the research that precedes draftsmanship, an indispensable requirement is an awareness of recent developments in the law. The Uniform Commercial Code (UCC) has made many important changes in the law, notably in the law of contract. The courts have begun to treat the Code as basically one of the Restatements, applicable to situations falling outside the Code, including land transactions. *Morse & Co. v. Consolidated Fisheries Co.*, 190 F2d 817, 822. The Uniform Land Transactions act, soon to be promulgated, tracks to a great extent with the UCC. Restatement of Property 2d also tracks with the UCC, Restatement of Property 2d introduces many almost revolutionary concepts into the law of real property, notably landlord and tenant law. Among the new concepts in Restatement of Property 2d is the concept that statutes are just as important as statements of a state's policy as court decisions, perhaps more so. Thus the Restatement takes a statutory proposition that is found on the books of a number of states and distills from these a new rule of property. Critics of the law of real property have pointed to its insularity. The real property law of each state stops at the state line. This is no longer possible. The real property lawyer must become familiar with trends in the statutes as well as the court decisions outside of his state. Of course, he must be familiar with the four sources of "new law" cited in this section.

The foregoing view of statutory law goes back at least as far as 1936 when Mr. Justice Stone said at the Harvard Tercentenary: "I can find in the history and principles of the common law no adequate reason for our failure to treat a statute much more as we treat a judicial precedent, as both a declaration and a source of law, and as a premise for legal reasoning." *The Common Law in the United States*, 50 Harv. L. Rev. 4, 13. This view will undoubtedly find increasing acceptance in the courts. It certainly emphasizes the need for real property lawyers to be aware of the UCC while ULTA waits in the wings. The Restatement of Contracts 2d (and to a much greater extent) Restatement of Property 2d, draw upon existing statutes as a source of Restatement law. Under this view, a statute has as much value as precedent as a court decision.

§ **11. Instant legal research.** Many citations to law review articles are included in the text. It is obvious that many of these articles represent careful legal research by scholars. Finding one such article may eliminate need for further research by the practitioner. Even a law library of modest size will have the *Index to Legal Periodicals*. Its section on *Periodicals Indexed* gives the address of all publishers of legal periodicals. Single issues are available for a modest price and are well worth the money. This brings to even smaller communities the resources of all the country's fine law schools.

3

Traps to Avoid

§ **12. In general.** When, in any complex deal, negotiations have been concluded and a compromise has been hammered out, lawyers rush to dictate its terms. The same thing occurs when a new, promising type of deal is contracted. Even in the highly flexible area of contract law, there are many limitations on what the parties can do. For example, if you assign exclusive territory or sign exclusive agents, you are going to run into anti-trust problems. Real property law bristles with requirements and prohibitions, some of which are considered anachronistic. The fact remains that they are still alive and well and must be reckoned with. Especially among the younger lawyers, whose law school careers may have given short shrift to the "unwitty diversities of the law of property," there are dangerous ignorance and disregard of the old learning.

§ **13. Perpetuities.** A good many shopping center leases were drafted with a term commencing "when the shopping center is completed." Then came *Wong v. DiGrazia*, 60 Cal. 2d 525, 386 P2d 817, 1964 Duke L.J. 645, 16 Hastings L.J. 470, 24 Md. L.Rev. 356, 12 U.C.L.A. L.Rev. 46, with its rude reminder that such leases could violate the rule against perpetuities. Indeed two earlier cases so held. It so happened that the lease in question was sustained but there is no guarantee that other courts will follow this liberal lead. Today we meet the threat by providing that the commencement shall be not more than five years from the date of the lease, otherwise the lease to be void. Many leases drafted since *Wong v. DiGrazia* lack the "escape hatch" clause. Ignorance of the law is the only explanation.

Options in gross, that is options not contained in leases, are subject to the rule against perpetuities. *United Virginia Bank v. Union Oil Co.*, 214 Va.48, 197 SE2d 174 (1973).

There is thinking that the rule against perpetuities ought not be applicable to commercial transactions. But we are not yet at that point.

§ **14. Covenants running with the land.** Countless agreements between adjoining buildings in different ownership provide that one building shall provide heat and air-conditioning for the other. Technically, this is an affirmative covenant, and to run with the land must comply with the ancient requirements regarding running covenants, one of them being "privity of estate." *Wheeler v. Schad*, 7 Nev. 204 (1871). Amazingly, few of such agreements comply with this requirement. In a few well-drafted agreements the building owners grant each other easements in the pipes and ducts that service the system, and the necessary privity of estate is supplied.

§ **15. Restraints on partition.** The law will not allow an indefinite restraint on the right of a co-owner to seek partition. 37 ALR3d 978. Yet many condominium statutes contain no provision like that in the Illinois statute that this rule is inapplicable to the condominium. This is necessary because the common elements are held in co-ownership and partition would be disastrous. If the statute contains no such provision, some ''escape hatch'' clause is needed.

§ **16. Easements.** Few lawyers seem to be aware of the rule that an easement cannot be used to serve non-dominant land, (Kratovil, *Real Estate Law* § 42) such as an additional contiguous parcel acquired by the owner of the dominant tenement some years after the creation of the easement. In actual experience, once a building is erected on the non-dominant land, the servient owner is in a position to demand an exorbitant price for permission to use the easement to service a new building. In the law of pipeline easements, there are a number of decisions holding that once the easement owner puts down a pipe, he has ''used up'' his easement. Additional pipes cannot be laid down. To be sure, there are also decisions to the contrary. Obviously, the draftsman must draft around this problem.

§ **17. Perpetual trusts.** There are one or two decisions holding that the rule against perpetual trusts (54 Howard L.Rev. 842) does not apply to business trusts because all interests are vested. *Wechter v. C.T.&T. Co.*, 385 Ill. 111, 52 NE2d 157. In states lacking such decisions, more often than not the problem is ignored.

§ **18. Sale of stock.** Purchases of all the stock of a corporation are commonplace. Rarely is thought given to the fact that a purchaser of *stock* is not a purchaser of *land*, and is therefore not protected by the recording acts. Whatever unrecorded instrument exists, executed by a corporation (easement running through the middle of the land, substantial mortgage, etc.) is good against the purchaser of the stock.

§ **19. Building ownership separate from ownership of land.** William Zeckendorf, of Webb and Knapp, is said to have invented the idea that you can separate ownership of the building from ownership of the land, and by piling lease upon lease, mortgages on the fee titles, and mortgages on the leaseholds, you can obtain legitimate financing substantially in excess of the total value of the land and building. He used to give an amusing talk in which he explained how the sum of the parts can be greater than the whole.

Getting the ownership of the building separated from the land is easy. *R* who owns the land and building, conveys to *E* the fee title to the land, ''excepting, however, the building presently located on said land.''

Then *E* leases the land to *R* on a long-term lease. The problem now is how to get fee ownership of the building transferred to *E* when the lease expires. Transferring fee ownership requires a deed of conveyance containing words of conveyance. It is only recently that this problem has been discovered and discussed and new language devised. The old language in the lease, that at its termination the building will belong to the landlord, is certainly an informal transfer of fee title. There is also an executary interest problem, a shifting use in the fee title to the building, and therefore a perpetuities problem.

The fact here that you have a "fee title" that lasts, not forever, but for a term of years, is something draftsmen have discussed only lately. Simes & Taylor, *Law of Future Interests* § 502.

§ **20. Options.** In options there is the problem of relation back. Kratovil, *Mortgages* § 325. It is easy to draft around the problem. Not one option in a thousand does so.

> **EXAMPLE:** *R* gives *E* an option, good for 20 years, to buy an office building. The option is recorded. *R* continues to make leases of office space. *E* exercises the option. Can he evict one of the tenants to make room for his own operation? In virtually every state the law on this point is unclear. Of course, the option can specify what kind of lease will survive and what kind will not. Few option draftsmen give this any thought.

Title companies are constantly badgered by requests to insure that exercise of the option will result in good title. Such an outright guarantee is impossible. The current thinking is that a landlord's trustee in bankruptcy might have the right to reject the option, since he has the right to reject "executory contracts." Moreover, an optionee is not a bona fide purchaser. A bona fide purchaser who is protected against unrecorded instruments and secret equities is one who acquires legal title for value without notice. The optionee has not acquired legal title. Neither has he paid the entire consideration.

§ **21. Installment contracts.** For reasons stated in the preceding section, a purchaser in an installment contract cannot be assured of receiving good title when he completes his purchase.

§ **22. Conclusion.** A complete list of risks to avoid would take an entire book. A few of the bad ones have been listed. Practical advice would be to keep an old property lawyer in the firm. He learned about perpetuities, covenants running with the land, and a lot more of the old law that the able young men of the law were never exposed to. Let him look over the documentation they prepare.

4

Canons of Construction

§ **23. In general.** You don't read a legal document the way you read a newspaper. The canons of construction peer over your shoulder as you read. Printed forms are construed against the party who supplies the form. This is especially true of contracts of adhesion. There is a constructional preference for a covenant rather than a condition, and for a condition rather than a determinable fee. General language has its teeth pulled by the doctrines of *ejusdem generis* and *noscitur a sociis*, and so on.

There are difficulties. One difficulty is that the law is scattered illogically in segregated areas of our law books. Under "Contracts" you will find a section on the rules of construction of contracts. The same is true of the sections on "Deeds," "Landlord and Tenant," "Mortgages," "Vendor and Purchaser," and "Easements." In point of fact, the compartments are simply not separable. Similar canons of construction are in many, perhaps most, areas applicable to all the important real estate documents.

The canons of construction are vitally important.

EXAMPLE: L leases to T on a long-term lease providing that "all" expense of rebuilding damaged or destroyed buildings during the lease falls on T. During the last year of the lease the building is gutted by fire. By the time T completes the restoration, the lease will be over and T gets no benefit from the restoration. But the word "all" admits of no exceptions. When the parties use the word "all," the courts assume they mean "all."

Another difficulty is that most inexperienced lawyers pay no attention to the canons of construction. Thousands of documents and memoranda are prepared in total disregard of the canons. Once the document becomes involved in litigation, the litigation counsel in the firm take over and start applying the canons of construction favorable to their cause, and their adversaries do likewise. It seems ironical that resort to the canons is deferred until litigation occurs. The young attorney ought to be apprised at the outset of his career that canons of construction exist, both as to documents and statutes, and that his documents will not pass muster unless they reflect an honest endeavor to apply the canons.

5

Grantor, Seller, Mortgagor, and Lessor

§ 24. In general. Special requirements with respect to *R* exist in different transactions. Nevertheless, there are many considerations that cut across transaction lines and are applicable to *R* whatever the nature of the transaction, whether contract, deed, lease or mortgage. The contract, whether it be a contract for sale, for lease, or commitment for mortgage, is referred to herein as the *contract.* As can be seen, technical and complex problems exist in this area. The attorney is encouraged to make his own analysis of these problems, but before the transaction is finalized the title insurer who will be called upon to insure the title should be consulted. It is suggested that the attorney read this chapter with other chapters in this book relating to specific documents.

§ 25. Executor. It is a common practice for today's draftsmen to state in a will that the executor has all the powers granted to the testamentary trustee in the comprehensive boilerplate as to trustee's powers. In many instances, it may be advantageous that the executor be selected as the party to act.

EXAMPLE: *T,* owner of Blackacre, dies leaving a will naming *R* as executor and trustee and giving both extensive powers. It becomes advisable to sell Blackacre while the estate is in probate. An executor who has a power to sell and mortgage can do so free and clear of possible claims of creditors against the estate, and, in many states, free and clear of the right of heirs to contest the will. *Smith v. Smith,* 168 Ill. 488, 48 NE 96. The testamentary trustee, on the other hand, cannot do this. The result is that if such a trustee sells while the estate is in probate, a title company will ask either for (a) a deposit of the purchase price to be retained by it until the time for filing claims and contest has expired, or (b) a surety bond, which may be difficult to obtain and expensive. Obviously, the executor should be named as seller in the contract and grantor in the deed. In some states an executor has a statutory power of sale.

From a title insurance standpoint, once a power of sale authorized by a will is exercised, a purchaser is not bound to inquire as to the necessity for the exercise of power. *See* 33 C.J.S. *Executors and Administrators* § 293, pp. 1322-1323. Further, a purchaser is not bound to inquire whether the sale is being made for a purpose other than that which the will authorizes the executor to sell. And the purchaser need not look to the application of the proceeds of the sale. *Wardwell v. McDowell,* 31 Ill. 364, 375; *Crozier v. Hoyt,* 97 Ill. 23, 31.

Where the transaction involved is a lease, there are special problems regarding the duration of the lease, since, *absent special clauses,* a trustee may not have power to execute long-term leases. Kratovil, *Mortgages*, § 339. Obviously an executor who is granted the same powers as the trustee faces the same problems.

§ **26. Foreign executor.** The question of the power of a foreign executor to act as *R* presents thorny problems. See *Foreign Fiduciaries* § 53.

§ **27. Trustee.** Business trusts, especially real estate investment trusts, have a trust name and the trust instrument authorizes it to do business in the trust name. Nevertheless, there is doubt in most states that the trust is an entity like a corporation. Hence, title is taken in the name of the trustees and the trustees become *R* in the contract of sale or mortgage. The trust instrument may authorize less than all the trustees to act. Nevertheless, all the trustees are named as *R* and their signatures are affixed by the authorized trustees, as is done where an agent acts under a power of attorney.

The trustee's power to engage in the transaction are determined by (a) the trust instrument and (b) state statutes granting general powers to the trustees. 3 A.B.A. Real Prop. Prob. & Tr. J. 273, 298. A contract may call for opinion of counsel, satisfactory to *E* and his title company, that the trustees do, indeed, have these powers.

All trusts end sometime. A testamentary trust for example, might end at the death of a life tenant. The trustee's powers after termination are different from his powers during the life of the trust, unless the trust instrument provides otherwise. Indeed, the trust instrument may be so drafted that at termination title automatically passes to the remaindermen. Hence, the contract calls for a certificate by *R* that at closing the trust has not terminated. The title company will insist on this.

§ **28. Recitals.** In all instruments executed by an executor or trustee, it is desirable that the instrument recite that it is executed pursuant to the powers granted by the will or other instruments. This is because of the ancient law regarding powers that an instrument exercising a power so recite.

§ **29. Foreign fiduciaries.** Where a trust or estate created in *State A* owns land in *State B*, difficult problems are presented. If the trust is a testamentary trust, in many states probate in *State B* will be necessary. Even if it is not a testamentary trust, the power of a foreign trustee to act creates problems. Some states attempt to forbid a foreign individual to act as trustee. This is probably unconstitutional. Bogert, *Trusts and Trustees*, § 132 (2d ed. 1965); 37 Va.L.Rev. 1119. All states limit the power of foreign corporate trustees to act in the state. For a covenient chart that will get you started on the problem, write to The American College of Probate Counsel, 10964 W. Pico Blvd. Los Angeles, California, 90064, and ask for the chart entitled "Rights of Non-resident Banks, Trust Companies, or National Banks Having Fiduciary Powers to Act as Fiduciary under the laws of the Various Other States without Qualifying to do Business."

Some foreign corporations "doing business" laws are broad enough in their definition and scope to include trusts, as, for example, in Michigan. 24 Corporation Journal 270. Other states (Arizona, for example) specifically require business trusts to qualify as a foreign corporation.

§ **30. Corporations.** Where *R* is a corporation, the contract requires that *R* produce at closing: (a) resolutions satisfactory to counsel and to *E's* title company, authorizing the transaction; (b) opinion of counsel satisfactory to *E* and *E's* title company that the transaction is a valid transaction and within the corporation's powers; (c) certificate by the secretary of state or other proper official, especially if *R* is a foreign corporation, that *R* is in good standing and has paid all its taxes.

In some states (Connecticut, for example) witnesses are required on a deed by a corporation. In some states (Indiana, for example) a deed by a corporation requires an endorsement as to payment of corporate taxes.

Some corporations require special attention. A non-pecuniary corporation may require a court order for leave to act as *R* in some states, *e.g.* New York. Religious corporations require special attention because their corporate records are often chaotic. If the corporation lacks an impression seal, one should be ordered immediately, for most title companies will require this to be affixed to the deed or other instrument.

Where the vendor is a corporation, its franchise or corporate tax for the current year may be a lien on the land although it may not fall due until the following year. The only satisfactory way to deal with this problem, from the purchaser's standpoint, is to insist that the title company give a clear title policy, leaving the title company and the vendor to work out the details of any indemnity deposit that may be required to assure the company that the tax will be paid. The contract should cover this point, if such taxes are in the picture. Such taxes cannot be prorated for obvious reasons. The franchise tax on a large corporation may exceed the sale price in the present transaction.

§ **31. Partnerships.** In a state where the Uniform Partnership Act is in effect, and the partnership has taken title in its partnership name, obviously such partnership must be named as *R*. The contract will call for (a) production of the partnership articles at or prior to closing; (b) certificate by the partners that as of date of closing the partnership is in existence and that no change has taken place in the partnership articles or the composition of the partnership; and (c) opinion of counsel satisfactory to *E* that the transaction is one in which the partnership may legally engage and was properly authorized by all the partners; (d) certificate by partners that as of date of closing no statutory liens exist against the partners or partnership in the place of their domicile or county where the land lies. The contract should call for all partners to sign the deed, lease or mortgage. Most title companies require this.

A certified copy of the partnership articles must be lodged with the title company. Some title companies require the articles to be recorded, in which case a proper acknowledgment must be affixed.

Generally speaking title companies require all the general partners to sign any deed, mortgage, or lease. This is especially true where title to the land is in the names of the partners, but it is also true where the land is owned in the partnership name. Where the partnership deals extensively in real estate, and all the partners are not readily available, then: (1) The articles of partnership must specifically authorize less than all of the partners to sign. (2) It is preferable to place some dollar limit on this authority. (3) The partnership articles should recite that purchasers, mortgagees, or lessees of the designated partner are protected against the claims of the other partners. (4) The partnership articles should be duly acknowledged and recorded to show the source of the designated partner's authority. (5) If title is in the names of the partners, all are named as grantors, and their names appear on the signature lines and in the certificate of acknowledgment, much as in the case of a deed executed under power of attorney. Kratovil, *Real Estate Law* § 89.

§ 32. Limited partnership. The requirements as to a limited partnership parallel those for a general partnership. In addition, where the transaction involves all the partnership assets, the contract should call for approval of the transaction by all the limited partners unless the partnership articles clearly permit the general partners to engage in the transaction without such approval. In the latter case, the contract calls for opinion of counsel satisfactory to *E* that the approval of the limited partners is not necessary.

A number of states have special requirements regarding foreign limited partnerships. 47 So.Calif. L. Rev. 1174 (1974). Obviously these must be complied with.

§ 33. Joint ventures. A joint venture is regarded as being subject to partnership law, for the most part. But there is doubt as to its existence as a legal entity, for, strictly speaking, the Uniform Partnership Act does not, explicitly, apply to joint ventures. Hence, the joint venturers should be named as *R*. Use of the joint venture name as *R* should be avoided. The title company will want a certified copy of the joint venture agreement and proof that it has not been amended. It may require that the agreement be recorded, in which case it must be duly acknowledged.

§ 34. Public body. Where *R* is a public body, there will usually be some local statute governing the transaction which should be followed. If no statute is found, consult the authorities, local and general. 3 Antieau, *Municipal Corporation Law* § 20.19, 10 McQuillin, *Municipal Corporations,* (1965) § 28.37 *et seq.* Where the sale involves dedicated land the complications are enormous. 3 Antieau, *Municipal Corporation Law,* § 20.19; 11 De Paul L.Rev. 61.

Where *R* is a public body borrowing money, local statutes, constitutions, and court decisions must be consulted. 11 ALR 828. Constitutional or statutory debt limitations exist in most states. The power to mortgage public property presents grave problems. 10 McQuillin, *Municipal Corporations* (1965) § 28.41.

Where *R* is a home rule municipality, all the problems that beset home rule are present. 22 De Paul L.Rev. 359.

Where *R* is a municipal corporation, the statutes and decisions should be consulted with respect to its power to make leases. 63 ALR 614; 129 ALR 1163; 86 ALR 1175; 47 ALR3d 19; 47 ALR3d 72.

§ 35. Payment provisions. Whenever any document calls for the payment of money, and all documents do, some provision should be made covering the situation where several people, co-owners for example, are entitled to receive payment and one of them dies. See § 276.

6

Grantee, Purchaser, Lessee, and Mortgagee

§ **36. In general.** The requirements here to some extent parallel those concerning *R* with some changes.

§ **37. Executor.** The executor under a will is rarely acting as *E*. If he holds a defaulted mortgage, he may take title in his name as executor by foreclosure, or deed in lieu of foreclosure, and convey it the same way. 110 ALR 1397. As to foreign executors, *see* § 29.

§ **38. Trustee.** A deed or other instrument to a trustee should clearly identify the trust. One never drafts a deed running simply to "John Smith, as trustee." 4 Scott, *Trusts*, § 297.3. Indeed, in some states the phrase "as trustee" is without any legal effect. 4 *id.* § 297.3. The deed should run to "John Smith, as trustee under Trust Agreement dated June 15, 1946, and known as the Pinecrest Liquidation Trust," or other proper designation.

The trustee's power to act as *E* is determined by the trust instrument and any state statute granting general powers to trustees. 3 A.B.A. Real Prop. Prob. & Tr. J. 273, 298. If the trustees are making a mortgage loan, their powers in this regard must also be verified. Opinion of counsel can be required. If the trust is being created at this time, be sure to include boilerplate giving the trustee ample powers and provide that no person dealing with the trustee need inquire into the trustee's powers, the propriety of his action, or the application of the funds received by him.

If the grantee is to be a business or Massachusetts trust, the draftsman has considerable homework to do. 2 Rowley, *Partnerships*, (1960) *et seq;* 156 A.L.R.22. If it is to be a real estate investment trust, again there is much to be learned before the deed is recorded. 16 Business Lawyer 900. As to foreign fiduciaries, *see* § 29.

§ **39. Corporations.** If a corporation is taking title, its charter should be checked and the name copied exactly and without the slightest deviation. For example, if the charter describes a corporation as "The Elite Hat Shop, Inc.," the draftsman does not omit the "The" and does not spell out the "Inc.,". If a corporation is being created to acquire the real estate, the draftsman should be sure that the corporation's charter has been issued and that all other formalities for corporate existence are complied with before the deed to the corporation is made out. In other words, the draftsman must be sure that he has an existing, legal grantee to whom to convey. To be sure, there are decisions sustaining a deed to a corporation if the corporation acquires a legal existence after the date of the deed. 4 Am. Law Property, § 18.47. And there are decisions holding that the grantor in the deed is estopped to question the grantee corporation's existence. 18 Am.Jur.2d, *Corporations*, § 78. But there are also decisions holding the deed void if the corporation grantee has no legal existence at the time the deed is delivered. *Allman v. Gatschet*, (Mo. 1969) 437 SW2d 70. Some states have enacted laws curing such defects. Basye, 636, 638.

Much the same problem arises with respect to a corporation that has been dissolved prior to the date of the deed. 20 ALR2d 1084.

If a foreign corporation is to be the grantee, obviously there are many technical problems relating to ''doing business'' laws. In some states, for example, mere acquisition of land in the state comes under the ''doing business'' laws. See Corporation Trust Co., *What Constitutes Doing Business* (1973) 103. Opinion of counsel should be required that the corporation has power to engage in the transaction. Corporate resolutions should be required. A foreign corporation should be required to display its certificate of authority at or before closing, also its certificate that it is in good standing in the state of its domicile. If a foreign corporation is lending money on local land, but lacks a local certificate of authority, it may be possible to employ the insulation theory. 25 Legal Bulletin (U.S. S.&L. League) 65 (1959); 14A CJ 1283. Agricultural corporations and corporations owned by aliens are subject to special legislation in some states, and this should be consulted.

In some states religious corporations are limited as to the acreage they may acquire. Here a certificate will be wanted at closing that this maximum has not been exceeded. Deeds to churches present thorny problems, *e.g.*, *Brady v. Reiner*, 198 SE2d 812.

Where *R* is a corporation having power to acquire land, the fact that it exceeded its authority in no wise affects the validity of its deed. Basye, § 300. And there are numerous statutes curing defective corporate deeds. Basye, Ch. 16.

Special care must be exercised where *E* is a charitable corporation. Otherwise problems arise, 130 ALR 1118; 96 C.J.S. 531; 50 Marq.L.Rev. 671; 24 Wash. U.L.Q. 1. A kindred problem arises in the law of wills. 19 B.U.L. Rev. 665; 40 Columb.L.Rev. 550; 53 Harv.L.Rev. 327. And a similar problem occurs in the law of charitable trusts. Bogert, *Law of Trusts and Trustees* § 46.

Where a recently formed corporation is involved, and is giving a mortgage, the question of possible evasion of the usury laws is present. 63 ALR2d 925.

§ **40. Partnerships.** A partnership may act as *E* where the Uniform Act is in effect. In other states title is taken in the name of the general partners. In some states partnerships must qualify to do business as foreign corporations. 24 Corporation Journal 267 (1965). If a foreign corporation is a general partner, it must qualify to do business if the partnership is doing business in the state. *Ashland Lumber Co. v. Detroit Salt Co.* 114 Wisc. 66, 89 NW 904: *Harris v. Columbia Water & Light Co.*, 108 Tenn. 245, 67 SW 811. If the state corporation law does not permit a corporation to become a partner (60 ALR2d 932) it may be possible to avoid this particular problem by setting up the deal as a joint venture. 60 ALR2d 936.

§ 41. Partnerships—death and other problems. Drafting articles of partnership is beyond the scope of this text. There are many books and articles on this subject. Death of a partner is a topic the articles treat in great detail.

References: 7 Baylor L.Rev. 291; 34 Chicago-Kent L.Rev. 169, 239, 41 Ill.B.J. 273; 44 *id.* 503; 45 Ky.L.J. 650; 62 Mich.L.Rev. 106; 23 Miss.L.J. 117; 20 Okla.L.Rev. 456; 11 Okla.L.Rev. 229; 14 U. of Fla.L.Rev. 176; 16 U. of Miami L.Rev. 92.

§ 42. Limited partnership. Before taking title in a limited partnership, be sure its partnership articles provide that the general partners may engage in all transactions, including those involving all the partnership assets, without consent of the limited partners. *Meissel v. Finley,* 95 SE2d 186. A clause that persons dealing with the general partners need not concern themselves with the rights of the limited partners is helpful. Where a limited partnership buys land outside of the state of its domicile, title companies require it to comply with local law, by filing a certificate that complies with local law, publishing notice as per local law, etc. To avoid questions as to possible creation of two different partnerships, it is best to include in the local partnership certificate a statement that it is the same partnership as was created in _____ (state) and evidenced by certificate of partnership recorded in _____ County in Book _____ page _____. In some states, limited partnerships must qualify to do business as foreign corporations.

Because of the requirement by the title companies that the Certificate of Limited Partnership be filed in each state in which the partnership operates, there should be a clause in the articles of partnership naming each of the general partners attorney-in-fact to execute and file such certificate and to do all acts and things necessary or convenient to enable the partnership to operate in any state.

A number of states have special statutory requirements regarding foreign limited partnerships. 47 So.Calif. L.Rev. 1174 (1974). Obviously these must be complied with.

§ 43. Joint ventures. A joint venture acting as *E* uses the names of the parties to the joint venture, not the name of the joint venture. As in the case of partnerships, if any party to the joint venture is a foreign corporation, and the joint venture is considered to be "doing business" in the state where the land lies, the corporation must qualify under the "doing business" laws. *Scott Co. v. Enco Const. Co.,* 264 So2d 409.

§ 44. Nominees. A nominee may act as *E*. The usual precautions are taken. Kratovil, *Real Estate Law* § 469.

§ 45. Sale to tenant. If you are selling to a tenant in possession, keep in mind that once the contract is signed, the lease comes to an end and the tenant becomes a purchaser in possession, paying no rent. The same is true when a tenant in possession exercises an option to purchase.

Once a lessee who has an option to purchase exercises his option the lease comes to an end, and thereafter the relation between the parties is that of seller and buyer, not landlord and tenant. *Cities Service Oil Co. v. Viering,* 404 Ill. 538, 89 NE2d 392. For example, rent is no longer due and the landlord cannot declare the lessee's rights terminated for non-payment of rent. *Crowell v. Brady,* 169 Cal.App.2d 352, 337 P2d 211.

Many lawyers feel that since merger is a question of intention, the following provision in the lease and contract will take care of the situation.

CLAUSE: The lease existing between the parties to this contract shall continue in full force and effect, and the buyer-lessee shall continue to pay rent and observe all the covenants of the lease until the closing of this sale and delivery of the deed to the buyer.

§ 46. Trust powers. Whenever *E* is to be a trustee, whether it be a real estate investment trust, *inter vivos* trust, or testamentary trust, the instrument should deal specifically with the manner in which title to the real estate will be held, consistent with state law. A common provision authorizes title to be taken in the name of the nominee. Trust powers are voluminous, with the usual provisions protecting persons dealing with the trustee, so that they need not inquire into the trustee's powers or fidelity in any given transaction. State statutes, including the Uniform Act on Powers of Trustees, may be helpful. 58 Ill. B.J. 654; 32 Law & Contemp. Problems 168; 31 *id.* 635; 32 *id.* 1; 41 Wash.L.Rev. 1, 801.

§ 47. Land trusts. Land trusts have been discussed elsewhere. Kratovil, *Real Estate Law* § 67. If a land trustee is to acquire ownership, the forms used should be those furnished or required by the trust company selected. Where title is taken in a trustee, it is possible, of course, to sell the beneficial interest at sale time instead of having the trustee make a deed of the land. As in the case of a sale of stock where a corporation owns the land, the purchaser of the beneficial interest in a trust does not receive the protection accorded a bona fide purchaser because he is not receiving legal title.

EXAMPLE: *B,* the beneficiary of a land trust directs *T,* the trustee, to place a mortgage on the land. This is done, but the mortgage is not recorded. *B* now sells the beneficial interest in the trust to *E.* The mortgage is good against *E.*

Since the land trust is confined to only a few states, the practitioner is referred to Kenoe, *Land Trust Practice in Illinois,* Illinois Institute for Continuing Legal Education, which can be procured from the Illinois Bar Center, Springfield, Illinois. This contains an excellent discussion of land trust practice.

§ 48. Postal Service. The United States Postal Service is authorized by law to take title to real estate in its own name as UNITED STATES POSTAL SERVICE. The Service will expect title insurance policies for its benefit to be written upon ALTA United States Form—1963, but requires certain modifications.

§ 49. Deed to HUD. The property conveyance should be made to the "Secretary of Housing and Urban Development of Washington, D.C., his successors and assigns." However, if a title company or title attorney will not insure or certify such a title, then the conveyance may be made as "(name the person) of Washington, D.C. as Secretary of Housing and Urban Development, his successors and assigns" to satisfy the particular requirements of the jurisdiction.

(1) *If the grantor is the mortgagee or mortgagor,* the deed should include covenants which warrant against the acts of the grantor and all claiming by, through or under said grantor. If the grantor is a party other

than the mortgagee or mortgagor, the special warranty covenants may be limited or amended to accord with the law of that particular jurisdiction. Nominal consideration may be recited if such a recital is adequate under the laws of the state in which the property is located, or else use such other consideration as may be necessary to support the deed. One deed covering a group of properties is satisfactory.

(2) *After conveyance of a home property to the Secretary,* forward as promptly as possible the title evidence showing the recordation of the deed together with a copy of the deed. This does not require awaiting the return of the original deed from the recorder nor including recording data on the copy of the deed. Forward the original deed as promptly as possible after receipt from the recording authority. If the original deed does not accompany the fiscal data, it must be identified by the FHA case number. All of the foregoing shall be forwarded as promptly as possible to the Office of the Comptroller, Department of Housing and Urban Development, Federal Housing Administration, Washington, D.C. 20412, Attention: Insurance Benefits Branch.

(3) *In order to save expense in recording,* the deed may be made directly to the Secretary from the mortgagor or other grantor. The mortgagee assumes the responsibility of the legality of such method of transfer. The Secretary is not responsible for the property until the deed is filed for record and he is so notified in accordance with the HUD-FHA regulations.

7

Drafting Survey Requirements— Reading the Survey

§ **50. In general.** Regardless of the nature of a real estate transaction, if a substantial amount of money is involved, a land survey will be required. A number of organizations have promulgated standards that surveys must meet to be acceptable to them. Some of these will be set forth and, thereafter, comments will be offered on these requirements.

§ **51. The American Title Association (now the American Land Title Association) and the American Congress on Surveying and Mapping.** The two organizations named in this section heading joined, in 1962, in promulgation of the following survey requirements, hereafter referred to as the "ATA requirements."

PREFACE

While the "Technical Standards for Property Surveys" adopted by the American Congress on Surveying and Mapping (ACSM) in 1946, are recognized as clear and concise technical standards for property-line surveys, and are so recommended, it is recognized that members of the American Title Association (ATA) have specific problems peculiar to title insurance matters which require particular information in detail and exactness for acceptance by title insurance companies when said companies are asked to insure title to land without exceptions as to the many matters which might be discoverable from survey and inspection and not be evidenced by public records. In the general interest of the public, the surveying profession, title insurers and abstracters, the American Title Association (ATA) and the American Congress on Surveying and Mapping (ACSM) now jointly promulgate and set forth such details and criteria for exactness. It is understood that local variations may require local adjustments to suit local situations and often must be applied. It is recognized that no professional surveyor can ethically undertake any project requiring prudent exercise of professional responsibility unless he is assured adequate compensation. It is recognized, equally, that in insuring title, title insurance companies are entitled to and should be able to rely on the evidence produced to it, as the basis for its insurance, being of the highest professional quality both as to completeness and accuracy.

STANDARD DETAIL REQUIREMENTS

For a survey of real property and the plat or map of the survey to be acceptable to a title insurance company for purposes of insuring title to said real property free and clear of survey questions (except those questions disclosed by the survey and indicated on the plat or map), certain specific and pertinent information must be presented for the distinct and clear understanding between the client (insured), the title insurance company (insurer) and the surveyor (the person professionally responsible for the survey). These requirements are:

1. The plat or map of such survey must bear the name, address and signature of the licensed land surveyor who made the survey, his official seal and license number (if any, or both), the date of the survey, and the caption "LAND TITLE SURVEY" with the following certification:

   "To (name of client) and (name of title insurance company, if known).

   This is to certify that this map or plat and the survey on which it is based were made in accordance with the "Minimum Standard Detail Requirements for Land Title Surveys" jointly established and adopted by ATA and ACSM in 1962.

   (Signed) . . . .(SEAL)"

   License No. . . . .

2. The title insurance company or the client, at the time of ordering a survey, should notify the surveyor that a "LAND TITLE SURVEY" is required, and furnish to the surveyor the record description of the property and the record easements or servitudes and covenants affecting the property, to which the "LAND TITLE SURVEY" must subsequently make reference. The names and deed data of all adjacent owners as available, and all pertinent information affecting the property being surveyed, should be transmitted to the surveyor for notation on the plat or map of the survey. If the area of the parcel is required, the title insurance company or the client shall so clearly indicate to the surveyor. If the plat or map of survey is to include thereon a note as to zoning classification of the property and indicate setback or building restriction lines (if such information can be platted on a map) the title insurance company or the client shall so clearly indicate to the surveyor. If applicable, the surveyor shall be informed by the title insurance company or client of any survey requirements of the Federal Housing Administration or Veterans Administration.

3. The surveyor's field work must be performed to locate the property corners accurately. The allowable positional tolerances of said corners may not be greater than

   (a) 0.02 ft. in urban area blocks wherein buildings can be erected along the property line, or where high land values so warrant.

   (b) 0.04 ft. in urban or suburban subdivision interior blocks and/or urban and suburban lots or parcels.

   (c) 1 ft. per 5,000 ft. of perimeter in rural areas except as follows:

   (i) closer tolerance is required where land value in rural areas is increased by adjacency to major highway intersections or thruway complexes, building congestion, oil or mineral rights or land value is increased for any other reason.

   (ii) when a parcel of land is extremely long or narrow, closer tolerance is required on the shorter narrow dimensions to qualify acceptable corner positioning in relation to the narrow width.

   The surveyor shall note on the plat or map of survey the following:

   "Maximum positional tolerance of corners is . . . ."

   When the surveyor has doubt as to the location on the ground of street or lot lines being within the tolerances cited above (for such reasons as street and lot lines being undefinable or indefinite because of insufficient monuments or markers in the ground or where errors are found to exist in the descriptions of legal or recorded plats or maps of streets and lots), the surveyor shall clearly indicate the nature of the difficulty or discrepancy and give his professional opinion as to range and scope of differences possibly involved and the effect, under the circumstances, of same on the surveyed positions. It is expected that the exercise of professional judgment by the surveyor will minimize differences of opinions with other professional surveyors exercising equally prudent judgment in such situation.

4. On the plat or map of a LAND TITLE SURVEY, the survey boundary should be drawn to a convenient scale, with that scale clearly indicated. If feasible, a graphic scale should be indicated. When practical, the plat or map of survey should be oriented so that North is at the top of the drawing. Supplementary or exaggerated scale diagrams should be presented accurately on the plat or map and drawn to scale. No plat or map drawing less than the minimum size of 8½" by 11" will be acceptable.

5. The plat or map of a LAND TITLE SURVEY shall contain, in addition to the items required already specified above, the following applicable information:

   (a) All data necessary to indicate the mathematical dimensions and relationships of the boundary represented, within a required mathematical closure not to exceed 1 part in 10,000; with angles given directly or by bearings; with the length of curve together with the radius chord and chord bearings. Bearings should refer to true North for the area, or to State Plane Coordinate North, or to some well-fixed bearing line so that the bearings may be easily re-established. All bearings around the boundary should read in a clockwise direction. The North arrow, preferably in the upper right quadrant of the drawing, must be referenced to its bearing base.

(b) When record bearings or angles or distances differ from measured bearings, angles and distances, both the record and measured bearings, angles and distances shall be clearly indicated.

(c) Measured and record distances from corners of parcel surveyed, to the nearest right of way lines or streets in urban or suburban areas, together with evidence of found lot corners, should be noted. Where conditions warrant, the distances to the intersecting streets in both directions from the surveyed premises, with the bearing of such streets, should be indicated. Names and legal lines and widths of streets, roads and avenues should be given. Where the surveyor has notice of changes in the lines of such streets or roads, the changes should be noted with the date of and authority under which the change was made.

(d) The identifying title of all record plats or filed maps which the survey represents wholly or in part must be shown with their filing dates, map numbers and the lot, block and section numbers or letters of the surveyed premises. Names of adjoining owners and/or recorded lot or parcel numbers, and similar information where known, must be shown. Interior parcel lines must clearly indicate contiguity, gores and/or overlaps.

(e) All monuments, stakes or marks, **found** or **placed,** must be shown and noted to indicate which were **found** and which were **placed.** All evidence of monuments, stakes or marks found beyond the surveyed premises, on which establishment of the corners of the surveyed premises are dependent, shall be indicated. The character of any and all evidence of possession must be stated and the location of such evidence carefully given in relation to the surveyed boundary lines. Where there is no physical evidence of possession along the record lines, the plat or map of survey must note along the line—"No physical evidence of line".

(f) The character and location of all buildings upon the plot or parcel must be shown and their location given with reference to boundaries. Proper street numbers should be shown where available. Physical evidence of easements and/or servitudes of all kinds, including but not limited to those created by roads; rights of way; water courses; drains; telephone, telegraph or electric lines; water, sewer, oil or gas pipelines, etc., on or across the surveyed property and on adjoining properties if they appear to affect the enjoyment of the surveyed property should be located and noted. If the surveyor has knowledge of any such easements and/or servitudes, not physically evident at time present survey is made, such physical non-evidence should be noted. Surface indications, if any, of underground easements and/or servitudes should also be shown. If there are no buildings erected on the property being surveyed, the plat or map of survey should bear the statement "No Buildings".

The character and location of all walls (independent, division, party or otherwise) and whether or not the same are plumb, buildings or fences within two (2) feet of either side of the boundary lines must be noted. Location of both sides of party walls and thickness should be shown. If the building on premises has no independent wall, but uses any wall of adjoining premises, this condition should be shown and explained. The same requirements apply where conditions are reversed. Physical evidence of all encroaching structural appurtenances and projections including but not limited to fire escapes, bay windows, windows that open out, flue pipes, stoops, eaves, cornices, area-ways, steps, trim, etc., by or on adjoining property or on abutting streets must be indicated with the extent of such encroachment or projection. Openings such as windows, doors, etc., in walls of adjoining premises within two (2) feet of the boundary lines being surveyed (other than street lines) should be shown. If the client or the title insurance company wishes to have same information as above, with regard to walls or buildings more than two (2) feet beyond the boundary lines of the premises being surveyed, the client or title insurance company will assume the responsibility of obtaining such permissions as are necessary for the surveyor to enter upon the adjoining property to make such determination. In the absence of such permissions, the surveyor will not be obligated to so enter.

Joint or common driveways and alleys must be indicated. Independent driveways along the boundary must be shown together with the width thereof. Encroaching driveways, strips, ribbons, aprons, etc., should be noted.

Cemeteries and burial grounds located within the premises being surveyed must be shown by actual location.

Springs, streams, rivers, ponds or lakes located, bordering on or running through the premises being surveyed must be shown by actual location.

Streets abutting the premises not physically opened should be so noted.

6. As minimum requirement, the surveyor shall furnish at least two sets of prints of the plat or map of survey to the title insurance company or the client. The prints should be on durable and dimensionally stable material of a quality standard acceptable to the title insurance company. At least two copies of legal boundary descriptions prepared from the survey shall be similarly furnished by the surveyor. For connecting record, reference to the date of the LAND TITLE SURVEY, surveyor's file number (if any), political subdivision, and similar information shown on the plat or map of survey shall be included and incorporated for documentation.[1]

* * *

§ 52. Illinois survey standards. The Illinois Land Survey Standards are set forth in 57 Ill. B.J. 327.

§ 53. New York survey standards. The New York State Land Title Association standards are available from any title company in that state.

§ 54. Florida survey standards. The Florida survey standards differ substantially from the other standards. They can be obtained from the Florida Society of Professional Land Surveyors, from the Florida Land Title Association, or contact a title insurance company.

§ 55. Chicago Title Insurance Company requirements. This company's requirements are as follows:

The surveyor shall furnish a plat of survey on tracing cloth (and three blueprints) accurately drawn to scale which shall show the following:

A. All dimensions and all angles of the lot or parcel of land surveyed, and the width of all streets on which it faces.

   NOTE: In the event there is a variance between the actual measured dimensions and angles and the recorded or deed dimensions or angles, the latter should also be shown.

   1. That wherever possible iron pipes of a minimum size of 1″ by 36″ have been set at all corners of the lot or parcel and at all points of curve or tangency.

   2. That wherever possible cross (+) notches also have been cut on even foot offsets in walks, curbs or alley pavements adjacent to said parcel.

   3. Any existing marks or monuments by other surveyors.

B. A detail sketch of the block in which the property is located with the actual measured dimensions and angles and, if there is variance, the recorded or deed dimensions and angles from and for each corner of the property surveyed to the block lines. If the property is not in a recorded subdivision, the distance shall be shown to the nearest quarter section or section line.

   NOTE: If there is a variance between actual and record or deed dimensions also show the occupation on the lines farthest from the property in question of the parcels or tracts of land *immediately adjoining* the surveyed property, so that it will appear whether the contiguous owners have the full amount of land called for in their deeds.

C. All improvements on the property surveyed, noting in detail:

   1. The dimensions, type of construction and material, number of stories and official and actual street numbers of all buildings.

   2. The location of all buildings and other improvements with reference to the lot lines, and any encroachments thereof onto adjoining premises.

   3. All party walls, the width thereof, and the center line thereof with reference to the lot lines. A detail sketch should be drawn showing the set backs and center line of the wall.

      NOTE: If a building is exactly on the lot line, the survey should so state, and should also indicate whether foundations extend beyond property lines and whether walls are plumb.

---

[1] Reprinted by permission of American Congress of Surveying and Mapping and American Land Title Association.

D. With reference to adjoining premises:
   1. If improvements on the immediately adjoining lands are within five feet of the property being surveyed, sufficient thereof should be shown to indicate the location of such improvements in relation to premises in question.
   2. If the adjoining premises are unimproved or used for other than building purposes (e.g., parking lot), so state.
E. All easements and similar matters indicating possible use by others of the premises in question, including:
   1. All passageways, walks, driveways, etc. on the property surveyed used by occupants of the adjoining property.
   2. All gates or entrances from adjoining property opening onto premises in question.
   3. All sewers or water lines in city records or found on the ground, and all conduits and wires from service poles crossing the property in question to serve other owners, and mutual steam lines, and utility lines whether overhead or underground, etc.
   4. Any and all encroachments which in any way affect the property surveyed, such as buildings, fences, retaining walls, private walks, public walks or street or alley pavements, eaves, cornices, etc.
   5. Any roadway, railroad tracks, and water courses or ditches.
F. A certificate by the surveyor, substantially as follows:
   "I hereby certify that this survey made under my supervision (*date*) correctly shows the relation of buildings and other structures to the property lines of the land indicated hereon; that the walls of said buildings are plumb and that there are no encroachments of adjoining buildings or structures onto said land, nor overlap of buildings or structures from said land, except as shown.

The Chicago Title Insurance Company, in some areas, requires a Surveyor's Report to be affixed to the survey, as shown in Form No. 1.

§ **56. AIA requirements.** The Architect's Handbook of Professional Practice indicates the following requirements for a survey:

A check list of data to be included in such a survey should include the following:
Boundaries of property, public walks, and planting strips.
Rights-of-way, easements, lampposts, electric wire posts, fire hydrants, manholes, manhole covers, and catch basins (with rim and invert elevations).
Sewers, water and gas mains (location, size, depth).
Interior roads, drives, walks, cultivated areas, fences, walls, pits, quarries, hedges, large boulders, ditches, culverts, cisterns, wells.
Water taps and service stubs (location, size, depth).
Location, size, and variety of trees within the site and nearby.
Elevations of tops of curbs, retaining walls, first floor and basement levels of buildings on or adjoining site, tops and bottoms of all exterior steps, and of surface at center lines of roads and ground at base of trees within the site.
Contour lines at specified intervals.
Location thickness, height and variation from plumb of party walls.
Establishment of a permanent bench mark for use during construction.
Establishment of all corners of the property with permanent stakes or monuments.
Record of subsoil investigations by means of rock soundings at specified intervals in each direction; or borings to rock at specified intervals in each direction; or soil samples at specified locations; or test pits of size and locations as specified.[2]

Subsequent to the adoption of the Architect's Handbook, the AIA developed form G 601, Land Survey requisition, as shown in Form No. 2.

---

[2] This checklist has been reproduced with the permission of the American Institute of Architects. Further reproduction is not authorized.

Form No. 1

ORDER NO:

SURVEYOR'S REPORT

I hereby report to Chicago Title Insurance Company that I have made an accurate survey of the premises situated at

City	County	State

known as Street Numbers_____
and shown on the accompanying map or plat of survey. In connection with such survey I made a careful inspection of said premises on_____, 19_____, and at the time of inspection I found to be in possession of said premises_____as._____
(tenant) or (owner)

    I made a specific examination with respect to the following items and report the existence of evidence of the following: (if none, state "none"):

1. Rights of way, including those for roads, lanes, driveways or walks across said premises serving other property:___ ..

2. Streams, ponds, or lakes located, bordering on or running through said premises:_____

3. Telephone, telegraph or electric power poles or wires overhanging or crossing said premises and serving other property or properties:_____

4. Underground installations such as sewers, water pipes, gas or oil pipe lines, conduits, across said premises:_____

5. Drainage ditches or underground drain tile across said premises: _____

6. Joint driveways or walkways; party or curtain walls; beam rights; porches, steps or roofs used in common or joint garages:_____

7. Encroachments, or overhanging projections (If our building or its eaves, fire escapes, bay windows, doors, flue pipes, stoops, or areaways, or signs affixed thereto, or our fences, walks, drives, gates or entrances encroach upon or overhang properties, or similar adjoining structures encroach upon or overhang our premises specify all such and if buildings are substantially on property lines indicate if walls are plumb and if foundations and footings are within lines): _____

8. Physical evidence of boundary lines on all sides (Be specific as to how boundary lines are evidenced, that is, by fences, plantings, etc. indicate whether same differ from deed lines and whether there is evidence of disagreement as to boundaries): _____

Civil Engineer or Surveyor

Form No. 2

LAND (BOUNDARY) SURVEY REQUIREMENTS: Property dimensions in both U.S.Std. and District Std.

    Error of closure of perimeter of property shall not exceed □ 1/5000 or □ _____

□ 1. Boundary lines, giving length and bearing on each straight line; interior angles; radius, point of tangency, and length of curved lines. Set iron pin (monument) at property corners where none exists; drive pin 18″ into ground, mark with wood stake; state on drawing whether corners were found or set and describe each.

□ 2. Legal description, including measurements in recorded deeds for comparison with observed.

□ 3. Area in square feet if less than one acre, in acres (to .001 acre) if over one acre.

☐ 4. Identity, jurisdiction and width of adjoining street and highways, width and how paved. Identity of landmarks.

☐ 5. Plotted location of structures on the property and on adjacent property within ___ feet. Dimension perimeters in ☐ feet and inches to nearest ½" ☐ feet and decimals to .05'. State character and number of stories. Dimension to property lines and other buildings. Vacant parcels shall be noted VACANT.

☐ 6. Encroachments, including cornices, belt courses, etc., either way across property lines.

☐ 7. Fences and walls; describe. Identify party walls and locate with respect to property lines.

☐ 8. Recorded or otherwise known easements and rights-of-way; state owner of right.

☐ 9. Possibilities of prescriptive rights-of-way and nature of each.

☐ 10. Anticipated street widenings.

☐ 11. Individual lot lines and lot and block numbers. ☐ Street numbers of buildings.

☐ · 12. Zoning of property; if more than one zone, extent of each. ☐ Zoning of adjacent property and property across street or highway.

☐ 13. Building line and setback requirements, if any.

☐ 14. Names of owners of adjacent property.

☐ 15. Reconciliation or explanation of any discrepancies between survey and recorded legal description.

TOPOGRAPHICAL SURVEY REQUIREMENTS: All lines of levels shall be checked by separate check level lines or on previous turning points or benchmarks.

☐ 16. Minimum of one permanent benchmark on site for each four acres; description and elevation to nearest .01'.

☐ 17. Contours at _____ foot intervals; error shall not exceed one-half contour interval.

☐ 18. Spot elevations at each intersection of a_____ foot square grid covering the property and if possible _____ grid interval(s) beyond.

☐ 19. Spot elevations at street intersections and at _____ feet on center on curb, sidewalk, and edge of paving including far side of paving. If elevations vary from established grades, state established grades also.

☐ 20. Plotted location of structures, man-made and natural features; floor elevations and elevations at each entrance of buildings on property.

☐ 21. Location, size, depth and pressure of water and gas mains, central steam, and other utilities serving or on the property.

☐ 22. Location of fire hydrants available to property and size of main serving each.

☐ 23. Location of electric and telephone services and characteristics of service available.

☐ 24. Location, size, depth and direction of flow of sanitary sewers, combination sewers, storm drains and culverts serving or on property; location of catchbasins and manholes and inverts of pipe at each.

☐ 25. Name of operating authority of each utility.

☐ 26. Mean elevation of water in any excavation, well or nearby body; flood level of streams.

☐ 27. Extent of watershed onto property. ☐ Probability of freshets overrunning the site.

☐ 28. Locations of test borings if ascertainable and elevation of top of holes.

☐ 29. Trees of _____" and over (caliper 3' above ground) locate within 1' tolerance and give species.

☐ 30. Specimen trees flagged by Owner or Architect (_____ in number): locate to center within 6" tolerance, give species and caliper and ground elevation on upper slope side.

☐ 31. Perimeter outline only of thickly wooded areas unless otherwise directed.[3]

---

[3] This checklist has been reproduced with the permission of the American Institute of Architects. Further reproduction is not authorized.

§ 57. Accuracy of field work. The standards are concerned with a diversity of matters. One of them is the accuracy of the field work. Obviously, no survey can be perfect. Some deviation from perfection must be expected. ATA and Illinois approach this problem quite realistically. They require a high degree of accuracy in high density areas where valuable buildings can be erected along property lines. Obviously, a skyscraper that extends over the property line presents a serious problem. The ATA Standards are fairly relaxed in "rural areas," because no one expects a farm fence to be exactly on the property line and moving it is no great problem. However, certain circumstances, such as adjacency to a major highway intersection, which shoots land values up, requires a "closer tolerance."

§ 58. Easements. The Illinois Standards illustrate the concern that is felt regarding easements. Thus the standards require the surveyor to show physical evidence of all easements.

The land surveyor must:

Depict and make reference to such record easements or servitudes and covenants and such other easements or servitudes and covenants shown on a recorded subdivision plat, if any, involving the subject property, if such information can be platted on a map.

Thus the surveyor is expected (1) on his own to find and depict the easements shown on the recorded subdivision plat (2) to depict all other recorded easements copies of which have been furnished him, and (3) to find and depict all physical evidences on the ground of possible easements whether recorded or not.

Thus the duties of the surveyor are in keeping with the law of property, which declares that the purchaser of land takes his title subject to:

(1) Recorded easements.
(2) Unrecorded possible implied easements.
(3) Unrecorded possible prescriptive easements.

Moreover these easements must be revealed to the purchaser because:

1. The existence of an easement not mentioned in the contract of sale renders title unmarketable and offers the buyer an opportunity to call off the deal, if he is so inclined.
2. Apart from this question, such easements materially affect building plans and make the buyer vulnerable to disastrous damage.

Note that the surveyor passes no legal judgment on the existence of easements. He depicts the physical facts, permitting the buyer's lawyer to draw the legal inferences.

Let us see how the surveyor's disclosures affect the sale transaction.

EXAMPLE: *A* and *B,* neighbors, verbally agree to construct a party driveway. This is a revocable license not an easement. Either party may terminate the arrangement at will. *Baird v. Westberg,* 341 Ill. 616, 173 NE 820. Here we are dealing not with an easement but with a physical fact that can lead to damage. The buyer's lawyer is entitled to know about it. He can advise his client to insist on a signed, written, easement agreement before the deal is closed if the contract so provides. See Chapter 10.

EXAMPLE: *A* owns two adjoining dwellings and constructs a party drive that services garages in the rear. There is no alley in the rear. *A* sells one of the houses to *B*. An implied easement is created. *Walters v. Gadde,* 390 Ill. 518, 62 NE2d 439. Note how this differs from the first example, where the driveway was constructed by verbal agreement between two property owners. Note that the surveyor has alerted the buyer's lawyer to a physical fact. The lawyer traces the drive back in time, and discovers it was erected at a time when *A* owned both lots. This is what makes this an easement, rather than a revocable license. Now, again, the lawyer advises his client. He now can assure the client that the driveway rights cannot be revoked by his neighbor. But he can also say that if the neighbor does not agree to sign a written driveway agreement and if the contract of sale makes no mention of the driveway easement, the client can still back out of the deal because the title is not marketable. The client may wish to do this because (1) he has changed his mind about the desirability of the deal or (2) because implied easements depend on proof of facts, and often cause trouble. Most of the litigation in easement law is about implied easements.

Most easements are recorded but a surveyor must also show physical evidence of easement use because this gives purchasers notice of the existence of an unrecorded grant of easement as efficaciously as recording of the easement grant.

1. Vehicle tracks crossing the property to reach adjoining premises. *Wallace v. Whitmore,* 47 Cal.App.2d 369 117 P2d 926.

2. Drainage ditch crossing the property to reach adjoining premises. *Harmon v. Rassmussen,* 13 Utah 2d 422 375 P2d 762.

3. A standpipe on adjoining land, near the property line, gave notice of underground pipe crossing the property. *Jones v. Harmon,* 175 Cal.App.2d 869, 1 Cal.Rptr. 192.

4. Pipe beneath basement ceiling crossing basement to reach adjoining house. *Pica v. Cross County Const. Corp.,* 18 N.Y.S.(2)470.

The New York Standards and Illinois Standards require the showing of surface indications of underground easements. A manhole cover, for example, discloses the presence of an underground installation and possible unrecorded easement therefor.

The ATA and Illinois requirements require the showing of windows and doors in adjacent properties, because a door that opens over our property or a casement window that opens over our property might reveal the existence of a prescriptive easement.

A common requirement is the showing of party wall, walks, and drives, for here again an unrecorded easement may be revealed.

If our building has no wall of its own but ties into a neighboring building, this indicates the need for an easement for this purpose if there is no recorded easement. If the converse of this situation exists, an unrecorded prescriptive easement may be revealed.

A common requirement for the showing of drains, electric lines, or telephone lines again smokes out possible unrecorded easements or rights.

§ 59. Encroachments. All the standards reveal a healthy preoccupation with encroachments. If any building extends over and upon your land or over and upon an adjoining street or alley, the title may be unmarketable. If your building encroaches upon my land, that also may render title unmarketable, and, in addition, if it has remained there long enough you have obtained ownership of the encroachment by adverse possession.

The requirements, for example, in New York, want adjoining buildings near the boundary line to be shown. If your building is close to my line, your footings may extend into my ground. Fire escapes, eaves, cornices, and gutters of adjoining buildings are commonly required to be shown, for prescriptive easements may be revealed thereby.

The New York Standards require the surveyor to show the perimeter of the tract as it would be were the deed descriptions to be followed. These are the "record lines" for they are taken from the deed records. Then they require the possession lines to be shown, for if my neighbor's fence or building encroaches on my land, I have either an encroachment problem or an adverse possession problem. If the fences of the land I am buying encroach upon neighboring land, I may be well-advised not to rest content with a deed that conveys only the record title. I may ask the seller for a quitclaim deed to the strip enclosed by the fences. This will give me ownership, if the fences have created title by adverse possession, or will help me acquire title by adverse possession through "tacking."

A common requirement calls for the showing of walks, streets, curbs, etc., for this may reveal the encroachment of an unrecorded public street on our property.

The ATA requirements call for the surveyor to plumb the walls of our building and adjacent buildings, for if our building wall is not plumb, it may encroach into my neighbor's air space, or vice versa.

§ 60. Contiguity. The New York Standards state that where the legal description consists of two or more tracts of land, the surveyor must indicate whether or not they are contiguous. Obviously, if you intend to improve the entire tract, you must be sure that all the pieces fit together. If they do, you can insist on a title company endorsement insuring contiguity, and that requirement belongs in the contract of sale. Alternatively the surveyor can furnish a "perimeter description" showing the entire tract, and this description can be used in the contract of sale. Then if the final survey shows outstanding strips or gores between the various parcels, the buyer is at liberty to rescind.

§ 61. Stakes. The Illinois, New York and ATA Standards require the surveyor to show all monuments, stakes, or marks found or placed at the survey corners. If a stake "placed" by the current surveyor is in a different location from a stake "found" there, a question arises. My neighbor's surveyor may have located his lines so as to enclose a portion of my property. This requires a conference with the current surveyor so as to iron out the inconsistency.

§ 62. Street deviations. If the street or highway on which the property abuts deviates from the lines set forth in the street dedication, it may be that a strip of land intervenes between my property line and the street line. I would lack access to the street. If an ALTA policy is used and the property abuts on only one street, the policy insures access to the street and the title company has assumed that risk. Hence it is a common requirement that the survey show such deviation. If the platted street has not been physically opened, that should also be shown, for it is possible that the public has not accepted the street, and the entire burden of paving and providing sewer and water would fall on the property owner.

§ 63. Rights of way over our property. Chicago Title Insurance Company

Surveyor's Report requires the showing of roads, lanes, driveways or walks across the surveyed property, for they may indicate the presence of unrecorded easements.

§ 64. **Reading the survey.** One should do his first survey reading under the tutelage of an experienced lawyer. The surveyors speak a technical jargon. Where the survey shows ''the East line of the property'' and ''brick 1.1 feet East of line,'' this does not mean that there is one brick at that point. It probably means that the East line of a brick wall encroaches 1.1 feet over the East boundary line of the property, a dangerous situation. It may show two roughly parallel lines, one labeled ''deed line'' or ''record line,'' the other ''occupation line.'' This means, for example, that the fence does not track with the deed line. If it is outside of the deed line, you want a quitclaim because title to the strip between the two lines may have been acquired by adverse possession. On the other hand, if the occupation line is inside the deed line, title to that strip may have been acquired by my neighbor's adverse possession. This, of course, poses several problems. First, does it adversely affect building plans? Second, can the construction lender live with it? Third, will a title company give insurance against the encroachment on the theory that the period for adverse possession has not run? Fourth, does the contract give the seller (mortgagor, lessor, etc.) the right to rescind without liability for damages if there is a material survey question, and if it does, should the parties renegotiate the deal to save it? For example, the sale price could be renegotiated and the seller given the right to except this objection in his warranty deed.

Naturally, the surveyor's legal description on the survey will be carefully checked against the description in the title policy, contract of sale, etc.

§ 65. **Surveyor's certificate.** In addition to his certification that he has surveyed the property, the surveyor should certify that the survey was made in accordance with the standards prescribed in the contract of sale, *e.g.*, ''the Illinois Land Survey Standards.'' If the survey is prepared for the seller, a question arises whether the surveyor is liable to the buyer or the buyer's mortgagee if an error in surveying comes to light. *Rozny v. Marnul,* 43 Ill. 2d 54, 175 NE2d 785 (1961) 64 NWUL Rev. 903. At a minimum, the surveyor should certify that the survey is intended for the benefit of the purchaser or any of his mortgage lenders, also their title companies. The certificate should bear a current date.

§ 66. **Caption of the survey.** The caption contains a legal description of the land surveyed. It should be checked against the seller's title policy.

§ 67. **Contract provisions.** It is best for the seller to include a clause in his contract of sale that defects revealed by a survey can be cured by the title company insuring over loss or damage by reason of said defects. Where the defects are minor, such as slight encroachments, title companies are quite willing to furnish an endorsement insuring over such defects.

§ 68. **Extended coverage.** A typical ALTA owner's policy will list survey questions, boundary disputes, and unrecorded easements as part of the printed exceptions. For an additional premium the company, if satisfied with the survey and the matters it reveals, will delete these exceptions by means of an endorsement. This places the burden of reading the survey on the title company. Many lawyers prefer to recommend this course to a purchaser-client.

§ 69. **The surveyor.** All the surveyors registered under local law are not uniformly competent. On large transactions, some lawyers representing a purchaser, want the contract of sale, in addition to specifying the applicable standards, to list the names of the surveyors who are acceptable to the buyer.

§ **70. Title company lists.** Some title companies have lists of acceptable surveyors.

§ **71. Contract requirements.** Obviously if *E* is expecting a survey that conforms to any of the standard requirements, the requirement for such a survey belongs in the contract or loan commitment.

§ **72. Common survey problems.** The survey requirements outlined in this chapter outline the common survey problems. Still, since they do so in technical language, it seems best to draw attention to the common problems:

EXAMPLE: Our buildings encroach on neighboring land or adjoining public or private streets, alleys, and ways. Adjoining buildings encroach on our land. Our buildings encroach on easements crossing our land. Encroachments exist in the air space above the surface of the ground, as where the walls are not plumb. Subsurface encroachments exist. Where the adjoining building is built to the boundary line, its footings may well extend into our property. Fences, walls, drives, cornices, eaves, window ledges, fire escapes, stoops, canopies, balconies, cross arms, or guy wires of utility poles, wires, and cables serving other property may encroach.

EXAMPLE: Buildings may extend over building lines established by private building restrictions (plats, deeds, etc.) or by zoning ordinances.

§ **73. FHLMC.** FHLMC requirements as to a survey are as follows:

The survey should show, among other things, (1) the location by courses and distances of (a) the plot to be covered by the mortgage, (b) the relation of the point of beginning of said plot to the monument from which it is fixed, (c) all servient easements, (d) the established building line, if any, (e) all easements appurtenant to said plot, and (f) the line of the street or streets abutting the plot and the width of said streets; (2) encroachments and the extent thereof in terms of feet and inches upon said plot or any easement appurtenant thereto; (3) all structures and improvements on said plot with horizontal lengths of all sides and the relation thereof by distances to (a) all boundary lines of the plot, (b) servient easements, (c) established building lines and (d) street lines. If the premises are described as being on a filed map, the survey shall contain a legend relating the plot to the map on which it is shown. The survey must disclose and provide assurance that the improvements erected lie wholly within the boundaries of the premises and that no part thereof encroaches upon or overhangs any easement or right of way or upon the land of others (other than permitted under 3.02(g) and (h), and that the improvements are wholly within the building restriction lines however established and that no adjoining structure encroaches upon the premises or upon any dominant easement appurtenant thereto. If there be any such encroachment, overhang or violation, the same should be clearly shown and will be subject to approval or waiver by FHLMC as set forth in Section 3.02 for home mortgages, or by FHLMC on a case by case basis for multifamily mortgages.

8

Describing the Land, Property, and Interests to Be Transferred or Reserved

§ 74. In general. In a large-scale transaction nothing less than a perfect, legal description is acceptable at all stages of the transaction, including the contract stage.

§ 75. Source of description. If a title policy, abstract, or Torrens certificate has been previously issued on the land that is being sold, and the land sold is identical with the tract mentioned in the title policy, abstract, or Torrens certificate (that is, there have been no subsequent conveyances of portions of the tract, and so forth), then the description may be copied from the title policy, abstract caption, or Torrens certificate, since such documents usually contain accurate descriptions. After the description has been copied into the contract, deed, mortgage, or lease form, the draftsman should have someone read it aloud to him while he follows the description in the title policy, abstract, or Torrens certificate, since even a miscroscopic error in typing may throw the whole description off.

§ 76. Role of surveyor and the title company. If the description is a new one, that is, something other than the identical description contained in a prior title policy, *E's* surveyor and title company should collaborate in the preparation of the description. Only experienced lawyers are equal to the task of carving a description out of a larger tract or assembling a description that includes a number of smaller, independently described parcels.

§ 77. Parts of lots. Care should be exercised in drafting descriptions of parts of lots.

EXAMPLE: A subdivision plat indicated that Lot 2 in block 3 is eighty feet wide. *R,* the owner, gives *E* a deed to the "east forty feet of Lot 2." When *R* sells the remainder of the lot, his description thereof should be "Lot 2, except the east forty feet thereof," and not "the west forty feet of Lot 2." The reason is obvious. Suppose Lot 2 is actually slightly more than eighty feet in width, as it well may be, for the land measurements are not perfectly accurate. Deeds of the east forty feet and the west forty feet of the lot would leave a small strip of land in the middle of the lot still owned by the seller.

When the lot is not a perfect square or rectangle, use of descriptions such as the "east half" or "north half" of the lot should be avoided, since the word "half" usually is considered to mean half by area, and the boundary line will be located with an equal number of square feet on either side thereof. This may result in an unequal division of the frontage of the lot.

A deed of a part of a lot that abuts on a diagonal street should use descriptions like the "northwesterly thirty feet" rather than the "north thirty feet," since if the diagonal street runs in a true northwesterly or northeasterly direction, it is difficult to determine which side of the lot is the "north" side. Cases will be found where two of the boundary lines may lay equal claim to begin the "north" line of the lot.[1]

Where R is selling part of a large tract he owns, E must be sure that local law does not require a plat of subdivision to be recorded. Laws relating to plat approval are commonplace. Attempts to evade these laws take the form of conveyances of part of larger tracts, often by use of metes and bounds descriptions. This is done in an attempt to avoid the requirements of donations of land for parks, schools, etc. now required of "subdividers." To block these evasions some laws define a "subdivision" as any division of land into two or more parts. Severe penalties attach to violation, including refusal of the recorder to accept the deed for recording.

Another problem, of course, is the adequacy of the description. Either a surveyor or a title company should approve it before it is used.

§ 78. Property conveyed. A clause used in a contract for improved property follows:

> Seller agrees to sell and convey to Buyer, who agrees to purchase all that certain land situated in the City of   , County of   , State of   , more particularly described as
>
> (LEGAL DESCRIPTION)
>
> (Which land is hereafter referred to as "the premises")
> Together with all buildings and other improvements erected thereon, fixtures, equipment and other personal property therein contained and used in the operation and maintenance thereof, including but not limited to, all lighting fixtures, electrical equipment, heating equipment and air conditioning equipment, and other specific property listed on Exhibit "A" attached hereto, initialed by the parties and made a part hereof, together with all right, title, and interest of Seller in and to any easements including easements for ingress and egress, drainage of surface and storm water and sanitary sewers, passageways, or rights of way appurtenant to the premises, as well as in and to the beds of streets, open or closed, public or private, existing or vacated, bordering upon the premises, and all awards in condemnation for damages of any kind to which Seller or Buyer may have become entitled or may hereafter be entitled by reason of the exercise of the power of eminent domain with respect to the taking of the premises or any part thereof, being all of the property owned by Seller, within the area described above as the premises.

Technically it is not necessary to describe the buildings on the premises being sold. A full legal description carries buildings because they are fixtures and part of the land. However, in recent times, ownership of the building has been separated from ownership of the fee. This is a tax gimmick for depreciation purposes. Hence, the prudent buyer will insist that the description of the premises sold also include a description of the building sold. Moreover, this is reassuring to a layman buyer. His view is that he is buying the building, and the contract reassures him when it describes it.

Where a mortgage covers after-acquired property, it should call for supplemental mortgages to be recorded to bring these into the chain of title.

---

[1] Copyright Kratovil *Real Estate Law* § 56 (6th ed. 1974). Reprinted by permission.

§ 79. Land assemblies. It is often necessary to acquire and assemble the lands of several adjoining landowners, for example, for a plant site. Here the danger is that the description used may leave small gaps between the parcels. *See* Kratovil, *Real Estate Law* § 468.

§ 80. Reference to prior deed. It is the custom of good lawyers to add after the description of the premises, "being the same premises conveyed to *R* by deed recorded in Book _____ Page __," but this clause must not be construed to reduce the estate to less than the full fee simple title." In the first place, a few states (Kentucky and Tennessee for example) require this recital as a pre-condition to recording of the deed. In the second place, it may cure an error in the description. In the third place, it helps the title examiner locate the property. One must be certain that the premises now dealt with are identical with, not merely a part, of the premises acquired by the described deed. It is also important to make sure that the earlier deed described conveyed the entire fee title, not merely some interest in the land, for otherwise questions arise as to whether the recital cuts down the interest presently dealt with.

§ 81. Adjoining owners. Lands are also described by reference to adjoining lands.

EXAMPLE: A deed described the land as follows: "Bounded on the east by a fifty-acre tract of land owned by G. B. Turner purchased by him from N. W. Rodden; bounded on the north by the right of way of the Texas and Pacific R.R.; and on the west by a fifty-acre tract owned by the said G. B. Turner and known as the J. F. Neal tract of land; bounded on the south by the Katie Moore Boham tract of land." *Cox v. Campbell,* 135 Tex. 428, 143 SW2d 361.

Such a description is unacceptable for any substantial deal. A proper survey must be made before any papers are signed. All corners must be monumented. Then the papers will employ the surveyor's description.

§ 82. Metes and bounds description. The subdividing of land is now carefully regulated. Land developers who wish to avoid these regulations (as to minimum lot size, streets, sewers, and so forth) simply do not prepare or record any formal plat. Instead they sell off each building site by a metes and bounds description. In many states, laws forbid the use of metes and bounds descriptions where the purpose is to avoid the legal safeguards surrounding the platting and subdividing of land. For this reason, *E* should not sign a contract or accept a deed that contains a metes and bounds description unless he is sure it does not violate some local statute. *Metzdorf v. Rumson,* 67 N.J.S. 121, 170 A2d 249. Many metes and bounds descriptions contain references to trees, fences, and other monuments that have long since disappeared. These descriptions are unacceptable on substantial deals and are handled as in the section on adjoining owners.

§ 83. Other indefinite descriptions. Many other descriptions are more or less indefinite, such as those calling for acreage. In substantial deals where big improvements are contemplated, the contract will use a specific description based on a current survey.

§ 84. Metes and bounds descriptions—FHLMC requirements. FHLMC requirements as to metes and bounds descriptions are as follows:

A metes and bounds description should comply with the following standards:
(1) The beginning point should be established by a monument located at the beginning point, or by reference to a nearby monument.

(2) The sides of the security should be described by giving the distances and bearings of each. In lieu of bearings it is equally acceptable to use the interior angle method, provided that the beginning point is located on a public street line or other properly fixed line or the course of the first side can be otherwise properly fixed.

(3) The distances, bearings and angles should be taken from a recent instrument survey, or recently recertified instrument survey, by a licensed Civil Engineer or Registered Surveyor.

(4) Curved courses should be described by data including: length of arc, radius of circle for the arc and chord distance and bearing. Exception—if deemed adequate locally by prudent institutional investors when a curved course is part of a public street or road line, that course may be described merely by indicating the distance and direction which that course takes along the street line from the end of the previous course.

(5) The legal description should be a single perimeter description of the entire premises. Division into parcels should be avoided unless a special purpose of the specific Loan is served. Division would be necessary, however, if the premises is located on two sides of a public way. It is also customary in many areas to describe an easement appurtenant to a fee parcel by using a separate parcel description.

§ 85. Land beyond deed lines—encroachments. At times R occupies land extending beyond the property lines described in the deed to R. For example, R may have fenced and farmed five or ten feet beyond his property line. He may have acquired title to this land by adverse possession. The survey will disclose this. He should be willing to agree to give a quitclaim deed to this land. If possession has not yet ripened into title, the quitclaim makes it easier for E to "tack" $R's$ possession to his own for adverse possession purposes.

SUGGESTED CLAUSE: If the survey reveals occupation by the seller of land beyond the boundaries of the property herein described, seller will, at closing, give buyer a quitclaim deed to the land so occupied.

Where the building encroaches on adjoining property, a decision must be made as to whether the land encroached upon will be included in the description, Patton, *Titles* § 161. R will prefer to exclude such land and agree only to give a quitclaim deed thereto. If it is included in the description, subsequent contract language may require R to include such land in the title policy, which the title company may decline to do.

§ 86. Lease descriptions—in general. The requirements as to the description to be used depend on the nature of the lease.

§ 87. Lease descriptions—ground lease or lease of entire building. Where the lease is a ground lease or lease of an entire building, the description must be a full legal description, taken from the owner's title insurance policy and accompanied by a survey. Danger is present in older areas where two contiguous buildings have a common entrance but no common foundations. Here use of a street address might create catastrophic uncertainty.

§ 88. Lease descriptions—lease of story of building. A lease of a story of a building leases the interior and outer surfaces of the outside walls of the building, the horizontal boundaries being the planes of the ceiling and floor extended outward. This is important, for if there is no other regulation of exterior signs, the tenant must keep his signs within the boundaries of the planes thus projected. Balconies, awnings, etc. falling within these planes are part of the leased premises. But such a lease does not include the roof, lobby, stairways, elevators, escalators, basement, or any other portions of the building, though implied easements may exist for their use. Obviously, if the tenant expects to use storage space in the basement this should be spelled out.

§ **89. Maps—colored boundary lines.** Often one encounters a description referring to areas outlined in various colors. This is usable in contracts of sale or other documents that are not to be recorded. The recorder photographs everything in black and white.

§ **90. Licenses.** A business that cannot be operated without license, *e.g.*, a tavern, hospital, convalescent home, is worthless to a purchaser who cannot procure a license. Many such licenses do not "run with the land," for they are granted or withheld depending on the moral character of the applicant. Obviously, a contract of sale of such property must be made contingent on the purchaser's ability to procure the license.

§ **91. Condemnation award.** The contract of sale may give *E* the right to rescind if condemnation proceedings are instituted before closing. If not, the contract should assign to *E* any condemnation award that may be made after the date of the contract.

§ **92. Farm and ranch requirements.** A contract of sale of farm or ranch land may need to call for transfer of crops (harvested or unharvested), hay or other feed, livestock, farm machinery, shares of stock in farm co-ops or other farm organizations, shares in a water company, livestock brands, etc. An attorney skilled in these matters is needed.

§ **93. Certificate of convenience and necessity.** There are decisions holding that a certificate of convenience and necessity is personal in character and cannot be assigned. 15 ALR2d 883. Obviously, one purchasing a business that requires such a certificate must take notice of this problem.

Obviously, if *E* desires to carry on such a business, a contract of sale must state as a pre-condition to closing, that such a certificate issues to *E* or that he has obtained satisfactory assurances that it will issue.

§ **94. Undivided interests.** Where a description includes an undivided interest, care must be exercised. For example, where an undivided interest is mentioned with respect to the first parcel, questions will arise as to whether this carries over to the subsequent parcels. Patton, *Titles* § 146. Problems are created where the quantum of the undivided interest as recited in the deed differs from the interest owned by *R*. 2 Devlin, *Deeds*, § 838a. Where *R* conveys an undivided interest in an undivided interest, the problem of double fractions arises. 11 S.W. L.J. 281.

§ **95. Exceptions and reservations.** Exceptions and reservations must be drafted with great care. 139 ALR 1339. Where a true exception exists, piling an exception on the exception is bad draftmanship.

EXAMPLE: Lot 20 except the west 50 ft. thereof, except the north 20 ft. thereof. It is hard to tell what this means.

Exceptions in favor of strangers are, of course, poor draftmanship, 24 Hastings L.J. 469.

§ **96. Development rights—transfer.** The sale of development rights is a modern development, as yet untested by the courts.

EXAMPLE: In its simplest form, building *A* is 40 stories high and is a historic landmark. If it were demolished a 50-story building could be erected. The owner of building *A* transfers his right to build the additional ten stories to a neighbor who will erect a building ten stories higher than would otherwise be permitted. 1 Real Estate Journal 163; 83; 82 Yale L.J. 338; 85 Harv.L.Rev. 574; 23 Miami L.Rev. 347.

§ **96a. Air space.** It has been held that a long-term lease of a building automatically carries the air space above the building. *Newport Associates Inc. v. Solow*, 30 N.Y. 2d 263, 332 N.Y.S. 2d 617, 283 NE2d 600. If the landlord has plans to develop the air rights, he must reserve them in his lease. Arguably, then, any deed, mortgage, or other transfer of a building (separated from ownership of the land) carries the air space above the building.

§ **97. Waters and water rights.** Where the land is bounded on waters, or where waters fall within the legal description, the good draftsman locates the boundary lines with special care. If the developer wants the descriptions to stop at the water's edge (so that he can control the lake) this must be done with care. Special mention may be made of the bed of a stream or non-navigable lake. Accretions, relictions, and filled land may be specially mentioned. The subject clause requires special attention. Rights of the public and state and federal government may be included in the subject clause. At times a factual determination may be needed before the description is drawn. For example, if a current exists, the body of water may be a stream rather than a lake. Swamp land is land, not water. Title does not pass by conveyance of the neighboring land. Moreover, local wetlands laws and regulations may belong in the subject clause as a precautionary matter at the least. The right to build on wetlands is subject to drastic regulation in some states.

In the arid states, the matter of water rights is one of considerable importance. Before the description can say anything regarding water rights, the parties must be clear in their own minds as to what *R* can convey.

In some of the water rights states, a water right passes with a deed of the land it serves. In other water rights states, they do not pass with a deed. In some water rights states, there are statutory procedures that must be complied with. Trelease, *Charges and Transfers of Water Rights*, 13 Rocky Mtn. Min. L. Inst. 507. Failure to follow statutory procedures for transfer of water rights may result in loss of the right of prior appropriation. 5 Powell, *Real Property* § 737.

Evidence of the existence, ownership, and abandonment of water rights is a complex affair. Ross, *Acquisition of Existing Water Rights*, 13 Rocky Mtn. Min. L. Inst. 477; Dewsnup, *Assembling Water Rights for a new Use*, 17 Rocky Mtn. Min. L. Inst. 613; Clark, *Waters and Water Rights* (1970) *passim*.

Exceptions or reservations of water and mineral rights should spell out the type of estate reserved. Bad draftmanship, for example, may result in the creation of a revocable license. 7 U.C.L.A.L.Rev. 383.

§ **98. Minerals.** Whether the sale should exclude or include mineral rights is an important decision. Obviously a careful investigation must precede the making of this decision. The same applies to reservations of minerals.

§ **99. Sewers.** *R* may own the sewers in the street or ways adjoining. 52 ALR2d 263; 9 U Fla.L.Rev. 225; 147 ALR 660. The decision must then be made whether *R* wishes to convey the sewer to *E* or to reserve it and merely grant *E* and easement to use it.

9

Street and Highway Requirements and Problems

§ **100. In general.** Whatever the character of the deal (purchase, lease, mortgage, etc.), if the land abuts on a highway intended as access to the development, special problems exist.

§ **101. Intervening strips—adjacency to the highway.** Obviously, the intended user requires access to the highway. If the legal description is such that a strip or gore intervenes between the land and the highway, disaster occurs. Therefore the intended user will stipulate in the contract for an opinion of an attorney satisfactory to him that the land abuts on the highway in question. Current ALTA policies insure "access" to the premises, but this requirement is satisfied if the land abuts on a side street, which, of course, is unsatisfactory to the intended user.

§ **102. Public, opened street.** The intended user wants to be sure that the highway is public, not private, and is presently being maintained by the public. Rather than relying on what meets the eye, let the opinion of counsel cover this point.

§ **103. Limited access highways.** If the land abuts on an existing or proposed limited access highway, it may be worthless to the intended user. He needs an opinion of counsel that the highway is not a limited access highway and an affidavit from the seller that he knows of no plans to convert to a limited access highway.

§ **104. Maps of future streets.** Under the laws of some states, public bodies file, in some public office, maps of future streets. 36 ALR3d 794; 22 Booklyn L.Rev. 17. Such streets may disturb the existing pattern of access, for example, by locating a limited access highway between the land and an intended destination. The intended user should try for opinion of counsel that no such plan exists. Of course, such a map may show a highway extending over the land itself, cutting it in two parts. The opinion of counsel should cover this point also.

§ **105. Title to existing public streets.** Whatever the character of the transaction, *E* wants a provision requiring *R* to agree to convey all his interest in abutting streets. For example, where a metes and bounds description is used, in some states this does not carry title to adjoining streets.

§ **106. Private streets.** If the premises abut on a "private street," this means that access by means thereof depends on the validity of a private easement, because a private street is merely an easement. It is indispensably necessary that the contract of sale call for title insurance that insures the right of access via the private street. The current ALTA policy insures only "access." It does not insure access via the street you see on the ground. If you can't get in and out, you are dead. *E* should require easement insurance. And *E* should require that the easement insurance run in favor of *all* the premises. It is truly amazing how many lawyers are unaware of the rule that an easement cannot be used to service non-dominant land. Kratovil, *Real Estate Law* § 42.

The rule applicable to a public road that a description of adjoining land runs to the center of the road is, in most states, applicable to land abutting on a private street or other private right of way, such as railroad, canal, ditch, or storm drain channel. *Rio Bravo Oil Co. v. Weed,* 121 Tex. 427, 50 SW2d 1080, 85 ALR 404; 11 C.J.S. 593; 1 Patton, *Titles* 381.

> **EXAMPLE:** The right of way of the West Surburban Railroad ran east and west through the center of *R's* land. *R* also owned the land in the right of way, subject to the railroad company's easement for street railroad purposes. He made a deed to *E* of the part of his land "bounded on the north by the West Surburban Railroad."

This description actually includes the south half of the right of way. *Talbot v. Mass. Mut. Life Ins. Co.,* 183 Va. 882, 14 SE2d 335.

In a few states this rule is not followed. *Stuart v. Fox,* 129 Me. 407, 152 Atl. 413. It is, therefore, preferable that a contract, deed, or other document relating to land bounded on private way make reference to the private way. Thus the description in a contract or deed of lot abutting on a private alley might conclude with a phrase like: "also the east half of the private alley lying west of, and adjoining, said lot."

§ **107. Land abutting vacated streets or alleys.** There is a conflict of authority as to the effect of a contract or deed that relates to land abutting on a vacated street or alley. 49 ALR2d 982, 1002. Some cases hold that the vacated street or alley does not pass unless mentioned in the deed. However, normally the grantee intends to acquire this area, and certainly it can do the grantor no good after he has conveyed. Describe the premises as "Lot 1 and the West half of vacated alley lying East of and adjoining Lot 1."

§ **108. Document provisions.** There is some tendency for lawyers to rely on boilerplate clauses following the property description like the following:

> **CLAUSE:** Together with mortgagor's present and future interest in all public or private ways and all vacated public ways on which the premises abut.

This is better than nothing but it is not good enough. Clearly the application for title insurance and the title policy will cover only the legal description contained in the mortgage or other instrument. Hence the necessity of getting into the instrument itself the appropriate language, as "Lot 1 and the West half of vacated alley lying East of and adjoining Lot 1."

10

Title Requirements—
Marketable Title—Subject Clause

§ **109. Marketable title—title insurance.** In general, R in a contract of sale will prefer not to be required to furnish a marketable title. He will argue that E should be satisfied with a title company policy. If E objects, R may offer to furnish a title company policy that insures marketability. $R's$ thinking here is that unless the policy provides that the title policy is in lieu of a marketable title or is conclusive evidence that the title is marketable, the law requires him to furnish a marketable title as well as a title policy. The danger to R is that if E wants to back out of the deal he can instruct his lawyer to comb the title looking for minor defects that title companies ignore but that nevertheless make the title unmarketable. Indeed, much of the law in marketable title arose in cases where the buyer was trying to back out of a deal. The buyer's lawyer, in such case, will focus on the recent history of the title. Suppose, for example, that O, the landowner, died a year ago and his heirs sold the property to R, the present owner and seller without going through probate of the estate. The title company would issue a clear policy to R even though the time for filing claims against the estate had not expired, the title company being furnished a surety company bond that protects it against claims against $O's$ estate. Just the same, the title is unmarketable. E can rescind unless the contract requires him to accept a title policy in lieu of marketable title. E, on the other hand, may want a marketable title, because even if he gets a title policy insuring that his title is marketable, he may, when he goes to sell, encounter a buyer who wants a marketable title as well as a title policy and he then has the same problem the seller was confronted with as outlined above. The problem is magnified where the buyer is planning to erect a substantial building. Defects a title company is willing to overlook for a policy of $25,000 look more substantial when a policy of $10,000,000 is requested, especially if litigation has been filed meanwhile. Perhaps a reasonable compromise is for the buyer to insist on a marketable title policy in the sum of $10,000,000, the seller paying only for insurance of $25,000, the buyer paying the balance.

Some contracts are ineptly worded and leave the inference that the title need only be marketable at the date when the evidence of title is furnished the buyer. To put this matter at rest the contract should make it clear that the title at closing will remain identical with the title at the earlier date. Then the buyer arranges for a formal or informal bring down of the title just before closing of the deal.

There are a number of decisions that treat title acquired by adverse possession as marketable title. *E* will therefore contract for a "marketable title of record" if he plans to insist on marketable title.

In some areas it is the practice to state in the contract that *R's* obligation with respect to title is satisfied "if a title company authorized to do business in this state is willing to issue its owners policy at its regular rates insuring *R* subject only to the objections set forth in this contract." The reference to "regular rates" excludes a policy which the title company is willing to issue because it has received an extra premium to overlook some defect of greater or less significance. This form is also adapted to the situation in some states where it is the custom for *E* to procure title insurance at his own expense.

In some states, it is the custom to state that, *with respect to the matters covered by the title policy*, the policy is conclusive that the title is good as therein stated. If the title policy is issued subject to printed exceptions, such as survey matters, the policy is, under this clause, not conclusive on the question of defects revealed by a survey.

§ 110. Title standards. Many states and even some counties have Title Standards outlining, in large part, the circumstances under which various title defects can be disregarded. They have no legal force, but since they represent the views of the local experts in property law, they are often persuasive.

§ 111. Mortgages. The most important title defect to be considered by the contract draftsman is the mortgage to be cleared at closing out of the purchase price. 53 ALR3d 678. This is considered elsewhere. *See* Chapters 16, 17 and 19.

§ 112. Restrictions. The printed objection "Building restrictions and conditions of record," found on house sales, is totally unacceptable in the large-scale transaction. If there is a restriction, it is set up specifically, *e.g.*, "Restrictions contained in Document 12345." A verbatim copy of this is furnished *E's* lawyer, who examines it before the contract is signed. The restriction might prohibit the building *E* plans to build or may show that the existing building violates the restrictions.

If a restriction exists, it may be unenforceable because of change of neighborhood. In such cases, *E* will insist on a title company endorsement that insures over enforceability of the restrictions, and this should be covered in the contract.

§ 113. Natural rights. Since natural rights, such as the right of riparian owners to the flow of a stream, are not encumbrances that render title unmarketable or breach a covenant against encumbrances, they need not be shown in the subject clause. *Kleinberg v. Ratett*, 252 N.Y. 236, 169 NE 289; *Ben-Hor Corp. v. Conant Realty Co.*, 107 N.J.Eq. 11, 151 A 554; 66 C.J. 923.

§ 114. Easements. The printed objection "easements of record," found in some house sales, is unacceptable in the large-scale deals. The easement might run through the middle of the land and effectively block any construction. Again, any easement is set up specifically and examined before the contract is signed.

§ 115. Drainage ditches and drain title. A farmer-seller may have a title policy subject to "drainage ditches and drain title" that extend over neighboring farms and drain adjoining land. A buyer intending to build cannot accept the objection. His building may block drainage and trigger lawsuits by the high ground adjoining. *E's* engineer must determine before the contract is signed whether a drainage problem exists.

§ 116. Violations of zoning and building ordinances. In some states, violations of zoning or building ordinances do not render title unmarketable. And the usual title policies do not insure against such matters. This leaves *E* totally exposed unless he insists that title will be conveyed free and clear of violations of zoning and building ordinances.

§ 117. Taxes. After the contract has been signed and evidence of title furnished *E*, *E* should check the taxes to see that they cover all interests in the property.

EXAMPLE: The tax records on the property showed the taxes as paid. However, the minerals had previously been conveyed separately, and the local law required a separate assessment of the minerals. Despite the tax records, there is a tax delinquency as to the minerals. *People v. O'Gara Coal Co.* 231 Ill. 172, 83 NE 140.

§ 118. Environmental controls. No law has emerged as yet concerning the impact of environmental matters on marketability of title. The enactment of a statute should not affect marketability. Where an environmental regulation is violated, the parties may have to consider the possible analogy of violations of zoning and building ordinances. Where a ''no development'' map has been filed (coastal zones, wetlands) a legal enigma exists.

§ 119. Miscellaneous title objections. In addition to those well-known, there are almost innumerable title objections a resourceful attorney for *R* will seek to find a home for in the subject clause, *e.g.;*

1. Concessions and licenses.

EXPLANATION: This is discussed in Chapter 21. Purely revocable licenses probably do not render title unmarketable. Today most licenses are contractual in nature and may be irrevocable by their terms. Concessions are common in discount houses, department stores, and even in apartment buildings.

2. Advertising leases.

3. Mineral rights.

EXPLANATION: In the West, the record will, in some instances, fail to reveal the existence of outstanding mineral rights. For example, where a patent has been issued pursuant to an Act of Congress requiring minerals to be reserved to the United States, the fact that the reservation is omitted in the patent is immaterial. The statute creates an outstanding mineral right.

4. Water rights.

EXPLANATION: In the West, the law of water rights is complex. Decisions are conflicting as to whether the existence of water rights over the land renders title unmarketable.

5. Drainage rights.

EXPLANATION: If the drainage rights are natural rights, such as the right under case law of high ground to drain over low ground, this does not render title unmarketable. It is part of the law of the land.

But if there are prescriptive drainage rights or drainage rights other than natural rights, they may render title unmarketable. Drainage rights created by recorded grant must go in the subject clause.

6. Rights of riparian owners in streams.

EXPLANATION: Again, if the only rights are those under case law of riparian owners to the flow of the stream, this is part of the law of the land, and need not be mentioned in the subject clause. But if riparian owners have acquired prescriptive rights to dam the stream, to pollute it, or to withdraw more water than the law allows, these matters may render title unmarketable. Such rights must go in the subject clause.

7. Rights of the United States, the public, or the State in land now or formerly covered by navigable water or tidewater.

EXPLANATION: This is touched upon elsewhere. *See* Chapter 21. It is a matter of importance. Especially where the land is known to be filled land, the right of the United States, for example, to compel removal of the fill goes on forever, even where the Corps of Engineers gave a permit to fill. All such permits are perpetually revocable.

8. Rights of the public in highways that cross the property.

EXPLANATION: This item is unnecessary in most states. The presence of open and used highways does not render title unmarketable. But careful draftsmen insert it because it has given rise to litigation.

9. Obvious easements.

EXPLANATION: This is a tangled area of the law. Some states say that obvious easements, if beneficial (*e.g.,* easements for public utilities) do not render title unmarketable. Other states limit this to obvious public easements. Some states say that any obvious easement, private or public, does not render title unmarketable. Needless to say, the draftsmen cover this point.

10. Encroachments on easements.

EXPLANATION: This is a common cause of unmarketable title and one often overlooked. The law is complex. Whether a building located over an underground cable easement is an encroachment is a subject on which authorities disagree.

11. Encroachment upon public ways, at, below, or above ground level.

EXPLANATION: Again the decisions are conflicting. Old-fashioned bay windows, extending into the air space above the street, render title unmarketable in some states, not in others. The same is true of steps or stoops.

12. Encroachments of improvements of adjoining landowners, including drive and walk encroachments.

13. Encroachment of improvements of premises in question upon adjoining land, including drive and walk encroachments.

14. Violations of building or zoning ordinances.

15. Violations of federal or state laws or regulations.

EXPLANATION: Novel areas of unmarketability are bound to arise, *e.g.*, violations of Securities Acts, energy crisis regulations, environmental control regulations, etc.

16. Maps of future streets.

EXPLANATION: The decisions are unsatisfactory as to whether official maps of future streets crossing our premises render title unmarketable.

17. Violation of acts relating to subdivision approval.

EXPLANATION: Here again there are novel problems. Probably some such violations render title unmarketable because each purchaser, under some laws, can rescind a purchase in an illegal subdivision.

18. Lack of access to public ways.

EXPLANATION: This problem is unresolved in most states.

19. Failure to comply with laws relating to recording.

EXPLANATION: Various laws today, few of them well-considered, state that no document shall be accepted by the recorder unless it contains the name of the draftsman, has typed signatures beneath the signatures, states the name of the party to pay real estate taxes, states the actual consideration, and so on. Nevertheless, the recorder accepts the document, since he (and many lawyers) are ignorant of the statutory requirements. One or two court decisions say such documents do not impart constructive notice. Arguably, then, you do not have a marketable title of record.

§ **120. Subject clause.** In analyzing the title to the property, attorneys for *R* and *E*, to some extent, cover the same ground. Both will look at the existing title policy. For example, *R* looks at it in order to list in his contract all the items to which the title is subject, for he dare not sign a contract for an unencumbered title if the title is, in fact, encumbered. *E's* attorney looks at the title policy to see if there is some unacceptable restriction or easement, for example, for there is not much point in negotiating a lengthy contract on a deal that will never close. The attorneys will check with the title company formally or informally for condemnation suits, or other litigation. There is not much point in going forward with a deal that is certain to be killed by pending litigation.

R's attorney in general, will be endeavoring to unearth any title objections (1) occurring since the date of the last title policy or (2) title objections covered by the "fine print" of the last title policy such as "easements not disclosed of record" or "survey questions." Both of these are common "fine print" exclusions in an owner's form title policy. *R's* attorney will not want to bind *R* to deliver a clear title if, in fact, the title is not clear.

R's attorney ought to check for recent violations of zoning or building ordinances that might render title unmarketable. He ought to check the premises for the presence of unrecorded easements. He takes the last existing survey along on this inspection trip to see if any physical change has taken place, for example, a new building on neighboring land that might encroach on our property. If any such new developments have taken place, he will have the surveyor come out to check if an encroachment exists. He inquires of *R* whether, since the last title search, there are any judgments, tax liens, or divorce proceedings against *R* that might cloud the title. He is then in a position to draft the clauses listing the defects or encumbrances to which the title is subject. These are always drawn in specific terms, not general terms. *See* Chapter 34 (Ground Leases) for a detailed subject clause.

The parties will draft the encroachments portion of the subject clause with great care. They will give thought to subsurface encroachments, such as footings. Encroachments in the air space (bay windows, building not plumb) are also considered. The question of encroachments upon easements is also given thought.

The subject clause in the deed will have to track with the subject clause in the contract of sale. Its office is to relieve the grantor of liability for the items listed. It is growing in importance as the decisions continue to weaken the doctrine that the contract of sale merges in the deed. In no case is the subject clause used to create rights, such as easements. *E* examines the subject clause carefully, both in the contract and deed. He may be estopped to deny the validity of an item appearing in the subject clause. 31 C.J.S. *Estoppel* § 38. *E* will wish to avoid the problem of reviving expired rights (such as building restrictions) which arises if the expired rights appear in the subject clause.

In preparing a subject clause, *R's* lawyer will include items that do not or may not render the title legally unmarketable. This is done in order to avoid controversies as to whether the title is or is not marketable.

EXAMPLE: A utility company has strung an electric line over the property, possibly under verbal permission from some prior owner. *R* will seek to have this included in the subject clause.

E's lawyer, of course, will take the opposite tack. If there are matters that could hamper *E's* plans, *E* doesn't want the property whether or not they render title unmarketable.

In the last example, it is quite possible that the existence of the electric line does not render title unmarketable. Yet if it runs through the middle of *R's* vacant land, *E* will have to struggle with the utility company to have the line moved. Quite often, courts will issue injunctions halting any attempt to remove the line while the utility company proceeds to condemn an easement. The reasons for this are obvious. Homeowners, hospitals, etc. cannot be deprived of power because of squabbles between landowners and utility companies. This is why *E* wants the survey to show all matters that could cause problems, whether or not they technically render title unmarketable. *See* Chapter 7. At this point *E's* lawyer should re-read Chapter 7, making particular point of the matters mentioned in the Surveyor's Report included therein. *E* will then try for a clause somewhat as follows:

CLAUSE: Without regard to questions of marketability of title or the legal right to maintain any of the following, it is agreed that *E* shall have the right to rescind if the survey or *E's* physical inspection of the premises reveal any of the following: (Here list items like those included as items 1 to 7 of the surveyor's report).

§ 121. Subject clause—leases and licenses. The Restatement of Property 2d lists a number of title objections (mortgages, possibilities of reverter, rights of entry, easements, running covenants, etc) that will enable T to terminate the lease prior to taking possession. Restatement of Property 2d § 4.2. This suggests the necessity of extreme care in preparing a subject clause for a substantial lease.

Where vaults beneath a street or other revocable licenses are transferred, it is best to include in the subject clause a statement regarding rights of revocation of such licenses (they are almost always revocable) to avoid any implication that the transferee will have any rights against the transferor if the license is revoked by the city.

§ **122. Subject clause—time problems.** Preparation of a subject clause on a substantial transaction involves problems. Technically, R ought to draft into the subject clause every burden on the title. Technically, further, this would require R to obtain: (1) a current title search, (2) a current survey (3) a current inspection of the premises, (4) a current certificate by the building manager as to existing leases, options, covenants to furnish heat, operating agreements, etc.

On the other hand, this will all have to be done over for E after the contract of sale is signed. Some compromises may be necessary. $R's$ attorney may be content to use $R's$ title policy as an accurate reflection of the condition of the title, especially if it is of recent date. R must be cross-examined by his attorney to determine if complications might be present, such as unpaid federal liens, placing of title in a subsidiary, etc., taking place after the date of the last policy.

If a fairly recent, good-quality survey is available, the surveyor can be given this survey and asked to give an informal opinion based on his examination of the premises, as to the possible existence of survey questions arising since the date of the survey. He can also be asked to give a preliminary surveyor's certificate as to utility wires serving other properties and other matters not covered explicitly in the old survey. Obviously, the building manager will co-operate in giving his information as to tenants, etc. He wants to keep his job.

§ **123. Title exceptions permitted by FHLMC.** FHLMC has listed certain title exceptions it deems unobjectionable. To the extent that this constitutes a sophisticated appraisal of these permitted exceptions, based in large part on the prior vast experience of FHA, these are illuminating provisions.

Waiver of Title Exceptions—Home Mortgages. The prior liens and encumbrances, listed below, to title of the real estate which secures a conventional home mortgage are acceptable under Section 2.1(b) of the Master Selling Agreement Conventional without express approval by FHLMC.

Note: Upon or prior to delivery of a conventional home mortgage, Seller must by letter request FHLMC to issue a written waiver of any other prior lien or encumbrance. Where Seller, in reliance on a general waiver set forth below, does not request a written waiver of an exception, Seller warrants that each condition stated in the general waiver (such as lack of interference with use) has been met. FHLMC considers it good practice for Sellers to document such factual determinations in the mortgage file by certification of the appraiser or surveyor, but FHLMC does not require written certification.

a. Any subsurface public utility easement for local residential distribution, such as for gas or water lines or electric, telephone or CATV cable, the location of which is ascertainable and fixed, provided that the exercise of the rights thereunder will not interfere with the use of any present or potential future improvements on the subject property.

b. Any surface easement for public utilities for local residential distribution along one or more of the property lines and extending not more than twelve feet therefrom, the location of which is ascertainable and fixed, provided that the exercise of the rights thereunder will not interfere with the use of any present or potential future improvements on the subject property or the use of that part of the property outside of the easement and not occupied by improvements.

c. Encroachment on an easement for public utilities by a garage or other improvement, other than those which are attached to or a portion of the main dwelling structure, provided such encroachment does not interfere with the use of the easement or the exercise of rights of repair and maintenance in connection therewith.

d. Agreements providing relief for cost, minimum size, architectural, aesthetic, building material or similar restrictions relating to the dwelling, or set-back restrictions (other than those imposed by zoning or other use restrictions) which do not provide for a penalty or reversion or forfeiture of title, or right to injunctive relief pending correction, or a lien of any kind for damages, so long as no violation of any such agreements exist.

e. Mutual easement agreement of record which establishes a joint driveway or a party wall constructed either partly on the subject property and partly on adjoining property, or wholly on the subject property, or wholly on the adjoining property, provided the easement agreement allows all future owners, their heirs and assigns forever, unlimited use of the driveway or party wall without any restriction other than restriction by reason of the mutual easement owner's rights in common and duties as to joint maintenance.

f. Fence misplacements of one foot or less on either side of the subject property line, provided that neither the misplacement nor a future correction thereof will interfere with the use of any improvements of the subject property or the use of the balance of the property not occupied by improvements.

g. Encroachments on the subject property by improvements on adjoining property where such encroachments extend one foot or less over the property line, have a total area of 50 square feet or less, do not touch any buildings, and do not interfere with the use of any improvements on the subject property or the use of property not occupied by improvements.

h. Encroachments on adjoining property by eaves or other projections attached to improvements on the subject property or by a driveway appurtenant to the subject property where such encroachments extend one foot or less beyond the property line, provided that as to a driveway encroachment there exists a clearance of at least eight feet between the buildings on the subject property and the property line affected by such encroachment.

i. Outstanding oil, gas, water or mineral rights which are customarily waived by local private institutional mortgage lenders, and will not result in damage to the property or impairment of the use of the property for residential purposes, provided that such rights only attach below 500 feet, that there are no rights of surface entry incident to such oil, gas, water or mineral rights, and that rights of subjacent support of the mortgaged premises are provided.

j. Restrictive covenants appearing of record in plat, deed or agreement, covering use, set-back, costs, and similar matters (other than single family use restrictions on 2-4 family properties), provided that there is no forfeiture or reversion in the event of violation thereof and no right to injunctive relief pending correction.

k. Liens for real estate or ad valorem taxes and assessments not yet due and payable.

11

Title Insurance—in General

§ **124. In general.** The great majority of substantial real estate deals involves the use of title insurance. The reasons for this are numerous and compelling; among them: (1) For large financial institutions the mere storage of bulky abstracts of title poses an economic problem. (2) Other forms of title evidence offer no protection against hidden risks, such as forgery of mortgage releases. Kratovil, *Real Estate Law* §§ 266, 267. This is a consideration not to be shrugged off, given the fact that in one year in Houston the operations of such a forger cost the title companies several million dollars. (3) Other forms of title evidence offer no duty to defend law suits attacking the title. (4) Title companies offer a wide variety of special coverages, *e.g.*, protection against existing violations of building restrictions, assurance of zoning compliance, and so on.

§ **125. Types of policies—title commitments.** There are a number of types of title policies. There is, first of all, the owner's policy. A contract for the sale of land calls for proof of good title in the form of a title policy. In practice, the contract calls for the issuance of a title company's commitment to insure. This commitment is issued to the buyer, in an amount equal to the purchase price. This is done so that if title objections appear (outstanding tax liens, mechanic's liens, dower rights, claims against a deceased estate, etc.), the seller is afforded an opportunity to clear these defects within the time permitted by the contract of sale. At times, the commitment will specify that the policy of a named title company is required. This occurs where the lawyers have done business with the named title company and can depend upon it not to raise frivolous objections. At times, the contract will state that the title policy must be one that the title company is willing to issue *at its regular rates*. This is done because title companies sometimes issue policies on defective titles on receipt of an additional premium. Cautious buyers object to this, simply because titles free of defects are easier to sell or mortgage. Almost invariably, the contract will provide that the title policy is accepted in lieu of a marketable title or is conclusive evidence of a marketable title. This is done because in the absence of this clause the purchaser is entitled to both a marketable title and a title policy. *New York Inv. Inc. v. Manhattan Beach Corp.*, 243 N.Y.S. 548, 30 Columb.L.Rev. 1215; 92 CJS *Vendor & Purchaser* § 191. This presents the seller with the problem of fly-specking or trivial objections that render titles unmarketable.

If the commitment reveals defects, it is up to the seller to remove them, which he does by procuring releases of liens, affidavits, and the like. At closing, the deed is delivered to the buyer, it is recorded by the title company, and after the title is searched to cover the date of recording of the deed, the owner's policy is issued to the buyer. Normally, this "later date" search is routine. The interval between the title company's commitment date (the contract of sale requires it to be dated at or after the date of the contract of sale) and the closing is a brief one, and the title company checks the deed for validity and insurability. If the buyer's attorney is unwilling to take the risk of defects against the seller's title (judgment liens, income tax liens etc.), intervening between the commitment date and the date of closing, he may insist on an escrow. Kratovil, *Real Estate Law*, Chapter 13. Or he may procure an oral commitment from the title company to insure the buyer's title. This is done by the title company making a quick, informal check of the title from the date of the commitment to the closing date. Once the title company accepts the deed for recording under such an arrangement, it is committed to issue a clear title policy to the buyer. Commonly, the commitment applied for requests an owner's policy for the buyer and a loan policy for his mortgagee.

There are two chief types of owner's policies. One insures the assured-buyer against loss by reason of defects in title not listed in the policy. The other type affords this coverage and in addition insures the assured-buyer against loss by reason of the title being held unmarketable.

EXAMPLE: *V* contracts to sell Blackacre to *P* and to furnish *P* a marketable owner's policy. This is done. Later, *P* contracts to sell the land to *E*, and a court holds that *E* can rescind because the title is unmarketable. The title company is liable for any loss. Actually this whole problem can be avoided if the seller's attorney is alert enough to include the standard provision that the title policy is conclusive evidence that the title is marketable. If you are curious as to how this situation arises, the answer is quite simple. Often a buyer repents of his decision to buy and pressures his lawyer to get him out of the deal. If the contract has no clause making the title policy conclusive evidence of marketable title, the buyer's lawyer checks the title himself looking for one of the innumerable defects that render titles unmarketable but are ignored by title companies because they are trivial. If you are confronted with this task. *See* 92 CJS, 23, *Vendor and Purchaser*, § 189 *et seq.* Be warned, however, that courts are growing less patient with the fly-specking process. And be wary of the risks involved. If the courts hold the title marketable and *E* has refused to accept it, *E* is liable for damages.

In most areas of the country, the policies issued are the current ALTA policies. These are standard forms prepared by the American Land Title Association. However, there are some geographic idiosyncrasies. In New York, for example, the policy commonly issued is the NYBTU policy. This must be read carefully, for, in general, the coverage is not as comprehensive as the ALTA policy.

In Texas and California also, and some other states, special types of policies are issued. There is no escape from the tedium of reading these policies in order to advise your client as to the coverage afforded. This also holds true for the other types of policies encountered, *e.g.*, the NBTU form, drafted by the National Board of Title Underwriters. In Ohio, there is a policy that simply insures the record title.

EXAMPLE: In Ohio the policy insuring record title gives no insurance against off-record risks, such as forgery of deed, forgery of release of mortgage, undelivered deed, etc.

It is realistically impossible to detail the differences in coverage, since these change from time to time. A good idea for the young lawyer is to sit down with his local title company *before* the contract of sale is signed and ask for an explanation of the various coverages available. All the title companies have old-timers who are more than willing to counsel with the young lawyer.

Some companies still issue their own policy forms.

§ 126. ALTA policies—in general. All of the ALTA policies follow the same format. The first page of the policy contains the primary contractual undertakings of the Company, that is, the insuring provisions, which undertakings are made subject to the provisions of the remainder of the policy. The remainder of the policy consists of four formal parts, to-wit: *Exclusions from Coverage, Schedule A, Schedule B, and the Conditions and Stipulations.*

The Exclusions from Coverage exclude from the coverage of the policy those matters which affect the title but which the title industry believes should not come within the framework of title insurance, *e.g.,* zoning ordinances.

§ 127. ALTA owner's policies. In all the ALTA owner's policies, Schedule A consists merely of identification material, setting forth the identifying number of the policy, the date covered by, and the amount of, policy, followed by the name of the party insured, the estate or interest in the land insured, *e.g.,* fee or leasehold, and in whom the title to such estate or interest is vested, that is, owned. This is necessary because at times one who is *not* the owner procures title insurance, for example, a contract purchaser obtains a policy insuring that his seller has clear title.

Schedule B shows the defects, liens, encumbrances, and other matters which affect the title and are excepted from the coverage of the policy and against which the policy gives no coverage. In Schedule B, those matters which are not insured against are separated into *General Exceptions and Special Exceptions.* The *General Exceptions* appear in printed form in most ALTA owner's policies and except from the title coverage matters against which a title company will not insure without a special investigation that discloses that such matters do not exist, for example, mechanic's liens, survey questions, and unrecorded easements. The *Special Exceptions* part lists title objections revealed by the title search, such as easements of record.

The last formal part of the policy, the Conditions and Stipulations, contains the definitions of certain items used in the policy, its duration and all the administrative provisions which control in the event a claim arises.

§ 128. ALTA policies—detailed analysis. Turning our attention to the insuring provisions shown on the first page of the Form A owner's policy, it is found that, subject to the exclusions from coverage, the exceptions contained in Schedule B and the Conditions and Stipulations of the policy, the Company insures against all loss or damage, not exceeding the amount stated in Schedule A, together with costs, attorneys' fees and expenses which the Company may become obligated to pay under the policy, sustained or incurred by the insured by reason of:

1. Title to the estate or interest described in Schedule A being vested otherwise than as stated in Schedule A, or, in other words, the estate in the land not being owned by the person the policy names as owner in Schedule B.

2. Defects in, or liens or encumbrances on such title, except those which are excluded by the language of the exclusions and general exceptions and those specifically shown as special exceptions in Schedule B.

3. Lack of right of access to and from the land.
4. And where a Form B, rather than a Form A, is being issued, Form B insures that the title is marketable.

Under paragraph 3(a) of the Conditions and Stipulations, the Company agrees, at its own cost and without undue delay to provide for the defense of an insured in all litigation asserting a defect, lien, or encumbrance insured against by the policy. Thus the insured is relieved from being required to pay the high cost of defending his title even if the court upholds the validity or marketability of his title.

One must go to paragraph 1 of the Conditions and Stipulations in either owner's loan policy to ascertain who the insured is under the policy. In the owner's policy the term is defined to mean the insured named in Schedule A and, subject to any rights or defenses the Company may have had against the named insured, those who succeed to the insured's interest by operation of law (*e.g.*, by death of an individual insured or by consolidation, merger, or dissolution of a corporate insured). In connection with the persons insured under the policy, it should be pointed out that the ALTA owner's policy does not specifically permit assignment. Hence, if a purchaser of property which has been previously insured desires insurance coverage, it is best that he have a new policy issued in his own name.

Although it is believed that Items 1 and 2 of the cover page of the owner's policy are self-explanatory, a brief explanation may be in order as to Item 3 on both the owner's policy and the loan policy. The coverage under Item 3 as to accessibility to and from the land basically insures that the property is not land-locked. It does not insure access via the street on which the land fronts.

Taking up next the "Exclusions from Coverage" appearing on the back of the front page of the owner's policy, the first exclusion relates to governmental limitations on the use and enjoyment of the land and violations thereof. It reads:

Any law, ordinance or governmental regulation (including but not limited to building and zoning ordinances) restricting or regulating or prohibiting the occupancy, use, or enjoyment of the land or regulating the character, dimensions, or location of any improvement now or hereafter erected on the land, or prohibiting a separation in ownership or a reduction in the dimensions or area of the land, or the effect of any violation of any such law, ordinance, or governmental regulation.

In general, land may be subject to two types of restrictions, that is, public restrictions and private restrictions. Public restrictions are those incorporated in zoning ordinances and building codes, while private restrictions are those we find in plats of subdivision, declarations of restrictions, and deeds. While the title companies always show private recorded restrictions in Schedule B as specific exceptions to title, the title industry has always excluded from the coverage of the policy, in the above general manner, public restrictions and violations thereof. The necessity for so doing is based on the very practical reason that the source of information as to ordinances and other governmental regulations is very seldom centralized and available from the public records. For example, in one case a zoning ordinance was found in the garage of a former village clerk.

The presence of this exclusion makes it necessary for *E* to provide his own protection as to public restrictions. His lawyer and architect will go over the plans of proposed buildings, carefully checking against the ordinances. In many cases, the clerk who will issue the permit is informally contacted and requested to make his own informal check. If an existing building is involved, it is also checked for violations. The offices where notices of violations are kept are also checked. In some cities, the title company is willing to do this. Some city building inspectors do a little moonlighting, and will check the building after office hours.

Exclusion 2 of the owner's policy excludes loss resulting from the exercise of police power or eminent domain in the following language:

> Rights of eminent domain or governmental rights of police power unless notice of the exercise of such rights appears in the public records at Date of Policy.

Exclusion 3 of the owner's policy principally removes from liability any loss or damage resulting from acts suffered by, or matters known to, the party insured, although it also clarifies further the primary contractual undertakings under the policy. It reads as follows:

> Defects, liens, encumbrances, adverse claims, or other matters (a) created, suffered, assumed, or agreed to by the insured claimant; (b) not known to the Company and not shown by the public records but known to the insured claimant either at Date of Policy or at the date such claimant acquired an estate or interest insured by this policy and not disclosed in writing by the insured claimant to the Company prior to the date such insured claimant became an insured hereunder; (c) resulting in no loss or damage to the insured claimant; (d) attaching or created subsequent to date of Policy; or (e) resulting in loss or damage which would not have been sustained if the insured claimant had paid value for the estate or interest insured by the policy.

Obviously, exclusions 3(a) and 3(b) are necessary and are acceptable to the insured. Clauses (a)(b) and (c) appear in identical form in the ALTA loan policy.

Obviously, if *E* has knowledge of any unrecorded title problem, he must communicate this fact to the title company. Some lawyers do this by conferring with the appropriate officer of the company, usually the title officer. This conference is followed by a letter addressed generally to the company and delivered to the title officer with a receipt therein and a copy for *E's* attorney. The officer signs the receipt and delivers the receipted copy to *E's* attorney. Other lawyers treat the matter more formally and request an endorsement to the policy insuring against loss or damage by reason of the defect in question. Suppose a lender has knowledge of a purchase contract that antedates his mortgage. Probably he should present this information to the title company. Let the title company decide whether it will rely on the subordination clause in the contract. If a tract development is involved, the letter to the title company can state that all contracts will have an identical subordination clause and the title company can respond that until *E's* lawyer is advised to the contrary, the title company will make no objection. This saves *E's* lawyer repeated trips to the title company, but protects the company if new legislation is enacted that requires a different form of subordination.

If *E* is a lender, he must exercise care in avoiding acts that might impair his coverage. For example, perhaps he ought not make a substantial modification of the mortgage if a junior lien has attached. If he is disbursing construction funds, perhaps he ought not disburse funds before the date they are due, for then they may become optional advances.

Exclusion 3(c) of the owner's policy would not appear to be necessary, since if no loss is caused to the insured there would be no liability under the very wording of the primary contractual undertaking. However, it does make it quite clear that the basic liability under the policy arises only in the event the insured suffered a loss or damage, so that even if an error were made on the examination of title but no actual loss or damage resulted therefrom, the company would have no liability. For example, if the policy omits a recorded mechanic's lien that later becomes outlawed, no loss has been suffered.

Exclusion 3(d) of the owner's policy appears even though such policies on their face insure only against defects and encumbrances existing at the date of the policy. Somewhat like the previous exclusion discussed, it clarifies further the contractual undertakings under the policy by confining liability thereunder only to loss or damage suffered from defects and encumbrances existing at the date of the policy and not shown as exceptions.

Exclusion 3(e) of the owner's policy is a most important exclusion. The exclusion, together with exclusion 3(b), is necessary to enable the company to take advantage of the protection that law affords an innocent purchaser for value against unrecorded interests and secret outstanding equities. These two exclusions permit the title company to assume that a person acquiring title to the property under examination is an innocent purchaser for value.

An Exclusion 4 appears on the Form A owner's policy but not on the Form B owner's policy. The reason for this is that in order to avoid insuring the marketability of title, the exclusion is essential. This immediately poses the question of why one would want the Form A owner's policy, which does not, by reason of the exclusion, insure marketability of title, when he can obtain the Form B owner's policy which does insure marketability. Simply stated, there are many matters which affect the marketability of title but do not in any way impair its soundness. For example, if the building on the property is five years old but extends two feet over a plat building line, this may make the title unmarketable even though age has made the violation harmless. Where requested to issue the Form B policy, the title insurer may wish to show such matters as exceptions to the marketability coverage of the policy, regardless of their triviality, and then extend affirmative insurance that their existence will not cause any loss or damage. The attorney for *E* may have difficulty explaining this to *E*.

Turning to Schedule A of the owner's policy, while the title, estate or interest insured by the policy and described under Item 1 is usually a "fee simple," it could be a life estate, a leasehold estate, or an easement, title to any of which title companies are willing to insure.

Title policies insure against many losses occasioned by "hidden risks," defects in title which are the results of matters which do not appear of record, such as false recitals of marital status, undisclosed heirs, lack of legal capacity of grantors, errors in the record and forgery. *See, e.g.,* 72 Dick.L.Rev. 35. Sound business practice, however, requires the elimination of certain unrecorded matters from the insurance where no investigation is made as to their existence. These matters are set forth by some companies in the first paragraph of the *General Exceptions* as follows:

(1) Rights or claims of parties in possession not shown by the public records.

(2) Encroachments, overlaps, boundary line disputes, and any matters which would be disclosed by an accurate survey and inspection of the premises.

(3) Easements, or claims of easements, not shown by the public records.

(4) Any lien, or right to a lien, for services, labor or material heretofore or hereafter furnished, imposed by law and not shown by the public records.

(5) Taxes or special assessments which are not shown as existing liens by the public records.

With respect to the first three general exceptions, a prudent purchaser obtains a survey and inspects the property before he buys it to determine if any of the matters referred to in the exceptions affect the property. If he does so, he may not wish to assume the additional expense of having the company also inspect the property and survey to verify his findings.

The next general exception is required, because under the law a secret lien is created on land in favor of persons improving that land or furnishing the material for the improvement thereof. This lien is imposed on the land in some states even before the work is done or the material is furnished simply by the execution of the contract with the workman or materialman, and, therefore, cannot be ascertained from an examination of the public records. Hence, it is obvious that the insurer, not being protected by the record, is in no position to insure against a secret lien created under the Mechanics' Lien Act without making a careful investigation and requiring affidavits from the owners and lessees of the property that there are no mechanics' liens, or, if there are, requiring the production of the waivers of such liens. To avoid this additional work and expense to the customer, the owner's policy is made subject to such secret liens, if any.

It should not be inferred from the foregoing that the insurer will not issue an owner's policy giving coverage over the aforesaid *General Exceptions*. All insurers give "extended coverage" by eliminating any or all of the first five *General Exceptions*. To do this, however, they require documentary evidence that such *General Exceptions* are not applicable to the property the title company is requested to insure. In other words, before the company gives such coverage it assures itself, by inspection, that there are no parties in possession holding adversely to the record owner; that an adequate survey reveals that there are no questions of survey; that there are no easements not on record; and that there is no possibility of mechanics' liens existing against the property. If this is not done, this burden falls on *E's* attorney. In his legal opinion given to *E*, he should explain the risks thus assumed by *E*.

§ 129. **The ALTA loan policy.** Turning now to the ALTA Loan Policy, it contains primary contractual undertakings on the cover page. Subject to the *Exclusions from Coverage*, the *Exceptions* contained in Schedule B and the *Conditions and Stipulations*, it insures those designated therein as insured against all loss or damage up to the amount of the policy, together with attorney's fees and expenses which under the policy the company may become obligated to pay, which the insured shall sustain by reason of:

1. Title to the estate or interest described in Schedule A being vested otherwise than as stated therein;

2. Any defect in or lien or encumbrance on such title;

3. Lack of a right of access to and from the land;

4. Unmarketability of such title;

5. The invalidity or unenforceability of the lien of the insured mortgage upon said estate or interest except to the extent that such invalidity or unenforceability, or claim thereof, arises out of the transaction evidenced by the insured mortgage and is based upon
    (a) usury, or
    (b) any consumer credit protection or *truth in lending* law;
6. The priority of any lien or encumbrance over the lien of the insured mortgage;
7. Any statutory lien for labor or material which now has gained or hereafter may gain priority over the lien of the insured mortgage, except any such lien arising from an improvement on the land contracted for and commenced subsequent to Date of Policy not financed in whole or in part by proceeds of the indebtedness secured by the insured mortgage which at Date of Policy the insured has advanced or is obligated to advance; or
8. The invalidity or unenforceability of any assignment, shown in Schedule A, of the insured mortgage or the failure of said assignment to vest title to the insured mortgage in the named insured assignee free and clear of all liens.

Summarizing in an affirmative manner these provisions, we find the first four extend to the lender the protection comparable to that extended to an owner under an owner's policy.

The remaining insurance provisions address themselves solely to the coverage with respect to the lien of the insured mortgage.

Exclusions 3 and 4 from the coverage extended by the primary contractual undertakings read as follows:

3. Defects, liens, encumbrances, adverse claims, or other matters (a) created, suffered, assumed or agreed to by the insured claimant; (b) not known to the Company and not shown by the public records but known to the insured claimant either at Date of Policy or at the date such claimant acquired an estate or interest insured by this policy or acquired the insured mortgage and not disclosed in writing by the insured claimant to the Company prior to the date such insured claimant became an insured hereunder; (c) resulting in no loss or damage to the insured claimant; (d) attaching or created subsequent to Date of Policy (except to the extent insurance is afforded herein as to any statutory lien for labor or material).
4. Unenforceability of the lien of the insured mortgage because of failure of the insured at Date of Policy or by any subsequent owner of the indebtedness to comply with applicable "doing business" laws of the state in which the land is situated.

Exclusions 1 and 2, excluding liability for loss or damage resulting from zoning laws and other governmental regulations and exercise of police powers and eminent domain are identical to those same exclusions appearing on the ALTA owner's policy.

Clauses (a), (b) and (c) of paragraph 3 are identical to the same exclusions which appear in and were already discussed in connection with ALTA Owner's Policy. Clause (d), like the corresponding exclusion in the owner's policy, again gives the traditional warning that the policy does not insure against loss or damage resulting from matters created after the date of the policy, but also contains language relating to mechanic's liens.

Taking up Exclusion 4, there is a great deal of question as to whether a foreign corporation not authorized to do business within the state can make a direct loan secured by a mortgage on local real estate. Kratovil, *Mortgages,* § 77. If an unqualified corporation makes a direct loan in such state secured by a mortgage on land here and assigns the mortgage to a corporation which is qualified to do business here, the assignee will be in no better position than its assignor. In most states in the event of default under such a mortgage, neither that mortgagee nor its assignee can bring an action to foreclose the mortgage in any court in this state or in the federal courts. The mortgagee is much better qualified than the title company to judge whether it is violating "doing business" laws. Often, the title company is requested to issue an endorsement deleting this exception, usually in reliance on the "insulation theory." Kratovil *Mortgages,* § 77.

A glance at Schedule B of the ALTA Loan Policy discloses it does not contain the *General Exceptions* which appear in Schedule B of the ALTA Owner's Policy. Therefore, the policy insures against (a) rights of parties in possession; (b) questions of survey; (c) unrecorded easements; (d) unrecorded mechanics' liens, and (e) the liens of taxes or special assessments not shown of record, unless they are typed or printed into the policy.

The laws of the various states vary widely as to the priority of mechanic's liens against construction mortgages, Kratovil, *Mortgages,* Chapter 17. Hence, it is impossible to set forth in detail the various devices that are employed to protect against mechanic's liens.

On large construction loans many title companies place on the commitment to issue a loan policy a "pending disbursement clause" somewhat along the following lines.

Pending disbursement of the full proceeds of the loan secured by the mortgage insured, this policy insures only to the extent of the amount actually disbursed but increases as each disbursement is made, up to the face amount of the policy. At the time of each disbursement of the proceeds of the loan, the title must be continued down to such time for possible liens, including mechanic's liens, and other objections, intervening between the date hereof and the date of such disbursement.

There are states where recording of the mortgage prior to the commencement of construction gives the lender priority over mechanics' liens. However, the priority may be precarious in some states. Kratovil, *Mortgages,* Chapter 17. Title companies in some of these states may give the following protection only:

The Company hereby insures the owner of the indebtedness secured by the mortgage or deed of trust hereby insured against loss, not to exceed the amount of this policy, which said insured shall sustain by reason of the establishment of the priority over said mortgage or deed of trust of any mechanic's lien which may be filed against said land, said priority being based upon the claim that building materials had been delivered to or upon said land or building operations had commenced thereon, prior to the recordation of said mortgage or deed of trust.

The title company should always be consulted as to the extent of the coverage it will give.

Paragraph 2 relates to the continuation of insurance after the acquisition of title by an insured mortgagee.

§ 130. **Specifying title insurance requirements.** Obviously in every transaction, *E* is interested in the quality of the title insurance he receives. First of all, in the substantial transaction a substantial title company is requested. The big lenders analyze the financial statements of all title companies, and on loans exceeding a sum determined by the title company, reinsure the risk with some other big insurance company. The operation varies from state to state. In some areas, the title companies *co-insure* so that each company has primary liability from the first dollar. In other situations, the *lead company* takes, say, $7,000,000 of the risk and reinsures with other companies as to the excess over $7,000,000. The title companies do this anyway, as a matter of sound underwriting, but some lenders have lower limits than the self-imposed limits of the title company. In the illustration given, *Life Insurance Company A* may instruct the lead company to reinsure everything over $5,000,000 instead of $7,000,000. Where reinsurance exists, some lenders demand *direct access agreements*. Ordinarily only the lead company has the right to sue the reinsurer, although the ALTA reinsurance policy has a provision for some direct access. In the outright direct access agreement, the reinsurer becomes primarily liable to the lender.

In any case *E* will wish to consider what endorsements he may wish to insist upon.

§ 131. Specifying title insurance requirements—marketable owner's policy. The landowner should insist on the marketable form owner's policy. For example, if he holds only ALTA Form A, and when he sells the property there are liens he is contesting, the title company need not clear up the liens. The landowner has a claim against the title company only after he has suffered a loss.

§ 132. Specifying title insurance requirements—extended coverage. The assured owner is always better off if he demands full extended coverage against all the general exceptions.

> **EXAMPLE:** A title policy issued subject to the usual printed "rights of parties in possession" clause. A tenant in possession under an unrecorded lease exercised an option to purchase contained in the lease. The owner was compelled to sell at a loss to the tenant. *Zale Corp. v. Decorama,* 470 SW2d 406.

§ 133. Duration of protection—warrantor protection. A landowner holding an ALTA policy may sell the land and give a warranty deed. Upon such sale the policy protects the assured against liability on his covenants of warranty.

§ 134. Letter to client where client refuses to buy title insurance. In a given situation, *E* may stubbornly refuse to incur the expense of buying title insurance. The lawyer representing such a client, to protect himself, must write a letter to his client and carefully preserve a copy. Indeed, it is better to deliver the letter and ask the client to receipt for it. The letter must explain that the client has decided to accept all the hidden risks that title insurance protects against and releases his lawyer from all liability for these matters.

§ 135. Leasehold coverage. In the case of the owner's policy, if there is a total loss of title, as where a deed in the prior chain of title is a forgery, the owner recovers the value of the land and building (not exceeding the face of the policy) and, by the better rule, value is fixed as of the date title is lost. 9 Appleman, *Insurance Law and Practice* § 5217 (1943); 6 Western ReserveL.Rev. 49, 59-61. In a leasehold policy, the measure of damages is more nebulous and is complicated by the various factors. Hence, many lessees demand a leasehold policy (insuring the leasehold estate) and an endorsement on the leasehold policy insuring against loss caused by relocating chattels and severable improvements, rental value collectible from the lessee by the true owner for the time the lessee was in occupancy, cost of reprinting business forms, and a variety of other damages. A lawyer representing a lessee or leasehold mortgage should request a specimen of this coverage, obtain a price quotation from the title company, and explain its value to his client.

§ 136. Special title reports. Title companies offer a vast diversity of title searches the attorney will find helpful.

EXAMPLE: The attorney for a foreclosing mortgagee will be furnished a title report giving the necessary parties for a judicial foreclosure, a later report covering the validity of service of process, a later report covering the insurability of the judgment or decree of foreclosure, and so on.

EXAMPLE: An attorney wishing to get rid of an easement will be furnished a title report giving the names of the persons who must sign the release, for this involves checking title to the dominant tenement or tenements, the liens thereon, etc.

EXAMPLE: Insurance of easements, options, contracts of sale, and running covenants is available in proper cases.

EXAMPLE: Where the property consists of a number of parcels, contiguity insurance is available. This saves *E's* lawyer the tiresome task of reading surveys and making his own judgment as to contiguity.

In short, in any situation involving land, whatever the problem, contact the title company to see if it can find a solution.

§ 137. Endorsements. Depending on the title company involved, an array of title endorsements is available to purchasers and lenders. Probably the most elaborate of the well-recognized endorsements are those approved by the California Land Title Association (CLTA). Almost any contingency a title company could possibly deal with is covered by one or more of these endorsements. Some can be anticipated and called for by the contract of sale or loan commitment.

EXAMPLE: In the sale or mortgage of a condominium apartment, *E* will want an endorsement that the condominium conforms to the local statute. *See* Chapter 41.

Other endorsements may be seen as a requirement only after the survey and title search have been completed.

EXAMPLE: The title search shows a plat building line of 20 feet and the survey shows the building 6 inches over the line. The contract can call for a title insurance company endorsement insuring over any building line violation, in which case the deal can close.

EXAMPLE: *E* may want the title company to insure compliance of the building with the zoning ordinance.

EXAMPLE: *E* may want insurance that some old reverter clause is unenforceable.

EXAMPLE: *E* may want insurance that no buildings encroach over the easements that run across the premises, for such may render title unmarketable.

Title companies furnish booklets describing the more common endorsements. These should be carefully studied.

§ 138. Endorsements—uniformity of endorsements. Unlike the title policies, endorsements have only limited uniformity. The CLTA endorsements, those approved by the California Land Title Association, are uniform throughout California, and are often used by the California companies when they or their subsidiaries insure out-of-state land. But other than that you will find various endorsements issued by different title companies. Many resemble the CLTA endorsements.

§ 139. California—CLTA policies. The California Land Title Association (CLTA) Policy was amended in 1973. It is modeled closely after the ALTA policies. Interestingly, it combines the owner's and the mortgage policies, so that in the typical land sale the buyer receives a duplicate of the policy as his owner's policy, and the lender receives a duplicate as his mortgage policy.

Exclusions from coverage. Among the exclusions from coverage not found in the ALTA policies are the following:

Proceedings by a public agency which may result in taxes or assessments, or notices of such proceedings, whether or not shown by the records of such agency or by the public records.

(a) Unpatented mining claims; (b) reservations or exceptions in patents or in acts authorizing the issuance thereof; (c) water rights, claims or title to water.

The proof of loss requirement contains the following, not found in ALTA:

When appropriate, state the basis of calculating the amount of such loss or damage.

The following coverage against mechanics' liens found in the ALTA loan policy is omitted from the CLTA form:

Any statutory lien for labor or material which now has gained or hereafter may gain priority over the lien of the insured mortgage, except any such lien arising from an improvement on the land contracted for and commenced subsequent to Date of Policy not financed in whole or in part by proceeds of the indebtedness secured by the insured mortgage which at Date of Policy the insured has advanced or is obligated to advance.

The CLTA policies are also used in Arizona, Idaho, Oregon, Utah, and Washington.

§ 140. Endorsement CLTA 100. A common endorsement requested for CLTA loan policies is the CLTA 100. It assures against loss or damage arising from a number of circumstances. It assures the insured that there are no covenants, conditions, or restrictions set forth in the policy under which the lien of the security instrument can be cut off, subordinated, or otherwise disturbed, and that there are no existing violations on the land insured of any enforceable covenants, conditions, or restrictions. Endorsement number 100 also insures against loss resulting from any future violations on the land of covenants, conditions, or restrictions. It also contains insurance against any loss which would be suffered if existing improvements, including lawns, shrubbery, or trees, are damaged by the exercise by the owner of the easement of his right to use the easement if the improvements encroach upon such easement. Outside of California, title companies often issue an endorsement much along the lines of CLTA 100.

§ 141. Use of ALTA policies in California. The ALTA policies are used to a limited extent in California. Where the ALTA loan policy is used, it is often accompanied by endorsement CLTA 100.

§ 142. NYBTU policy. The policy form commonly used in New York is the New York Board of Title Underwriters Form 100 D. It must be read in connection with the *Commitment for Title Insurance,* because this commitment lists many items of general exclusion that will be included in the policy, particularly items 1 to 7.

§ 143. New York ALTA forms. The only ALTA policy authorized for use in New York is the ALTA Loan Policy of 1946. It differs from the Standard ALTA policies. If *E's* lawyer is asked to accept this policy, he should consult the title company and have the policy explained to him.

§ 144. Ohio policies. The ALTA Loan Policy is issued in Ohio, but is known as the OTIRB Loan 1972. The owner's policy (also designated OTIRB) contains marketability coverage, and is comparable to the ALTA B form. A policy called a *Title Guaranty* is issued in Ohio. Of particular interest is the fact that it insures only the title as shown by the public records. It does not insure against off-record defects, such as forgeries.

§ 145. The United States policies. Special forms of title policies designed especially for the United States as owner are employed.

§ 146. Title evidence HUD. If the title and title evidence are such as to be acceptable to prudent lending institutions and leading attorneys generally in the community in which the property is situated, such title and title evidence will be satisfactory to the HUD Secretary and will be considered by him as good and marketable. If more than one property is involved, furnish evidence for each property individually. Include map or diagram showing property location with reference to public streets or roads. If restrictions or easements exist, furnish a verbatim copy together with evidence that restrictions have not been violated and that easements are so located as not to interfere with the residential use of the property. One of the following types of title evidence showing recorded title to the Secretary is satisfactory.

(1) *Fee or owner's title policy*—A fee or owner's policy of title insurance, a guaranty or guarantee of title, or a certificate of title, issued by a title company duly authorized by law and qualified by experience to issue such instruments. If an owner's policy of title insurance is forwarded, it shall show title in the Secretary and inure to the benefit of his successors in office.

(2) *Mortgagee's policy of title insurance*—If the mortgagee's policy of title insurance is furnished, supplemented by abstract and attorney's certificate covering the period subsequent to the date of the mortgage, the terms of the policy shall be such that the liability of the title company will continue in favor of the Secretary after title is conveyed to him. The policy may be drawn in favor of the mortgagee and the Secretary of Housing and Urban Development "as their interest may appear," or the policy may be assigned to the Secretary with the consent of the title company endorsed thereon.

(3) *Abstract and legal opinion*—An abstract of title prepared by an abstract company or individual engaged in the business of preparing abstracts of title and accompanied by the legal opinion as to the quality of such title signed by an attorney at law experienced in examination of titles. If title evidence consists entirely of abstract and attorney's certificate of title, the search should extend for at least forty years prior to the date of the

certificate to a well-recognized source of good title. Use FHA Form
No. 2319 (Figure 3), Attorney's Certificate of Title.

(4) *Torrens or similar certificate*—A Torrens or similar title certificate.

(5) *Title standard of U.S. or state government*—Evidence of title conforming to the standards of a supervising branch of the government of the
U.S. or of any state or territory thereof.

Special Instructions. The following documents are to be forwarded with the title
evidence: (1) a deficiency judgment, if any, duly and separately assigned or endorsed by
the mortgagee to the Secretary without recourse; (2) a survey, if available; and (3) in the
states where required an abstract of title in the possession of the mortgagee. The original
credit and security instruments are not to be forwarded.

§ **147. Legal opinions.** As is pointed out elsewhere, both buyers and lenders often
request a legal opinion as to the title. *See* Chapter 43. Commonly, a lawyer giving such
an opinion states that his opinion is based on a described policy. But he then continues
with a statement of the risks not covered by the policy.

EXAMPLE: The lawyer may state that the policy insures access, but not access to the highway
on which the policy fronts. Access via a side street satisfies the policy.

EXAMPLE: On an owner's policy the opinion will set forth the general exceptions (*e.g.,* survey
questions, boundary disputes, unrecorded easements) often encountered in the owner's policy. The
opinion will then go on, for example, to state that the lawyer has examined a described survey, and
from his examination of *that survey* only the following survey questions appear, setting forth the
survey problems shown by the survey.

EXAMPLE: On a loan policy issued to a foreign corporation the opinion will state that the loan
policy does not insure against "doing business" problems, but that the lawyer has examined the
certificate of authority of the lender to do business in the state, and that is regular in all respects.

EXAMPLE: On a loan policy the lawyer may state that the policy does not insure that usury is not
present, but that he has examined certain loan documents (describing them) and from *those
documents* it is his opinion that usury is not present. He cannot state categorically that usury is not
present because there is a risk, however slight, of other circumstances that might create a usury
problem. The opinion must not be given without careful thought. The fact that the mortgagor is a
corporation does not dispose of the usury problem if the corporation was recently formed just to evade
the usury laws.

EXAMPLE: The opinion will state that the title policy does not insure zoning, but that the lawyer
has examined a certified copy of the zoning ordinance (describing it) and from his examination of *that*
copy he is of the opinion that the building on the land and its use do not violate the zoning provisions of
that ordinance.

As can be seen, in big deals especially, the lawyers play a very important role in title
matters. *See also:* Chapter 43.

§ **148. Specimens.** Specimen copies of all title insurance forms can be obtained
from title insurers.

12

Title Insurance—Texas

§ **149. In general.** The forms of the Texas policies are prescribed by the State Board of Insurance of that state, and deviation therefrom is not permitted. They differ from all other policy forms and should be studied by *E's* attorney.

§ **150. Procedural rules.** Procedural rules adopted by the State Board of Insurance are binding on title companies and are as follows:

SECTION IV—PROCEDURAL RULES AND DEFINITIONS

IN NO EVENT MAY ANY POLICY OR ENDORSEMENT FORMS CONTAIN COVERAGES NOT EXPRESSLY AUTHORIZED BY THESE RULES AND/OR THE STATE BOARD OF INSURANCE OF THE STATE OF TEXAS.

P-1. Definitions

a. Land—The land described, specifically or by reference, and improvements affixed thereto which by law constitute real property.

b. Company—Any company holding a certificate of authority to transact the business of title insurance in the State of Texas and/or an authorized agent thereof.

c. Board—The State Board of Insurance of the State of Texas.

d. Policy—Any contract of title insurance, the form for which is prescribed by the Board.

e. Title Examination—The search and examination of the title to determine the condition of the title to be insured.

f. Closing the Transaction—The investigation made by the Company, just prior to the actual issuance of the policy, to determine proper execution, acknowledgment and delivery of all conveyances, mortgage papers, and other title instruments which may be necessary to the consummation of the transaction. It also includes the determination that all delinquent taxes are paid, all current taxes, based on the latest available information, have been properly prorated between the purchaser and seller (in the case of an Owner Policy), the consideration has passed, all proceeds have been properly disbursed, a final search of the title has been made and all necessary papers have been filed for record. The foregoing definition does not prevent voluntary assistance rendered by the Company as a convenience to a party to the transaction, although not necessary to the closing of the transaction and issuance of the policy (such as receiving and disbursing money for the mortgagee, furnishing copies of restrictions, prorating insurance and rents, etc.), so long as the same does not violate the provisions of Article 9.30, Texas Title Insurance Act, 1967, prohibiting rebates, discounts, etc. The Company may specify the requirements necessary for the issuance of title insurance, but it is the responsibility of the applicant for the insurance to meet such requirements. It is not the responsibility of the Company to cure defects of title, nor to perform escrow or other services extraneous to closing the transaction. The premium does not include the cost of legal services performed for the benefit of anyone other than the Company. Legal services, as here referred to, are those constituting the practice of law, and shall, accordingly, be performed only by Attorneys at Law, licensed to practice law in Texas.

g. Insuring Around—Refer to Rule P-11 for definition.

h. Title Insurance Agent—A person, firm, association or corporation owning, or leasing, and controlling an abstract plant, or a participant in a bona fide joint abstract plant operation, and authorized in writing by a title insurance company to solicit insurance, collect premiums and issue and countersign policies in its behalf.

i. Abstract Plant—Refer to Rule P-12 for definition.

j. Endorsement—The form promulgated by the Board for use in amending policies as prescribed by the rules.

P-2. Elimination of Exception as to Area and Boundaries, Etc.—In either an Owner or Mortgagee Policy, when Insured desires to have eliminated the exception as to area and boundaries, etc., the Company may, if it considers the additional hazard insurable, eliminate such exception upon being paid all expense in connection with a survey made by a surveyor of its selection, and in that event shall certify to the elimination of such exception upon the payment of said expense, and the premium prescribed in Rule R-16 in the case of an Owner Policy.

P-3. Exception to "Rights of Parties in Possession"—In an Owner or Mortgagee Policy, where Insured waives inspection, and is satisfied to accept the policy subject to the Rights of Parties in Possession, the Company shall have the right to make a general exception as to "Rights of Parties in Possession". In all such cases, the Company must obtain written waiver from Insured, which waiver must be retained and preserved by the Company.

P-4. Restrictive Covenants Exception—When the examination does not disclose that restrictive covenants affect the applicable land, lien or estate, the Company may indicate "None of Record" after the restrictive covenant exception prescribed in policy forms. When such are disclosed, the Company may indicate, following the prescribed exception, the words "None of record except the following:—" and refer thereto by giving specific reference to the volume and page where each appears of record.

When examination of title discloses that restrictive covenants have expired by their terms, or if in the opinion of counsel, the restrictive covenants are void and unenforceable by statute, have been effectively released, or have been cancelled by final judgment of a court of competent jurisdiction binding upon all of the property owners and lienholders affected by said restrictions, the Company may indicate "None of Record" after the restrictive covenant exception prescribed in the policy forms.

P-5. Special Exceptions—With the knowledge of the Insured, it shall be permissible for the Company to insert such special exception(s) as shall develop from the examination of the title under consideration. Such special exception(s) shall in all cases specifically describe the particular item(s) excepted to, and shall not be general in its terms.

P-6. Co-Insurance—Should a Company elect to issue a policy for a lesser amount than the whole risk, it may do so by causing other Companies qualified to do business in Texas to co-insure the excess. Each Company issuing a policy under the above provision shall insert in Schedule B thereof the following:

"This policy is issued contemporaneously with Policy No. _____ of (Name of Title Insurance Company(ies)) for $_____. The liability of the Company hereunder is hereby limited to (proportion) of any loss, but said liability shall not exceed the face amount of this policy."

P-7. Loans Guaranteed by HUD, FHA or VA—When the Department of Housing and Urban Development, the Federal Housing Administration or the Veterans' Administration, or as their names may be changed from time to time, is guaranteeing the payment of loans, or portions thereof, the Secretary of Housing and Urban Development or the Administrator of Veterans' Affairs, or as their names may be changed from time to time, may be included as one of the Insureds.

P-8. Issuance of Policies Prior to Completion of Improvements

a. Owner Policy

(1) When an Owner Policy is issued in an amount to include the cost of immediately contemplated improvements, the Policy must contain the following exception in Schedule B:

"Completion of improvements on said land and any and all liens arising by reason of unpaid bills or claims for work performed or materials furnished in connection with improvements placed, or to be placed, upon the subject land. However, the Company does guarantee that no such liens have been filed with the County Clerk of _____ County, Texas, prior to the date hereof."

AND THE FOLLOWING "LIABILITY" PARAGRAPH:

"Liability hereunder at the date hereof is limited to $_____. Liability shall increase as contemplated improvements are made, so that any loss payable hereunder shall be limited to said sum plus the amount actually expended by the Insured in improvements at the time the loss occurs. Any expenditures made for improvements, subsequent to the date of this policy, will be deemed made as of the date of this policy. In no event shall the liability of the Company hereunder exceed the face amount of this policy. Nothing contained in this paragraph shall be construed as limiting any exception or any printed provision of this policy."

(2) Upon the completion of the improvements on said property, the owner's acceptance thereof, and satisfactory evidence to the Company that all bills for labor and materials have been paid in full, only the "Liability" paragraph set out in "a(1)" of this rule may be eliminated from the policy by the issuance of the promulgated Endorsement form containing the applicable promulgated language covering said elimination.

In addition to the above elimination, if a satisfactory survey made after the completion of improvements is furnished to the Company, survey coverage may be provided as set out in Rules R-16 and P-2, using the promulgated Endorsement form and containing the applicable promulgated language.

b. Mortgagee Policy

(1) When a Mortgagee Policy is issued prior to completion of improvements made under a mortgage given in whole, or in part, for the cost of improvements, the policy must contain the following exception under Schedule B:

"Completion of improvements on said land and any and all liens arising by reason of unpaid bills or claims for work performed or materials furnished in connection with improvements placed, or to be placed, upon the subject land. However, the Company does guarantee that no such liens have been filed with the County Clerk of _____ County, Texas, prior to the date hereof."

AND THE FOLLOWING "PENDING DISBURSEMENT" PARAGRAPH:

"Pending disbursement of the full proceeds of the loan secured by the lien instrument set forth under Schedule A hereof, this policy insures only to the extent of the amount actually disbursed, but increases as each disbursement is made in good faith and without knowledge of any defects in, or objections to, the title up to the face amount of the policy. Nothing contained in this paragraph shall be construed as limiting any exception under Schedule B, or any printed provision of this policy."

(2) Upon the completion of the improvements on said property, the owner's acceptance thereof, and satisfactory evidence to the Company that all bills for labor and materials have been paid in full, the exception plus the "Pending Disbursement" paragraph in "b(1)" above may be eliminated from the policy and mechanic's and materialmen's lien coverage amended by issuance of the promulgated Endorsement form containing the applicable promulgated language covering said elimination and amendment.

In addition to the above elimination, if a satisfactory survey made after the completion of improvements is furnished to the Company, survey coverage may be provided as set out in Rules R-16 and P-2, using the promulgated Endorsement form and containing the applicable promulgated language.

P-9. Endorsement of Mortgagee Policies

a. Assignment of Mortgage to Government Agencies—Where a mortgagee Policy has been issued covering the lien securing an indebtedness, and such indebtedness and lien have been subsequently sold, transferred, and assigned to Government National Mortgage Association and/or Federal National Mortgage Association and/or Administrator of Veterans' Affairs and/or Secretary of Housing and Urban Development, or as their names may be changed from time to time, the Company which issued the original policy may issue an Endorsement thereto to show the Government National Mortgage Association and/or Federal National Mortgage Association and/or Administrator of Veterans' Affairs and/or Secretary of Housing and Urban Development, or as their names may be changed from time to time, as a party insured. As a condition to the issuance of the Endorsement, the Company may require a showing from the assignor that such assignor has not accelerated the maturity of the indebtedness, or if he has, that there has been a proper reinstatement of the obligation. It shall be permissible for the Company to show the current owner of the fee simple title to the property in the said Endorsement.

b. Assignment of Mortgage to Others—*Except as to those loans secured by one-to-four family residential properties,* the Endorsement provided for in Rule P-9a may also be issued to any assignees other than those set out in said Rule P-9a.

c. Partial Release, Release of Additional Collateral, Modification Agreement, Reinstatement Agreement, and/or Release from Personal Liability—When a Mortgagee Policy has been issued covering the lien securing an indebtedness, and the holder of such Mortgagee Policy desires to release a part of the land described in Schedule A of said policy, and/or to release additional collateral securing indebtedness described in said Schedule A, and/or modify the terms of payment of said indebtedness secured by said mortgage or deed of trust by entering into a Modification Agreement, and/or reinstate said mortgage or deed of trust by entering into a Reinstatement Agreement, and/or the Mortgagor(s) is being released from personal liability, the title insurance company which issued the original policy may issue an Endorsement thereto to show that the original Mortgagee Policy is still in effect as to the remaining security and unimpaired, notwithstanding the modification, reinstatement or release. It shall be permissible for the Company to show in said Endorsement the current owner of the fee simple title to the property. The issuance of this Endorsement is prohibited if by the terms of the Modification Agreement the final maturity date of the indebtedness is extended beyond the original maturity date of the indebtedness, plus the period of limitation then applicable to such indebtedness calculated from such maturity.

P-10. Facultative Reinsurance—Unless any Company submits to the Board a form such Company proposes to use, the American Land Title Association Facultative Reinsurance Agreement Form, 1961, is hereby adopted and is to be used by all title insurance companies authorized to do business in Texas. If the Board approves the form submitted by any such Company, then such form may be used by the submitting Company after it has been approved by the Board.

Permission is hereby given any title insurance company using the American Land Title Association Facultative Reinsurance Agreement to modify Paragraph No. 4 of the Conditions so as to provide that an action can be brought thereon against the reinsurer either in the state of reinsurer's domicile or the state in which the property covered by the policy which is being reinsured is situated. The Maximum Liability which may be assumed by any title insurance company hereunder is governed by Article 9.19 of the Texas Title Insurance Act—1967.

P-11. Insuring Around—Article 9.08 of the Texas Title Insurance Act—1967, defines "Insuring Around" as follows:

" 'Insuring Around' is defined as the willful issuance of a title binder or title insurance policy showing no outstanding enforceable recorded liens while the issuer knows that in fact a lien or liens are of record against the real property, and shall be prohibited, except under circumstances as the State Board of Insurance under its rulemaking powers shall approve."

Pursuant to the authority and instruction given the Board by the Legislature as above stated, the Board hereby sets forth the following rule to be followed by all title insurance companies and title insurance agents in complying with such Article 9.08, viz.:

a. "Willful issuance" shall be defined as the issuance of a title insurance policy or binder with intent to conceal information by suppressing or withholding title information, the consequence of which could result in a monetary loss either to the title insurance company or to the Insured under the policy or binder.

b. "Insuring Around" shall not be construed as prohibiting the issuer of a title insurance policy or binder from issuing a policy or binder without taking exception to a specific lien, or liens, of record when sound underwriting standards and practices would not otherwise prohibit such issuance. Specifically, but not limited to, the term "insuring around" shall not include the issuance of a title insurance policy or binder under the following circumstances:

(1) Where liens securing obligations which, though not released of record, have been discharged to the satisfaction of the title insurance company or agent, and the title insurance company or agent has evidence in its file that the lien has been paid in full;

(2) Where funds are in escrow to pay same, and a recordable release is forthcoming and will be filed for record in the ordinary course of business;

(3) Where liens, in the opinion of counsel, are barred by the statute of limitation;

(4) Where liens are inchoate and sufficient indemnity executed by a financial institution regulated by State or Federal Government, such as a bank, savings and loan association, life insurance company or surety company has been delivered to, and accepted by, the title insurance company, or where sufficient funds have been deposited with the title insurance company or its agent to assure the ultimate payment and release of record of the liens; provided the written consent of the Insureds (owner and mortgagee) shall be delivered to the title insurance company and retained in its file;

(5) Where a sufficient indemnity executed by a financial institution regulated by State or Federal Government, such as a bank, savings and loan association, life insurance company or surety company is delivered to, and accepted by, the title insurance company, or where sufficient funds have been deposited with the title insurance company or its agent to protect against mechanic's liens by affidavits which are being contested or disputed; provided the written consent of the Insureds (owner and mortgagee) shall be delivered to the title insurance company and retained in its files;

(6) Where a title insurance company has previously issued a policy without taking exception to a specific lien and is called upon to issue a new policy and is already obligated under such prior policy, and will not increase its liability or exposure to the lien by the issuance of such new policy; provided the written consent of the Insureds (owner and Mortgagee) shall be delivered to the title insurance company and retained in its files;

(7) Where a title insurance company has erred as in (6) above, and another title insurance company discovers the error in preparing to make a subsequent issuance, the second title insurance company may rely upon an indemnity agreement and/or an agreement to defend by the first company, and insure against such lien; provided the written consent of the Insureds (owner and mortgagee) shall be delivered to the title insurance company and retained in its files;

(8) When issuing a Mortgagee Policy insuring the validity and priority of a lien, the issuer shall not be required to itemize liens which are subordinate to the lien insured, either by express subordination or by operation of law, unless requested so to do by the Insured; however, when issuing a Mortgagee's Title Policy Binder on Interim Construction Loan, the Company shall be required to show all subordinate liens in Schedule B of said binder, but a statement may be made therein that such lien(s) is subordinate.

(9) In instances where federal estate taxes and state inheritance taxes have not been paid, but the title insurance company:

(a) Examines a balance sheet of the estate and determines that the estate will have no difficulty in paying its estate and inheritance taxes, and the title insurance company takes an indemnity from responsible persons protecting itself against loss due to unpaid estate and inheritance taxes, or

(b) Requires sufficient money or other securities to pay estate and inheritance taxes to be left in escrow with it pending payment of such taxes, or pending the receipt of waivers of lien from the taxing authority or authorities, or

(c) Examines the balance sheet of the estate and determines the estate will have no difficulty in paying its inheritance and estate taxes, and the title insurance company obtains a letter from a responsible person agreeing to see that such taxes are paid out of the assets of the estate.

P-12. Abstract Plants

a. Definition: An abstract plant used as the basis for issuance of title insurance policies in the State of Texas shall consist of fully indexed records showing all instruments of record affecting lands within the county for a period of at least 25 years immediately prior to the date of search. The indices pertaining to land shall be arranged in geographic order (i.e.: Lot and Block for subdivided lands, and by Survey or Section Number for acreage tracts). Miscellaneous alphabetical indices shall be maintained according to name. Said indices, land and miscellaneous, may be stored in a computer, and as to land, be subject to retrieval by reference to description of the property under search. The records of the abstract plant shall be maintained to current date, and shall include, but not be limited to, plat or map records, deeds, deeds of trust, mortgages, lis pendens, abstracts of judgment, federal tax liens, mechanic's liens, attachment liens, divorce actions, wherein real property is involved; probate records; chattel mortgages attached to realty and financing statements relating to items which are, or are to become, attached to realty, if available for indexing from the office of the County Clerk of the county which is covered by said plant.

b. Leased Abstract Plants: A lessee is not necessarily excluded from the phrase "owning and operating an abstract plant" as used in Article 9.30 of the Texas Title Insurance Act—1967, but will be so excluded unless in actual, exclusive, physical possession and control of an abstract plant meeting the requirements of paragraph "a" above, operating it under the terms of a bona fide lease agreement, which places the lessee in exclusive possession and control of such abstract plant facilities for a determinable period and for a fixed rental.

c. Joint Abstract Plants: Two or more Companies may combine their operation into a single abstract plant for the purpose of increasing the efficiency and speed of producing title evidence for examination purposes. In such event, if the base plants owned or leased by the individual participants are not merged into a single plant, then the base plants and the joint abstract plant, when considered as one, must meet all of the requirements of an abstract plant as set forth under paragraph "a" above. Ownership of such joint abstract plant may be by corporate ownership, joint venture or partnership agreement, but ownership must rest with the Company participants.

P-13. Truth-In-Lending—The disclosures required in "CONSUMER CREDIT PROTECTION ACT," "TRUTH-IN-LENDING," and similar acts are duties imposed on lenders and constitute no part of the issuance of title insurance policies. Therefore, title insurance companies and agents may not prepare or pass judgment on disclosure documents and notice of right of rescission documents as required by such acts or make any computation as required thereunder. However, this rule shall not prohibit said title insurance companies or agents from performing the ministerial act of inserting in loan disclosure statements, prior to the delivery of same and at the request of and under the direction of creditors, items or figures, not readily ascertainable by creditors prior to the actual closing of the transaction, which items are not a part of the financing charge; nor shall it prohibit said title insurance companies or agents from presenting said disclosure statements and notices of rights of rescission to borrowers and having said borrowers properly acknowledge and sign said statements. All of the foregoing shall be applicable, either fully or to the extent that it is not contrary to superior law, but in no event shall the title insurance company be liable, or its policy provide such liability, to an Insured in respect of such matters, except as expressly provided and authorized by this rule.

P-14. Owner Title Policy Commitment to the Texas State Highway Department—The Owner Title Policy Commitment to the Texas State Highway Department shall be issued only as follows:

a. The Commitment shall be issued only to the Texas State Highway Department.

b. There will be no additional premium, over and above that ultimately collected for the Owner Policy.

c. The term "negotiation of said warrant" in said form is hereby defined to include the right of the Company to refuse to negotiate the warrant in the event the release of existing liens cannot be obtained, or in the further event adverse matters affecting the title become known to it subsequent to the date of the Commitment.

d. The issuance of such Commitment to the State Highway Department, in those cases where there are outstanding and enforceable recorded liens which have been previously or contemporaneously disclosed to said Department, shall not be construed a violation of Rule P-11, "Insuring Around".

P-15. Mortgagee Information Letter (MIL)—The Mortgagee Information Letter (MIL) shall be issued only as a preliminary instrument in instances in which the Company has a bona fide order for its regular Mortgagee Policy, to be issued within 30 days from date of the MIL. The MIL shall be effective for not more than 30 days, and shall be used only to enable the proposed Insured to obtain information concerning title requirements, contents of proposed policy and information necessary for preparation of loan documents. In no event shall such MIL be used in lieu of a Mortgagee Policy, either on permanent or short term loans, or in lieu of a Mortgagee's Title Policy Binder on Interim Construction Loan.

P-16. Mortgagee Title Policy Binder on Interim Construction Loan (Interim Binder)—The Mortgagee Title Policy Binder on Interim Construction Loan (Interim Binder) shall be used only with respect to interim construction loans in which it is contemplated in good faith that the Company issuing Interim Binder shall be asked to issue its Mortgagee Policy on a permanent loan covering the identical property (on one or more parcels) when improvements are completed, but which permanent loan may be made by mortgagee other than the mortgagee named in the Interim Binder. The use of such Interim Binder shall be limited to interim construction loans and pledges of the interim construction notes and liens.

The Interim Binder shall not be issued on vacant lots or tracts, except in connection with the immediate construction of improvements thereon, nor shall such Interim Binder be issued after completion of improvements to which it relates, but this does not prohibit the issuance of Extensions after completion of improvements. In all cases not specifically enumerated in this rule, a Mortgagee Policy shall be used.

The Company shall be required to show all subordinate liens in Schedule B of the Interim Binder, but a statement may be made therein that such lien(s) is subordinate.

P-17. *Foreclosure Information Letter and Foreclosure Binder*

a. Foreclosure Information Letter—At the request of an existing lienholder, whose lien was insured by a Mortgagee Policy, contemplative of foreclosure, the Company may issue to such lienholder a Foreclosure Information Letter, reflecting condition of title and requirements necessary to obtain a Foreclosure Binder insuring good and indefeasible title in the lienholder, if such lienholder is the purchaser at foreclosure sale, or to the Secretary of Housing and Urban Development or the Administrator of Veterans' Affairs, or as their names may be changed from time to time.

The Foreclosure Information Letter shall be issued only as a preliminary instrument in instances in which the Company has a bona fide order for its Foreclosure Binder to be issued within 90 days from date of the Foreclosure Information Letter. Such Foreclosure Information Letter shall not be used for any other purpose.

b. Foreclosure Binder—The Foreclosure Binder, which is available only when the foreclosed lien has been previously insured by a Mortgagee Policy, shall be issued to the purchaser at foreclosure, or to the Secretary of Housing and Urban Development or to the Administrator of Veterans' Affairs, or as their names may be changed from time to time, if title is conveyed to either after foreclosure, for the amount of the existing indebtedness at the time of foreclosure of the lien set out in the Foreclosure Information Letter, or for the amount of debentures, whichever is greater.

These rules are self-explanatory. Of special significance is the rule forbidding waiver of mechanic's liens until the building is completed and paid bills for work and material are produced.

13

Abstracts

§ 151. In general. In parts of the country, mostly in agricultural areas, the abstract is still used to evidence title. In large transactions, the lender is likely to insist on title insurance, and for a very good reason.

EXAMPLE: *R* contracts to sell land to *E* for $1,000,000. *E* obtains a commitment from a lender to make a mortgage loan for $700,000. An abstract is prepared and shows clear title in *R*. One of the recent transactions revealed in the abstract is a mortgage for $700,000 and a release or satisfaction thereof. After the current transaction is consummated, it develops that the release of mortgage was forged, so that the land is legally subject to the earlier mortgage of $700,000. This, of course, is disastrous. Title insurance protects against these "off record" risks which lenders are unwilling to assume. In recent memory, title companies lost several million dollars in one year on just such a situation, involving not one, but a number of forged releases, all the product of one forger. Of course, he went to jail, but this did not eliminate the financial loss.

§ 152. The abstracter. If abstracts are universally accepted in the locality, the buyer and lender will accept this form of title evidence. Care should be exercised in selecting the abstracter, if there are several in the area. Don't be bashful about requiring "errors and omissions" insurance. After all, if the abstracter negligently omits a mortgage of $50,000 from his abstract, it is comforting to know that a big insurance company will make good the loss. And if the abstracter does not carry adequate "errors and omissions" insurance, the buyer or lender can insist on title insurance. The requirement for adequate "errors and omissions" insurance belongs in the loan commitment. If *R* is unwilling or unable to comply with the requirement, the attorneys for buyer and lender discuss this with their clients. If their clients are willing to go along without adequate insurance, letters are written to the clients warning of the risk they have willingly assumed. Copies of the letter are preserved. Malpractice suits against lawyers are growing more common.

Incidentally, some states require an abstracter to put up a surety bond. Usually this is not adequate to cover large deals.

Before the deal is finalized, *R's* abstract should be given preliminary scrutiny. Often such abstracts consist of various "continuations" made by various abstract companies, some of which may be out of business. In any case, these prior companies have no liability to the current buyer or lender, for "privity of contract" is lacking. The current abstracter must be required to certify the entire abstract and his certificate must explicitly run to the benefit of the current buyer and lender, for there is still some barbarous law to the effect that if the seller buys the abstract, other parties cannot sue on it, for "priority of contract" is lacking. This requirement of certification belongs in the loan commitment.

While the question of merchantability of an abstract does not often arise, and must not be confused with the merchantability of title, occasional decisions deal with the merchantability of an abstract. *Whitfield v. Clendon,* 38 So2d 856.

Reference: Liability of abstracter to third parties. *William v. Polgar,* 215 NW2d 149 (1974).

14

Clearing Title Objections

§ 153. In general. Many title insurance commitments show items that are objectionable to *E* and must therefore be removed or "waived" by the title company. The procedure for accomplishing this tends to be more or less standard. It is of utmost importance that the contract of sale be consulted repeatedly. It will set forth "permitted objections." It will set forth time limits and procedures for clearing objections that are not permitted.

§ 154. Contract provision. A clause used in Illinois relative to curing objections is as follows:

If the title commitment, survey or inspection of the premises by *E* reveals objections other than those listed as permitted objections, then the following provisions are applicable:

If the title commitment or plat survey (if one is required to be delivered under the terms of this contract) discloses either unpermitted objections or survey matters that render the title unmarketable (herein referred to as "survey defects"), Seller shall have 30 days from the date of delivery thereof to have the exceptions removed from the commitment or to correct such survey defects or to have the title insurer commit to insure against loss or damage that may be occasioned by such exceptions or survey defects, and, in such event, the time of closing shall be 35 days after delivery of the commitment or the time expressly specified for closing, whichever is later. If Seller fails to have the objections removed or to correct any survey defects, or in the alternative, to obtain the commitment for title insurance specified above as to such objections or survey defects within the specified time, Purchaser may terminate this contract or may elect, upon notice to Seller within 10 days after the expiration of the 30-day period, to take title as it then is with the right to deduct from the purchase price liens or encumbrances of a definite or ascertainable amount. If Purchaser does not so elect, the contract shall become null and void without further action of the parties.

All title company requirements for furnishing extended coverage against general exceptions must be complied with on or before _____ and the title commitment must reflect the fact that this has been done.

§ 155. Mortgages and other liens. If the title commitment shows a recorded mortgage or other lien, it is quite customary to pay off the lien at closing, by use of part of the purchase price. *See* § 228.

Where a purchaser is paying off the mortgage, he must pay to the right party. He comes under the *payment rule* rather than the *release rule*. Kratovil, *Mortgages*, Chapter 37. Where the mortgage is a deed of trust running to a corporate trustee, a release deed by the corporate trustee is usually acceptable. Where the trustee is an individual, the title company will ask to see the cancelled deed of trust and note. At times the deed of trust and note cannot be produced. They have been destroyed or mislaid. In such case, the title company or purchaser will usually demand a surety company bond. Who knows, for example, who is holding a bearer note secured by a deed of trust? If, however, the deed of trust secures a note running to a well-known lending institution, a corporate trustee will issue its release deed on proof furnished by the lending institution that the institution never sold, pledged, or otherwise disposed of the papers and that the debt was paid in full.

If the party holding the mortgage or other lien cannot be paid in full, usually because the amount of his lien is larger than the sale price, he may be willing to give a partial release of his lien as to the property sold. This is a release in ordinary form coupled with a statement that the release is confined to the particular land described. Obviously a *satisfaction of mortgage* cannot be used in this situation. That form is used only where the debt is paid in full.

In some cases a lienor may be willing to subordinate his mortgage to the new mortgage, in which case a subordination of lien is employed. *See* Chapter 36.

§ **156. Assignment of rents.** A common fault in clearing title where an assignment of rents has been given as additional security for a mortgage, is to procure a release of the mortgage but forget about obtaining a release of the assignment of rents. This makes it necessary to obtain and record a release of the assignment of rents. Before you do this, check the mortgage. Some mortgages contain a provision that a release of the mortgage automatically releases the assignment of rents.

§ **157. Waiver of defenses.** Where a mortgage is assigned, the value of the assignee of the waiver of defenses (also called estoppel certificate) is well understood. It is sometimes obtained at the time the mortgage is executed, but retained undated until the assignment is made and then dated contemporaneously with the assignment. However, where a possible claim of usury is involved, the title company will insist on watching the mortgagors sign a fresh waiver of defenses at the time of the assignment. Kratovil, *Mortgages* §§ 185, 193. Some title companies follow this last practice on all waivers of defenses.

§ **158. Judgments.** In most states a judgment against a person owning an interest in land is a lien on the land. Where the landowner is *Oscar Schultz* and the records reveal a judgment against a person having that name, it becomes necessary to obtain proof that the judgment is not against *R*, whose name is *Oscar Schultz*. All title companies have forms for this purpose. They call for information as to *R's* residence and business address for a period of time, so that this can be checked against the court files. *R* might quite innocently give an incorrect affidavit that there are no judgments against him, for example, where a judgment is rendered by confession. Where the name is a common one, *John Smith*, for example, it is usually impractical to list all the judgments against that name. But if the name is an uncommon one, *Robert Kratovil*, for example, the title company will want the affidavit to list any judgment against that name, so that *E's* attention is drawn to that particular judgment when he signs the affidavit. This brings up a time problem. The attorney for *R* can select one of three dates for having *R* sign that affidavit:

(1) The date he is first called into the deal. *R* is usually co-operative at this time. The wrangling that sometimes takes place over what items go with the building has not yet taken place. But it is not known at that time what judgments will be encountered.

(2) The date the attorney for *R* receives the title commitment. He can then discuss with *R* suspicious judgments (like those showing a line of business in which *R* is engaged). The affidavit can be used to clear the affidavit from the title commitment.

(3) The date of closing. Where the deal is closed outside of escrow, some attorneys for *E* want an affidavit dated as of the date of closing. This covers the "gap period" between the date of the title commitment and the date of closing. Often there is no alternative except to have *R* sign two affidavits, one to clear the title commitment and one to satisfy *E's* closing attorney. Alternatively, *R's* attorney may refer the title company to other recent files where *R* has furnished the title company an affidavit on other properties, as where *R* is an active builder. Then one affidavit at closing will suffice.

The affidavit often covers other matters such as divorces, bankruptcies, work or materials that could result in mechanics' liens, period of *R's* occupation of the premises, chattel security instruments, etc., as in the first of the affidavits shown.

A similar affidavit may be required of the purchaser. For example, if there are prior judgments against the purchaser, his mortgagee lender will want them cleared. Title companies and legal stationers supply these forms.

§ 159. Judgment in fact against seller. At times, the title search reveals a judgment that *R* acknowledges is against him. Typically this is cleared by *paying* the judgment or arranging for judgment creditor to be present at closing and receiving payment then. The judgment creditor gives a *Satisfaction of Judgment.* Often the local court clerk has a form for this item. If not the local legal stationers do. The satisfaction is often entrusted to the title company on written direction to deliver to *E* for filing when the title company has received a check for the amount of the judgment. The satisfaction must also be signed by the judgment creditor's attorney, to release his attorney's lien. The judgment creditor also signs, though where absolutely full payment is being made, the judgment creditor's attorney may sign for him.

Some attorneys prefer to have the judgment creditor sign in all cases. The firm of attorneys that presented the judgment creditor may have changed in membership after the judgment was rendered. This creates an obvious problem.

If the judgment is too large to be handled in this way, the judgment creditor, rather than blow the deal, in which ca: e he receives nothing, will often consent to issue a release of the lien of the judgment as to the land sold on receipt of a specified sum of money. This is handled much like the satisfaction of judgment. *See* Form No. 3.

Alternatively, if only a new mortgage is involved, the judgment creditor may be willing to subordinate his judgment to a new first mortgage, though some lenders object to junior liens and others are legally bound to so object. *See* Form No. 4.

Form No. 3

* FORM 3080—CHICAGO TITLE INSURANCE COMPANY STANDARD FORM RELEASE OF LIEN OF JUDGMENT

CHICAGO TITLE INSURANCE COMPANY

ORDER NO:

RELEASE OF LIEN OF JUDGMENT

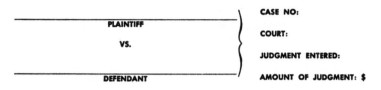

_____ PLAINTIFF	CASE NO:
VS.	COURT:
	JUDGMENT ENTERED:
_____ DEFENDANT	AMOUNT OF JUDGMENT: $

This release, made between plaintiff in the above suit (the judgment creditor) and defendant in the above suit (the landowner)

Witnesseth, that whereas the judgment creditor named above recovered a judgment as set forth above, as will by the record thereof in said court more fully appear, and is still the owner of said judgment,

Now therefore, said judgment creditor in consideration of $ in hand paid, does hereby release unto the landowner all interest acquired by said judgment, so far as the same is a lien or charge upon the following described premises, to wit:

But it is understood and agreed that this instrument shall operate as a release, satisfaction and discharge of said judgment as to the Real Estate above described, and none other.

In witness whereof, the said judgment creditor has hereunto set his hand and seal the   day of

A.D.

_____(Seal)

_____(Seal)

_____(Seal)
(Attorney for judgment creditor)

(Add acknowledgment as on deed)

Form No. 4

FORM 3082 (10-83)—CHICAGO TITLE INSURANCE COMPANY STANDARD FORM SUBORDINATION

CHICAGO TITLE INSURANCE COMPANY

ORDER NO.

COUNTY

STATE

SUBORDINATION

WHEREAS, the mortgagors

by   mortgage dated   and recorded in the Recorder's
Office of   County,   in Book   Page   as
Document   , did mortgage unto

certain premises in   County   , described as:

to secure a debt in said mortgage described; and

WHEREAS, the undersigned ha   some right, interest and claim in and to said premises by reason of:

but are willing to subject and subordinate   right, interest and claim to the lien of the above
mentioned mortgage.

NOW THEREFORE, the undersigned in consideration of the premises and of the sum of ONE DOLLAR ($1.00) paid to the undersigned, receipt of which is hereby acknowledged, do hereby covenant and agree with the said mortgagee that the right, interest and claim of the undersigned is and shall be and remain at all times subject and subordinate to the lien of the said mortgage for all advances made or to be made under the provisions of said mortgage or on the debt secured thereby and for all other purposes specified therein; hereby releasing and waiving all rights under and by virtue of the appraisement and homestead exemption laws of the state aforesaid.

(Insert in above space any language required by this state law in mortgages of real estate)

WITNESS the hand and seal of the undersigned this   day of
A.D. 19

WITNESSES:_____   _____(Seal)

_____   _____(Seal)

(ADD ACKNOWLEDGMENT BELOW)

SUBROGATION

AGREEMENT

Form No. 5

FORM 1025

KNOW ALL MEN BY THESE PRESENTS, THAT, WHEREAS, THE UNDER-
SIGNED, IS THE HOLDER
OF THE LEGAL TITLE TO THE PROPERTY HEREINAFTER DESCRIBED, WHICH PROPERTY IS LEGALLY DESCRIBED AS: -

AND
WHEREAS,

EXECUTED A TRUST DEED DATED AND RECORDED

AS DOCUMENT NO. TO AS TRUSTEE, TO SECURE THEIR NOTE FOR

DOLLARS, DUE YEARS AFTER DATE, WITH INTEREST AT % PER

ANNUM, PAYABLE SEMI-ANNUALLY; AND
WHEREAS,

EXECUTED A TRUST DEED DATED AND RECORDED ON

AS DOCUMENT NO. TO AS TRUSTEE, TO SECURE THEIR NOTE FOR

DOLLARS, DUE YEARS AFTER DATE, WITH INTEREST AS % PER

ANNUM, PAYABLE SEMI-ANNUALLY; AND
WHEREAS, THE MONEY SECURED BY TRUST DEED RECORDED AS DOCUMENT NO.

HAS NOT YET BEEN ADVANCED BUT IS TO BE ADVANCED BY THE LEGAL HOLDER AND OWNER OF THE INDEBTEDNESS

AND NOTE SECURED BY SAID TRUST DEED AND TO BE APPLIED TO THE PAYMENT AND CANCELLATION OF THE RE-

MAINDER OF THE INDEBTEDNESS SECURED BY THE TRUST DEED RECORDED AS DOCUMENT NO. ;

NOW THEREFORE, IN CONSIDERATION OF THE PREMISES AND OF ONE DOLLAR ($1.00),

THE UNDERSIGNED DO HEREBY AUTHORIZE AND EMPOWER THE LEGAL HOLDER AND OWNER OF THE NOTE SECURED BY

THE TRUST DEED RECORDED AS DOCUMENT NO. TO DISBURSE THE FUNDS SECURED BY SAID

TRUST DEED AND TO APPLY THE SAME TO THE PAYMENT AND CANCELLATION OF THE INDEBTEDNESS SECURED BY

THE TRUST DEED RECORDED AS DOCUMENT NO. , AND UPON SUCH PAYMENT AND CANCELLA-

TION, THE OWNER OF THE INDEBTEDNESS SECURED BY THE TRUST DEED RECORDED AS DOCUMENT NO.

SHALL BE AND HE IS HEREBY SUBROGATED TO ALL RIGHTS AND PRIVILEGES WHICH BEFORE SUCH PAYMENT

AND CANCELLATION WERE VESTED IN THE OWNER OR LEGAL HOLDER OF THE INDEBTEDNESS SECURED BY THE TRUST

DEED RECORDED AS DOCUMENT NO. AND THE TRUST DEED RECORDED AS DOCUMENT NO.

UPON SUCH PAYMENT AND CANCELLATION, SHALL BE TO ALL INTENTS AND PURPOSES A FIRST

VALID LIEN, SUBROGATED AS AFORESAID, UPON THE PREMISES ABOVE DESCRIBED.

WITNESS OUR HANDS AND SEALS THIS DAY OF A.D. 19

_____
(SEAL)

STATE OF ILLINOIS) SS
COUNTY OF COOK)

I, , A NOTARY PUBLIC IN AND FOR SAID COUNTY AND STATE
AFORESAID, DO HEREBY CERTIFY THAT PERSONALLY KNOWN TO ME TO BE THE SAME
PERSON WHOSE NAME IS SUBSCRIBED TO THE FOREGOING INSTRUMENT, APPEARED BEFORE ME THIS DAY IN PER-
SON AND ACKNOWLEDGED THAT SIGNED, SEALED AND DELIVERED SAID INSTRUMENT AS OWN FREE
AND VOLUNTARY ACT FOR THE USES AND PURPOSES THEREIN SET FORTH,

GIVEN UNDER MY HAND AND NOTARIAL SEAL THIS DAY OF
A.D. 19

_____
(NOTARY PUBLIC)

§ 160. Subrogation agreement. In some instances, the title company will be willing to rely on the doctrine of conventional subrogation. Kratovil, *Mortgages*, Chapter 22.

EXAMPLE: Blackacre is subject to a first mortgage paid down to $20,000 and now due. It is also subject to a second mortgage of $5,000, and the junior mortgagee is unwilling to release his junior mortgage in order to allow the landowner to put a new first mortgage on the land to refinance the old first mortgage. The landowner puts a new first mortgage on the land in the sum of $20,000. The entire proceeds are used to pay off the old first mortgage. The mortgagor and mortgagee in the new mortgage execute a subrogation agreement to the effect that the new mortgage succeeds to the priority of the old first mortgage. The new mortgagee retains the old first mortgage papers, preferably uncancelled, to put in evidence if the junior mortgagee challenges his priority. See subrogation agreement, Form No. 5.

§ 161. Corporate resolutions. Where a close corporation is involved, the requirement for corporate resolutions authorizing a sale, lease, mortgage, etc. is easily complied with. 53 Boston U.L.Rev. 101.

EXAMPLE: John Smith certifies that he is Secretary of *XYZ Corporation,* and as such is custodian of the records of said corporation; that the records of such corporation reveal that on _____ (date) at a joint meeting of all directors and stockholders of said corporation, the following resolution was unanimously adopted and has never been modified or repealed.

"Be it resolved that Blackacre be sold to *ABC Corporation* at the price of $10,000 and on the terms set forth in contract of sale attached to and made part of this resolution and that the officers of this corporation are authorized to do all things necessary or convenient to consummate said transaction."

Section 44 of the Model Business Corporation Act (2d) contains the following provision, some version of which exists in some states:

Unless otherwise provided by the articles of incorporation or by-laws, any action required by this Act to be taken at a meeting of the directors of a corporation, or any action which may be taken at a meeting of the directors or of a committee, may be taken without a meeting if a consent in writing, setting forth the action so taken, shall be signed by all of the directors, or all of the members of the committee, as the case may be. Such consent shall have the same effect as a unanimous vote.

See, for example, Ill. Rev. Stat. Ch. 32 § 157.147.1.

To comply with this statute is relatively simple.

EXAMPLE: "John Smith hereby certifies that he is the Secretary of *XYZ Corporation* and as such is the custodian of the records of said corporation; that the records of said corporation show that on _____ (date) a consent in writing was lodged with him as such Secretary, as follows:

"The undersigned, being all of the directors of *XYZ Corporation,* do hereby consent that the following action shall be taken by said corporation:

(Here set forth the action)

_____
Henry Brown,

_____
John Jones

_____
Alfred Smith

"He does further certify that the signatories are all of the directors of said corporation and the consent bears their genuine signatures; also that said consent has never been modified nor repealed."

The statutes must be carefully checked before this type of action is taken. Alabama permits it only if the corporate charter provides for it. Arkansas and California require that it be provided for in the charter or by-laws. Delaware and New Jersey require it to be in the charter and by-laws. Pennsylvania requires it to be in the by-laws. Many lawyers will put it into the by-laws, even if the statute doesn't require it.

Informal action by the stockholders proceeds along the same lines, if the statute permits it.

§ **162. Easements.** It is not enough to say that the title is subject to a recorded easement. It must be examined before the deal is firmed up.

EXAMPLE: Pipeline companies have a habit of going to a farmer and getting him to grant a pipeline easement over his farm. When the time comes to develop the property, the pipeline company must be approached and a modification agreement must be executed and recorded defining the precise boundaries of the easement. You can't have a pipeline easement that could run through the middle of a shopping center.

§ **163. Restrictions and violations of restrictions.** Non-reverter restrictions of the general plan variety can be eliminated for a variety of reasons. Kratovil, *Real Estate Law*, Chapter 28. Again this is a risk *E* will want a title company to assume. The mechanics are not complicated.

EXAMPLE: A subdivision has a plat restriction calling for two-story residences, a common restriction in the "twenties," when some developers thought that bungalows cheapened an area. Builders erect a great many ranch homes in the subdivision. The title company will send out an inspector, and if he reports a sufficient number of violations, the title company will waive the restriction.

In many states Marketable Title Acts or other laws exist that outlaw state restrictions. Kratovil, *Real Estate Law*, Chapter 28.

Violations of restrictions constitute defects in title separate and apart from the restrictions. Thus a contract of sale that is "subject to restrictions of record" does not require the buyer to accept the property if there are material violations of the restrictions. However, a title company will insure against loss or damage by reason of such violation if it is old enough so that enforcement is barred by laches or some state limitations law. Again, this is a title company risk. It is best for *R* to put a clause in his contract requiring *E* to accept title company coverage against this violation.

§ **164. Covenants.** Covenants present a variety of problems.

EXAMPLE: A life insurance company is asked to make a mortgage loan on land in Mississippi. Under the laws of the state where it was chartered, it can only lend on *first* mortgages. This is a common statute. The title research reveals a prior recorded covenant in a deed that the grantee and his successors should bear all of the expenses incidental to the future paving of an adjacent street and sidewalk. Under the law in Mississippi and some other states, this covenant creates a lien on the land superior to the lien of any subsequent mortgage. *Mendrop v. Harrell,* 183 So2d 418 (Miss. 1958); Restatement, Property § 540, Comment C; 2 Am. L. Ppty. 386. If possible, this lien should be subordinated to the lien of the mortgage.

§ **165. Conditions.** If the title policy reveals a condition, that is, a reverter type restriction, obviously this must be disposed of before the deal is firmed up. Arrangements can include one of the following:

(1) A release of the reverter is procured from its owner. The offer of money for the release can be sweetened by an offer to continue the restriction in non-reverter form. For example, if the reverter is limited to *sale* of intoxicating liquor on the premises, as many are, and *E* is about to erect a shoe factory, he couldn't care less about selling liquor on the premises. But he is very much concerned over the fact that many institutional lenders are forbidden by law to loan on any property burdened with a reverter right.

(2) The owner of the reverter may be willing to give a subordination of the reverter right to the lender.

(3) The reverter instrument may include a clause that the reverter is subject to "any present or future mortgages on the property to an institutional lender." Here, if the title company or the lender's lawyer is willing to state that this protects the lender, the deal can go forward. The answer depends on the state law. These "blanket subordinations" are suspect in some states.

(4) On occasion, a title company will insure against damage by reason of a reverter right. Or a lawyer may give an opinion that it is dead. Many states have Reverter Acts, Marketable Title Acts, or other laws that outlaw stale conditions.

§ **166. Deeds by minors.** Every once in a while you run into a situation where a vacant lot or cheap house is being sold by the heirs of a former owner.

EXAMPLE: *D* died leaving his children *A, B,* and *C* as his heirs. They contract to sell his vacant lot to *E* for $1500.00. *C* is 17 years old, a minor. If a guardianship is put through, his share of $500 will be almost completely consumed by court costs. The title company may be willing to accept his deed and a surety bond of $1000.00 to protect against the minor's right of disaffirmance. The cost is roughly $20.00. To obtain the bond, *A* and *B* must sign an agreement to indemnify the title company. *C* never disaffirms, for if he does, he subjects his brothers to liability for loss.

§ **167. Power of attorney.** Where the deal is closed by an attorney-in-fact acting for *R,* problems arise.

EXAMPLE: *R* is taking an around-the-world cruise. He may, in fact, be dead when the deal is closed, in which case the deed is void. By force of circumstance, *E* may sometimes have to accept a cable from *R* advising that he is alive and has not revoked the power of attorney. The shortcomings of this procedure are obvious. Anyone can send a cable. It is best to let the title company take this risk.

§ **168. Death of joint tenant or tenant by the entireties.** Where, since the last title search, a joint tenant or tenant by the entireties has died, the fact of his death must be established. This is done by producing an affidavit and death certificate. Also it must be established that no inheritance or estate tax will be payable. The affidavit can be used for this purpose, but some states require a summary proceeding to establish that fact, also a summary proceeding to establish title in the survivor. In the case of tenancy by the entireties, you need information that they had not divorced each other, for that would convert the tenancy into a tenancy in common. You also need information as to any

Form No. 6

FORM 3081- (11-63)—CHICAGO TITLE INSURANCE COMPANY STANDARD FORM AFFIDAVIT AS TO JOINT TENANCY OR TENANCY BY THE ENTIRETIES

CHICAGO TITLE INSURANCE COMPANY

AFFIDAVIT AS TO JOINT TENANCY OR TENANCY BY THE ENTIRETIES FOR CHICAGO TITLE INSURANCE COMPANY

STATE OF _____ } s.s.   ORDER NO:

COUNTY OF _____   COUNTY:

     STATE:

On this_____ before me personally appeared_____
     (insert date)

to me personally known, who being duly sworn on oath did say that:

1. Affiant resides at the address given below affiant's signature;

2. Affiant makes this affidavit for the purpose of inducing Chicago Title Insurance Company to issue its *Title Insurance Policy*, insuring title to the premises described as follows:

3. Affiant is_____;
    (state interest of affiant in the above premises as "owner," "son of owner," etc.)

4. Said premises were formerly owned as joint tenants or as tenants by the entireties by_____

    _____and_____;

5. Said_____
    (fill in name of co-tenant who died)

    died on_____

    leaving_____will;
    (insert "a" or "no"; if will left, attach a copy)

6. The total value of the taxable estate of said deceased including joint tenancies, tenancies by the entireties, individual ownerships of both real and personal property, and insurance does not exceed the sum of $_____ and to the best of affiant's knowledge there is no estate or inheritance tax liability by reason of the death of said decedent;

7. Where this affidavit relates to a tenancy by the entireties, were the parties ever divorced? _____

    (If answer is "Yes," identify the divorce proceedings:

    _____);

8. Affiant's relationship to the deceased was_____.

Subscribed and sworn to before me by the affiant

this _____   Signature:_____
    (insert date)

     Address: _____

_____
    Notary Public

divorces before the parties acquired ownership, for if any such divorce is involved, and is invalid, the new couple are not husband and wife because one is considered still married to another, and no tenancy by the entireties exists. You also need information as to any will made by the decedent because of the obscure doctrine of *election*.

EXAMPLE: *H* and *W* are joint tenants as to Blackacre, and *H* makes a will by which he gives $10,000,000 to *W* and gives Blackacre to *X*. Obviously, *W* may legally choose to take Blackacre as surviving joint tenant. But if she finds the $10,000,000 more attractive, and takes that, she has made an "election," and must give up Blackacre to *X*. This is a great rarity. See Affidavit Form No. 6.

§ **169. Death of sole owner or tenant in common.** Where a sole owner or tenant in common dies, in many states probate is necessary. In a testate estate, probate is necessary to establish the will. In an intestate estate, probate is necessary to establish heirship. In both cases, administration is needed to dispose of claims of creditors, payment of death taxes, right of surviving spouse to renounce will, widow's award, right of contest, etc.

In a very few areas, title companies are willing to handle this without probate.

EXAMPLE: *T,* a widower who is a sole owner, dies leaving *A* and *B* his children, as his only heirs. He leaves a will by which he gives them all his property in equal shares. His only asset of importance is his residence, worth $10,000.00. The title company may be willing to accept the following:

(1) Affidavit of heirship by *A* or *B*.

(2) Death certificate.

(3) Photostat of will, the original to be deposited with Probate Court Clerk as many statutes require.

(4) Affidavit as to value of estate. In many states, the exemptions from inheritance tax are far greater than this estate. Obviously, there is no estate tax here.

(5) Paid bills showing undertaker's bill and expenses of last illness paid, supported by affidavit of *A* or *B* that there were no other debts.

(6) Statement from Old Age Assistance Department showing that *T* was not receiving such assistance, for in some states that is a claim against his estate or a lien on his land. This is also supported by affidavit.

(7) Surety bond protecting the title company against claims. Alternatively the title company may charge an extra premium to assume this risk and take a personal undertaking from the heirs to protect it. This requirement is dispensed with if the sale takes place after expiration of the time limit for filing claims against an unprobated estate, for example 3 years in Illinois.

The affidavit must not state conclusions like "Rose Jones died leaving as her only heirs _____, _____, and _____." It must state facts, exactly as if the affidavit were testifying in the Probate Court. Form of such affidavit follows.

Form No. 7

(a) A form of Affidavit of Heirship
Re: Commitment for Title Insurance
Number 60—15—90

STATE OF ILLINOIS)
) SS.
COUNTY OF COOK)

AFFIDAVIT OF HEIRSHIP

FRANK J. JONES, of the City of Chicago, Cook County, Illinois, being first duly sworn upon oath, deposes and says as follows:

1. That he is the son of ROSE JONES, who died on February 17, 1972, in Chicago, Cook County, Illinois, leaving a Will, a copy of which is attached hereto, and he makes this Affidavit for the purpose of inducing CHICAGO TITLE INSURANCE COMPANY to issue its Commitment for Title Insurance, free and clear of the interest of Rose Jones, Deceased.

2. That Rose Jones was married to Jack Jones who died before her on January 24, 1960, and she was not previously or thereafter married to anyone else.

3. That the following children were born to ROSE JONES and JACK JONES and no other children were born to or adopted by either of them.

   a. Elizabeth Brown, sister of the Affiant, who is of legal age and sound mind and is married to John Brown and who resides at

   b. Rose Taylor, sister of Affiant, who is of legal age and sound mind and who is a Widow and not since remarried and who resides at

   c. Frank J. Jones, the Affiant, who is of legal age and sound mind and who is married to Catherine Jones and who resides at

4. That the total value of the Estate of ROSE JONES, which was owned by her at the time of her death including both real property and personal property, did not exceed the sum of $10,000.00 and consisted only of the property in question, which is described in the above referenced Commitment for Title Insurance.

_____

FRANK J. JONES

Subscribed and sworn to
before me this _____
day of _____
1975.

_____

    Notary Public

§ 170. Probated estate—sale by executor under power of sale.

Where an estate is in probate and the decedent's executor has a power of sale under the will, he may wish to sell the property immediately after the will has been admitted to probate, for example, the decedent's house, now vacant and subject to vandalism. In all states, his sale under the power gives the purchaser title free and clear of the claims of the creditors of the estate, their claims attaching to the proceeds of sale. In many states, the sale is also free of the right to contest the rights of disinherited heirs again attaching to the proceeds of sale. While the common law was otherwise in some states, many statutes now provide that an *administrator de bonis non* succeeds to the power of sale if the executor dies, resigns, or fails to qualify. The sale does not cut out the rights of the surviving spouse to renounce the will, but if she has moved in with one of the children, she wants the house sold and will give a deed to the purchaser. The attorney for the estate will sit down with an officer of the title company and make a frank disclosure of the assets of the estate. Often he has represented the decedent for years and is intimately familiar with his affairs. On this basis, an estimate can be formed of the outside limit of the anticipated death taxes and this amount is deposited with the title company, with a modest cushion. This is returned to the executor upon proof of payment of death taxes.

    The title company prefers to have the personal representative file an inventory before the deal is closed, for this is additional assurance as to the extent and value of the estate.

Usually, the local statute requires the personal representative to post an additional surety bond to cover the proceeds of this sale, and the title company checks to see that this has been done.

§ 171. Sale by personal representative by court proceedings. In some states, the personal representative has no testamentary power of sale. In all states, he has a statutory right to sell land where anticipated claims will exceed the personal property available to pay them. In some states, he has the power to do this even though the personal property is adequate but the sale will be convenient for the estate. This requires a court proceeding. The title company will furnish the following services:

(1) It will give a title report listing the necessary parties for the proceeding.

(2) After the petition has been filed and service of process obtained, it will furnish a report that approves the sufficiency of the petition and service of process, for title insurance purposes.

(3) After the decree or judgment of sale has been entered, it will issue a report covering the sufficiency of the decree or judgment.

(4) After the sale has been made, confirmed, and deed issued, the title company insures the title of the purchaser.

Such a sale automatically is clear of claims of creditors and the right to contest the will, if any. Usually the surviving spouse is asked to give a deed to the purchaser. Part or all of the proceeds of sale are deposited with the title company to protect against death taxes.

§ 172. Estate tax. In large estates, where an estate tax will be payable, or a sale is to be made before closing of the estate, the lien thereof can be released by furnishing the I.R.S. the following.

(a) Certified copy of letters testamentary or of administration.

(b) Certified copy of will.

(c) Certified copy of inventory.

(d) Three copies of I.R.S. form describing the sale.

Then if the premises sold constitutes one-third or less in value of the gross estate, I.R.S. will furnish immediately a release of its lien as to the premises being sold.

Alternatively, if the I.R.S. has issued its Estate Tax Closing Letter showing no tax due, the objection can be waived.

§ 173. Forfeiture of installment contract. In a number of states, an installment contract can be extinguished by forfeiture for default. This is one of the most difficult tasks of title clearance. The title company must always be consulted. It is folly for *E* to rely on a forfeiture where title insurance is not furnished. The risks are too great. As a rule, the procedure follows the following lines:

(1) A separate notice ("notice of intention to declare forfeiture") is served on each of the purchasers listing all the defaults and stating categorically

that all defaults must be cured on or before _____ (date) or the contract and all of the purchaser's rights thereunder will be forfeited. As to the time, this should never be less than the time for notice specified in the Forcible Detainer Statute. Most lawyers add about a ten-day's cushion to avoid arguments over the date the notice was received. Many lawyers use a process server. Whoever serves the notice attaches an affidavit of service to a duplicate original of the notice. If the notice is served by registered or certified mail, check to see that the contract explicitly permits this. Otherwise use personal service. If the contract does not contain an acceleration clause, the notice cannot call for payment of the entire contract price.

(2) After the time for curing defaults has elapsed, you serve on each of the purchasers a declaration of forfeiture reciting the existence of the defaults, the service of notice to cure defaults, the fact that the defaults were not cured, and declaring a forfeiture of the contract. A demand for possession is included where the state law requires this. Affidavits of service of the declaration and of the notice of intention to declare forfeiture are appended to a duplicate original. A certificate of acknowledgment is appended. If the contract has been recorded, or if the contract calls for recording of the declaration of forfeiture, it must be recorded. Otherwise it is simply delivered to the title company.

(3) If the purchasers have placed a mortgage on their contract interest or if other liens exist against them, the notice to cure defaults and the declaration of forfeiture should also be directed to them, describe their interest, and be served upon them.

(4) The purchasers must be evicted. If they are permitted to remain as tenants, this act of kindness may backfire. When you later seek to evict them as tenants, they will claim that the forfeiture was defective.

(5) An affidavit is furnished the title company showing all the foregoing facts and the amounts paid on the contract by the purchasers. If the purchasers paid $99,000 on a contract price of $100,000, you can be sure of an attack on the forfeiture.

§ 174. Title standards. In many states the real property bar has drafted *Title Standards*, outlining the standard rules and procedures governing real estate deals as the sophisticated practioners see them. Every attorney should be familiar with these standards, for they often contain an exposition of the local law and set forth customs that other lawyers in the deal are likely to insist upon. Such standards set forth many circumstances that, under the standards, warrant the waiver of title objections.

§ 175. Clearing mechanic's liens—in general. Ridding the title of mechanic's lien objections in construction loans is one of the most difficult problems facing the construction lender and the title company. Practices differ from state to state, depending on the state law. Also, the practice on big loans differs from those on small loans.

§ 176. Clearing mechanic's liens—big loans. On big loans the objective is to

Form No. 8

FORM 3056—CHICAGO TITLE INSURANCE COMPANY STANDARD FORM MECHANIC'S LIEN AFFIDAVIT—UNIMPROVED PROPERTY

CHICAGO TITLE INSURANCE COMPANY

ORDER NO:

MECHANIC'S LIEN AFFIDAVIT—UNIMPROVED PROPERTY

STATE OF

} s.s.

COUNTY OF

_____

being first duly sworn on oath deposes and says as follows:

1. That he is thoroughly familiar with all the facts and circumstances concerning the premises described as follows:

2. That during the six months last past the only work or materials furnished in connection with the mentioned premises were as follows:

a. Architect (give name of architect, how much paid, and how much still due):

b. Surveyors (give name of surveyor, how much paid, and how much still due):

c. Demolition (give name of party doing the demolition, how much paid, and how much still due):

d. Engineer (give name of engineer, how much paid, and how much still due):

e. Soil tests (give name of party doing soil tests, how much paid, and how much still due):

f. Fabrication of any construction or building materials (give name of fabricator, nature of material, how much paid, and balance due):

g. Installation of water, utilities, sewer or other drainage, or grading or paving of streets, alleys or other ways.

h. Other:

3. That the only contracts for the furnishing of *future* work or materials to said premises including work or materials for any of the purposes specifically stated above are as follows:

4 This affidavit is given to induce Chicago Title Insurance Company to issue its title insurance policy or policies.

Subscribed and sworn to before me this   day
of   A.D., 19   _____

_____
Notary Public

NOTE: Use this form for vacant land where substantial improvements are about to be erected.

determine at all stages of disbursement who is doing the work, how much they have done and are entitled to be paid, how much is still due each party, whether extras or change orders have crept in, and that the balance of the loan kitty suffices to complete construction. Sometimes the documentation has the sanction of statute, so that if the lender relies on the documents, he is protected against mechanic's liens. In most states, the documents merely provide the best available assurance that all the bills will be paid where a general contractor is involved. One starts by getting an affidavit from the landowner as to the work he has ordered from others than his general contractor. See Form No. 8.

Then on each draw the general contractor submits a detailed verified statement of work done and to be done. Procure form from title company.

The careful lender chooses to pay the subcontractors directly, to protect himself against forged lien waivers and lien waivers purchased by the general contractor with rubber checks. As to each such payment made, a three-part form is obtained. The first part is a payout order signed by the owner and his architect. After all, it's the owner's money that the lender is paying out. The money was loaned to the owner by the lender. Nevertheless, the money is that of the owner. The architect signs to show that he has approved the work. The subcontractor signs a partial waiver of lien, covering work done to the date of disbursement. On all disbursements up to the final one, the parts in brackets are deleted, because the subcontractor is unwilling to waive his lien for future work. He also signs an affidavit that reveals the names of persons who furnished lienable work and materials to him, and a similar three-part form is obtained from them as they are paid by the lender. On final disbursement, the parts in brackets remain unbracketed, for if the subcontractor is called back to repair defective work, which he must do to be entitled to payment of the retention, he is not entitled to additional compensation. See Form No. 9.

§ 177. **Clearing mechanic's liens—small deals.** On smaller deals, where the house has been completely constructed, the title company may be content with a form as Form No. 10.

Reference: Basye, *Clearing Land Titles* (2d ed.)

Form No. 9

FORM 3057—CHICAGO TITLE INSURANCE COMPANY STANDARD FORM LIEN WAIVER, PAYOUT ORDER, AND SUBCONTRACTOR'S AFFIDAVIT

CHICAGO TITLE INSURANCE COMPANY

PAYOUT ORDER

TO:

You are hereby authorized to pay to_____

contractor_____Dollars for_____

_____and charge same to my loan account on building situated at_____

_____
                                        Street Address

for work and/or material delivered on said building according to sworn statements given to you.

Statement of Account

Original contract_____

                                                                    _____
                                                                                    Owner

Approved additions_____

                                                                    Approved,

Approved deductions_____

                                                                    _____
                                                                        Architect or General Contractor

Net contract_____

                                                                    Received payment in the above amount,

Previous payments_____

                                                                    _____

This payment_____

Balance_____

WAIVER OF LIEN

To all whom it may concern:

The undersigned in consideration of _____ $1.00 and other valuable considerations, the receipt whereof is acknowledged, and in order to induce the making of one or more mortgage loans on the real estate hereinafter described and the issuance of mortgage or owner's policies of title insurance on said real estate, do hereby waive and release to the owners or hereafter thereon, or upon the monies or other considerations due [or to become due] from the owner, said liens or right to liens being on account of labor or services, material, fixtures, or apparatus heretofore furnished [or which may be furnished at any time hereafter] by the undersigned. The premises as to which said liens or right to liens are hereby released are described as follows:

Signed, sealed and delivered this_____day of_____, 19_____

                                                    Signed_____(Seal)

                                                    _____(Seal)

Form No. 9 (Continued)

| COUNTY OF | } SS | ORDER NO: |
| STATE OF | | |

CONTRACTOR'S AFFIDAVIT

TO WHOM IT MAY CONCERN:

THE undersigned, being duly sworn, deposes and says that he is_____

_____ _____ _____ ⌐ _____

of the_____ _____ _____ _____ ___ _____who is the

contractor for the_____ _____ _____ _____ _____work on the

building located at_____ ___ _____ _____

owned by_____ _____ _____ _____ _____

That the total amount of the contract is $_____of which he has received payment of $_____

That all waivers presented herewith are true, correct and genuine and delivered unconditionally and that there is no claim either legal or equitable to defeat the validity of said waivers. That the following are the names of all parties who have furnished material or labor, or both, for said work and all parties having contracts or sub contracts for specific portions of said work or for material entering into the construction thereof and the amount due or to become due to each, and that the items mentioned include all labor and material required to complete said work according to plans and specifications:

	CONTRACT PRICE	EXTRAS OR DEDUCTIONS	AMOUNT PAID	BALANCE DUE
Name: What for:	$	$	$	$
Name: What for:				
Name: What for:				
Name: What for:				
Name: What for:				
Name: What for:				
			TOTAL $	

That there are no other contracts for said work outstanding, that there ` nothing due or to become due to any person for material, labor or other work of any kind done or to be done upon   connection with said work other than above stated, and that no chattel mortgages, conditional sale contracts,   agreements, financing statements, retention of title agreements, or personal property leases have been given or are now outstanding as to any materials, fixtures, appliances, furnishings, or equipment placed upon or installed in or upon the aforesaid premises or the improvement thereon by the affiant.

Signed this_____day of_____, 19____.

_____

Subscribed and sworn to before me this_____day of_____, 19____.

_____

Form No. 10

FORM 3083—CHICAGO TITLE INSURANCE COMPANY STANDARD FORM OWNER'S AND CONTRACTOR'S FINAL AFFIDAVIT AND INDEMNITY AGREEMENT

CHICAGO TITLE INSURANCE COMPANY

ORDER NO:

AFFIDAVIT AND AGREEMENT

STATE OF ⎱ s.s.

COUNTY OF ⎰

On this_____day of_____, 19_____ before me personally appeared

_____,

owners of property, and_____, General Contractor, to me personally known, who, being duly sworn on their oaths, did say that all of the persons, firms and corporations, including the General Contractor and all sub-contractors, who have furnished services, labor, or materials, according to plans and specifications, or extra items, used in the construction or repair of buildings and improvements on the real estate here-

inafter described, have been paid in full and that such work was fully completed on or before_____ and accepted by the owners, free and clear of any mechanic's lien whatever, all such liens or claims for lien being hereby expressly waived.

Affiants further say that no unsatisfied claims for lien or payment have been made to either of the affiants by, nor is any suit now pending on behalf of, any contractor, sub-contractor, laborer, or materialman, and further that no chattel mortgages, conditional sale contracts, security agreements, financing statements, retention of title agreements, or personal property leases have been given or are now outstanding as to any materials, fixtures, appliances, furnishings, or equipment placed upon or installed in or upon the aforesaid premises or the improvement thereon, and all plumbing, heating, lighting, refrigerating, and other equipment is fully paid for, including all bills for the repair thereof, except as follows: (if none, state "none")

Affiants, parties hereto, hereby request Chicago Title Insurance Company to issue its policy or policies of title insurance upon said real estate without exception therein as to any possible unfiled mechanics' or materialmen's liens, and in consideration thereof, and as an inducement therefor, said affiants do hereby, jointly and severally, agree to indemnify and hold said Chicago Title Insurance Company harmless of and from any and all loss, cost, damage and expense of every kind, including attorneys' fees, which said Chicago Title Insurance Company shall or may suffer or incur or become liable for under its said policy or policies now to be issued, or any reissue, renewal or extension thereof, or new policy at any time issued upon said real estate, part thereof or interest therein, arising, directly or indirectly, out of or on account of any such mechanics' or materialmen's lien or liens or claim or claims or in connection with its enforcement of its rights under this agreement. All representation, agreements of indemnity, and waivers herein contained shall inure also to the benefit of any party assured under any policy issued by Chicago Title Insurance Company and any action brought hereon may be instituted in the name of Chicago Title Insurance Company or said assured or both.

Continued on Reverse Side

Form No. 10 (Continued)

The real estate and improvements referred to herein are situated at_____

_____in the County

of_____, State of _____, and are described as
follows to-wit:

This affidavit is given to induce Chicago Title Insurance Company to issue its title insurance policy or policies.

NOTE: Where the premises are owned by two
or more owners, both should be named as affiants and both should sign. Where corporations
are involved, the names of the affiants and the
signatures should be those of officers of the corporations, preferably the Presidents.

_____
Owner of Property

_____
Owner of Property

_____
General Contractor

Subscribed, and sworn to before me the day and year above written.

_____
Notary Public

For use with corporate landowner and/or corporate contractor:

_____

a corporation of the State of_____joins in the execution of this instrument for the purpose of
adopting all the representations of fact made in the foregoing affidavit and hereby joins in all the agreements of indemnity
and waivers therein contained.

_____
(Name of Corporation)

By:_____
President

Affix corporate
seal here.

By:_____
Secretary

15

Deeds

§ **178. In general.** Probably over 99 percent of the deeds recorded in this country are on forms, printed locally, that comply with local law. Nevertheless, substantial problems remain and it will be the purpose of this chapter to point out the problems and offer some suggestions.

The legal requirements for deeds have been discussed elsewhere. Kratovil, *Real Estate Law*, Chapter 7; 8A Thompson, *Real Property* (1963 Replacement) §§ 4360 *et. seq.* (state by state).

§ **179. Form of deed.** Usually there is a contract for the sale of land. The deed draftsman should determine if the contract specifies the form of deed to be given and follows the contract.

Special forms are needed for a conveyance by a trustee, corporation executor, sheriff, etc.

§ **180. Grantor.** The grantor's name must be spelled the same way as in the deed by which he acquired title. If a woman acquires title by her maiden name and subsequently marries, a deed by her should show both names: *Mary Jones, formerly Mary Smith.* Any examiner of the title will thus find a connected chain of title to the land. Title companies are likely to insist on this practice. In some states, statutes make this practice mandatory. *Pucetti v. Girola*, 20 Cal.2d 574, 128 P2d 13, 41 Mich.L.Rev. 980.

The grantor's marital status should be given: *bachelor, spinster, widower, divorced are not remarried.* Some title examiners object to the word "unmarried." They feel this could conceal a divorce. Of course, if a grantor has been divorced, the title examiner must check the divorce carefully for validity and disposition of property rights. If the grantor is married, his spouse must also be named as grantor in some states and their marital status given, *e.g., John Smith and Mary Smith his wife.* A married woman or widow should never be described as "Mrs. John Jones." Her legal name is "Mary Jones." 38 Am.Jur. *Name* § 9. The grantor should not be described as "R. John Smith." The middle name or middle initial is no part of a name in many states. 38 Am.Jur. *Name* § 5. Hence, the vendor should describe himself as "Robert J. Smith."

If the grantor is a surviving joint tenant it may be necessary to record with the deed the death certificate of the decedent, as, for example, in Michigan. *See* Mich.Rev.Stat. § 26.564.

Of course, all the landowners should join in the deed or give separate conveyances to the purchaser. Because of technical rules relating to married persons (*e.g.*, husband and wife must join in the same deed to release homestead rights), it is best, and often necessary, to have husband and wife join in the same deed.

Other matters relating to the grantor are discussed in Chapter 5.

§ **181. Grantee.** The grantee's marital status should be given. The reason for this is obvious. If a deed runs to ''John Smith and Mary Smith,'' they might be husband and wife, or brother and sister. If no marital status is indicated, a title examiner, finding a conveyance out by ''John Smith and Mary Smith his wife,'' is uncertain as to whether this Mary Smith is the same Mary Smith as was named grantee. If two or more persons are acquiring title, the names of all must be shown in the deed. If they are taking title as joint tenants, the draftsman uses a joint tenancy form deed. Following the names of the grantees in this printed form is a phrase reading somewhat like this: *as joint tenants with the right of suvivorship and not as tenants in common nor as tenants by the entireties.* Of course, the deed must follow the contract of sale as to the parties who are to be the grantees, and the contract must be checked for this purpose. If, however, the contract permits E to designate a nominee to receive title, this is permitted and a written designation furnished to R. If the contract has been assigned by E and the contract does not forbid assignment, the deed runs to the assignee.

Other matters relating to the grantee are discussed in Chapter 6.

§ **182. Deeds involving husband and wife.** In creating either a joint tenancy or a tenancy by the entireties, the old cases tended to insist on the ''four unities,'' under which the joint tenants had to acquire title by the same deed.

EXAMPLE: *H,* a landowner, conveys the land to *H* and *W,* (himself and wife) as joint tenants. Under the old law, this would be a tenancy in common.

Pointless technicalities of this sort are going out of style and many states have abolished them. But in creating a joint tenancy or tenancy by the entireties, the draftsman should determine whether the old technical rules persists in his state. If they do, he should run a deed from H and W to X, a nominee, who then conveys to H and W as joint tenants. If it is desired to create a joint tenancy, it is not sufficient, in many tenancy-by-the-entirety states, to run a deed to a husband and wife ''in joint tenancy.'' In most of such states, this will create a tenancy by the entireties. 161 ALR 470. Hence the need to negative the intention to a tenancy by the entireties.

While in most tenancy-by-the-entireties states, a deed to a husband and wife creates a tenancy by the entireties if no other type of tenancy is clearly indicated, in Kansas, Kentucky, Massachusetts, and perhaps other states laws have been passed stating that the deed must show on its face an intention to create a tenancy by the entireties. 52 Mich.L.Rev. 804.

There are other residual problems in conveyances from husband to wife, or *vice versa.*

EXAMPLE: *H* and *W* own land in joint tenancy. They are about to separate, though divorce is not contemplated. *H* makes a deed to *W.* In a state where curtesy, dower, or some statutory marital right exists, *H's* signature will still be needed on the deed by *W* to a purchaser.

A number of other husband-wife deed problems remain. The local law should be checked before an interspousal conveyance is executed. *See,* for example: 14 U. of Miami L.Rev. 638, 658, discussing the homestead morass in Florida.

§ **183. Addresses.** Quite a number of states require the deed to state the street address of both parties or of the grantee, for example, Arkansas, Colorado, Florida, Hawaii, Illinois, Massachusetts, Missouri, Montana, New Hampshire, New York, North Carolina, South Dakota, and Tennessee. 30 Mo.L.Rev. 164. Some states require the deed to state the address where the tax bill is to be sent.

§ **184. Consideration.** Every deed should recite a consideration. Some states (Massachusetts, Nebraska, and New Jersey, for example) require the true consideration to be stated.

Deeds by trustees and other fiduciaries should always recite the true consideration.

§ **185. Words of grant.** Every printed form of deed contains words of grant. It is not necessary to tamper with these.

§ **186. Subject clause.** If the grantor in a warranty deed wishes to avoid personal liability, he should include in the subject clause all defects in title, such as mortgages, unpaid taxes, existing leases, restrictions, and so forth. One should keep in mind the rule that the grantee's knowledge of a lien or defect does not relieve the grantor of liability of his covenants if the lien or defect is not mentioned in the deed. *Sterling v. Blackwelder,* 302 F.Supp 1125. The contract of sale usually specifies the objections to which the title will be subject when it is conveyed to the buyer. The seller, in preparing the deed, has no right to add items to this list. In a quitclaim deed, a subject clause is unnecessary and inappropriate.

§ **187. Recital as to source of title.** In Kentucky the deed must recite the source of the grantor's title. K.R.S. 328.090, 382.110. This is also the law in Tennessee. T.C.A. 64.2410, 64.2411. Other states also have this rule. It is a good practice to follow even when the law does not require it.

§ **188. Mortgages.** If the land is being sold subject to a mortgage that the grantee is to assume and agree to pay, let the deed so state.

SUGGESTED FORM: Subject to a mortgage recorded in Book 100, Page 101, as Document No. 999, which the grantee herein assumes and agrees to pay.

Of course, if the grantee is not to be personally liable for payment of the mortgage, the deed should state that the grantee does *not* assume the mortgage.

In either case, the contract of sale must be consulted to determine which way the deed should go. Obviously, the well-drafted contract will spell this out clearly.

Where the grantee is paying part cash and giving back to the seller either a mortgage or a mortgage deed of trust for part of the purchase money, it is better that the deed contain a recital somewhat as follows:

As part of the consideration for this transaction, the grantee herein has this day executed to _____, as trustee, a deed of trust of even date herewith, securing a promissory note in the sum of $_____, which represents part of the purchase price for said premises.

This is particularly desirable where a mortgage deed of trust is involved, since if *A* sells and conveys land to *B*, and *B* simultaneously executes a mortgage deed of trust to *C*. as trustee, the public records do not clearly show that the deed of trust was given as part of the purchase deed of price unless the deed contains the suggested recital. Of course the trust deed or mortgage should also contain a recital that:

This deed of trust is given to secure payment of part of the purchase price of said premises.

These precautions are desirable to protect the priority of the mortgage against earlier judgments against the grantee. *Curtis v. Root*, 28 Ill. 367.

§ 189. Statement of purpose of deed. Inclusion of a statement of the purpose for which the deed is given is a very dangerous practice. If you add in your deed phrases like "to be used for road purposes," the result may be to create a grant of an easement out of what started to be a deed of the land. 136 ALR 379; 6 ALR 3rd 973.

§ 190. Reservation of life estate. The reservation of a life estate, common in deeds, between a parent and child, needs careful drafting to give the grantor adequate protection.

CLAUSE: Grantors reserve to themselves, and to the survivor of them, an estate in the above described premises for their lives and for the life of the survivor of them, and also reserve to themselves, and to the survivor of them, the power to sell, mortgage or otherwise dispose of the fee simple title to said premises, and to retain proceeds of such sale, mortgage or other disposition as the sole and absolute property of the grantors or survivor of them.

Simple reservation of a life estate does not give the grantor adequate protection. The state law should be checked. A broad power such as in the suggested clause may create problems in some states. 28 Am.Jur. 2d *Estates* § 83.

At times, especially in a deed between parent and child, the grantor wishes to reserve a right of occupancy.

CLAUSE: Grantor reserves to himself as a right personal to himself the exclusive right of occupancy of the second floor apartment of said premises during his lifetime, with right of access thereto, terminating, however on his removal from said premises, for whatever reason, with no liability for taxes, mortgage payment or other duties whatever except that of ordinary maintenance of said apartment. No alterations shall be made of said apartment during grantor's occupancy. The recorded affidavit of the landowner that the grantor's occupancy has ceased or that he has died shall be conclusive evidence of that fact in favor of any grantee or mortgagee of the premises.

§ 191. Vendor's lien. *E* will want a clause negating the existence of a vendor's lien if part of the sale price remains unpaid.

§ 192. Alterations. It is unwise to make erasures or alterations in a deed. Such may even render title unmarketable. *Tesdel v. Haines*, 248 Ia. 742, 82 NW2d 119. They may prevent the grantee from being a bona fide purchaser. *Marsh v. Marsh*, 261 A2d 540.

§ 193. Name of draftsman. Quite a few states (Florida, Indiana, Kentucky, Michigan, New Jersey, and Wisconsin, for example) require the deed to state the name and address of the draftsman. If the statute goes on to say that the deed shall not be recorded if this requirement is not met, possibly it will not impart notice even if the recorder accepts it.

§ 194. Waiver of dower and homestead. Almost without exception, deed forms prepared by local stationers include the necessary waivers of dower and homestead rights.

§ 195. Date. It is the custom to date all deeds.

§ 196. Signature. The draftsman should be sure that the signature of the grantor is identical with the spelling in the body of the deed, since even trivial variations are frequently objected to by title examiners. The draftsman types the name of the grantor beneath the signature line and directs him to sign exactly as his name is typed. This is required by statute in some states.

§ 197. Seal. If a seal is needed on deeds of land in the particular state, deed forms printed in the state will show a seal on the signature line. The corporate seal should be affixed on deeds made by corporations even if the state law does not require a deed to be sealed. The corporate seal creates a presumption that the officers had authority to sign.

§ 198. Taxes. In some states, real estate taxes must be paid before the deed can be recorded.

§ 199. Documentary stamps. The necessary documentary tax stamps should be attached where the state law requires this.

§ 200. Witnesses. The draftsman should have two or more witnesses sign the deed if any grantor has signed by mark. If all grantors are able to write, their signatures need not be witnessed unless the state law requires witnesses. Some states require that all deeds be witnessed.

§ 201. Acknowledgment. The printed form will have the local acknowledgment form. It should be properly filled in, and signed and sealed by a notary. If the deed is signed by an attorney-in-fact, a special form of acknowledgment is needed. A comprehensive annotation of the sufficiency of the certificate of acknowledgment is found in 25 ALR 2d 1124.[1]

§ 202. Recitals. The matter of recitals in deeds has been competently covered elsewhere. Basye, Chapter 3.

§ 203. Correction deeds. When an error has been detected in a deed, the question that arises is whether a correction deed should be given. The problem, of course, is that the grantee may be affected and his signature may not appear on the correction deed. Obviously, it is best that the grantee sign and acknowledge the correction deed. Patton, *Titles* § 82; 3 Am.L.Ppty. § 1285. The problem of intervening rights is too obvious to require discussion. Bona fide purchasers take free of the equity of reformation and a correction deed is reformation by act of the parties.

---

[1] Copyright Kratovil, *Real Estate Law* (6th ed. 1974), Chapter 7. Prentice-Hall, Inc. Reprinted by permission.

16

Contract of Sale—
Residential Transactions

§ **204. In general.** Many articles, many of them quite good, have dealt with the subject here discussed. Most have been local in flavor, thus enhancing their value to local practitioners. Some suggestions, however, have more or less general application. These are offered here with the hope that they will suggest some fresh insights into the problem and with the warning that they only scratch the surface of a complex problem. *See, e.g.,* Friedman, *Contracts and Conveyances of Real Property* (1963).

§ **205. Form of contract—the contract as a blueprint for closing of the deal.** The contract of sale is the blueprint for the closing of a real estate deal. Whenever, in the course of a deal, a question arises as to the rights of the parties, we turn to the contract. Hence plans for closing the deal must be made before the contract is signed, for once the contract is signed, the shape of the deal is set, and rights and liabilities are crystallized. Before the contract is signed, the following, for example, must be considered: (1) If the land is vacant, are there any zoning ordinances that will prevent use of the land for the purposes contemplated by the purchaser? If there is a building on the land, but the purchaser expects to remodel it, are there any ordinances that will prohibit such remodeling? For example, the building may be a non-conforming use (which under the law cannot be enlarged), or constructed under a variance that forbids enlargement. (2) If the land is vacant, and the contract is a printed form requiring the buyer to take subject to "building restrictions," what do these building restrictions provide? Do they prohibit use of the land for the purpose contemplated by the purchaser?

§ **206. Form of contract—printed forms.** On the really big deals, the contracts, of course, are tailor-made. *See* Chapter 17. On anything less, it is probable that a local printed form, often one supplied by a title insurance company, can be employed as the basic document. A good lawyer, of course, comes to know the weaknesses of the form and adds riders as needed. But there is something so comforting, so commanding of acceptance, in the familiar form furnished by a respected business establishment, that it disarms suspicion and reduces sales resistance that a completely typed contract might encounter. A rider, oddly enough, seems to arouse little hostility. Every deal is unique in some respects, the other party reasons, and a rider is obviously needed to deal with such features.

§ 207. **Necessity for detailed contract provisions.** Probably over 99% of real estate sales are closed without literal conformity with contract provisions. Most people are people of good will and gladly do things they are not legally obligated to do. Some of the suggestions made herein fall in this category. For example, a vendor, who has no intention of up-dating his old survey will usually make it available to the purchaser for whatever it is worth. On the other hand, at times the parties quarrel bitterly during the transaction, often over trivial matters. At that point the warring parties take the position that nothing will be done that is not there "in black and white." It is a matter of sound business judgment to decide what gets left out. If either party is strongly of the view that he is driving a good bargain, his lawyer should resolve doubts against insisting on a lengthy rider. Clauses in riders ought to be as brief as possible and legal jargon avoided, if possible. The shorter it is, the easier it is to sell.

§ 208. **Completeness.** In order to be enforceable, a contract must be complete in all its parts. All the terms of the contract must be settled, and none must be left to be determined by future negotiation. Numerous examples of contracts held unenforceable for lack of completeness are given in Kratovil, *Real Estate Law* §§ 177, 178.

§ 209. **Binders and receipts.** Some sellers and real estate offices may request the buyer to sign a binder or may request the seller to sign a receipt that describes the intended sale briefly. Obviously intending sellers and buyers should be warned against signing such documents. No one should sign anything but a contract that adequately protects his rights.

§ 210. **Seller and buyer.** Of course the names of seller and buyer should be given accurately. The seller's name should be identical in spelling with the deed by which he acquired title. Seller's spouse should join. Other requirements are found in Chapters 5 and 6. Cotenancy problems are discussed in Chapter 17.

§ 211. **Property sold—chattel clause:** Most deals involve a transfer of chattels as well as title to land. These items often lead to controversy. A suggested list of items is given below.

Together with the following chattels for which a bill of sale will be given at closing:

Air conditioning equipment, awning, bar and bar stools, bookcases, cabinets, carpets (particularly stair carpets), chandeliers and lighting fixtures, clothes washer and dryer, crops, curtains, curtain rods, draperies and other interior decorations, electric fans, electrical equipment, fireplace grates and andirons, dishwasher, doorbells and chimes, fuel, furniture, garbage cans, garbage disposal, gas logs, high fidelity or stereo equipment that has been built in, ironing boards, kitchen cabinets, lamps, lawn mowers and garden equipment, linoleum, mirrors, refrigerators, rugs, screen doors, shelves, space heaters, sprinkling equipment, storm doors and windows, stoves, supplies, TV antennas and masts, tools and equipment (particularly janitor's tools), water softener, trade fixtures, venetian blinds, ventilators, wash tubs, washers and driers, water heaters, towel racks and bars, water meter, window shades, window screens, stokers, security systems, garage door openers and car units.

§ 212. **Land description.** The contract must contain a reasonably certain description of the land sold. It must be sufficiently definite to identify the land sold with reasonable certainty. 23 ALR2d 6. There is a conflict as to whether the description in the contract must be as specific as the description in a deed. Friedman, *Contracts & Conveyances of Real Property* (1963) 35. *See* Chapter 8.

§ 213. Land description—quitclaim of premises occupied by vendor beyond the deed lines. Quite commonly a vendor occupies land extending beyond the property lines described in his deed. For example, a vendor-farmer may have fenced and farmed five or ten feet beyond his property line. He may have acquired title to this land by adverse possession. The survey will disclose this. He should be willing to agree to give a quitclaim deed to this land. If possession has not yet ripened into title, the quitclaim makes it easier for the purchaser to ''tack'' the vendor's possession to his own for adverse possession purposes.

§ 214. Land description—streets and private streets. Careful attorneys for purchasers want the contract to require the vendor to convey his interest in public and private ways adjoining the property, including vacated streets and alleys. Decisions conflict as to whether such interests pass by mere conveyance of the abutting land. *See* Chapter 9.

§ 215. Assignment of service contracts. The purchaser should include a clause requiring vendor to deliver and assign to purchaser existing service contracts, (exterminators, scavenger, and the like) and guarantees (roof guarantee, heating guarantee, etc.). Some vendors refuse to assign or to contract to assign service contracts. They feel they will remain liable if the purchaser fails to pay for services performed.

§ 216. Assignment of warranties. The seller may have warranties in his favor of the building, the roof he had installed or appliances that go with sale of the property. The contract should call for assignment thereof to buyer.

§ 217. Acreage shortage or unusable land. There are endless arguments as to the effect of a shortage in area where the sale is by acre. Hence it is best for the parties to agree in advance. Arguments also ensue as to land the buyer cannot use. This also should be covered. The following is a suggested clause:

Price on acreage: At a price of $_____ per usable acre, but if survey reveals acreage of less than _____ usable acres, buyer shall have the right to rescind within _____ days after delivery of copy of survey to seller. Areas falling in (1) open or dedicated public streets or ways, (2) in recorded private easements of ingress, or (3) in areas fenced by adjoiners are not deemed usable acres. All other acres are deemed usable.

§ 218. Purchase price—manner of payment. There is no problem as to the dollar figure of the sale price. Where the seller is taking back a purchase money mortgage or the buyer is assuming an existing mortgage, great care is needed. One good form uses this language.

Purchaser has paid $_____ as earnest money to be applied on the purchase price, and agrees to pay or satisfy the balance of the purchase price, plus or minus prorations, at the time of closing as follows: *(strike language and subparagraphs not applicable).*

(a) The payment of $ _____

(b) The payment of $_____ and the balance payable as follows:
to be evidenced by the note of the purchaser (grantee), providing for full prepayment privileges without penalty, which shall be secured by a part-purchase money mortgage, the latter instrument and the note to be in the form hereto attached as Schedule B, and by a security agreement (as to which

Purchaser will execute or cause to be executed such financing statements as may be required under the Uniform Commercial Code in order to make the lien created thereunder effective), and an assignment of rents, said security agreement and assignment of rents to be in the forms appended hereto as Schedules C and D. Purchaser shall furnish to Seller an American Land Title Association loan policy insuring the mortgage issued by _____ Title Insurance Company.

(c) The acceptance of the title to the real estate by Purchaser subject to a mortgage or trust deed of record securing a principal indebtedness (which the Purchaser (does/does not) agree to assume) aggregating $_____ bearing interest at the rate of _____% a year, and the payment of a sum which represents the difference between the amount due on the indebtedness at the time of closing and the balance of the purchase price.

§ 219. Payment by cashier's check. Some lawyers for buyers state that purchase price shall be payable in cash. This gives them the right to state what substitute shall be accepted. Others prefer to state that price will be paid in cashier's check or certified check.

§ 220. Earnest money in escrow: There is no objection to having the earnest money held in escrow by a responsible individual or corporation. But if R insists on some individual whom E does not know, E should insist on the following:

The earnest money shall be held by _____ for the mutual benefit of the parties. Inasmuch as the escrowee of the earnest money has been designated by the seller, the seller agrees to be responsible for return of the deposit to the buyer if he becomes entitled thereto under the terms hereof.

§ 221. Marketable title. If title insurance is not used, the seller will be obliged to furnish a marketable title. It appears that a title which rests upon adverse possession is "marketable." Therefore most buyers will wish to stipulate for a marketable title of record, for where it appears that the parties intended a title of record to be conveyed, the purchaser will not be required to take a title resting only on adverse possession. In any case the seller will want to include a provision that if the examination of title reveals defects or encumbrances that the contract does not permit, he can cure these defects by tendering a title policy free and clear of such defects or encumbrances.

§ 222. Marketable title—restrictions. Often the use to which a tract of land may be devoted is restricted by building restrictions contained in recorded deeds or subdivision plats. Unless the contract provides otherwise, the buyer is not required to accept a title encumbered with restrictions as to the character of the buildings that may be erected, the use to which the property may be put, and so on, even though such restrictions actually enhance the value of the property.

Suppose the contract requires the buyer to accept title subject to "building line and building restrictions," but it appears that the building on the property violates existing restrictions. The buyer may decline to go through with the deal, for a violation of a restriction is a defect or encumbrance separate and distinct from the restriction itself.

A buyer should never be permitted to sign a contract which states that title will be subject to "restrictions of record." This obligates the buyer to take title subject to any restriction, no matter how absurd, even a restriction that the only building permitted on the land is a chicken coop. If the seller's title insurance policy or previous abstract and opinion is available, examine it, if it shows a restriction, go to the title company or the recorder's office and read the restriction. If you have no objection to it, let the contract read that title will be "subject to restriction recorded as Document No. 123456." Where the contract must be signed at a time when information as to existing building restrictions is not available and the land is improved with a building that is the principal subject matter of the sale, you might employ the following clause:

Subject to covenants and restrictions of record, provided same are not violated by the existing improvements or the use thereof.

When you are buying vacant land you must insist on reading the restrictions in full before signing the contract.

There are a few cases concerning the enforcement of contracts which failed to mention restrictions which were against the property to be sold. A New York decision (*Bull v. Burton*, 227 N.Y. 101, 124 NE 111), following a line of four or five decisions that developed elsewhere, (See *Hall v. Risley*, 213 P.2d 818 (Ore.).) held that if the building restrictions are identical to the provisions of a zoning ordinance, then the failure to mention the restriction in the contract would not render the title unmarketable. There are two recent cases where the contract failed to mention restrictions which had become unenforceable because of a substantial change in the neighborhood. In *Anness v. Freeman*, 294 S.W. 2d 77, the Kentucky court held that the title was marketable. In *Javna v. Friederichs*, 125 A.2d the New Jersey court held the title unmarketable. Obviously, *E* will want the contract to say that title must be conveyed "free and clear of all building restrictions, covenants, or conditions except those listed as *permitted objections*, and free of violations thereof."

§ 223. Permitted objections—encumbrances. The seller should see that he has listed in the contract all the encumbrances or other defects in title that he does not propose to clear before the deal is closed. Most contract forms contain a printed list of common encumbrances, such as leases or building restrictions, but it is intended that the seller will add to this list as necessary. Suppose, for example, that the seller's title is subject to an easement. Is it mentioned in the contract? If not, and the buyer changes his mind and decides to back out of the deal, he may be able to do so because the title, as finally examined before the deal is closed, must reveal no encumbrances other than those listed either in general or in specific language in the contract.

The buyer should carefully analyze every encumbrance listed by the seller. For example, if in the contract he agrees to take subject to "existing leases," he must accept the property subject to any lease, no matter how ridiculously low the rent may be. If the contract says that the buyer will accept title subject to "building and other restrictions of record," and "mineral rights," as many printed forms provide, will any of these restrictions, easements, or mineral rights interfere with his building program, assuming that he is buying land to build on? Moreover, will some easement document to which the land is subject obligate the buyer in some way as owner of this land? For example, an easement for road purposes may obligate me to keep my neighbor's road in repair. Similar personal liability provisions may be contained in restriction documents.

The following expressions in capitals are common permitted objections found in contracts:

Subject to:

1. EXISTING LEASES EXPIRING _____.
2. ROADS AND HIGHWAYS, IF ANY.

Both of these are usually deleted by the purchaser when sale of a residence is involved.

Where apartments are involved, often you find this clause:

3. EXISTING LEASES AS PER SCHEDULE ATTACHED HERETO IDENTIFIED BY INITIALS OF PARTIES HERETO, NONE OF WHICH LEASES IS IN DEFAULT OR CONTAINS AN OPTION TO PURCHASE OR RENEW EXCEPT AS STATED IN SAID SCHEDULE. NO PREPAYMENTS OF RENT HAVE BEEN MADE EXCEPT CURRENT RENTS AS PER LEASE AND NO CONCESSIONS HAVE BEEN GRANTED.

4. PARTY WALLS AND PARTY WALL RIGHTS.

Most lawyers do not bother to change this one.

5. SUBJECT TO EASEMENTS OF RECORD.

This is objected to by many attorneys for purchasers. They say that the buyer would have to take the title even if there were a 50-foot easement running through the middle of the house. Some attorneys will accept a general objection if the land is improved, but they change it to read:

CUSTOMARY UTILITY EASEMENTS OVER REAR 10 FEET OF SAID PREMISES.

They use the word "customary" to show that a high-voltage transmission easement would be objectionable.

On a sale of vacant land some attorneys insist that the objection be changed to read:

EASEMENT CREATED BY INSTRUMENT RECORDED IN BOOK _____ PAGE _____.

Then they read it before the client signs the contract.

6. SUBJECT TO BUILDING, BUILDING LINE AND USE OR OCCUPANCY RESTRICTIONS, CONDITIONS AND COVENANTS OF RECORD.

This is objected to by some attorneys for buyers as being too broad. The buyer would have to accept title to burdensome or ridiculous restrictions.

On vacant land some attorneys insist on deleting this in favor of a clause giving the specific document creating the restriction, *e.g.;*

SUBJECT TO RESTRICTIONS CREATED BY INSTRUMENT RECORDED IN BOOK _____ PAGE _____.

The theory is that a lawyer cannot permit his client to contract to buy restricted vacant land unless he reads the restrictions and knows what it provides.

Some lawyers will permit a buyer to sign a contract if the land is improved, and the following language is added:

PROVIDED SUCH RESTRICTIONS, CONDITIONS, OR COVENANTS ARE NOT VIOLATED BY EXISTING IMPROVEMENTS OR EXISTING USE THEREOF AND CONTAIN NO REVERTER CLAUSE.

Other attorneys add a requirement that:

AND TITLE INSURANCE COMPANY IS WILLING TO ISSUE ITS RESTRICTIONS EN-DORSEMENT NUMBER _____.

This endorsement protects the insured against any violations of restrictions or conditions.

7. INSTALLMENTS NOT DUE AT THE DATE HEREOF OF ANY SPECIAL TAX OR ASSESS-MENTS FOR IMPROVEMENTS THERETOFORE COMPLETED.

This should be unacceptable to the prudent buyer. If a sewer or street has been put in under special assessments, the enhanced value of the property is reflected in the sale price. There is no reason why the buyer should pay twice for the improvement, once to the seller and the second time to the city.

§ 224. **Special assessments.** This problem ought not be resolved in technical terms. The statutes and cases are in bewildering disagreement as to the date on which a special assessment "becomes a lien." Even more chaotic are the decisions on supple-mental assessments, being those levied where the improvement costs more than the original assessment. There are decisions that the lien of supplemental assessments "relates back" to the lien date of the original assessment. The real point at issue is who should pay if the improvements have already been installed. If they have, the sale price reflects the added value, and the seller ought to pay the assessments. If the final amount has not yet been finally determined, an escrow can be made with a bank, trust company or title company. If the title company can be persuaded to give an endorsement insuring against the special assessment, this is the best solution for the buyer, for it leaves the title company with the decision as to the size of the deposit it must exact from the seller. In situations where the amount cannot be calculated, the title company may refuse the burden, since it will alienate the seller if it asks for too large an amount and will suffer loss if it takes a deposit that is too small.

§ 225. **Evidence of title—the abstract.** Abstracts at times consist of various segments each certified by different abstracters. The last abstracter to certify has no liability for omissions of prior abstracters unless he certifies the entire abstract. And his certificate should be in form satisfactory to the buyer. For example, if the abstracter's certificate states that he does not certify as to federal court proceedings, since the federal court does not sit in his county, the buyer may wish him to amend this certificate and cover such proceedings. *See* Chapter 13.

The following is a suggested abstract clause:

Form of Abstract: Abstract shall be by an abstracter satisfactory to buyer and all continuations found in such abstract shall be certified by such abstracter to date of abstract with certificate in form satisfactory to buyer.

Substitution of Title Policy for Abstract. Where the contract calls for the seller to furnish an abstract of title, this does not permit the seller to substitute a policy of title insurance. *Cobb v. Nau,* 12 SW2d 594 (Tex. Civ. App. 1929).

When, as occasionally occurs, seller agrees to deliver an abstract or title insurance he may not after delivery of an abstract, supply title insurance instead of correcting defects appearing in the abstract. *Giddens v. Moore,* 348 S.W.2d 404 (Tex. Civ. App. 1961).

Hence the contract should be quite specific on this point. For example:

The seller shall, within twenty (20) days from the date hereof, deliver to the buyer or at the office of _____ an abstract of title by competent abstracters showing all instruments of record affecting said property from the United States Government to this date, with the usual certificates as to bankruptcy, taxes, judgments, and mechanics' liens. Subsequent acceptance of abstract by the buyer shall be a waiver of time of delivery. The buyer shall have ten (10) days after such delivery of abstract to examine it. If there are objections to the title, the buyer shall specify the objections in writing, to be delivered to the office of _____. The seller shall have any defects in the title corrected and shown on the abstract within thirty (30) days from date of delivery of such objections. The abstract shall become the property of the buyer.

In lieu of furnishing such abstract of title, or in lieu of correcting such objections the seller may furnish the buyer an Owner's Title Insurance Policy in the amount of the purchase price from a company authorized to insure titles in this state, insuring a merchantable fee simple title in the buyer as of the date of recording the deed. The seller may, within twenty (20) days from the date hereof or the date of receipt of objections to said title, deliver to the buyer or at the office of _____ a commitment for said policy. The seller shall have an additional thirty (30) days to make any corrections in the title required by said company. In case such defects in title are not rectified within the time specified, or the title insurance commitment is not delivered, this contract shall be null and void, unless the buyer elects to waive such objections, and the money deposited aforesaid shall be returned to the buyer and the abstract returned to the seller.

§ 226. Title policy in lieu of marketable title. The law of marketable title is a quagmire, made up, in substantial part, of decisions in cases where the purchaser was seeking to extricate himself from a contract he later regretted signing. Hence it is to the vendor's advantage to include a provision that any title commitment or title policy of _____ Company shall be conclusive evidence of good title as therein shown as to all matters insured thereby. This precludes the purchaser from raising "fly-speck" objections to the title and contending that they render title "unmarketable." In the absence of the quoted clause, the buyer in a contract calling for a title policy is entitled to marketable title and a title policy.

§ 227. Chattel liens. If the sale includes valuable chattels, the seller may be required to furnish a Uniform Commercial Code search showing that the chattels are free of filed liens. If abstracts are used the buyer may want the seller to furnish a search on fixture liens if the abstracter's certificate indicates that he does not search for Code filings. Most likely, where title insurance is used, the title company covers fixture filings under the Code, but if it does not, the contract should call for a fixture filing search.

§ 228. Mortgage problems—existing mortgages. Unless the contract provides otherwise, the purchaser has the right to demand a title free and clear of all mortgages, tax liens, judgments liens, mechanics' liens, and all other liens. It is not sufficient for the vendor to offer to deduct the amount of such liens from the purchase price. The purchaser may reject the title unless it is actually cleared of such liens. Suppose, however, that there is a mortgage or other lien on the property, and the vendor can arrange to have the mortgagee present at the closing of the deal, so that, at the closing of the deal, the mortgage will be paid in full out of the purchase money due the seller and the mortgagee will deliver a release of the mortgage to the buyer. Must the purchaser go through with the deal in this manner if the contract does not require him to do so? In quite a number of states, the answer is in the affirmative. The vendor's title is not considered unmarketable if he can arrange to have the owner of the mortgage, judgment, or other lien present at the closing of the deal, ready to turn over proper releases to the buyer on receiving payment of the amount due from the buyer. In other states, a contrary rule is followed. Any mortgage or other lien not mentioned in the contract must be cleared before the deal is closed. Many lawyers feel that where the contract requires good title to be established by title insurance, by inference this requires the vendor to produce to the purchaser a title company policy or commitment free and clear of any existing mortgage. Inferentially, the contract obviously contemplates that the title company must, *before the deal is closed* be satisfied with documents produced to discharge the mortgage. A form that has been suggested to deal with this problem is as follows:

If at the date of closing there is any mortgage encumbrance which the vendor is obligated to pay and discharge, the vendor may use any portion of the balance of the purchase price to satisfy the same, provided the vendor shall at the closing, either (1) deliver to the purchaser an instrument in recordable form sufficient, in the judgment of purchaser's title company, to satisfy such encumbrance of record, or (2) deposit with the purchaser's title insurance company sufficient money required by it to insure the recording of such satisfaction and the issuance of title insurance to the purchaser free of any such encumbrance, together with the mortgagee's letter indicating its willingness to accept such payment.

It is usually impossible to obtain a provision as formal as this. Most small deals close in reliance on the mortgagee's payoff statement, which indicates the amount required to pay off the mortgage. If the mortgage is held by some institutional lender or the payoff letter is given by his mortgage banker correspondent, it may state that it is "subject to audit." In this case the parties must decide whether or not they will gamble on the correctness of the letter or try to figure out a "re-proration clause" to cover possible variations in the final figures.

If there is a mortgage on the land and the buyer is to accept the land with the mortgage remaining unpaid, the contract should specify: (1) that the land is being sold subject to such mortgage; (2) the amount remaining unpaid thereon; (3) whether or not the buyer assumes and agrees to pay the mortgage, since if he does, he becomes personally liable to the mortgagee for the mortgage debt. If he does not assume and agree to pay the mortgage, he may lose the land by foreclosure should he default in his mortgage payments, but no personal judgment can be rendered against him. If the contract calls for the buyer to take the land subject to a mortgage but misdescribes the mortgage, the buyer can back out of the deal. *Crooke v. Nelson,* 195 Ia. 681, 191 NW 122. *See also* Chapter 17.

If a purchase money mortgage is to be given by the buyer as part payment, the contract should state the amount thereof, the rate of interest, how principal and interests shall be payable, whether or not monthly deposits are to be made to cover taxes, any other special provisions to be inserted in the mortgage, and the form of mortgage to be employed. Great care should be exercised in drafting the purchase money mortgage provision, since it is on this particular point that many contracts have been held too vague and uncertain to be enforced. Once again it must be emphasized that courts cannot enforce a contract unless the parties have clearly set forth therein the terms of their agreement. If the contract calls for a purchase money mortgage, but fails to specify a due date or an interest rate thereof, the contract is incomplete and cannot be enforced, 60 ALR 2d 251. The contract should also specify who is to pay for the recording of the purchase money mortgage and the cost of bringing down the abstract or title policy thereon. It should also state what prepayment privileges are to exist, what tax and insurance escrow payments are to be made, and what late charges are to be made.

If there is already a first mortgage on the land to which the purchase money mortgage will be subject, it is customary to provide that the purchase money mortgage will be subject to any extension or replacement of the existing first mortgage. This is done to make it possible for the buyer to obtain a new mortgage to pay off the existing first mortgage when it falls due.

§ 229. **Contract contingent on buyer getting financing.** One common fault with contingent clauses is that they often fail to give details of the mortgage, such as interest rate, time of payment, and so forth. A seller may procure a mortgage loan of the desired amount for the buyer and the buyer rejects it in horror because the interest rate is too high. Obviously, all such details should be covered in the clause.

The seller should tie the contingent clause into the printed clause of the contract form. The contract may give the buyer thirty days in which to procure a mortgage of a specified amount. Yet the printed portion of the contract may state that seller must deliver to the buyer evidence of seller's good title within twenty days of the date of the contract. Why should seller have his title examined when he does not even know that he has a deal with the buyer?

In addition, there is danger to the seller that the buyer may make only half-hearted efforts to procure the loan if he decides that he does not really want to go through with the deal. It is therefore desirable from the seller's viewpoint that the clause give the buyer a specified time in which to procure the loan, and in case of his failure so to do, the seller is given a further period of time in which to procure the loan for the buyer.

§ 230. **Surveys—contract provisions.** Whether the contract should call for the seller to furnish a survey is a matter of business judgment. For example, if I am buying a forty year old dwelling where the fences have also been up for that length of time, it is unlikely that any encroachment trouble will develop. Age has set the matter at rest. If on the other hand you were buying a relatively new house, you should consider requiring a survey. The survey will show whether your driveway encroaches on the neighbor's land or whether his driveway encroaches on your land. Fence and garage encroachments will be revealed. Encroachments of the residence over building lines established by plat restrictions, deed restrictions or zoning ordinances will also be revealed. *See* Chapter 7.

R will try to get his contract subject to "questions of survey" or "survey matters disclosed by survey" (describing it). *E* will resist this and, indeed, will ask for title insurance insuring that there are no survey problems.

§ 231. **Surveys—curing survey questions.** There is a special problem with objections such as survey questions. Title objections can be cleared by obtaining quitclaim deeds or releases of liens. Buildings cannot be moved to remove survey objections. But the vendor can negotiate with a title company for the issuance of special coverage against loss or damage by reason of the survey objection. For example, if the building on the premises sold has encroached on the adjoining land for well over twenty years, the title company may be willing to issue special coverage on the theory that the matter has been set at rest by adverse possession. For this reason it is best for the contract of sale to have a clause permitting the seller to cure such objections by having the title company give an endorsement insuring against loss or damage by reason of such objections, for example:

> If the title commitment or plat of survey (if one is required to be delivered under the terms of this contract) discloses either unpermitted exceptions or survey matters that render the title unmarketable (herein referred to as survey defects), Seller shall have 30 days from the date of delivery thereof to have the exceptions removed from the commitment or to correct such survey defects or to have the title insurer commit to insure against loss or damage that may be occasioned by such exceptions or survey defects.

§ 232. Leases—assignment of leases.

Commonly the contract calls for assignment of the seller's interest in all leases. This is done because the deed to the buyer automatically transfers to him the right to enforce covenants running with the land, but the benefit of covenants that do not run passes only by assignment from lessor to buyer. The contract may call for a warranty and representation at closing by seller that leases in the contract schedule remain in force, that there are no defaults and no advance payment of rent. If any lease might expire before closing, another clause is needed:

> If any apartment leases expire prior to closing, seller may lease same for not less than the existing rentals and for a period not exceeding one year.

§ 233. Delinquent rents.

There is no really satisfactory way of handling uncollected rents. *See* Chapter 17.

§ 234. Leases—advance payments of rent, security deposits.

The contract should state what advance payments of rent or security deposits have been made by tenants and how vendor proposes to give purchaser advantage of same. If a deposit of securities exists, vendor should agree to procure a written consent by the tenant to transfer of same to purchaser, if the lease makes no provision for this.

§ 235. Leases—sale to tenant.

If you are selling to a tenant in possession, keep in mind that once the contract is signed, the lease comes to an end and the tenant becomes a purchaser in possession, paying no rent. The same is true when a tenant in possession exercises an option to purchase.

Many lawyers feel that since merger is a question of intention, the following provision in the lease and contract will take care of the situation.

> The lease existing between the parties to this contract shall continue in full force and effect, and the buyer-lessee shall continue to pay rent and observe all the covenants of the lease until the closing of this sale and delivery of the deed to the buyer.

§ 236. Seller's documents—documents in possession of vendor and his mortgagee.

The contract can require that the vendor will make available to purchaser or his agent within a specified number of days, for examination and copying, documents in the vendor's possession relating to the property. Simultaneously vendor shall be required to deliver to purchaser an order on vendor's mortgagee to exhibit to purchaser or his agent all documents relating to the property in which vendor has an interest, at closing all such documents to be delivered to purchaser. This picks up quite a mixed bag of documents. The only survey of the premises may be in the mortgagee's possession, likewise policies of hazard insurance, and title policies. Some documents held by the mortgagee belong to him (*e.g.* mortgagee's title policy on his mortgage) and he is under no legal obligation to exhibit them to the purchaser. However, he is likely to do so anyway, hoping to get a savings deposit from the vendor or a mortgage loan application from the purchaser. Having a title policy as a "starter" shortens the time for searching title. A fairly recent survey is helpful when supplemented by a physical inspection showing no physical changes on the ground. The purchaser will wish to verify that vendor has a certificate of occupancy, showing that the building complied with zoning and building codes when built. If there are marquees, vaults, or other structures extending into streets, city permits for these purposes should be checked and ultimately retained by purchaser. Obviously all leases must be examined and checked for rent, rent concessions and options to renew or purchase. Paid tax bills and bills for insurance premiums make it possible to start the work of prorating. A vendor may wish to list specifically the items he is willing to have the purchaser inspect, since some items (vendor's contract to buy the property at time of his acquisition) are items the vendor may not wish to reveal. A suggested provision is as follows:

Seller shall allow reasonable inspection of the premises by the buyer (and his financing agent) and furnish any pertinent information requested by them.

§ 237. Risk of loss. It is suggested that, for the buyer's protection, the contract provide that if there is substantial damage to the building or if a condemnation suit is filed before the deal is closed the buyer shall have the option of rescinding. After all, he's buying a house to live in, not a claim against an insurance company.

Many attorneys cover the buyer by phone-call to the insurance company as soon as the contract is signed.

§ 238. Builder's implied warranties. The law has recently undergone a complete revolution in the area of builder's warranties. Beginning in 1964 the courts began to throw the old rules of caveat emptor overboard. They began to hold that in every sale of a residence by a builder-seller there is an implied warranty that the home was built in a workmanlike manner in accordance with laws and ordinances and is fit for habitation. The philosophy here is that the average buyer of a home is ill-equipped to detect the defects and shortcomings of jerry-built construction. It is likely that all states will come around to this point of view in time. Probably a disclaimer of such warranties would not stand up. Some builders are giving the buyer a detailed warranty that explains what is and what is not covered. *See* Kratovil, *Real Estate Law*, § 491.

§ 239. Warranty in existing construction. Because the doctrine of caveat emptor still exists with respect to sales of apartments and used homes, warranties and representations are needed as to matters one cannot readily detect on inspection. Perhaps a word or two can be added as to the form of this clause. The words of warranty are added, because if a warranty is made that automatically becomes a material matter, and one doesn't need to argue about the materiality of a misrepresentation. A suggested clause is as follows:

Seller represents and warrants that the building on said premises is not located on filled ground and is free from termite or other insect infestation, from wood-destroying fungus and from flooding or water seepage, that roof does not leak and that heating plant, cooling, and electrical systems are in working order and will so remain at closing, as a condition of closing.

Where the Seller is selling an old building and wishes to make no warranties the following Seller's "as is" clause should be used.

The Purchaser hereunder represent(s) that he or his representative fully examined the premises herein before described and the improvements thereon, prior to the execution hereof, and that he know(s) and is satisfied with the physical condition thereof in all respects and that the same are acceptable to him "as is" and said Purchaser agree(s) and admits that no representations or statements have at any time been made by the Seller or its agents as to the physical condition or state of repair of said premises in any respect, which have not been expressed in this agreement.

§ 240. Misrepresentation clause. The typical boilerplate some sellers use to the effect that no representations have been made except as set forth in the contract may be a waste of time. No court today will permit the seller to protect himself with this type of clause if a verbal misrepresentation has, in fact, been made.

§ 241. Building code and zoning violations. If the seller is to furnish a formal, official report as to zoning and building code violations, cover this, including time allowed for this purpose. The buyer should endeavor to have the contract provide:

Seller warrants the building on said premises is now and at the date of closing will be free and clear of all violations of laws and ordinances, and for breach of this warranty buyer may rescind this contract, before or after closing, or, at his election, may sue for damages.

Obviously the seller's lawyer will resist inclusion of this clause.

§ 242. Certificate of occupancy. Quite a number of contracts that, in the main, call for closing after completion of the building, give the seller a grace period. This complicates the problem of obtaining a certificate of occupancy. For example, one contract provides:

In the event that the dwelling or its environs shall not be fully completed at the time set by the Seller for the closing of title, the same shall not constitute an objection for such title closing provided the lending institutions or the F.H.A. or the V.A. as the case may be, shall issue an Inspection Report and an escrow fund be deposited by the Seller with the lending institution if required under said report.

A prudent buyer might well ask himself if the deal should indeed be closed if a certificate of occupancy is not available. Obviously, many such closings take place.

§ 243. Closing—escrow closing. If either party may wish to close in escrow an appropriate clause is needed in the contract, such as:

At the election of Seller or Purchaser upon notice to the other party not less than 5 days prior to the time of closing, this sale shall be closed through an escrow with _____ Title Insurance Company, in accordance with the general provisions of the usual form of Deed and Money

Escrow Agreement then in use by _____ Title Insurance Company, with such special provisions inserted in the escrow agreement as may be required to conform with this contract. Upon the creation of such an escrow, anything herein to the contrary notwithstanding, payment of purchase price and delivery of deed shall be made through the escrow and this contract and the earnest money shall be deposited in the escrow. The cost of the escrow shall be divided equally between Seller and Purchaser.

§ **244. Prorating provisions.** The authorities on prorating clauses fall into three groups, namely: (1) One group of cases states that there is no legal right to prorate unless this is stated in the contract. For example, if the seller has ten tons of coal in his basement at closing, the buyer need not buy it. (2) The next group of cases say that all customary items shall be prorated whether or not the contract so provides. (3) The final group says that in the absence of a contract provision certain items will be prorated, rents, for example, but not others. Schwartz, *Real Estate Manual*, §§ 76-86,333.

Hence, the contract should contain a fairly detailed itemization of items to be prorated, including rents, advance rents, tax and insurance escrows, and the like. On taxes it is not uncommon to find that this is to be prorated on the basis of 110% of the last tax bill, the assumption being made that taxes always go up. This is preferred by some lawyers to the provision that taxes shall be reprorated after the tax bill issues, for this requires an additional operation that is sometimes forgotten, and chasing someone to collect the balance due.

§ **245. Prorating tax escrows.** Mortgages held by banks on homes often require the mortgagor to deposit moneys with the mortgagee sufficient to accumulate funds to pay taxes and occasionally insurance and other charges. At the time of sale these deposits may range from several hundred to, perhaps, a thousand dollars. Where this is so, the contract should make provision for giving seller credit for this amount.

§ **246. Prorating the building manager's commission.** If the property is multi-tenant and large enough to be managed by an agent the apportionment of rent should be after deduction therefrom of agent's commission.

§ **247. Prorating the insurance.** If an insurance policy is a "Homeowner's Policy," i.e., one which covers personal property, personal liability and other matters, in addition to fire, the seller may have no choice but to cancel the policy. The purchaser should know of this sufficiently in advance to have his own insurance in time.

§ **248. Prorating provisions—miscellaneous.** Where the building employs staff, some provision should be included indicating how staff costs are to be prorated. For example, vacations are usually considered part of the janitor's pay. If he takes his vacation in the summer and the deal is closed in the spring the buyer will take the position that the greater part of the vacation represents compensation that really ought to be borne by the seller.

There may be service contracts, such as scavenger contracts, elevator maintenance, burglar alarm service, and so on. Since closing often occurs during the period when these services are being rendered, the seller should be charged his proportionate share of the service charge even though it is billed and paid after closing.

Fuel on hand, oil or coal is purchased by the buyer and the sale price debited to the buyer in the settlement sheet. The same is true of other supplies, such as janitor's supplies. The contract ought to cover this point. It ought to indicate that the building superintendent's statement as to the amount due for such items will be accepted for prorating purposes. At times a suspicious buyer wants this item limited to quantities ordinarily and customarily kept on hand. He doesn't want the seller to buy a ten year's supply of cleaning supplies from his brother-in-law.

§ 249. **Affidavit of title.** The contract should require the vendor to furnish an affidavit of title at closing. *See* Chapter 14.

§ 250. **Possession clauses.** If nothing to the contrary is stated the buyer is entitled to possession the moment he receives the deed to the property. 56 ALR2d 1272. Some sellers like to underscore this proposition by including the following clause:

> Legal possession shall be delivered to buyer at closing by handing him the deed to the property and the keys to the building.

This makes it clear that the buyer assumes liability for injuries on the premises at that moment.

Another seller, however, may need additional time to move out. For him an occupancy clause is needed, a suggested clause is as follows:

> Seller may retain occupancy after closing but not beyond _____. He shall pay for such occupancy the sum of $_____ per day. To insure timely surrender of the premises to the buyer, the sum of $_____ shall be deducted from the sale price and held by _____, for the benefit of both parties. No cause whatever shall prolong the seller's right of occupancy beyond the date specified. The seller does not become the buyer's tenant and agrees that he can be ousted by forcible detainer proceedings. In such proceedings buyer shall also recover a reasonable attorney's fees.

It's important that the occupancy amount provided above be sufficient to encourage the Seller to vacate the premises and be sufficient to cover buyer's cost of lodging during any holdover period.

E would like a deposit of part of the purchase price to be held in escrow until *R* vacates. The expenses *R* will pay (utilities, for example) during his occupancy should be set forth, also *R's* duties (lawn mowing, etc.)

§ 251. **Type of deed.** A contract is enforceable even though it does not specify the type of deed to be given. Nevertheless, the type of deed should be specified.

§ 252. **Merger.** There is always a question as to what matters survive closing. To put the matter at rest the buyer may argue for a non-merger clause:

> All representations and warranties made herein are intended to survive closing and shall not be merged in the deed. The contract shall not be cancelled at closing.

However, the seller may argue for an addition to this clause. He does not want the buyer complaining at closing, for example, about the quality of the title he received. He may ask for an addition to this clause as follows:

> However, all contractual obligations of the seller, other than express representations and warranties, terminate with closing.

§ 253. **Brokers.** Sophisticated sellers put the "no deal, no commission" clause in the broker's listing. This clause provides that "commission is payable only if and when deal is closed and sale price is paid to seller." Kratovil, *Real Estate Law* § 147. Where this is the case, the contract clause calling for payment of commission to broker should also contain the quoted language. Also add the following:

> *Broker's commission.* Buyer represents that negotiations for this contract were conducted exclusively by _____, as broker, and that no other broker participated in these negotiations. Should a claim for commission be made by any other broker, buyer will hold seller harmless against such harm and defend any litigation relating to such claim at his own expense.

In addition, for the Seller's protection from conflicting claims from other brokers, the Seller should require the following broker's undertaking be attached to the contract of sale:

> The undersigned, a licensed real estate broker, hereby makes claim for the broker's commission on the sale if the foregoing offer be accepted and consummated, and, to induce the seller to pay the commission to the undersigned, represents to the seller that the undersigned is the only broker involved in the foregoing offer and the the undersigned was the procuring cause thereof. The services of the undersigned were rendered with knowledge: (a) that the seller will pay a commission at the rate of _____%; (b) that the seller will pay the commission to the broker only who was the procuring cause of the offer, and then only in case the offer be accepted by the seller and the sale completed; (c) that the sale shall not be considered as completed unless payment to the seller of the purchase price be made; (d) that if the purchaser shall fail to complete the sale the seller assumes no obligation to the broker to take any legal action to enforce any rights the seller may have against the purchaser; (e) that the seller will pay the commission only upon condition that if thereafter any other brokers make claim for the commission the undersigned broker shall indemnify and save the seller harmless from all such other claims.

§ **254. Assignment of contract.** Some sellers want a clause in the contract forbidding assignment of the contract without the seller's written consent. The seller has checked the buyer to see that the buyer is ready, financially able and willing to buy. He argues that he ought not to be compelled to look for performance to a party concerning whom he has no knowledge. This is a must if the buyer is to give a purchase money mortgage.

§ **255. Witnesses.** In some states, a contract for the sale of a homestead must be witnessed or acknowledged.

§ **256. Delivery of contract.** Suppose you list your land with a broker for sale and he finds a buyer interested in its purchase but who does not wish to pay the price you are asking. The buyer prepares and signs a contract of sale stipulating a lower price. This is an offer. He hands the contract to the broker, who hands it to you. You sign the contract and return it to the buyer. This is an acceptance. The contract is now in force. Suppose, however, that you simply hold on to the contract, hoping that a higher offer will appear, and refuse to answer the buyer's telephone calls. This last situation poses problems.

To avoid this problem the buyer signs both duplicates of the contract to the seller but retains a carbon copy, so that he can always prove his nonliability if he fails to receive a signed duplicate within a specified time. A suggested clause is as follows:

> This contract is conditional upon return to buyer, within _____ days of the date this contract bears of a duplicate hereof signed by seller, with no modification of terms herein set forth, otherwise this contract to be void.

§ 257. Recording of contract. The seller likes to see a clause declaring that the contract will become void if it is recorded. The thinking here is that the buyer, if he changes his mind about going through with the deal, may record the contract, hoping thereby to cloud the title and to force the seller to give him back his earnest money.

§ 258. Default, notice and rescission. The contract will likely have some clause along the following lines:

Every act required to be performed by seller or buyer has been set forth herein, and the time for performance has also been stated. It is expressly agreed that time is of the essence. In the event of failure of either party to perform within the time specified, the other party has the right to elect to rescind and may do so by depositing in the U.S. Mail, certified or registered mail, postage prepaid, a notice to that effect, addressed to the party at his address given in this contract, which notice shall be effective whether or not received.

§ 259. Time limits—clearing title objections. The contract must carefully set time limits for every act, and all these time limits should create a consistent and workable pattern:

(1) There should be a time limit on the seller's furnishing evidence of title, survey, and chattel lien search..

(2) There should be a time limit on the buyer's procuring of financing, but the seller should not be required to furnish evidence of title until the buyer has procured his financing.

(3) There should be a time limit on the buyer's pointing out unacceptable objections to the title, whether they be objections revealed by the title records or the survey of the property.

(4) There should be a time limit on the seller's curing of objections pointed out by the buyer.

(5) There should be a time limit on the buyer deciding whether he will take the title "as is" or rescind because the seller cannot cure defects in his title.

The Real Estate Sale Contract forms printed at Appendix 1-A and 1-B are good examples of contracts with carefully conceived time limits. *See* pages 134-137. These contracts have many virtues, namely:

1. The form at Appendix 1-A does not make the mistake of requiring the seller to furnish the buyer any title evidence until the buyer's financing has been firmed up. The form at Appendix 1-B, since it is not used on single-family dwellings, is not made contingent on the procuring of financing.

2. Both forms permit the seller to use the buyer's money to clear title objections. This is not permitted as a matter of law unless the contract so provides.

3. Both forms eliminate all controversy about marketable title by making the title commitment conclusive evidence of title.

4. Under both forms, if the seller cannot in good faith, clear his title the buyer must take the title as is or release seller's liability for damages.

5. The form at Appendix 1-B permits the seller to cure survey objections by having the title company insure against loss by reason of survey defects.

6. Both forms permit either party to insist on escrow closing.

7. Both forms tell each party exactly what he must do and when he must do it.

§ 260. **Rental property.** Where rental property is involved, the buyer may want the contract to provide: (1) That the seller will furnish him letters to tenants advising them to pay future rent to buyer; (2) That seller will assign mortgagee's escrow funds at closing if mortgage remains after closing; (3) That leases will be delivered to buyer at closing with assignment of buyer's interest hereunder; (4) That seller will turn over to buyer existing survey, paid and cancelled mortgage notes (if mortgage secures several notes), last tax bill, last paid water bill, hazard insurance and assignment thereof (other than Homeowners Policies, which may not be assignable). (5) That if the conveyance is subject to mortgage, the mortgagee at closing will furnish its estoppel certificate showing the amount due on the mortgage debt and that no defaults exist.

§ 261. **Sell-and-build contracts.** The sell-and-build contract has been discussed elsewhere. Kratovil, *Real Estate Law* § 481.

§ 262. **Express warranties—JAG—NAHB.** Warranties of residence suggested for purchase of home by military personnel (8 JAG L.Rev. 40) are as follows:

In addition to any warranties of materials and workmanship which may be required of the seller by the lending agency, FHA, or VA the seller specifically warrants:

1. That the building or buildings are free from termites and dry rot.
2. That the basement is dry.
3. That all appliances and fixtures are in proper working order.
4. That the roof does not leak.
5. That the septic tank, if any, and underground sewer pipes are in good working order.
6. That all trees and shrubbery on the premises are alive.
7. That the walls, floors, and ceilings of the building or buildings are not subject to bulging or cracking other than hairline cracking which is not indicative of substantial structural defects.
8. That all fireplaces and flues draw properly.
9. That all windows and doors are free moving and do not stick.
10. That all land is fully settled.
11. That the structure's wiring, plumbing and heating are in compliance with all applicable building regulations and codes.
12. That all conditions warranted to exist in 1 through 11 above will continue to exist at the time of closing and under normal conditions for a period of _____ months after closing except that the warranty on appliances shall extend for a period of only _____ months after closing. After date of closing this warranty shall not cover damages caused by fire, windstorm, flood, earthquake, or other casualty or damage resulting from negligent use, care or maintenance, or to noncompliance with building codes and regulations resulting from changes in such regulations or codes after the date of closing. Seller's liability under the above warranties, if there has been no deliberate misrepresentations, shall not exceed $_____ as to any individual warranty or a total of $_____ on all warranties given.

The National Association of Home Builders sponsors a warranty for new homes. It costs $2.00 for each $1,000 of coverage. For one year after completion, the builder will replace or repair faulty work or material. For two years after completion, the builder is liable for major defects, such as badly sagging floors, also defects in heating, air conditioning, plumbing and electrical systems. From the third to the tenth year, a national insurance program takes over and pays for repair of major structural defects.

§ 263. **The installment contract.** The installment contract has been discussed elsewhere. Kratovil, *Real Estate Law* § 214.

Additional references on installment contracts. 21 UCLA L.Rev. 477; 9 *id*. 608; 19 U. Miami L.Rev. 550; 12 Wayne L.Rev. 391; 54 Mich. L.Rev. 929.

Appendix 1-A (Form No. 11) and Appendix 1-B (Form No. 12) follow on pages 134 to 137.

APPENDIX 1-A—Form No. 11

Real Estate Sale Contract

1. _____ (Purchaser)

agrees to purchase at a price of $ _____ on the terms set forth herein, the following described real estate

in _____ County, Illinois:

(If legal description is not included herein at time of execution, _____ *is*

authorized to insert it thereafter.)

commonly known as _____ , and

with approximate lot dimensions of _____ x _____ , together with the following personal property presently located thereon:

(strike items not applicable) (a) storm and screen doors and windows, (b) awnings; (c) outdoor television antenna; (d) wall-to-wall, hallway and stair

carpeting; (e) window shades and draperies and supporting fixtures; (f) venetian blinds; (g) electric, plumbing and other attached fixtures as installed; (h)

water softener, (i) refrigerator)s); (j) _____ range(s); and also

2. _____ (Seller)

(Insert names of all owners and their respective spouses)

agrees to sell the real estate and the property, if any, described above at the price and terms set forth herein, and to convey or cause to be conveyed to

Purchaser or nominee title thereto (in joint tenancy) by a recordable _____ deed, with release of dower and homestead rights, and

a proper bill of sale, subject only to: (a) covenants, conditions and restrictions of record; (b) private, public and utility easements and roads and highways,

if any; (c) party wall rights and agreements, if any; (d) existing leases and tenancies; (e) special taxes or assessments for improvements not yet completed;

(f) installments not due at the date hereof of any special tax or assessment for improvements heretofore completed; (g) mortgage or trust deed specified

below, if any; (h) general taxes for the year _____ and subsequent years; and to

3. **Purchaser has paid $** _____ (and will pay within _____ days the additional sum of $_____) as earnest money to be

applied on the purchase price, and agrees to pay or satisfy the balance of the purchase price, plus or minus prorations, at the time of closing as follows:

(strike subparagraph not applicable)

(a) The payment of $ _____

(b) The acceptance of the title to the real estate by Purchaser subject to a mortgage (trust deed) of record securing a principal indebtedness (which the

    Purchaser [does] [does not] agree to assume) aggregating $ _____ bearing interest at the rate of _____ % a year, and the

    payment of a sum which represents the difference between the amount due on the indebtedness at the time of closing and the balance of the

    purchase price.

4. This contract is subject to the condition that Purchaser be able to procure within _____ days a firm commitment for a loan to be secured by a

mortgage or trust deed on the real estate in the amount of $ _____ , or such lesser sum as Purchaser accepts, with interest not to exceed

_____ % a year to be amortized over _____ years, the commission and service charges for such loan not to exceed _____ %. If, after making

every reasonable effort, Purchaser is unable to procure such commitment within the time specified herein and so notified Seller thereof within that time,

this contract shall become null and void and all earnest money shall be returned to Purchaser; provided that if Seller, at his option, within a like period of

time following Purchaser's notice, procures for Purchaser such a commitment or notifies Purchaser that Seller will accept a purchase money mortgage

upon the same terms, this contract shall remain in full force and effect. *(Strike paragraph if inapplicable.)*

5. The time of closing shall be on _____ , or 20 days after notice that financing has been procured if above paragraph 4 is

operative, or on the date, if any, to which such time is extended by reason of paragraph 2 of the Conditions and Stipulations hereafter becoming

operative (whichever date is later), unless subsequently mutually agreed otherwise, at the office of _____ or

of the mortgage lender, if any, provided title is shown to be good or is accepted by Purchaser.

6. Seller shall deliver possession to Purchaser on or before _____ days after the sale has been closed. Seller agrees to pay Purchaser the sum of

$ _____ for each day Seller remains in possession between the time of closing and the time possession is delivered.

7. Seller agrees to pay a broker's commission to _____

in the amount set forth in the broker's listing contract or as follows: _____

8. The earnest money shall be held by _____

for the mutual benefit of the parties.

9. Seller agrees to deliver possession of the real estate in the same condition as it is at the date of this contract, ordinary wear and tear excepted.

10. A duplicate original of this contract, duly executed by the Seller and his spouse, if any, shall be delivered to the Purchasers within _____ days

from the date below, otherwise, at the Purchaser's option, this contract shall become null and void and the earnest money shall be refunded to the

Purchaser.

This contract is subject to the Conditions and Stipulations set forth on the back page hereof, which Conditions and Stipulations are made a part of this

contract.

Dated _____

Purchaser _____   (Address) _____

Purchaser _____   (Address) _____

Seller _____   (Address) _____

Seller _____   (Address) _____

*Form normally used for sale of residential property other than property improved with large multi-family structures.

Form No. 11 (Continued)

CONDITIONS AND STIPULATIONS

1. Seller shall deliver or cause to be delivered to Purchaser or Purchaser's agent, not less than 5 days prior to the time of closing, a title commitment for an owner's title insurance policy issued by the Chicago Title Insurance Company in the amount of the purchase price, covering title to the real estate on or after the date hereof, showing title in the intended grantor subject only to (a) the general exceptions contained in the policy, (b) the title exceptions set forth above, and (c) title exceptions pertaining to liens or encumbrances of a definite or ascertainable amount which may be removed by the payment of money at the time of closing and which the Seller may so remove at that time by using the funds to be paid upon the delivery of the deed (all of which are herein referred to as the permitted exceptions). The title commitment shall be conclusive evidence of good title as therein shown as to all matters insured by the policy, subject only to the exceptions as therein stated. Seller also shall furnish Purchaser an affidavit of title in customary form covering the date of closing and showing title in Seller subject only to the permitted exceptions in foregoing items (b) and (c) and unpermitted exceptions, if any, as to which the title insurer commits to extend insurance in the manner specified in paragraph 2 below.

2. If the title commitment discloses unpermitted exceptions, Seller shall have 30 days from the date of delivery thereof to have the exceptions removed from the commitment or to have the title insurer commit to insure against loss or damage that may be occasioned by such exceptions, and, in such event, the time of closing shall be 35 days after delivery of the commitment or the time specified in paragraph 5 on the front page hereof, whichever is later. If Seller fails to have the exceptions removed, or in the alternative, to obtain the commitment for title insurance specified above as to such exceptions within the specified time, Purchaser may terminate this contract or may elect, upon notice to Seller within 10 days after the expiration of the 30-day period, to take title as it then is with the right to deduct from the purchase price liens or encumbrances of a definite or ascertainable amount. If Purchaser does not so elect, this contract shall become null and void without further actions of the parties.

3. Rents, premiums under assignable insurance policies, water and other utility charges, fuels, prepaid service contracts, general taxes, accrued interest on mortgage indebtedness, if any, and other similar items shall be adjusted ratably as of the time of closing. If the amount of the current general taxes is not then ascertainable, the adjustment thereof shall be on the basis of the amount of the most recent ascertainable taxes. All prorations are final unless otherwise provided herein. Existing leases and assignable insurance policies, if any, shall then be assigned to Purchaser. Seller shall pay the amount of any stamp tax imposed by law on the transfer of title, and shall furnish a completed Real Estate Transfer Declaration signed by the Seller or the Seller's agent in the form required pursuant to the Real Estate Transfer Tax Act of the State of Illinois.

4. The provisions of the Uniform Vendor and Purchaser Risk Act of the State of Illinois shall be applicable to this contract.

5. If this contract is terminated without Purchaser's fault, the earnest money shall be returned to the Purchaser, but if the termination is caused by the Purchaser's fault, then at the option of the Seller and upon notice to the Purchaser, the earnest money shall be forfeited to the Seller and applied first to the payment of Seller's expenses and then to payment of broker's commission; the balance, if any, to be retained by the Seller as liquidated damages.

6. At the election of Seller or Purchaser upon notice to the other party not less than 5 days prior to the time of closing, this sale shall be closed through an escrow with Chicago Title and Trust Company, in accordance with the general provisions of the usual form of Deed and Money Escrow Agreement then in use by Chicago Title and Trust Company, with such special provisions inserted in the escrow agreement as may be required to conform with this contract. Upon the creation of such an escrow, anything herein to the contrary notwithstanding, payment of purchase price and delivery of deed shall be made through the escrow and this contract and the earnest money shall be deposited in the escrow. The cost of the escrow shall be divided equally between Seller and Purchaser. *(Strike paragraphs if inapplicable.)*

7. Time is of the essence of this contract.

8. All notices herein required shall be in writing and shall be served on the parties at the addresses following their signatures. The mailing of a notice by registered or certified mail, return receipt requested, shall be sufficient service.

APPENDIX 1-B—Form No. 12

Real Estate Sale Contract

1. _____ (Purchaser)
agrees to purchase at a price of $ _____ on the terms set forth herein, the following described real estate
in _____ County, Illinois:

commonly known as _____ , and with approximate lot dimensions of
_____ x _____ , together with the following property presently located thereon:

2. _____ (Seller)
agrees to sell the real estate and the property described above, if any, at the price and terms set forth herein, and to convey or cause to be conveyed to
Purchaser or nominee title thereto by a recordable _____ deed, with release of dower and homestead rights, if any, and a proper
bill of sale, subject only to: (a) covenants, conditions and restrictions of record; (b) private, public and utility easements and roads and highways, if any;
(c) party wall rights and agreements, if any; (d) existing leases and tenancies (as listed in Schedule A attached); (e) special taxes or assessments for
improvements not yet completed; (f) installments not due at the date hereof of any special tax or assessment for improvements heretofore completed; (g)
mortgage or trust deed specified below, if any; (h) general taxes for the year _____ and subsequent years; and to

3. Purchaser has paid $ _____ as earnest money to be applied on the purchase price, and agrees to pay or satisfy the balance of
the purchase price, plus or minus prorations, at the time of closing as follows: *(strike language and subparagraphs not applicable)*

(a) The payment of $ _____

(b) The payment of $ _____ and the balance payable as follows:
_____
_____
_____

to be evidenced by the note of the purchaser (grantee), providing for full prepayment privileges without penalty, which shall be secured by a
part-purchase money mortgage (trust deed), the latter instrument and the note to be in the form hereto attached as Schedule B, or, in the absence of
this attachment, the forms prepared by _____ and identified as Nos._____ ,** and
by a security agreement (as to which Purchaser will execute or cause to be executed such financing statements as may be required under the Uniform
Commercial Code in order to make the lien created thereunder effective), and an assignment of rents, said security agreement and assignment of
rents to be in the forms appended hereto as Schedules C and D. Purchaser shall furnish to Seller an American Land Title Association loan policy
insuring the mortgage (trust deed) issued by the Chicago Title Insurance Company.

(**If a Schedule B is not attached and the blanks are not filled in, the note shall be secured by a trust deed, and the note and trust deed shall be in
the forms used by the Chicago Title and Trust Company.)

(c) The acceptance of the title to the real estate by Purchaser subject to a mortgage or trust deed of record securing a principal indebtedness (which the
Purchaser [does] [does not] agree to assume) aggregating $ _____ bearing interest at the rate of _____% a year, and the
payment of a sum which represents the difference between the amount due on the indebtedness at the time of closing and the balance of the
purchase price.

4. Seller, at his own expense, agrees to furnish Purchaser a current plat of survey of the above real estate made, and so certified by the surveyor as having
been made, in compliance with the Illinois Land Survey Standards.

5. The time of closing shall be on _____ or on the date, if any, to which such time is extended by reason of paragraph 2 of the
Conditions and Stipulations hereafter becoming operative (whichever date is later), unless subsequently mutually agreed otherwise, at the office of
_____ or of the mortgage lender, if any, provided title is shown to be good or is accepted by the purchaser.

6. Seller agrees to pay a broker's commission to _____
in the amount set forth in the broker's listing contract or as follows: _____ .

7. The earnest money shall be held by _____
for the mutual benefit of the parties.

8. Seller warrants that Seller, its beneficiaries or agents of Seller or of its beneficiaries have received no notices from any city, village or other
governmental authority of zoning, building, fire or health code violations in respect to the real estate that have not been heretofore corrected.

9. A duplicate original of this contract, duly executed by the Seller and his spouse, if any, shall be delivered to the Purchaser within _____days from
the date hereof, otherwise, at the Purchaser's option, this contract shall become null and void and the earnest money shall be refunded to the Purchaser.

This contract is subject to the Conditions and Stipulations set forth on the back page hereof, which Conditions and Stipulations are made a part of this
contract.

Dated _____

Purchaser _____   (Address) _____

Purchaser _____   (Address) _____

Seller _____   (Address) _____

Seller _____   (Address) _____
*Form normally used for sale of property improved with large multi-family structures or of commercial or industrial properties.

Form No. 12 (Continued)

CONDITIONS AND STIPULATIONS

1. Seller shall deliver or cause to be delivered to Purchaser or Purchaser's agent, not less than 5 days prior to the time of closing, the plat of survey (if one is required to be delivered under the terms of this contract) and a title commitment for an owner's title insurance policy issued by the Chicago Title Insurance Company in the amount of the purchase price, covering title to the real estate on or after the date hereof, showing title in the intended grantor subject only to (a) the general exceptions contained in the policy, (b) the title exceptions set forth above, and (c) title exceptions pertaining to liens or encumbrances of a definite or ascertainable amount which may be removed by the payment of money at the time of closing and which the Seller may so remove at that time by using the funds to be paid upon the delivery of the deed (all of which are herein referred to as the permitted exceptions). The title commitment shall be conclusive evidence of good title as therein shown as to all matters insured by the policy, subject only to the exceptions as therein stated. Seller also shall furnish Purchaser an affidavit of title in customary form covering the date of closing and showing title in Seller subject only to the permitted exceptions in foregoing items (b) and (c) and unpermitted exceptions or defects in the title disclosed by the survey, if any, as to which the title insurer commits to extend insurance in the manner specified in paragraph 2 below.

2. If the title commitment or plat of survey (if one is required to be delivered under the terms of this contract) discloses either unpermitted exceptions or survey matters that render the title unmarketable (herein referred to as "survey defects"), Seller shall have 30 days from the date of delivery thereof to have the exceptions removed from the commitment or to correct such survey defects or to have the title insurer commit to insure against loss or damage that may be occasioned by such exceptions or survey defects, and, in such event, the time of closing shall be 35 days after delivery of the commitment or the time expressly specified in paragraph 5 on the front page hereof, whichever is later. If Seller fails to have the exceptions removed or correct any survey defects, or in the alternative, to obtain the commitment for title insurance specified above as to such exceptions or survey defects within the specified time, Purchaser may terminate this contract or may elect, upon notice to Seller within 10 days after the expiration of the 30-day period, to take title as it then is with the right to deduct from the purchase price liens or encumbrances of a definite or ascertainable amount. If Purchaser does not so elect, this contract shall become null and void without further action of the parties.

3. Rents, premiums under assignable insurance policies, water and other utility charges, fuels, prepaid service contracts, general taxes, accrued interest on mortgage indebtedness, if any, and other similar items shall be adjusted ratably as of the time of closing. If the amount of the current general taxes is not then ascertainable, the adjustment thereof shall be on the basis of the amount of the most recent ascertainable taxes. All prorations are final unless otherwise provided herein. Existing leases and assignable insurance policies, if any, shall then be assigned to Purchaser. Seller shall pay the amount of any stamp tax imposed by law on the transfer of the title, and shall furnish a completed Real Estate Transfer Declaration signed by the Seller or the Seller's agent in the form required pursuant to the Real Estate Transfer Tax Act of the State of Illinois.

4. The provisions of the Uniform Vendor and Purchaser Risk Act of the State of Illinois shall be applicable to this contract.

5. If this contract is terminated without Purchaser's fault, the earnest money shall be returned to the Purchaser, but if the termination is caused by the Purchaser's fault, then at the option of the Seller and upon notice to the Purchaser, the earnest money shall be forfeited to the Seller and applied first to the payment of Seller's expenses and then to payment of broker's commission; the balance, if any, to be retained by the Seller as liquidated damages.

6. At the election of Seller or Purchaser upon notice to the other party not less than 5 days prior to the time of closing, this sale shall be closed through an escrow with Chicago Title and Trust Company, in accordance with the general provisions of the usual form of Deed and Money Escrow Agreement then in use by Chicago Title and Trust Company, with such special provisions inserted in the escrow agreement as may be required to conform with this contract. Upon the creation of such an escrow, anything herein to the contrary notwithstanding, payment of purchase price and delivery of deed shall be made through the escrow and this contract and the earnest money shall be deposited in the escrow. The cost of the escrow shall be divided equally between Seller and Purchaser. *(Strike paragraph if inapplicable.)*

7. Time is of the essence of this contract.

8. Any payments herein required to be made at the time of closing shall be by certified check or cashier's check, payable to Seller.

9. All notices herein required shall be in writing and shall be served on the parties at the addresses following their signatures. The mailing of a notice by registered or certified mail, return receipt requested, shall be sufficient service.

17

Contracts of Sale—
Large-Scale Transactions

§ **264. In general.** While there are obvious differences between the large-scale sale and the sale of residential properties, nearly all of the material in the chapter on residential contracts of sale is applicable to large-scale transactions.

The law of contracts generally has undergone great changes in recent memory, and the real property bar must be aware of them. *See* § 10. In addition to the concepts of good faith and unconscionability introduced by UCC and ULTA, both codes recognize the right of a party to a contract to recover consequential damages and to shape the remedies to be afforded by the courts. Moreover, the old notion that impossibility of performance does not excuse performance of a contract is weakened, something the courts were doing anyway. 6, Corbin, *Contracts* § 1320 *et seq.* (1962). The "new law" also gives its explicit blessing to the doctrine of frustration. And a series of detailed warranties of quality and title will be found in ULTA. All this introduces a new dimension into contract draftsmanship. This text can only sound a warning. Each practitioner must plot his own landmarks. A few suggestions concerning provisions are: (1) Exclusion of "consequential damages, so called," with examples of types of damage not recoverable. For example, the buyer of a shopping center site may make extensive commitments (construction contracts, lease contracts, etc.) in reliance on the contract, but the seller will not want to be liable if something happens that prevents delivery of good title, for example, as an actual case, a suit by an unsuccessful bidder as a taxpayer to set aside sale of the property by a city to the contract seller. *Futterman-Marott Corp. v. City of Ft. Wayne*, 248 Ind. 503, 230 NE2d 102 (1967). Experience reveals that a buyer who wants this protection must be prepared to up his price. (2) Draft a liquidated damages clause, if possible, with an explanation of how the parties arrived at the figure. As to earnest money, to be treated as liquidated damages under the new law, include a provision that in view of the difficulties of predicting actual damages, it is an agreed liquidated damages clause. *See* 40 Yale L.J. 1013. (3) Contract recitals and provisions reciting equality of bargaining power and full negotiation of contract price, to pull the teeth of an attack on the contract terms or price as unconscionable. (4) *Force majeure* clause is still necessary. (5) Provision still necessary that change in zoning of vacant land prior to closing gives buyer right to rescind. This is especially important in light of the new decisions that permit zoning provisions to lock an owner of swamps or wetlands into the existing use, such as berry-picking. Kratovil, *Real Estate Law* (6th ed. 1974) § 516. (6) Include a clause that contract merges into deed at closing, because ULTA abolishes this rule and the courts have been moving this way anyway. Kratovil, *supra,* § 210. Spell out explicitly *in the deed* what obligations remain on seller after closing, *e.g.,* paving of roads when weather permits. (7) Be explicit as to what seller warrants and does not warrant as to quality of building or land and freedom from violations of zoning or building ordinances. (8) Try to anticipate and deal with contingencies that should or might relieve the buyer of the obligation to close, *e.g.,* filing of condemnation suit, introduction of zoning amendment, class action by tenants, suits or defenses by tenants claiming the benefit of the new landlord and tenant law (Kratovil, *supra* § 637 *et. seq.*), environmental protection regulation or ruling, etc.

Also the old contract drafting problems are still with us, mainly the fact that even experienced lawyers fail to think in terms of possible breach and what rights, liabilities, and remedies then arise. For example, (1) What consequences result from breaches of the various contract covenants? Does a particular breach give a right to rescind or only a right to damages? (2) What remedies are to be available where breach occurs? For example, should retention of earnest money be an exclusive remedy if buyer defaults? (3) What defects in performance are tolerated and how do they affect the specified compensation? This is the problem of substantial performance (4) Where performance is less than substantial, what payment should be made for benefits conferred? (5) What notices should be given and in what manner?

§ 265. **Parties—seller and purchaser.** Considerations relating to the parties to the contract have been considered elsewhere. *See* Chapters 5 and 6.

§ 266. **Buyer as a nominee.** There is no *legal* objection to having the buyer insist that his nominee or "straw party" be named as purchaser. The seller, of course, must realize that he may be giving up the personal liability of the real buyer. If the sole purpose is to relieve the buyer of personal liability on the mortgage needed to complete the purchase, there are two alternatives: (1) let the real buyer be so named and get the mortgagee to agree on a waiver of personal liability, which is often easily obtained; or (2) the buyer can agree to perform all the nominee's covenants except for liability for the mortgage debt. This problem crops up when the buyer does not want to show the mortgage as a personal liability on his financial statements.

§ 267. **Corporation partnership, or trust to be grantee in deed.** *E* may insist on a clause giving him power to direct *R* to convey to a corporation or partnership designated by *E*. There is no objection to this. If *E* wants power to direct *R* to convey to a trust, *R* should refuse if the deed will operate, in part, as the creation of a new trust. *R* can agree to convey to a nominee, who can convey to *E's* trust. *R* is selling, not creating trusts.

§ 268. **Property sold in general.** Discussion of land descriptions and street and highway problems is found elsewhere. *See* Chapters 8 and 9.

§ 269. **Property sold—easements.** Especially where part of the seller's land is being sold, the buyer may need easements of access, utilities, service, water, etc. The buyer's contractor or engineer tells the buyer's lawyer what is needed, and the buyer drafts it into the contract. *See* Chapters 38 and 39. Even where the tract is serviced by an easement created long ago, the easement should be included in the description of the property sold. In easement situations you usually set the description up as follows:

PARCEL I

Lot 1 in Block 1 in Sheffield's Addition to Chicago in Section 1, Township 1 North, Range 14 East of the Third Principal Meridian in Cook County, Illinois.

PARCEL II

Perpetual easement for ingress and egress over the North twenty feet of Lot 2 in Block 1 aforesaid, appurtenant to Lot 1 and created by grant recorded July 1, 1973 as Document 12345 in the Recorder's office of Cook County, Illinois.

Or if the easement is to be created at closing, the concluding language runs:

"By grant of easement to be delivered by Seller to Buyer contemporaneously with the delivery of deed hereunder."

Of course, if the seller will need easements over the land conveyed to the buyer, that also must be provided for.

§ 270. Property sold—land assemblies. Where the project will work out only if several parcels of land are assembled, the contract of sale must state as a pre-condition that no liability shall attach or closing take place unless and until all deals are ready for closing and consummation. The techniques of land assemblies have been discussed elsewhere. PLI *Real Estate Law Handbook* 35 (1971); Kratovil, *Real Estate Law* Chapter 25.

§ 271. Property sold—other references. Much of the material relating to the property and interests to be sold is covered in Chapter 8.

§ 272. Property sold—fixtures and chattels. It is, of course, elementary law that a contract of sale automatically entitles E to receive all fixtures existing at the date of the contract, for they are, in law, part of the real estate. The description of the land in the contract of sale and deed automatically carries them. This is not particularly helpful in larger deals. For one thing, R and E may differ as to what items are fixtures and what items are chattels. Even a temporary removal may interrupt an operation E intended to run from the date of closing. The fact that he may win a damage suit a year later against, possibly, a corporation that has since dissolved is no comfort to E. Moreover, even if R and E do not disagree as to the nature of the articles, R may attempt to remove, before closing, items of value such as machinery. Therefore, it is important to describe in the contract all items that are bargained for as passing in the deal, whether chattels or fixtures. General descriptions expose E to risk.

EXAMPLE: A contract for the sale of an industrial plant states that it includes all machinery installed therein as of the date of the contract. As of the date of closing E contends substitutions have been made. In the absence of a detailed list this may be hard to prove. Couple a detailed list with a right in E to inspect prior to closing, and the possibility of substitution is minimized.

If the property contains valuable chattels, the contract must describe them in some way, for a contract for the sale of land does not carry chattels. Detailed descriptions are better than general descriptions, because they help prevent substitution of inferior chattels between date of contract and date of closing. If some items are of doubtful status (could be chattels or fixtures) include them in the chattels clause.

The list of chattels to consider, of course, includes items in Chapter 16. But it also should include transformers, switchboards, conveyors, machinery, and many other items. It is best to provide for a bill of sale to be given at closing.

If seller wishes to remove machinery or other articles that could be regarded as fixtures, that right must be reserved in the contract.

Title insurance is not available to insure title to chattels being sold. But the concept of marketable title exists as to chattels, and the contract should require *R* to convey marketable title to the chattels included in the deal. The contract should make *R's* books available to *E* so that *E* can ascertain that the chattels were in fact paid for.

At various places in the text there are discussions of the party entitled to chattels, fixtures, and articles that fall into the gray area between fixtures and chattels. Falling in a gray area from the draftsman's viewpoint is something that is almost certainly real estate, such as a steel bank vault and door, but which will be costly to remove if *E* plans to devote the premises to a different use. A clause is needed requiring *R* to remove this at his expense within a stated time.

§ 273. Property sold—name of building and trade names—land to be developed—soil tests. The property conveyed should include *R's* interest in the name of the building and all other trade names used in connection with *R's* operation.

Other matters to be furnished by seller.

On or before _____ seller will furnish to purchaser on land to be developed the following documents:

(1) A soil test report by an engineer satisfactory to purchaser showing to seller's satisfaction soil conditions satisfactory for the construction of _____ by means of customary construction methods, without resort to extraordinary subsurface procedures.

(2) Environmental control approval, and any other report or approval required by law (other than a building permit) reflecting purchaser's right to acquire the property and improve and sell or otherwise deal with it in accordance with buyer's intention, notice of which is hereby given seller to _____

────────────────────────────────────

(HERE DESCRIBE PURCHASER'S INTENDED PURPOSE)

(3) Opinion of counsel satisfactory to purchaser that purchaser has the legal right, subject to payment of hookup charges, to connect and to use sewer, water, utilities and other facilities required for purchaser's intended use.

§ 274. Purchase price. The seller wants the earnest money in the form of a cashier's check. There have been instances of forged certifications, so that certified checks are somewhat suspect. Likewise, the balance of the purchase price should be payable in cashier's checks and cash. Some strict sellers require payment in "cash." This enables the seller to call the buyer's bank at closing and verify the genuiness of the cashier's check and the solvency of the bank. Most buyers object to this. However, any check the seller accepts is subject to the possibility of the bank's insolvency. Alternatively, the seller can list the banks whose checks he will accept. The buyer will argue for a cashier's check drawn on any member of the Chicago Clearing House, for example. This will not be acceptable to the prudent seller. In no case will the seller accept a personal check or a check of some third party. A check endorsed to the buyer is particularly dangerous.

§ 275. Purchase price—real and personal property. If the purchase price covers both real and personal property, the contract ought to have a double aspect. The amount allocated to real property ought to be stated separately from the amount allocated to personal property. In the first place, differences exist for federal and state tax purposes. In the second place, the law as to real property is different from the law as to personal property. For example, retention of earnest money is possible as to real property if *E* defaults, but not as to personal property, the latter being governed by the U.C.C.

§ 276. Purchase price—payment provisions where a cotenancy exists. Payment provisions where the sellers are cotenants are a neglected area. Few contracts make adequate provision for payment.

Where a husband and wife enter into a contract to sell their land, and one of them dies before the purchase price is fully paid, questions arise as to who gets the balance of the purchase price, the surviving spouse or the estate of the decedent. Where the sellers held the land in joint tenancy or tenancy by the entireties some courts hold that the right to the money goes to the survivor just as though there were a right of survivorship as to the contract price. *Watson v. Watson,* 5 Ill.2d 526, 126 NE2d 220 (1955); *Hewitt v. Biege,* 183 Kan. 352, 329 P2d 872 (1958); *DeYoung v. Mesler,* 373 Mich. 499, 130 NW2d 38, 41 (1964). *In re Maguire's Estate,* 296 NYS 528; 18 *Miami L. Rev.* 825.

EXAMPLE: *H* and *W*, joint tenants, enter into a contract to sell their land to *X*. After a few payments are made on the contract, *H* dies leaving a will giving all his property to children by a former marriage. *W* will get the entire remainder of the purchase price.

There are cases taking a contrary view.

EXAMPLE: *H* and *W*, joint tenants, entered into a contract to sell land. *H* dies. His heirs got his share of the sale price. In a few states sale proceeds are treated as though held in tenancy in common. *Register of Wills. v. Madine,* 242 Md. 437, 219 A2d 245; *In re Baker's Estate* 78 NW2d 863 (Iowa), 55 *Mich. L. Rev.* 1194, 33 *Notre D.L.Rev.* 246; *Buford v. Dahike,* 158 Neb. 39, NW2d 252. These cases are poor law.

Of course once the money has been paid by the buyer to the sellers, the cash money, even if held intact by the sellers in a joint safety deposit box, is owned by them in tenancy in common. *Ill. Public Aid Commission v. Stille,* 14 Ill.2d 344, 153 NE2d 59.

Suppose that the sellers are tenants by the entireties. They give a deed to the buyer and take back a purchase money mortgage. Some states hold that the mortgage is owned as tenants by the entireties. *Ciconte v. Barba,* 19 Del. Ch. 6, 161 Atl. 925. Others hold that the mortgage is owned in tenancy in common. *Webb v. Woodcock,* 134 Ore. 319, 290 Pac. 751; 64 ALR2d 8. Similar problems arise as to the sale price where no mortgage has been given the sellers.

EXAMPLE: *H* and *W*, tenants by the entireties, entered into a contract to sell land. *H* died. His heirs got his share of the purchase price. *Panushka v. Panushka,* 349 P2d 450 (Ore), 14 *Vand. L. Rev.* 687, 36 *Notre D. Law Rev.* 203. This result is dictated by the rule in some tenancy by the entireties states which do not recognize this type of tenancy in money or *personal property.* 41 *Cornell L.Q.* 154.

Community property states present special problems.

EXAMPLE: In a community property state, *H* and *W*, joint tenants, entered into a contract to sell land. The proceeds of sale are community property. *Smith v. Tang,* 100 Ariz. 196, 412 P2d 697.

The problem also exists with respect to the proceeds of fire insurance policies. 41 *Cornell L. Q.* 154.

The better rule is that the money goes to the survivor. Had the parties been asked about this when they received their deed, virtually all would have been astonished to hear any question raised as to the right of the survivor to get the money. This intention ought to be controlling. 41 *Cornell L.Q.* 154.

SUGGESTION: Let the contract read that the price is payable to the sellers *as joint tenants with the right of survivorship and not as tenants in common nor as tenants by the entireties nor as community property.*[1]

CAUTION: Some community property states do not recognize joint tenancies.

It must be remembered that some states do not permit a tenancy by the entireties in personal property. 64 ALR 2d 8. However, even in those states language of survivorship should create a right of survivorship.

§ 277. Earnest money. The larger the earnest money deposit, the more uneasy E becomes over its return. One solution is to provide for its deposit with a bank, title, or trust company in a *joint order escrow*. This escrow simply calls for payment of the money on the joint direction of R and E. It may take litigation to pry the money loose if the parties have a falling out, but E is protected against $R's$ defalcation or insolvency.

§ 278. Title insurance requirements. A form for requiring title insurance is as follows:

Title Report and Insurance Commitment. Not later than 19_____, or not later than _____ days after Buyer has obtained his financing under Paragraph _____ hereof, whichever date is later, Seller will deliver to the Buyer a commitment by _____ Title Insurance Company, dated as of the date of this agreement, showing title in the Seller subject only to the permitted exceptions and committing the title company to insure the title in the Buyer as of the date of the recording of the deed to the Buyer, subject only to the permitted exceptions, such policy to be an ALTA marketable form Owner's Policy with extended coverage against all general exceptions.

§ 279. Survey. A form used for requiring a survey is as follows:

Survey. At least _____ days prior to the date of settlement, as set forth herein, Seller shall deliver to Buyer a survey of the premises obtained at Seller's expense and prepared by a registered land surveyor acceptable to Buyer, which survey shall be in accordance with the Minimum Standard Detail Requirements for Land Title Surveys as adopted by the American Title Association and American Congress on Surveying and Mapping. If such survey reveals any condition or state of facts adversely affecting the marketability of title hereunder, Seller will be deemed in default hereunder, and Buyer shall have all remedies as set forth in Paragraph _____ hereof. If said survey reveals that the premises make use of any other premises as a means of ingress or egress, or for any other purpose that ordinarily would be made pursuant to an easement, the title commitment in the title policy furnished by the Seller to the Buyer will specifically insure such easements as easement appurtenant to the premises, subject only to the permitted exceptions and current real estate taxes not delinquent as of the date of the title policy.

§ 280. Deed—form of deed. A contract is enforceable even though it does not specify the type of deed to be given. Nevertheless, since there is a vast difference

---

[1] Copyright, Kratovil, *Real Estate Law* (6th ed. 1974). Prentice-Hall, Inc. Reprinted by permission.

between a quitclaim deed and warranty deed, the contract should specify the type agreed upon. If the contract is silent regarding the type of deed to be given, in most states the vendor need only give a quitclaim deed or deed of bargain and sale. Kratovil, *Real Estate Law* § 179. This does not excuse the seller from giving a marketable title. It simply means that once the title has been shown to be marketable, the vendor may deliver a quitclaim deed or deed of bargain and sale and be rid of any possibility of future worry regarding presently unknown title defects. It is best for the purchaser to insist that the contract call for a general warranty deed. However, local custom may force the buyer to accept a special warranty deed. In a number of states, the mere fact that the buyer is content to take a quitclaim deed is enough to keep him from being a bona fide purchaser, and he will take the land subject to unrecorded deeds, mortgages, liens, and so forth. Patton, *Titles* § 16. There are some decisions holding that even in the absence of a contract provision for warranty deed, the vendor must give a warranty deed. 55 Am. Jur. *Vendor & Purchaser*, § 315.

Every once in a while you encounter a contract that calls for a "good and sufficient deed." This is a bad phrase to use. In some states, the courts construe this to call for a general warranty deed. *Seabord Air Line Ry. Co. v. Jones*, 120 S.C. 354, 113 SE 142; *Fleming v. Harrison's Devisees*, 5 Ky. (2 Bibb) 171. In other states, the courts will not so construe the requirement. *Tyman v. Linski*, 16 N.Y.2d 293, 213 NE2d 661. Obviously, you avoid use of this phrase and state what kind of deed is wanted.

If the contract calls for a warranty deed, the purchaser need not accept a warranty deed from the vendor's grantee. 57 ALR 1507. If the purchaser rejects the warranty deed from the vendor's grantee, the grantee must reconvey to the vendor, who will then give his warranty deed. *Norman v. William Koch Motors Inc.* (Ky. 1961) 342 SW2d 392. Even if the contract does not call for a warranty deed, the purchaser is entitled to receive the personal deed of the vendor. He need not accept a deed from a third person. 55 Am. Jur. *Vendor and Purchaser*, § 317. For this reason, if the vendor does not wish to give his personal deed, the contract should state that the vendor will convey "or cause to be conveyed."

§ 281. Deed—recordable deed. Of course the contract should require the seller to give a "valid and recordable deed." But the lack of sophistication on this proposition is truly amazing. In many states there are numerous requirements that must be met for a deed to be entitled to recording, and failure to meet the requirements makes the deed "unrecordable" even if the recorder accepts it and records it.

§ 282. Sale subject to existing mortgage. The subject has been discussed elsewhere. *See* Chapter 16. Some additional suggestions are in order for the large-scale transaction. For example, the suggestions applicable to paying off the seller's mortgage at closing are applicable to the "payoff letter." Obviously, before the contract is signed, *E* must read the mortgage carefully if he expects to take title subject to the existing mortgage. At the worst, it might contain a "due-on-sale" clause, making the sale itself an event giving rise to a right of acceleration. Or it might provide that the presence of a junior lien gives rise to a right of acceleration, a provision common in corporate mortgages. This would be disastrous where the buyer needs junior financing. Or a corporate mortgage might require the mortgagor to furnish the mortgagee an annual financial statement. How a purchaser could comply with this is difficult to understand.

It is customary to include in the contract of sale and deed a covenant by the grantee to make all the payments due and observe all the covenants of the mortgage. This is one of the "no merger" covenants. *E* sometimes adds that this clause is for *R's* benefit only.

Sometimes the contract provides that if the mortgagee insists on assumption, *E* will sign an assumption agreement, and other documents required by the mortgage, and will pay all assumption fees.

E, of course, will argue for a clause that he does not assume or agree to pay the mortgage debt or accept any personal liability for it, by indemnity or otherwise.

Where *E* is buying subject to an existing mortgage he will want *R* to include in the contract a clause somewhat as follows:

CLAUSE: *R* represents and warrants that there are no defaults or breaches of covenant under said mortgage, and as a pre-condition to closing this will remain true at the date of closing; also that the mortgagee has not asserted or indicated, orally or in writing, that there are possible uncured defaults or breaches of covenant; that there have been no modifications of said mortgage since the recording thereof and that, as a condition of closing, this will be true at time of closing. *R* also covenants that he will endeavor to deliver to *E* at closing the mortgagee's certificate, running to *E* or to whom it may concern, as to the truth of *R's* representations and warranties in this paragraph set forth.

§ 283. **Existing mortgages to be cleared at closing.** In addition to the clauses suggested elsewhere (*see* Chapter 16), where existing mortgages are to be cleared at closing, *R* may ask for a clause as follows:

If request is made within a reasonable time prior to the date of closing, *E* will use its best efforts to provide at the closing separate checks, as requested, aggregating the balance of the purchase prior, to facilitate the satisfaction of any existing mortgages or other liens.

Where an existing mortgage is to remain as a lien after the sale is closed, other problems arise:

(1) The problem arises initially when the contract of sale is signed. If the language of the *contract* is sufficient, under local law, to create a third party beneficiary right in the mortgagee to hold the buyer personally liable, it may be impossible to alter this liability by tinkering with the language of the *deed*. Kratovil, *Mortgages,* Chapter 14. Hence, if the buyer wishes to disclaim such personal liability, the *contract* reference to the mortgage states "which the buyer does not assume or agree to pay." For a much more elaborate clause, *see* 17 *Practical Lawyer* #7, page 15. The same language is included in the deed.

(2) If the buyer is to assume some personal liability, it must first be decided whether he wishes to be liable to both the seller and the mortgagee. If the contract and deed merely recite that the buyer "assumes and agrees to pay the mortgage," the buyer will wind up with liability to both the seller and the mortgagee, though the liabilities will differ in legal effect. If the parties so agree, the contract and deed may provide that the buyer's promise runs only for the benefit of the seller.

CLAUSE: Buyer covenants as a direct and primary obligation that he will pay the mortgage payments as they come due and perform all the covenants of said mortgage, but this clause is not intended to create any obligation to the holder of said mortgage. Should the buyer default in this regard, seller may declare an acceleration of said mortgage debt, but only for the purposes of this covenant.

For what it's worth, it gives the seller the right to seek a personal judgment against the buyer, and to apply his own pressures against the buyer, for institutional lenders are, at times, reluctant to apply such pressures.

(3) If the buyer is content to be liable to both the seller and the mortgagee, the contract and deed can simply recite that the buyer-grantee assumes and agrees to pay the mortgage debt.

(4) Since R is saved from paying the prepayment penalty, E may request a credit therefor.

§ 284. Purchase money mortgages—seller's requirements—partial releases. When R is selling vacant land to E for development, he will take back a purchase money mortgage. E cannot pay all cash. That would deplete his capital. Among the requirements R makes are these: (1) The price per square foot to release part of the land from the mortgage must always be greater than the cost or value of the land. This is a matter of negotiation. Some lawyers think a release price twice the cost or value of the land is about right. (2) The parcels released must always be at the boundary of the tract left under the mortgage. Releasing scattered parcels of land under the mortgage is out of the question. (3) For the same reason, the tracts released should be contiguous. (4) Arrangements must be made for easements to be created, as needed when a release is given. If the release leaves the land under the mortgage with an access problem, the giving of the release and the creation of needed easements take place simultaneously. (5) If the land under the mortgage varies in value, a schedule should be prepared listing the release prices in the various parts of the mortgaged land. (6) E prepares and submits the releases to R. (7) No partial release is given while E is in default under the mortgage. (8) Partial release payments are applied on the last maturing installments of the mortgage. This is the opposite of the provision that E asks for. (9) If the tract under the mortgage is large, R may want to split the mortgage into two or more parts. This makes the separate mortgages more salable. Provision must be made for this. (10) E pays the expense of $R's$ title policies on the mortgage. Form of policy must be specified.

§ 285. Purchase money mortgages—buyer's requirements—partial releases. Among the provisions E wants in the purchase money mortgage clause on vacant land are these: (1) E can file a scheme of building restrictions and R will subordinate his mortgage to the restrictions. Homebuyers will want $R's$ land bound by the restrictions if he forecloses, (2) If rezoning is necessary, R will join in the application for rezoning. (3) R will join in or consent to $E's$ plat of subdivision. (4) R will join in $E's$ grants of utility easements. (5) Payments for releases are applied to next accruing principal payments. (6) Like any other contract, a contract for partial releases is enforceable only if it is complete and certain. The best way to achieve this is to attach a copy of the mortgage and note forms to the contract. (7) Where the sale is subject to an existing first mortgage, the contract should contain some representation as to the amount that will be due thereon at the closing of the deal. (8) Detailed provision for subordination to construction mortgages, keeping in mind that such provisions cannot be enforced unless details are given. Kratovil, *Mortgages*, Chapter 21.

§ 286. Leases, tenancies, and rents. R should agree to keep in force all existing leases, without modification or prepayment of rent, until closing or normal expiration of the lease, whichever event first occurs. He should agree to keep and perform all landlord's covenants in said leases.

If an existing tenant's lease has legally terminated when the deal is closed and no periodic tenancy has taken its place, the buyer is not protected by his contract against a wrongful holdover by the tenant. The contract contains a clause stating that title will be delivered subject to:

Existing leases and tenancies as per schedule attached hereto marked "Exhibit A."

The schedule will show the expiration date of leases and tenancies, and the buyer is stuck with this list if it is accurate.

In other words, the seller has no duty to evict his tenant wrongfully holding over. The buyer, of course, would like a provision that:

The seller will put the buyer in possession on or before _____, evicting existing tenants at his expense, where necessary, and if the tenant has not been evicted by the stated date, buyer to have the right to rescind.

Such a clause is necessary, for example, where the buyer has an existing lease that is expiring and he needs to move to the purchased property by a certain date. Or a tenant buying a building might have a mortgage commitment that expires at a stated date. If such a clause is included, it might be well to include a provision that if the tenant is in wrongful occupancy at closing, the deal will be closed in escrow to facilitate restoration of the status quo if the tenant cannot be evicted by the stipulated date.

Security deposits by tenants reposing in seller's hands must be disposed of in the contract. If tenant's consent to transfer is needed (as it well may be because it is his property), seller should agree to procure it. Advance payments of rent should also be covered in the prorating. Percentage leases require special treatment.

The contract should list all services being furnished tenants, cost thereof during the preceeding year, and any revenue received by seller, for example, for sale of electricity to tenants. The buyer may wish seller to represent that all decorating due tenants for the year has been done and paid for, and, if not, what remains.

The seller should agree to notify the tenants of the sale of the building when the deal has been closed. It suffices if he furnishes signed notices, which the buyer can mail or deliver.

There is no really satisfactory way of handling uncollected rents. If the tenants have been paying promptly, and the deal is closed near the first of the month, the tenant rent checks may still be in the mail. Or one or more tenants may be about to default. Some lawyers try to close the deal as of the last day of the preceding month. The building manager is then instructed not to bank the tenants' checks but to endorse them without recourse to the seller. The theory here is that when a contract says that rents will be prorated to date of closing, this must mean collected rents. You cannot prorate something that doesn't exist. The other side argues that the landlord has the right to the rents as of the first of the month and that he should bear the risk of loss if the rents are not collected. This appears to be the better rule. Schwartz, *Real Estate Manual*, 110, 523; Friedman, *Contracts and Conveyances*, 476.

Some thought should be given to the problem of substantial alterations or repairs, especially those needed to retain tenants, intervening between the date of contract and the closing date. A clause giving E the right to rescind in such case is not necessarily the answer. The buyer may want to go through with the deal. The contract may expressly provide that the expense of alterations or repairs required by the tenant shall be borne by R. If the operation is substantial, E will want to supervise it, for fear R will lack a sense of responsibility and R will object to supervision by E, because he can't be sure the deal will close. One solution would be to provide that the job will be done by a contractor approved by both parties, with E's obligation to close the deal being contingent on an architect's certificate that the work was properly done. R, if he does his job, should agree to furnish documentation, satisfactory to E, that all bills have been paid.

E will want R to represent and warrant as of the date of closing the entire situation existing with respect to himself as landlord and his tenants. This requires R to state that, except as disclosed in the contract or its schedules:

(1) No other leases or tenancies exist.

(2) No modifications, extensions, renewals, options to renew or purchase exist.

(3) No concessions have been given tenants, all rents are as per contract and its schedules, no free gas, electricity, or other utility is furnished.

(4) All decorating and all repair or other work legally owing to tenants has been furnished by landlord and landlord will remain in compliance as of closing. Last painting done on _____.

(5) The following appliances are in the apartments:_____, _____ and _____ are owned by R free of any liens, and same are in good order and repair.

(6) To the best knowledge of R and his building manager, no disputes exist between R and his tenants as regards performance of R's duties to his tenants in general, and, in particular with respect to implied warranties, if any, of R.

(7) No violations exist with respect to rent control laws or regulations, if any, and all tenants are receiving all services to which they are entitled under rent control laws.

(8) No lease brokerage is or will be due from E.

§ 287. Lease approval. R at times will insist on a lease approval clause:

CLAUSE: At least _____ days prior to closing R will furnish E for examination the leases to be assigned to E hereunder and, if E approves same, E will indicate his approval by placing his initials thereon.

§ 288. Approval of documents other than leases. Where documents other than leases are to be assigned to E at closing, a clause similar to the lease approval clause can be used.

§ 289. Assignment by buyer. R can legitimately contend for a clause forbidding assignment by E without his written consent. After all, R has, to some extent, selected E and is content to do business with him. If E was found by a broker, the rule is that R has a right to look him over to see that he is ready, able, and willing to buy. "Willing" means willing to sign a binding contract and "able" means financially able to swing the deal. Why should R be forced to conclude the deal with some one else? Of course, if R is taking back a purchase money mortgage, this clause is a must. If there is no purchase money mortgage, R can agree to convey to E "or his nominee."

The clause may go on to state that any consent by the seller to an assignment, whether or not the assignment includes an assumption of liability by the assignee, nevertheless, leaves E a party primarily liable on the contract. Otherwise, some court could hold that E is then liable only as a surety, with the surety's usual defenses, for example, in case the contract is modified by R and assignee.

Where R consents to an assignment he normally requires that the assignee assume and agree to perform the contract. The consent states that any further assignment also requires the seller's consent.

E, on the other hand, will want a clause in the assignment under which the assignee agrees to perform all E's obligations under the contract, and, in addition will hold E harmless against liability to R under the contract.

Some buyers like a clause in the contract that the seller's consent to the assignment will not be unreasonably withheld if the assignee is willing to assume the buyer's obligations under the contract. Obviously, if the buyer has in mind a quick turn-over of the property at a profit, probably to a buyer he has already lined up, this enables him to do so without using his money or borrowing. Seller cannot "reasonably" object to assignment to a giant corporation.

Both seller and buyer sign the assignment, the buyer doing so because he is assuming liabilities.

The assignment is recorded to give the world notice of the assignee's rights.

It is a good idea to have the contract provide that the seller's consent will be included in the assignment in recordable form, so it also becomes a matter of record.

§ 290. Conveyance by seller before closing—escrows. Because cash sale contracts are rarely recorded, E has a legal risk that R may convey to another purchaser before the deal is closed, especially a purchaser who offers a substantially higher purchase price. This is a good reason for requiring that the deed go into escrow as soon as the contract is signed, with R's deed being recorded immediately. There is no danger to R here, because E also deposits a reconveyance deed, which the escrowee records if the deal does not go through. There is no problem about liens against E clouding R's title. Title companies waive these liens on the theory that in escrow deals, E acquires no title, or, at best a defeasible title, which becomes perfected only when the terms of the escrow are met.

§ 291. Death of seller prior to closing—escrows. If E worries about an individual seller dying before closing, as he should, there is no dependable alternative to going into escrow as soon as the contract is signed. Then the doctrine of "relation back" protects the purchaser. Kratovil, *Real Estate Law* § 257. Anything else is fraught with danger. The seller's will might be contested, for example. The problems of claims, death taxes, etc. pile up. It is comforting to have a corporate seller, or a trustee, or even a partnership.

§ 292. Zoning—rezoning. The matter of contracts contingent on obtaining rezoning has been discussed elsewhere. Kratovil, *Real Estate Law* § 196.

§ 293. Zoning change. A given purchaser may want a provision under which he agrees to proceed with dispatch to apply for a building permit and to proceed with construction, but that if zoning is changed before the property has achieved nonconforming use status, the purchaser shall have the right to rescind. The reason for this is obvious. In many areas, land development is no longer welcome. Environmentalists may seek an adverse change in zoning once the project is announced.

§ 294. Building code violations. If it is the law or custom to procure some official search or certificate for building code violations, this should be provided for.

§ 295. Annexation. If contract is to be conditioned on annexation of the land to a municipality, that should be provided for and a time limit included.

§ 296. Plats and rezoning. *R* does not want the land conveyed by the contract platted of record except as to parts conveyed to buyer; a clause is as follows:

CLAUSE: *E* agrees not to record any plat of subdivision of the land except such parts as have been conveyed by *R* to *E,* unless *R* consents in writing.

A provision requiring *R* to join in plats or rezoning applications may be as follows:

CLAUSE: It is understood and agreed that Purchaser is in the land development and construction business. The land is now unimproved farm land. Seller agrees to execute any documents or plats, upon request of Purchaser, in order to subdivide the land or rezone the same or any part thereof for annexation to a municipality. The cost of the preparation of such documents or plats, and of the engineering involved, shall be borne completely by Purchaser. Seller agrees to cooperate with Purchaser in securing such rezoning or subdivision, and approval of the Land by the Federal Housing Authority or Veteran's Housing Authority, but all the costs, expenses and attorney's fees involved in such proceedings shall be at Purchaser's sole cost.

If *E's* project depends on the obtaining of plat approval, *E* may insist that plat approval be a pre-condition to closing or the deal can be closed subject to *E's* obtaining plat approval. In the latter case, a time limit should be stated and the purchase price held in escrow meanwhile.

§ 297. Risk of loss. Typically *E* presses for a clause giving him the right to rescind if the premises are destroyed or materially damaged before closing. Some buyers want this right if a condemnation suit is filed or notice of proposed condemnation is served before closing. *E* may want a clause that on his demand *R* will assign to *E* any condemnation award made after the date of the contract if he elects not to rescind.

R will also want protection if he has agreed to deliver the premises at closing substantially in the condition that existed at the date of the contract, for the possibility exists that he will be unable to comply with this provision, considering the delay normally incidental to settling with the insurance companies. *R* may wish to reserve the right to rescind in such case. *E* will object to this where the existing structure is one *E* intends to demolish.

If *E* agrees to assume risk of loss pending closing of deal, he needs several things: (1) a statement in the contract or separate document certifying as to existing policies. (2) An agreement by *R* to have *E's* name added as additional assured on all policies where this is possible. (3) An agreement by *R* to keep the policies in force until the deal is closed and to refrain from doing any acts that might impair coverage. (4) Insurance binders on all areas of loss where *R's* policy is not assignable.

§ 298. Lateral support. Where *R* is selling off part of his land, and part of his land is vacant and part improved, he may wish to deal with problems of lateral support. 87 ALR2d 710; 36 ALR2d 1253; 139 ALR 1267; 1956 Law Forum 646; 14 Temp. U.L.R. 243; 77 U.Pa.L.Rev. 77; 33 Mich.L.Rev. 812; 15 Chi-Kent L.Rev. 137. Shoring up the building while construction takes place on the vacant, should be covered. 24 Minn.L.Rev. 852; 50 Yale L.J. 1125.

§ 299. Representations and warranties. If *E* wants representations and warranties, the contract must provide for them, *e.g.*, representations and warranties as to income, expenses, etc. Some buyers like a representation as to ownership of chattels in the rented spaces, but a careful buyer will endeavor to check this representation with the tenant. *E* will want a representation and warranty that the building complies with existing zoning and building ordinances, environmental and energy crisis laws and regulations, and, without limitation, all police power laws and regulations, and will so comply at closing; also that seller has received no notices of violation, or if he has, that same have been corrected. *R* will argue for a narrower clause. Also a representation and warranty should be given that *R* has no knowledge of proposed condemnations. *E* wants a representation and warranty that the building is not a non-conforming use, because most ordinances forbid expansion of such uses. *E* may seek a representation that heating system will heat to _____ degrees in zero weather and cooling system will cool to _____ degrees in hot weather. *E* will want a representation and warranty that the building complies with all building restrictions. Alternatively, *E* may ask for a title company endorsement insuring against zoning or restriction violations. *See* Chapter 11.

R may be quite willing to include a representation that heating, electrical systems, and air conditioning are in working order and will so remain at closing and 90 days thereafter. *E* must ask himself whether this is adequate protection. If a 20-year-old heating plant fails the day after the deal is closed, *E's* damages against *R* might be microscopic. After all *R* has only represented that a 20-year-old heating plant will work for a stated period of time. He has not contracted to replace it with a new plant. This point is well-illustrated by the old cases on removal of heating plants:

EXAMPLE: *R* mortgages his house to *E*. It has an old furnace. *ABC Furnace Company* sells *R* a new furnace on credit. It removes the old furnace and junks it. It installs the new furnace, but removes it when *R* defaults his payments. It is pointless for *E* to sue *ABC Furnance Company*, though he has a legal right to do so. What would a jury award in damages for a 20-year-old furnace?

E will want a representation and warranty as to agreements other than leases and tenancies.

CLAUSE: *R* warrants and represents that there are in existence, and as a condition of closing will then be existing, only the contracts, agreements, advertising leases, concessions, relating to the premises sold, including, without limitation, agreements relating to scavenger service, elevator maintenance, escalator maintenance, sale or purchase of utilities, extermination & pest control, building management agreements, agreements relating to furnishing of steam or air conditioning, coin-operated appliances, licenses or franchises of any kind, including those for maintenance of vaults or other structures extending into public ways, permits, including permits for fill of land formerly under navigable or public water and permits relating to environmental matters, or labor union agreements, set forth in Schedule B.

What representations and warranties are to survive the closing is a matter of negotiation. *E* will want a clause that all warranties and representations survive the closing. Any agreement by *R* to perform work after closing should survive closing. Any penalties for retention of possession beyond the agreed date should survive closing. *R* will argue for a clause as follows:

CLAUSE: It is intended that all representations made herein are to be verified by buyer prior to closing of deal and are not to survive closing.

R should warrant that he has made all contributions to date of closing with respect to pension, profit sharing, medical care, or health funds for his employees.

R should warrant that the only union agreement is that furnished to *E* and that no union problems (strikes, strike notices, work stoppages, claims by union, etc.) exist or are pending to his knowledge.

E may insist that *R* warrant and represent that sewers, water mains, and utilities are installed, operating, and serving the property, and that no third party claims any rights in such facilities.

E will want *R* to warrant that sewer and water lines are available at the property line of the premises, and that same are adequate to service the premises for the purposes stated in this contract, also that the property has legal access to all streets adjoining the property.

§ 300. Access to premises. To avoid complications, the contract should give the purchaser reasonable access to the premises for purposes incident to the transaction. This permits entry by the purchaser's surveyor or purchaser's architect or inspector checking for building code violations or defects in heating plant, etc. This should include permission to inspect just before settlement to see whether the seller or some tenant facing ouster has pillaged the property, removed plumbing fixtures, chandeliers, etc.

§ 301. Collective bargaining agreements. A purchaser of a business may not be automatically bound by the seller's collective bargaining agreement with a labor union. But he may have a duty to bargain with the union that has the agreement. *Nat. Labor Re. Bd. v. Burns Inc. Sec-Services Inc.*, 32 L.Ed. 2d 61 (1972). The collective bargaining agreement should be checked before the contract is signed.

It may, in terms, bind any purchaser. In any event negotiating a different contract presents obvious difficulties.

If the contract has been negotiated by an office building association to which both *R* and *E* belong, *E* has no alternative but to continue with the existing contract.

§ 302. Non-competition agreement. If *E* wants a non-competition agreement from *R*, that provision belongs in the contract of sale or in a separate, contemporaneous contract. The local law is checked to see what restraints are permitted.

§ 303. Fees—documentary taxes. All fees should be covered. State who pays recording fee for deed and purchase money mortgage, if any; fees for title insurance for buyer's owner's policy and seller's mortgage policy if he is taking back a purchase money mortgage; documentary taxes on deed and purchase money mortgage; surveyor's charges, fees for transfer of vault permits, fees for certificate as to building code violations, termite inspection fee; fees for Uniform Commercial Code Searches, etc.

§ 304. Copies. Neither *R* nor *E* can insist upon copies or duplicates unless the contract calls for them. As to Torrens properties, routinely the contract calls for the deed and mortgage to be executed in duplicate, for the Torren's office keeps one set and *E* and his mortgagee want duplicates for their own use. A general clause is helpful.

CLAUSE: Each party hereto will furnish to the other copies or duplicates of any closing document where request therefor has been made a reasonable time prior to closing and the party requesting is willing to bear the reasonable expense therefor.

§ 305. Third-party beneficiaries. There may be aspects of the contract that are intended primarily for the benefit of *R* for example, but that might incidentally benefit other landowners, such as an agreement by *E* to install sewers, water or utilities in public streets that abut land retained by *R* and his neighbors. Careful lawyers like to include a clause to the effect that the contract is not intended for the benefit of any parties other than the parties to the contract.

§ 306. Brokers. Some provision is needed as to brokers' commissions. One solution is to provide that *R* and *E* represent and agree that *X* is the only broker involved in the transaction, that *R* will pay his commission, and that if any other broker claims a commission, the party whom the broker claims to represent will indemnify the other party against all liability for broker's commissions. *See* Chapter 16.

§ 307. Liability of vendor for injuries after closing. *R* may continue to have some liability for personal injuries occurring after closing. 44 Minn.L.Rev. 144; 24 Tenn.L.Rev. 1170; 48 ALR3d 1027. This may call for a representation and warranty by *E* that he has made a full inspection of the premises and absolves *R* of any such liability and will hold *R* harmless against actions brought by tenants. The insurance company should be consulted to make sure that either *R* or *E* has coverage against actions by third parties based on these pre-existing defects. *R* must remember that he today faces the new concept of ''products liability.'' Insurance is available to *R* to protect him against these liabilities. Kratovil, *Real Estate Law* § 492.

§ 308. Integration. The parol evidence rule is pretty liberal these days in permitting proof of ''collateral agreements.'' Hence many lawyers press for a clause stating that the contract expresses all of the agreements between the parties and that no collateral agreements exist.

§ 309. Securities acts. Both federal and state laws and regulations regarding securities affect many aspects of large-scale transactions. They are beyond the scope of this text.

§ 310. Default and termination clause. In all large-scale contracts, default and termination clauses are detailed. Obviously, provisions relating to *R's* right to terminate are different from those relating to *E's* right to terminate. And a tendency remains to differentiate between termination rights where the other party is *at fault* from those where no fault is involved.

EXAMPLE: Where the soil fails to pass the soil tests, *E* should have a right to terminate, but no right to sue *R* unless he has made representations as to soil conditions.

With respect to title, agreement must be reached as to liability if the title does not conform to the contract. *R* is often able to persuade *E* to accept a clause limiting *E* to a return of his deposit plus payment of stipulated expenses, such as title or survey charges borne by *E*, otherwise *E* to accept title ''as is.'' The title commitment may show a lien of a stated amount. The contract should cover this. *E* wants a clause giving him the right to pay this and deduct the amount from the sale price. If *R* wants to contest the lien he may want a clause giving him the right to deposit an amount in escrow while he litigates the lien.

If it turns out that the leases differ substantially from those described in the contract, most likely *R* is seriously at fault. *E* may want the right to rescind, and recover his earnest money and sue for damages. Other representations and warranties may fall in this category.

EXAMPLE: *E* is engaged in a land assembly. *R*, who owns one of the parcels, represents and warrants that he has no notice of any proposed condemnation. *E's* investigation reveals that *R* has been served with notice of a highway condemnation on his tract. *E* may suffer serious damage if the deal falls through for this reason.

One way of handling this is to state that *E's* right to maintain against *R* an action for damages for breach applies only to paragraphs _____, listing the paragraphs agreed upon.

R's remedies for breach on *E's* part should also be spelled out.

EXAMPLE: The contract gives *E* four months to obtain rezoning. *E* covenants to proceed with diligence to obtain rezoning. *E* does nothing. Perhaps the contract should provide that if *E* does nothing, it shall be conclusively deemed that rezoning could have been obtained, that *R's* damages are difficult to determine accurately, and he shall be entitled to liquidated damages of $_____ in addition to the earnest money and *R's* other expenses.

Of course, the local law of liquidated damages must be kept in mind at all times.

§ 311. Time limits. Time limits should be set for every act to be done, *e.g.*, furnishing of survey, furnishing of Uniform Commercial Code search, furnishing of title evidence, clearing of title objections, closing, giving of possession, etc.

§ 312. Closing—prorations. Describe fully all items to be prorated, and how prorations are to be made. Payments may be due tenants for repairs or alterations. Vacation pay and payroll should be apportioned. Supplies on hand should be paid for.

§ 313. Closing—pre-conditions to seller's duty to close. *R* will need to insist on pre-conditions to his duty to go forward and *E* may wish to insist on time limits. Other provisions may be needed where other pre-conditions exist.

EXAMPLE: A corporate seller may need a condition relating to approval of sale by stockholders or members.

EXAMPLE: Where *R* is selling pursuant to judicial proceedings he must insist on a pre-condition that the court approve the sale to *R*. *E* will insist on a condition that the proceedings be checked and approved by the title company. Both *R* and *E* must deal with the following problems: (1) The right to set aside court orders within term time. (2) Rights of parties served by publication, which may extend for a period as long as a year. (3) Rights of appeal. As a generalization, even a third-party purchaser takes subject to (1) and (2), and in many states takes subject to (3) if the sale is consummated before appeal time has expired.

§ 314. Closing—escrows for minor liens. It is indispensably necessary for the seller's protection to permit him to deposit money in escrow with the title company to clear minor liens. An unexpected mechanic's lien, for example, may pop up just before closing. The seller, obviously, will need time to clear up this lien if it is debatable or inflated. Meanwhile, the buyer can rescind, unless the escrow provision is present.

§ 315. Closing—seller's closing documents. A clause used with respect to seller's closing documents follows:

At the time of settlement Seller shall execute and deliver to the Buyer the following:

(a) Special Warranty Deed to the premises in recordable form, so as to vest in the Buyer a good fee simple marketable title thereto, insurable as set forth in paragraph _____ hereof at regular rates under a policy excepting only the permitted exceptions.

(b) All contracts setting forth the terms and conditions under which service is rendered to the premises and assignments thereof.

(c) An assignment of the lessor's interest in all leases on the premises.

(d) Certified copies of Resolutions of all the Directors of Seller, as well as all the stockholders thereof, authorizing the execution and delivery by Seller of this Agreement and of the instruments required herein to be so executed and delivered.

(e) An opinion of Seller's counsel dated as of the date of settlement that all persons signing this Agreement and all other instruments on behalf of Seller, were duly authorized and said instruments constitute valid acts and binding obligations of the Seller and do not violate any of the provisions of Seller's Charter, By-Laws, or any contract or commitment of the Seller known to Seller's counsel.

(f) If requested by Buyer, an assignment in proper form assigning and transferring to Buyer the exclusive use of the Seller's trade name and all goodwill associated therewith.

(g) All plans and specifications presently in possession of Seller covering the improvements which were constructed on the premises.

(h) Letters to all tenants signed by the Seller that the premises have been sold to Buyer or to Buyer's successor, and directing the tenants to make future rental payments to said Buyer, his successor, or to a party designated by Buyer.

(i) If any lease does not provide for transfer of the security deposit to a buyer, the Seller will deliver to Buyer a consent by the tenant to such transfer.

(j) Any guarantees or warranties heretofore received by Seller from any contractors, subcontractors, or suppliers still in force at the time of settlement and assignment thereof.

(k) A written statement of the holder of the mortgages stating substantially that said mortgages are in good standing, in accordance with their original terms; that no uncured defaults have been committed thereunder, or under obligations which they secure; that the conveyance of the premises as herein set forth will not constitute a default thereunder or cause any acceleration of the principal debts thereof, and that no more than $_____ of the principal debt remains unpaid as of the date of settlement.

(l) An estoppel certificate from each tenant stating that their leases are in full force and effect, without modification, that they are unaware of any defaults thereunder, and the date to which rent has been paid.

(m) A statement of profit and loss for the period from the date of this Agreement to the date of settlement. Said statement will show no material adverse change in the operation of the premises.

(n) An assignment to Buyer of all awards in condemnation for damages of any kind to which Seller or Buyer may have become entitled, or may hereafter be entitled by reason of the exercise of the power of eminent domain with respect to the taking or damaging of the premises, or any part thereof.

18

Closing Check List— Before Contract Is Signed

§ 316. **In general.** The contract of sale is the blueprint for the closing of a real estate deal. Whenever, in the course of a deal, a question arises as to the rights of the parties, we turn to the contract. Hence plans for closing the deal must be made before the contract is signed, for once the contract is signed, the shape of the deal is set, and rights and liabilities are crystallized.

Before the contract is signed, the following should be considered:

1. If the land is vacant, are there any zoning ordinances that will prevent use of the land for the purposes contemplated by the buyer? If there is a building on the land, but the buyer expects to remodel it, are there any ordinances that will prohibit such remodeling? For example, the building may be a non-conforming use (which under the law cannot be enlarged), or constructed under a variance that forbids enlargement. A contract cannot be rescinded because of the buyer's ignorance of such ordinances. Also the contract should require the seller to deliver the building free of violations of building codes or zoning ordinances, for it is not clear that such violations would permit the buyer to reject the title as "unmarketable."

2. If the land is vacant, and the contract is a printed form requiring the buyer to take subject to "building restrictions," what do these building restrictions provide? Do they prohibit use of the land for the purpose contemplated by the buyer? Like considerations apply where the contract is to be subject to "easements of record" or some specific easement. An easement running through the center of vacant land can play havoc with building plans.

3. Has the seller listed in the contract all the encumbrances or other defects in title which he does not propose to clear before the deal is closed? Most contract forms contain a printed list of common encumbrances, such as leases or building restrictions, but it is intended that the seller will add to this list, as necessary. Suppose, for example, the seller's title is subject to an easement. Is it mentioned in the contract? If not, and the buyer changes his mind and decides to back out of the deal, he can do so because the title as finally examined before the deal is closed must reveal no encumbrances other than those listed either in general or specific language in the contract. If the contract is subject to "existing leases," the rental and duration of the leases should be set forth, also whether the leases contain options to renew or purchase. The buyer should consider whether he wants assurances in the contract that there are no revocable permits, such as permits to maintain a marquee over the sidewalk.

§ 317. **Mining country.** In mining country, you will encounter the problem of unpatented mining claims, severance of surface and mineral estates, mineral leases and reservations of minerals contained in federal or state statutes but not set forth in the patent by federal or state government. The latter requires brief explanation. Some laws require the reservation of minerals to the government. Government agencies have issued thousands of patents making no reference to these statutory reservations. Yet they exist as though set forth in the patent. Abstracts fail to show them. *U.S. v. Frisbee,* 57 F.Supp. 299. Title policies may include them in printed exceptions. Obviously *E* must seek counsel as to these rights.

§ 318. **Arid land.** In arid land, supply of water is crucial. *E* will want *R* to warrant the validity of his water rights, and these must be set forth in the contract and deed. *E* may wish a supporting legal opinion. *E* may want affidavits as to peaceful enjoyment by *R* of his water rights and the actual physical existence of an adequate flow of water. In the "prior appropriation" states *E* may want affidavits as to the facts of prior appropriation. Kratovil, *Real Estate Law* (3rd ed. 1958) § 659. State permits will be needed for digging new wells. If *E* plans to change the use of the land, he should have a legal opinion as to the effect of such change on his water rights. *E* may need to have *R* contract to transfer to *E R's* stock in a water supply company. *E* may wish to inquire as to what water rights cross the land.

§ 319. **Grazing permits and leases.** If *E* plans to continue *R's* grazing use in a ranch sale, he must ascertain what *R's* rights are and must arrange for transfer of these rights, permits, and leases to *E*.

§ 320. **Insurance requirements before contract is signed.** *E* will wish to know, before he signs the contract of purchase, that he can obtain hazard insurance that pays to *rebuild* the building, not simply to *pay for loss*. *E* wants insurance money that will demolish what must be demolished and reconstitute the structure as it was before the fire damage occurred. Adjusting fire damage on the standard fire policy without *completion insurance* can be a serious problem.

In recent times, especially where inner city problems exist, insurers have begun to "red line" areas where they refuse to write insurance. Before *E* signs a contract to purchase or *E* agrees to loan money, there must be a firm understanding and preferably verbal coverage, with an authorized insurance agent. Before *E* accepts risk of loss in reliance on existing hazard policies, an inspection of the building should be made to unearth policy violations (sprinkler not working, no watchman on duty, etc.) *Holz Rubber Co. Inc. v. General Acc. & L. Assur. Corp.,* 111 Cal. Rept. 883.

§ 321. **Landlord and tenant problems.** Before *E* signs the contract of purchase, he and his attorney must decide whether *E* can live with the new developments greatly expanding the rights of tenants. *E* must also consider his possible "products liability."

§ 322. **Building codes—violations.** *R* and *E* should settle between themselves who will be liable for building code violations existing at the date of closing.

§ 323. **State regulation and zoning.** In addition to the usual check of *local* zoning and building ordinances, *E* must now consider regulations and zoning imposed by the *state*. 56 Minn.L.Rev. 869.

§ 324. **Flood plains.** Where vacant land is scheduled for development, *E* must determine, before the contract is signed, whether it falls in a flood plain.

Construction is forbidden in some flood plain ordinances. United States related or regulated mortgage lenders are required to carry flood insurance in areas subject to flooding as shown on official maps.

§ **325. Sewage and solid waste disposal.** Water pollution and waste disposal are major problems. Both existing and planned uses must be checked against state and local legislation. Usually there is a local board to consult.

§ **326. Security service.** In these days, security protection against crimes is important. *R's* protection should be checked for adequacy, and transfer of his security contract and equipment arranged for. In some institutions, this is a big-figure item.

§ **327. Check list of matters before contract is signed.**

1. *Electricity*. Check to see that lines of sufficient voltage exist.

2. *Sewers and drains*. Check to see that sewers, drains, and waste disposal facilities are adequate and are not likely to encounter environmental regulation problems, for example, where effluent is being discharged into a stream or lake.

3. *Access*. Check to see if heavy trucks can use the abutting streets and that spur tracks exist and will be serviced by the railroad. Check to see if highway is a limited access highway.

4. *Loading platforms*. Check adequacy of loading platforms and space.

5. *Parking*. Check adequacy of parking areas for customers and employees.

6. *Vaults*. Check to see if there will be any problems on getting a license to use necessary vault space or parking space beneath adjoining public streets. If there are, or are to be, curb cuts, marquees, etc., check to see if permits are in existence or available.

7. *Mapped streets*. Especially where vacant land is being sold, the appropriate public office should be checked for maps of future streets, for the buyer may be denied compensation if he builds over such streets and condemnation is later filed. 36 ALR3d 794, 26 Am.Jur. 2d 843; 112 U. Pa.L.Rev. 774; 66 W.Va.L.Rev. 73.

8. *Tax aspects*. The tax consequences to seller and buyer should be explored.

9. *Access to premises*. Obtain permission to enter
   (a) for soil tests.
   (b) to check carrying capacity of floors, columns and beams.
   (c) to check for ordinance violations, city inspections, elevators, electric wiring, boilers, heating plant, plumbing, all other equipment.
   (d) to check sewer capacity.
   (e) for inspection reports by insurance underwriters.

10. *Governmental body as seller*. If some governmental body is the seller, the buyer should obtain opinion of counsel as to the powers of the officers he is dealing with, the need for public sale, etc.

11. *Party wall*. If buyer means to hook on to a party wall, he must determine that it is adequate for his needs from an engineering point of view. Also, can buyer obtain permission to extend the wall, if necessary?

12. *Historic landmarks*. It is best to determine at an early date whether the building is a historic landmark. Most laws forbid alterations of such buildings.

13. *Existing easements*. Check texts of easements, building restrictions, heating agreements, etc. that seller proposes to list in his contract. Can the buyer live with them?

14. *New easements*. Will the buyer want new easements over, or restrictions upon, seller's remaining land? Is he willing to so contract? How about a non-competition agreement with seller?

15. If sale is of part of seller's land, check to see whether implied easements might result.

16. *Mortgages*. R considers whether he will have to pay a prepayment fee to retire the existing mortgage. E considers the amount of a possible assumption fee if he takes over the existing mortgage and possible increase of interest under compulsion of a "due on sale" clause.

17. *Civil rights—racial discrimination*. R must consider possible consequences of racial discrimination in rejecting E.

18. *Termination of lease*. If termination of such a lease is a matter of concern to E, as where E plans to demolish the building, the lease will be examined for an explicit right of termination, and if none exists, require opinion of counsel before the contract is signed. Keep in mind that some lessees

are not above using their technical rights to extort payment of compensation. If there is any doubt, the lessee may have to be contacted and a cancellation agreement procured, contingent on closing of the deal.

19. *Survey as a source of information.* In checking the physical aspects of the land prior to signing the contract, it is well to keep in mind the requirements for surveys outlined in Chapter 7. These are good reminders of legal and practical problems that should be considered by a prospective buyer.

20. *Environmental control.* Environmental control is of such overwhelming importance today that no contract should be signed by the buyer until he has opinion of counsel that his operations will not bring him into conflict with present or projected regulations relating to environmental control. The fact that he plans to continue the seller's operations is inconclusive. Controls are getting tighter.

21. *Energy crisis controls.* Energy crisis controls must be considered before the contract is signed.

22. Before any contract is signed, *E* must consider the possible impact of any of his construction plans on his neighbors.

EXAMPLE: An electric sign was constructed so that its bright lights illuminated *P's* hotel rooms facing the lights. The court ruled this could be stopped as a nuisance. In another case, night baseball games interfered with use of adjacent school property, particularly the dormitories. The court stopped the games. On the other hand, the Eden Roc was not successful in blocking an addition to the Fountainbleau that put the Eden Roc's swimming pool in the shade. The Sears Building in Chicago prevailed in litigation alleging interference with TV reception. 22 De Paul L.Rev. 870 Litigation of this sort can be costly.

23. *Senior citizen exemption. E* should determine whether *R* has a special senior citizen tax exemption and whether *E* will be entitled to same. This also affects the prorating of taxes if next year's taxes will be without benefit of the exemption.

24. *Curb cuts.* A check should be made of local ordinances on curb cuts. Narrow curb cuts may block your development.

19

Closing Steps—After Contract Is Signed

§ **328. Documents.** The following documents should be assembled immediately after contract is signed:

1. Existing title evidence—title insurance or abstract. If contract requires *R* to bring down title, he should immediately attend to this. If *E* is to obtain his own title evidence, *R's* attorney may deliver *R's* title evidence on "trust receipt" to *E's* attorney. *E's* attorney will use this as a "starter." For example, if *R* has a title policy dated in 1970, but *E* intends to use a different title company, *E's* title company will use *R's* title policy as a "starter," thus giving faster service. The title company or abstractor must be given a time limit for completion of their work prior to the date set in the contract for establishing condition of title.

EXAMPLE: Contract requires *R* to place a title commitment in *E's* hands on or before 20 days from the date of contract. The title company should be told, when the title company search is ordered, that the title commitment must be in *R's* hands at least five days before the deadline. This gives *R* the opportunity to clear any objections or otherwise cause the title commitment to conform to contract.

Sometimes the contract where an abstract is involved, requires the abstracter to certify the entire abstract. This should be done before the abstract is tendered to *E.*

EXAMPLE: The present abstract consists of three parts, the original portion one by *Company A,* the second continuation by *Company B,* the third continuation by *Company C, Company A* and *Company B* are now out of business. If *Company C* is to prepare the present continuation, it should certify to the correctness of the work done by these companies.

2. Existing survey. If *R* is to up-date the survey under the contract, he will probably use the same surveyor, and if so, the survey need only be shown to surveyor, who will then check his records of surveys, and furnish an up-dated survey. If a new surveyor is to be used, he can be given the old survey on a "trust receipt." The surveyor should be given his time limit for furnishing the survey, as in the case of title evidence.

3. Last tax bill, which will be needed for prorating.

4. Insurance policy, and paid bill therefor, which will be needed for proration and assignment to buyer if contract so provides.

5. Deed to *R,* which both lawyers will wish to examine.

6. Copies of all building restrictions, which *E's* lawyer will check for possible violations when down-dated survey is available.

7. Copies of any easements over the property or in favor of the property. If the easement is over the property, *E's* lawyer will (a) Check to see that it does not go beyond its description in the contract; for example, if contract mentions a "utilities easement," *E's* lawyer will object to an easement "for railroad purposes," (b) Check for proper location of easement after up-dated survey comes in, for

example, a paved driveway should fall within the strip assigned to it in the easement grant, else a title problem is present, (c) See if there are encroachments on the easement, which may also render title unmarketable.

8. Party wall agreement, if any. If *E* is buying vacant land, he may have to pay for the right to tie into party wall.

9. Corporation tax bill, personal property tax bill, water tax bill, sewer tax bill, and any other tax bill for taxes that could create a lien on the land or be needed in prorating.

10. Mortgage pay-off statement, preferably with clause indicating that mortgagee is prepared to accept payment and issue release on receipt of amount indicated and omitting any recital that "statement is subject to audit."

11. All leases for inspection by buyer's attorney and assignment at closing, also all guarantees by third parties of leases.

12. Permits for curb-cuts, awnings or signs over sidewalks, marquees, vaults beneath sidewalks, permits for underground parking space beneath sidewalks.

13. Duplicate Torrens certificate to be delivered at closing.

14. Service contracts (scavenger, management, elevator maintenance, snow removal, etc.) for assignment at closing or cancellation.

15. Certificate of occupancy under zoning ordinance, also variances if building does not comply with zoning ordinance.

16. Mechanic's lien waivers for any recent work done, also contractor's affidavits and other mechanic's lien documents.

17. Insurance policies to be assigned or cancelled at closing.

18. Contractor's warranty of house, warranties of roof and heating plant, etc. to be assigned to *E* at closing.

19. If vacant land involved, all subdivision reports required by state or federal law.

20. Paid bills for condominium assessments or planned unit development assessments.

21. Agreement between *R* and union of employees.

22. Federal lien search. Whenever personal property figures in the transaction, a federal lien search must be made where *R* resides.

§ 329. Matters to consider after the contract is signed, but before closing time:

1. *R* should give lender notice to make payoff letter on the seller's existing mortgage available at closing. Many lenders and some mortgages require notice of intention to prepay, and this requirement must be also complied with.

2. After the title has been brought down to date, both *R* and *E* will want to check to make sure that all title objections have been cleared, so that the title will be good as specified in the contract. From *R's* viewpoint this should be done, for if his title is not clear by the time allowed by the contract for showing clear title, *E* will be entitled to rescind where "time is of the essence," as most contract forms provide. From *E's* viewpoint this should be done, for once the deal is closed all questions of marketability of title are at an end and *E's* only protection is under the covenants of warranty if he has received a warranty deed. If the contract calls for an abstract of title, normally documents clearing defects in the title (quitclaim deed, affidavits, and the like) should be recorded and covered by the abstract, for *E* is entitled to clear title as shown by the abstract.

3. If the personal property to be transferred is valuable, as in a hotel or furnished apartment, *E* should make a search for financing statements under the Uniform Commercial Code covering such property. In some situations, also, it may be necessary to comply with the Bulk Sales provisions of the UCC.

4. *E* should check the survey for encroachments. These may occur at the surface of the earth, or above or below it. For example, if an adjoining building is tilted, its upper stories may encroach upon the air space of the land being sold. Footings often encroach over property lines. The building on the property being sold may extend over adjoining streets, alleys, or private property; or adjoining buildings may extend over and upon the land being sold. All these encroachments must be considered, for they may render title unmarketable. Be sure the survey shows fences, driveways, drainage

ditches, manhole covers, power lines, etc. And be sure the survey is a current one. A survey made ten years ago, for example, may fail to reflect current conditions. If the survey reveals that *R* has been occupying beyond his property line (a fence encroachment, for example) *E* should, if he finds the encroachment unobjectionable, endeavor to procure a quitclaim deed from *R* to the part so occupied.

5. If possible *E* should check to determine whether the building materially violates zoning ordinances. For example, the building may be closer to the lot lines than is allowed by the ordinances. If the plat of survey is checked against the ordinance, such violations will be revealed. Of course, if the building antedates adoption of the ordinance it may be a valid nonconforming use.

6. *E* should check to determine whether the building materially violates local building ordinances. For example, there may be illegal partition walls, illegal apartments in the basement, living quarters that lack required exits, and the like.

7. *E* should check to determine whether the building violates private building restrictions, such as building lines created by subdivision plats. A violation of a building line can be detected by checking the plat of survey against the recorded restrictions. In this connection all recorded restrictions should be read in full. Naturally the danger is greater where the violated restriction is in the form of a condition, for complete loss of title results where a condition is enforced. If the restriction does not have a reverter clause, violations are less serious, for the right to compel compliance may be barred by laches. It should be remembered that even if the contract requires *E* to take subject to "building restrictions," he is not required to take subject to violations of restrictions. Such violations constitute a separate and distinct defect in title.

8. *R* should determine from *E* what broker interested him in the property. This should be done so that after *R* has paid *Broker A*, he will not be confronted with a claim by *Broker B* that *Broker B* was in fact the procuring cause of the sale.

9. If possible, *E* should check with local authorities for drainage assessments or other assessments that may not have been confirmed by a court of record.

10. Where the evidence of title reveals defects not permitted by the sale contract (or permitted by the contract only where title insurance thereover is available), the parties may choose to avail themselves of title insurance coverage afforded against the potential loss or damage which could be incurred by the existence of such defects. Title companies offer a variety of endorsements to the title policy which extend such coverage. By way of illustration, the following are some of the endorsements issued by Chicago Title Insurance Company in such situations:

a. *Encroachment Endorsement 1.* This form of endorsement is issued to protect *E* against any loss resulting from a mandatory injunction compelling removal of an encroachment of our building on adjoining land. Normally, the Company will issue the endorsement where the encroachment is so trivial that it is highly improbable that a successful action to obtain the injunction could be maintained or the encroachment is protected against removal by reason of over twenty years of adverse possession.

b. *Encroachment Endorsement 2.* This endorsement is issued to protect *E* against any loss resulting from a mandatory injunction to remove encroachment of an improvement on the land over a private easement crossing our land. As in the case of Encroachment Endorsement 1, it is issued by the Company where the triviality of the encroachment or adverse possession would defeat any action to remove the encroachment.

c. *Restriction Endorsement 1.* This endorsement can be used to provide protection where a deed in the chain of title contains a restriction with a reverter clause and the building violates the restriction but the violation is barred by the Reverters Act.

d. *Restriction Endorsement 4.* This is used where a restriction exists and is violated by our building but the violations are trivial or the restriction has become unenforceable because of other nearby violations or changes in neighborhood.

e. *Restriction Endorsement 4A.* This is used where our building violates a building line.

11. There are situations where *E* desires or needs more title insurance protection than is afforded by the standard types of owners title insurance policies. Title companies often can and do amend their standard policies in certain areas by endorsements insuring against loss or damage arising from some common situations. Illustrative of some of these endorsements furnished by the Chicago Title Insurance Company are:

a. *Restrictions Endorsement 1.* This form of endorsement furnishes assurance to *E* that the improvements on the land are in conformity with existing private restrictions affecting the land.

b. *Restrictions Endorsement 5.* This form of endorsement furnishes assurance to the buyer of vacant land that a contemplated improvement in violation of one or more restrictions affecting the land will not furnish a basis for injunctive relief against the construction or maintenance of the improvement. It is normally issued where the restrictions being violated have become unenforceable by reason of changes in the neighborhood or abandonment.

c. *Special Endorsement 1.* This form of endorsement extends assurance to a buyer of a condominium apartment that the condominium was created in conformity with the Condominium Property Act.

d. *Location Endorsement 1.* This form of endorsement informs E as to the location of the land by a reference to its distance from an identified street or alley and, if available, to its street address. It extends assurance to E that the contract describes the land he intends to purchase and such land is covered by the title policy.

e. *Location Endorsements 2 and 3.* These endorsements are similar in purpose to Location Endorsement 1, but Endorsement 2 is issued where the sale involves a condominium unit, while Endorsement 3 is used where the sale involves a town house.

f. *Location Endorsement 4.* This form of endorsement assures the buyer that two or more parcels of land described in his contract and in the policy which he intends to improve are contiguous.

§ 330. Matters to consider when the deal is ready for closing:

1. If the deal is not closed in escrow, an informal check should be made of the records to cover the period or "gap" between the date of the abstract or title search and the date of the closing of the deal. Judgments or other liens may attach during this interval, and will, of course, be good against E. Of course, if the deal is closed in escrow, all danger from this source is obviated. If, by agreement, R is to clear certain objections after closing, E should retain part of the purchase price (usually double the amount of the lien involved) to insure performance on the part of R.

2. If this has not been done in advance of closing, E should check the deed to see that it conforms to the contract. For example, if it is a warranty deed, the subject clause should not list any items that were not included in the subject clause of the contract. The description should also be checked against the title insurance commitment. It should be determined that the deed is properly signed and acknowledged. The deed should also conform to the statutes.

EXAMPLE: Statutes may require (1) Deed to state name of draftsman. (2) Deed to show payment of state taxes. (3) Deed to state party to whom tax bills are to be sent. (4) Deed to show true consideration or sale price. (5) Deed to have all signatures typed beneath signatures.

If the contract calls for R to do some act after closing (pave a driveway, for example) this covenant should be included in the deed to prevent a later claim that the contract was *merged* in the deed.

3. If this has not previously been done, all leases should be checked. Normally the contract contains a schedule of all leases, their duration, rent and a statement that they contain no options to renew or purchase, or if options exist, they also are set forth. The leases should be checked for conformity to the schedule.

4. E should call for production of paid water bills. If all water bills have not been paid, E may have trouble getting service.

5. Prorations or adjustments should be computed, and a closing statement prepared. In computing prorations, it is often convenient to use a prorating table or chart. Such tables facilitate computation of the usual prorations.

6. The balance due according to the closing statement should be paid, and the documents to which each party is entitled delivered to him. If the existing mortgagee is present at the closing he will give a release deed at this time.

7. If disputes arise in the process of closing the deal, in the Chicago area solution of the problem may be facilitated by referring to the *Uniform Rules for Closing Real Estate Sales* adopted by the Brokers Division of the Chicago Real Estate Board and the Committee on Real Estate Probate and Trust Law of the Chicago Bar Association. Other such rules exist. These rules, of course, have no

legally binding force. They are merely an expression of what experienced persons consider a fair and reasonable method of closing deals.

§ 331. The closing statement. In preparation of the closing statement, showing the prorating or adjustment of the various items other than sale price that enter into a real estate deal, the following are the usual credits due *E:*

1. Earnest money.

2. Existing mortgages if the sale is for part cash and balance by assumption of existing mortgages.

3. Interest accrued and unpaid on existing mortgages that are to be assumed by *E.*

4. Amount of purchase money mortgage if *R* has agreed to receive such mortgage as part of the purchase price.

5. Unearned rents that have already been collected. Rents are usually collected on the first of the month, and if the deal is closed after the first of the month, *E* is, under most contracts, entitled to his proportionate part of the current month's rent collections. Taxes for the current year (if these have not already been paid), are prorated and contracts usually so provide.

6. Items based on meter readings, such as water tax, electricity and gas, if same are not paid in advance.

7. Wages and other charges accrued and unpaid, such as janitor's salary, scavenger service, etc.

8. Release fee and recording charge, where *E* will record or obtain release of mortgage which seller should have removed from his title.

And the following are usual credits due R:

1. Full purchase price.

2. Unearned insurance premiums.

3. Fuel on hand. Where oil heat is involved, have the tank filled just before closing so that *E* pays for a full tank.

4. Any items paid by *R* in advance, as water tax (if same has been so paid), prepayments on exterminator or other service contracts, prepayments of taxes and insurance made by *R* to mortgagee under the terms of the mortgage, where such mortgage is to be assumed by *E.*

§ 332. Items and documents to be obtained by *E* at closing:

1. Deed, also supporting corporation resolutions if grantor is a corporation.

2. Real estate transfer declaration stating the full consideration for the transfer or other local deed tax documents.

3. Abstract, title policy, or other evidence of title and paid bills for same.

4. Bill of sale of personal property, with warranty of title and freedom from encumbrances.

5. Survey.

6. All paid notes on existing mortgages, which *E* assumes, since these notes will be needed in obtaining a release deed; also any mortgage and mortgage notes that have been paid in full and the release or satisfaction of the mortgage, if such release has not yet been recorded.

7. Estoppel certificate by mortgagee showing amount due on existing mortgage, so that the mortgagee cannot thereafter assert that any greater amount remains due. This applies where *E* is taking the land subject to an existing mortgage or his mortgagee will retire the existing mortgage with funds reserved from the sale.

8. Insurance policies and assignments thereof.

9. Leases including leases of advertising space or advertising signs.

10. An assignment of all major leases and estoppel certificates. A lease is both a contract and a conveyance, and some of the provisions of the lease may not be covenants running with the land. For this reason, a lawyer representing a purchaser of leased land may wish to receive an assignment of

the lessor's interest in the lease, including the benefits of all contracts, agreements, and covenants on the lessee's part. Past due rent can be included if the purchaser is to receive the same under the contract of sale. The right to a tenant's security deposit may not pass by the deed in some jurisdictions 52 CJS *Landlord & Tenant* § 473(2). A separate assignment of the deposit can be used, to which the tenant's consent can be appended. The deposit belongs to the tenant, after all, and he has a right to choose to whom he will entrust it. The tenant in a major lease should also be asked to give *E* an estoppel certificate stating that the lease is valid and subsisting, that there are no unrecorded modifications or assignments exist.

11. Copies of restrictions, easements, or covenants that *E* will have to comply with.

12. Letter by seller to tenants advising them to pay future rent to *E*.

13. Letter by *R* to *R's* building manager or rental agent advising him of sale of building and of termination of his authority.

14. Statement by *R* as to names of tenants, rents paid and unpaid, due date of rents, and that no rents have been paid in advance except for current month.

15. Service contracts such as exterminator contract, if they are to be assigned to *E* with assignment thereof.

16. Last receipts for taxes, special assessment, gas, electricity, and water.

17. *R's* affidavit of title, which states (among other things) that there are no judgments, bankruptcies, or divorces against him, no unrecorded deeds or contracts, no repairs or improvements which have not been paid for, that *R* knows of no defects in his title, and that he has been in undisputed possession of the premises. The affidavit of title has several functions: (1) In many cases, the abstract or title search covers only the date of the contract, and the deal is closed at some later date. The affidavit covers the period between the date of title search and the date of closing. (2) Some defects in title are not revealed by a title search, for example, a divorce obtained in some other state. Indeed, the only way in which one can be assured of the seller's marital status is by procuring an affidavit relative thereto. Other defects such as mechanic's lien for work or material furnished in the building, may likewise not be revealed by the title examination. (3) The warranty deed gives *E* the right to sue for damages if a defect in title is later revealed. But the affidavit may give *E* the right to have the seller prosecuted criminally for obtaining money through false pretenses.

18. Securities deposited by tenants as security for payment of rent and money deposits by tenants made as security for payment of rent for last months of lease. But if lease does not provide that on any sale of property the deposit shall go to *E*, the tenant's consent should be obtained to a transfer of the deposit.

19. Permits for signs, vaults, marquees, water tanks and other structures that require city or village permits, also certificate of occupancy under the zoning ordinances where a new building is involved.

20. Assignment of any written warranty of the building held by *R*, also any other warranties or guarantees, such as warranties of roof, heating plant etc.

21. Termite inspection certificate, if inspection was made.

§ 333. **Payment of purchase price.** At closing *R* should obtain balance of purchase price. Typically *E* brings to the closing a cashier's check for an amount less than the prorations will show as due from him and cash ample to pay any balance. If a purchase money mortgage is to be given, *R* receives the purchase money mortgage also the note thereby secured. He then retains the hazard insurance policies.

§ 334. **Other contracts and documents to be transferred at closing-office buildings.** In office buildings there are a number of contracts that are transferred at closing:

(1) Elevator and escalator maintenance contracts.

(2) Contracts for cleaning and window washing.

(3) Rubbish removal contract.

(4) Contracts for furnishing of steam or air conditioning as between neighboring buildings.

(5) Contract for electricity where building has wholesale rate and sells to tenants at higher rate.

(6) Contracts for fuel delivery.

(7) Termite and extermination contracts.

§ 335. Surrender of leases.

Where a substantial lease is to be terminated at closing by agreement between *L* and *T*, the title insurance company should be requested to make a special search for this purpose. The title company will cover a number of items lawyers often overlook, namely:

(1) Judgments or other liens against *T*. *T* cannot defeat their rights by surrendering his lease.

(2) Assignments and subleases of the lease.

(3) Corporate resolutions.

(4) Execution and recording of surrender agreement.

(5) Cancellation of originals of lease.

See § 370.

§ 336. Other documents for closing:

(1) If *part* of *R's* land is the subject of sale, at closing both *R* and *E* receive executed duplicates of documents needed for division of real estate taxes.

(2) Consent by *T* to transfer of *T's* security deposit held by *R*.

(3) Security deposits on garage door openers (common in office building leases).

(4) If new mortgage requires this, subordination of existing leases to new mortgage.

(5) Collective bargaining agreements. In the case of office buildings there may be a master agreement between the Building Managers Association and the office building employees, which may be automatically binding on *E* under its terms.

(6) Permits from city for vaults beneath streets, marquees, etc. and bond accompanying same.

§ 337. Sale subject to mortgage.

Whether or not the mortgage requires the lender's consent to a sale, *E* should contact the lender and have his name substituted for *R's* name in the lender's books. This assures *E* that he will receive notice of payments due, that he can obtain statements as to amount due on the mortgage, etc., that *E* will be credited with *R's* tax escrow, etc. The charge is small. It is worth it.

§ 338. Closing letter.

After closing *E's* lawyer writes *E* a letter listing the documents he is furnishing *E*, listing documents *E* will later receive (such as deed after same has been recorded, insurance policies, and consents to assignment, etc.) and steps *E* should take on his own, *e.g.*, serving notice on tenants to pay rent to *E*.

20

Options

§ 339. In general. Options are often drafted poorly. The obvious reason is, of course, that in most instances the draftsman has not troubled to look up the law of options.

§ 340. Lack of detail. A common fault is the lack of detail. To cover a sale adequately, a lawyer may draft a 20-page contract. The same details belong in an option, because, once notice of exercise of the option is given, the option becomes a contract of sale. But options are often very skimpy as to detail. Thousands of options have been executed without any mention of the title objections which the optionee must accept. In other words, the optioner is called upon to give a marketable title free of any objections, such as building restrictions, easements, party walls. Such titles are extremely rare. The *subject clause* is just as important in the option as it is in the contract.

The option ought to treat the matter of evidence of title in detail, as it does in the case of a contract of sale. Possession, default, prorations, mortgage terms, all the provisions found in the contracts of sale, belong in the option. The requirements of completeness and certainty are present. 31 ALR3d 522; 2 ALR3d 701. The optioner's spouse should join. When an option to purchase is exercised, the parties often negotiate and execute a contract of sale. A common omission in options is failure to deal with risk of loss. 44 N.C.L. Rev. 63. Failure to comply with homestead waiver requirements is another fault. *Strempler v. Peterson,* 206 NW2d 629 (Neb.1973).

§ 341. Relation back. When an option is exercised, the title acquired by the optionee relates back to the date of the option for some purposes but not others. 50 ALR 1314; 66 CJ 487; 91 CJS *Vendor and Purchaser* § 13.

EXAMPLE: *R* gives *E* an option, which is recorded. Thereafter, *R* places a mortgage on the premises, which is recorded. *E* exercises his option. There is a decision that title "relates back" to the time of the option, and the mortgage is extinguished. *Kansas State Bank v. Bourgeois,* 14 Utah 2d 188, 380 P2d 931.

Obviously, the option ought to cover this point. If the optioner wishes to reserve the right to mortgage his fee title, the option should so state, and should provide that the optionee's title will be subject to the mortgage. The option should state the upper limits of the mortgage debt and interest and state the details of the mortgage in much the same fashion as where a lease requires the landlord to join in the leasehold mortgage so as to bind the fee title. If the optionee is unwilling to take title subject to $R's$ mortgage, the option should provide that upon exercise of the option any mortgage by R shall be extinguished and shall attach to the proceeds of sale. This is likely to discourage lenders. Or the option could provide that any mortgage is prepayable on exercise of the option and the mortgage will so state. The optionee will have his own financing. Doubt exists as to the validity of a provision forbidding R to mortgage the land. The rule forbidding restraints on alienation creates this doubt.

Another problem relates to leases made by R during the option period.

EXAMPLE: During the option period R makes a lease to a tenant. The lease still has ten years to run when E exercises his option. One decision holds that E must take subject to a lease given by R to a third party during the option period even though the option was recorded. *Durfee House Furnishing Co. v. Great Atlantic Pacific Tea Co.* 100 Vt. 204, 136 A 379, 50 ALR 1309 (criticized in Corbin, Contracts § 272) *See also* 75 U. Penna.L.Rev. 791; 27 Columb.L.Rev. 749. Since E may be exercising his option because he wants to take possession immediately, this certainly creates an awkward situation. The option should state whether exercise terminates leases, and, if not, how long the leases can run. A schedule of rents and terms can be attached to the option.

§ 342. Eminent domain. A further matter most options leave unanswered is the matter of subsequent condemnation. Some decisions do not permit the optionee to share in the award, feeling that an option creates no interest in the land. 85 ALR2d 588. One would think the courts would honor an option provision for reduction of the option price in the event of partial condemnation.

§ 343. Perpetuities. The rule against perpetuities applies to options in gross but not to options in leases. 53 Mich.L.Rev. 147; 13 U. of Fla.L.Rev. 214. The application of the rule to options in gross causes few problems. Options in gross almost invariably run for short periods of time. If a long period of time is contemplated, the usual ''perpetuities escape clause'' is used, as:

In no event shall this option extend beyond twenty years after the date of the death of the last living descendant of the late Senator Robert Kennedy. 8 U. of Richmond L.Rev. 845, 850.

§ 344. Bankruptcy. $R's$ trustee in bankruptcy may be able to reject the option as an ''executory contract.'' 26 Bus. Law. 1391. You can try a liquidated damages clause that gives liquidated damages in the event R refuses to convey for the difference between the option price and value fixed by the customary three-man appraisal, and then go on to provide that if $R's$ trustee in bankruptcy disaffirms the option, E will have a claim against the bankrupt estate for the liquidated damages. Since the trustee will reject the option only because the land has gone up in value, this clause may operate as a deterrent, even though it may not stand up.

Where T has erected a building pursuant to a covenant in the lease that requires L to reimburse T for this expense, $L's$ trustee in bankruptcy, in rejecting the lease, must reimburse T for this expense before he can oust T. *In re N.Y. Investors Mut. Group*, 153 F. Supp. 772, aff'd 258 F2d 14. This may discourage the trustee in bankruptcy from disaffirming the lease.

§ 345. Exercise of option. An option is an irrevocable offer. Notice of exercise of the option is an acceptance of the offer. In contract law, the rule is that when I accept an offer, I must not deviate from the terms of the offer even slightly. Thus, if *E* writes that he exercises the option, "the deal to be closed at my office ten days from this date," he is, in legal effect, changing the contract, and the notice may be void. *Morris v. Goldthorp*, 390 Ill. 186, 60 NE2d 857; *Standard Reliance Ins. Co. v. Schoenthal*, 171 Neb. 490, 106 NW2d 704. The manner in which the option is to be exercised should be covered in detail. Where an option runs in favor of two or more optionees, all must join in the exercise of the option.

It is best that *E* himself sign the exercise of the option. In some states, a notice signed by *E's* agent is not valid unless the agent has written authority to sign. *Welsh v. Jakstas*, 401 Ill. 288, 82 NE2d 253.

§ 346. Options in leases. An option cannot be exercised after the lease has been terminated for default in payment of rent. *Sandra Frocks, Inc. v. Ziff*, 397 Ill. 497, 74 NE2d 669, 10 ALR2d 884. However, if the notice is given after default in payment of rent, but before the landlord has decided to terminate the lease because of such default, the option is validly exercised. *Jader v. Costello*, 405 Ill. 181, 90 NE2d 778; 10 ALR2d 884. *Contra: Helberg v. Bonsness*, 227 Wisc. 52, 227 NW 634. Obviously, the option should cover this point, perhaps by a provision that an exercise after default must be accompanied by tender of the purchase price.

A difficult question arises where a lease contains an option to purchase the property and also contains an option to extend the term or renew for an additional period. The various states are not in agreement as to the proper rule to be followed. In some states, the option to purchase property continues during the extended or renewal period. *Wanous v. Balaco*, 412 Ill. 545, 107 NE2d 791; *Hindu Incense Mfg. Co. v. MacKenzie*, 403 Ill. 390, 86 NE2d 214; *Didriksen v. Havens*, 136 Conn. 41, 68 A2d 163. However, in Maryland, Pennsylvania, and some other states, the option to purchase ends with the original term of the lease and does not continue into the renewal period. 37 ALR 1245, 163 ALR 711. The option should cover this point.

Where a lease contains an option to purchase, and at the expiration of the lease *T* holds over and *L* accepts rent, so that a tenancy from year to year is created, the authorities are once more divided as to whether the option continues into the tenancy from year to year. In some states, it is held that the option to purchase ends with the lease. *Wanous v. Balaco*, 412 Ill. 545, 107 NE2d 791. However, in Colorado, Indiana, New Jersey, and perhaps other states, the option to purchase continues into a tenancy from year to year. The option should cover this point.

If a lease is assigned by the lessee, the option to purchase is assigned as part of the lease and may be exercised by an assignee, 45 ALR2d 1036, but if the lease is not assignable, then the option likewise is not assignable. Whether the option can be separated from the lease and separately assigned is debatable. 51 CJS *Landlord & Tenant* § 85(2).

§ 347. Pre-emption type options. Many lease options give *T* the "first privilege to buy," "the first right to buy," or "the first refusal" options. Often such options have been held by the courts to be conditional on *L's* wish to sell. In other words, if *L* decides to keep the property and not place it on the market at all, *T* cannot compel a sale of the property to himself. It is only where *L* decides to sell the property while the lease is in effect that *T* must be given the first right to buy. 34 ALR2d 1158. A difficulty exists where a mortgage on the property is foreclosed. Some courts hold that the foreclosure sale is a sale that the optionee can match by offering to buy at the foreclosure sale. Other courts hold to the contrary. 17 ALR3d 962. Obviously, you can draft around this problem. Simply provide that a foreclosure sale or any other forced sale does not trigger the pre-emption option. Where the optioner receives an offer for a tract of land that includes the leased land, problems arise. 170 ALR 1068. This point should be considered and covered. Also cover an offer for *part* of the leased land.

§ 348. **Options to renew in leases.** Many leases contain an option or privilege of some sort to renew or extend the lease for an additional period, and such provisions have evoked considerable controversy. The following are some points to consider:

1. When the lease gives *T* the "first right" or first privilege" of receiving a new or extended lease, this simply gives the existing tenant a prior right if *L* decides to continue renting the property. *T* has no right if *L* decides to take the property off the rental market. 6 ALR2d 820.

2. When the lease contains a true option to renew, but says nothing about *T* giving *L* notice of his exercise of this option, it is sufficient in most states if *T* simply remains in occupancy after the lease has expired. His remaining adequately exercises the renewal option, but it is a poor practice. *Basler v. Warren,* 159 F2d 41. To avoid controversy, *T* should give notice well in advance of the expiration of the lease.

T, as has been stated, should give *L* written notice of his exercise of the renewal option. In some states, such notice is legally necessary. 51 CJS 593. Nowadays, most leases specifically require that notice be given *L* a certain number of days before the end of the lease that *T* is exercising his renewal option. Naturally, such provisions must be strictly complied with.

3. Unless the lease specifically authorizes the notice of exercise of option to be given by mail, it should be personally served upon the landlord.

4. It is best that the notice be signed by *T* personally. If the notice is signed by an agent for *T,* some states require that the agent have written authority to bind *T.*

5. Since the notice is technically an acceptance of an offer, you must keep in mind the rule of contract law that when you accept an offer you must not add to, subtract from, or in any way change the terms of the offer. About all you can safely say is "I hereby notify you that I hereby exercise the renewal option set forth in Paragraph X of our lease."

6. Where the lease runs to two or more tenants, all must join in the notice of exercise. *Kleros Building v. Battaglia,* 348 Ill. App. 445, 109 NE2d 221.

7. An option to renew does not continue into the renewal period. Successive renewals are not permitted unless the lease specifically provides for them. Were the rule otherwise, the tenant could renew the lease forever. *Hindu Incense Mfg. Co. v. MacKenzie,* 403 Ill. 390, 86 NE2d 214.

§ 349. **Termination clauses in leases.** Commonly a lease will provide that in case of destruction of the building and failure to rebuild within a specified time, the lease will terminate. Such termination will terminate the options contained in the lease. *E* may wish to structure the option in such a way that destruction does not terminate his options.

§ 350. **Leasehold mortgages.** If a tenant has an option to purchase and places a mortgage on his leasehold, and then exercises his option to purchase the fee, quite likely the fee title thus acquired would "feed" the leasehold mortgage and be covered by it. *Garner v. Union Tr. Co.,* 45 A2d 106, 163 ALR 431 (Md.); *Chinn v. Sheridan,* 229 Ore. 123, 336 P2d 321; *Chapman v. Great Western Gypsum Co.,* 216 Cal. 420, 14 P2d 758, 85 ALR 917. But good draftmanship dictates that this be spelled out in the lease.

§ 351. **Assignment of option.** Unlike other offers, an option is assignable, Corbin, *Contracts* § 271. But the parties may limit the option to the optionee only and may forbid assignment thereof. Corbin, *Contracts* § 271; 45 ALR2d 1034. Whatever the parties decide, ought to be stated in the option. As a rule an option in a lease passes with an assignment of the lease. 38 ALR 1163, 45 ALR2d 1036. Good draftsmanship suggests that the assignment mention both the lease and the option. There is some law to the effect that the option can be sold and assigned separately from the leasehold. *But see* 51 CJS *Landlord & Tenant* § 85(2). Obviously, this should be covered in the option. Do not depend on the lease clause forbidding assignments as applying to the option, though it probably does. 45 ALR2d 1034.

A lessee may assign a geographic part of the lease. 49 Am.Jur. 2d 413; 99 ALR 220. Whether an assignee of a part can exercise the option is doubtful. 45 ALR2d 1034. Obviously, the lease should cover both points, *i.e.*, whether an assignment of part is permitted, and, if so, what happens to the option.

§ 352. **Mortgages of options.** Whether an option can be mortgaged is a question on which there is little law. 45 ALR2d 1034. One would prefer to have this covered in the option.

§ 353. **Death of optionee.** Where an optionee dies, some cases pass an option to purchase to the personal representative and others pass the option to the heirs. 45 ALR2d 1034. If it is split by going to the heirs, problems arise. Putting the option in a corporation would help solve the problem of who may exercise the option.

§ 354. **Death of optioner.** Problems arise where the optioner dies. *Weintz v. Baumgarner*, 434 P2d 712; 172 ALR 438, 91 CJS *Vendor and Purchaser* § 867. Putting the title to the land in a corporation or trust would help solve the problem.

§ 355. **Tender of purchase price when option is exercised.** Tender of the purchase price need not accompany exercise of the option unless the option so provides. If the optioner wants his money promptly, he can provide for a time limit after exercise, within which the deed and the optionee's purchase money and mortgage must be placed in escrow with a selected title company in its usual form sale escrow.

§ 356. **Deed by optioner.** The option should provide that any deed by the optioner to a third party shall be expressly subject to the option. In most states, there are no court decisions or statutes on whether an option is recordable, although it certainly ought to be. *Daniel v. Kensington Homes*, 232 Md. 1, 192 A2d 114; 38 ALR 1166.

§ 357. **Expiration of option period.** There are statutes that make the record of an option ineffective after a stated period of time from its expiration. Basye, § 133. Some are pretty drastic.

EXAMPLE: In New York, the record of an option expires 30 days after the expiration date of the option unless the optionee records notice of exercise of the option within that period. Basye, § 133.

Conversely, an expired option continues to cloud the optioner's title. 78 ALR 24, 92. Hence, a clause is needed that the option ceases to impart notice—months after its recorded expiration date unless notice of its exercise has been recorded within that period.

§ 358. **Payment of option price.** Under the general theory that one who has recorded his interest in the land has no duty to check the records subsequent to that time, it has been held, probably improperly, that an optionee can exercise his option, pay the optioner, and take a deed from him without checking the title for intervening recorded deeds by the optioner. *Connally v. Des Moines*, 68 NW2d 320. Perhaps a precautionary provision should be included to the effect that the optionee is charged with notice of all duly recorded matters occurring after the date of the option.

§ **359. Risk of loss.** The problem of risk of loss arises in connection with options. 23 ALR 1225. Obviously, the option should cover this point, including the optionee's rights in the hazard insurance. This is particularly important in the period between exercise of the option and the closing of the deal, because during that period the option has been converted into a contract.

§ **360. Easements.** An option to purchase an easement is valid. *Lacy v. U.S.* 216 F2d 223.

§ **361. Option to acquire lease.** An option to acquire a lease is valid. Restatement, Property (2d) § 2-5.

§ **362. Suggested option clauses:**

CLAUSE: *R* reserves the right to make leases of the premises or any part thereof during the option period but no such lease shall have a duration (including renewals and extensions) of more than _____ years.

CLAUSE: *R* reserves the right to make leases of the premises or any part thereof during the option period, but any such lease and any periodic tenancy hereafter created shall terminate _____ days after service of notice of exercise of the option on *E* or on the tenant, whichever is later.

CLAUSE IN LEASE: *E* has no right to exercise any option contained in this lease while *E* is in default on payment of rent or has breached any of the other covenants or conditions on his part herein contained and such breach has not been cured. Service on *E* of valid notice of forfeiture by *R* automatically terminates all options herein contained.

CLAUSE IN LEASE: The option to purchase herein contained terminates on _____, the date when the term of this lease terminates as above specified. It does not continue into the period of any renewal or extension or into periodic tenancy that may be created after the stated termination of this lease.

Reference: As to bankruptcy, see § 685. 40 ALR3d 920; 44 ALR2d 342.

21

Miscellaneous Real Estate
Documents and Clauses

§ 363. In general. So much has been written on the major documents involved in real estate transactions (contract of sale, deed, lease and mortgage) that the other documents involved in real estate transactions are all but forgotten. These documents, however, must not be neglected. Care must be exercised in preparing supporting documents and in determining what supporting documents are needed. Existing documents that will continue to affect the land after the deal has been closed must be carefully examined in the light of the applicable law.

§ 364. Affidavits. Almost instinctively the real property lawyer seems prone to resort to an affidavit to clear sundry defects in title. Yet in the absence of statute, the hearsay character of this document diminishes or destroys its value in some jurisdictions. Basye, *Clearing Land Titles* (2d ed. 1970) §§ 31, 39. Statutes permit the use of affidavits for some purposes in some states. 4 American Law of Property 632, 708, 832. In some states decisional law permits the use of the affidavit for some title clearance purposes. *Atteberry v. Blair*, 244 Ill. 363, 91 NE 475; *Lamotte v. Steidinger*, 266 Ill. 600, 107 NE 858. The decisions are conflicting. 57 ALR 1481. The moral of course is that the attorney representing a purchaser or lender must be aware of the local law when he accepts such a document. Where an affidavit is to be accepted, it is important that it comply with local statutes or court decisions as to form and recording. See, *e.g.*, *Ewing v. Plummer*, 308 Ill. 585, 140 NE 42; *Clark v. Jackson*, 222 Ill. 13, 78 NE 6.

§ 365. Estoppel certificates. Estoppel certificates are employed in a variety of circumstances:

(1) Land is sold subject to a mortgage. Here the purchaser invariably insists upon an estoppel certificate by the mortgagee reciting the amount due on the mortgage and the absence of any default or breach of covenant. 90 ALR 1432.

(2) Mortgaged land is sold and under the contract of sale the mortgage will be paid out of the proceeds of sale. If the mortgagee is not to be represented at the closing, his estoppel certificate should be given the purchaser reciting that the mortgagee remains the owner of the mortgage, the amount due thereon including interest to the date of closing and indicating (in the absence of an unconditional prepayment privilege) that the

mortgagee will accept payment of the stated amount and issue its release or satisfaction. 90 ALR 1432.

(3) An assignment or mortgage of a leasehold is taking place. Here the assignee or mortgagee will ask for an estoppel certificate from the landlord reciting that rent is not in default and that there are no breaches of covenant on the tenant's part. If the leasehold derives its value from the existence of a major sublease, the assignee or mortgagee of the leasehold may endeavor to procure from the subtenant a certificate that the sublease is valid and subsisting, that no unrecorded modifications or breaches of covenant exist, and that rent has not been prepaid.

(4) A sale of leased land is taking place. The tenant in a major lease may be asked to give an estoppel certificate to the purchaser of the fee stating that the lease is valid and subsisting, that no unrecorded modifications, concessions, or assignments exist, that the only subleases are as stated in the certificate, and that rent has not been paid in advance. Schwartz, *Lease Drafting in Massachusetts,* 447.

(5) A permanent lender is about to disburse funds to retire interim financing. Here he may insist on estoppel certificates from the tenants reciting, among other things, that they have accepted the demised premises and that there are no breaches of covenant on the landlord's part.

(6) A mortgage is to be executed or assigned. Many institutional lenders will not make or buy a mortgage unless the mortgagor furnishes an estoppel certificate reciting the amount due and that he has no defenses to the enforcement of the mortgage. This serves, through estoppel, virtually to impart the quality of negotiability to the mortgage. 2 Jones, *Mortgages,* § 792 (8th ed. 1928): 59 CJS *Mortgages* § 369; 31 CJS *Estoppel* § 81.

Whether such documents will be forthcoming on request is another matter. There seems to be a trend toward providing in other documents that the estoppel certificate will be furnished on request. For example, a lease of premises on which the landlord will construct a building can require that the tenant will give an estoppel certificate on completion of construction. Otherwise, the landlord may be faced with sincere objections by the tenant. He may ask: "How can I tell at this time that there are no latent defects in construction?" Or specious objections may be raised. The tenant may think, "what advantages can I extract from this landlord who needs my estoppel certificate to show the takeout lender?"

§ 366. Release and assumption of covenant liability. Where a lessor sells and conveys his fee, his deed to the purchaser will not relieve him of liability on his lease covenants unless the lease expressly so provides. The contracts in the lease remain binding on him because contract duties are not assignable. 2 American Law of Property § 9.5. In other words the lessor-grantor is in the uncomfortable position of remaining liable on his covenants while being unable to prevent their breach by his grantee. *Ibid.* He can seek a release of such liability from the lessee. In return for giving this release, the lessee may demand that the grantee expressly assume the lessor's covenants. However, the grantee will exclude from his assumption liability for any breach of covenant by the lessor existing prior to the date of his assumption.

In documents drafted in recent times you will encounter provisions terminating all of a party's liability in the event of a bona fide transfer of his interest in the property.

§ 367. Notices. When it comes to the question of notices one is immediately confronted with an embarrassment of riches. Only a few can be mentioned:

(1) One who buys leased premises must immediately give actual notice of the purchase to the tenants. Else any seasonable payment of rent made to the former landlord will be a good payment against the purchaser. 36 C.J. 367.

(2) Similarly upon any sale and assignment of a leasehold, notice should be given the subtenants.

(3) Upon any assignment of a mortgage, notice should be given the landowner to make future payments to the assignee. Otherwise mortgage payments made thereafter to the assignor may be good against the assignee. Kratovil, *Real Estate Law* § 416.

(4) An assignee of a leasehold estate should immediately serve notice of his purchase and his name and address to the landlord. Substantial leases typically provide that notice of default and notice of termination for breach need only be given to the tenant at the address stated in the lease unless another name and address is furnished the landlord. The same precaution should be taken by a mortgagee of a leasehold estate.

(5) Some leases contain a clause giving the landlord the right to terminate the lease in the event of a sale of the fee. Such a clause is included in those instances where it is likely that any such purchaser would wish to have immediate possession of the premises. Obviously the notice should be given promptly. It must be exercised in connection with the sale. *112 E. 36th St. Co. v. Daffos*, 78 NYS2d 31 (notice served two years after sale held too late): *United Cigar-Whelan Stores Corp. v. Basiliko Inv. Corp.*, 54 A2d 857. Some questions arise as to service of termination notices. If the lease states that in the event of sale of the leased premises by the lessor *he* shall have the right to terminate this lease, the contention may be advanced, for example, that a notice given by the purchaser is fatally defective. *Gates v. Norton*, 228 Ill. App. 96. But the clause may be so drafted that the purchaser has the right to serve the notice. *Mitchell v. Tyles*, 332 Ill. App. 577, 76 NE2d 237; 163 ALR 1019. If the language of the lease leaves in doubt the identity of the party who is to serve notice, there is no harm in having both vendor and purchaser serve separate notices.

(6) A lease may give the tenant a pre-emptive option. This is a clause giving the tenant the ''first refusal'' of the property in case the landlord decides to sell the property. Obviously proper notice should be given the tenant, so that the period given him by the lease to exercise his option expires before the landlord is firmly committed to the purchaser.

(7) Often vacant land is purchased by one intending to build. He will routinely serve his neighbors with notice of his intention to do so. This is

done so that the neighbors may take precautions by shoring up their buildings. In some localities this is a statutory notice and the statute or ordinance should be complied with. Failure to give this notice may result in negligence liability for damage occasioned by withdrawal of support as excavating takes place.

(8) A contract of sale usually fixes the date and place of closing, but not the time of day. Especially where the other party is giving indications of a reluctance to go through with the deal it is best to serve a notice on him stating the hour at which you propose to close. This is usually accompanied by a statement that you will assume this time is satisfactory unless you are notified within a stated time that the other party prefers a different time.

So far as manner of service of notice goes, it is difficult to lay down general rules. If a statute calls for "service" of notice, anything less than actual personal service is apt to be fatally defective. *Liese v. Hantze*, 326 Ill. 633, 158 NE 428. The same may be true if a document calls for "service of notice." If a document specifies the manner of service of notice, obviously these requirements should be scrupulously observed. If the document calls for service by U.S. mail, perhaps it would be best to send notice by regular mail, and, if desired, supplement this by service by certified mail. Some people routinely reject certified mail on the theory that it always contains bad news. The contention may then be advanced that notice should have been given by regular mail.

§ 368. **Consent and assumption.** A lease may contain a clause forbidding assignment without the landlord's consent. Obviously this consent must be obtained. He may choose to terminate the lease if it is not procured. As a condition of consenting, he may request the assignee to assume personal liability. This is a reasonable request. This may open the door to negotiations for a new lease, which can be advantageous for both parties.

§ 369. **Consent, assumption, and novation.** A clause common in mortgages is one giving the mortgagee the right to accelerate if the mortgaged land is sold without his consent. If a deal is closed on the basis of the purchaser taking subject to an existing mortgage, and it is thereafter discovered that the mortgagee is in a position to accelerate, the situation is apt to be embarrassing for the purchaser's attorney. Obviously it was his professional duty to read the mortgage—all of it—before the contract of sale was signed. Assuming that this clause was discovered before the contract of sale was signed, the mortgagee's consent to the sale would be solicited. Routinely the mortgagee will ask for an assumption of personal liability by the purchaser. This is a reasonable request. The seller may ask the mortgagee simultaneously to release his personal liability. If the document takes the form of a release of the mortgagor and an assumption of personal liability by the purchaser, it is a novation.

§ 370. **Surrender of lease.** Where a substantial lease is given up by a tenant, it is best to have the landlord and tenant enter into a recordable instrument stating that the lease is thereby surrendered. Commonly the document contains assurances by the tenant that he owns the leasehold estate, free of liens, and that there are no outstanding assignments or subleases. Title is searched to recording of surrender. *See* § 335.

§ 371. Declaration of merger. Where a recorded easement exists but both the dominant and servient estate become vested in the same person, it is customary, in some areas, for such person to execute a recordable declaration of merger to clear the record of the easements. This seems less awkward than having the party execute a release to himself.[1]

§ 372. Assignment of seller's rights under substantial leases. On all big deals, the buyer will want an assignment of the vendor's rights under existing leases. The theory is explained in Kratovil, *Possession. Rents, and Mortgagee Liability*, 11 DePaul L.Rev. 1 (1971) as follows (p. 11):

> Occasionally one hears it said that a deed of leased property gives the grantee all the contractual rights ("privity of contract") the lessor enjoyed as against the grantee. 55 L.R.A. (n.s.) 190, 211 (1915). This is supposed to be by virtue of an Act of Parliament passed during the reign of Henry VIII. *Ibid.* This is open to question. It is more likely that this venerable law was addressed to King Henry's special problems with confiscated church lands, and did not concern itself with transfer of contractual rights. 2 Powell, Real Property 315 (1950); 1 Tiffany, Landlord & Tenant 833 (1910). American laws patterned after this Act of Parliament present the same problem. Because of this doubt a buyer of leased land will often insist that the seller give the buyer an assignment of the seller's rights under the leases. If a buyer needs this protection, it is obvious that a mortgagee has even greater need for the protection, for his rights are never as comprehensive as those of a buyer.

§ 373. Servicing agreement. The agreement between a mortgage banker and the investor for whom it acts as loan correspondent is called a servicing agreement. It contains detailed warranties by the servicer with respect to the validity of the mortgage and accompanying documents and spells out the servicer's duties as to insurance, taxes, etc. Because it places many onerous burdens on the servicer, it should expressly disclaim any intention to benefit third parties such as the mortgagor. *Honaker v. Farmers Mort. Ins. Co.*, 313 A2d 900.

§ 374. Pledges. In connection with corporate mortgages by corporations having few shareholders, it is not uncommon for the mortgagee to demand that the shareholders pledge their stock as security for payment of the mortgage debt. The document employed is a "collateral note," which is a combination of promissory note and pledge agreement. It is buttressed by undated resignations signed by all officers and directors and given to the mortgagee with written permission to employ them at its pleasure.[2] An officer of the mortgagee corporation is placed on the board of directors. Its virtue lies in the fact that when default occurs, the pledge can be quickly foreclosed without court proceedings. The mortgagee can thus step in as owner of all the stock, elect its own officers and directors, and operate the property while the process of foreclosure continues for the purpose of extinguishing junior liens. This device has obvious additional advantages in states which will not permit a mortgagee to take possession until the period of redemption has expired. Many attorneys consider this arrangement as helpful in blocking bankruptcy proceedings that can delay foreclosure. In case trouble threatens, the mortgagee moves in, so that the old directors cannot vote for bankruptcy.

---

[1] © Copyright Kratovil, *Miscellaneous Documents and Clauses, Lawyers Supplement* published by Chicago Title Insurance Co. (1972). Reprinted by permission.

[2] © Copyright Kratovil, *Miscellaneous Documents and Clauses*, Chicago Title Ins. Co. Lawyers Supplement (1972). Reprinted by permission.

§ **375. Pledges of other stock or securities.** *R* may own other stock and securities, including, but not limited to, stock of a subsidiary corporation. A decision should be made whether these are to be pledged as security for the mortgage debt.

§ **376. Pledges—form of pledge.** In preparing pledge forms one can borrow language from the "collateral note" used in ordinary pledges of corporate stock.

§ **377. Pledges—notice provisions.** The typical printed collateral note allows foreclosure of the pledge without notice to the pledgor. Delete this clause. Courts often set aside a pledgee's sale if this notice is omitted. The law of unconscionability makes such provisions archaic.

§ **378. Pledges—place of sale.** The typical collateral note allows the pledgee to hold the sale in his office. Today's law of unconscionability makes it prudent to select some more public place, such as the traditional "court house steps."

§ **379. Pledges—purchase by pledgee.** The typical collateral note permits the pledgee to purchase at his own sale. Perhaps it would be better to provide that the pledgee may designate some third party to hold the sale and give all the necessary notices. Today's law of unconscionability suggests the wisdom of avoiding a purchase at one's own sale.

§ **380. Concessions.** A great variety of "concessions" exist today. Even in an apartment building, the washing machines may be operated by a concessionaire. In hotels, department stores, and discount house concessions are commonplace. Whether a purchaser will be able to oust the concessionaire depends on the amount of space involved, whether the location is fixed or subject to be changed at the pleasure of the landowner, the nature of the document, and the views of the local courts. The decisions are quite numerous. *Beckett v. City of Paris Dry Goods Co.*, 14 Cal. 2d 633, 96 P2d 122 (right to conduct optical department in department store held to be a lease); *Belvedere Hotel v. Williams*, 137 Md. 665, 113 A335 (barber shop and manicure concession in hotel held to be a lease); *R. H. White Co. v. Jerome H. Remick & Co.*, 198 Mass. 41, 84 NE 113 (sheet music concession in department store held to be a license): *Pratte v. Balatsos*, 99 N.H. 430, 113 A2d 492 (exclusive right to operate a jukebox held to be an equitable servitude); *People v. Horowitz*, 309 N.Y. 426, 131 NE2d 715 (vending concession in movie theater held a license); *Lamken v. Miller*, 181 Wash. 544, 55 P2d 190 (food concession at race track held to be a license); *In re Owl Drug Co.*, 12 F.Supp. 439 (toilet goods concession in drug store held to be a lease); *see* 1A Thompson, Real Property § 223.[3]

§ **381. Advertising leases.** Often an advertising company will pay a landowner for the privilege of using the wall or roof of his building for displaying an advertising sign. Sometimes the sign is simply printed on the wall of the building. Sometimes a massive structure is erected on the roof. Usually the landowner gives the company a "lease" for this purpose. Whether a purchaser will be bound by such a lease depends on the size and nature of the sign, the language of the document, and the views of the local courts. In different states, different views have been taken of these advertising "leases."

1. When it is clear that the company is given more or less exclusive possession of

---

[3] Copyright Kratovil, *Miscellaneous Documents and Clauses* Chicago Title Ins. Co. *Lawyers Supplement* (1972). Reprinted by permission.

the area, as is true of the large signs, many courts hold that a true lease exists. The parties are landlord and tenant. Landlord and tenant law governs, and, of course, the landlord cannot revoke the lease. 17 Tex.L.Rev. 409; 19 Cornell L.Q. 138.

2. When the document simply gives "permission" to erect and maintain the sign, and particularly when the sign is simply painted on or attached to a wall or is of ordinary size, courts often hold the document, though labelled a lease, a license. Therefore in many states the landowner can revoke it at will. *Lewis v. Baxter Laundries*, 254 Mich. 216, 236 NW 239; *Bielzoff v. Beam*, 3 Ill. App.2d 530, 123 NE2d 135; 53 CJS 819.

3. In more recent times, courts have been so dissatisfied with the revocability notion involved in the license theory that they have tended more and more to regard the "lease" as creating an easement in gross. Easements are not possessory interests, and therefore the court can still say that the landowner retains possession of the wall or roof of his building, which is logical. But easements are not revocable, and this gives the advertising company the protection it has paid for and is entitled to receive. *Baseball Pub. Co. v. Bruton*, 302 Mass. 54, 18 NE2d 362.

§ 382. Certificate of convenience and necessity. There are decisions holding that a certificate of convenience and necessity is personal in character and cannot be assigned. 15 ALR2d 883. Obviously one purchasing a business that requires such a certificate must take notice of this problem.

§ 383. Variances. A zoning variance can be granted in terms making it personal to the landowner who applies for it. *Maki v. Town of Yarmouth*, 163 NE2d 633. Obviously any purchaser is on notice that he may not receive a variance or may receive a less favorable one.

§ 384. Licenses. A business that cannot be operated without license, *e.g.*, a tavern, is worthless to a purchaser who cannot procure a license. Many such licenses do not "run with the land", for they are granted or withheld depending on the moral character of the applicant. Obviously a contract of sale of such property must be made contingent on the purchaser's ability to procure the license.

§ 385. Conditions. Despite their objectionable features, conditions are still encountered from time to time. At the very least, the grantee in a deed containing a condition must insist on the clause providing that the reverter right is subject and subordinate to all mortgages thereafter placed on the premises. Any condition in the prior chain of title that has not yet been barred by a Reverters Act (*Trustees v. Batdorf*, 6 Ill. 2d 486, 130 NE2d 111) or by a Marketable Title Act (71 ALR2d 846) must also contain a similar cause. Otherwise mortgage financing is impossible.[4]

§ 386. Covenants—creation of covenants between fee owners. Covenants to perform an act are known as affirmative covenants. 20 Am.Jur. 2d 609; 24 Cornell L. Q. 133. An example is a covenant by a landowner to furnish heat or air conditioning to adjoining premises. Such covenants can run with the land. 119 ALR 982. But privity of estate must be present. *Wheeler v. Schad*, 7 Nev. 204. Hence, an agreement between the adjoining owners may not create a running covenant, because a mere agreement does not create privity of estate. *Ibid.* However, if the agreement creates cross-easements in the pipes or ducts that furnish or receive the heat or air, this will suffice, since easement

---

grants create privity, American Law of Property § 9.11. This is why party wall agreements can contain running covenants. 2 American Law of Property, § 9.13. The cross-easements of support created by the agreement supply privity of estate. The party who is to furnish the heat or air likes to see a provision terminating any liability on his part after he has parted with ownership of the land. Otherwise, the agreement stands as an indeterminate contract on his part with no release of his duty to perform upon his conveyance of the land.

The drafting of covenants that run with the land as to benefit and burden parallels the drafting of appurtenant easements. For example, the benefited tract of land is specifically described and it is stated that the benefit of the covenants runs with this parcel, and the covenants are enforceable by X, its present owner, his heirs, successors, and assigns. The burdened parcel is specifically described, and the covenants are stated to be enforceable against Y, the present owner, his heirs, successors and assigns. It is stated that the covenant is intended to run with the land, both as to benefit and burden.

Less well understood is the problem of dividing covenants, as where the burdened or benefited properties are divided or where either parcel goes into cotenancy, for example, by death. 5 Powell *Real Property* § 680; 1 Patton, *Titles* § 161; 2 Am. L. Ppty. 359; 25 Ky. L. J. 142.

§ 387. Permits. Some permits are invariably revocable. For example, a permit to place fill in navigable waters is issued by the Corps of Engineers subject to the absolute right to revoke. *Miami Beach Jockey Club v. Dern*, 83 F2d 715. Some pretty substantial structures are erected on such fill. One buying riparian land abutting on navigable water must check to see what consequences would ensue were such valuable improvements erected in reliance on such permit and were such permit to be revoked. There is no constitutional requirement that the landowner be compensated for loss ensuing from revocation of the permit. *U.S. v. 87.30 Acres of Land*, 430 F2d 1130. If a title insurance policy has issued and includes filled land within its description, it probably will contain an exception relating to the federal navigational servitude of the United States or some similar exception. Much has been written on the subject of the federal navigational servitude. 44 Notre Dame Lawyer 236; 48 Oregon L.Rev. 1; 25 Wash & Lee L.Rev. 323. Obviously when filling has been completed and buildings have been erected, a physical inspection of the property may offer no evidence as to the original location of the shoreline. There is a similar state navigational servitude in some states. 19 Case Western L.Rev. 1116; 4 Land & Water L.Rev. 521.

Permits to erect structures in public streets (theater marquees, for example) are quite likely to be revocable. 3 McQuillin, *Municipal Corporations* (3rd ed.) § 26.155. In practice they are seldom revoked.

No procedure has been evolved that can prevent revocation of these revocable permits. The problem must be decided on a case-by-case basis, viewing each situation from the standpoint of business risk. Where a lawyer knows a situation as this is legally vulnerable, but his client insists on going through with the deal, the lawyer may feel inclined to write a letter to his client, describing the risk, and retaining a copy in his permanent files. Conversations are often forgotten.[5]

Obviously, in many contracts *E* will want, as a pre-condition to closing, satisfactory assurances that the property is not involved in any filled-land permits. The surveyor should be consulted, for his maps will show the property as it was in the past.

Environmental control permits present a thorny problem, beyond the scope of this text.

§ 388. Oil delivery contracts. Oil delivery contracts were formerly routine matters. Today *E* must give thought to who his next supplier should be, what the new prices are likely to be, and whether there will be any difficulty in obtaining heating oil. Alternative sources should be considered, and the cost thereof given careful thought.

§ 389. Electricity. Any large building, such as an office building, may have a contract with a utility under which it buys power wholesale and sells it to tenants on a metered basis. This is a valuable, revenue- producing asset, and should be considered in fixing a contract price and should be assigned to *E*.

§ 390. Steam and air conditioning. A large building, such as an office building, may sell or buy steam or air conditioning from a neighboring building. The contract should be analyzed before the contract is signed. It may be a liability or an asset. If the building is buying steam or air conditioning the term of the contract must be considered. It will usually be assignable, and should be assigned. If it is not renewable by its terms, a question must arise as to the new terms when it expires. If the lines are underground and cross a city street, there will be a revocable city permit for this purpose and a price charged periodically for its renewal. These arrangements are seldom disturbed by the city unless it has plans for a subway. It is unlikely that *E* will refuse to buy a building serviced in this manner because of the remote contingency of trouble with the city, but the careful attorney for *E* will advise *E* of the problem before the contract is signed and will make specific reference to the problem in his closing letter, simply so that he can say "I told you so" if trouble arises.

§ 391. Elevators and escalators. There will be elevator and escalator maintenance contracts in many office buildings. They may be non-cancellable and will have to be assigned. Usually they pose no problems. However, the costs should figure in the sale price.

§ 392. Inspection certificates. Unless the elevator, escalator, boiler, etc. have been examined by the city to a recent date, an effort should be made to get new certificates close to the closing date.

§ 393. Cleaning contracts. Contracts for cleaning, window washing, etc. usually have a cancellation clause and pose no problems.

§ 394. Scavenger service. Most big buildings have contracts for scavenger service and *E* will wish to continue with this service.

§ 395. Termites. Termite infestation is common in many areas and can create a serious problem. *R* should be required to give a warranty against termite infestation and a satisfactory termite certificate by a company that performs this service must be required. Sellers have been known to conceal termite infestation. *Beagle v. Gagwell*, 169 So2d 43. And there are two or three ill-considered cases holding that even if the seller is aware of the situation, he is protected by the doctrine of caveat emptor. Granting that this doctrine is disappearing, it has not yet disappeared. These requirements belong in a contract or loan commitment.

§ 396. Union contract. Where *R* has a contract with a labor union, this may affect the rights of *E*.

EXAMPLE: *Lockheed* hired *Wackenhut* to furnish security service. *Wackenhut* entered into a collective bargaining agreement with its employees, who were represented by Union Local. When *Lockheed's* contract with *Wackenhut* expired, *Lockheed* entered into a new contract for security service with *Burns*. *Burns* hired a majority of the *Wackenhut* employees. The United States Supreme Court held that the collective bargaining agreement between *Wackenhut* and its employees did not automatically bind *Burns*, but because the agreement had not yet expired, *Burns* had a duty to bargain with the Union Local. *NLRB v. Burns Internal Security Service*, 406 U.S. 272, 48 Notre D. Law. 978.

§ 397. Letter of credit. In lieu of using money deposits as a guarantee of performance, parties often resort to the letter of credit.

EXAMPLE: *R* wishes to sell or mortgage land on which *X* has filed a mechanic's lien claim of $10,000, which *R* wishes to contest. *R* deposits an irrevocable letter of credit from *B* bank in the sum of $12,000 with the title company which issues its policy free of the lien. The advantage to *R* is that he pays a small premium for the letter of credit and his money is not tied up. Of course, if the lien claim begins to look serious the title company will call on the bank to deposit cash, at which time *R* must start paying interest at the going rate. The advantage to *R* is that he pays only a small annual fee until he is forced to call on the bank for money.

It is important to see that the letter of credit is irrevocable and unconditional, so that the title company is free at any time, to call on the bank for funds, on simple demand for same.

The advantage to *R* is that the fee charged by the bank is small until and unless it is forced to advance its funds.

Obviously, for the recipient of the letter of credit, the important precaution is a good tickler system. An expired letter of credit is worthless. All such letters have an expiration date.

§ 398. Deed in satisfaction of mortgage debt. Where a mortgagor who is hopelessly in default makes a deal to sell his equity to the mortgagee in satisfaction of the mortgage debt, the deal is vulnerable to attack. Kratovil, *Mortgages* § 28. Some mortgagees put a clause in the deed to forestall attack by the mortgagor. Kratovil, *Mortgages* § 34. Other mortgagees opt for a formal contract that tends to show the transaction was a voluntary transaction on the borrower's part. Kratovil, *Mortgages*, § 36. Get form from title company.

§ 399. Holding agreements. In California and some other southwestern states, the parties to a real estate deal may not wish to take title in a corporation, partnership, or joint venture. In such case they may choose to put title in a stakeholder, often a title or escrow company under a holding agreement. California, Land Security § 20-15. All the learning on this subject is a California monopoly. A good discussion will be found in *Proceedings, California Land Title Association, 62nd Annual Convention*, May 21-23, 1969, discussing, among other things, *Schriber v. Alameda East Bay*, 156 Cal.App.2d 700 and the *Lucky Investments Case*, 183 Cal.App.2d 462. The California practice followed by title companies operating with a holding agreement is described in detail in CLTA Manual, *Holding Agreements* 26 D.01 *et seq.* A practitioner wishing to acquaint himself with this useful document should consult with one of the California title companies, obtain a thorough briefing on what the holding agreement will and will not do.

§ 400. Appraisal. On big deals, a common document is the appraisal. This is a lengthy document. A lender looking at this document has much more expertise than his lawyer. The lawyer's role is minimal. However, he should see that the appraiser is given exact copies of all easements, building restrictions, etc. The appraisal should describe them and state that the appraiser has considered them in reaching his opinion. Obviously, an easement running through the land will affect the value of the property. A careful party will also want a copy of the survey to be given the appraiser and considered by the appraiser. For example, if my neighbor's building encroaches on my land, wrongfully or rightfully, that affects the value of the land.

§ 401. Letter of intent. The letter of intent is a document used when parties wish to express an intention to enter into a contract but have not gone far enough to be sure of the terms on which they wish to be bound. It does not create a legal obligation. *Sonesta Int. Hotels, v. Colony Sq. Co.* 482 F2d 281; *Forbes v. Wells Beach Casino Inc.*, 307 A2d 210; *Itek Corp. v. Chicago Aerial Inc.*, 274 A2d 141.

§ 402. Guarantees. There are many kinds of guarantees. Because a guarantor may be discharged by various events (38 Am. Jur. 2d 1086) a document labeled "guarantee" sometimes contains a primary or unconditional promise to pay. 38 Am. Jur. 2d 998. Such a document is not a guarantee. Perhaps a parent of a mortgagor corporation could be persuaded to give such a "guarantee." It would appear, however, on a financial statement as an absolute liability and resistance may be encountered on this score. Somewhat less strong is the absolute guarantee of payment. 38 Am. Jr. 2d 1019. But it is still a guarantee, and the danger of discharge is present. Then there is the guarantee of collection, which is weak because the creditor must first attempt to collect from the debtor. 38 Am. Jur. 2d 1021. A guarantee on a mortgage loan may provide that it will become void after the mortgage debt is reduced to a stated amount which the lender feels provides an ample equity. Because some early cases call in question the assignability of a guarantee, it should expressly recite that it is assignable. In a mortgage loan guarantee, it should provide that it passes without assignment to any holder of the mortgage, though it is still usual to specifically assign the guarantee when the mortgage is assigned. Especially on lease guarantees, it must be provided that modifications of the lease do not discharge the guarantor. On lease guarantees, a special form is made necessary by the bankruptcy problem. Kratovil, *Mortgages* § 410. The guarantor should waive rights in securities held by the creditor. *Combs v. Heirs,* 366 F. Supp 851.

See also Chapter 22.

§ 403. Agreement between life tenant and remainderman. Where a parent conveys to a child reserving a life estate, only the clause reserving the life estate is placed in the deed. But a side agreement is signed by the parties setting forth in detail who makes the mortgage payments, how the payments are divided if the life tenant pays interest only, who pays taxes, who make repairs, who carries hazard insurance and in what amount and form, who pays for repairs, etc. Some of this is covered by case law, but the parties should be forced to think about these matters. It saves arguments later.

§ **404. Partnership liability disclaimer.** In various documents (percentage leases, mortgage participation, mortgages where mortgagee is sharing in profits through subsidiary or otherwise) it is customary for the parties to disclaim an intention to create a partnership or joint venture.

§ **405. Disclaimer of warranties.** Because implied warranties are sometimes read into documents (*e.g.*, by use of the word "demise," in lease), some transferors state that there are no warranties except as specifically set forth in the document.

§ **406. Renewals and extensions.** Wherever a document is required, whether it be a lease, mortgage, UCC document, assignment of rents, lease guarantee, option to purchase, etc., some disposition must be made of the problem of extension of time or renewal.

> **EXAMPLE:** Does a lease guarantee continue into the renewal period provided by a renewal option? This should be covered.

§ **407. Bond for street work.** In the process of construction, the builder may excavate the street to hook up sewers, etc. A permit and bond for repairing are required by the city.

§ **408. Security system.** There may be a contract for an existing security alarm system. This should be assigned at closing.

§ **409. Restraints on competition.** Where you are buying part of a parcel of land for development, you should try for a covenant restraining competition with your development by the seller or his grantees on the remainder of the parcel. 25 ALR3d 897.

22

Mortgage Applications and Commitments—Construction Loans

§ 410. In general. In all mortgage transactions, there should be a formal, binding contract between R and E outlining the terms upon which they are entering into the transaction. The contract is important to R, for once the contract is finalized, E dare not welsh on it. He cannot come back to the borrower and say, for example, that he misread the loan market and should be getting a higher rate of interest. *Leben v. Nassau S & L Assn.*, 337 N.Y.S.2d 310. In addition, it is important to E that a binding loan contract exist. For most purposes, the mortgage, even though recorded, is vulnerable to other liens unless it is an "obligatory advance" mortgage. This means that the mortgagee must be legally obligated to make a loan. Kratovil, *Mortgages* § 115; 41 Tenn.L.Rev. 311.

Finally, in the large scale transaction there are a large range of points to be negotiated and revolved. As might be surmised, the requirements are largely those specified by the lender.

§ 411. Types of loan agreements. There are three types of loan agreements, namely: (1) Application and commitment. (2) Loan agreement. (3) Construction loan agreement.

In brief, $R's$ application for a loan, when followed by $E's$ commitment to make it, creates a loan contract on the simple contract principle that offer plus acceptance equals contract. More often, the commitment departs substantially from the application, and is therefore a counter-offer. R, in turn, accepts the counter-offer, and a loan contract exists.

In large-scale transactions it is simpler for R and E to enter into a formal loan agreement, setting forth the terms on which the loan is to be made. Just as a contract of sale provides the blueprint for all later steps in the sale transaction, including the closing, the loan agreement provides a blueprint for the loan transaction, including the closing.

In construction loans, the construction loan agreement is, of course, a form of formal loan agreement, but with elaborate provisions designed to assure the lender that the building will be completed in apt time according to plans and specifications, free of mechanic's liens, and that the tenants whose rentals generate cash flow to retire the mortgage debt, will accept and occupy the leased premises. Or alternatively, the application and commitment cover the principal loan terms, call for a title search and survey, and when these prove satisfactory, the application and commitment require the parties to enter into a construction loan agreement on *E's* usual form or in form attached to the commitment.

§ 412. **Application and commitment—in general.** Although the law is the same in both instances, the small lender and the big lender tend to approach the problem of loan application and commitment differently. The small lender looks at the application as a source of information, which it is. The applicant is asked for information concerning his employment, his wife's employment, place of residence for the past 10 years, assets, purpose of loan, contract price if a sale is involved, etc. Often the small lender does not give a formal commitment. The big lender takes a different approach. He regards the application and commitment as creating a contract for a loan, which it is. As such, it is likely to be quite detailed.

If the borrower does not bind himself to borrow the money on the terms stated in the commitment and pays nothing for the commitment, it is a revocable offer only, despite its statement that it is irrevocable for a stated period of time. *Stanish v. Polish Roman Cath. Union,* 484 F2d 713. But if the borrower obtains the commitment for an end loan to induce an interim lender to furnish construction funds, the end loan lender is bound under the rule of "promissory estoppel." *Ibid.*

§ 413. **Requirements similar to sale contract.** Many, though not all, of the requirements of a contract for sale or lease are requirements that also belong in the loan commitment. It would be folly to duplicate this ground. It is assumed that the attorney for the lender will read the remainder of this book and incorporate appropriate requirements in the loan application. Obviously, for example, the lender wants the protection of a termite certificate or proper survey just as much as a buyer or lessee does. However, where the requirements differ, they are discussed, either in this chapter or elsewhere. For example, the coverage of a title policy given the lender varies from that given an owner. This is discussed in the chapter on title insurance. But the knowledge thus obtained must be employed in drafting the loan commitment. Title requirements are set forth in Chapter 11. It is customary to provide that evidence of title (abstract, title policy, etc.) will remain in *E's* possession, likewise hazard insurance, survey, etc.

§ 414. **Institutional lenders.** Institutional lenders are regulated by law. Such a lender must not commit to make an unauthorized loan. A commercial loan may, on its face, seem regular. Yet if the institution has already loaned up all its permitted commercial loan funds, it cannot make the commitment. Some institutions cannot make leasehold mortgages. Those that can may be confined to leases of a specified duration. The loan must be within the institution's permitted lending area.

§ 415. **Documents.** The commitment will have attached or specify the forms of mortgage documents the borrower is to sign, *e.g.,* mortgage, mortgage note, assignment of leases and rents, chattel security instrument, guarantee of payment, etc.

§ 416. **Commitment terms.** The terms of the commitment will be given, *e.g.,* payment of commission, acceptance within time specified, restriction against assignment of commitment, form of mortgage title policy to be given, name of title company, time for issuing title insurance commitment, which time should be measured from date of borrower's notification of acceptance. The appraisal is described, as well as time allowed for furnishing the same.

§ 417. Title requirements. The lender will want the condition of title to be described, objections to be set forth specifically, not generally, all as in Chapter 11.

§ 418. Loan terms. Loan terms are set forth in detail, including payment privileges.

§ 419. Equity participation. Equity participations are set forth in detail.

§ 420. Loan closing terms. The terms on which the loan will be closed are set forth, *e.g.*, requirements of opinions of counsel, delivery of lease security deposits, etc.

§ 421. Corporate borrower. In states that permit a corporate borrower to waive its right of redemption, the lender should insist on such a waiver. This requirement belongs in the loan commitment. The commitment will have the lender's mortgage form attached or will refer to it. The corporate form should be used. This will have the usual corporate provisions forbidding secondary financing, requiring financial periodic statements, etc. But the waiver of redemption may have to be typed in, since only a few states provide for this. Care should be exercised to name the corporation the lender wants as borrower. Parent and subsidiary often have similar names. If the lender wants the financial resources of the parent, it is that corporation he should name.

§ 422. Leases. Where the land is leased to high-credit tenants, the loan commitment may be issued by *E* and accepted by *R*, "subject to" approval of the terms of the leases as satisfactory to the lender. This is done where *E* does not want to incur the trouble and expense of examining the leases until the loan contract has been finalized by appraisal approval, etc. "Satisfaction" clauses such as these are valid. *Matthei v. Hopper*, 330 P2d 625, 47 Calif.L.Rev. 752. Since the construction lender is counting on the permanent lender to "take out" the construction loan, and the permanent lender's commitment is contingent on his approval of leases, the construction loan commitment will be contingent on approval of major leases by the takeout lender.

§ 423. Leasehold mortgage. It is difficult to give a commitment for a leasehold mortgage until the contents of the lease have been agreed upon. The commitment can then be contingent on signing of the lease and collateral documents.

§ 424. Certainty and completeness. A developer often seeks to steer customers to his mortgage lender for end loans and likes to assure his prospective purchasers that mortgage money will be available. The commitment or contract by the lender tends to be indefinite at times.

EXAMPLE: A contract by *E* to consider loan application in the future according to his "then existing policy" was too indefinite to be enforced. You need more detail. *Wimbleton Develop. Co. v. Travelers Ins. Co.*, 206 NW(2) 222 (1973).

§ 425. Borrower protection. *R* must endeavor to introduce into the commitment such clauses as are needed for his protection.

EXAMPLE: *R* procured from *E* a commitment for loan funds for construction of a motel. He paid a commitment fee of $25,000.00. Later a building permit was refused because the state had decided to condemn the land for a highway. *R* sued *E* for return of the $25,000. The court held for *E*. Like any other contract, a loan commitment comes under the rule that impossibility of performance is no excuse unless the contract so provides. *Hawkins v. First F. S. & L. Assn.*, 280 So.2d 93 (1973).

§ **426. Pre-conditions.** The construction commitment, as has been stated, is subject to a variety of pre-conditions. There are pre-conditions to *CL's* (*CL* is construction lender) obligation to proceed at all. There are pre-conditions to making the first advance. And there are pre-conditions to making advances after the first advance and to making the final advance. To recapitulate:

The commitment lists the documents that are to be furnished as pre-conditions to *CL's* obligation to proceed somewhat as follows:

1. Financial statements of borrower.
2. Plans and architect's approval of plans.
3. Satisfactory appraisal.
4. Zoning ordinance.
5. Survey acceptable to *CL* and title company.
6. Building permit and all other governmental authorizations.
7. Title company commitment and verbatim copies of restrictions and other documents listed as exceptions.
8. Leases and assignments thereof, also security deposits.
9. Construction contract.
10. Opinion of counsel as to validity and priority of mortgage.
11. All corporate documents (charter, resolutions, etc.). All partnership documents if borrower is a partnership. All trust documents if borrower is a trust.
12. Payment of commitment fees, legal fees, etc.
13. Acceptance of commitment by borrower.
14. Buy-sell agreement.

Pre-conditions to *CL's* obligation to make the first loan advance include:

1. Receipt by *CL* of documents including note, mortgage, guarantee, title insurance commitment, hazard and other insurance, contractor's bonds, chattel liens search, chattel lien documents, etc.
2. Architect's certificate as to work and material in place and in compliance with contract, also statement that balance of loan proceeds are sufficient to complete the building.
3. Down-dated survey to show building complies with restrictions, ordinances, no encroachments.
4. Lien waivers for all work in place, supporting affidavits, all other lien documents required by law.

Pre-conditions to subsequent advances include:

1. No default or breach of covenant.
2. Down-date of title search.
3. Down-date of survey.
4. Architect's certificates, lien waivers, etc.

Pre-conditions to final disbursement may include:

1. Satisfactory proof that "punch-list" items were all taken care of. (Any deviation from construction contract).

2. Architect's certificate that building complies with plans, ordinances, restrictions.
3. Certificate of occupancy.
4. Final lien waivers by all trades, also filed notice of completion if required by lien law.
5. Down-date of title search certifying all liens waived.
6. Down-date of survey.
7. Estoppel certificate by major tenants.
8. Approvals by fire underwriters.
9. Hazard and other insurance (*e.g.*, shift to standard fire from builder's risk).
10. Approval and acceptance by takeout lender.
11. Consent by bonding company to release of retentions.

§ 427. Construction loan commitment—outline. The pattern of a construction loan commitment is as hereafter stated. For convenience, the construction lender is described as *CL* and the end loan lender as *TL* (takeout lender):

1. The amount of the mortgage and note should be stated at a figure that completes the estimated cost of construction plus a reasonable margin, with a provision that the total amounts advanced are not to exceed the cost of construction. This is done because some state laws state that the amount of the mortgage lien will not exceed the stated principal. On the other hand, local mortgage taxes suggest that the margin be kept within reasonable bounds. If junior financing is to be prohibited, that should be stated.

2. The interest should be stated, usually payable "according to the tenor of the construction loan agreement." Principal amount is followed by the phrase "or so much thereof as may from time to time be advanced under construction loan agreement."

3. The commitment must contain a timetable for construction of the project, including commencement date, a detailed breakdown of construction loan disbursements (that ties into the stages of construction stated in the construction contract) and final loan maturity that provides time to meet *TL's* end loan requirements. It must be stated how disbursement is to be made, *e.g.*, to the general contractor on production of waivers by the subcontractors, or to the subcontractors directly, or to a bank or title company in escrow for payment to the various trades. The commitment may give *CL* the option to go either way. If architects' certificates are to be required this is stated. Also give details of retentions.

4. Provide for submission to *CL* of cost analysis, showing all trades, amounts to be paid, expenses, legal fees, architect fees etc. This should be complete and detailed, so that it can be seen that funds are adequate to complete. An item marked "estimated" means no firm subcontract exists. This item calls for a business judgment by *CL*.

5. The commitment identifies the contractor, calls for the construction contract, plans, shop drawings and specifications (or duplicates) to be lodged with *CL* together with a security assignment thereof. This enables *CL* to go forward with construction if *R* becomes insolvent. It enables a new contractor to go forward if the original contractor walks off the job. Note that the AIA architect's agreement makes him the owner of the plans and this will have to be modified. And this enables *CL* to check with the contract,

plans and specifications furnished *TL*, for if there are differences (as has happened) *TL* may refuse to take out *CL*.

6. It is required that *R's* contract with the architect be lodged with *CL*, together with a security assignment thereof. This helps if *R* becomes insolvent.

7. To the greatest extent possible the commitment should have pre-conditions patterned after the end loan commitment, for example, with respect to firming up of key leases.

8. Requirements as to the identity of guarantors and form of guarantee are stated.

9. Time limits for the compliance with commitment requirements are stated, with an outside date for final completion. Two duplicates of the commitment are delivered to *R* with a requirement stating that one be returned to *CL* within _____ days bearing *R's* acceptance.

10. It should be provided that *R* pays *CL's* expenses, including attorney's fees, loan commission, appraisal fees, survey costs, etc. and state when these are payable. These are payable whether or not the project gets off the ground, and it is stated that the mortgage is security for all such expenses. Otherwise, they are merely an unsecured claim. The mortgage should provide that it secures performance of and sums due under construction loan agreement.

11. The commitment may be expressly non-assignable together with a provision forbidding conveyance of the property during construction. There is doubt as to the validity in some states as to the restraint on conveyance, though the states that permit reasonable restraints on alienation will sustain it. It can be phrased in terms of an option to *CL* to discontinue disbursements if a conveyance is made.

12. The form of construction loan agreement is attached, with requirements for its execution, with a time limit. The loan agreement should not conflict with the commitment. If both are on *CL's* forms, this possibility is minimized. Obviously, some of the provisions suggested for the commitment can be placed in the loan agreement.

13. Since *CL* must be certain of the takeout, the commitment will require proof of the existence of the takeout.

14. Insurance requirements are set forth, with provision for mortgagee loss clause wherever possible.

15. Any requirements as to contractor's surety bonds are stated, or, alternatively, requirements for title company completion of building service.

16. If a chattel security is to be given, that is provided for.

17. Copies of the mortgage, note, and assignment of leases and rents are attached. If these are on forms supplied by *TL* it facilitates consummation of the end loan. It should be stated which leases are to be specifically described in the assignment. When the assignment comes in, notice thereof, including a copy of the assignment are served on tenants other than the minor tenants.

18. Extras and change orders are treated in detail. There is the usual prohibition against extras or change orders without written consent of *CL*. Some lenders require a separate statement at the time of each disbursement listing any extras or change orders. It

is stated that payments of unauthorized extras or change orders do not waive the requirement for written approval on subsequent disbursements. Cash deposits by R for extras and change orders are spelled out. Anticipated time delay caused by change orders should be spelled out. This fixes party liable for delay.

19. Since many mechanic's lien laws provide protection for the "landowner" who relies on documents furnished by the general contractor, the commitment calls for a document signed by R designating CL as his agent to receive such documents.

20. If the mortgaged property is a ground lease it must be stated whether the lessor is to subordinate his interest to the mortgage or join in the mortgage.

21. As a pre-condition to first disbursement, a document regarding R may be required, *e.g.*, corporate charter, certificate of authority to do business in this state, certificate of good standing in state of incorporation, partnership articles, certificate of limited partnership, financial statements of R and his guarantor, etc.

22. CL should reserve the right to approve or reject any borrowing entity other than R.

23. It is common to call for opinion of counsel at closing that R is a valid legal entity, that the documents are all valid and duly authorized and that no violation of the usury or doing-business laws is present.

24. A pre-condition to first disbursement is the furnishing of a legal opinion that the project conforms to zoning and an architect's certificate that the contract, plans, and specifications conform to local codes and statutes.

25. Provide for satisfactory soil tests, engineering reports on drainage, etc. as pre-condition to first disbursement.

26. As a pre-condition to first disbursement, R must furnish license to operate, *e.g.*, convalescent home, hospital.

27. Appraisal requirements are set forth, same to be based on a building conforming to construction contract, plans and specifications.

28. As a pre-condition to first disbursement, R must show he has complied with environmental development and energy crisis requirements. CL may wish to insist on opinion of counsel.

29. The amount of work to be done by R before disbursement of loan funds begins should be stated. Customarily CL accepts his inspection of building and lien waivers as proof that the work was done and paid for. CL may wish to verify payment to the trades before he accepts the waivers, and the commitment should permit this.

30. The commitment may be conditioned on continuance of the existing zoning until $R's$ disbursements have made it impossible for the city to amend its ordinances so as to make the project an unlawful one. The building does not achieve non-conforming use status until expenditures are made in reliance on the building permit.

31. The commitment requires CL to keep the loan *in balance*, that is the loan kitty must at all times be adequate to complete construction. Some lenders require the architect to sign such a certificate to this effect at the time of each disbursement, or to state an estimate of remaining cost of construction.

32. The commitment defines "work in place" for disbursement figures. Materials delivered to the site but not yet incorporated in the building may not be included. They may never get into the building. If materials delivered are to be included, provision for watchman is included. Diversion of construction funds to other costs (annexation costs, for example) is forbidden, and best policed by direct payment by *CL* to the trades. Some non-construction costs are payable out of disbursements, *e.g., CL's* expenses, surety bond premiums, title insurance costs, etc.

33. Commitment should call for an initial title commitment, satisfactory to *CL*. Certified copies of building restrictions and easements are furnished *CL* and a legal opinion may be required that the project does not violate them. If title is to be brought down before each disbursement, that is provided for.

34. The survey requirements are set forth, together with any date-down requirements as construction progresses, to show any violation of ordinances building restrictions or easements before they get out of hand.

35. At a minimum, the commitment should require as a pre-condition to any disbursement, a statement by *R* that he has no knowledge or notice of (1) any change in zoning or building ordinances that would affect the structure; (2) any violations of building restrictions or easements; (3) any complaints of invalidity by other landowners; (4) any threatened action that might imperil the project, including condemnations, environmental control, energy crisis restriction, etc.

36. Where funds are to be wired, it is a matter of convenience to so state and give the bank account number, and bank officer in charge.

37. If there are to be escrows during construction, for example, for taxes, insurance, etc., these should be set forth.

38. Provision should be made for reserves for installation of chattels needed to operate, as in motel or hotel, and written assurance should be given by some reliable supplier that he will furnish the chattels at a stated figure.

39. A partial release provision may be included, for example, on a condominium. This contains conditions, *e.g.,* that the building has been completed, that _____% of all units are sold under binding contracts, that sale price will be used to reduce principal, etc.

40. In connection with the final disbursement, including release of retentions, special conditions are applicable, for example, certificate of occupancy, estoppel letters by tenants, certificate of completion according to plans by architect, final survey, final title report, consent by bonding company, etc.

41. The loan commitment and mortgage will call for Uniform Commercial Code filings and renewal thereof on the chattels the lender wants as security for the loan. On all construction loans, the Amendments to the Code require the construction mortgage to state that it is a construction loan, whereupon it obtains priority over fixture liens created during the course of construction. Also, wherever the Uniform Code Uniform Amendments are in effect, its requirements as to financing statements are followed, that is both mortgagor and mortgagee sign the mortgage, and give their addresses. Thereupon the

mortgage operates as a code filing as to fixtures to be installed, but not subject to the five-year limitation imposed by the Code in other cases.

42. Gap or bridge loan. The end loan commitments may be such, particularly with respect to leases, that *R* may be required to pay *CL* before the end loan pays out. *R* will be compelled to get a standby commitment for a loan that pays the construction loan and bridges the period until the end loan is payable. This plays havoc with the combined construction loan end mortgage and weakens the priority of the end loan, for example, as to mechanic's liens and UCC filings. This is because the end-loan becomes a second-stage subrogation document.

§ 428. Guarantees. The commitment should stipulate what guarantees are to be forthcoming. The manufacturer of roofing material may be willing to give you a roof guarantee. An item of great potential risk is glass. A very large skyscraper has been vacant and unoccupied for several years because the panes of glass pop out. Another large building leaks because of the curving glass exterior. Other buildings are difficult to air-condition because of glass exterior. Blame is difficult to apportion. The mortgagee would like to see a detailed guarantee by a responsible general contractor, incorporated in the general contract and covered by the surety company performance bond covering every possible glass defect. If the general contractor turns this down, the subcontractor's guarantee can be considered, if it in turn, is covered by a very ample surety bond that protects landowner and lender. In either case, the guarantee should spell out what damages are recoverable, *e.g.*, loss of rents, loss of leases, etc. The energy crisis will diminish glass expanses, but will not eliminate them. *See* also: §§ 402, 605.

§ 429. Reserves and retentions—loan in balance. There is a common misconception that the retentions from funds due the prime contractor and major subs are some sort of security protecting the owner. This will not withstand analysis. These are moneys earned by the contractors, due them if they do their jobs right. To be sure, there is a security of sorts, in that the lender can hold on to the retentions until all defects are corrected. But to protect himself against rising prices, extras and change orders, the lender needs a contingency reserve in addition to the other reserves. These days it had best be substantial. And the borrower must keep the "loan in balance." Each disbursement's documents must show that the balance of the loan funds will complete the building. Many lenders now require, in addition to the traditional documents, that the architect or supervising engineer certify on each draw that the loan funds suffice to complete the building according to filed plans.

A reserves clause follows:

There shall be reserved from the construction loan proceeds, before the first disbursement to any contractor or sub-contractor, sufficient monies to pay and discharge the following items, to-wit:
  (a) All unpaid loan charges, commissions, standby fees and appraisal fees.
  (b) The balance of Lender's attorney's fees, if any.
  (c) An estimated amount to be reserved and used for the payment of interest on construction payouts made from time to time.
  (d) An estimated amount to be reserved for the payment of real estate taxes against the premises, insurance premiums, and other accrued items of expense anticipated during the period of construction.
  (e) An estimated amount to allow for construction extras and contingencies.

(f) An estimated amount to be reserved for payment of Interim Title Insurance Binders, later date continuation fees, and the issuance of the ALTA Mortgage Title Guaranty Policy on completion of the buildings and for the issuance of the plat of survey.

And the parties hereto covenant and agree that after setting aside the aforesaid Reserves, the balance of the construction loan proceeds must then be sufficient to pay, in full, the charges of all contractors, sub-contractors and materialmen in accordance with the Construction Contracts and Sworn Contractor's Statements heretofore described, for the full and total completion of all buildings and improvements, required hereunder; with the further proviso that should the balance of the loan proceeds be insufficient for such purpose or purposes, Borrower shall immediately deposit with _____ a sum of money, which together with the balance of loan proceeds, will be sufficient to accomplish such purposes. At that time and upon the deposit of such additional money, this construction loan shall be considered in balance, and the first construction disbursement shall be eligible for payment.

At all times thereafter, Borrower agrees to keep the loan in balance, so that the funds remaining in the construction loan shall, at all times, be sufficient to complete the buildings and related improvements and appurtenances in accordance with the terms hereof, free and clear of mechanic's lien or other claims; and should Borrower make or undertake any approved changes in construction resulting in an increase in the cost thereof, said Borrower shall immediately deposit with _____ sufficient monies to pay for the same, and will not commence any such additional construction unless such funds are deposited as aforesaid. It is the intention of the parties hereto that this loan shall, at all times hereafter, be and remain in balance up to and including the time of final disbursement; and the parties agree that failure to deposit such additional monies, at any time, so as to keep the loan in balance, shall constitute a default hereunder as well as a default under the Mortgage delivered hereunder.[1]

§ 430. Pre-conditions—suggestion to construction lender.

Make the construction loan commitment subject to the same conditions as those contained in the takeout commitment. That is, if the permanent lender is making requirements, for example, as to key leases that he wants signed, the construction loan commitment should be subject to the same requirements, so that all these are met before disbursement is to begin. A key lease can be signed by the mortgagor and his tenant (subject of course, to completion of the building before it becomes effective), and this lease can be approved by the permanent lender before disbursement of the construction loan begins. It is a good idea to have all documents required by the permanent lender approved by him to the greatest extent possible. This will avoid the pitfall of running into an insoluble difference with the permanent lender, thus forcing you to look elsewhere for a permanent lender. Some permanent lenders will furnish their mortgage, note and other forms to the interim lender. The interim loan documents are on forms, in consequence, that the permanent lender has prepared and is willing to accept. Of course, the promissory note then has a double aspect. It will call for payments (usually interest only) during the course of construction "according to the tenor of the construction loan agreement," and thereafter in installments as set forth in the commitment for the permanent loan. Incidentally, this will reduce mortgage tax fees and recording fees involved in the use of different documents for the interim and permanent loans. It is customary to provide in the mortgage and note that default by the mortgagor in performance of his construction loan agreement covenants is a default giving rise to a right of acceleration under the mortgage. The permanent loan commitment should be checked with care. For example, if it expires in one year, and the building will take two years to complete, the interim lender cannot commit. The interim lender needs a margin of at least 30 days after construction ends to

---

[1] Reprinted by permission of Abert Marks of the Chicago Bar.

get the papers ready for delivery to the permanent lender. Since construction completion dates are rarely met, it is also wise to provide for extensions of the permanent loan commitment on payment of agreed fees. It probably is a sensible precaution for the construction lender to make certain that the building plans he is checking are the same as those furnished the permanent lender. The permanent lender will turn down the loan if the building is not completed according to plans he has been given, and this means that the construction lender must determine that they are identical with his plans.[2]

§ **431. Damages.** The usual contract damages rules are applicable to loan commitments.

EXAMPLE: *E* committed to loan funds to *R* in connection with an apartment development. Later *E* refused to make further disbursements, and, in consequence, the project collapsed. *R* sued *E* for the profits he lost as a result of collapse of the project. The court refused to award such damages. Where lost profits are purely a matter of speculation, contract law refuses to award damages for loss thereof. *Standish v. Polish Roman Catholic Union,* 484 F2d 713 (1973).

§ **432. Construction commitment and permanent commitment.** Since the construction lender depends on the permanent lender to "take him out," the construction loan commitment is given only after the end loan commitment has been given and a key provision in the construction loan commitment is that the borrower agrees to do nothing, or omit anything that will or might cause a termination of the end loan commitment.

§ **433. Anti-merger provision.** Since the *commitment* for the construction loan contains provisions that are intended to continue after the construction loan *agreement* has been signed, it is customary to place either in the commitment or construction loan agreement a clause stating that the provisions of the *commitment* continue in force after the construction loan *agreement* is signed.

§ **434. Timing of construction lender's initial disbursements.** Obviously, *R* does not want *CL* to spend a lot of money which he is to be charged until he knows, in general, the project will be approved. Thus, if he can get the appraisal toward the top of the list of items to be approved he will be in a position to avoid further expenses if the appraisal is rejected by *CL*

§ **435. Commitment for combined construction and permanent loan—standby commitment.** There is a problem in construction lending in that once the project has been constructed and its prospects for profitable operation seem bright, the borrower can get permanent financing elsewhere on better terms than those outlined in the permanent loan commitment he obtained before construction had begun. At that time he may balk at signing the permanent loan documents. To forestall this, the interim and permanent lenders at times contrive a commitment given by the construction lender to the borrower which has a dual aspect. It sets forth the terms that will govern disbursement and repayment during the construction period. And it also sets forth the terms of the permanent financing. Once the borrower has signed the mortgage documents, he is firmly committed, and cannot seek permanent financing elsewhere. Obviously, this is an awkward sort of document. An alternative is provided in the construction loan commit-

---

[2] © Copyright, Kratovil *Modern Mortgage Law and Practice* (Prentice-Hall Inc. 1972). Reprinted by permission.

ment for a substantial "stand-by" fee, which is to be retained by the construction lender if closing of the permanent loan does not take place because of any action by *R*, otherwise to be refunded to *R*.

There is a measure of convenience in using the permanent lender's mortgage form as the basic mortgage and attaching the construction lender's form with a provision that the construction form governs during the period of construction and the permanent form governs after takeout.

§ 436. Standby commitment. If *R* wishes to proceed with construction before he has firmed up his end loan commitment, he will probably procure a standby commitment. This is a commitment for a loan that will take out the interim loan, but is on terms less liberal to *R* than the terms of the end loan lender. Moreover the standby lender charges a commitment fee, often a substantial one. This charge does not make the loan usurious even if it takes *E's* yield over the usury limit. Kratovil, *Mortgages,* § 164. Because *R* hopes that he will not be compelled to resort to the standby commitment, but have only the option to resort to it if more favorable financing is not available, the commitment is drafted like an option, that is, *E* is bound, but *R* is not until *R* gives notice of exercise of his option.

At times the standby commitment is for a number of mortgages.

EXAMPLE: *R* has a construction loan for a condominium apartment. He may wish to procure a standby commitment for those unit purchasers who are unable to procure their own financing. This commitment is a little unusual because it calls for loans to third persons, not to *R*. If *R* exercises his option when a given unit is sold, *E* may be confronted with a possible liability to the unit purchaser as a third-party beneficiary. For example, if *E* welshes on his commitment, the unit purchaser may lose his down payment. The parties should give thought to this. If *E* decides that he does not want to be liable to unit purchasers, the usual clause negativing liability to third-party beneficiaries is included, usually stating that the contract is for the benefit of the parties thereto only and not for the benefit of any third parties.

§ 437. Refundable loan commitment fee. In an effort to prevent *R* from welshing on his end loan commitment because he can then get better terms from some other permanent lender, end loan commitments sometimes provide for a refundable loan commitment fee. The fee is paid by *R* at the time the loan commitment is given. It is refundable only if *R* consummates the end loan committed. It is sufficiently large to deter *R* from seeking a different end loan. The difficulty is that the legal philosophy has not been worked out as yet. The device seems similar to the earnest money deposit customary in land sales. There is no agreement as to the form the provision should take. 23 Bus. Law. 1065; 33 Mortgage Banker 29. In the Business Lawyer it is suggested that the fee be characterized "as part of the consideration for the issuance of this commitment and for the lender's obligation to loan the money in question." In the Mortgage Banker the fear is expressed that this seems to give *R* the option of not going through with the end loan as long as he is willing to sacrifice the commitment fee. The Mortgage Banker suggests additional language to the effect that the moneys so paid "do not permit the borrower the option of not completing the loan transaction." On balance, it would seem that the size of the commitment fee is the key to the situation. If it is large enough, it should be an adequate deterrent.

Instead of using money deposits, many parties, including borrowers, are trying to substitute letters of credit. *R*, instead of depositing cash for a refundable commitment fee, may seek to substitute a letter of credit. This enables *R* to avoid tying up cash.

§ **438. Bridge loan.** After construction has been completed, the interim lender will wish to be paid off. The conditions of the permanent loan commitment as to full occupancy and possession by tenants, may not as yet have been satisfied. Hence *R* may need a standby commitment by another lender to make a "bridge loan" that pays off the construction lender and is in turn paid off by the permanent lender when the terms of the permanent commitment have been met. Hence, the construction commitment will provide that *R* will keep the standby commitment in force and execute the bridge loan documents and otherwise perform all the terms of the standby commitment. The interest rates on standby loans are high enough to encourage *R* to obtain the permanent loan but its rental space requirements, obviously, are less rigorous than those of the permanent lender.

§ **439. Assignment of construction contract.** The construction commitment or construction loan agreement will call for a duplicate of the construction contract to be delivered to *E* at closing of the construction loan together with an assignment thereof, so that *E* can step in to complete if *R* defaults.

§ **440. Certificate of occupancy.** There may be difficulties about obtaining a certificate of occupancy. Tenants who do their own interiors will not finish until long after the rest of the building is completed. "Punch list" items (work that needs to be completed or done over) may hold up the certificate. In some states, the certificate does not issue for the building as a whole, but only to each tenant. This makes it desirable for *CL* to provide to *TL* some satisfactory substitute for a certificate of occupancy.

§ **441. General conditions.** In lieu of providing for a construction loan agreement to be signed, the commitment may contain *General Conditions* stating the terms customarily found in the Construction Loan Agreement.

§ **442. Escrow for improvements—suspense letter.** After *E* has examined the property, he may wish to hold back part of the loan proceeds for specified repairs or improvements. This belongs in the commitment. *E* may wish to attach a copy of the *suspense letter* under which this money will be held back and disbursed.

§ **443. Securities Act.** A mortgage commitment is a "security" under the federal Securities Act. If a commitment fee is procured with no intention of providing the funds committed, the penalties of the Securities Act attach. *U.S. v. Austin,* 462 F2d 724.

§ **444. Expiration date.** The date the commitment expires is stated.

23

Mortgage Applications and Commitments—Takeout Lenders

§ **445. In general.** The takeout lender (hereafter *TL*) here discussed is one who will acquire the construction mortgage or refinance it. Often the construction mortgage is drafted with a double aspect, one aspect dealing with the construction period and the other dealing with the period after construction has been completed and the *TL* steps in. Quite commonly the construction lender will use the *TL's* mortgage and note form, and this obviously satisfies the *TL's* requirement that the mortgages and note be satisfactory in form to the *TL*.

§ **446. Validity of the mortgage.** Obviously, *TL's* first concern is that the mortgage is valid and that a title company is willing to insure its validity. *TL* will include in his commitment to buy the loan a requirement that he receive at the date of the assignment to the *TL* an ALTA loan policy (unless the state law precludes this) with the assignment of the mortgage insured on the cover page of the policy, subject only to stated defects. These defects can be ascertained by referring to the defects and encumbrances listed on the title policy furnished the construction lender.

§ **447. Defects not covered by the loan policy.** *TL* must satisfy himself in some way as to matters not covered by the ALTA policy. Usury is an example. There are several ways of dealing with the problem. The commitment may, for example, require that the title company give special usury coverage. This the title company may be willing to do, for example, where the mortgagor is a corporation and state law exempts corporate mortgagors from the usury laws. It would be most unwise to conclude that such insurance is unnecessary. The title company is buying the risk that the corporation was not formed with intent to evade the usury laws. Or if the state statute exempts "business loans" from the usury laws, the title company is taking on the risk that the loan is indeed a business loan. Likewise, the answer is far from clear where various other exceptions to the usury laws are involved, because many of these are shrouded in doubt. Kratovil, *Mortgages*, Chapter 14. Or *TL* may insist that the construction lender furnish an opinion of counsel selected by *TL* that the loan is not usurious. The legal opinion method will probably also be used to cover the title company's refusal to insure against violation of the Truth-in-Lending laws. Probably it will also be used to cover the possibility that the construction lender has been guilty of a violation of the ''doing business'' laws directed against foreign corporations.

§ 448. Collateral documents—assignment of leases and rents. Obviously, *TL* will want an assignment of leases and rents and an assignment thereof to *TL*. Again, the construction lender will have procured this on a form used by *TL*. Accompanying the assignment will be estoppel certificates by key tenants accepting the premises as completed to their satisfaction.

§ 449. Collateral documents—assignment of mortgage. The assignment of mortgage will be on *TL's* form and his commitment will so provide. The commitment, of course, requires that the assignment be accompanied by physical transfer of the mortgage, the mortgage note duly endorsed, and all collateral documents.

§ 450. Collateral documents—insurance policies. Some notion of *TL's* requirements as to insurance requirements can be gleaned from Kratovil, *Mortgages*, Chapter 17. It is best to have separate assignments of each of the policies and consents by each insurer to the assignment. Also let the attorney's opinion certify that the coverage has been validly transferred to *TL*. Where there is a lease that antedates the construction mortgage and it requires that the landowner's insurance be applied to reconstruction of the building, *TL* takes subject to this right of the tenant.

§ 451. Collateral documents—architect's certificates. The loan commitment will call for an architect's certificate that the building was completed according to the plans installed by the construction lender and *TL*. If possible, this should be accompanied by a certificate of occupancy issued by the zoning commission. If operation is permitted only if some *environmental agency* has certified the development as being in compliance, *TL's* commitment must be subject to issuance of such a certificate.

§ 452. Collateral documents—licenses to mortgagor. If the structure is a hospital, nursing home, tavern, or other enterprise that can be operated only after a license to operate has issued, *TL's* commitment must be conditioned on the procuring of such a license.

§ 452A. Collateral documents—survey. *TL's* commitment will call for a survey to be issued covering the completed structure. The type of survey may depend on local standards. Both *TL* and the title company will read the survey, looking for encroachments, encroachments upon easements, violations of private restrictions, violations of zoning or building ordinances, etc.

§ 453. Takeout lender—inspections of building during construction. *TL* has a copy of the plans and specs. His commitment reserves the right to inspect during construction to make sure the building is constructed according to plans and specs. Alternatively, both interim lender and takeout lender can agree on inspections made by a mutually acceptable architect or engineer.

24

Mortgages—Residential

§ **454. In general.** The typical pre-consumerism residential mortgage seems vulnerable to attack today for a number of reasons, namely: (1) There is inequality of bargaining power as between the homebuyer and the lender. (2) The mortgage is a contract of adhesion. (3) The courts have already begun the process of reshaping the mortgage by resort to the concept of unconscionability.

EXAMPLE: A typical due-on-sale clause provides that the mortgagee could accelerate if the mortgagor sold the property without written permission of the mortgagee. The mortgagor sold the property and the lender accelerated. The court set the acceleration aside on the ground that the clause could not be invoked if the buyer was sufficiently responsible to qualify for the loan. *Tucker v. Pulaski Fed. S. & L. Assn.,* 481 S.W.2d 725 (Ark. 1972).

To be sure much of the law relating to the unconscionable contracts is found in contracts relating to chattels. 18 ALR3d 1305. But it has made its appearance in the law relating to real estate documents. *Rego v. Decker,* 482 P2d 834 (Alaska 1971) (lease with option to purchase); *Weaver v. American Oil Co.,* 276 NE2d 144 (Inc. 1971) (lease).

There is something to be said, from the lender's point of view, therefore, for drafting a mortgage form that is sufficiently consumer-oriented so that courts will be tempted to enforce it as written. In other words, the courts will undoubtedly tinker with the old pre-consumerism pro-lender mortgage. They might very well leave the consumer-oriented mortgage alone.

The history of the process just described took a dramatic turn when FNMA and FHLMC proposed to enter the conventional mortgage market on residential loans. Attorneys for the two organizations summoned to Washington a group of technical advisers, including this author. A form of mortgage covenants (herein referred to as "uniform covenants") was drafted that could be used in all fifty states, with special added clauses to accommodate the special statutory requirements that exist in each state. A number of consumer advocates, including Senator Proxmire and Ralph Nader criticized the forms as pro-lender. Representatives of various interested groups, including this author were called to state their views in public hearings in Washington. As a result a new form emerged that gave substantial protection to the mortgagor. Thus, we can use this form as a model of a pro-consumer mortgage and discuss its provisions. The FNMA varies slightly from the FHLMC version. These differences will be commented upon. The form as it existed prior to the Washington hearings will hereafter be referred to as the original FNMA form.

§ 455. The chattel clause. The original FNMA form contained a broad chattel clause. The philosophy behind inclusion of this clause still seems sound to many lenders. Where a conventional loan is made on a relatively new house, it is quite likely that part of the value on which the loan is made consists of various items in the package kitchen, for example, stove, refrigerator, dishwasher, and the like. Often these are built-in or special order items, making for an efficient and attractive kitchen. These items are so commonly considered as "going with the house" that most builder-sellers do not dream of giving the homebuyer a bill of sale. The law on the nature of these articles is unclear. The possibility remains that some courts will continue to view these articles as chattels. True fixtures, such as the building itself, the sink, toilet, bathtubs etc., are real estate and pass by the mortgage. Chattels are not included in the mortgage security unless (1) the mortgage expressly covers them, or (2) a special chattel security document covers them. If a mortgagor defaults and foreclosure occurs, removal by the mortgagor of these items harms the lender. In the first place, the lender has lost part of the security he counted on. In the second place, these special-order items are difficult to replace. Nevertheless consumer advocates carried the field in Washington, and the final draft covers only "fixtures," a meaningless addition because every mortgage automatically carries fixtures.

Possibly the best solution for the lender is to use the FNMA final draft, but to supplement this by a chattel filing under the Uniform Commercial Code covering all items installed by a builder-seller. This can be defended on the ground that these items were intended to "go with the house" and removal thereof leaves the lender with a kitchen that is unsaleable. Where, however, the house contains no builder-furnished items, as would be true with many older residences, and the kitchen is of the old-fashioned variety, the lender might well omit the chattel clause and the chattel security. Where the security is an older residence with a remodeled kitchen, the use of a chattel security becomes a matter for negotiation. If the value added by the remodeled kitchen is a significant part of the value on which the loan is made, the loan commitment should require that the mortgagor sign a chattel security. It would be best to avoid inclusion of this type of requirement in the printed part of the loan commitment. It should be typed in, preferably in capitals, so that there can be no question about the borrower understanding what he is agreeing to.

§ 456. Prepayment privilege. Inclusion of an across-the-board prepayment privilege is fine for the borrower and bad for the lender. The lender cannot increase the mortgage interest rate when interest rates go up. But the borrower can refinance at the lower rates if interest rates go down. On the other hand, the borrower can legitimately argue for some sort of prepayment privilege when he sells his house, a decision that is often forced on the borrower by an employee transfer, retirement, or illness. The FHLMC mortgage continues to retain a prepayment privilege penalty if and only if the borrower prepays with money borrowed from another lender. This is logical because the lender ought to be compensated for the cost of putting the loan on his books. FNMA has completely eliminated the prepayment penalty. Where FNMA buys an FHLMC mort-gage, it does not enforce the prepayment penalty as long as it owns the mortgage.

Different considerations are applicable to the situation where a mortgagor occa-sionally makes a payment of two or three times the required monthly payment under a mortgage provision permitting him to do so. Here the issue is whether this should give the mortgagor the right to a moratorium when he suffers adversity. Up to the present time the court decisions have held that the mortgagor is not entitled to a moratorium and that, in effect, the prepayments are applied to the final payments due under the mortgage. *Smith v. Renz*, 122 Cal.App.2d 535, 265 P2d 160. Some modern decisions tend to revise this view. *Bradford v. Thomas*, 470 SW2d 633. (Tex. 1971.)

Interestingly the FHLMC and FNMA notes state that "any partial prepayment shall be applied against the principal amount outstanding and shall not extend or postpone the due date of any subsequent monthly installments or change the amount of such installments, unless the holder hereof shall otherwise agree in writing." Thus this consumer-oriented mortgage resolves this problem in favor of the older pro-lender view.

In both the hazard insurance and eminent domain clause a like point of view is taken. In both of these mortgage provisions it is stated that application of such funds to the principal does not extend the due date of the monthly payments or change the amount thereof.[1]

§ 457. Acceleration clause. The acceleration clause in the note should not conflict with the acceleration clause in the mortgage. For example, if the note says that acceleration may be declared if a default continues for thirty days, the mortgage should also specify thirty days.

You will see many negotiable mortgage *notes* that permit acceleration only for default in payment of principal or interest. The clause in the *mortgage* is much broader, permitting acceleration for breach of any of the mortgage covenants, which include matters such as payment of real estate taxes, maintenance of hazard insurance, and the like. This introduces a problem. To understand the problem, let us first state an obvious proposition of law, namely: the function of the mortgage note is to create a personal liability for payment on the part of the mortgagor, while the function of the mortgage is to create a lien on the mortgage land. Obviously these are two distinct matters. Neverthe-less, it is traditional with mortgagees in many jurisdictions to seek in one action, i.e., the foreclosure suit, foreclosure of the lien of the mortgage and also a deficiency decree or judgment against the mortgagor for any unpaid balance remaining after the foreclosure sale has resulted in the customary *pro tanto* satisfaction of the mortgage debt. If an acceleration is declared for breach of a mortgage covenant, for example a breach of the covenant to pay real estate taxes, and a comparable event of default permitting accelera-tion of the mortgage note is not set forth in such note, in many states the mortgagee can foreclose his mortgage but he cannot obtain a deficiency judgment. Likewise, there is a problem if the mortgage contains an acceleration clause but the note does not. All courts hold that in case of default the acceleration clause in the mortgage can be invoked and the

---

[1] © Copyright, Kratovil, *Residential Mortgages in the Age of Consumerism*, Chicago Title Insurance Co., Lawyer's Supplement (1973). Reprinted by permission.

mortgage may be foreclosed for the full amount of the mortgage debt. However, some courts hold that the mortgagee cannot obtain a deficiency judgment because by its terms the *note* is not yet due. *Connerty v. Richsteig*, 379 Ill. 360, 41 N.E.2d 476. Other courts will permit the entry of a deficiency judgment in such case. *Bollenbach v. Ludlum*, 84 Okla. 14, 201 Pac. 982; 34 A.L.R. 848. These courts regard the mortgage and note as part of one contract. To meet this situation you can set forth *in the mortgage note*, as an event authorizing acceleration, a breach of any of the covenants of the mortgage, setting them forth *in extenso*. This may be done under the Uniform Commercial Code, as long as the note sets forth the covenants and does not attempt simply to incorporate the covenants of the mortgage by reference.

Another trap to be avoided is the automatic or *ipso facto* acceleration. Some acceleration clauses state simply that in case of default or breach of covenant the mortgage debt shall become due. A number of courts take this quite literally. If a default occurs, the mortgage debt becomes due. 88 U. of Pa.L.Rev. 94, 95, 108. Considering the likelihood that most mortgagors will occasionally be late with their payments, this is something of a nuisance. Moreover, in some states a default under such a mortgage starts the statute of limitations running on enforcement of the mortgage. Obviously the clause should state that acceleration takes place at the option of the mortgagee.

Occasionally you will encounter a clause providing that foreclosure of the mortgage from time to time as to part or parts of the debt then due shall not impair the right to foreclose as to the remainder. This clause may be helpful where the mortgagor deliberately defaults, hoping to coerce the mortgagee into accelerating the entire mortgage debt. This the mortgagor might hope to do, for example, where the mortgage lacks a prepayment privilege and commands an interest rate substantially higher than the current rate. It would be to the mortgagor's advantage to refinance and to the mortgagee's advantage to prevent this. Here, also, the *ipso facto* acceleration clause would work to the disadvantage of the mortgagee.[2]

There is an aspect of acceleration that has attracted considerable interest recently. A mortgage may contain a clause giving the mortgagee the right to accelerate if the mortgagor sells or conveys the land without the written consent of the mortgagee. Such clauses are valid. *Baker v. Leight*, 91 Ariz. 112, 370 P2d 268; *Coast Bank v. Minderhout*, 61 Cal.2d 311, 44 Los Angeles Bar Bulletin 64 (1968); *Jones v. Sacramento Sav. & Loan Ass'n.*, 56 Cal. Reptr. 741, *Jacobson v. McClanahan*, 43 Wash.2d 751, 264 P2d 253; *Gunther v. White*, 289 SW2d 529; *Walker Bank & Tr. Co. v. Neilson*, 490 P2d 328; *Malouff v. Midland F. S. & L. Ass'n.*, 509 P2d 1240 (clause used to raise interest rate); *Mutual F. S. & L. Ass'n. v. Wisconsin Wire Works*, 205 NW2d 762. But other cases are appearing holding the clause can be used only where it is equitable to do so. *Tucker v. Pulaski F. S. & L. Ass'n.*, 481 SW2d 725. Statutes to this effect are also appearing.

The FNMA form of mortgage has dropped the due-on-sale clause but FHLMC continues it in a fairly mild form. FNMA does not enforce the clause where it holds a FHLMC mortgage.

---

[2] © Copyright, Kratovil, *Mortgage Draftsmanship*, Chicago Title Insurance Co., *Lawyer's Supplement* (1969). Reprinted by permission.

Up to the present time, in most states it was unnecessary to give the mortgagor notice of intent to accelerate and a grace period to cure defaults. A few states, either by statute or court decision require notice and provide a grace period. The final draft provides for a notice of not less than 30 days time period to cure defaults. This is something a consumer-oriented court might be likely to require, particularly where the lender has been in the habit of accepting late payments without protest. A clause along these lines belongs in the consumer-oriented mortgage.

On the other hand, the chronic delinquent poses a real problem to lender. It seems reasonable to provide that opportunity to cure defaults after notice given cannot be exercised more than once in any five-year period, as the Illinois statute provides. Ill. Rev. Stat. Ch. 95 § 57.

The final FNMA form has a more lenient provision on curing defaults. It provides as follows:

BORROWER'S RIGHT TO REINSTATE. Notwithstanding Lender's acceleration of the sums secured by this Mortgage, Borrower shall have the right to have any proceedings begun by Lender to enforce this Mortgage discontinued at any time prior to entry of a judgment enforcing this Mortgage if; (a) Borrower pays Lender all sums which would be then due under this Mortgage, the Note and notes securing Future Advances, if any, had no acceleration occurred; (b) Borrower cures all breaches of any other covenants or agreements of Borrower contained in this Mortgage; (c) Borrower pays all reasonable expenses incurred by Lender in enforcing the covenants and agreements of Borrower contained in this Mortgage and in enforcing Lender's remedies as provided in paragraph 17 hereof, including, but not limited to, reasonable attorney's fees; and (d) Borrower takes such action as Lender may reasonably require to assure that the lien of this mortgage, Lender's interest in the Property and Borrower's obligation to pay the sums secured by this Mortgage shall continue unimpaired. Upon such payment and cure by Borrower, this Mortgage and the obligations secured hereby shall remain in full force and effect as if no acceleration had occurred.

§ **458. Insurance.** The pro-lender insurance clause confers the following rights upon the lender: (1) the right to select the insurer; (2) the right to select the types and amounts of coverage to be provided; (3) payment of premiums by borrower often by additions to the monthly mortgage payments of 1/12th the annual premium as estimated by the lender, and to hold the policy; (4) the right to accelerate the mortgage debt in the event of material injury to or destruction of the building; (5) the option to apply insurance proceeds to repair of the building or to apply the same in reduction of the mortgage debt; (6) if the lender decides in favor of applying the insurance proceeds to the mortgage debt, the right to receive in its own name the proceeds of the insurance, thus eliminating the problem of disagreement where the check is made payable to borrower and lender; (7) the right to make proof of loss.

The final draft does several things, namely:

(1) It gives the borrower the right to select the insurance carrier subject to approval by the lender, approval not to be unreasonably withheld. This is a somewhat innocuous concession, since few borrowers have access to commercial services that give ratings to insurance carriers, and in the great majority of the cases the lender will continue to select the insurance carrier as heretofore. Where a lender has been sending insurance business to one carrier, there is an advantage to the lender where a loss has to be adjusted. Obviously the carrier will resolve doubts in favor of the assured in determining the amount of the claim.

(2) The lender shall not require the amount of coverage to exceed the amount due

on the mortgage. Thus, if the lender forecloses, he will have to increase the insurance at his own expense.

(3) The borrower is given the option of paying premiums directly to the insurance carrier. This takes the monthly deposits out of the lender's hands. It also requires an additional operation whereby the borrower is notified when renewal time comes up and following up to see that the renewal premium is paid. This is a nuisance and it is doubtful that a court would consider omission of this borrower's privilege unconscionable.

(4) There is no acceleration clause as such in case of damage to the building, but the provision that if restoration is not economically feasible, the insurance proceeds shall be applied to the mortgage debt is an acceleration clause of sorts. This is pro-lender, since in the absence of such clause, some decisions require the lender to hold the insurance proceeds and apply them to the monthly payments as long as no other event of default occurs. *Fergus v. Wilmart,* 117 Ill. 542, 7 NE 508; *Gordon v. Ware Savings Bank,* 115 Mass. 588; *Naquin v. Investment Assn.,* 95 Tex. 313, 67 SW 85; *Thorp v. Croto,* 79 Vt. 390, 65 Atl. 562; *Zeigler v. Federal Bank* (Tex.Civ.App.), 86 SW 2d 864; 88 U. of Pa.L.Rev. 347.

(5) Unless lender and borrower agree in writing, the final form provides that insurance proceeds shall be applied to restoration or repair provided such restoration is economically feasible. And if borrower and lender cannot agree on economic feasibility, the determination of feasibility, the final form says, shall be made by an independent appraiser at lender's expense. This takes from the lender the right under pro-lender forms to make this decision. It is anyone's guess whether the old pro-lender clause would now be held unconscionable. There will always be judicial sympathy for the borrower who has no place to go for money to repair his home when the security is going to be a second mortgage on a fire-damaged home.

The forms add a requirement that in addition to economic feasibility, the security of the mortgage is not to be impaired. This addition certainly cannot be criticized by the courts. This clause is as follows:

CLAUSE: Unless Lender and Borrower otherwise agree in writing, insurance proceeds shall be applied for restoration or repair of the Property damaged, provided such restoration or repair is economically feasible and the security of this Mortgage is not thereby impaired. If such restoration or repair is not economically feasible or if the security of this Mortgage would be impaired, the insurance proceeds shall be applied to the sums secured by this Mortgage, with the excess, if any, paid to Borrower. If the Property is abandoned by Borrower or if Borrower fails to respond to Lender within 30 days after notice by Lender to Borrower that the insurance carrier offers to settle a claim for insurance benefits, Lender is authorized to collect and apply the insurance proceeds at Lender's option either to restoration or repair of the Property or to the sums secured by this Mortgage.

§ 459. Eminent domain. The pro-lender mortgage gives all condemnation awards to the lender with the right to apply them to the mortgage debt or rebuilding. An unreasonable decision by the lender, as in the comparable situation of fire damage could hurt the borrower. Here is where today's courts might well invoke the doctrine of unconscionability. The final draft deals with this problem as follows:

CLAUSE: Condemnation. The proceeds of any award or claim for damages, direct or consequential, in connection with any condemnation or other taking of the Property, or part thereof, or for any conveyance in lieu of condemnation, are hereby assigned, and shall be paid, to Lender.

In the event of a total taking of the Property, the proceeds shall be applied to the sums secured by this mortgage, with the excess, if any, paid to Borrower. In the event of a partial taking of the Property, unless Borrower and Lender otherwise agree in writing there shall be applied to the sums secured by this mortgage such proportion of the proceeds as is equal to that proportion which the amount of the sums secured by this mortgage immediately prior to the date of taking bears to the value of the Property immediately prior to the date of taking, with the balance of the proceeds paid to Borrower. If Borrower and Lender are unable to agree as to the value of the Property immediately prior to the date of taking, such value shall be established by independent appraisal at Lender's expense.

If the Property is abandoned by Borrower or if after notice by Lender to Borrower that the condemnor offers to make an award or settle a claim for damages, Borrower fails to respond to Lender within 30 days of the date of such notice, Lender is authorized to collect and apply the proceeds at Lender's option either to restoration or repair of the Property or to the sums secured by this mortgage.

Unless Lender and Borrower otherwise agree in writing, any such application of proceeds to principal shall not extend or postpone the due date of the monthly installments referred to in paragraphs 1 and 2 hereof or change the amount of such installments.

The FHLMC form omits the language about the independent appraiser.

§ 460. **Warranties of title.** The old pro-lender mortgage contains a warranty that the title is free and clear of all liens and encumbrances. This is commonly done by use of statutory language like "mortgage and warrant." In commercial and industrial mortgages the subject clause is often drafted with care. In the residential mortgage, a subject clause is given no attention. In consequence, if there is an encumbrance on the title, the lender is technically at liberty to accelerate immediately upon the signing of the mortgage because nearly all titles are subject to building restriction, utility easements, etc., and the acceleration clause permits acceleration if there is breach of any covenant. Probably no courts today would permit this. Surely no lender would ever attempt it. Acceleration because of defects in title seldom occurs as long as the mortgage is not in default. After default, acceleration can take place for that reason alone. The bickering about this clause, in consequence, was somewhat unrealistic. But the final draft contained a rather realistic clause:

CLAUSE: Borrower covenants that Borrower is lawfully seized of the estate hereby conveyed and has the right to mortgage, grant and convey the Property, that the Property is unencumbered, and that Borrower will warrant and defend generally the title to the Property against all claims and demands, subject to any easements and restrictions listed in a schedule of exceptions to coverage in any title insurance policy insuring Lender's interest in the Property.

§ 461. **Tax and insurance escrow.** The pro-lender mortgage provides that the borrower shall pay each month 1/12th of the amount of the taxes and insurance as estimated by the lender. It specifies no depository. It gives no interest to the mortgagor on the deposits. Consumer advocates made an issue of this. A number of statutes have been enacted as a result. The final form covered this situation as follows:

FUNDS FOR TAXES AND INSURANCE. Subject to Lender's option under paragraphs 4 and 5 hereof, Borrower shall pay to Lender on the day monthly installments of principal and interest are payable under the Note, until the Note is paid in full, a sum (herein "Funds") equal to one-twelfth of the yearly taxes and assessments which may attain priority over this mortgage, and ground rents on the Property, if any, plus one-twelfth of the yearly premium installments for hazard insurance, plus one-twelfth of the yearly premium installments for mortgage insurance, if any, all as reasonably estimated initially and from time to time by Lender on the basis of assessments and bills and reasonable estimates thereof. Lender shall hold the Funds in an account which is insured by a Federal or State agency and shall apply the Funds from said account to pay said taxes, assessments, insurance, premiums and ground rents. Lender shall make no charge for so holding and applying the Funds, analyzing said account or verifying and compiling said assessments and bills. Borrower and Lender may agree in writing at the time of execution of this mortgage that interest on the Funds shall be paid to Borrower, and unless such agreement is made, Lender shall not be required to pay Borrower any interest on the Funds. Lender shall give to Borrower, without charge, an annual accounting of the Funds showing credits and debits to the Funds, interest, if any, paid to Borrower on the Funds and the purpose for which each debit to the Funds were made. The Funds are pledged as additional security for the sums secured by this mortgage.

If the amount of the Funds held by Lender, together with the future monthly installments of Funds payable prior to the due dates of taxes, assessments, insurance premiums and ground rents, shall exceed the amount required to pay said taxes, assessment, insurance premiums and ground rents as they fall due, such excess shall be, at Borrower's option, either promptly repaid to Borrower or credited to Borrower on monthly installments of Funds. If the amount of the Funds held by Lender shall not be sufficient to pay taxes, assessment insurance premiums and ground rents as they fall due, Borrower shall pay to Lender any amount necessary to make up the deficiency within 30 days after notice from Lender to Borrower requesting payment thereof.

Upon payment in full of all sums secured by this mortgage, Lender shall promptly refund to Borrower any Funds held by Lender.

If under paragraph 17 hereof the Property is sold or the Property is otherwise acquired by Lender, Lender shall apply, no later than immediately prior to the sale of the Property or its acquisition by Lender, any Funds held by Lender at the time of application as a credit against the sums secured by this mortgage.

The FHLMC form is somewhat different as to the institutions in which these funds must be kept.

So much heat has been generated by this situation, that it seems prudent to use a clause along these lines, modifying it if local statutes require that tax bills and insurance premiums be furnished the borrower or that interest is to be paid the borrower on the deposits.

Where the mortgage or note calls for monthly deposits to pay real estate taxes, hazard insurance, etc., the mortgage or note will "pledge" these deposits to the lender, and give him the right, in case of default, to apply these sums in payment of the mortgage debt.

§ 462. Inspection. Consumer groups objected to the unfettered right of inspection by the lender in the original drafts. The notion of the lender using this right to harass a borrower by untimely inspections is unrealistic to anyone familiar with the mortgage business. Mortgage lenders have their hands full taking care of their legitimate concerns. The villain of the old-time dramas could not stay in the first mortgage business today. Perhaps this is the notion that makes the consumer position unrealistic. Mortgage lenders are not vicious predators preying on unsuspecting, unsophisticated borrowers. First mortgage lending is a highly competitive, strictly regulated business, with sensitive concern for its image. At all events, the final draft contained a clause every lender can live with:

CLAUSE: Inspection. Lender may make or cause to be made reasonable entries upon and inspections of the Property, provided that Lender shall give Borrower notice prior to any such inspection specifying reasonable cause therefor related to Lender's interest in the Property.[3]

---

[3] © Copyright, Kratovil, *The Residential Mortgage in the Age of Consumerism*, Lawyer's Supplement, Chicago Title Insurance Company (1974).

§ **463. The mortgage debt.** Of course, every good draftsman will take care to describe the mortgage debt accurately in the mortgage. Some jurisdictions are more particular about this than others, and will deprive a recorded mortgage of its priority over subsequent liens if it falls short in this respect. Thus it has been held that where a mortgage failed to state the amount of the mortgage debt, subsequent purchasers and lienors were not charged with notice of the recorded mortgage. *Bullock v. Battenhousen*, 108 Ill. 28. It has also been held that where the mortgage recited that it secured a certain note for a certain sum of money, and the mortgagor owed the money but no note had been executed, the mortgagee lost all priority over subsequent lienors because of this technical misdescription of the mortgage debt. *Ogden v. Ogden*, 180 Ill. 543, 54 NE 750. Granting that this is a rather technical holding, there is nevertheless solid authority for the proposition that the character and amount of the debt must be defined with reasonable certainty. *Bowen v. Ratcliff*, 140 Ind. 393, 39 NE 860. Where the mortgage is an open-end mortgage, that is, one securing optional future advances, the mortgage should in some way describe the future advances. To be sure there is some law for the proposition that the mortgage need not state the upper limit of the future advances. 81 ALR 631. However, legislation on open-end advances will now be found in a number of states, (for example, Connecticut, Kentucky, Maryland, North Dakota, and Rhode Island) and, whether by legislation or court decision, there appears to be some tendency to require greater particularity in the mortgage description of open-end advances. Of course, any other requirement of the statute should be complied with. To achieve broad open-end lending authority, the mortgage will provide that the advances may be made to the mortgagors or either of them or to their successors in title or any of them. *Walker v. Whitmore*, 165 Ark. 276, 262 SW 678; 38 Minn.L.Rev. 507. When the advance is made, an appropriate document should be executed by the borrower acknowledging that it is an advance made under the mortgage, so that the mortgagee has something that can be introduced in evidence in the event of foreclosure.

§ **464. The promissory note.** Whenever possible the obligation secured by the mortgage should be a negotiable note. Where the mortgage secures a negotiable note, the great weight of authority is that a negotiation of the note to a holder who takes it in good faith, for value, and without notice before maturity, i.e., a holder in due course, to whom the mortgage is then formally assigned, will take the mortgage as he takes the note, free from defenses that would have been available to the mortgagor against the mortgagee. Kratovil, *Mortgages* §§ 185, 19359 CJS. Mortgages, § 369. The advantages offered by this rule are so important that it is difficult to understand why so many mortgage lenders persist in using non-negotiable obligations. The need for preparing a negotiable note requires study of the Uniform Commercial Code, where the modern rules of negotiability are set forth. The Code provides that the statement (commonly occurring in mortgage notes) that the note is secured by a mortgage does not render the note non-negotiable. UCC § 3-105(1)(e). Where the note is executed by a partnership or a trustee, the note is negotiable even though payment is limited to the assets of the partnership or trust. UCC § 3-105(1)(h). But to make the note payable only out of *the land mortgaged* and not out of the entire assets of the partnership or trust leaves the note non-negotiable. *Ibid.* While the Code requires the note to be payable at a definite time, a

note that is "subject to any acceleration" complies with that requirement. UCC §
3-109(1)(c). This is liberal language. One would think that the note could list events of
default that would subject the note to acceleration in a form as comprehensive as the
events of default spelled out in the mortgage. However, the note must not refer to the
mortgage for the events of default, for the Code states that a promise is not negotiable if
the instrument states that it is subject to or governed by any other agreement. UCC §
3-105(2)(a).

§ 465. Description of the mortgaged property. An accurate description of the
mortgaged land is of great importance. Even greater care must be exercised in this regard
than is necessary in the case of deeds. A purchaser usually goes into possession of the
land under his deed and thereby gives all the world notice of his rights, since possession
imparts constructive notice, whereas a mortgagee rarely goes into possession and
therefore depends entirely on the recording of his mortgage to give all subsequent
purchasers and mortgagees notice of his rights.

§ 466. Easement provisions. When *A* owns Lots 1 and 2 and mortgages Lot 1 to
B, he may, at *B's* insistence, include in the mortgage a grant of easement over part of Lot
2. Such a clause may run somewhat as follows: *And as further security for payment of the
debt above described, the mortgagor mortgages and grants to the mortgagee, his heirs
and assigns, as an easement appurtenant to Lot 1 aforesaid, a perpetual easement for
ingress and egress over, under and across the south ten feet of Lot 2 in the subdivision
aforesaid.*

When *A* owns Lots 1 and 2 and is mortgaging Lot 1 to *B*, *A* may wish to reserve, for
the benefit of Lot 2, an easement over part of Lot 1. In such case, an appropriate clause of
reservation may be included in the mortgage.

The foregoing illustrations show how a mortgage can *create* an easement. When
such a mortgage is foreclosed, ownership of the dominant and servient tenements passes
into separate hands, and the real existence of the easement begins. Suppose, however,
that *A* owns a lot that enjoys the benefit of a *previously created* easement. He mortgages
the lot, and in the mortgage nothing is said concerning the easement. The mortgage is
foreclosed. The purchaser at the foreclosure sale enjoys the benefit of the easement, for
an appurtenant easement runs with the land even though it is not mentioned in the
mortgage or in the foreclosure proceedings. 38 Cal.L.Rev. 426. Despite this well-
understood and well-established rule, mortgage lenders tend to require that a mortgage
on land that enjoys the benefit of a previously created easement describe the easement.
There is no harm in complying with this requirement. In such case one can conveniently
divide the mortgage description into two parcels. The fee title is set forth in the first
paragraph and is captioned *Parcel I*. The easement is set forth in the second paragraph of
the description and is captioned *Parcel II*. It usually reads somewhat as follows:

PARCEL II

*Easement for the benefit of Parcel I created by easement grant dated—and recorded on—in
Book—Page—for ingress and egress over, under, and across the following described premises:*
A description of the easement tract follows the quoted language.
This procedure simplifies the ordering of the mortgage title insurance policy, which should
contain parcel descriptions identical with those in the mortgage.

§ 467. Extensions. It is best to include a provision that any extension of time granted by the mortgagee to any purchaser of the mortgaged land shall not release the personal liability of the mortgagor. This is because of the rule that an extension of time granted to an assuming grantee may release the personal liability of the mortgagor. 41 ALR 277.

SUGGESTED CLAUSE: This mortgage shall secure any and all renewals, or extensions of the whole or any part of the indebtedness hereby secured however evidenced, with interest at such lawful rate as may be agreed upon and any such renewals or extensions or any change in the terms or rate of interest shall not impair in any manner the validity of or priority of this mortgage, nor release the Mortgagor from personal liability for the indebtedness hereby secured.

§ 468. Foreclosure provisions-deeds of trust-successor trustee clauses. This chapter focuses primarily on the smaller mortgages. There is room here for a word or two of advice on foreclosure provisions helpful where non-judicial foreclosure is contemplated. The discussion will proceed in terms of the *deed of trust* (also called *trust deed*), for it is this instrument that is most often used where non-judicial foreclosure is to take place by exercise of a power of sale. The deed of trust that contains a power of sale will, of course, recite in some detail the events of default that will give rise to foreclosure and exercise of the trustee's power of sale. Provision will also be made in the deed of trust for publication and posting or mailing of a notice of the public sale that the trustee is to hold. The trustee's deed to the purchaser at the foreclosure sale will, in turn, recite the events of default that occurred and that requisite notices were published, and posted or mailed. The recitals in the trustee's deed normally established a rebuttable presumption of the truth of the facts recited therein. 32A CJS. *Evidence,* § 767. However, the deed of trust may contain a clause that such recitals are *conclusive evidence* of the truth of the statements therein contained, and some decisions sustain the validity of such a provision. *Ibid.* Such provisions, of course, are common in trust instruments. *Eisel v. Miller,* 84 F2d 174 (CCA 8th 1936). Absent such a provision the recitals in the trustee's deed may be effective only as to purchaser subsequent to the original purchase at the foreclosure sale. 59 CJS. *Mortgages,* § 594. In some states statutes exist concerning the effect of recitals in trustee's deeds, *e.g.,* West's Calif. Civil Code Annot., § 2924 (1967 pocket part); Vernon Mo. Stat. Annot., § 443. 380. Obviously the deed of trust should contain a strong clause as to the conclusiveness of the recitals in the trustee's deed. Parenthetically, this aspect of the law is bound to assume increasing importance as more and more states sanction power of sale foreclosure as a means of reducing foreclosure costs. In recent times a number of states have enacted such legislation. Idaho (1957), Oregon (1959), Utah (1961), Montana (1963), Nebraska (1965), and Washington (1965). Other states using this method are Alabama, Alaska, California, Colorado, District of Columbia, Mississippi, Missouri, Nevada, New Mexico, North Carolina, South Carolina, Tennessee, Texas, Virginia, and West Virginia. A federal statute is before Congress.

Some state laws now call for the recording of a notice of default at a specified interval of time before the holding of the foreclosure sale under the power. There is no harm in including a provision in the deed of trust that recitals in such notice shall be conclusive in favor of the purchaser at the sale.

Since by far the great majority of mortgages are paid in full, it is common practice to name an employee of the lender as trustee in the trust deed. When the debt is paid he can execute a release or discharge of the deed of trust at no cost to the lender. However, if default occurs so that exercise of the power of sale becomes necessary, a somewhat awkward conflict of interest arises. The trustee is trustee for both borrower and lender and ought to act with impartiality toward both. 3 Jones, Mortgages 798 (8th ed. 1928). Hence it renders the sale less vulnerable to attack if the deed of trust contains a clause authorizing the lender to substitute trustees, which power should be exercised before foreclosure, so that a disinterested third party is named to conduct the sale. In a few states this must be done. 138 ALR 1013, 1022. Care should be exercised to confer the power of substitution on any holder from time to time of the mortgage note, for if the power is conferred in so many words on the present owner of the note, it cannot be exercised by a subsequent owner. *Webb v. Biles*, 192 Miss. 474, 6 So2d 117. Moreover, the clause should provide that substitution can be effected without notice to the mortgagor. *Blaustein v. Aiello*, 229 Md. 131, 182 A2d 353. *See* 98 ALR 1132, 1141.[4]

§ **469. Master mortgage.** The master mortgage has been discussed elsewhere. Kratovil, *Mortgages* § 58. See Form No. 13.

The back of the form contains the mortgage covenants.

§ **470. Assignment of mortgage.** A mortgage can be assigned with or without covenants by the assignor. Obviously, *E* wants an assignment with covenants and *R* prefers an assignment without covenants. An assignment covenants clause follows:

CLAUSE: And the assignor covenants that there is now owing upon said mortgage, without offset or defense of any kind, the principal sum of $ _____ with interest thereon at eight per centum per annum from the day of _____ AD 1974.

§ **471. Waiver of defenses.** In a minority of the states the rule that a negotiable note imparts the quality of negotiability to the mortgage is not followed. 138 ALR 566, 576. Even in states that follow the majority rule, events may occur that may deprive the assignee of the benefits of negotiability. For example, installment notes are commonplace today. In some states the fact that at the time of the purchase of the note some prior installment was unpaid may prevent the purchaser from being a holder in due course. 170 ALR 1029. For these reasons the mortgagee's attorney will probably require the mortgagor to sign a *waiver of defenses*, also sometimes called an *estoppel certificate*. This document is commonly addressed *To All Whom It May Concern*, and recites that the mortgagor has no defenses to the enforcement of the mortgage or mortgage note. This constitutes a representation made to any subsequent purchaser of the note, is intended to be relied upon by the purchaser, and when so relied upon creates an estoppel. 2 Jones, Mortgages, § 792 (8th ed. 1928); 59 CJS Mortgages, § 369; 31 CJS Estoppel, § 81; 51 ALR2d 886, 894. Thus, through the operation of estoppel, defenses good between the mortgagor and mortgagee, such as the defense of absence of consideration, are unavailing as to the assignee. Local law should always be consulted as to the scope of the estoppel created. With respect to the defense of usury, for example, in some

---

[4] © Copyright Kratovil, *Mortgage Draftsmanship*, Chicago Title Insurance Co., *Lawyer's Supplement* (1969). Reprinted by permission.

Form No. 13

RECORDING REQUESTED BY

AND WHEN RECORDED MAIL TO

NAME
ADDRESS
CITY &
STATE

Title Order No._____ Escrow No._____

——————— SPACE ABOVE THIS LINE FOR RECORDER'S USE ———————

DEED OF TRUST AND ASSIGNMENT OF RENTS WITH REQUEST FOR NOTICE

By This Deed of Trust, made this   day of   , 19   , between

, herein called Trustor,

whose address is _____
        (number and street)   (City)   (State)   (Zip Code)

and CHICAGO TITLE INSURANCE COMPANY a Missouri corporation, herein called Trustee, and

, herein called Beneficiary,

Trustor grants, transfers, and assigns to trustee, in trust, with power of sale, that property in
County, California, described as:

Trustor also assigns to Beneficiary all rents, issues and profits from said real property reserving, however, the right to collect and use the same so long as there is no existing default hereunder and does hereby authorize Beneficiary to collect and recover the same in the name of Trustor or his successor in interest by use of any lawful means.

FOR THE PURPOSE OF SECURING: (1) Payment of the indebtedness evidenced by one promissory note of even date herewith in the principal sum of $, payable to Beneficiary or order; (2) Payment of any additional sums and advances hereafter made by Beneficiary or his assignee to Trustor or his successor in ownership of the real property encumbered hereby; (3) Performance of each agreement of Trustor herein contained.

TO PROTECT THE SECURITY OF THIS DEED OF TRUST, TRUSTOR AGREES that all of the provisions of Section A, Paragraphs 1 through 5, and IT IS MUTUALLY AGREED that all of the provisions of Section B, Paragraphs 1 through 10, both of that certain Fictitious Deed of Trust recorded on the date, as the instrument number and in the book and at the page of Official Records in the office of the county recorder of the county where said property is located, noted below opposite the name of such county, viz.:

COUNTY	RECORDING DATE	INST. NO.	BOOK	PAGE	COUNTY	RECORDING DATE	INST. NO.	BOOK	PAGE
Kern	5-20-68	30035	4162	480	Santa Barbara	5-20-68	16024	2232	955
Los Angeles	1-12-67	1159	T-5220	910	San Diego	1-12-67—Series 8		1967	5000
Orange	1-12-67	6275	8151	422	San Luis Obispo	5-20-68	9567	1476	459
Riverside	1-12-67	3020			Ventura	1-12-67	1498	3092	378
San Bernardino	1-12-67	453	6757	41					

(which provisions, identical in all counties, are printed on the reverse side hereof) are hereby incorporated herein and the parties hereto agree to be bound thereby as though fully set forth herein. All references to property, obligations and parties in the provisions of said Fictitious Deed of Trust are the property, obligations and parties set forth in this deed of Trust.

The undersigned Trustor requests that a copy of any notice of default and any notice of sale hereunder be mailed to him at the address set forth above.

In accordance with Section 2924b, Civil Code, request is hereby made by the undersigned TRUSTOR that a copy of any Notice of Default and a copy of any Notice of Sale under Deed of Trust recorded_____

In Book_____, Page_____, Official Records of_____County, California, as

affecting above described property, executed by_____ . _____

as Trustor in which_____

is named as Beneficiary, and_____as Trustee,

be mailed to_____

whose address is_____
        (City)   (State)   (Zip Code)

jurisdictions the waiver of defenses is effective only if procured at the time the assignment of mortgage is made. At that time, of course, the mortgagor is under no pressure to sign the document and signs it voluntarily, if at all. Some title companies always require this when asked to issue a policy to an assignee of the mortgage. Where one is dealing with a mortgage that falls within the ambit of consumer protection laws, one had better check to see how such law curtails the protection of an assignee.

A customary form of waiver of defenses is appended (Form No. 14).

§ 472. Truth in lending. The truth in lending law requires the lender to disclose the actual interest to the borrower. All lenders have a form for this purpose. Borrower and lender will have duplicates of this, lender's copy receipted by borrower.

§ 473. Mortgage escrows. Since a mortgage given to secure a debt does not become a lien until a debt exists, mere recording of a mortgage does not create a lien. Liens attaching to the land prior to the time that the mortgage money is disbursed to the mortgagor are sometimes held to be superior to the lien of the mortgage. This would not be true where the mortgagee has given the mortgagor a binding commitment to make the loan, as has been discussed in connection with the mortgage debt. Where a binding commitment to loan money exists, the lien of the mortgage relates back to the date of the

Form No. 14

FORM 3088—CHICAGO TITLE INSURANCE COMPANY STANDARD FORM WAIVER OF DEFENSES OR ESTOPPEL CERTIFICATE

CHICAGO TITLE INSURANCE COMPANY

ORDER NO.

COUNTY

STATE

WAIVER OF DEFENSES

To Whom It May Concern:

This is to certify that the mortgage or trust deed dated

and recorded   in Book   Page

in the above County and the note or notes thereby secured are good and valid and in all respects free from all defenses, both in law and in equity, and that said note together with the interest thereon, will be fully paid when and as the same becomes due in accordance with the terms thereof, and that any person purchasing said note or otherwise acquiring any interest therein, may do so in reliance upon the truth of the matters herein recited.

This certificate is made for the purpose of better enabling the legal holder or holders of said instruments to sell, pledge or otherwise dispose of the same, freely at any time, and so as to insure the purchaser or purchasers, pledgee or pledgees thereof against any claim of defense thereto by the maker or makers thereof, their heirs, personal representatives or assigns

Dated this   day of   19

To be signed by
makers of note
and mortgage.

_____

_____

recording of the mortgage. Also, if the mortgagee deposits his mortgage money in escrow, with directions to pay the money over to the mortgagor if an examination of title shows the mortgage as a first lien on the date of its recording, then immediately upon the recording of the mortgage its position as a first lien is established. Not only has the mortgagee obligated himself to make the loan, but he has also parted with control over the mortgage money. Indeed, it is certainly arguable that the mortgagee has disbursed the mortgage money by paying it over to the escrowee. In such case the priority of the mortgage over liens accruing after its recording is assured. Thus there are *mortgage escrows* as well as *sale escrows*.

There are mortgage attorneys who push this thinking one step further. Under their procedures the mortgagee in a construction loan, for example, issues his check for the loan proceeds to the borrower, who immediately endorses it to the mortgage lender's special construction loan account set up for the particular loan. As long as it is clear that the funds are held in trust for the borrower, some courts regard this as a disbursement as of the date the original check issues. *Home Hardware Co. v. Denbigh*, 17 Del.Ch. 234, 152 Atl. 130; *Whilan v. Exchange Trust Co.*, 214 Mass. 121, 100 NE 1095. Obviously it would be unsafe to rely on such a procedure in the absence of satisfactory local decisions sanctioning it. Using a third party corporate escrowee is certainly a far safer practice.

Again, there are cases where a buyer is borrowing money to complete his purchase. The mortgagee does not want his money paid out until title shows clear in the buyer, who is the mortgagor. The seller will not want to part with title until and unless he is assured of receiving the purchase price. This difficult situation is easily taken care of through an escrow. The deed, mortgage, and mortgage money are deposited with the escrow holder under written instructions to record the deed and mortgage and pay the mortgage money to the seller if the title examination shows the mortgage as a first lien. The interests of all parties are protected.[5]

§ 474. **Substitution of trustee.** Where a deed of trust goes into default and the trustee is an employee of the corporation that holds the mortgage debt, it is necessary in some states to appoint a substitute trustee who is disinterested. Kratovil, *Mortgages* § 85. Every well-drafted deed of trust provides for this.

§ 475. **Request for notice.** Increasingly, as due process requirements become more stringent, legislation is appearing along the lines of the California statute permitting junior lienors and others to lodge with the trustee in a deed of trust or to record in the Recorder's office a request to be notified of default and sale under the deed of trust. Form No. 15.

§ 476. **Request for release of deed of trust.** When the last installment is paid, the landowner will go to the trustee in a deed of trust and request a release or reconveyance. The trustee insists on a formal, written request, plus production of the cancelled papers.

§ 477. **FHLMC—insurance requirements.** The FHLMC insurance requirements on homes are as follows.

---

[5] © Copyright, Kratovil, *Mortgage Draftsmanship*, Chicago Title Insurance Company, *Lawyer's Supplement* (1969).

Form No. 15

Request for Notice
UNDER SECTION 2924b CIVIL CODE

In accordance with Section 2924b, Civil Code, request is hereby made that a copy of any Notice of Default and a copy of any Notice of Sale under the Deed of Trust recorded as Instrument No._____ on_____ _____, in book_____, page_____, Official Records of_____ County, California, and describing land therein as

Executed by_____, as Trustor, in which_____is named as Beneficiary, and_____, as Trustee, be mailed to_____ at_____
          Number and Street

          City and State
Dated_____

Insurance coverage in the following kinds and amounts is required on property covered by a home mortgage:

The scope of coverage shall be equal to or greater than Fire and Extended Coverage and shall be at least equal to that customary in the geographical area in which the mortgaged premises are located, *and* the amount of coverage shall in any case be sufficient, except for deductibles as permitted below, so that in the event of any damage or loss to the mortgaged premises, which damage or loss is of a type covered by the insurance, the insurance proceeds shall provide at least the lesser of: (i) compensation equal to the full amount of damage or loss, or (ii) compensation to the first mortgagee under the mortgage equal to the full amount of the unpaid balance of the mortgage. All buildings valued at $1,000 and over must be insured.

Such insurance must be in effect on the date of delivery of the mortgage, and the expiration date of each policy must be more than 30 days after the date of delivery.

Where Seller is aware that a mortgaged property is exposed to any appreciable hazard against which Fire and Extended Coverage does not afford protection, Seller shall advise FHLMC of the nature of such hazard and the additional insurance coverage, if any, which Seller has obtained against such hazard. If adequate insurance has not been obtained against such hazard, FHLMC may require Seller to obtain such coverage prior to accepting the mortgage for purchase.

Policies containing a deductible clause up to $200 applicable to either Fire or Extended Coverage, or both, are acceptable in States or areas where such provisions are mandatory or customary. When policies contain a Fall of Building Clause, such clause must be waived.

§ 478. FHLMC insurance requirements—multi-family dwellings. The requirements on multi-family dwellings are as follows:

With respect to each multi-family mortgage sold to FHLMC, hazard insurance must be in effect meeting all requirements above applicable to home mortgages except as follows:

Fire coverage and extended coverage must be issued by the same carrier.

The Deductible Clause may be in an amount up to $1,000 per loss on policies in excess of $1,000,000 in areas where such provision is mandatory or customary.

If there is a steam boiler in operation in connection with the mortgaged property, there must be in force boiler explosion insurance evidence by the standard form of boiler and machinery insurance policy and providing as a minimum $50,000 per accident per location.

There must be in force rent loss insurance covering abatement in rent caused by fire or any other casualty insured under a fire and extended coverage policy, in the amount of the gross rentals for a period of at least (i) 6 months in the case of a garden-type apartment building (not more than 3 stories), or (ii) 12 months in the case of all other multi-family projects.

Mortgagee Clauses must be endorsed expressly to name FHLMC (c/o Servicer at Servicer's address).

§ 479. Mortgage insurance. Private mortgage insurance exists and is available from a number of companies. 48 Calif. St. Bar. J. 684.

§ 480. FNMA environmental requirements. A mortgage banker selling a mortgage to FNMA must warrant with respect to environmental problems as follows:

Neither the mortgaged property nor appurtenances thereto, nor the subjection thereof to use and enjoyment for the purposes intended, is, or will be, violative of any applicable law, rule or regulation, existing at the time of Seller's delivery of the mortgage to FNMA, relating to or governing the protection of the environment; that all outstanding requirements of such laws, rules and regulations have been complied with respecting said property and use thereof; that there is no pending case or proceeding directly involving such property in which compliance with any such law, rule or regulation is an issue; and that nothing further remains to be done to satisfy in full all requirements of each such law, rule or regulation constituting a prerequisite to such use and enjoyment of said property; provided, however, that this warranty shall be deemed not to have been made if a title policy affording, in substance, the same protection to FNMA is furnished by Seller.

§ 481. Forms. There is a pronounced trend toward use of the FNMA and FHLMC forms on all residential transactions. There is a different form for each state. The multi-family differs from the single-family form.

§ 482. Documents of the loan file. The mortgagee's loan file should include the following papers:

1. Application for loan, signed by borrower, and copy of mortgagee's letter of commitment.

2. Plat of survey.

3. If loan is made to finance purchase of property, the mortgagee should have a copy of the contract of sale in his files. This will prove helpful in checking appraisal of property.

4. Appraisal of property.

5. Mortgage, mortgage note, chattel lien on personal property in building, and assignment of rents and leases.

6. Assignment of mortgage and waiver of defenses if loan was purchased from original lender.

7. Operating statement showing borrower's profit and loss figures for last fiscal year, also audited financial statement. These help in determining borrower's financial responsibility on bigger loans.

8. Insurance policies, with mortgagee loss clauses attached.

9. Mortgage title policy, abstract and opinion, Torrens certificate, or other evidence of title.

10. Mortgagor's affidavit as to judgments, divorces, recent improvements, and other pertinent facts.

11. Copy of escrow agreement, if loan was closed in escrow.

12. Loan closing statement, including receipt for loan proceeds signed by borrowers.

13. If loan was a refinancing loan, the canceled mortgage and note that was taken up by the new loan.

14. Waiver of encroachments by FHA, and all other FHA documents when loan is FHA-insured.

15. Loan guaranty certificate and other documents needed in case of VA insured loans or copies of such documents.

16. Subordination of reverter if one was obtained. If any other prior mortgage or other lien was subordinated to the current mortgage, the subordination agreement, of course, should also be in the loan files.

17. Certified copy of corporate resolutions if mortgage was made by corporation. If property mortgaged is all, or substantially all, of the assets of corporation, resolutions by both directors and stockholders may be necessary.

18. Will, trust indenture, or other trust instrument, or copy of these, if mortgagor is a trustee.

19. Full copy of building restrictions affecting the mortgaged premises, particularly if loan is a construction loan.

20. Leases to key tenants and assignments thereof to mortgagee.

21. Where a franchised chain is involved, e.g., a Holiday Inn, the mortgage should give the lender the right to declare the mortgage debt due if the franchise is revoked. It should also provide that the mortgagee can expend any sums needed to retain or revive the franchise and add these sums to the mortgage debt. Likewise, the mortgagee should have a side agreement with the chain that in case of foreclosure the chain will franchise the mortgagee as an operator and will render technical aid to bring the operation up to chain standards.[6]

---

[6] © Copyright, Kratovil, *Mortgage Draftsmanship*. Chicago Title Ins. Co., Lawyer's Supplement (1969).

25

Mortgages and Deeds of Trust in Large-Scale Transactions

§ **483. In general.** The law and practice relating to mortgages have been discussed elsewhere. Kratovil, *Mortgages, passim.*

§ **484. Mortgagor and mortgagee.** Requirements as to *R* and *E* are discussed elsewhere. *See* Chapters 5 and 6.

§ **485. Description of mortgaged property.** Requirements as to description of mortgaged property are also discussed elsewhere. *See* Chapters 8 & 9.

§ **486. Title, title insurance and survey requirements.** Requirements as to title, title insurance and surveys are covered in the mortgage loan contracts (application and commitment, for example) and are also discussed elsewhere. *See* Chapters 10 to 14, Chapters 21 to 23.

§ **487. Residential mortgages.** Most of the discussion of residential mortgages is also relevant to mortgages in large scale transactions. *See* Chapter 24.

§ **488. Lease provisions in lease that primes mortgage.** Where a mortgage is placed on leased land, obviously the rights of the lessee are paramount to those of the mortgagee. The mortgagee makes the same analysis of the lease that an intending purchaser would make.

EXAMPLE: An existing ground lease requires that the proceeds of hazard insurance will be used to rebuild a destroyed building. Obviously, the mortgagee's requirement that the hazard proceeds be applied in reduction of the mortgage debt do not square with this provision. Likewise, a mortgage provision requiring insurance policies to be lodged with the lender could conflict with provisions in the ground lease.

Perhaps a problem like this could be settled by a lease modification that would put the insurance proceeds in the hands of an institutional lender to disburse for rebuilding provisions, with a mortgage clause making a like provision.

The lease must be checked for a provision forbidding mortgages on the fee while a leasehold mortgage exists.

Because a lease that antedates the mortgage is binding on the mortgagee, he will scrutinize it carefully, noting: (1) whether the rent is adequate in his opinion; (2) whether the computations of percentage rent and minimum rentals are satisfactory; (3) whether the rent can be diminished in any way, for example, by partial condemnations, too liberal abatement of rent provisions in case of fire damage, etc.; (4) whether the lease contains an option to purchase, for if it does, this must be subordinated to the mortgage; (5) whether the tenant had been given too liberal a right to terminate the lease, *e.g.*, in case of fire damage; (6) whether the lease imposes obligations on the lessor that the mortgagee would find objectionable if he became the landlord by foreclosure; or (7) whether the lease is too liberal in giving the lessee the right to remove buildings, fixtures, etc., erected or installed by him. The fee mortgagee checks the lease especially carefully to see if it provides for abatement of rent, *e.g.* where premises become untenantable because of fire. Obviously, any lender would be concerned with such loss of revenue. If such a clause is used, it should specifically provide that it does not apply if any fee mortgagee becomes the owner by foreclosure or deed in lieu of foreclosure.[1]

Only big tenants are likely to be able to obtain abatement clauses. Even for such tenants it should be possible to obtain some agreement by T to pay a proportionate share of debt service and taxes to avoid default.

Obviously, this is a situation that calls for bargaining. Where elevator service breaks down, T will want a rent abatement good even against a mortgage lender, and for strong tenants the lender may choose to live with it.

§ 489. General observations on clauses in large-scale transaction. As one studies the forms in large-scale transactions, one notices several matters: (1) There are provisions for maintenance of $R's$ corporate status. (2) The clause describing the mortgaged property is detailed. *See* Chapters 8 and 9. (3) The warranties of title are elaborate. (4) There are provisions for liens on chattels. (5) Requirements for $R's$ financial statements are elaborate. (6) Requirements are included that R will cause to be released all future liens that prime the mortgage or obtain equal lien. Even junior liens are often forbidden. (7) Provisions limit the use of the premises, so that laws and ordinances are not violated and insurance rates are not increased. (8) Provisions as to insurance requirements and deposit of insurance and eminent domain proceeds thereof are detailed. (9) Provisions are included governing manner in which R will be allowed to contest real estate taxes. (10) E usually reserves the right to inspect the premises from time to time. (11) Special provisions needed in leasehold mortgages are detailed. (12) In mortgages of the fee, $E's$ rights with respect to leases are set forth in the mortgage and in the assignment of leases and rents. (13) Events of default are set forth in great detail. (14) The rights of E to possession and rents in case of default are detailed and, of course, vary from state to state. (15) Provisions for acceleration are detailed. (16) Where permitted by local law, $R's$ right of redemption is waived. (17) Items that should be added to the mortgage lien are covered in great detail, for example, real estate taxes or hazard insurance premiums paid by E, advances by E to complete construction, advances by E for repairs. (18) Where the mortgage is, in form, a deed of trust, the duties and rights of the trustee are spelled out and provisions for substitution of trustees, successor trustees, are elaborate. (19) A clause is included forbidding structural alterations except as

---

[1] © Copyright Kratovil, *Modern Mortgage Law & Practice*, Prentice-Hall, Inc. (1972). Reprinted by permission.

required by law. (20) Elaborate provisions are included regarding the mortgagee's rights in the event of probate or bankruptcy proceedings involving the mortgagor, condemnation proceedings or other litigation involving the mortgaged land, including the right of mortgagee to defend the proceedings or otherwise appear and protect its interests, including the addition of court costs and attorney's fees to the mortgage debt. (21) Provisions concerning foreclosure are elaborate, including provision for title searches, abstracts of title, etc., the expense of which is to be added to the mortgage debt. (22) Provisions regarding foreclosure sale are detailed. Sale *en masse* is permitted. Adjournment of sale without new publication of notice is permitted. (23) The mortgage will usually forbid any alterations in the building, the nature of the occupancy, or in the zoning without the mortgagee's written consent. (24) Provisions, or related documents relating to participation in the equity. In a period of tight money and rapidly rising interest rates, lenders tend to exact onerous terms from borrowers. Quite apart from the usury laws, mortgage law imposes a limit on what the lender is permitted to exact.

EXAMPLE: Contemporaneously with the mortgage the borrower gave the lender an option to purchase the land. The court declared the option invalid. The lender must not take advantage of the borrower's necessities by exacting "collateral advantages." *Humble Oil Refining Co. v. Doerr,* 123 N.J.S. 530, 303 A2d 898 (1973). This case cites many texts and court decisions. In the older decisions, this is commonly spoken of as "clogging the equity." Historically, the doctrine arose in England, when brewers loaning mortgage money to tavern keepers tried to insert clauses requiring the tavernkeeper to buy all his beer from the brewer-lender. This "tie in" clause was declared invalid. Today the courts will sweep this under the modern rule forbidding unconscionable contract provisions.

E will, at the time the loan is made, require in its loan commitment various devices to enable it to obtain control of the mortgagor-corporation if things begin to go wrong. *E* may require *R's* shareholders to pledge their stock to *E.* Often this is accompanied by undated resignations of *E's* officers and directors. Or *R's* stock can be placed in a voting trust. 98 ALR2d 376; 42 N.Y.U.L.Rev. 349. Or *E* can demand an irrevocable proxy from *R's* shareholders. 36 Calif.L.Rev. 281; 41 Temple L. Q. 480; 98 U. Pa.L.Rev. 401. To implement these devices the mortgage forbids any increase or change in stock or merger with another company. If *R* is a partnership, provision is included for removing the developer's manager and substituting a manager acceptable to *E.* 39 Fordham L.Rev. 579, 634. The partnership agreement may be amended to include a "buy-sell" provision enabling *E* or its subsidiary to buy out the developer. Of course, with control come the problems that inhere in control. A majority stockholder must not freeze out or otherwise oppress a minority stockholder. 70 Columb.L.Rev. 1079; 1959 Duke L. J. 436; 74 Harv.L.Rev. 1630. Owning 5 percent or more of the voting shares of a registered corporation subjects the shareholder to the reporting requirements of the Williams Act. *GAF Corp. v. Milstein,* 453 F2d 700. Problems of insider trading arise (*Feder v. Martin Marietta Corp.,* 406 F2d 260) also problems of insider information, as in *SEC v. Texas Gulf Sulphur Co.,* 401 F2d 833. If *E* obtains control, he cannot sell his control to the prejudice of the minority, for example, to one who will pillage the corporation. *Sevinney v. Keebler Co.,* 239 F.Supp.216. The directors *E* puts on *R's* board must exercise care and skill at pain of personal liability. In a limited partnership *E* must avoid exercising control in a fashion that will cause it to assume general partner liability. If E uses a subsidiary, it must be a bona fide subsidiary.

It is obvious that many of the clauses E requires must appear in the recorded mortgage, so as to impart constructive notice to subsequent purchasers and lienors, for example, the *future advances clause* and the *after-acquired property* clause. It is equally obvious that many clauses E requires are matters strictly between R and E. These matters can be relegated to an unrecorded Loan Agreement. This also cuts down recording fees. Thus all the representations and warranties by R as to corporate existence and capacity, compliance with laws and ordinances, proper corporate action to authorize the making of the loan documents, the fact that the loan does not violate earlier corporate indentures, the warranty of accuracy of the financial statements furnished E, the non-existence of other financial commitments that would affect R's financial status, the representation that all corporate taxes are paid, the warranty of non-existence of any litigation affecting R, all of these find their way into the Loan Agreement. Also found there are representations as to compliance with federal and state laws and regulations, *e.g.*, Securities Acts. Negative covenants are often found in the Loan Agreement. These are covenants not to permit junior liens or not to incur other debt, not to execute guarantees that might drain off R's assets, not to declare unusual dividends, to maintain net worth at a stipulated figure, not to change the character of its corporate business, not to sign leases as tenant calling for rentals exceeding a stipulated figure, to maintain its records at an office conveniently available to E, and so on. The Loan Agreement permits acceleration for breach of these covenants, representations and warranties, and is referred to and incorporated by reference into the real estate mortgage for this reason.

§ **490. Debt description.** The debt description is elaborate, including (1) Description of the mortgage note in detail, with late charges, prepayment penalties, after maturity interest, etc. or set forth the note verbatim (2) Construction loan agreement. (3) Amounts lender may, but need not, advance, including, taxes assessments, insurance, repairs, cost of completing buildings, all whether or not same exceed amount of stated principal. (4) Attorney's fees, title searches, foreclosure costs, and all expenses of foreclosure. (5) If the lender is to participate in borrower's gross revenues, that is set forth in detail and gross revenues are defined. (6) Future advances.

§ **491. Future advances.** Every big mortgage should contain broad future advance clauses somewhat as follows:

That it is the intent hereof to secure payment of said note whether the entire amount shall have been advanced to the Mortgagor at the date hereof or at a later date, or having been advanced, shall have been repaid in part and further advances made at a later date. It is understood that at any time before the cancellation and release of this mortgage, the note and mortgage, including the terms of repayment thereof, may from time to time be modified or amended in writing thereon by the parties liable thereon and the holder thereof to include any future advance or advances for any purpose made by the holder, as its option, to or for said parties liable thereon. Mortgagors covenant and agree that this mortgage secures any and all such future advance or advances whether the same are of the same or a different kind or quality as the original advances, and whether or not related to the original advances together with the specified interest thereon as well as the hereinbefore described principal and interest now evidenced by said note, the total principal secured hereby not to exceed _____ Million _____ Dollars at any one time. The term "note" as used in this mortgage includes said principal promissory note hereinabove described as so modified or amended, if the same shall be modified or amended, and nothing contained in this paragraph shall be considered as limiting the interest which may be secured hereby or the amount or amounts that shall be secured herein when advanced to protect the security.[2]

§ 492. Covenant to pay principal and interest—usury—prepayment.

§ 492. Covenant to pay principal and interest—usury—prepayment. Because of the need to accelerate the mortgage in case of default in payment of principal or interest and recover a deficiency decree in the foreclosure suit, the mortgage should contain a covenant to pay principal and interest as set forth in the promissory note.

For what it is worth, it is wise to include the usury-escape clause. This provides, in substance, that the parties intend no violation of the usury laws and that borrower is entitled to a premium-free credit for any sum paid that exceeds the usury limit. *Terry v. Teachworth*, 413 SW2d 918; *State v. Standard*, 414 SW2d 418; *Nevels v. Harris*, 102 SW2d 1046.

The ordinary prepayment clause will not be construed to apply to involuntary prepayment, *e.g.*, by condemnation or total destruction by fire. Some lenders, therefore, include an involuntary prepayment clause calling for a prepayment penalty in such cases.

§ 493. The acceleration clause. The acceleration clause is detailed, often spelling out numerous "events of default" that will lead to acceleration. The clause often provides that by agreement of the parties an acceleration can be rescinded without consent of junior lienors or other parties interested in the premises.

§ 494. Conventional subrogation. Routinely, every big mortgage takes advantage of the doctrine of conventional subrogation. See Kratovil, *Mortgages*, Chapter 22. This is of particular importance to a takeout lender seeking to be subrogated to the construction lender's priority over mechanic's liens.

CLAUSE: That should the proceeds of the loan made by the Mortgagee to the Mortgagor, the repayment of which is hereby secured, or any part thereof, or any amount paid out or advanced by the Mortgagee, be used directly or indirectly to pay off, discharge, or satisfy, in whole or in part, any prior lien or encumbrance upon said premises above described, or any part thereof, then the Mortgagee shall be subrogated to such other lien or encumbrance and to any additional security held by the holder thereof and shall have the benefit of the priority of all of same.[3]

§ 495. Anti-marshalling clause—holding parties secondarily liable. It is necessary to protect the mortgagee against the doctrine of marshalling of assets. Kratovil *Mortgages*, Chapter 18. It is also necessary to prevent the discharge of parties secondarily liable (guarantors, for example) by acts of the mortgagee, for example, extensions of time. Kratovil, *Mortgages*, Chapter 12. Hence the following clause is used:

CLAUSE: That Mortgagee, without notice, and without regard to the consideration, if any, paid therefor, and notwithstanding the existence at that time of any inferior liens thereon, may release any part of the premises or any person liable for any indebtedness secured hereby, without in any way affecting the liability of any party to the Note and Mortgage and without in any way affecting the priority of the lien of this Mortgage, to the full extent of the indebtedness remaining unpaid hereunder, upon any part of the security not expressly released, and may agree with any party obligated on said indebtedness or having any interest in the security described herein to extend the time for payment of

---

[2] © Copyright *Commercial Real Property Practice*, Ill. Continuing Legal Education (1972). Reprinted by permission.

[3] © Copyright Ill. Continuing Legal Ed., *Mortgages and Foreclosures* § 1.60 (1973). Reprinted by permission.

any part or all of the indebtedness secured hereby. Such agreement shall not, in any way, release or impair the lien hereof, but shall extend the lien hereof as against the title of all parties having any interest in said security which interest is subject to said lien.

In the event the Mortgagee (a) releases, as aforesaid, any part of the security described herein or any person liable for any indebtedness secured hereby; (b) grants an extension of time for any payments of the debt secured hereby; (c) takes other or additional security for the payment thereof; (d) waives or fails to exercise any right granted herein or in said Note, said act or omission shall not release the Mortgagor, subsequent purchasers of the said premises or any part thereof, or makers or sureties of this Mortgage or of said Note, or endorsers or guarantors thereof under any covenant of this Mortgage or of said Note, nor preclude the Mortgagee from exercising any right, power, or privilege herein or intended to be granted in the event of any other default then made or any subsequent default.[4]

§ 496. Multistate mortgage clause. Multistate mortgages require a special clause:

CLAUSE: The note secured by this mortgage or deed of trust is secured by mortgages and/or deeds of trust conveying lands and other property in the States of _____, _____ and _____, all of which instruments, including this instrument, being hereafter referred to as "the mortgage instruments." Wherever in this clause the word "mortgagee" occurs, it shall be deemed to include, as the context indicates, an assignee of the mortgage or other holder of the mortgage note, the trustee under a deed of trust, or a state or county officer engaged in any aspect of the enforcement of the lien of any of the mortgage instruments.

A default or breach of covenant under any of the mortgage instruments is a default or breach of covenant under each of the other mortgage instruments, and in consequence of such default or breach of covenant, the mortgagee may accelerate the mortgage debt and foreclose any or all of the other mortgage instruments or resort to any of his other remedies thereunder.

It is understood and agreed that all of the properties of all kinds conveyed by the mortgage instruments are security for the debt evidenced by said note without allocation of any one or more of the parcels or portions thereof to any portion of the mortgage debt less than the whole amount thereof.

It is specifically covenanted and agreed that the mortgagee may proceed, at the same or at different times, to foreclose said mortgage instruments, or any of them, by any proceedings appropriate in the state where any of the land lies, and that no event of enforcement taking place in any state including, without limiting the generality of the foregoing, any pending foreclosure, judgment or decree of foreclosure, foreclosure sale, rents received, possession taken, deficiency judgment or decree, or judgment taken on the said note, shall in any wise stay, preclude or bar enforcement of the mortgage instruments or any of them in any other state, and that the mortgagee may pursue any or all his remedies to the maximum extent permitted by state law until all the debt now or hereafter secured by any or all of the mortgage instruments has been paid and discharged in full.

Neither the mortgagor, nor any person claiming under him, shall have or enjoy any right to marshalling of assets, all such right being hereby expressly waived as to the mortgagor and all persons claiming under him, including junior lienors. No release of personal liability of any person whatever and no release of any portion of the property now or hereafter subject to the lien of any of the mortgage instruments shall have any affect whatever by way of impairment or disturbance of the lien or priority of any of said mortgage instruments. Any foreclosure or other appropriate remedy brought in any of the states aforesaid may be brought and prosecuted as to any part of the mortgaged security, wherever located, without regard to the fact that foreclosure proceedings or other appropriate remedies have or have not been instituted elsewhere on any other land subject to the lien of said mortgage instruments or any of them.

The mortgages and/or deeds of trust securing said note are as follows:

(Here describe all the mortgages).

In case of default in payment of principal or interest when due or in case of breach of covenant in this mortgage or any other mortgage securing said note, the entire principal may, at the option of the holder of the note, be declared immediately due and payable.

---

[4] © Copyright Ill. Continuing Legal Ed., *Mortgages and Foreclosures*, § 1.62 (1973). Reprinted by permission.

This last clause also goes into the note.

§ 497. Construction loans—incorporation of construction loan agreement.
Every construction loan mortgage should make reference to the construction loan agreement and incorporate it by reference.

Mortgagor acknowledges that the proceeds of the Note are intended to finance the construction of improvements on the premises and further covenants and agrees that:

A. The improvements to be erected on the premises shall be completed in accordance with the provisions of a certain Building Loan Agreement dated of even date herewith by and between Mortgagor and Mortgagee (Building Loan Agreement).

B. Upon default in any of the terms, provisions or covenants in the Building Loan Agreement contained, the holder of the Note may (but need not):

(1) declare the entire principal indebtedness and interest thereon due and payable.

(2) complete the construction of said improvements and enter into the necessary contracts therefor. All monies so expended shall be so much additional indebtedness secured by this Mortgage, and any monies expended in excess of the Note, shall be payable on demand with interest at the rate applicable in the Note.

The holder of said Note may exercise either or both of the aforesaid remedies.

C. All advances and indebtedness arising and accruing under the Building Loan Agreement from time to time whether or not the total amount thereof may exceed the face amount of the Note, shall be secured hereby and said Building Loan Agreement is fully incorporated in this Mortgage to the same extent as if fully set forth herein. The occurrence of any event of default under said Building Loan Agreement shall constitute a default under this Mortgage entitling the holder of the Note to all of the rights and remedies conferred upon the said holder by the terms of this Mortgage (including those set forth in sub-paragraph "B" of this paragraph), or by law, as in the case of any other default. In the event of the conflict between the terms of this Mortgage, the Note and the terms of the Building Loan Agreement, those of the Building Loan Agreement shall govern and prevail over those of the Mortgage and the Note.

It is contemplated that after whole or partial disbursement of the loan this Mortgage and the Note secured hereby will be purchased by _____ (hereinafter referred to as Permanent Investor). From and after such purchase the foregoing provisions of this paragraph 19 and all subparagraphs thereof shall be terminated and no longer effective, and thereafter no defenses, offsets, or counterclaims available to the Mortgagor, its beneficiaries, successors and assigns, arising out of said Building Loan Agreement shall be valid or effective as against the indebtedness evidenced by the Note, and as against the Permanent Investor, its successors or assigns, all said defenses, offsets, and counterclaims are waived insofar as the said indebtedness and Permanent Investor, its successors and assigns are concerned, and no party to said Building Loan Agreement shall thereafter look to this Mortgage for any right or remedy under said Building Loan Agreement nor shall any provision of said Building Loan Agreement thereafter operate to modify, limit, impair or prejudice any right or remedy hereunder, which may be had or exercised by said Permanent Investor, its successors or assigns.[5]

In some jurisdictions (New York, for example) it is necessary to record the construction loan agreement with the mortgage. This is sound practice everywhere.

§ 498. Construction loans—takeover of construction clause.
Perhaps the most important clause in the construction mortgage is that giving *E* the right to take over and complete construction in case of *R's* default. One form follows:

SUGGESTED CLAUSE: In the event of a material failure of performance by the borrower, the lender may perform borrower's obligations hereunder by taking possession of the premises together

---

[5] © Copyright, Illinois Continuing Legal Education, *Mortgages and Foreclosures* § 1.55 (1973). Reprinted by permission.

with all materials, equipment, and improvements thereon, whether affixed to the realty or not, and performing any and all work and labor necessary to complete the improvements substantially according to the plans and specifications.

To implement the rights of the lender under this paragraph, the borrower hereby constitutes and appoints the lender its true and lawful attorney in fact with full power of substitution in the premises to complete the improvements in the name of the borrower and to pay all bills and expenses incurred thereby and hereby empowers the lender as his attorney as follows: to use any funds of the borrower, including any balance which may not have been advanced, for the purposes of completing the improvements; to make such additions, changes, and corrections in the plans and specifications as may be necessary or desirable to complete the improvements in substantially the manner contemplated in the plans and specifications; to employ such contractor's agents, architects, and inspectors as shall be required; to pay, settle, or compromise all existing bills and claims which may be or become liens against the premises or as may be necessary or desirable for completion of the improvements or for the clearance of title; to execute all applications, certificates, or instruments in the name of the borrower which may be required by any governmental authority or contract; and to do any and every act which the borrower might do in its own behalf. It is further understood and agreed that this power of attorney shall be deemed to be a power coupled with an interest and cannot be revoked. The abovementioned attorney shall also have power to prosecute and defend all actions and proceeding in connection with the construction of the improvements on the premises and to take such action and require such performance under any surety bond or other obligation or to execute in the name of the borrower such further bonds or obligations as may be reasonably required in connection with the work.

Anything herein to the contrary notwithstanding, it is specifically understood and agreed that all funds furnished by the lender and employed in performance of the obligations of the borrower under this agreement shall be deemed advanced by the lender under an obligation to do so regardless of the identity of the person or persons to whom such funds are furnished. Funds advanced by the lender in the reasonable exercise of his judgment that the same are needed to complete the improvement or to protect his security are to be deemed obligatory advances hereunder and are to be added to the total indebtedness secured by the note and mortgage and said indebtedness shall be increased accordingly.

Any requirement of this contract not otherwise specifically set forth in detail shall be deemed to call for performance that is reasonable under the circumstances. In the event that a requirement of reasonable performance shall nevertheless be deemed too vague or uncertain as to admit of legal enforcement, such requirement shall be deemed null and void, but without other effect on the enforceability of this contract.

The provisions of this paragraph shall prevail over inconsistent provisions of this agreement.[6]

§ 499. Construction loans—mortgage note in construction loans. The note secured by a construction mortgage should differ from the ordinary mortgage note. There are several reasons: (1) Under the rule that the mortgage documents must describe the mortgage debt as accurately as possible, certainly the mortgage note should describe the true character of the debt. Otherwise one is left with the inference, if an ordinary mortgage note is used, that *R* owes and agrees to repay the entire principal amount of the note, which of course, is inaccurate. (2) The note agrees to repay only the amounts actually advanced. (3) The interest is payable only on the amounts actually advanced and then only from the date of the advance. Otherwise you could run into usury. (4) The acceleration clause should be tied to the events of default recited in the construction loan agreement.

§ 500. Default clause. The default clause is detailed, and in addition, includes:

---

[6] © Copyright, Kratovil, *Modern Mortgage Law & Practice* § 211 (Prentice-Hall Inc. 1972). Reprinted by permission.

MORTGAGEE'S RIGHT OF POSSESSION IN CASE OF DEFAULT

In any case in which under the provisions of this Mortgage the Mortgagee has a right to institute foreclosure proceedings, whether before or after the whole principal sum secured hereby is declared to be immediately due as aforesaid, or whether before or after the institution of legal proceedings to foreclose the lien hereof or before or after sale thereunder, forthwith, upon demand of Mortgagee, Mortgagor shall surrender to Mortgagee and Mortgagee shall be entitled to take actual possession of the premises or any part thereof personally, or by its agent or attorneys, as for condition broken, and Mortgagee in its discretion may, with or without force and with or without process of law, enter upon and take and maintain possession of all or any part of said premises, together with all documents, books, records, papers and accounts of the Mortgagor or the then owner of the premises relating thereto, and may exclude the Mortgagor, its agents or servants, wholly therefrom and may as attorney in fact or agent of the Mortgagor, or in its own name as Mortgagee and under the powers herein granted, hold, operate, manage and control the premises and conduct the business, if any, thereof, either personally or by its agents, and with full power to use such measures, legal or equitable, as in its discretion or in the discretion of its successors or assigns may be deemed proper or necessary to enforce the payment or security of the avails, rents, issues, and profits of the premises, including actions for the recovery of rent, actions in forcible detainer and actions in distress for rent, hereby granting full power and authority to exercise each and every one of the rights, privileges, and powers herein granted at any and all times hereafter, without notice to the Mortgagor, and with full power to cancel or terminate any lease or sublease for any cause or on any ground which would entitle Mortgagor to cancel the same, to elect to disaffirm any lease or sublease made subsequent to this Mortgage or subordinated to the lien hereof, to make all necessary or proper repairs, decorating, renewals, replacements, alterations, additions, betterments and improvements to the premises as to it may seem judicious, to insure and reinsure the premises and all risks incidental to Mortgagee's possession, operation and management thereof and to receive all of such avails, rents, issues and profits.

APPOINTMENT OF RECEIVER

Upon or at any time after the filing of any bill to foreclose this Mortgage, the Court may, upon application, appoint a receiver of said premises. Such appointment may be made either before or after sale without notice, and without regard to the solvency or insolvency, at the time of application for such receiver, of the person or persons, if any, liable for the payment of the indebtedness secured hereby and without regard to the then value of the premises or whether the same shall be then occupied as a homestead or not, and without bond being required of the applicant. Such receiver shall have the power to take possession, control and care of said premises and to collect the rents, issues and profits of said premises during the pendency of such foreclosure suit and, in case of a sale and a deficiency, during the full statutory period of redemption, whether there be redemption or not, as well as during any further times when the Mortgagor, its heirs, administrators, executors, successors or assigns, except for the intervention of such receiver, would be entitled to collect such rents, issues and profits, and all other powers which may be necessary or are useful in such cases for the protection, possession, control, management and operation of the premises, during the whole of said period. The Court from time to time may authorize the receiver to apply the net income in his hands in payment in whole or in part of: (i) the indebtedness secured hereby or by any decree foreclosing this Mortgage, or any tax, special assessment, or other lien which may be, or become superior to the lien hereof, or of such decree, provided such application is made prior to foreclosure sale; (ii) the deficiency in case of sale and deficiency. Any such proceedings shall in no manner prevent or retard the collection of said debt by foreclosure otherwise.

APPLICATION OF PROCEEDS OF FORECLOSURE SALE

The proceeds of any foreclosure sale of the premises shall be distributed and applied in the following order of priority: First, on account of all costs and expenses incident to the foreclosure proceedings, including all such items as are mentioned in the paragraph 33(b) hereof; second, all other items which under the terms hereof constitute secured indebtedness additional to that evidenced by the Note, with interest thereon as herein provided at the Post Maturity Rate; third, all principal and interest remaining unpaid on the Note; fourth, any overplus to Mortgagor, its successors or assigns, as their rights may appear.

RESCISSION OF OR FAILURE TO EXERCISE OPTION OF ACCELERATION

That the failure of the Mortgagee to exercise the option for acceleration of maturity and/or foreclosure following any default as aforesaid or to exercise any other option granted to the Mortgagee hereunder in any one or more instances, or the acceptance by Mortgagee of partial payments hereunder shall not constitute a waiver of any such default, except as may be provided by law, nor extend or affect the grace period, if any, but such option shall remain continuously in force. Acceleration of maturity, once claimed hereunder by Mortgagee, may, at the option of Mortgagee, be rescinded by written acknowledgment to that effect by the Mortgagee, but the tender and acceptance of partial payments alone shall not in any way affect or rescind such acceleration of maturity except as may be provided by law nor extend or affect the grace period, if any.[7]

There may also be a clause that *R* will not participate in any modification of the first mortgage or any existing lease, will not participate in any lease cancellation, accept advance rentals, or grant any rent concessions.

E may insert a clause requiring *R* to carry rent insurance or business interruption insurance.

The acceleration clause may include a "due on sale" clause. It may even permit acceleration if change of management occurs.

§ **501. Junior mortgages.** Junior mortgages are of all kinds.

EXAMPLE: *R* sells an orange grove to *E,* a builder. *R* takes back a purchase money mortgage, covenanting to subordinate it to construction loans.

EXAMPLE: *R* sells land subject to an existing first mortgage and takes back a purchase money mortgage.

EXAMPLE: *R* owns a business subject to a first mortgage and borrows on a junior mortgage to obtain additional working capital.

EXAMPLE: A wrap-around mortgage.

Certain covenants are common to all junior mortgages: (1) a covenant to pay on the first mortgage and perform all its covenants, breach to result in acceleration: (2) a covenant not to permit other mortgages or liens to attach to the premises; (3) a covenant to give the lender any notices received by the mortgagor from the first mortgagee. (4) the right reserved to the mortgagee to cure defaults or breaches under the first mortgage, sums so expended to become part of the mortgage lien and debt, even where they bring the debt over the face amount of the mortgage.

Often a clause is inserted:

CLAUSE: Promissors covenant that no sums whatsoever except said principal amounts and interest due thereon are due and payable under said notes and first mortgage which secures said note and that no default has occured or exists under said note or said mortgage which secure said note. Promissors agree that said notes and the mortgages which secure said notes will not be modified or amended without the prior written consent of note holder.

Routinely there is a clause providing for subordination of the junior mortgage to refinancing of the existing first mortgage.

---

[7] © Copyright Ill. Institute for Continuing Legal Education, *Mortgages and Foreclosures* §§ 1.71–1.75 (1973).

And there may be a clause providing that if the principal amount of the first mortgage is increased, the junior mortgage will immediately be reduced by a payment in that amount, so that the value of the equity remains the same.

Especially where a senior mortgage and junior mortgage are recorded simultaneously, it is essential that the junior recite that it is subordinate to the senior mortgage. Obviously, the senior mortgage cannot claim the benefit of prior recording in such cases. The recital is usually dispositive of the question of priority. *Tippett v. Frank*, 238 So.2d 671 (1970).

Local statutes must be consulted, such as those requiring junior mortgages to be conspicuously so labeled or statutes regulating junior lenders.

A junior mortgagee should always attempt to obtain an agreement from the first mortgagee that the latter will give notice to the former of any default with the right to cure same, and notice of the time and place of the foreclosure sale. The junior mortgagee should pay at least a nominal consideration for this agreement. Lacking this, the junior mortgage should require mortgagor to furnish like information to junior mortgagee.

Some junior mortgages assign to the mortgagee all proceeds of the foreclosure sale on the first mortgage, up to the amount due on the junior mortgage. This prevents payment of such proceeds to the mortgagor.

If a junior mortgage is made that is paramount to later leases that the first mortgagee would consider valuable as *revenue generator*, the first mortgagee may wish to include a clause giving him the right to accelerate if such a junior mortgage is executed.

§ 502. Partial releases. Where R takes back a purchase money mortgage from E, a developer, the partial release clause requires careful drafting. Among the factors to consider are: (1) The dollar figures, when and how much. Some lawyers take a rough figure of two dollars to release one dollar's worth of land. (2) The time limits for permitting partial releases. After all, there ought to be some program that liquidates the entire debt in some reasonable time. (3) The minimum amounts to be released. The mortgagee should not agree to partial releasing of minor areas. Every partial release should take out a reasonable area of land and reduce the mortgage debt in a substantial amount. (4) The geography of the released areas is important. You can run the areas releasable from the road to the rear, leaving viable, contiguous areas of unreleased land. You can't partial-release the premises into a checkerboard. This means that every new release will be contiguous to previously released land.

The provision for partial release may provide for including in the release E's rights in the streets abutting the released tract; may provide for access over the released area; may provide that no implied easements or dedications are created by the partial release; may call for a survey of the tract to be released; will call for payment of interest on the release price up to date of delivery of release.

In giving a release as to part of the mortgaged land, E must always consider whether his release may destroy his FHA insurance, VA guarantee, or the insurance given by a private mortgage insurance company. Such insurers have rights in the mortgage land which must not be impaired by any action E might take.

Obviously, the contract of sale provides the blueprint for partial releases. *See also* Chapter 17.

§ 503. Participations. It is common for an institutional lender to buy a participation in a mortgage originated by another lender. Kratovil, *Mortgages*, Chapter 16.

§ 504. Extension agreements. Where *R* seeks an extension of the time of payment of his mortgage debt, he must be prepared to make the concessions *E* demands. Thus, the extension agreement may bring chattels under the lien of the mortgage, give any condemnation award to *E,* expand the acceleration clause, and so on. The mortgage should contain an explicit provision regarding extensions. *See* § 467. Else any attempt to increase the interest rate will fail as against junior lienors. Kratovil, *Mortgages* § 134.

§ 505. Consolidations. Especially in New York, because of the high mortgage tax, it is the practice not to release the old mortgage when a new and larger loan is needed. Instead the new lender buys the old mortgage. Then a new mortgage is made and is consolidated with the old mortgage.

EXAMPLE: *R* owns land subject to a mortgage paid down to $500,000.00. He needs an additional $100,000.00. *R* could get a new mortgage of $600,000.00, and use $500,000.00 to pay off the old mortgage. But the mortgage tax would have to be paid on the new debt of $600,000. Instead *E,* the new lender, buys the old mortgage and an assignment is recorded. Or the old lender agrees to make an additional advance of $100,000. In either case, a new mortgage of only $100,000.00 is recorded, and a tax is paid on that amount. Then *R* and *E* enter into a consolidation agreement that, in effect, converts the two mortgages into one mortgage. If *E* wants additional security, the mortgage lien may also be "spread" to other property owned by *R*. This is another case where tax laws contribute to the complexity and absurdity of real estate documents.

§ 506. Parity clause. Where one mortgage secures several notes and the notes are sold to different persons, various states have different rules governing the relative priority of such notes.

1. In a number of states, (Florida, Illinois, Iowa, Kansas, Missouri, and Wisconsin, for example), there are court decisions to the effect that a mortgage given to secure two or more notes maturing at different dates must be considered as if there were as many different successive mortgages as there are notes. In other words, the various notes enjoy priority of lien in the order of their maturity. If the mortgage secures five notes, one due each year after the date of the mortgage, there would be, in effect, not one, but five mortgages. The first note falling due would be a first mortgage on the land; the second note due, a second mortgage; and so on. *In re Estate of Lalla,* 362 Ill. 621, 1 NE2d 50.

2. An entirely different rule is followed for example, in Alabama, Georgia, Oklahoma, Virginia, and West Virginia. These states follow the rule that when a mortgage secures a number of notes and the mortgagee originally holds all of them, thereafter selling and assigning one or more of the notes but retaining the remainder, the mortgagee thereby automatically makes the notes that he retains subject and subordinate to those that he has sold. *Lawson v. Warren,* 34 Okla. 94, 124 Pac. 46, 42 L.R.A.N.S. 183.

3. However, the rule followed in most states is that where a mortgage secures a number of notes, absent a contrary provision, all the notes have equal lien regardless of their maturity dates or the dates of their assignment.

Special or local rules differing from the above exist in a number of states. Whenever a mortgage secures more than one note, it is important that the mortgage contain a clause to the effect that all notes are equally secured by the mortgage without any preference or priority by reason of time of maturity, negotiation, or otherwise. This is known as the *parity clause* or *preference and priority clause*. Under such a clause, all notes have equal lien. Failure to understand these rules has led to much trouble. Many printed mortgage forms are intended for use only when the mortgage secures but one note; hence no parity clause appears. If such a form is used to secure several notes, particularly if the notes are to be owned by different people, the draftsman should be aware of the need for making appropriate changes.

SUGGESTED FORM: All notes secured by this mortgage are equally secured thereby without any preference or priority of one over the other by reason of priority of maturity, negotiation or otherwise.[8]

§ 507. Application of insurance proceeds or condemnation award clause:

All monies coming into the mortgagee's hands or to which the mortgagee may become entitled in connection with said premises and not applied to reconstruction or repair of improvements on said premises may be applied in reduction of the mortgage debt. All such monies and all prepayments of the mortgage debt shall be applied in reduction of the last maturity installments of said debt. Such application does not extend or reduce mortgage payments due hereunder.

The foregoing clause is needed to forestall arguments that money coming into *E's* hands gives *R* the right to a moratorium on mortgage payments.

§ 508. Mortgage escrows. Since a mortgage given to secure a debt does not become a lien until a debt exists, mere recording of a mortgage does not create a lien. Liens attaching to the land prior to the time that the mortgage funds are disbursed to the mortgagor are sometimes held to be superior to the lien of the mortgage. This would not be true where the mortgagee has given the mortgagor a binding commitment to make the loan. Where a binding commitment to lend money exists, the lien of the mortgage relates back to the date of the recording of the mortgage. Also, if the mortgagee deposits his mortgage money in escrow, with directions to pay the money over to the mortgagor if an examination of title shows the mortgage as a first lien on the date of its recording, then immediately upon the recording of the mortgage its position as a first lien is established. Not only has the mortgagee obligated himself to make the loan, but he has also parted with control over the mortgage money. Indeed, it is certainly arguable that the mortgagee has disbursed the mortgage money by paying it over to the escrowee. In such case, the priority of the mortgage over liens accruing after its recording is assured. Thus, there are mortgage escrows as well as sale escrows.

§ 509. Commercial mortgage insurance. Insurance on residential mortgages is, of course, well understood. Typically, the commercial insurers issue coverage more quickly and with less red tape than FHA. FNMA requires commercial insurance in many cases, notably on condominium loans. Less known is the insurance that is available on mortgages of commercial property. One of the large companies will insure

---

[8] © Copyright Kratovil, *Mortgage Draftsmanship.* Chicago Title Insurance Company, *Lawyer's Supplement* (1969). Reprinted by permission.

loans up to $5,000,000.00. Normally, you can get a commitment two weeks after application.

§ **510. Other references.** Obviously, the chapters on leases and leasehold mortgages must be checked for material bearing on the mortgaging of leaseholds. Lease clauses of all kinds are important to the mortgagee who holds a mortgage on the fee title. Many important mortgage documents are discussed in Chapter 21. The split fee is a problem to the mortgagee. *See* Chapter 31. Building construction problems are important to the construction lender. *See* Chapter 22.

Reference: Mortgage Default Clause, PLI *Real Estate Law & Practice,* Course Handbook 105, page 25.

26

Assignment of
Leases and Rents

§ 511. Incorporation of assignment of rents. In some states an assignment of leases and rents is regarded as basically a chattel instrument, and therefore it imparts no notice though recorded in the land records. 75 ALR 261. This can be overcome by the following clause in the mortgage, which, is of course a recordable instrument:

> Simultaneously with the execution of this Mortgage, Mortgagor, as additional security for the payment of the indebtedness described in and secured hereby, has by virtue of that certain instrument executed by Mortgagor, captioned Assignment of Lessor's Interest In Lease, dated of even date herewith (hereinafter "Assignment"), a duplicate of which is appended hereto marked "Exhibit A," the terms and conditions of which are hereby expressly incorporated by reference, sold, transferred and assigned to Mortgagee, all of its interest in a certain Lease(s) demising all or a portion of the premises.

> Mortgagor expressly covenants and agrees that if it as Lessor thereunder fails to perform and fulfill any term, covenant, condition or provision in the Lease(s), on its part to be performed or fulfilled, at the times and in the manner therein provided, which failure results in a termination of one or more of the Lease(s), or if it suffers or permits to occur any breach or default under the provisions of the said Assignment, then in any such event, at the option of the Mortgagee and without notice to Mortgagor, such breach or default shall constitute a default hereunder.

§ 512. Form of assignment. The form of the assignment and leases and rents has been discussed elsewhere. Kratovil, *Mortgages* § 303 and Kratovil, *Real Estate Law*, § 411. Form No. 16 is a form of assignment of lease.

§ 513. Filing under the Uniform Commercial Code. In some states, an assignment of rents is recorded as a security assignment of a chose in action, namely, rents that are deemed personal property. In these states, the assignment need not conform to the Uniform Commercial Code and a financing statement need not be filed. *In the Matter of Bristol Associates Inc*, CA-E.D. Pa. Nov. 1974.

Reference, PLI *Real Estate Law & Practice*, Course Handbook 105, page 21.

Form No. 16

ASSIGNMENT OF LEASE

(Individual Form)

By this instrument made _____, 19____, the undersigned, _____

_____

(hereinafter called the "Assignor"), for value received, hereby assigns, transfers and sets over to DOVENMUEHLE, INC., an Illinois corporation (hereinafter called the "Assignee"), all interest of the undersigned in the leases (or extensions or renewals thereof) described in the schedule herein between the Assignor (or its predecessor) as lessor and the lessees named in said schedule (hereinafter called "Lessees") together with all rights against any guarantors (hereinafter called "Guarantors") of the Lessees' obligations under said leases, including the Guarantors under the guarantees described in said schedule, which leases demise and lease all or portions of the premises legally described as follows:

SCHEDULE OF LEASES AND GUARANTEES ASSIGNED HEREBY

LEASES

Name of Lessee	Date of Lease

GUARANTEES

Name of Guarantor	Date of Guarantee	Name of Lessee Whose Performance Is Guaranteed

together with all rents payable under said leases and all benefits and advantages to be derived therefrom, and from said guarantees, if any, to hold and receive them unto the Assignee.

Form No. 16 (continued)

The Assignor does hereby empower the Assignee, its agents or attorneys, to collect, sue for, settle, compromise and give acquittances for all of the rents that may become due under said leases and avail itself of and pursue all remedies for the enforcement of said leases and guarantees and Assignor's rights in and under said leases and guarantees as the Assignor might have pursued but for this assignment.

The Assignor warrants that said leases and guarantees are in full force and effect, that it has not heretofore assigned or pledged the same or any interest therein, and no default exists on the part of the Lessees, or the Assignor, as lessor, in the performance on the part of either, of the terms, covenants, provisions or agreements in said leases contained; that no rent has been paid by the Lessee for more than one installment in advance, and that the payment of none of the rents to accrue under said leases has been or will be waived, released, reduced, discounted or otherwise discharged or compromised by the Assignor; that no security deposit has been made by Lessees under any of said leases. The Assignor waives any rights of set-off against the Lessee. Assignor further warrants that, except as shown in the schedule of leases herein, said leases and guarantees have not been amended or modified, nor have any of the rights of the lessor therein been waived. All of the foregoing warranties are hereby reaffirmed as of the time of each disbursement of proceeds of said loan.

The Assignor agrees:

(a) that said leases shall remain in full force and effect irrespective of any merger of the interest of the lessor and lessee thereunder; and that it will not transfer or convey the fee title to said premises to any of the Lessees without requiring such Lessees, in writing, to assume and agree to pay the debt secured hereby in accordance with the terms, covenants and conditions of the note and mortgage hereinafter described;

(b) that if the leases provide for the abatement of rent during repair of the demised premises by reason of fire or other casualty, the Assignor shall furnish rental insurance to the Assignee, the policies to be in amount and form and written by such insurance companies as shall be satisfactory to the Assignee;

(c) not to terminate, modify or amend said leases or any of the terms thereof, or grant any concessions in connection therewith, either orally or in writing, or to accept a surrender thereof without the written consent of the Assignee and that any attempted termination, modification, or amendment of said leases without such written consent shall be null and void;

(d) not to collect any of the rent, income and profits arising or accruing under said leases in advance of the time when the same become due under the terms thereof;

(e) not to discount any future accruing rents;

(f) not to execute any other assignments or instruments having the legal effect of assignments, or suffer or permit assignments to occur by operation of law, of said leases or the reversions therein or any interest therein or any of the rents thereunder, except, subject hereto, to a purchaser of the mortgaged premises;

(g) to perform all of Assignor's covenants and agreements as lessor under said leases and not to suffer or permit to occur any release of liability of the Lessees, or any right to the Lessees to withhold payment of rent; and to give prompt notices to the Assignee of any notice of default on the part of Assignor with respect to said leases received from the Lessees thereunder, and to furnish Assignee with complete copies of said notices;

(h) if so requested by the Assignee, to enforce said leases and guarantees and all remedies available to the Assignor against the Lessees and Guarantors, in case of default under said leases by the Lessees, or under said guarantees by Guarantors;

(i) that none of the rights or remedies of the Assignee under the mortgage shall be delayed or in any way prejudiced by assignment;

(j) that notwithstanding any variation of the terms of the mortgage or any extension of time for payment thereunder or any release of part or parts of the lands conveyed thereunder, the leases and guarantees and benefits hereby assigned shall continue as additional security in accordance with the terms hereof;

(k) not to alter, modify or change the terms of any guarantees of any of said leases or cancel or terminate such guarantees without the prior written consent of the Assignee, or suffer or permit to occur any release of liability of the Guarantor or Guarantors under such guarantees; not to omit to be done anything which may be requisite to keep in effect or render enforceable any guarantee; promptly to advise the Assignee of any notification or other knowledge or information received by the Assignor or coming to the Assignor's attention of any defenses or claims of non-liability, in whole or in part, of any Guarantor under such guarantees;

(l) not to consent to any assignments of said leases, or any subletting thereunder, whether or not in accordance with their terms, without the prior written consent of the Assignee;

(m) not to request, consent to, agree to or accept a subordination of said leases to any mortgage or other encumbrance or lease now or hereafter affecting the premises, or suffer or permit conversion of any of said leases to subleases; and

(n) not to engage in any so-called sale and leaseback transaction, or in any other way to lease all or portions of the mortgaged premises under any lease which is subject or subordinate to any of the leases assigned hereby without the prior written consent of the Assignee.

This assignment is given as additional security for the payment of the note of the Assignor of even date herewith, in the sum of $_____, and all other sums secured by the trust deed or mortgage (herein referred to as "Mortgage") of even date herewith from the Assignor to the Assignee as Mortgagee, conveying premises of which those demised in said leases form all or a part. The security of this assignment is and shall be primary and on a parity with the real estate conveyed by said Mortgage and not secondary. All amounts collected hereunder, after deducting the expenses of operation of the demised premises and after deducting the expenses of collection, shall be applied on account of the indebtedness secured by said Mortgage, or in such other manner as may be provided for in the Mortgage, or in any general assignment of rents relating to said premises. Nothing herein contained shall be construed as constituting Assignee a trustee or mortgagee in possession.

Upon issuance of a deed or deeds pursuant to foreclosure of the Mortgage, all right, title and interest of the Assignor in and to said leases and guarantees shall, by virtue of this instrument, thereupon vest in and become the absolute property of the grantee or grantees in such deed or deeds without any further act or assignment by the Assignor. Assignor hereby irrevocably appoints Assignee and its successors and assigns, as its agent and attorney in fact, to execute all instruments of assignment or further assurance in favor of such grantee or grantees in such deed or deeds, as may be necessary or desirable for such purpose.

In the exercise of the powers herein granted the Assignee, no liability shall be asserted or enforced against the Assignee, all such liability being hereby expressly waived and released by the Assignor. The Assignee shall not be obligated to perform or discharge any obligation, duty or liability under said leases, or under or by reason of this assignment, and the Assignor shall and does hereby agree to indemnify the Assignee for and to hold it harmless of and from any and all liability, loss or damage which it may or might incur under said leases or under or by reason of this assignment and of and from any and all claims and demands whatsoever which may be asserted against it by reason of any alleged obligations or undertakings on its part to perform or discharge any of the terms, covenants or agreements contained in said leases and guarantees. Should the Assignee incur any such liability, loss or damage under said leases or under or by reason of this assignment, or in the defense of any such claims or demands, the amount thereof, including costs, expenses and reasonable attorneys' fees, shall be secured hereby, and the Assignor shall reimburse the Assignee therefor immediately upon demand.

Although it is the intention of the parties that this instrument shall be a present assignment, it is expressly understood and agreed, anything herein contained to the contrary notwithstanding, that the Assignee shall not exercise any of the rights or powers herein conferred upon it until a default shall occur under the terms and provisions of this assignment or of the note or Mortgage, but upon the occurrence of any such default the Assignee shall be entitled, upon notice to the Lessees, to all rents and other amounts then due under the leases and guarantees and thereafter accruing, and this assignment shall constitute a direction to and full authority to the Lessees and Guarantors to pay all such amounts to the Assignee without proof of the default relied upon. The Lessees and Guarantors are hereby irrevocably authorized to rely upon and comply with (and shall be fully protected in so doing) any notice or demand by the Assignee for the payment to the Assignee of any rental or other sums which may be or thereafter become due under said leases and guarantees, or for the performance of any of Lessees' undertakings under the leases and shall have no right or duty to inquire as to whether any default under the Mortgage has actually occurred or is then existing.

This assignment is intended to be supplementary to and not in substitution for or in derogation of any assignment of rents contained in the Mortgage or in any other document.

This assignment shall include any extensions and renewals of the leases and any reference herein to the said leases shall be construed as including any such extensions and renewals.

This instrument shall be binding upon and inure to the benefit of the respective successors and assigns of the parties hereto. The words "Assignor," "Assignee," "Lessees," and "Guarantors," wherever used herein, shall include the persons named herein and designated as such and their respective successors and assigns, and all words and phrases shall be taken to include the singular or plural and masculine, feminine or neuter gender, as may fit the case.

27

Wrap-Around Mortgage

§ 514. In general. The "wrap-around mortgage" and the legal problems it creates are described in Kratovil, *Mortgages*, § 393 as follows:

EXAMPLE: *R* has mortgaged a shopping center to *E* for $5,000,000 at 6% interest. The loan has been paid down to $4,000,000. He now would like to borrow an additional $5,000,000 to expand the center. The going rate of interest in the area on commercial loans is 10% and this rate is permitted by law on business loans. *R* makes a second mortgage to *X* of $9,000,000 at 10% interest. *X* advances only $5,000,000. However, the mortgage provides that *R* will make all his payments to *X* and *X* will make the mortgage payments to *E*. *R* will pay interest at 10% on the money actually loaned to him by *X* and on the advances *X* makes to retire the mortgage to *E*. But *X* pays *E* only 6% interest. The result is a yield to *X* greatly in excess of 10%. *R* should not be in a position to complain, it is argued, because he is paying 6% on his old mortgage and 10%, as agreed, on his new mortgage. Healey, *A Legal View of "Wrap-Around" Mortgages,* N.Y. Law Journal (October 14, 1970).

A number of questions arise. One is the question of usury. Of course, if the borrower is exempt (e.g., borrower is a corporation), or the lender is exempt (e.g., lender is a bank and local law exempts bank lenders from usury loans), or the loan is exempt (e.g., the loan is a business loan and is exempt under local law), no problems arise. But if there is no local exemption, the question of usury may arise in states that consider usury is present if the lender *receives* more than the statutory maximum. *Mindlin v. Davis,* 74 So2d 789.

Another question that arises is that of intervening liens. If, for example, *R* places a third mortgage on the property, does this obtain priority over subsequent advances made by *X*? In wrap-around mortgages, it is uncommon for *X* to obligate himself to make all the advances. Hence he does not have the protection of obligatory advances rule. And the third mortgagee will no doubt notify *X* of his third mortgage, so that *X* seems, at first blush, to suffer the exposure to risk and loss that is involved in making optional advances.

Actually, this last risk can be eliminated by resort to (a) the doctrine of conventional subrogation and (b) the rule that a junior mortgagee who pays on a prior encumbrance enjoys the same priority as to these advances as was enjoyed by the original junior mortgage when it was recorded.

§ 515. Conventional subrogation. The doctrine of conventional subrogation, which is relied upon to preserve the wrap-around's priority over intervening liens, is explained in Kratovil, *Mortgages*, § 256.

§ 516. Payment of prior encumbrance by junior mortgagee. The proposition that a junior lienor who, to protect his lien, makes payments on the prior lien, is entitled to add the amounts so paid to his lien and enjoy at least on a parity with the priority of his original junior lien is well established. *Ager v. Murray*, 105 U.S. 122, 126; *Mosier v. Norton*, 85 Ill. 59, 525; *Harper v. Ely*, 70 Ill. 581, 584; 55 Am.Jur.2d, *Mortgages* § 259. Thus, the wrap-around mortgagee may pay on the first mortgage and add these payments to his junior mortgage, enjoying, as to such payments, a lien at least as good as the lien of his original mortgage, and the mortgage should so provide.

§ **517. Wrap-around covenants.** A necessary covenant is that *R* pays to *E*, not to the first mortgagee, the required payments on the first mortgage, as well as the payments on the wrap-around debt, and *E* makes payments to the first mortgagee. An important covenant in the wrap-around forbids prepayment by *mortgagor* of the first mortgage, since it is the presence of the low-interest first mortgage that creates the attractive yield on the wrap-around. Prepayment of the wrap-around is postponed for like reasons.

§ **518. Wrap-around—other provisions.** The wrap-around mortgagee may find it desirable to extend or modify the first mortgage. The wrap-around mortgage should require *R* to execute such documents so long as they do not increase his liability.

§ **519. Other requirements and problems.** The mortgage will track with the first mortgage as to covenants so that the mortgagor will owe to the wrap-around mortgagee, the identical performance he owes to the first mortgagee. In addition, the mortgagor notifies the first mortgagee that he will receive future payments from the wrap-around mortgagee. In this connection, however, note that some first mortgages expressly provide that "no other party (than the mortgagor) shall in any manner be permitted or allowed to make the payments required on the indebtedness secured hereby." In such case, the wrap-around mortgage should give the mortgagee power, as a power coupled with an interest to make such payments, as the mortgagor's agent. It would be extremely helpful if the first mortgage were to contain a prepayment privilege, so that in case of default the wrap-around *mortgagee* could pay off the first mortgage and acquire owner- ship by foreclosure. This would get around the problem created by probable merger of the wrap-around mortgage in a decree of foreclosure, thus destroying the benefit of all the protective covenants therein contained. It has been suggested that the wrap-around mortgagee ask for a deposit of the pre-payment privilege money, but this is going to be hard to get. Of course, any institutional lender must exercise care to avoid making a junior mortgage wrap-around where that is forbidden by his regulatory statute. See *e.g.*, Opinion of Ohio Attorney General 75-005, stating that a building and loan association cannot make a wrap-around mortgage.

§ **520. Title insurance requirements.** One title company lists its wrap-around mortgage requirements as follows (Forms No. 17, No. 18, No. 19):

1. The wrap-around mortgage should expressly provide that all additional payments made thereunder by the mortgagee to protect the lien created thereby would constitute additional indebted- ness secured by the mortgage for which the wrap-around mortgagee would be subrogated to the rights of the prior mortgagee.
2. The wrap-around note should contain the express agreement of the holder thereof to make the payments on the prior mortgage.
3. A formal subrogation agreement should be executed by both the mortgagor and the wrap- around mortgagee and recorded.
4. Reference to such recorded subrogation agreement should be made in the wrap-around mortgage.

Where the foregoing conditions are met, the title company will issue its loan policy insuring the lien of the wrap-around mortgage for the stated amount thereof, limiting its liability by an endorsement, however, to the amount of money actually disbursed at the time the policy issues, but agreeing in the endorsement that the amount of the policy shall increase *pro tanto* as additional payments are made by the wrap-around mortgage solely from the mortgagee's own funds and not from any monies received by it from the mortgage.

The form that (1) the wrap-around mortgage, (2) the note secured thereby, (3) and the subrogation agreement, are to assume is illustrated by Exhibits A, B, and C.

References: Beverly Hills Bar Journal (Jan.–Feb. 1973) p. 31; 2 Real Estate Review 35; Healey, A Legal View of Wrap-Around Mortgages, N.Y. Law Journal (Oct. 14, 1970). 1972 Duke L.J. 785; 4 ABA Real Ppty., Probate and Trust J. 315, 323 (1969).

EXHIBIT A (Form No. 17)

(Language to be inserted in the mortgage)

The mortgaged premises are subject to the lien of the following described mortgage (hereinafter for convenience referred to as "senior mortgage"):

(here describe the existing first mortgage
and any note or notes secured thereby)

Mortgagor covenants and agrees to comply with all of the terms and provisions of said senior mortgage (except the requirement to make the payments of principal and interest thereon), and upon compliance by mortgagor with the terms and provisions contained in said senior mortgage and contained herein, mortgagee will pay the installments of principal and interest from time to time due under said senior mortgage in accordance with its terms. Nothing contained herein shall require the holder of the note secured hereby to perform the terms or provisions contained in said senior mortgage required to be performed by mortgagor, its successors and assigns, except the payment of installments of principal and interest but only in accordance with the terms and provisions hereof. If mortgagor shall default in the performance of any term or provision contained in this mortgage, mortgagee shall not be obligated to pay any principal or interest under the senior mortgage.

Mortgagor covenants and agrees that, to the extent mortgagee pays any installment of principal or interest or any other sums due under the senior mortgage, mortgagee shall become entitled to a lien on the mortgaged premises hereunder but equal in rank and priority to the senior mortgage and, in addition, to the extent necessary to make effective such rank and priority: (i) mortgagee shall become subrogated to, receive and enjoy all of the rights, liens, powers and privileges granted to the senior mortgagee under the senior mortgage, and (ii) the senior mortgage shall remain in existence for the benefit of and to further secure the debt and other sums secured, or that hereafter become secured, hereunder. Contemporaneously herewith the parties hereto have executed a subrogation agreement to which reference is hereby made for the terms thereof.

In case of default hereunder, in addition to any other rights and remedies available to mortgagee, mortgagee may, but need not, make any payment or perform any act herein required of mortgagor in any form and manner deemed expedient, and may, but need not, make full or partial payments of principal or interest on the senior mortgage, other prior encumbrances, if any, and purchase, discharge, compromise or settle the senior mortgage, any tax lien or other prior lien or title or claim thereof, or redeem from any tax sale or forfeiture affecting said premises or contest any tax or assessment. All moneys paid for any of the purposes herein authorized and all expenses paid or incurred in connection therewith, including attorneys' fees, and any other money advanced by mortgagee to protect the mortgaged premises and the lien hereof, shall be so much additional indebtedness secured hereby, and shall become immediately due and payable without notice and with interest thereon at the rate of _____ percent (_____%) per annum. Inaction of mortgagee shall never be considered as a waiver of any right accruing to it on account of any default on the part of mortgagor.

EXHIBIT B (Form No. 18)

(Language to be inserted in the wrap-around note):

The owner and holder hereof agrees to make payments of principal and interest from time to time as they become due on the following described mortgage:

(here describe the senior mortgage and
the note or notes secured thereby)

but only in accordance with the terms and provisions of the mortgage securing this note.

EXHIBIT C (Form No. 19)

This indenture made between _____ of the City of _____, County of _____, and State of _____, (hereinafter referred to as the "mortgagor") and _____, of the City of _____, County of _____, and State of _____, (hereinafter referred to as the "Mortgagee"),

WITNESSETH THAT:

WHEREAS, the mortgagor is the owner in fee simple of the following described premises, to-wit:

(which premises are hereinafter referred to as "the mortgaged premises"); and

WHEREAS, the mortgagor has heretofore executed a mortgage dated _____ and recorded _____ as Document No. _____ to _____ to secure its note for _____ Dollars and interest and the other charges therein described; and

WHEREAS, the mortgagor has executed contemporaneously herewith a mortgage (referred to herein as the "current mortgage") dated _____ to secure its note for _____ Dollars, and interest and the other charges therein described, which note is held by mortgagee, and

WHEREAS, all of the money secured by the current mortgage has not yet been advanced but is to be advanced by the legal holder and owner of the indebtedness and note secured by said mortgage pursuant to the terms thereof, and to be applied from time to time to the payment of the remainder of the unpaid indebtedness secured by the mortgage recorded as Document No. _____;

NOW, THEREFORE, in consideration of the premises and of the making of the current mortgage the mortgagor does hereby authorize and empower the legal holder and owner from time to time of the note secured by the current mortgage to disburse the funds secured by said mortgage and to apply the same from time to time to payment of part or all of the principal and interest secured by the mortgage recorded as Document No. _____, and it is expressly covenanted and agreed by the parties hereto that upon each such payment, the owner of the indebtedness secured by the current mortgage shall be and he is hereby subrogated to all rights, liens, and privileges which before such payment were vested in the owner or legal holder of the indebtedness secured by the mortgage recorded as Document No. _____ and upon such payment the current mortgage shall be to all intents and purposes and to the extent of payments so made a first and valid lien, subrogated as aforesaid, upon the premises above described.

This agreement is binding upon the successors and assigns of the parties hereto.

WITNESS our hands and seals this _____ day of _____, A.D. 19_____.

_____   _____
            (Seal)   (Seal)

(Acknowledgement clauses to be added for mortgagee and mortgagor for recording purposes.)

28

Net Leases—Lease of Entire Building—Sale and Leaseback— Active Assignment of Rents

§ 521. History of lease as a financing device. In early times, probably before 1200, the lease was used as a financing device to evade the church's prohibition of usury.

EXAMPLE: *L,* a landowner, borrowed money from *T*. In return *L* gave *T* a lease of the land sufficient to provide *T* a return of his money and a profit. On its face it looked like a lease for a lump sum. Plucknett, *A Concise History of the Common Law* (4th ed. 1948) 141.

Thereafter, this function disappeared, and leases of land, as we know them, began to appear.

Later, the ground lease, which is a method of financing construction of substantial improvements made its appearance. *See* Chapter 34.

In Maryland, their peculiar ground rent system of financing is used extensively. *Jones v. Magruder,* 42 F. Supp. 193. *See* Chapter 34.

However, it is in the area of "layering" net leases that the greatest ingenuity has been shown in modern times in developing new financing techniques:

An example of this type of layering is the Graybar Building at 420 Lexington Avenue in New York City. The land and building are owned by the Penn Central Transportation Company. Despatch Shops, Inc., a subsidiary of Penn Central Transportation, is holder of a "grant of term" from its parent of the land and building. Despatch leases the land and building to Metropolitan Life Insurance Company under a long-term net "ground lease." Metropolitan Life subleases the land and building under a long term net "sandwich lease" to Graybar Building Associates, a partnership headed by Lawrence A. Wien. Graybar sub-sub-leases the land and building under a long term net "sandwich lease" to Precision Dynamics Corporation. Precision Dynamics sub-sub-sub-leases the land and building under a long-term net "operating lease" to Harry B. Helmsley d/b/a Graybar Building Company. Mr. Helmsley operates the building and sub-sub-sub-sub-leases space therein to tenants for their own use and occupancy. Ground leases, sandwich leases and operating leases are often bought and sold just as fee title is bought and sold. For example, in the Graybar Building, Metropolitan Life purchased its position from Webb & Knapp, Inc.; Graybar Building Associates acquired its interest by assignment from Lawrence A. Wien, and Precision Dynamics Corporation bought its lease from Webb & Knapp, Inc. with numerous mesne assignments. 26 Bus. Law 1391.

239

Under the *pineapple theory* fathered by William Zeckendorf, of Webb and Knapp, leases and mortgages thereon can be layered in such a fashion that the sum of the values of the interests thus created can exceed the value of the land and building appraised at its fair market value. In condemnation however, the award is going to be fair market value. Drafting the condemnation clauses for layered leases presents almost insuperable problems.

§ 522. Drafting suggestions—in general. It is obvious that every lease represents a compromise reached by negotiation. Beyond that, however, it seems necessary to point out the dangers of a scissors-and-paste approach to clauses that have not been fought over. Many of the form book clauses or printed form clauses leave much to be desired. And the various lease clauses must track with each other.

EXAMPLE: Lease gives *T* a year to construct a building on the property. Another clause says if the building is destroyed, *T* must rebuild within 30 days. This is inconsistent.

EXAMPLE: Lease says all betterments erected by *T* become the property of *L*. Another clause requires *T* to carry the insurance on the betterments. Actually he has an insurable interest in the use value of the betterments for the term of the lease. That is not quite the same as insurance on the betterments.

§ 523. Structure of net lease. When draftsmen became aware of the fact that a net lease could be used as a financing device, they turned to the oldest financing device for guidance. They looked at the real estate mortgage. Both documents, it is evident, produce a "net return." And just as a mortgage places all the burden of ownership and operation on the mortgagor (payment of real estate taxes, hazard insurance, repairs, etc.), so can the net lease place all these burdens on *T*. But this can be done while preserving some very substantial advantages for *L*: (1) If default occurs under a net lease, *L* can quickly and inexpensively oust *T* and terminate *T*'s interest in the property by short notices and the inexpensive, informal eviction proceedings used to oust tenants. There is no cumbersome mortgage foreclosure, no foreclosure sale, and no redemption period. (2) Just as the mortgagee retains the right to obtain a deficiency judgment, *L*, by means of the survival clause (Kratovil, *Real Estate Law* § 659), can oust *T* and still retain the right to sue *T* for a personal judgment for the rent due and to become due under the lease. But structurally, the net lease continues to borrow from the real estate mortgage. The covenants for payment of real estate taxes, hazard insurance, etc. strongly resemble those found in the real estate mortgage. As in the case of a large mortgage, the net lease typically deals with an entire building.

Some tenants under long term leases fail to maintain the mechanical equipment in the last years of the lease, in accordance with the lease requirements. Accordingly, some landlords insist upon a clause in all long term net leases wherein *T* covenants and agrees to maintain a service contract for the heating and air conditioning systems. A copy of the contract is sent to *L* and all renewals are likewise sent to *L*. In other words, the lease treats a service contract in the same manner as it treats the obligation to maintain insurance policies. By using this device it is believed that the maintenance of the mechanical systems will be made on a higher level, and properties will be turned over in better condition than otherwise.

The net lease contains many clauses designed to insure the continuance of payment of net rent. Draftsmen have given attention to a number of matters, namely:

(1) The affirmative obligations of *T* in general, such as payment of taxes. (2) The affirmative obligations of *T* to pay and perform all covenants of the existing mortgage, except, in some cases, payment of principal and interest, the idea being that *L* is relieved of all such payments and *T's* rentals pay the principal and interest. Rental cash flow must be adequate to provide mortgage debt service. (3) Clauses dealing with *T's* failure to perform his affirmative obligations, including (a) *L's* right to make payments, as on taxes, and add such amounts to rent due by *T* (b) *L's* right to declare a forfeiture of the lease and regain possession of the premises expeditiously. (4) Clauses dealing with protection of *L* and his mortgage lender should the premises, or part thereof, be condemned. (5) Clauses requiring *T* to repair and rebuild in case of damage or destruction so that *L* and his mortgage lender can always count on a building, in full repair, being in existence to continue the cash flow needed to retire the mortgage debt. (6) Requirements as to *T* procuring insurance, so that funds will be available to cause the building to be repaired or restored. (7) Covenants requiring *T* to bear the burden of complying with laws, ordinances, and regulations, so that this burden does not fall on *L* or his mortgage lender. (8) Clauses protecting *L* against claims by third parties or governmental bodies for accidents, injuries, or damage of any kind, including insurance requirements. (9) Restrictions on *T's* transfer of the lease.

§ 524. Steps prior to signing lease—zoning. In a lease of an entire building *T* will be more meticulous as to zoning. If the leased building contains a diversity of uses, the check of zoning must be very carefully done. *T* may want *L* to furnish a copy of the zoning ordinance and furnish opinion of counsel that this is an accurate copy of existing zoning. *T's* own attorney will determine if the building is a lawful non-conforming use, but if it is indeed a non-conforming use, *L* should warrant the date of construction of the building, for this is the key date that determines whether the building is a lawful non-conforming use. Then *T's* lawyer will certify, if necessary: (1) whether wings can be added? (2) whether stories can be added? (3) whether zoning building lines prevent any additions? (4) whether new and larger machinery or equipment can be added? (5) whether uses by prospective subtenants will violate zoning?

§ 525. Steps prior to signing lease—building restrictions. *T* will want *L* to furnish verbatim copies of building restrictions and a title company endorsement that the building conforms to the restrictions. Prospective uses by subtenants should be considered for possible violation of building restrictions.

§ 526. Steps prior to signing lease—mortgages—prior mortgage. Before a net lease is signed, the title is checked and any prior mortgage is carefully analyzed. The lease cannot permit *T* to do anything forbidden by the mortgage, for example, alterations forbidden or not permitted by the mortgage. If *T* plans alterations he must get the mortgagee's permission. The lease may, if desired, leave the burden of paying principal and interest on the mortgage with *L* (for, after all, he got the money and should pay it back), but all other sums required by the mortgage to be paid by mortgagor are made part of the rent payable by the tenant in the net lease. Where *L* wants a return that is completely "net" to him, without the bother of making mortgage payments, the lease may require *T* to make principal and interest payments on the mortgage, but after the mortgage debt has been satisfied, *T's* payments step down *pro tanto*. *T* will not want to pay any "balloon" at the end of the loan. (A "balloon" is a large, final payment.)

§ 527. Steps prior to signing lease—general suggestions. The same precautions are taken prior to signing as are taken in any large-scale transaction. *See* Chapter 18.

§ 528. Property demised—entire building. The net lease is made with respect to an entire building. *See* Chapter 8.

§ 529. Property demised—fixtures and equipment. The property demised clause often covers fixtures and equipment now attached or installed in the building or useful in operation of said property including, without limitation, machines, motors, elevators, radiators, awnings, shades, screens, plumbing, heating, ventilating, refrigerating, incinerating, air-conditioning equipment, and any replacements thereof, whether similar to or different from the existing equipment, all of which are or shall become *L's* property. Absent such a clause, courts give *T* liberal rights of removal of fixtures he installs.

§ 530. Property demised—subreversions. The subreversions under existing and future subleases are included in the demise, much as in ground leases.

§ 531. Property demised—exceptions from demised property. The lease expressly excepts from the property demised articles installed by *T* that would be deemed trade fixtures as between a landlord and tenant and all *T's* furniture and stock in trade used in connection with conduct of a business on said premises.

§ 532. Subject clause. The "subject clause" is compiled as in any other large-scale transaction. *See* Chapter 10.

§ 533. Name of building. *T* should be given the right to change the name of the building on said premises to _____.

EXPLANATION: *T* cannot change the name of the building without *L's* consent. 52 Am. Jur. *Trademarks and Trade Names* § 31 p. 525. On the other hand, *L* wishes to control the name of the building to some extent.

§ 534. Rent. The net lease spells out in great detail the fact that the lease is a net lease and that all burdens fall on *T*. At times the lease will divide the rental into two categories, the *basic rent,* which is the money rent *T* agrees to pay, and the *additional rent,* which consists of the amounts *T,* in later covenants, agrees to pay in the form of taxes, insurance, etc. This is coupled with a provision that no event whatever will in any way diminish the liability of *T* to pay these amounts. One such form follows:

ADDITIONAL RENT. Lessee will also pay, as additional rent, all other amounts, liabilities and obligations which Lessee herein assumes or agrees to pay, and, in the event of any failure on the part of Lessee to pay any of the same, Lessor shall have all rights, powers and remedies provided for herein or by law or equity or otherwise in the case of non-payment of the Basic Rent. Lessee will also pay Lessor on demand, as additional rent, interest at the rate of 6% per annum on all overdue installments of Basic Rent and on all other amounts, liabilities and obligations as are payable to Lessor and are not paid within 10 days of the date of demand, from the due date thereof or from the date of such demand, as the case may be, until payment.

NO COUNTERCLAIM, ABATEMENT, ETC. The Basic Rent and such additional rent shall be paid without notice, demand, counterclaim, setoff, deduction or defense, and without abatement, suspension, deferment, diminution or reduction by reason of, and the obligations and liabilities of Lessee under this Lease shall not be affected by, any circumstance or occurrence whatsoever including, without limitation, (a) any damage to or destruction of the Leased Property or any part thereof (except as provided in section) (b) any restriction or prevention of or interference with any use of the Leased Property or any part thereof, (c) any Taking of the Leased Property or any part thereof (except as provided in section) or any change of grade affecting the same, (d) any title defect or encumbrance or any eviction or prospective eviction from the Leased Property or any part thereof by title paramount or otherwise, (e) any bankruptcy, insolvency, reorganization, composition, adjustment, dissolution, liquidation or other like proceeding of or on the part of Lessor or any assignee of Lessor's equity in the Leased Property or any action taken with respect to the Lease by any Trustee or Receiver of Lessor or any such assignee or pursuant to order of Court in any such proceedings, (f) any change, extension, waiver, indulgence or other action or omission in respect of any obligation or liability of Lessor, or (g) any claim which Lessee has or might have against Lessor; whether or not Lessee shall have had any notice or knowledge of the foregoing. Except as specifically provided herein, Lessee waives all rights now or hereafter conferred by statute or otherwise to quit, terminate or surrender this Lease or the Leased Property or any part thereof, or to any abatement, suspension, deferment, diminution or reduction of Basic Rent or additional rent, on account of any such occurrence.

See also § 5.

Whenever the lease calls for periodic appraisals and then keys rent to appraised value, the method of appraisal must be carefully spelled out. *Plaza Hotel Assn v. Wellington Assoc. Inc.* 34 N.Y.S.2d 796. The various techniques and formulas for variable rentals have been discussed elsewhere. 72 Columb.L.Rev. 625.

There should be a strong covenant to repair and maintain. *L* wants the building back just as it was when the lease was made.

The provision in a net lease that taxes, repairs, cost of reconstruction, etc. are additional rent is a salutary provision. *Rent, per se,* is compensation for the use of land. It is only when the parties so contract that additional payments become rent. When they do so contract, the speedy remedy of forcible detainer becomes available when default occurs. Friedman, *Leases* § 5.204. Otherwise, the clumsy time-consuming remedies for breach of contract must be resorted to. Likewise, it is probable that for income tax purposes the rent agreed upon is tax-deductible rent if the parties so agree.

Standard clauses requiring *T* to comply with all present and future laws, ordinances and regulations and to pay all costs in connection therewith as part of the basic rent require thought. Some limits are needed for *T's* protection. An environmental control regulation might require substantial expenditure beyond *T's* contemplated financial commitments. And if the regulations put *T* out of business, he may also need an escape hatch.

§ 535. **Repairs and maintenance.** The provision calling for *T* to provide repairs and maintenance is apt to be sweeping.

§ 536. **Maintenance and repair.** Clause follows:

Lessee is fully familiar with the physical condition of the Leased Property and at its expense will keep the Leased Property and all sidewalks, curbs, vaults and vault space adjoining or appurtenant to the Leased Property (to the extent that the owner or occupant of the property be legally obligated to maintain such adjoining or appurtenant property) in good order and condition (ordinary wear and tear excepted) and promptly make all necessary and appropriate repairs, replacements and renewals thereof whether interior or exterior, structural or non-structural, ordinary or extraordinary, foreseen or unforeseen. All repairs, replacements and renewals shall be equal in quality and class to the original work. Lessee will not do or permit any act or thing which might impair the value of usefulness of the Leased Property or any part thereof, or commit or permit any waste of the Leased Property or any part thereof. Lessor makes no representation or warranty with respect to the condition of the Leased Property or its fitness or availability for any particular use and neither Lessor nor any Assignee shall be liable for any latent or patent defect therein.

§ 537. **Alterations.** *L,* as a rule, wants the demised building to return to him at the termination of the lease in much the same form as at the time of the lease. For example, he does not want it attached to an adjoining building owned or rented by *T*, possibly with the elevators in the adjoining building. The clause permitting alterations by *T* must prohibit such a result. Where a net lease authorizes major alterations, subject to *L's* consent, the clause goes on to provide much the same completion and mechanic's-lien protection for *L* as are found in a ground lease where *T* is to construct a building.

The lease may permit *T* to make alterations up to a stated amount without *L's* consent. This provision will be fairly liberal to *T*. If there is a prior mortgage on the fee that forbids alterations without the written consent of the lender, either his consent must be obtained or the mortgage must be modified. If the alterations exceed the stated amount, the lease will require *L's* consent and will require *T* to obtain all necessary permits.

§ 538. Taxes and insurance—prorating. Inasmuch as a net lease involves the transfer to *T* of a substantial interest in the land, it will provide for prorations of insurance premiums to date of commencement of term, much as in the case of a sale of land. Prorating of taxes will also be provided for. And, again, when the term ends, a substantial interest in the land is relinquished, and a transfer of insurance takes place, with prorating of taxes and insurance premiums. But in the case of a sale and leaseback, the similarity to a loan situation is such that there is no prorating. *T* simply continues to carry the burdens as tenant that he carried as a fee owner.

A provision for prorating taxes at the end of the lease should use the word "ends" rather than "expires" to indicate that ending by condemnation etc. is also intended. Friedman, *Leases* § 5.2.

§ 539. Special assessments. *T* expects a clause requiring him to pay all real estate taxes. As to special assessments, he may argue for some relief where the assessment is levied in the last two or three years of the lease, contending that he will receive no benefit from the improvements. *T* may argue for a clause that if an assessment occurring in the last two or three years exceeds a stated amount, he is to have the option of terminating the lease. *L* will resist this. If the assessment is payable in installments, *T* agrees to pay only those installments falling due during the term of the lease and any renewals thereof. The tax clause is a broad one, covering governmental charges of every kind, present or future, foreseeable and unforseeable.

§ 540. Eminent Domain. The provision regarding condemnations is a difficult one to draft.

If *all* of the leased premises is condemned, the lease obviously must come to an end. Some leases simply require *T* to pay rent up to the date the condemnor is entitled to take possession. *L* will argue that he should then receive the entire award. *T* will argue for some compensation for improvements he has constructed. The clause should cover a deed given under the threat of condemnation.

If there is an existing mortgage, *L* will want the award applied to extinguishment of the mortgage. The mortgage requires this anyway. *L* may want the award next applied to the value of his land and the value of the building that existed at the commencement of the lease, so that he gets out of the award such value as he contributed to the award. *T* will participate in the award after *L* and his lender are compensated in this fashion, possibly on the basis of the value of the leasehold and the value of improvements he has contributed.

Where there is a partial condemnation it is difficult to generalize as to the contents of the condemnation clause. *See* Friedman, *Leases*, Ch. 13.

If there is a prior mortgage on the fee, again the mortgage gives the lender rights in the award, and the mortgagee may have the right to apply the award on the mortgage debt or to make the award available for restoration. Obviously the lease must recognize the mortgagee's rights in this regard. A side agreement with the mortgagee may be needed to make insurance funds available for rebuilding.

Reconstruction after partial taking involves architect's certificates, lien waivers, etc. as in the case of accidental destruction. This can be combined with the insurance clause.

§ 541. Options to renew. Options to renew occur at times in net leases. The problem is one of fixing the rental to be paid during the renewal period. *L* and *T* will not see eye to eye on this point. *L* will certainly argue for a rent not less than that during the last year of the term. A compromise may permit the rent to be fixed by a three-man appraisal, or by arbitration.

There have been situations with AAA tenants where the rental under the initial term (say, 20-year term) is fixed at a figure so that *L* will get all his money back, plus— percent, over the 20-year term. In addition, the amount of the rental is sufficient to pay off the debt service on the original mortgage so that at the end of the lease term *L* will have received the return indicated aforesaid and in addition will have his building free and clear of mortgage debt service. Under these circumstances, the rental for the renewal period will actually be reduced because there are no debt service payments to be made.

§ 542. Burdens personal to *L*. Burdens personal to *L*, such as franchise taxes, income tax, inheritance or estate taxes, always remain as a burden on *L*. It is sometimes provided that if in the future a tax is levied on the rentals in lieu of a real estate tax, this will be borne by *T*.

§ 543. Mortgage subordinations. If *L* is insisting on a clause subordinating the lease to any future mortgage placed on the fee by *L*, all the problems inherent in such subordination are present. Probably *T* will want the clause to be limited to institutional mortgages, for they are apt to be conservative in their terms. *T* will want limits on the amount of the mortgage and will want the amortization payments to be limited to an amount not greater than the rentals under the lease. *T* may argue that his lease should not be subordinated unless he obtains a non-disturbance clause. *See* Chapter 36.

§ 544. Assignments and subleases. In a ground lease, the building is erected by *T* and this contribution of value entitles him to a lease with unfettered right to assign and sublease. In the ordinary net lease, the building has been contributed by *L*. Moreover, in some instances *L* is relying on *T's* high credit to generate revenue. Thus you are likely to find in the net lease, restrictions on the right of *T* to assign or sublease. *L's* consent may be required for a sublease of the entire building. Where the net lease permits assignment, it sometimes provides that the liability of *T* for rent continues after assignment, which is the opposite of what you expect to find in a ground lease. In some sale-and-leasebacks you will find a clause that after the investor's investment has been reduced by lease payments, *L* will not unreasonably withhold his consent to an assignment, and *L* will often agree not to withhold consent to an assignment by *T* to a corporate affiliate or to an assignment resulting from a merger.

§ 545. Indemnification—condition of premises. A suggested indemnity clause is as follows:

Section 1. The Lessee agrees to indemnify and save the Lessor harmless against and from any and all claims by or on behalf of any person or persons, firm or firms, corporation or corporations, arising from the conduct or management of or from any work or thing whatsoever done in or about the demised premises and will further indemnify and save the Lessor harmless against and from any and all claims arising during the term of this lease from any condition of the buildings or other structures, sidewalks, driveways, or parking areas and facilities on the demised premises or any street, curb, or sidewalk adjoining the demised premises, or of any vaults, passageways, or spaces therein or appurtenant thereto, or arising from any breach or default on the part of the Lessee in the performance of any covenant or agreement on the part of the Lessee to be performed, pursuant to the terms of this lease, or arising from any act of negligence of the Lessee or any of its agents, contractors, servants, employees, or licensees, or arising from any accident, injury, or damage whatsoever caused to any person, firm, or corporation, occurring during the term of this lease, in or about the demised premises, or upon or under the sidewalks, vaults, and the land adjacent thereto, and from and against all costs, counsel fees, expenses, and liabilities incurred in or about any such claim or action or proceeding brought thereon; and in case any action or proceeding be brought against the Lessor by reason of any such claim, the Lessee upon notice from the Lessor covenants to resist or defend such action or proceeding by counsel reasonably satisfactory to the Lessor.

Section 2. The Lessee is fully familiar with the physical condition of the demised premises and the buildings, improvements, fixtures, and equipment thereon. The Lessor has made no representations of any nature in connection with the condition of the demised premises or of the buildings, improvements, fixtures, or equipment thereon, and the Lessor shall not be liable for any latent or patent defects therein. The Lessee shall be presumed to have accepted possession of the demised premises under this lease on the first day of the term hereof, and such acceptance of possession by the Lessee shall be conclusive evidence as against the Lessee that said premises were in good and satisfactory condition when possession of the same was so accepted.

Section 3. The Lessee covenants and agrees to pay, and to indemnify the Lessor against, all legal costs and charges, including counsel fees, lawfully and reasonably incurred in obtaining possession of the demised premises after default of the Lessee or upon the expiration or earlier termination of the term of this lease or in enforcing any covenant or agreement of the Lessee in this lease contained.[1]

A careful landlord will require *T* to defend all lawsuits at his expense on matters falling within the indemnity clause. A careful tenant will be reluctant to indemnify against liability he cannot cover by insurance.

§ 546. Damage to or destruction of building—insurance. The clause concerning damage or destruction will be detailed, *e.g.:*

Section 1. The Lessee further covenants and agrees that in case of damage to or destruction of any building on the demised premises or the trade fixtures, lighting fixtures, and motors and machinery located therein, by fire or otherwise, it will promptly at its sole cost and expense repair, restore, and rebuild the same as nearly as possible to the condition they were in immediately prior to such damage or destruction or with such changes or alterations as may be made in conformity with Article VIII, such repair, restoration, or rebuilding to be completed within eighteen months after the date of such damage or destruction (subject, however, to delays occasioned by fires, explosions, strikes, lockouts, acts of God, inability to obtain labor or materials, governmental restrictions, or similar causes beyond the control of the Lessee) and the value of the demised premises, upon such completion, to be at least equal to their value prior to such damage or destruction.

Section 2. No damage or destruction, as enumerated in Section 1 of this Article, of any or all buildings on the demised premises, by any casualty whatsoever, shall be taken to entitle the Lessee to surrender possession of the demised premises and to terminate this lease nor shall there by any suspension or abatement of the rent provided for herein as a result of such damage or destruction.

---

[1] © Copyright Ill. Continuing Legal Ed., *Commercial Real Property Transactions*, p. 2–147 (1972). Reprinted by permission.

Section 3. Lessor and Lessee agree to assign and deliver all proceeds of insurance recovered on account of the damage or destruction, as enumerated in Section 1 of this Article, less the cost, if any, of such recovery, to the Lessee, or such depositary as may be agreed by the parties hereto, for the payment of the cost of repair, restoration, or rebuilding. If the proceeds of insurance shall be insufficient to pay the entire cost of said repair, restoration or rebuilding, the Lessee agrees to pay the deficiency. If there shall be a balance of insurance money after the whole cost of the work shall have been defrayed from such insurance money, then in each such case all remaining insurance money collected as a result of such loss shall be the property of the Lessee.

Section 4. The Lessor shall not be responsible for the collection or non-collection of any insurance money in any event, but only for such insurance money as it may receive as Lessor, and the Lessor agrees that in the event it fails to collect any proceeds of insurance the Lessee shall be and hereby is subrogated to and shall at all times, so long as it is not in default, have any and all rights of the Lessor in and to any and all insurance monies, for the purpose of repairing, restoring, or rebuilding the demised premises or any portion thereof.[2]

T may argue for some relaxation of this burden, for example, where destruction occurs in the last two or three years of the lease, and where *T* would derive little benefit from the rebuilding. *T* will argue that he should have the right to terminate in such case as long as insurance money is available to rebuild. *L* will argue that he and his lender make their deal in the expectation of cash flow from *T* for the entire life of the lease.

Of course *T* will be required to carry insurance to cover every contingency in adequate amounts to repair, rebuild, and take care of claims of third parties. Any existing mortgage must be checked to see that all insurance required by the lender is also required by *L*, including insurance the lender may "hereafter" require. *L* will want the insurance to run to him, rather than to *L* and *T*, so that he does not need *T*'s consent to an adjustment of loss with the insurance company. *L* will want hazard policies to run in favor of his mortgage lender also with the standard mortgage clause if any such mortgage exists, and the policies are to be lodged with his lender. Disposition of hazard insurance proceeds in such a way that any rebuilding that takes place is a problem. At times, it is provided that insurance proceeds are to be escrowed with a bank or trust company, which will undertake the rebuilding on production of architect's certificates and mechanic's lien waivers, with reasonable retentions, as in the case of construction under a construction mortgage or ground lease. If the existing mortgage permits the mortgagee to apply hazard insurance proceeds in reduction of the mortgage debt, the mortgage should be modified or a side agreement obtained that the insurance money will be applied to rebuilding. This is apt to be a complex clause, requiring architect's certificated, surety bonds, etc., much like the provisions in construction loans and ground lease. *See* Chapters 22 and 34. If there is any danger that destruction of the improvements may imperil *T*'s ability to continue paying rent, *L* may require *T* to carry rent insurance payable to *L*.

L may want a clause calling for periodic appraisals to make sure that the insurance is adequate.

§ 547. Damage and destruction—short term net leases. At times a net lease of a store or warehouse runs for a short term, say ten years. In those cases, the lease will be something less than a fully net lease.

---

[2] © Copyright Ill. Continuing Legal Ed., *Commercial Real Property Transactions*, 2–148 (1972). Reprinted by permission.

Requiring rebuilding of a destroyed building or even requiring extensive alterations to conform to law (*e.g.*, installing a sprinkler system in the last year of the lease) might be unreasonable. Hence, the lease is modified to protect *T* against unreasonable expenditures. Thus, there are leases that are not fully "net." Indeed, in the real estate business they talk colloquially about "net leases," "net-net leases" and "net-net-net leases."

§ 548. Demolition of existing building and construction of replacement structure. A net lease may provide that *T* shall have the right to demolish the existing building and construct a replacement structure. This is in recognition of the fact that an existing structure may become obsolete. In addition to all the usual problems involved in new construction, this involves the problem of describing a building that will be satisfactory to *L*. This must be done in the lease itself, since *T* will not want to go back to give *L* too much control over the situation at the time he makes the decision to demolish and construct. The new construction is governed by clauses requiring lien waivers, etc. like those governing accidental demolition and reconstruction.

§ 549. Default, remedies, and survival clause. In drafting net leases, some landlord lawyers place stress on the survival clause under which liability for rent continues after abandonment of the premises by *T* or eviction of *T* for default. A tenant having substantial assets is unlikely to abandon the premises where such a clause is present. An aspect of the survival and abandonment clauses that must not be forgotten is the distinction between *rent,* which is a property law concept, and *damages,* which is a contract law concept. Rent issues out of the land, according to the old rules. *T* can agree to pay any *rent* that *L* and *T* can agree upon. But if *T* is ousted for default or abandons the premises, his liability, if any, thereafter, is a *contract liability* for damages, and is subject to the rules of contract law forbidding *L* recovery for avoidable damages, also the contract law rules regarding liquidated damages. Kratovil, *Mortgages* § 332.

A form of default clause follows:

Default and remedies. Section 1. If, during the term of this lease, (a) the Lessee shall make an assignment for the benefit of creditors, or (b) a voluntary petition be filed by the Lessee under any law having for its purpose the adjudication of the Lessee a bankrupt or the extension of the time of payment, composition, adjustment, modification, settlement, or satisfaction of the liabilities of the Lessee or to which any property of the Lessee may be subject or the reorganization (other than a reorganization not involving the liabilities of the Lessee) or liquidation of the Lessee, or (c) an involuntary petition be filed against the Lessee under any law having for its purpose the adjudication of the Lessee a bankrupt or the extension of the time of payment, composition, adjustment, modification, settlement, or satisfaction of the liabilities of the Lessee or to which any property of the Lessee may be subject or the reorganization (other than a reorganization not involving the liabilities of the Lessee) or liquidation of the Lessee and such petition is not dismissed within sixty days, or (d) a permanent receiver be appointed for the property of the Lessee by reason of the insolvency or alleged insolvency of the Lessee, or (e) a temporary receiver be appointed for the property of the Lessee by reason of the insolvency or alleged insolvency of the Lessee and such temporary receiver is not discharged or removed within sixty days, or (f) any department of the state or federal government or any officer thereof, duly authorized (other than as provided in (d) and (e) above), shall take possession of the business or property of the Lessee by reason of the insolvency or alleged insolvency of the Lessee, or (g) the Lessee is adjudicated a bankrupt, the occurrence of any such contingency shall be deemed a breach of this lease and the Lessor, at its option, may terminate this lease and upon such termination the Lessee will quit and surrender the demised premises to the Lessor, but the Lessee shall remain liable as hereinafter provided.

Section 2. If, during the term of this lease, (a) the Lessee shall make default in fulfilling any of the covenants of this lease (other than the covenants for the payment of the basic rent, additional rent, or other charges payable by the Lessee hereunder), or (b) the demised premises shall be used for any unlawful business, or (c) the demised premises shall be left vacant or unoccupied or be deserted for a period of thirty days, or (d) this lease shall be assigned or transferred otherwise than as permitted in Article XII or shall by operation of law pass to or devolve upon any third party (except any personal representative or distributee of a deceased individual assignee of this lease), the Lessor may give to the Lessee notice of any such default or of the happening of any contingency in this Section 2 referred to, and if at the expiration of thirty days after the service of such notice the default or the happening of the contingency upon which said notice was based shall continue to exist, or in the case of a default or contingency that cannot with due diligence be cured within a period of thirty days, if the Lessee fails to proceed promptly after the service of such notice and with all due diligence to cure the same and thereafter to prosecute the curing of such default with all due diligence (it being intended that in connection with a default not susceptible of being cured with due diligence within thirty days, the time of the Lessee within which to cure the same shall be extended for such period as may be necessary to complete the same with all due diligence), the Lessor at its option may terminate this lease and upon such termination the Lessee will quit and surrender the demised premises to the Lessor but the Lessee shall remain liable as hereinafter provided.

Section 3. If the Lessee shall make default in the payment of the basic rent expressly reserved hereunder, or any part of the same, and such default shall continue for fifteen days after notice thereof by the Lessor, or shall make default in the payment of any item of additional rent or any other charge required to be paid by the Lessee hereunder or any part of the same, and such default shall continue for thirty days after notice thereof by the Lessor, or if this lease shall be terminated as in Section 1 or Section 2 of this Article XIX provided, the Lessor or the Lessor's agents and servants may immediately or at any time thereafter reenter the demised premises and remove all persons and all or any property therefrom, either by summary dispossess proceedings or by any suitable action or proceeding at law or by force or otherwise, without being liable to indictment, prosecution, or damages therefor, and repossess and enjoy said premises together with all additions, alterations, and improvements, without such reentry and repossession working a forfeiture of the rents to be paid and the covenants to be performed by the Lessee during the full term hereof. Upon the termination of this lease by reason of the happening of any of the events described in Section 1 or Section 2 of this Article XIX, or in the event of the termination of this lease by summary dispossess proceedings or under any provision of law now or at any time hereafter in force by reason of or based upon or arising out of a default under or breach of this lease on the part of the Lessee, or upon the Lessor's recovering possession of the demised premises in the manner or in any of the circumstances hereinbefore mentioned or in any other manner or circumstances whatsoever, whether with or without legal proceedings, by reason of or based upon or arising out of a default under or breach of this lease on the part of the Lessee, the Lessor shall use reasonable diligence to relet the demised premises or such part or parts thereof as may be practicable, for the account of the Lessee or otherwise, and receive and collect the rents therefor, applying the same first to the payment of such reasonable expenses as the Lessor may have incurred in recovering possession of the demised premises, including legal expenses and attorneys' fees, and in putting the same into good order or condition or preparing or altering the same for re-rental, and all other expense, commissions, and charges paid, assumed, or incurred by the Lessor in or about reletting the premises, and then to the fulfillment of the covenants of the Lessee hereunder. Any such reletting herein provided for may be for the remainder of the term of this lease as originally granted or for a longer or shorter period. In any such case and whether or not the demised premises, or any part thereof, be relet, the Lessee shall pay to the Lessor the basic rent and all other charges required to be paid by the Lessee up to the time of such termination of this lease, or of such recovery of possession of the demised premises by the Lessor, as the case may be, and thereafter, the Lessee agrees to pay the equivalent of the amount of all the basic rent reserved herein and all other charges required to be paid by the Lessee, less the net avails of reletting, if any, and the same shall be due and payable by the Lessee to the Lessor on the several rent days above specified, that is to say, upon each of such rent days the Lessee shall pay to the Lessor the amount of the deficiency then existing. In any of the circumstances hereinabove mentioned in which the Lessor shall have the right to hold the Lessee liable to pay to the Lessor, upon the several rent days herein specified, the equivalent of the amount of all the basic rent and all other charges required to be paid by the Lessee less the net avails of reletting, if any, the Lessor shall have the election, instead of holding the Lessee so liable, forthwith to recover against the Lessee, as damages for loss of the bargain and not as a penalty, an aggregate sum representing, at the time of such termination of this lease or of such recovery of possession of the premises by the Lessor, as the case may be, the then present worth of the excess, if any, of the aggregate of the basic rent and all other charges payable by the Lessee hereunder that would have accrued until the end of the lease term over the aggregate rental value of the demised premises during such term.

Section 4. If this lease shall be terminated by reason of the occurrence of any contingency mentioned in Section 1 of this Article XIX, the Lessor shall be entitled, notwithstanding any other provision of this lease or any present or future law, to recover from the Lessee or its successors and assigns (in lieu of the equivalent of the amount of all the basic rent unpaid at the date of such termination), as damages for loss of the bargain and not as a penalty, an aggregate sum representing, at the time of such termination of this lease, the then present worth of the excess, if any, of the aggregate of the basic rent and all other charges payable by the Lessee hereunder that would have accrued until the end of the lease term over the aggregate rental value of the demised premises for such term, unless any statute or rule of law governing the proceeding in which such damages are to be proved shall limit the amount of such claim capable of being so proved, in which case the Lessor shall be entitled to prove as and for liquidated damages by reason of such breach and termination of this lease the maximum amount that may be allowed by or under any such statute or rule of law. Nothing herein contained shall limit or prejudice the Lessor's right to prove and obtain as liquidated damages arising out of such breach or termination the maximum amount allowed by any such statute or rule of law that may govern the proceedings in which such damages are to be proved, whether or not such an amount be greater, equal to, or less than the amount of the excess of the basic rent over the rental value referred to above.

Section 5. The Lessee hereby expressly waives the service of notice of intention to reenter as provided for in any statute, and also waives any and all right of redemption in case the Lessee shall be dispossessed by a judgment or by warrant of any court or judge. The Lessee also waives and will waive any and all right to a trial by a jury in the event that summary proceeding shall be instituted by the Lessor. The terms "enter," "reenter," "entry," or "reentry" as used in this lease are not restricted to their technical legal meaning.[3]

§ 550. Warranties and representations. As in the case of a sale of a substantial building, a net lease contains warranties, for example, warranties that the heating and air conditioning system are in operating condition. Warranties of installers held in *L's* files should be assigned to *T*. Representations are not unlike those in a sale of a substantial building. For example, *L* represents that he knows of no disputes or threats of litigation with neighbors, no threatened condemnation, etc. *See* Chapter 42.

§ 551. Miscellaneous clauses. There are a number of miscellaneous clauses of a semi-routine nature, including; (1) Remedies are cumulative. (2) No merger clause, like that in a ground lease. *See* Chapter 34.

§ 552. Sale and leaseback—in general. A sale and leaseback invariably involves a net lease. Some investors require monthly payments of taxes and insurance as in mortgages.

§ 553. Sale and leaseback—mortgage nature of sale and leaseback. The single great legal problem with respect to a sale and leaseback is whether it can be construed as a mortgage. In this respect a multitude of circumstances are weighed, including:

1. The intention of the parties as expressed and as evidenced by the economic realities of the transaction.

2. If the grantee-lessor is a lending institution, this is a minor circumstance tending to indicate a loan transaction. Many such parties also have the right to invest in land and the line between lender and investor becomes blurred.

---

[3] © Copyright Ill. Continuing Legal Ed., *Commercial Real Property Transactions*, P.2—150 *et. seq.* (1972). Reprinted by permission.

3. Disparity between sale price of the property and the fair-market value of the property. But if the rent is attractive to the grantor-lessor, this waters down the importance of inadequate sale price.

4. An option to repurchase that, in economic effect, compels the lessee to exercise the option because it is far below the value of the property, is some evidence that a loan was intended. This is the doctrine of *economic compulsion*. Of course, a covenant by *T* to exercise the option goes a long way toward establishing the mortgage nature of the transaction. The same result is achieved, it is argued, if the economics of the situation compel *T* to exercise the option.

5. Application of rentals. If the rentals are applicable to the option price, rather than to pure rental income, this tends to show a loan intention, since the lessee is building up an equity by paying "rent."

§ 554. Sale and leaseback—tax aspects.

The tax aspects of a sale and leaseback have been ably discussed elsewhere. 2 Real Estate L. J. 664 *et. seq.*

It is interesting to note that whatever the parties agree upon among themselves, or indeed, whatever the courts decide concerning the nature of the transaction, the IRS has its own rules governing the tax consequences of the transaction.

References: 24 U. of Miami L.Rev. 642; 48 Calif. B.J. 555 (1973); 1972 Duke L.J. 1221; PLI Real Estate Financing 329 (1970).

§ 555. Sale and leaseback—suggested clauses:

It is covenanted and agreed between the parties hereto as follows:

(a) Each of the parties hereto is represented by able counsel and each of the parties fully understands the legal and economic aspects of this transaction.

(b) This instrument is what is commonly known as a lease and the relation between the parties is that of landlord and tenant. There is no intention to create a security interest of any kind, a joint venture, a partnership, or any relationship other than that of landlord and tenant.

(c) No inequality of bargaining power is present and neither party has taken advantage of or exercised any coercion upon the other.

(d) The rents reserved herein represent the fair, market rental value in the circumstances of this transaction.

(e) The option price stated herein represents the fair, market option price in the circumstances of this transaction.

(f) Should either party hereto, or his successor, unsuccessfully assert in litigation that this transaction is other than a lease, the other party shall receive a reasonable attorney's fee as part of the costs.

§ 556. Sandwich lease.

A sandwich lease is a lease of the entire property by *L* to *T*, followed by a sublease by *T* to the actual operator. The return to *T* is the difference between the rent he pays to *L* and the rent he receives from his subtenant. The sublease may be "sweetened" by giving the subtenant an option to purchase *T*'s leasehold. *L* shifts the burden of operation to a qualified tenant-operator. When *L* mortgages the fee, the lender must be sure he procures from *T* an assignment of the subreversions in all the major occupancy leases. The sandwich lease should contain a covenant requiring this. *L* would be well advised to require an attornment agreement from the major subtenants. It is always possible that *T* will fold up, and *L* and his mortgagee will want to hold the subtenants.

Where the premises are subject to an existing mortgage, the rentals should be adequate to meet debt service and provide income to *L* over and above mortgage payments.

§ 557. Active assignment of rents.

Another form of net lease that developed out of the sale and leaseback concept involves the active assignment of rents.

EXAMPLE: *D* a developer, forms a shell corporation, *D Corporation,* and in its name acquires land suitable for use by *T,* a high-credit corporation (or an option to purchase the same.) *T* gives *D* a commitment to accept a lease conditioned on erection of a building to *T's* specifications. *D Corporation* now goes to *E,* an institutional investor, and obtains a commitment under which *E* will advance 100 percent of the construction funds. As security, *D Corporation* gives *E* a mortgage on the land, and included therein, or in a separate assignment, an assignment of *D Corporation's* interest in the lease, contemporaneously executed by *D Corporation* to *T,* and all rents accruing thereunder. The assignment provides that *E* will immediately step in as a mortgagee in possession collecting all the rents from *T* under the lease. The rent from *T* under the fully net lease is adequate to pay the mortgage payments. There is no risk to *E.* Indeed the focus is on the assignment. The mortgage is there to complete the customary, well understood, package of mortgage with mortgagee in possession under an activated assignment of rents, good in all states.

It is important, especially in lien theory states, that the mortgagee immediately acquire the status of mortgagee in possession. This is a respectable, venerable status, recognized universally, and unassailable.

CLAUSE: It is agreed that immediately upon the first payment of rent by said tenant to said mortgagee, the mortgagee shall acquire the status of a mortgagee in possession.

It is best to reinforce this by language in the assignment of leases and rents.

CLAUSE: It is expressly covenanted and agreed that, in addition to the other rights and titles vested in the mortgagee by the said mortgage and by this assignment, the mortgagee has the rights and status of a mortgagee in possession.

Because in some states the ridiculous rule is entertained that an assignment of rents relates to a chose in action and is, therefore, not recordable as an instrument relating to real estate, the mortgage, which is clearly recordable everywhere, should contain a clause that incorporates the assignment and pulls it into the chain of title. 75 ALR 261.

CLAUSE: This mortgage and the assignment of rents therein contained is supplemented and implemented by an Assignment of Lease and Rents from _____ to _____ dated _____ and recorded simultaneously herewith, to which reference is made for the terms thereof, all of which are incorporated herein.

And because in some states one must take precautions against prior unrecorded assignments of rents, valid in that state without recording, a further clause is needed.

CLAUSE: Mortgagor represents and warrants that this is the only mortgage on the mortgaged premises and that there is no assignment of leases or assignments of rents other than that herein described.

And as part of the rights assigned to the mortgagee, the covenants in the lease should be assigned:

CLAUSE: This mortgage also assigns to the mortgagee the benefit of all covenants in said lease binding on the lessee or its successors and necessary or convenient for the enforcement of the interests of the mortgage hereby created.

And the mortgagor's interest in the lease must also be assigned in and by the assignment of rents to the mortgagee.

CLAUSE: As security for payment of the debt aforesaid, the mortgagor irrevocably assigns, transfers and sets over to the mortgagee, its successors and assigns, as a present and primary fund, of equal dignity with the conveyance of the land as security as in said mortgage set forth all of the mortgagor's right, title and interest in, to, and under the lease, and all of the mortgagor's reversion, including, without limitation the full amount of the Basic Rent and the Additional Rent in said Lease described.

Another clause is needed in the assignment.

CLAUSE: This assignment shall not be merged or extinguished by any foreclosure of the mortgage herein described.

And a final clause is added to the assignment.

CLAUSE: This assignment of lease is and is intended to be and create a security interest separate and distinct from the mortgage aforesaid. Foreclosure of the mortgage shall not, by merger or otherwise, extinguish any rights or interests created by this assignment. The title and rights hereby created shall continue through and during any redemption period existing with respect to said mortgage.

§ **557a. Net leases.** A suggested Landlord's Form Insurance clause for net lease follows:

14. INSURANCE:

(a) So long as this Lease remains in effect, *T,* at its expense, will maintain, or cause to be maintained with insurers approved by *L:* (1) insurance with respect to the Improvements against loss or damage by fire, lightning, and other risks from time to time included under extended coverage endorsements, in amounts sufficient to prevent *L,* or *T* from becoming a co-insurer of any partial loss under the applicable policies, but in any event in amounts equal to 80 percent of the full replacement value of the Improvements (exclusive of the cost of foundations and excavations), less physical depreciation, as determined at the request of *L* and at *T's* expense by the insurer or insurers or by an expert approved by *L,* as the case may be; (2) comprehensive general liability insurance applicable to the Premises with limits of liability of not less than $500,000 per person and $1,000,000 per occurrence for injury to persons including death resulting therefrom, and $100,000 per occurrence for damage to the property of others with not more than $5,000 deductible; (3) explosion insurance in respect of any boilers and similar apparatus located on the Premises in an amount of $100,000; and (4) war risk insurance, when and to the extent available and usually maintained, and in the amounts usually carried, by persons operating like or similar properties in the vicinity of the Premises; (5) rent, or use and occupancy or rental value insurance in an amount at least sufficient to meet the payments for one year of the fixed rental provided for in Section 5(a), the Impositions provided for in Section 8(b) and the debt charges on any Permitted Encumbrance, which insurance shall be payable to *L, T,* and the holder of any Permitted Encumbrance, as their interests may appear, but which policies shall be delivered to and held by *L* or the holder of such Permitted Encumbrance and, in the event that the Improvements or any substantial portion thereof, shall be destroyed or seriously damaged, *T* shall assign to *L* the interest of *T* in said policies and all proceeds thereunder, which proceeds, when collected in cash by *L,* shall be held in trust and applied to the payment of any debt charges then due and payable under any Permitted Encumbrance, and to the performance by *T* of all the covenants, agreements, terms and provisions of the Lease until the repair, restoration, or reconstruction of the Improvements shall be completed as provided for in Section 15 hereof; and (6) such other insurance on the Improvements and in such amounts as may from time to time be reasonably required by *L* against other insurable hazards which at the time are commonly insured against in the case of premises similarly situated.

(b) All insurance required to be maintained pursuant to Section 14(a) shall: (1) except for comprehensive general liability insurance, name *L* and *T* as insureds, as their respective interests may appear; (2) provide that all insurance proceeds shall be adjusted with *L* and *T* by *T* and shall, except in the case of comprehensive general liability insurance, be payable to *L* and *T,* as their respective interests may appear and (3) provide that no cancellation thereof shall be effective until at least 10 days after receipt by *L* and *T* of written notice thereof. Any insurance required to be maintained by *T* pursuant to this paragraph 14 may be evidenced by blanket insurance policies covering the Premises and other property or assets of *T,* provided that any such policies of the type referred to in subdivisions (1) and (3) of paragraph 14(a) shall specify that portion of the total coverage of such policy that is allocated to the Premises and shall, in all other respects, comply with the requirements of this Section 14. All insurance proceeds paid to *T* and *L* shall be held in trust by *L* for application in the manner provided in paragraph 15.

(c) All insurance policies covering the Premises shall expressly waive any right on the part of the insurer to be subrogated to any rights of *L* against *T* and to any rights of *T* against *L.*

(d) *T* will promptly upon request deliver to *L* the originals or certified copies of all insurance policies (or, in the case of blanket policies, certificates thereof) with respect to the Premises which *T* is required to maintain pursuant to this Section 14 and Section 12(g).

15. CASUALTY:

(a) If, at any time during the term of this Lease, the Improvements or any part thereof, shall be damaged or destroyed by fire or other casualty (including any casualty for which insurance coverage was not obtained or obtainable) of any kind or nature, ordinary or extraordinary, foreseen or un-foreseen, *T,* at its sole cost and expense, and whether or not the insurance proceeds, if any, shall be sufficient for the purpose, shall proceed with reasonable diligence (subject to Unavoidable Delays and a reasonable time allowance for the purpose of adjusting such loss) to repair, alter, restore, replace or rebuild the same as nearly as possible to its value, condition and character immediately prior to such damage or destruction, subject to such changes or alterations as *T* may elect to make in conformity with the provisions of Section 12 hereof. Such repairs, alterations, restoration, replacement or rebuilding, including such changes and alterations as aforementioned and including temporary repairs or the protection of other property pending the completion of any thereof, are sometimes referred to in this Section as the "Work."

(b) Except as otherwise provided in this Section, the conditions under which any repairs, alterations, restoration, replacement or rebuilding Work are to be performed and the method of proceeding with and performing the same shall be governed by all of the provisions of Section 12 hereof,[4] except subsections (a) and (h) of said Section.

(c) All insurance money paid to *L* on account of such damage or destruction under the policies of insurance provided for in Section 14 hereof, less the cost, if any, incurred in connection with the adjustment of the loss and the collection thereof (herein sometimes referred to as the "insurance proceeds"), shall be held by *L* in trust and applied exclusively to the payment of the cost of the Work to the extent such insurance proceeds shall be sufficient for the purpose, and shall be paid out to or for the account of *T* from time to time as such Work progresses. All sums so paid to *T* and any other insurance proceeds received or collected by or for the account of *T* (other than by way of reimburse-ment to *T* for sums therefore paid by *T*) shall be held by *T* in trust for the purpose of paying the cost of such Work.

Upon receipt by *L* of evidence reasonably satisfactory to it that the Work has been completed and paid for in full and that there are no liens on the Premises as a result thereof, *L* shall pay to *T* any remaining balance of said insurance proceeds. If the insurance proceeds received by *L* shall be insufficient to pay the entire cost of the Work, *T* shall supply the amount of any such deficiency and shall first apply the same to the payment of the cost of the Work before calling upon *L* for the disbursement of the insurance proceeds held by *L.*

Under no circumstances shall *L* be obligated to make any payment, disbursement or contribution toward the cost of the Work except to the extent of the insurance proceeds actually received by *L.* If *T* shall fail to comply with any of the provisions of subsections (a) or (b) above, *L* shall notify *T* of such default and thereafter *L,* in addition to any other remedies *L* may have, may refuse to make any payment hereunder and may apply the insurance proceeds in any order *L* may elect toward the payment of the cost of the Work or the payment of any fixed rental or percentage rental in default.

(d) In no event shall *T* be entitled to any abatement, allowance, reduction or suspension of rent because part or all of the Premises shall be untenantable owing to the partial or total destruction thereof, and anything herein to the contrary, no such damage or destruction shall affect in any way the obligation of *T* to pay the fixed rental, percentage rental, and other charges herein reserved or required to be paid, nor release *T* of or from any obligation imposed upon *T* under this Lease.

---

[4] Relates to architect's certificates, etc.

29

Lease Outline—Check Lists and Suggestions—Lease Clauses

§ **558. I. Demised premises.** What goes with premises demised, *e.g.*, vaults beneath sidewalks, pipes and conduits crossing leased premises.

§ **559. II. Condition of demised premises.** *L* should agree to put premises and entrances into usable condition and free of building code violations before term begins.

§ **560. III. Repairs.**

A. For *L*, lease should acknowledge premises are now in good repair or *T* accepts them as they are.

B. *T* should not covenant to repair any damage covered by *L's* insurance, including *L's* all-risk casualty policy. In a net lease, *L* does not insure.

C. If *L* covenants to repair, *L* should be sure his obligations are all covered by insurance.

D. *L's* covenant to repair:

1. *T* wants *L's* duty to extend to walks, drives, parking areas, etc.

2. Exculpate *L* where statute, ordinance, or regulation forbids such repairs.

3. *L's* duty should be conditioned on prior notice from *T* to make repairs in *T's* premises.

4. No obligation to repair damage caused by *T* or by his occupancy.

5. *T* to provide ordinary maintenance for items (air conditioners, etc.) entirely within the store premises. *T* will wish to exclude replacement.

6. Exculpate *L* for liability for consequential damages, *e.g.*, *T's* business interruption, also for personal injuries to *T*, invitees, licensees. *T* can cover this by insurance.

7. Clause should require *L* to proceed with dispatch.

E. *T's* covenant to repair or maintain:

    1. *T* should have no duty to repair where *L* has insurance coverage. *T* should permit access for insurance adjustment and repairs.

    2. If *T* has duty to repair, require him to carry insurance to provide funds for repairs.

    3. *L* should not allow *T* to have right to exercise judgment as to need for repairs.

    4. *T* should not extend covenant to common areas except those immediately adjoining.

    5. Cover liability of *T* for injuries to third parties owing to failure to make repairs or negligent repairs. Require *T* to carry liability insurance. A big claim could bankrupt *T*.

    6. Pinpoint time at which *T* is to make repairs.

    7. Distinguish between gross lease and net lease. In net lease, *T* has complete duty to repair and carries insurance.

    8. Determine whether *T* should covenant to repair pipes and other common facilities running through demised premises.

    9. Clause requiring *T* to *maintain in good condition* requires *T* to replace damage of ordinary deterioration unless wear and tear are excluded. It may include an obligation to install facilities not present when lease is made. *Holtz Rubber Co. Inc. v. General Acc. & L. Assur. Corp.*, 111 Cal. Rep. 883.

    10. The covenant by *T* to *make repairs* is a troublesome one. In some states, a covenant to *"repair"* does not require *T* to replace a defective item, such as a compressor for air conditioning. A good clause is apt to be lengthy. Most repair items in commercial leases that are not net leases should fall on *L*.

    11. What does covenant to "maintain" mean, for example, with respect to heating system? Replacement included?

§ 561. IV. Damage or destruction generally.

    1. Must cover rent abatement during period when weighing decision to terminate. If rent abates, there is a negative cash flow, and mortgagee will insist on rent insurance. After all, mortgagee counts on rent to pay debt service.

    2. Negate *T's* duty to rebuild except in fully net lease.

    3. Where *L* has duty to rebuild, should this include betterments installed by *T*?

    4. Whichever party has decision to terminate, fix a time limit.

    5. If *L* has right to terminate, this is a boon when rents are rising. If *T* has the right, it's a boon to him when rents are falling.

6. If *T* is given right to terminate on *destruction* define *destruction*. Define *untenantable*. *T's* premises may remain "tenantable" though hopelessly out of reach because of destruction of the story beneath. "Untenantable" is a slippery word.

§ 562. V. Services.

A. Who provides services such as heat?

B. Is there an Acts of God Clause, in case it is impossible to furnish service? Does it include voluntary compliance with government policy statements not amounting to law?

§ 563. VI. Yield up and surrender clause.

A. *T* should avoid clause requiring him to yield up in good condition if premises were in bad condition at inception of lease.

B. If clause to yield up in condition that existed at inception of lease, *T* should consider commercial photographs.

C. *T* should negate liability for conditions due to normal wear and use.

D. If only clause is that requiring *T* to "surrender" or "yield up" in good repair, this does not require repairs prior to end of lease term. *Gallup Gamerco Coal Co. v. Irwin*, 515 P2d 1277.

E. Yielding in good condition does not require *T* to dismantle his alterations, signs, mosaic titles, etc., which may be costly. Consent of mortgagee may be needed on big items. They may be fixtures and part of the land. Also cover removal of *T's* chattels, and his failure in this regard.

F. Duty to rebuild may be qualified by yield up clause which relieves *T* of duty in case of Acts of God.

G. Watch out for exculpatory provisions in yield up clause, *e.g.*, clause requiring *T* to yield up in good condition except fire damage.

H. Assignee or subleasee doesn't know conditions *at inception of lease* and should beware of yield-up clause that mentions this period.

§ 564. VII. Uses.

A. *T's* uses defined and other uses forbidden.

B. Check whether permitted use violates building restrictions or ordinances or exclusive of another tenant. If it is a valid nonconforming use, lease cannot require rebuilding in case of destruction, for the ordinance forbids this.

C. Forbid structures or uses on adjoining premises controlled by *L* and, harmful to *T*.

§ 565. VIII. Common areas and facilities.

A. *L* will reserve right to enter to replace pipes, conduits, etc., that serve other areas.

B. *L* will reserve right to make changes in entrances, etc. that do not harm *T*.

§ 566. IX. Insurance.

A. *L* should be required to carry hazard insurance in amounts sufficient to rebuild. In net lease, *T* carries the insurance due with an assignment in lease of insurance proceeds to *L* for rebuilding purposes.

B. *L* and *T* as co-insured parties.

   1. Insurance company can have no subrogation against either if both *L* and *T* are the assured. *T* does not want liability to insurance company. Keep in mind *T*, though occupying one store, could be liable for destruction of the entire building if due to his negligence. Many policies now contain waiver of right of subrogation.

   2. Spell out who pays premium.

   3. Spell out how insurance proceeds are shared.

   4. You need clause in policy that acts of one will not invalidate insurance as to other.

   5. Law permits either to sue other for negligence.

   6. Drawbacks of having joint assureds include: (a) both must join in proof of loss, and one party may seek to make this a tactical advantage. (b) death, insanity, etc. complicate proof of loss. (c) Not always clear who owns what, where *T* invests in "betterments."

C. Liability.

   1. O L & T does not cover "assumed liability", that is liability assumed by contract. If *T* has assumed liability for escalators, sidetracks, etc., try to get insurance to cover *T*, possibly comprehensive liability. There is fire liability insurance to cover negligence liability for fire damage.

   2. Policy should cover *L* and *T*.

D. Interior damage. If *T* is responsible for interior, *L* should not carry insurance for this, but *T* should.

E. If use of adjoining premises controlled by *L* or his tenants increases *T's* insurance costs, *L* should agree to pay for this increase. But if *T's* operations increase *L's* insurance costs, *T* should agree to pay.

F. Mortgages.

   1. Must mortgagee be considered in adjustment of loss?

   2. Watch out for situations in which insurance money goes to mortgagee, leaving no funds to rebuild.

G. Bankruptcy.

Fire may put a party in bankruptcy and his insurance proceeds go to his trustee in bankruptcy. Trustee is not interested in rebuilding. If *T* is to carry insurance, consider clause that if a receiver or trustee in bankruptcy is appointed, all *T's* rights in proceeds of hazard insurance pass to *L*.

H. If lease provides that *T* is not liable for fire damage caused by his neglect, *L*'s existing policy should be endorsed with company's consent. This may violate subrogation clause in insurance policy. Or let the company waive subrogation.

I. Measure of damage for failure to insure.

1. Loss sustained?

2. Amount of insurance premium?

J. Negligence liability of *T* to *L* for loss may continue though lease requires *L* to insure.

K. Periodic appraisals to keep insurance coverage equal to value.

§ 567. X. Improvements and betterments by *L* and *T*.

A. *T* to have right to enter an adjoining premises controlled by *L* to make improvements.

B. *L* to have right to enter demised premises to make improvements on adjoining land.

C. If *L* is to construct shell and *T* to do all interior work, lease should be detailed as to who does what.

D. It is always necessary to state who owns what; necessary for insurance proof of loss, for example. Avoid *"T's* improvements become *L's* property at termination of lease." *T's* improvements, called *betterments* in insurance circles are of a permanent nature. If they are to belong to *L* at termination, let him own them as part of the building during lease. Then, whoever, has the burden of restoring the building restores the betterments. *L's* covenants to restore the "building" may not extend to betterments owned by *T*. In sale and leaseback, *T* wants to *own* the building.

E. *T's* trade fixtures are personal property, removable at termination of lease, and are therefore different from *T's* betterments, which are not removable.

F. A landlord's covenant to erect additional buildings for the tenant is objectionable to a mortgage lender. If he acquires title by foreclosure he is stuck with a requirement to construct a building for which he has reserved no funds and which would not meet his appraisal requirements.

§ 568. XI. Alterations by *T*.

A. Alterations should not cause architectural change, weaken structure, decrease rental value.

B. Procure existing mortgagee's consent (mortgage forbids alterations without his consent).

C. *L* may wish to require his consent to alterations where *L* wants *T* to make a substantial investment as a hedge against default by *T;* or where *T's* remodeling would be costly to take out were *T* to become insolvent; or where alterations would affect other tenants.

D. *L* may wish to forbid *structural alterations.*

E. *L* wants protection against mechanic's liens. A triple-A tenant's covenant to pay all liens may suffice.

§ 569. XII. Ordinance and statute violations.

A. *L* covenants no ordinance or statute considerations exist and will take no action to cause any.

B. Who is liable for future ordinance and statutory changes that require alterations, and remedies if default?

C. *L* no liability for police power action not due to his act or neglect.

D. *T* will not permit violations, but special provision for big expense items.

§ 570. XIII. Indemnity clause. To hold *L* harmless from loss, damage, liability, or expense suffered by *T* or any third person and caused by any:

1. Act or neglect of *T.*
2. Use or misuse by *T* of gas, water, steam, electricity, pipes, sprinklers.
3. Use or misuse by *T* of machinery, apparatus, signs, awnings, stairways, elevators, escalators, approaches.

§ 571. XIV. Nonclaim clause. All property of *T* is at sole risk of *T* and *L* not liable for any damage or destruction, including that caused by fire, water, and any other cause whatever, whether or not caused in part or whole by *L. T* will resist.

§ 572. XV. Taxes. State who is to pay taxes.

§ 573. XVI. Lease tracking with other documents. The lease should track with the other relevant documents.

EXAMPLE: *T* agrees to a broad clause indemnifying *L* against all loss. *T* cannot procure comprehensive liability insurance against *all* the losses *L* might suffer. Is *T* really willing to indemnify *L* against uninsured losses?

§ 574. Demised premises. Some description is needed of what is included in, or excluded from, the demised premises, *e.g.,* the demised premises include balconies, awnings, interior partition walls, interior washrooms and plumbing fixtures but not outside walls, roof, airshafts, gutters, facilities serving other areas (including pipes, ducts, conduits and the like) basement, cellars or vaults. If *T* is to have use of basement space that should be specifically described.

§ 575. Demised premises—appurtenances. A lease automatically carries with it a mixed bag of rights denominated "appurtenances."

EXAMPLE: A lease of a building carries to the center of the street adjoining, as is true of contracts, deeds, and mortgages.

EXAMPLE: A lease of an office creates implied easements over the halls, stairs, elevators, etc.

EXAMPLE: A lease of a store may carry the landlord's license rights in the vault space beneath the sidewalk if used exclusively for the store.

There really is no alternative to checking the situation carefully in the light of existing law. Friedman, *Leases* § 3.2. Then those rights that are of importance ought to be set forth specifically. However, *L* may wish to state that he demises the appurtenances without warranty and that revocation by the city of licenses shall not result in a reduction of rent. Rights that are really important, such as parking easements, may call for a title policy insuring such easement rights.

§ 576. Demised premises—chattels. If *L* owns substantial chattels that *T* will need in his operation, the demise should include the chattels in the demise.

Sometimes *L* and *T* will enter into what has become known as a "turn-key lease." This is a lease where *L* does everything by way of construction to both the exterior and interior, including all cosmetic work as well as other structural matters. In some cases, *L* even stocks the facilities with the initial inventory of personal property necessary to operate the specific business of *T,* such as hospitals, convalescent homes, hotels, motels, restaurants, etc. In such a lease, adequate provision should be made for one of the parties (as agreed) to pay for all replacements of worn out personalty included in the original demise. It is customary for these replacements to be made by *T.*

§ 577. Percentage leases. From time immemorial, tenant-farmers have entered into share-cropping arrangements with their landlords. This is the historical antecedent of today's percentage lease. The rise of the chain store introduced a new element into the rental bargaining between landlord and tenant. Ultimately, a rental tied basically to sales volume emerged as a sound substitute for the old "location rental." The problems of draftsmanship are complex. They are discussed elsewhere.

References on percentage leases: *The Percentage Lease* Building Managers Association of Chicago; *Percentage Leases for 80 Types of Retail Business in Manhattan,* Management Division, Real Estate Board of New York; *Percentage Leases,* National Institute of Real Estate Brokers of NAREB; 36 Boston U.L.Rev. 190; 19 Chicago Kent L.Rev. 384; 51 Minn.L.Rev. 1139; 60 N.W.U.L.Rev. 677; 38 ALR2d 1113; 58 ALR3d 184.

§ 578. Office buildings—check lists. Excellent check lists are found in the *Practical Lawyer*, December, 1970, p. 69, and March, 1971, #3, p. 79, both by Philip G. Meyers, of the Chicago Bar.

§ 579. Office buildings floor area. In office buildings, the lease may call for rental per square foot of area computed according to a formula promulgated by the local Building Managers Association. Whether corridors are included in "rentable area" is an important item. Special provisions are encountered for support columns, washrooms, elevator shafts, steps to basement, etc.

§ 580. Office buildings—floor load. Before lease is signed, *L* determines whether *T's* planned installations create floor-load problems.

§ 581. Office buildings—option in *L* to relocate *T*. In office buildings *L* likes to retain an option to relocate a small tenant to make it possible to rent a whole floor to a big tenant, *L* to pay moving expenses, carpeting etc.

§ 582. Services by landlord. Drafting of *L's* covenants as to services he has to perform (heat, water, gas, air-conditioning, trash removal, snow removal, painting, cleaning, termite eradication, decorating corridors, lobbies, etc.) was formerly a matter involving no great skill. Today, with the energy shortage, problems arise. *L* might be unable to procure energy sufficient to heat or air-condition the building on weekends. Even during the week he may be unable to go over 68° in the winter or below 80° in the summer. *L* cannot agree to achieve the impossible. So-called "voluntary controls" pose an obvious problem. Another matter, that of security, seems indispensable today. The type and cost of security service is a matter of negotiation.

Particular care must be exercised in preparation of lease covenants involving special services to be rendered by *L*. This is particularly true in case of leases for computer using tenants where *T* requires special provisions for constancy of temperature levels and continuous flow of power to operate the sophisticated machinery to be installed in the premises. Sometimes computer companies will want *L* to install rather expensive and ornate standby power plants which trigger into operation in case of a failure of public utility companies. Obviously, the cost of these facilities becomes reflected in the rent.

§ 583. Repairs and maintenance. Structural maintenance directly affecting the leased premises is a matter of negotiation. This includes roof repair, exterior walls, (tuck pointing, etc.), walls between tenants, foundations, footings, replacing broken glass. In the lease of a department store, the burden will fall on *T*, as it does in any lease of an entire building.

T will want *L* to agree to repair promptly and maintain all the facilities in the premises that are under *L's* control such as water pipes, sewer pipes, ducts, utilities. Other facilities, such as washrooms, lighting fixtures, etc., that are basically under *T's* control present a matter for negotiation. If *L* has a maintenance crew and *T's* operation does not warrant such an expense, the answer is obvious. If we are dealing with an ordinary store lease, it makes sense to have *T* assume all repairs in the store itself that cost under a stated figure, say $100.00. Calling in *L* for minor items is too irritating and expensive. In a fully net lease, where the mortgage lender is relying on the rental income, the answer is obvious, *T* pays for all repairs.

Except in the net lease, *T* will want a clause requiring *L* to replace worn out or defective equipment furnished by *L*, such as air conditioners.

At all times, the attitude of *L's* lender must be kept in mind. He does not like burdens that will fall on him if he is forced to take over the operation.

While the attitude of the lender must be kept in mind, it should be recognized that there are certain customs and usages with which lenders are familiar. For example, lenders recognize that in a typical retail store lease, L may be obligated to replace worn out parts of mechanical systems, which under the terms of the lease T may be obligated to maintain. Also, in many instances where T is obligated to repair or restore any damage or destruction caused by fire or other casualty, there is customarily reserved to T the right to abstain from repairing and the right to cancel the lease if the damage occurs within the last two or three years of a long term lease. Mortgagees are accustomed to seeing this kind of covenant and will normally accept it.

T will want L to agree to promptly repair and maintain facilities outside the leased premises that are not under tenant control, such as parking areas, malls, walks, drives, elevators, escalators, lobbies, sewer, water and utility lines, etc. T will want some general agreement that L will maintain in good condition, substantially as at the date of the lease, the project of which the leased premises are a part, whether it be a shopping center, etc. The parties must keep the mortgage lender in mind while drafting such clauses. All landlord burdens fall on a lender who forecloses. He wants few landlord burdens in the lease.

Some triple-A tenants, chain stores for example, can expect to obtain fairly broad agreements by L to make repairs that are needed in the project and even a mortgage lender must reconcile himself to these agreements if he must take over the project.

If the duty to repair or maintain falls on T, L will require language that repairs and maintenance will take place within a reasonable time after occasion for such actions arises, since delayed action can affect other tenants injuriously. If the only clause is one that T will "yield up" the premises in good repair, this could enable T to procrastinate until the end of the term. However, if the duty rests on T to *maintain* or *not to suffer waste*, the addition of the *yield up* clause may not permit T to delay repairs until the end of the term. Where T has the burden of repair, including, for example, replacement of equipment, he will want to consider the possibility of a substantial defect arising toward the end of the lease. Replacement will be of little benefit to T. If L will not agree to a cancellation clause, perhaps he will agree to assume this burden during the last years of the lease.

T will argue for an abatement of rent while L is repairing damage caused by fire, etc., or by a partial taking under the power of eminent domain. Present and future mortgage lenders object to rent abatements.

Wherever T is to assume the burden of repairing, rebuilding, etc., he must expect L to insist that he use union labor, if that is the practice in the community. L does not want trouble with his own union employees. If L is insisting on a surety bond to protect against mechanic's liens, T had better check with some surety company to see whether he is an acceptable risk, since the surety company will look to T for reimbursement if it is compelled to complete the job. The surety company may require collateral.

The lease may require T to keep all glass in repair and to carry plate glass insurance. T will argue for an exception where L is required to carry insurance that covers this damage also. Both parties should not cover the same risk.

Whether L or T agrees to repair and maintain, he will like to see a provision excepting ordinary wear and tear, Acts of God, such as storm damage and other matters beyond his control.

Where the burden of repair or replacement falls on *T*, he will want some agreement as to enforcement of warranties and guarantees the landlord has obtained from various contractors, such as roof warranties, air-conditioning warranties.

Some leases require *T* to surrender the premises at the end of the lease *in good condition*. Questions then arise whether there was an implied agreement by *T* to improve the premises if they were leased to him in bad condition. It is better for *T* to agree to surrender the premises in the same condition as existed when *T* took possession, ordinary wear and tear excepted, and without liability for necessary damage caused by *T's* lawful removal of his installations.

§ 584. Landlord's work—work list—incorporation in lease. Agreements by *L* to do work must be supported by consideration, like other contracts. Hence, the work letter or other agreement should be referred to and made part of the lease.

§ 585. Damage and destruction. Some agreement must be reached as to the effect of destruction in the project outside the leased premises, *e.g.*, fire damage affecting a major tenant in a shopping center. Obviously, a fire that puts a key department store temporarily out of business, affects the patronage of a shopping center. One solution is to go to a percentage rent until repairs are completed.

If the burden of repairing falls on *L*, it is often agreed that if the premises become "untenantable," rent and other charges payable by *T* will abate, at least as to the damaged parts, until the premises have become tenantable. If *T* can stay in business as to part of the premises, he can agree to pay a percentage rent. At times there is a further provision giving *T* the right to cancel out if the premises remain untenantable for a stated period of time. A common period stated is 60 days, which is rather unrealistic when we consider how slowly insurance companies sometimes act to settle claims. *L* will argue for a longer period, if he makes a reasonable start during that time on the actual work or repair and will try to tie the period to his insurance policies. If the building is destroyed, *T* will want to be relieved of his liability for rent. He will want a clause terminating the lease in such event, unless the lease is a net lease.

The mortgage lender's needs must be kept in mind. Lenders who count on cash flow from tenants oppose rent abatement clauses.

The clause for abatement of rent should take account of rents paid in advance. If part of the rent abatement falls in the period for which rents were paid in advance, *L* should agree to refund a pro-rata part of such advance payment.

Where the lease is of such magnitude that the mortgage lender is looking to the rental cash flow to amortize the mortgage debt, *L* will raise objection to any right on *T's* part to cancel because of damage to the building, since mortgage lenders object to such clauses.

§ 586. Tenant liability—subrogation. *L* may try for a clause obligating *T* to pay for any loss or damage caused by the tenant's negligence. This raises several questions. *L* may have insurance against this contingency, in which case, if the insurer compensates *L*, it will insist on being subrogated to *L's* right to sue *T*. If *T* insists on being a party assured under the policy, this right to subrogation is extinguished, because the insurer must compensate both *L* and *T*, and if *T* can compel the insurer to settle, his liability to *L* will come to an end. But *L* objects to this solution because *T*, being a party assured, can cause the policy coverage to terminate by his own act, such as arson. Also, in big buildings you cannot add the names of all tenants to the hazard policies. Many policies now contain a waiver of the right of subrogation against the tenant. One would think that a clause in the lease requiring the insurance policies, including existing policies, to contain a waiver of the right of subrogation would do the trick.

§ 587. Building to be constructed. Where *L* leases space in a building to be constructed by *L*, he will wish to exculpate himself and to hold *T* liable despite delays in completion. Despite this, the court may allow the tenant to rescind after a reasonable time has passed. *Harting v. 6465 Realty Co.*, 324 N.Y.S.2d 567. Obviously, time limits should be specified.

§ 588. Shopping center leases. Shopping center leases have been discussed elsewhere.

References: XXIX Brooklyn L.Rev. 56; 1 Real Estate Rev. 12; 28 Rocky Mt. L.Rev. 460; 16 Practical Law 31 (No. 5); 2 ABA Real Property, Prob. & Tr. J. 222; 9 U. Kan. L.Rev. 379; 35 Notre D. Law. 184; XVI Baylor L.Rev. 1; 1955 Law Forum 62.

§ 589. Assignments and subleases. Many commercial leases contain a restriction against assignment or sublease without *L's* consent. It is necessary to add a provision that *L's* consent to an assignment or sublease does not dispense with the necessity of consent on subsequent transactions, else the requirement of consent is totally waived in some states. Friedman *Leases* § 7.3.

An assignee automatically becomes liable to *L* for rent and breach of covenants running with the land because of the privity of estate created by an assignment. This liability ends when the assignee, in turn, assigns. This rule has limited application, however, because *L* will often insist, as a condition to permitting assignment that the assignee "assume" all the obligations of *T* under the lease. *L* will insist that his consent, and the assignee's assumption are one document, so that there is no doubt of the assignee's liability to *L*. Now the assignee has liability that is contractual, and this liability continues even after the assignee assigns.

Whether the assignee's assumption is retroactive and includes liabilities of *T* prior in time to the assignment depends on the language of the assumption. Normally it is not retroactive. But if the assignee assumes "with the same force and effect as if he had executed the lease as tenant", assignee's liability is retroactive. Friedman, *Leases* § 7.501c2(a).

When a geographic portion of the leasehold is assigned, a *pro tanto* division of the rent occurs unless the assignment provides otherwise. Friedman *Leases* § 7.402. Obviously, the division of rent ought to be thought out and negotiated.

An assignment or sublease does not destroy *L's* right to terminate the lease for default or breach of covenant. Obviously, this leaves in a vulnerable position any subleasee or assignee of part of the leased premises. Default by some one else may extinguish his rights. Of course, the parties can draft around this with *L's* consent and joinder.

If *T* subleases to *X* for the entire balance of the term, this is an assignment, not a sublease. The consequences are serious. *X* becomes liable to *L* for rent and this liability continues even if he pays rent to *T*. Friedman, *Leases*, § 7.4.

If the lease states that *L* will not "unreasonably" withhold his consent to the assignment, the cases are a morass. Few lawyers are familiar with the conflicting and bizarre decisions as to what is "reasonable." Friedman, *Leases* § 7.304c.

It is imperative that any lawyer dealing with these problems be thoroughly familiar with the excellent exposition of the subject in Friedman, *Leases*.

The commercial lease to a high-credit tenant forbids any assignment or sublease of all or part of the demised premises or any device (concession, transfer of stock of lessee corporation, merger or dissolution of lessee corporation occupancy of all or part of the premises by one other than the lessee) without *L's* written consent. Kratovil, *Mortgages* § 321; 46 Chicago Bar Record 140. But some leeway is needed where, for example, *T* is a partnership that admits a new partner, where *T* is a corporation that merges into a corporation of greater net worth, etc. *T* argues for a clause that where *L* consents to an assignment, *T's* liability under the lease terminates. *L* is likely to require that the assignee assume personal liability. If *T* cannot obtain a provision for release of his personal liability, the documentation becomes complex. *T* may want *L* to agree to give him notice of the assignee's default. *T* may want a clause in the assignment giving *T* the right to terminate the assignment and to re-enter if the assignee fails to cure defaults. And *T* will want the assignment to include an indemnity provision, perhaps bolstered by a security deposit.

T always argues for a provision that *L's* consent to an assignment or sublease will not be withheld unreasonably.

If *T* wishes to retain the right to assign or sublease, *L* may want this clause conditioned on his right to receive any increase in rent paid by the subtenant. Friedman, *Leases* § 7. In the heyday of the office building boom in New York, you often encountered several subleases of the same office space each at a rent greater than the preceding sublease, all before the building was even completed. Where the assignment or sublease requires *L's* consent, which shall not unreasonably be withheld, both parties must be aware of the wealth of case law defining "reasonableness" in this context. Friedman, *Leases* § 7.304c.

In an assignment of a leasehold the subject clause will also include: (1) Terms and provisions of the lease. (2) Right of the lessor and all those claiming under him. (3) Existing mortgages on the fee as follows: _____ (4) Existing attornment agreements. (5) Existing mortgages on the leasehold as follows _____ (6) Subleases, tenancies, occupancies and concessions, and rights of parties claiming thereunder.

§ 590. Subordination of lease to mortgages. Many commercial lease forms contain a printed clause subordinating the lease to all present and future mortgages on the property. This facilitates refinancing the existing mortgage or placing a mortgage on the property in connection with a sale of the property. It eliminates going to a host of tenants for specific subordinations where the lender is insisting that his mortgage prime all leases. Some observations are in order; (1) Some prime tenants, such as national chains, will not agree to such a clause. (2) Some title companies are unwilling to rely on this clause because of the hostile court decisions on blanket subordinations. (3) Some tenants will agree to the clause only if it limits the aggregate of the mortgages to some specific principal amount or some percentage of the appraised value of the property.

Some institutional lenders will reject clauses calling for an automatic subordination where *T* is a "prime" lessee. Most lenders prefer the subordination clause to be "the mortgagee's option." Remember that the tactical position of the mortgage lender is improved where the lease is superior to the mortgage. Kratovil, *Mortgages* § 301.

In connection with subordination, some tenants will only agree to subordinate providing the mortgagee executes a "non-disturbance letter" of some kind so as to insure *T's* right of possession so long as *T* faithfully abides by the terms of the lease. *See* Chapter 36.

§ 591. Eminent domain—termination of lease. All commercial leases deal with the matter of taking by eminent domain, distinguishing between complete and partial taking, and covering the matter of abatement of rent where the taking is partial. *See* ABA Real Property, Probate and Trust Journal, 226 (1968).

With the possible exception of the insurance clauses, the next most difficult subject in leases is the eminent domain clause. The covenants of this clause are a matter of negotiation. So far as the mortgage lenders are concerned, most of them are prepared to accept a clause which calls for the termination of the lease in case the entire premises are taken by condemnation or eminent domain. They take the same point of view, generally, where the taking is of such a substantial nature that the demised premises cannot be reasonably used for the purposes for which they were demised.

From that point on it is strictly a matter of negotiation.

In certain special instances, some tenants will insist that the slightest taking (for example, the parking area in a drive-in restaurant) constitutes such a taking as to warrant the termination of the lease. Sophisticated lenders are aware of this attitude and will go along. See § 596.

§ 592. Shell lease. A shell lease, like other important leases, should spell out who is to pay the taxes, real and personal property, assessed against the property. This will not be binding upon the assessor, who is obliged to follow the state law. But *L* and *T* can sit down after the tax bills issue and decide who pays what.

Any covenant by *L* to rebuild or repair in case of destruction or damage should be confined to the shell.

§ 593. Signs. *T* wants the right to install signs advertising his business and *L* needs control over signs so installed. *T* often agrees to indemnify *L* against all losses caused by the erection or maintenance of signs and to include insurance against loss in the liability policies he carries. *L* may wish to require *T* to install a sign, as where *T* is a national tenant whose sign will attract other business. In a shopping center, *L* may want the Merchants Association to approve the signs.

§ 594. Security deposit. *T* will want his securities representing a security deposit held by a bank or trust company. *L,* though financially responsible, may transfer the reversion to some irresponsible person.

§ 595. Lease and build-to-suit. Investors, at times, enter into a lease with a high-credit tenant coupled with a contract to construct a building according to the tenant's plans. This is a hybrid contract. Just as a sell-and-build contract is both a contract of sale and a construction contract, so this lease is both a lease and a construction contract. Presumably the courts will apply the doctrines of substantial performance and waiver of defects as developed in the law of construction contracts.

However, additional problems arise. There will be the usual clause extending the time for performance or excusing performance by *L* occurring through Acts of God. And there will be a clause excusing *L's* delay or failure to perform where caused by *T's* acts, such as excessive change-orders. And there will be the usual disputes as to who was at fault. And it will be unclear how the law of landlord and tenant affects the problem. *L* is stuck with a building he may find it difficult to rent to others. Hence, *L* may argue for a clause making a damage suit *T's* exclusive remedy. And *T*, if he needs occupancy by a certain date, will not be content with a damage suit. He may wish to terminate the lease altogether. *L* may have loan commitments that have time limits. There is no simple solution. Probably, a limit should be placed on change orders. Architects are able to estimate the delay caused by a change-order. Perhaps this should be provided for. No change-orders should be valid if they push completion beyond a date that will enable *L* to keep his loan commitments with a reasonable time margin to spare. *L* will usually covenant to assign and deliver to *T* all contractor's warranties received by *L*.

T may insist on passing on various phases of the construction, including soil tests, approval of shop drawings, etc.

§ 596. Eminent domain. The problem of eminent domain where a lease exists presents aspects of great complexity.

ABA Real Property, Probate and Trust Journal (Fall 1968) p. 226; 43 Ia. L.Rev. 279; 44 Ill. B. J. 835; 14 Prac. L.Rev. 27 (May 1968); 1957 Law Forum 302; 4 U. of Kan. L.Rev. 339; 48 Va. L.Rev. 477; 54 Va. L.Rev. 1246, 67 W.Va.L.Rev. 101; 3 Williamette L. J. 39. *See* § 591.

§ 597. Exculpatory clauses. Exculpatory clauses in leases present legal problems of great complexity.

49 ALR 3d 321; 1972 Wisc. L.Rev. 520; 14 Vand. L.Rev. 1211.

§ 598. Shopping centers—additional construction. *L* and *T* in a shopping center will seldom see eye to eye on the question of future construction by *L*.

EXAMPLE: *L* leased to *T* a store in an attractive location as a book store. *L* later erected a department store in the center that left *T* with an unattractive location. The lease had a clause permitting *L* to add improvements in the center as long as *T's* right of access was not interfered with. *T* was stuck with the altered center because of this clause. *MNS Brandell Inc. v. Roosevelt Nassau Co.,* 345 NYS2d 608.

T should have argued for a clause that added improvements would not adversely affect his business. *L* will resist this.

§ 599. Shopping centers—restraint of trade. A major store in a shopping center may seek to exercise considerable control over the center. The Federal Trade Commission frowns on this as being in restraint of trade. Order Docket 8885, entered January 30, 1974, against a major store as follows:

ORDER

I.

[*Definitions*]

For purposes of this Order, the following definitions shall apply:

A. The term "respondent" refers to XYZ Corporation, its operating divisions, its subsidiaries, and their respective officers, agents, representatives, employees, successors or assignees.

B. The term "shopping center" refers to a planned development of retail outlets which has a total floor area designed for retail occupancy of at least 200,000 sq. ft. excluding, however, such a development consisting of one major tenant and less than 50,000 sq. ft. designed for retail occupancy by tenants other than the major tenant.

C. The term "tenant" refers to any occupant or potential occupant of retail space in a shopping center, whether as lessee or owner of such space, but not as a developer of a shopping center.

D. The term "retailer" refers to a tenant which sells merchandise or services to the public.

E. The term "major tenant" refers to a tenant providing primary drawing power in a shopping center.

F. The term "respondent's pro rata share of lineal feet" refers to the number of lineal feet in a shopping center determined by dividing 50% of the total lineal feet of nonmajor tenant mall store frontage by the number of major tenants in the shopping center.

II.
[Lease Provisions]

A. It Is Ordered that respondent, in its capacity as a tenant in a shopping center, cease and desist from making, carrying out, or enforcing, directly or indirectly, an agreement or provision of any agreement which:

1. grants respondent the right to approve or disapprove the entry into a shopping center of any other retailer;

2. grants respondent the right to approve or disapprove the amount of floor space that any other retailer may lease or purchase in a shopping center;

3. prohibits the admission into a shopping center of any particular retailer or class of retailers, including, for purposes of illustration:

  (a) other department stores,
  (b) junior department stores,
  (c) discount stores, or
  (d) catalogue stores;

4. limits the types of merchandise or brands of merchandise or service which any other retailer in a shopping center may offer for sale;

5. specifies that any other retailer in a shopping center shall or shall not sell its merchandise or services at any particular price or within any range of prices;

6. grants respondent the right to approve or disapprove the location in a shopping center of any other retailer;

7. specifies or prohibits any type of advertising by other retailers, other than advertising within a shopping center;

8. prohibits price advertising within a shopping center by retailers or controls advertising within a center by retailers in such a way as to make it difficult for customers to discern advertised prices from the common area of such shopping center; or

9. prevents expansion of a shopping center.

B. It Is Further Ordered that respondent, in its capacity as a tenant in a shopping center, shall not enter into or carry out any conspiracy, combination or arrangement with any other tenant to exclude any tenants from a shopping center or to grant respondent or another tenant any control over the admission of other tenants to the shopping center.

III.
[Permitted Activities]

A. It Is Further Ordered that when respondent is the first major tenant to agree with a developer or landlord of a shopping center to become a tenant in such center, this Order shall not prohibit respondent from terminating its agreement to become a tenant in such center if such developer or landlord does not obtain the agreement of one major tenant acceptable to respondent to operate a store in the center.

B. It Is Further Ordered that this Order shall not prohibit respondent from negotiating to include, including, carrying out, or enforcing provisions in any agreement (a) with a developer or a landlord of a shopping center, or (b) if respondent shall be the owner of the building in which its store is located within a shopping center or land in a shopping center on which it intends to erect such a building, then with the owners of other buildings and land in such shopping center, which:

1. permit respondent to establish reasonable categories of retailers from which the developer or

the landlord may select tenants to be located in the area immediately proximate to respondent's store; provided that such categories shall not include specification of (a) price ranges, (b) price lines, (c) trade names, (d) store names, (e) trademarks, brands or lines of merchandise of retailers, or (f) identity of particular retailers, including the listing of particular retailers as examples of a category; and further, provided, that such area shall not exceed 150 lineal feet of mall store frontage with respect to respondent's department stores and 200 lineal feet of mall store frontage with respect to respondent's Smith's Fifth Avenue stores, immediately proximate to the mall frontage of respondent's store, on each level, provided that such area does not exceed respondent's pro rata share of lineal feet.

2. require the developer or the landlord to maintain reasonable standards of appearance, signs, maintenance and housekeeping of and in the shopping center;

3. prohibit occupancy of space in the shopping center by clearly objectionable types of tenants, including, for purposes of illustration, shops selling pornographic materials;

4. approve or grant to respondent the right to approve an initial layout of the shopping center, which layout may (a) designate respondent's store, (b) set forth the location, size and height of all buildings, (c) locate parking areas, roadways, utilities, entrances, exits, walkways, malls, landscaped areas and other common areas, and (d) establish a proposed layout for future expansion of the shopping center; and

5. require that any expansion of the shopping center not provided for in the initial layout:

(a) shall not interfere with efficient automobile and pedestrian traffic flow into and out of the shopping center and between respondent's store and perimeter and access roads, parking areas, malls and other common areas of the shopping center;

(b) shall not interfere with the efficient operation of respondent's store, including its utilities or its visibility from within the shopping center or from public highways adjacent thereto;

(c) shall not result in a change of (i) the shopping center's parking ratio; (ii) the location of a number of parking spaces reasonably accessible to respondent's store determined by the application of such parking ratio to the number of square feet of floor are of respondent's store; (iii) the entrances and exits to and from respondent's store and any malls; and (iv) those parking area mall entrances and exits which substantially serve respondent's store;

(d) shall be accomplished only after any and all covenants, obligations and standards (for example, construction, architecture, operation, maintenance, repair, alteration, restoration, parking ratio, and easements) of the shopping center, exclusive of the expansion area (i) shall be made applicable to the expansion area and (ii) shall be made prior in right to any and all mortgages, deeds of trust, liens, encumbrances, and restrictions applicable to the expansion area, and (iii) shall be made prior in right to any and all other covenants, obligations and standards applicable to the expansion area.

IV.

It Is Further Ordered that respondent shall forthwith distribute a copy of this Order to each of its operating divisions.

It Is Further Ordered that respondent shall:

(1) within thirty (30) days after service of this Order upon respondent, notify each developer of shopping centers in which respondent occupies floor space, of this Order by providing each such developer with a copy thereof by registered certified mail, and

(2) within sixty (60) days after the date of issuance of this Order, file with the Commission a report showing the manner and form in which it has complied and is complying with each and every specific provision of this Order.

V.

It Is Further Ordered that respondent shall notify the Commission at least thirty (30) days prior to any proposed change in the corporate respondent such as dissolution, assignment or sale resulting in the emergence of a successor corporation, the creation or dissolution of subsidiaries, or any other change in the corporation which may affect compliance obligations arising out of this Order.

A careful study of the permitted actions will give you an idea of what major stores want in shopping center controls.

§ 600. Zoning problems. The lease draftsmen must pay careful attention to zoning problems. A check list follows:

(1) Is the tenant's proposed use permitted under all existing housing and zoning ordinances?
   (a) Is the zoning map you are relying upon up-to-date?
   (b) Have you examined the entire zoning ordinance, not just the section on the district in question?
   (c) Does the tenant plan aerials or signs prohibited by height restrictions in the zoning ordinances?
(2) If the building is a "prior nonconforming use" under the zoning ordinance, what will happen if the building is destroyed by fire or other casualty and the zoning ordinance prohibits rebuilding?
   (a) Should the lease provide for cancellation?
   (b) Should there be a provision for payment of liquidated damages?
(3) If stricter ordinance enforcement prohibits tenant from continuing his use, what are the respective rights of the parties?
   (a) Should the tenant be allowed to adapt the premises to a lawful use?
   (b) Should the tenant be allowed to cancel the lease?
(4) If an ordinance is amended during the term of the lease, to provide for amortization of a new prohibited use of the building, what are the respective rights of the parties?
   (a) When the amendment is passed, may the lease be cancelled?
   (b) When the right to continue tenant's use expires, may the lease be converted?
(5) Where the relocation of a street, or the establishment of one-way streets, or the establishment of a limited access expressway restricts access to the premises, what are the respective rights of the parties?
   (a) When can lessee cancel the lease?
   (b) Can the rental be adjusted?
(6) If alterations or additions to the building are required by a new ordinance to permit tenant to continue his business, what are the respective rights of the parties?
   (a) Who pays for: outside stairways or entrances; building-wide alarm systems; automatic sprinkler systems; additional bathrooms; additional inside electrical wiring; additional outside electrical wiring; installation or removal of room partitions?
   (b) Should tenant pay for all expense incurred to put property in compliance with ordinance in effect at the time of lease?[1]

§ 601. Improvements by tenant—endorsing the hazard policy. Where *T* is to make substantial improvements on the leased premises, (betterments), some attorneys prefer that the hazard policy be endorsed along the following lines:

"When insurance under this policy covers improvements and betterments, such insurance shall cover the improvements and betterments to the building described on the first page of this policy.

"The word 'lease' wherever used in this form shall mean the lease or rental agreement, whether written or oral, in effect as of the time of the loss.

"The term 'improvements or betterments' wherever used in this policy, is defined to be fixtures, alterations, renovations, installations, additions, any related expense involving any of these, which have been made or added to the building described in this policy, at the expense of the lessee (assured), in such a manner and under such legal conditions, so as to constitute a permanent part of such realty (building) and in which the assured retains an interest under one or more of the following conditions:

"In the event that under the conditions of the lease, improvements or betterments remain the property of the lessee, or the lessee is liable for the replacement of improvements and betterments and such improvements and betterments are damaged by insured perils, this Company shall be liable for the replacement value of such improvements or betterments.

"In the event that under the conditions of the lease the improvements or betterments become the property of the lessor, either by operation of law or contract, this Company agrees to recognize the interest of the lessee (assured) to be the use of such property and in the event of loss or damage to

---

[1] © Copyright, Illinois State Bar Association, April, 1958. Reprinted by permission.

the building herein described by insured perils, (whether or not such improvements or betterments are actually damaged) which results in a cancellation of the lease contract, this Company's liability for such interest shall not exceed that proportion of the lessee's (assured's) original cost of altering the building for the assured's use, that the unexpired term of the lease at the time of the damage bears to the unexpired term of the lease when the improvements or betterments were added to the building.

"In the event that under the conditions of the lease the improvements or betterments become the property of the lessor by operation of law or contract, and in the event of loss or damage, by insured perils, to the improvements or betterments (during the term of the lease) or any extension thereof, which loss or damage does not cause cancellation of the lease and the lessee (assured) restores the improvements or betterments for his continued occupancy of the demised premises (building), this Company's liability shall be the replacement value of such improvements and betterments at the time of the loss."[2]

§ 602. Real estate investment trust—rental income. To prevent loss of IRS advantages, a lease by a real estate investment trust may contain a "safety valve" clause as follows:

So long as the Landlord shall be a real estate investment trust, the term "Gross Rentals" shall not include any amounts referred to in this subsection (b) which, if included in the definition of "Gross Rentals" would result in any part of the fixed rental or percentage rental otherwise payable to the Landlord hereunder being held not to constitute "rent from real property" as that term is defined in Section 856 (d) of the Internal Revenue Code of 1954 and the Regulations issued thereunder, as the same may from time to time be amended.

§ 603. Recording. On any substantial lease, *T* should seek the protection recording affords. For example, this protects his easement rights and gives notice to subsequent purchasers of *L's* covenants that run with the land. The lease should be in recordable form, with proper acknowledgements, name of draftsman as required by local law, etc. A rather unsophisticated practice has sprung up in recent times of recording a "memorandum of the lease." This is probably ineffective legally except in the few states that provide for such instruments. This situation is complicated by the presence in a number of states requiring leases of a stated duration or length to be recorded. It is unwise to ignore these statutes. However, in actual practice commercial leases are rarely recorded.

---

[2] © Copyright, 7 The Forum 130 (1972) published by the ABA Section of Insurance, Negligence, and Compensation Law, author John T. Even of the John Marshall Law School faculty. Reprinted by permission.

30

Lease Clauses—Landlord's
Clauses and Tenant's Clauses

§ **604. Landlord's clauses—default clause—termination clauses.** Perhaps the most important clause from the landlord's point of view is the default clause. Except in a ground lease or other mortgageable lease, the default clause should be detailed. The ABA Real Property, Probate and Trust Committee offers a good form and discussion. ABA Section of Real Property Probate and Trust Law, Proceedings Aug. 10–13, 1964, p. 104 *et seq.*

L will want the lease to cover all contingencies that might lead to a contention by *T* that *T* has a right to terminate the lease.

EXAMPLE: Under prior law, if *part* of the leased premises is condemned, the lease does not terminate. However, under the "new law," the lease terminates if the taking "significantly interferes with the use contemplated by the parties." Restatement, Property 2d (Tentative Draft No. 2) § 7.1.

Under the "new law" (see § 10), there are many situations in which *T* is at liberty to terminate the lease prior to taking possession of the premises if any paramount title or interest exists that could terminate the lease.

EXAMPLE: If there is a condition subsequent, *e.g.*, one forbidding sale of intoxicating liquor, or a building restriction restricting the use of the land, or a mortgage on the fee, for example, *T* may terminate the lease at any time before taking possession. Restatement Property 2nd (Tentative Draft No. 2) § 4.1.

And if a non-man-made force or the Act of a third party renders the building unsuitable for the use contemplated by the parties, *T* may terminate the lease.

EXAMPLE: Premises consist of a residence and two-car garage. An arsonist causes destruction of the garage. *T* may terminate the lease. Restatement Property 2d (Tentative Draft No. 2) § 5.2.

And if premises are leased for a purpose that later becomes illegal, *T* may terminate the lease. Restatement Property 2d (Tentative Draft No. 2) § 8.2.

EXAMPLE: Premises are leased at a high rent as a tavern. A law or ordinance makes this use illegal. *T* may terminate the lease.

Many other examples are cited in the Restatement.

If a net lease is involved, or a lease on the faith of which mortgage credit is to be extended, it is important that the lease cover *all* events that could terminate the lease and negate them in explicit language.

The "new law" draws attention to many items of damages recoverable by *T* where *T* has the right to terminate the lease, *e.g.,* moving costs, compensation for *T's* expenditures on the leased premises, loss of profits, attorney's fees. Restatement Property 2d (Tentative Draft No. 2) § 9.2. *L* will want a provision fixing liquidated damages in the event *T* rightfully terminates the lease. Where *T* sues for damages without terminating the lease, the lease should require him to mitigate damages.

§ 605. Landlord's clauses—guarantee of rent. *L* may insist that some third party, for example, the parent of a subsidiary corporation tenant, guarantee the payment of rents. Because a true guarantee will not survive termination of the lease by *T's* trustee in bankruptcy, some landlords insist that the "guarantee" contain a primary obligation by the "guarantor" to pay in cash the present cash value of the rent stipulated in the lease in case of bankruptcy. Kratovil, *Mortgages,* § 410. Or the guarantee may provide that in such event the guarantor becomes the tenant under the lease. At all events, the guarantee should read that the guarantor guarantees the payment of the stipulated amounts as its own debt and that, in case of default, it may be proceeded against without first suing the tenant. Thus the guarantee is one of payment rather than of collection. *EAC Credit Corp. v. Wilson,* 187 SE2d 752; *National Bank of Washington v. Equity Investors,* 506 P2d 20. The guarantee should provide that it extends to rent and other charges under any modification of the lease. This prevents discharge of the guarantee by such modification. *Essex International Inc. v. Clamage,* 440 F2d 547. The guarantee should be contemporaneous with the lease, so that the lease creates consideration for the guarantee. And the guarantee should state that it runs in favor of the landlord and all those claiming under him, there being some law that a guarantee is not assignable.

§ 606. Landlord's clauses—guarantee of rent by commercial insurance company. Especially in shopping centers, mortgage lenders have preferred to see national tenants of great financial stability. Rents pay the debt service. In recent times the small but stable local tenant has been able to procure attractive policies by commercial insurance companies that insure payment of rent and performance of lease covenants by the tenant. This practically puts the tenant on a par with a national chain. A mortgagee clause is available just as in the case of hazard insurance. Extended coverage is available to cover the expense of lease brokerage if the landlord finds it necessary to evict the tenant and to cover the expense of restoring the premises to rentable condition in such case. The policy provides that coverage can be increased as rent escalates.

§ 607. Landlord's clauses—exceptions from the demised premises. *L* wishes to retain control over pipes, ducts, airshafts, elevators, and all other facilities serving other tenants, even though they run through the demised premises. *T* can agree to this as long as the exception relates to the facilities as they are at the date of the lease. *L* will also wish to reserve the right to enter to inspect and repair the excepted facilities.

§ 608. Landlord's clauses—rent escalation. Operating expenses tend to rise rapidly these days. Hence *L* will argue for an escalation clause. If a fixed dollar amount is stated as rent, some landlords want that dollar amount to increase periodically as prices increase, perhaps according to the Consumer Price Official United States Index of prices published by the Bureau of Labor of the Department of Labor. This is done because the purchasing power of the dollar paid by the tenant decreases as prices go up. *T* may argue for a more favorable price index, such as some wholesale price index. *T* will argue that the factors may go down as well as up, and that downward fluctuations should reduce his payments as long as they don't go below the rent for the base period. A leasehold mortgagee of ground leases worries about escalating rent, because if he forecloses, the leasehold mortgagee must pay the escalated rent and operation of the property may be thereby rendered unprofitable.

Usually the tenant of a ground lease is building on the property and needs mortgage money. Both the construction lender and permanent lender are involved in this problem, since the permanent lender will not "take out" the construction lender if he cannot live with the rent escalation. Some clause probably can be negotiated limiting the amount of escalation that will be good against lenders. *See* 3 Real Estate Review 46. *See also* discussion under Tenant's Clauses.

§ 609. **Landlord's clauses—alterations—landlord's approval of contractors.** If *T* is to engage in construction or alteration, *L* may wish to reserve the right to approve the general contractors and subcontractors, and *T* will argue for a provision that such approval will not be unreasonably withheld. *T* may be suspicious of *L's* choice but be perfectly willing to hire a triple-A contractor.

§ 610. **Landlord's clauses—alterations—landlord's alterations.** *L* may wish to reserve the right to make alterations, such as changes in stairways and entrances. *T* will wish to condition this right on the doing of the job without unreasonable inconvenience to *T*.

§ 611. **Landlord's clauses—alterations—tenant's duty at end of term.** If the lease gives *T* the right to make alterations, some disposition should be made of *T's* duty at the end of the term. Should he be obligated to restore the premises to the condition that existed when the lease began? Should *L* have the option of waiving this right? Obviously the parties would be well advised to keep blueprints or other evidence as to the condition that existed when the lease began. *T* will argue for any delay being excused if caused by acts beyond the tenant's control, such as strikes, etc.

§ 612. **Landlord's clauses—alterations—zoning.** *L* should forbid any alterations by *T* that would cause the building to lose its non-conforming use status, if it is a non-conforming use.

§ 613. **Landlord's clauses—alterations—surety bond.** *L* may want to require surety bonds if *T* is to do substantial work, but triple-A tenants will resist this requirement.

§ 614. **Landlord's clauses—construction of building—estoppel certificate of acceptance of premises.** Where *L* is building for *T*, he wants *T* to agree, on completion, to give his estoppel certificate accepting the premises as completed as per lease agreements. This is a document *L* needs to display to his mortgage lender, who is lending in reliance on cash flow from key tenants. *T* will seek to exclude latent defects, which is not acceptable to the landlord's lender.

§ 615. **Landlord's clauses—contractual lien for rent.** *L* will argue for a clause in the lease that he has a lien for delinquent rent or other charges payable by the tenant under the lease on all property of T, of all kinds, located on the demised premises and that if L serves notice of such lien on T, removal of any such property from the demised premises shall be unlawful. The clause may provide that the lien can be enforced under the Uniform Commercial Code, which, of course, can be done only as to chattels. An appropriate Code filing should be made. The lease should be executed so as to be effective as a Code security agreement. Consideration should be given to making the lien subordinate to mortgages, including leasehold mortgages.

§ 616. Landlord's clauses—additional rights to enter. In addition to reserving a right to show the premises to other tenants toward the end of the term, L will need the right to enter during the term at reasonable times to make repairs or alterations for the benefit of other parts of the building, to inspect the premises, to show the premises to prospective purchasers, tenants, or mortgage lenders, or to enter and make repairs on the premises which L is obligated to make or which T is obligated to make but has not made. For example, failure of T to replace a broken window in a high-class structure requires action by L regardless of who is at fault.

§ 617. Landlord's clauses—options to renew. If T insists on an option to renew, L should insist on the notice of exercise being given not later than some stated time before the lease expires and allow a period that will give L reasonable opportunity to procure a new tenant if T fails to renew.

§ 618. Landlord's clauses—restriction on assignment of sublease. In a ground lease of vacant land, probably it is best in some cases to include a restriction on assignment of a geographic part of the leased premises. Division of the rent creates problems. *See* § 689.

A restriction on subletting *the premises* may not prevent a sublease of *part* of the premises. This point should be covered. Also, a declaration of trust of the sublease should be prohibited.

Even transfer by operation of law can be controlled by the assignment clause, for example, death or bankruptcy of the tenant, or the filing of arrangements under the Bankruptcy Act, appointment of receivers or statutory liquidators, sheriff's sale etc.

Probably some provision should be included covering the death or addition of a partner where the lessee is a partnership.

§ 619. Landlord's clauses—use of premises—continuous operation. In some states T is under no obligation to use and occupy the premises if the lease is silent. Obviously an unoccupied store hurts the rental value of L's adjoining stores. The lease must require T to use and occupy the premises at all times during the life of the lease. It may specify the hours and days of the week T is to be open for business. But T must be expressly restricted to the uses permitted by the lease. Else he may devote the premises to an offensive use should he wish to break the lease. Since use clauses are often stated broadly, such as "uses usual in ABC supermarkets," there must be provision against illegal uses, *e.g.*, anything that violates the certificate of occupancy or environmental control, energy crisis, or building regulations. Also uses that violate exclusives given other tenants should be forbidden. Likewise uses that violate insurance policies are prohibited. Uses that could damage the premises, such as those involving excessive floor loads are forbidden.

As to a major tenant (*e.g.*, department store in a shopping center), L will require T

to operate continuously at the specified use, T to be liable to L for consequential damages to the center if T ceases operations. Obviously revenue will drop sharply if a major attraction closes down.

§ 620. Landlord's clauses—indemnity—defense of litigation. L may not be content with the more or less standard indemnity covenant by T. Such a covenant usually requires T to hold L harmless from a claim that has been reduced to judgment. A broader clause would require T to defend at his expense where the loss falls within the indemnity clause. If there is a dispute as to whether the loss falls in the indemnity clause, $T's$ insurance carrier may wish to defend under a reservation of rights.

§ 621. Landlord's clauses—common facilities. Where the building is a multi-occupancy facility, L will routinely include a clause reserving exclusive control of common facilities. L will wish to reserve the right to relocate in a reasonable manner facilities used by the tenants in common. T will resist this, arguing that common facilities are not to be relocated except as required by law.

§ 622. Tenant's clauses—events at the beginning of the term—putting tenant in possession. In many states, the landlord has no duty to put a tenant in possession. The tenant, at his expense, must oust a previous tenant who holds over.

As attorney for the new tenant, you should require the landlord to put your tenant in possession at his expense, using your tenant's name as plaintiff, if necessary, but bearing all expense of eviction. Provision should be made for abatement of rent until tenant is in possession. Your tenant may wish to reserve the right to cancel out if possession is not given him within a specified time. Consider, for example, the fact that if your tenant's existing lease elsewhere is expiring, your tenant must have quarters to move to. And consider that if your tenant plans to demolish the building and erect a new one, his construction mortgage commitment may expire while the landlord bickers with the old tenant. Whether the landlord shall be liable for damages for failure to deliver possession is a matter for negotiation.

§ 623. Tenant's clauses—events at the beginning of the term—putting the building in proper condition. T wants a clause obligating L to put the premises in proper condition for $T's$ use, all in accordance with laws, ordinances, and regulations before T is obligated to accept possession or begin performance of his obligations under the lease, and with a right to terminate if this is not done within a specified time. L will not agree to this if he is planning to use the lease to obtain mortgage credit, for mortgage lenders object to such clauses. A mortgage lender wants T unconditionally bound to perform under the lease.

§ 624. Tenant's clauses—events at the beginning of the term—chattels installed by prior tenant or landlord. A new tenant may consider requiring that the existing tenant, or if he refuses, L, will furnish a list of items the existing tenant installed and which he may seek to remove, such as electrical transformers or air conditioners. If the existing lease states that all tenant installations, whether permanent in nature or trade fixtures, become the landlord's property at the end of the lease, there is no harm in having the landlord agree to serve notice on the existing tenant that he will enforce this existing right, but where there is bad blood between the landlord and existing tenant, the tenant may become pretty vindictive. The new lease should expressly lease such items to the tenant, for a lease does not include the landlord's chattels unless it says so.

§ 625. Tenant's clauses—events at the beginning of the term—restoration of damage to premises by prior tenant. A prior tenant moving out may play havoc with the premises. Such a tenant may even remove door knobs, lighting fixtures, air conditioners, etc. A new tenant may wish to consider requiring that *L* agree that as a condition of the lease the premises will be in the condition they were when his lease was made, ordinary wear and tear excepted, also damage incidental to remove fixtures that the prior tenant could lawfully remove, such as trade fixtures.

§ 626. Tenant's clauses—removal of tenant's installations at end of term. In the absence of other agreements, *T* may remove only his trade fixtures at the end of the lease. This is a loose rule that has led to litigation. A big restaurant tenant may install a false ceiling, lighting system, elaborate booths, ventilating system, built-in cooking equipment, including equipment in the dining area, built-in refrigeration equipment, built-in tropical fish tanks, built-in glassed-in areas for swimming displays, stages for entertainers, ornamental fireplaces, dining terraces, murals by famous artists, and a multitude of other things that have never been the subject of litigation. Likewise, as to a bank tenant who installs computers, elaborate teller's cages, and security systems. Specific provisions should cover these items.

Falling into some gray area of law, are those improvements by *T* that seem permanent in character but that he insists on removing.

EXAMPLE: *L* leases store premises to *T*, a national chain, with *L*'s consent to construction by *T* of a distinctive store front used by the chain nationally. When *T* vacates, the will want lease permission to remove the old store front, simply because *T* does not want others to use the chain store front. It is useless to speculate as to the legal nature of such improvements. Simply spell out *T*'s rights and let *T* exercise them.

§ 627. Tenant's clauses—rent—escalation clauses. *T* cannot legitimately object to rent escalation based on ordinary increase in rent estate taxes based in proportion to the space he occupies, though he can insist upon being furnished a copy of the tax bill reflecting the additional taxes. He can also insist that the rent escalation be computed on the basis of the project as it existed when the lease was made. If part of the tax increase reflects buildings added to the project after the lease was made or modernization of an existing building, this should require a re-computation of *T's* proportion of the taxes. Likewise, on new construction, the tax assessment is something of an unknown factor. Some tenants argue for a tax escalation base determined on the basis of a "base period" such as the average of the first three years of the lease. One reason for this is the part that the tax assessor's opinion plays as to the precise date when the building was completed, and therefore fully assessable. *L* will wish to check to see that no part of the base period includes a tax-exempt year (new construction, etc.).

The lease should indicate clearly whether the tax escalation is that attributable only to the percentage of area occupied by the demised premises or extends also to common areas, such as the parking lot.

L will want the escalation to include increases in operating costs. Wages, for example, always go up. *T* will fight to exclude "non-operating items" from the escalation, such as broker's commission on leases, landlord's accounting and legal fees, advertising costs, etc.

§ 628. Tenant's clauses—real estate taxes—other charges. If *T* agrees to pay real estate taxes, as in true net leases, he needs an agreement that he can contest any tax increase whose validity he questions, though *L* may want a clause requiring the disputed tax to be deposited in escrow with some bank pending disposition of the tax litigation. *L* may argue for *T* to pay his attorney's fees in the litigation or to allow *L* to contest the taxes in his own name.

Often, as in a fully net lease, *T* agrees to pay the real estate taxes. But at the beginning and end of the term, *T* may occupy the premises for only part of the year. Some tax prorating clause is needed.

If *T* agrees to pay other charges, such as electricity, heat, and air conditioning, furnished by *L*, he will want some protection against arbitrary increases in the charges for these items, such as a limitation based on actual increase in cost to *L*, to be properly documented at *T's* request. Some charges present difficulties that must be negotiated. If the building converts to automatic elevators, for example, *L* will have no escalation privilege because his labor costs go down. But he should be entitled to compensation for the improved service. For *T's* protection some ceiling is needed. The small tenant, barber shop, for example, ought not to be involved in complex escalations of this sort.

§ 629. Tenant's clauses—notice of default. Because of numerous instances of "computer error," *T* will want notice to cure even a default in payment of rent. Other breaches of covenant (*e.g.*, failure to maintain insurance) routinely provide for notice to cure breach before a forfeiture can be declared by *L*.

§ 630. Tenant's clauses—use of the premises. *L*, obviously, will insist on a clause limiting the use to which the premises can be devoted. But *T* must give careful thought to the limitation. If he has power to sublease, he must give thought to the uses prospective subtenants may make. If he means to concession out parts of his floor space, he must consider the uses potential concessionaries might make. *L*, on the other hand, will be sensitive to the needs of other tenants, especially those having, or later to have, exclusives. This is apt to be a difficult clause to draft.

The lease may contain hidden limitations on the use the tenant may make of the demised premises such as clauses that forbid uses that increase insurance rates, uses that may cause damage to the building, uses that increase the cost of maintenance or operation, offensive uses, etc. If any such clause could prohibit the use to which the tenant or a prospective subtenant would make of the premises, the tenant would like some blanket clause stating that no provision in the lease shall be construed to forbid the use the tenant or subtenant plans to make.

A clause that *T* will engage in no use now or hereafter forbidden by law sounds innocuous, but as environmental and energy crisis regulations multiply, *T* may find that he is out of business. He will argue for a clause that if any law or regulation makes his contemplated use unlawful, he may terminate the lease without further liability for rent. This would be objectionable to a mortgage lender. It is difficult to envision a satisfactory compromise.

§ 631. Tenant's clauses—easements. Even where the lease is silent, *T* enjoys a multitude of implied easements. But the careful lawyer will ask for a clause in the lease, granting for the duration of the term, as easements appurtenant to the leasehold estate, easements over the remainder of the development necessary or convenient for the enjoyment of the leased premises, including, without limiting the generality of the foregoing, use of the parking area as it existed at the date of the lease, all access rights, including use of walks, drives, malls, sewer and water pipes, utilities, etc. In a big lease, the tenant will want the title company to insure specified easements. *L* may wish to reserve rights to relocate facilities, double-deck the parking lot, etc., but *T* should argue for some provision that all such work must be promptly completed without unreasonable interference with *T's* rights.

§ 632. **Tenant's clauses—traffic pattern clauses.** In some cases, particularly leases involving gasoline service stations, drive-in quick service restaurants, and other business operations directly dependent upon the flow of traffic at the door of the facility, the tenant will insist upon a clause which recites that in case the street grade is materially changed, or the direction of traffic is permanently changed or detoured, or the street is made a one-way thoroughfare, the tenant may have the right, at its option, to cancel the lease. From a tenant's point of view, of course, this is of extreme importance.

With respect to mortgage lenders, they are now quite accustomed to the inclusion of "traffic pattern" clauses in major oil company leases and accordingly, it can be expected that such a clause will not materially affect the mortgageability of the leasehold facility.

§ 633. **Tenant's clauses—shopping center leases.** A major chain will seek tenant protection clauses in shopping center leases. Some such clauses follow:

Default clause. If lessee shall make default in the payment of the rent hereinbefore reserved, or any part thereof, when the same falls due under the provisions hereof, and such default shall continue for thirty (30) days after notice thereof from Lessor by registered mail to Lessee, then it shall be lawful for Lessor, at its election, to declare said term ended and to re-enter the demised premises, or any part thereof, either with or without process of law and to expel, remove and put out Lessee, and all persons occupying under it, using such force as may be necessary in so doing, and again to repossess and enjoy said premises, including said building or buildings, as in its first or former estate. Should Lessor elect to re-enter and repossess the demised premises as herein provided, Lessor may either terminate this lease or it may, without terminating this lease relet said premises or any part thereof for such rent and upon such terms as to Lessor may seem fit, and if a sufficient sum shall not be thus realized monthly after paying the expenses of such re-letting and collecting to satisfy the rent hereby reserved, Lessee agrees to satisfy and pay all deficiency monthly during each month of the remaining term of this lease.

In case the Lessee shall fail or neglect to keep and perform any of the covenants and agreements in this lease contained on the part of the Lessee to be kept and performed other than the failure to pay rent, the Lessor, in addition to all other remedies now or hereafter afforded by law, may at its election, and after 20 days written notice to the Lessee to cure the specified default, perform such covenants or agreements on behalf of such Lessee or make good any default, and any amount or amounts which the Lessor shall advance on that behalf shall be repaid by the Lessee to the Lessor on demand, together with interest thereon at the rate of 6% per annum from the date of such advance to the repayment thereof in full. If Lessee's default is of such character that same cannot be cured within 20 days after written notice from Lessor, such default shall nevertheless be deemed cured and waived, if Lessee takes prompt steps within said 20 day period to cure same and prosecutes such steps with due diligence and continuity; any default cured within said grace period shall be deemed waived.

Bankruptcy clause. If a petition in bankruptcy shall be filed by the Lessee or the Lessee shall be adjudicated bankrupt or if the Lessee shall make a general assignment for the benefit of creditors or if in any proceeding based upon the insolvency of the Lessee a receiver of all of the property of the Lessee shall be appointed and shall not be discharged within ninety (90) days after such appointment, or if Lessee shall abandon or vacate the premises for a period of sixty days (except if Lessee vacates premises due to fire or other cause beyond its control), then the Lessor may terminate this lease by giving notice to the Lessee of its intention so to do; but neither bankruptcy, nor insolvency, nor an assignment for the benefit of creditors nor the appointment of a receiver, nor abandonment or vacation of the premises shall, however, affect the lease or permit its termination so long as the covenants on the part of the Lessee to be performed are being performed by the Lessee or someone claiming under it or the then owner of the demised term.

Common area maintenance charges. Lessee agrees to reimburse Lessor on a semi-annual or quarterly basis for Lessee's share of the shopping center parking lot and common area maintenance costs prorated in the proportion that the total square foot ground floor area of Lessee's store is to the total square foot floor area of all other buildings in this development, provided, however, that Lessee's share of such costs shall not exceed $_____ per square foot of ground floor of its store building per annum. Said parking lot and common area shall include parking areas, service areas and drives, and sidewalks. Said parking lot and common area costs shall include reasonable charges for minor repairs, restriping the parking lot, lighting, cleaning, snow removal and liability insurance. Lessor shall maintain said parking lot and common area in good condition and repair and shall furnish Lessee with an audited or certified statement of prorations together with a statement showing detailed expenditures made by Lessor for parking lot and common area maintenance. The failure of Lessor to include any expenditure in a statement to Lessee within twelve (12) months of the date of such expenditure shall be deemed a waiver by Lessor of Lessor's right to demand payment by Lessee of Lessee's proportionate share thereof.

Lessor agrees to indemnify and hold Lessee harmless for any and all claims for injury to or death of persons and/or damage to property arising out of the use of said parking or common areas.

Lessor covenants and agrees to obtain and maintain in force during the term of this lease or any extensions thereof a policy of general comprehensive liability insurance covering all of the parking lot and common areas of the total development herein contemplated, or any future additions thereto, and naming Lessee as an additional insured party, with limits of not less than $200,000.00 for each person, and $500,000.00 for each occurrence and $100,000.00 for property damage. Lessor also agrees to provide Lessee with a certificate of issuance of said insurance and of each and every renewal thereof. The aforesaid policy shall also provide that same may not be cancelled or altered except on ten (10) days prior written notice to Lessee.

Indemnity. Lessee agrees to indemnify and save harmless the Lessor from and against any and all claims and demands on account of any injury or death or damage to property occurring:

(a) Upon a part of the leased premises which is in the exclusive possession of Lessee, or
(b) Because of the acts of Lessee, its contractors, invitees, agents, servants, or employees,

except, however, in both a) and b) above, Lessee shall not so indemnify and hold harmless the Lessor:

(a) If Lessor, his contractors, licensees, agents, servants or employees are negligent and such negligence causes the happening or event giving rise to such claims, or
(b) If Lessor fails to perform any of the obligations to be performed by Lessor hereunder and such failure causes the happening or event giving rise to such claims, or
(c) If injury or death to any person and/or property damage results from a risk covered either by an insurance policy in which the Lessor is an insured party or a risk against which the Lessor is obligated to insure by the terms of the herein lease, or
(d) For injury or death of any person and/or damage to property resulting from the use or intended use of the parking areas or common areas, or
(e) For injury or death of any person and/or property damage resulting from fire, casualty or other causes beyond the control of Lessee.[1]

§ 634. Tenant's clauses—assignment clauses.

In ground leases, there must be no provision forbidding assignment. In the first place, this might block mortgaging of the leasehold. Kratovil, *Mortgages*, § 345. In the second place, a leasehold mortgagee who forecloses wants to be able to freely dispose of the leasehold. Any restraint on

---

[1] © Copyright Chicago Bar Association 1971. Reprinted by permission from 52 Chicago Bar Record 345, author Bennet I. Berman of the Chicago Bar.

assignment makes the leasehold unmortgageable. For obvious reasons there must be no restraint on subleases. The ground lessee builds a building, as described in the lease, but subleases it to tenants.

The commercial lease, particularly the shopping center store lease, contains rigid controls on assignments and subleases. Kratovil, *Mortgages*, § 321. But the tenant can argue for a clause permitting an assignment that takes place by lessee's merger or consolidation with another corporation.

§ 635. Tenant's clauses—alterations. *T*, in the absence of agreement otherwise, has no right to make alterations in the premises unless the lease explicitly or implicitly authorizes this. Obviously, if *L* leases an old theater to *T* "for use only as a savings and loan association," he implicitly agrees to alterations. But knocking out interior walls is a doubtful matter. Obviously, *T* needs permission in the lease to make all necessary alterations. If *T* has an architect's synopsis of the layout he means to have, this can be appended to the lease, with additional permission to change the layout during the term of the lease. In any lease permitting *T* to make alterations, *L* will demand provisions against mechanic's liens, *e.g.* contractor's bonds.

§ 636. Tenant's clauses—building laws. *T* routinely expects *L* to insist on a clause requiring *T* to observe all laws, ordinances, and regulations. Today this requires some thought. Environmental regulations are creating some pretty expensive requirements. An industrial building that has been dumping effluent in a body of water must expect to be compelled to provide some expensive substitute. However, because ultimate liability *to the city* for building ordinance violations will rest on *L,* he will reserve the right to enter the leased premises, after due notice to detect and correct building code violations.

§ 637. Tenant's clauses—renewal options. Obviously *T* will want renewal options. Income tax aspects materially affect the tenant's renewal options. I.R.C. Sec. 178.

§ 638. Tenant's clauses—holding over. The tenant in smaller leases will want a clause that a holding over creates a tenancy only from month-to-month. This is for the reason that a tenant cannot always move out on time and does not wish to be held as a tenant from year-to-year. However, *L* will insist, in turn, that the rent be, perhaps, double the previous rent because of the inconvenience and delay to *L* in placing a new tenant in possession.

§ 639. Tenant's clauses—erection of new structures by landlord. *T* would like to see a clause forbidding the erection by *L* of structures that block off *T's* windows or otherwise impair or depreciate the value of *T's* occupancy.

§ 640. Tenant's clauses—liability of tenant for injuries in common areas. *T* will want *L* to protect *T* in all damage suits for injuries on the parking lot or other common areas.

§ 641. Tenant's clauses—warranties by landlord. *T* may seek to exact warranties of the landlord. If the lease requires *L* to maintain all mechanical equipment (air conditioning, heating, etc.) in good condition, such a warranty is not necessary. But if a big tenant is about to accept responsibility for taking care of mechanical equipment servicing his premises, he may want *L* to warrant that the equipment is in good condition as of the date of the lease.

In an industrial park, *T* may want *L* to warrant that applicable zoning permits the use specified in the lease and may ask for opinion of counsel to this effect. *L* may resist this on the ground that he lacks precise knowledge of all details of *T's* operations. The tenant in a big lease may want *L* to agree to furnish him a certificate of occupancy when the building is completed. *T* will want warranties that building restrictions, if any, permit his intended use. Indeed, *T* will look ahead and try to obtain warranties as to the uses possible subtenants would make.

Warranties as to hidden defects are a matter of negotiation. *L* can warrant that to his knowledge no hidden physical defects exist in the leased premises or in the common areas the tenant has the right to use. But a defect may exist unknown to *L*. Even good soil tests do not always reveal bad soil conditions that can cause serious wall cracking and settling. Even in a fully net lease it seems unjust to stick *T* with hidden defects of which *L* had knowledge, but the difficulty is that the mortgage lender, lending in reliance on a fully net lease, will object to any provision for abatement of rent or set-off. Even if *L* accepts responsibility for defects in new construction that crop up within one year from date of completion, the problem can crop up later. Probably the net-lease tenant, like one in a free-standing building, is stuck with this problem, though he can argue for a guarantee by *L's* contractor to be liable for all defects known to the contractor and not visible on ordinary inspection. The contractor will know whether, for example, oversize footings were used on filled land or whether he encountered quicksand or underground streams.

§ 642. Check list for tenant's lawyer. Another check list for tenant's lawyer follows:

(1) Have you obligated the lessor to provide heat, refrigeration, steam, electric power, without providing saving clauses such as machinery breakdown, strikes, riots and other causes beyond his control?

(2) Have you imposed on the lessor an obligation for the replacement of improvements and betterments?

(3) Have you imposed on the lessor the obligation to rebuild and other conditions which would detract from the value of the demised premises from a prospective buyer's viewpoint?

(4) If the improvements or betterments are to be installed by the lessee, who has the ownership during the lease term of such improvements?

(5) If the improvements or betterments are destroyed by any peril and the lease is not cancelled, who has the obligation to replace them?

(6) If the lessee is to maintain the heating boiler, what is intended?
    (a) only to provide fuel?
    (b) to make all repairs and replacements needed for the upkeep of the boiler?
    (c) Does this obligation include the insuring of the boiler, and if so, for what limits?
    (d) If there is a heat failure in the building and other tenants' property is damaged thereby, does the lessee incur an obligation to the other tenants?

(7) Has the lessee obligated himself to maintain air conditioning and refrigeration equipment? What did the parties agree to do?
    (a) replace any equipment if damaged by any peril.
    (b) provide current for the operating of the unit.
    (c) provide supervision and service contracts for the operation of the unit.

(8) If the lessee has to maintain automatic sprinkler equipment, what did the parties agree to do?
    (a) make any necessary repairs or replacements.
    (b) maintain system in service.
    (c) incur any responsibility for sprinkler equipment failure and as a result, complete destruction of the building by fire.

(d) Has the liability of the parties for damage or destruction by fire been limited in the event the sprinkler system fails?

(9) If the lessee is to maintain the elevator, what is meant?
   (a) make repairs.
   (b) provide inspections.
   (c) replace if elevator is damaged by collision or other perils.

(10) In fire clauses, is the time needed to replace the demised premises by the lessor (30, 60 or 90 days) adequate under modern construction practice?

(11) Does the lease provide for the abatement of the rent during the period of untenantability?

(12) If the lessee agrees to return building at termination of the lease,
   (a) what perils are to be excluded—fire, fire and extended coverage, boiler, elevator, all risk perils?
   (b) What arrangements have been made in the lease to protect tenant against lessor's insurers subrogation actions?

(13) If the tenant agrees to keep the building in repair, what is meant?
   (a) against damage by any peril?
   (b) perils other than what the lessor insures?
   (c) Is there an intention to include boiler, air conditioning or other mechanical devices?

(14) If the tenant agrees to insure building, what are his duties?
   (a) For what amount shall building be insured?
   (b) Should it be on a replacement or actual cash value basis?
   (c) What perils are to be included in the policy?
   (d) Should policy contain Co-Insurance Clause?
   (e) Who has the duty in long-term leases to keep the reconstruction cost of the building current?
   (f) Have you specified unrealistic specific amounts, which, as a result of inflation, will always be inadequate?

(15) If the lessee is to pay a substantial amount of rent in advance, what provisions have been made for return of this money if building is destroyed and the lease is cancelled?

(16) Have you obligated tenant to perform duties which are difficult to interpret and practically impossible to insure, such as:
   (a) not to commit waste.
   (b) maintain interior of building.
   (c) maintain exterior of building.
   (d) maintain the roof.

(17) Have the words "repair," "restore," "replace" and "maintain" been used without checking the legal meaning of these words as determined by the courts in your state?

(18) In fire clauses, have ambiguous terms such as the following been used?
   (a) other casualty.
   (b) Acts of God.
   (c) unavoidable accident.
   (d) catastrophe loss.
   (e) things beyond tenants' control.

(19) In providing for the procurement of insurance and the insuring of indemnity agreements contained in the lease, have we specified dollar limits which are unrealistic for individual accidents?

(20) Has sufficient consideration been given in the preparation of the duties and responsibilities of the parties to provide for changing philosophies in the insurance industry?

(21) If the tenant has permission to install improvements and betterments, what lease provisions have been made to protect lessor against mechanic lien laws and other claims?[2]

---

[2] © Copyright. 7 The Forum 130 (1972) published by the ABA Section of Insurance, Negligence and Compensation Law, author, John T. Even of the John Marshall Law School Faculty. Reprinted by permission.

31

The Split Fee

§ **643. The split fee—in general.** For tax reasons beyond the scope of this text, it is common today to separate the ownership of the fee title from the ownership of the building.

EXAMPLE: *R* conveys land improved with an office building to *E,* excepting title to the building. *E* then makes a long-term lease of the land to *R.* The documents provide that on termination of the lease, ownership of the buildings passes to *E.*

§ **644. The split fee—deed clause.** The early forms of this transaction called for excepting and reserving to the grantor ownership of the building but made no provision for transfer of ownership of the building to the fee owner at the termination of the lease. The transfer of ownership of the building was provided for in the lease. The current thinking is that this probably will hold water but is poor draftsmanship. It is the function of a deed, not a lease, to transfer ownership, whether it be ownership of land or ownership of a building. Thus you are likely to encounter a deed conveying as follows:

Lot 1 in Block 1 in Sheffield's Addition to Chicago in Cook County, Illinois:
Excepting and reserving to the grantor all buildings and improvements located thereon (including, without limitation all fixtures and equipment located therein or associated therewith) and all leases executed by the grantor as lessor for occupancy of such buildings or improvements or part thereof. This exception and reservation is subject to the terms of a certain lease of even date herewith between the Grantee, as lessor, and the Grantor, as lessee, and the rights and title of the Grantor so excepted and reserved shall terminate on the termination of the lease term, whether by expiration of the lease term or otherwise, and such buildings, improvements and occupancy leases, including those hereafter executed are thereupon conveyed to and shall become the property of the Grantee, its successors and assigns, and this provision shall be deemed a conveyance on the terms herein set forth. The buildings and improvements shall be and remain real property.

Thus there are more formal words of conveyance than in the early transactions of this sort. Moreover, the faint possibility that the building could become personal property by constructive severance is eliminated by express provision.

§ **645. The split fee—lease clause.** The lease clause is likely to be along the following lines:

EXAMPLE: Ownership of Improvements. In accordance with the terms of a certain Warranty Deed from the Lessee as grantor to the Lessor as grantee bearing even date herewith, the Lessee has reserved and excepted title to the improvements. Notwithstanding such reservation and exception, the terms of this Lease shall govern the use, operation and transfer of the Improvements and the exercise of the Lessee's rights with respect thereto. On termination of the Lease Term, whether by expiration of time or otherwise, title to the Improvements shall be surrendered to and the Improvements shall become the full and absolute property of the Lessor, his successors and assigns without further action by the Lessor or the Lessee. The Lessee's interest in this Lease and all of the Lessee's right, title and interest in and to the Improvements shall be non-separable and any attempt to transfer, mortgage, assign, convey or otherwise encumber in whole or in part either of such interests shall be void and ineffective (whether by act of the Lessee, judicial decree, judgment or otherwise) unless there shall be a complete transfer, mortgage, assignment or encumbrance to the same party of the Lessee's interest under this Lease and the Lessee's interest in the Improvements. Any severance resulting from the Lessee's reservation of title to the Improvements and the Lessee's conveyance of title to the land shall not change the character of the improvements as real property.

§ 646. The "split fee"—air space problems. The "air space" problem of the ownership of the building separated from the ownership of the land has been discussed elsewhere. Kratovil, *Mortgages,* § 395. For a good current discussion *see* Frankel and Runk, *Real Estate Togetherness,* 27 Record 556 (Nov. 1972). This publication is by the Bar of the City of New York, 42 W. 44th St., New York, New York, 10036. A condensation appears in 3 Real Estate Review 52.

§ 647. "Split-fee"—drafting theories. Of course, different draftsmen adopt differing approaches to the "split fee." Thus in 7 ABA Real Property, Probate and Trust Journal 785 (1972), the following differing approaches are commented upon:

(1) Deed conveys land "together with the improvements" and lease acknowledges ownership of building in Developer with provision for building "to revert back" to Investor on termination of lease. The author brands this approach unacceptable.

(2) Developer deeds land to Investor, with no mention of building (it would pass to grantee by operation of law) and lease contains provision acknowledging Developer's ownership of building, with provision for automatic passage of title to building to investor on termination of lease. The author regards this approach as unacceptable.

(3) Developer deeds land to Investor, reserving title to building, with provision in deed that title to building will vest in Investor on termination of the lease. The author fears the Rule against Perpetuities endangers this approach.

(4) Deed of land and building from Developer to Investor reserves estate for years in Developer. Both deed and lease provide that on termination of the lease, estate of Developer in the building ceases. The author sees problems here.

In point of fact, there is no ideal solution to the "split fee" problems.

32

Sale of Fee Subject
to Substantial Leases

§ 648. In general. A prospective buyer of property subject to substantial leases will check the lease *before* he signs the contract of purchase, because once he signs he is stuck with the lease no matter how unfavorable it is to the landlord. In general, he is looking at the lease just as if he were about to sign it as landlord. However, a few reminders are included here for ready reference:

Rent. As to rent, the buyer will check: (1) Whether the rent is adequate in his opinion; (2) whether the computations of percentage rent and minimum rentals are satisfactory; (3) whether the rent can be diminished in any way, for example, by partial condemnations, too liberal abatement of rent provision in case of fire damage, etc.

Termination rights. He will check for termination rights. If he is buying because he wants the rent revenue coming in, he may decide against buying if the lease gives the tenant the right to terminate if part of the premises are condemned or destroyed by fire, for example.

Ownership of the building. If a ground lease tenant erected the building, the buyer wants to check ownership of the building, ownership at termination of the lease, options of the parties, (option of lessor to buy the building, option of tenant to buy the fee).

Burdensome covenants. The buyer looks for burdensome covenants, such as a covenant to rebuild a building, to repair all fire damage within 60 days, replace betterments, provide heat, power, etc., with no escape clause for strikes and other causes beyond the landlord's control.

Tenant's covenants. The tenant's covenants should be checked for completeness and certainty, for example, the tenant's duty to replace worn out or damaged boilers, air conditioning, elevators, escalators, sprinklers, etc.

§ 649. Assignment of the reversion. It is well established that after executing a lease the lessor's interest in the land is a reversion to which the right to receive rents is attached as an incident. A transfer of the reversion carries with it the benefit and burden of lease covenants which run with the land, also the right to receive rents under an existing lease unless specifically reserved. *Anderson v. Island Creek Coal Co.,* 297 F.Supp. 283; 51c CJS *Landlord & Tenant,* § 285(2). But a lease is both a contract and a conveyance, and some of the provisions of the lease may not be covenants running with the land. A rather conspicuous area, for example, of doubt as to the running nature of covenants occurs with respect to covenants to pay money. 2 *American Law Property* § 9.13. Another muddy area relates to covenants not to compete. 2 *American Law of Property* § 9.13. Of course, other such areas exist. For this reason, a lawyer representing a purchaser of leased land may wish to receive an assignment of the lessor's interest in the lease, including the benefit of all contracts, agreements, and covenants on the lessee's part. Past due rent can be included if the purchaser is to receive the same under the contract of sale. The right to a tenant's security deposit may not pass by the deed in some jurisdictions. Friedman, *Contracts & Conveyances of Real Property*, § 8.4; 1 *American Law Property*, 335; 52 CJS *Landlord & Tenant* § 473 (2). A separate assignment of the deposit can be used, to which the tenant's consent can be appended. The deposit belongs to the tenant, after all, and he has a right to choose to whom he will entrust it.

Similarly, where a sale and assignment of a leasehold is taking place and there is a major sublease, the tenant under the ground lease may be asked to assign his sub-reversion to the assignee of the ground lease and the subtenant will be notified. Such an assignment will require the subtenant to pay future rent to the assignee of the ground lease.

Requirements for such assignments belong in the contract of sale.

§ **650. Modification of lease.** *E* will want the contract to forbid modification of existing leases pending the closing of the deal.

§ **651. Guarantee.** Many leases, especially those by a subsidiary corporation, are backed by a guarantee, often by a parent corporation. Any sale of such leased land makes provision for assignment of the guarantee to the purchaser.

§ **652. Advance payments of rent, security deposits, etc.** The contract should state what advance payments of rent or security deposits have been made by tenants and how *R* proposes to give *E* advantage of same. Any advance payment of rent other than as specified in the lease is forbidden by the contract. If a true deposit of securities exists, *R* should agree to procure a written consent by the tenant to transfer of same to his purchaser, if the lease makes no provision for this.

§ **653. Warranty as to lease covenants.** Where the premises sold are occupied by tenants under valuable leases, *E* may insert the following with respect to the warranty deed to be given:

CLAUSE: Which deed will expressly warrant that no breaches exist of covenants or conditions in existing leases whether such breach be that of the landlord or the tenant.

The theory is that *R* has intimate knowledge of controversies existing between tenants, for example, a contention by one tenant that another is violating an exclusive. Or there may be a contention by a tenant that the landlord is in violation of a lease provision.

§ **654. Notice to tenants.** One who buys leased premises must immediately give actual notice of the purchase to the tenants. Else any seasonable payment of rent made to the former landlord will be a good payment against the purchaser. 36 CJ 367. Obviously, the notice must be signed by *R* and the contract should call for this.

§ 655. **Estoppel certificate by tenant.** The tenant in a major lease may be asked to give an estoppel certificate to the purchaser of the fee stating that the lease is valid and subsisting, that no unrecorded modifications, concessions or assignments exist, that the only subleases are as stated in the certificate, and that rent has not been paid in advance. The lease may require the tenant to give such a certificate, where appropriate. The contract should require *R* to procure such a certificate to be delivered to *E* at closing.

§ 656. **Preemption rights.** A lease may give the tenant a pre-emptive option. This is a clause giving the tenant the "first refusal" of the property in case the landlord decides to sell the property. Obviously, proper notice should be given the tenant, so that the period given him by the lease to exercise his option expires before the landlord is firmly committed to the purchaser. Many leases are drafted requiring *R* to serve this notice. Obviously, the contract should require him to do so.

§ 657. **Modifications—side agreement with lender.** Where mortgage financing takes place subject to an existing lease, the mortgagee occasionally enters into a side agreement modifying the lease in some respect, but only as to the lender. While this is common enough, it creates a problem whenever refinancing takes place. Hence, it is better for the modification to take place between landlord and tenant.

33

Subleases in Large-Scale Transactions

§ 658. In general. The chief task of the sublessee is to stay alive if the lessee goes down the drain. Forfeiture of the ground lease automatically terminates all subleases, unless documentary provisions are provided to the contrary.

§ 659. The ground lessee. Obviously, the sublessee will make a careful check of the financial stability of the ground lessee who will be his landlord. This is done to assure that the ground lessee is substantial enough so that he will not default under the ground lessee. This, however, offers limited protection only, for the ground lessee is free to assign the leasehold to less responsible parties.

§ 660. The ground lease. The proposed sublessee carefully scrutinizes the ground lease before the sublease is signed. The terms ought to be such that in all probability the ground lessee will be able to pay the rent and perform the covenants of the lease. Moreover, since the sublessee may wind up as tenant under the ground lease, (*see* Chapter 36), the covenants ought to be such that the sublessee can perform them without undue hardship. The ground lease may make elaborate provisions regarding a mortgage on the ground lease. It may, for example, provide that subleases are subject to the prior approval of the leasehold mortgagee. The leasehold mortgagee may contain a comparable clause. In such case, the leasehold mortgagee ought to be consulted informally at an early stage. The final draft of the sublease should be contingent on formal approval by the leasehold mortgagee.

The ground lease will also be examined to see if it has adequate provisions for protection of the leasehold mortgage, such as requiring notice of default to the leasehold mortgagee and his right to cure defaults. If the ground lessee encounters adversity, no doubt he will endeavor to sell and assign the lease. If he is unsuccessful, the leasehold mortgagee will have to step in, cure defaults, and foreclose, in which case the sublessee has a new landlord but is still in business under the non-disturbance clause. *See* Ch. 36.

The ground lease and leasehold mortgage should contain a non-disturbance clause, under which the possession of the subtenant will not be disturbed by the leasehold mortgagee as long as the sublessee continues full performance under the sublease. (*See* Chapter 36). This will be coupled with a provision that if notice of default has been served on the ground lessee, he has failed to cure defaults, and the leasehold mortgagee has begun paying rent to and performing lease covenants for the landlord, the sublessee will attorn in writing to the leasehold mortgagee and accept him as his landlord. *See* Chapter 36.

§ 661. Checking the sublease by leasehold mortgagee. The leasehold mortgagee coming in after subleases have been made will check the subleases to see if they contain any covenants he cannot live with, for some day he may become the landlord in the sublease. Attornment and recognition or non-disturbance clauses or agreements are required in order to keep the good tenants in occupancy after foreclosure of the leasehold mortgage. *See* Chapter 36. Absent some provision in the documents, foreclosure of a leasehold mortgagee that wipes out the ground lessee also wipes out his subtenants. The ground lease may provide that if the ground lease is forfeited as to the tenant, it will continue as to the leasehold mortgagee or that the leasehold mortgagee will be given an identical lease for the balance of the term. The sublease should tie into this clause so that the sublease continues in effect under the new lease. *See* Chapter 36.

§ 662. Defaults in ground lease. The sublease can provide that if notice of default is served on the ground lessee, and the leasehold mortgagee begins performing under the ground lease, the leasehold mortgagee shall serve notice of such facts on the sublessee, who shall thereupon attorn in writing to the leasehold mortgagee, and that service of such notice is conclusive evidence of these facts in favor of the sublessee, all future liability of the sublessee to the ground lessee being expressly waived. A ground lessee who is in default cannot expect to continue to collect revenue from the premises. *See* Chapter 36. And the leasehold mortgagee ought to have a source of revenue to pay the rent to the fee owner.

§ 663. Title requirements and title insurance. The big sublessee is just as interested as the ground lessee in the condition of the title and title insurance. There will often, then, be a contract for sublease. The title requirements will be drawn after examination of the ground lessee's title policy and the title commitment will be examined before the sublease is signed. If there is to be a mortgage on the sublease, the contract will call for a mortgage title policy on the subleasehold. A survey may well be in order. *See* Chapters 7 and 11. Probably the building restrictions and easements on the ground lessee's title policy should be checked before too much time is spent in negotiating the sublease. If recorded building restrictions forbid any of the uses planned by the sublessee, this may kill the deal. If any recorded easements interfere with the sublessee's plans this might have a like effect.

§ 664. Sublease covenants. Some provision is needed in the sublease that the sublessee will do nothing that could cause a forfeiture of the ground lease and will perform all the ground tenant's covenants if the sublease is of the entire building.

§ 665. Options to renew in ground lease. If the ground lease contains options to renew, and the renewal term is of importance to the sublessee, he can, if the option so permits, require in his contract for sublease that the ground lessee exercise this option. If this is not feasible, the attornment agreement can permit the sublessee to exercise the option if the ground tenant fails to do so.

34

Ground Leases—
Mortgageable Ground Leases

§ **666. History.** The first use of the long term lease in this country took place in Maryland. 2 Powell, *Real Property* § 249. Since 1900 use of the long term lease has increased because of its utility as a financing device for development of urban land. *Ibid.*

§ **667. In general.** The chief characteristic of the ground lease is that it is either a lease of vacant land or a lease of improved property where the improvements are obsolete and to be demolished or where the improvements are to be substantially remodeled. The security to L lies in the investment of capital by T in improvement of the premises.

The lease in a sale-and-leaseback transaction bears a superficial resemblance to the ground lease, but since it involves a net lease of improved property to a high-credit tenant its structure is considered elsewhere.

Among the reasons for using a ground lease rather than a sale are: (1) The owner refuses to sell, usually because he wishes his children and grandchildren to benefit by appreciation of the value of the land. (2) The lessee is not required to make the larger investment entailed in purchase of valuable land. (3) Tax considerations, for example, if the land has appreciated greatly in value, a sale would involve substantial income tax.

Among the disadvantages of a ground lease are: (1) Subleases are not as attractive to tenants as leases of fee title. Keeping subleases alive if the ground lease is terminated poses problems. (2) A leasehold estate is not as easy to mortgage as a fee title. (3) T can make favorable subleases as the property appreciates in value, but the problem of subleasing grows more sticky in the closing years of the lease.

No attempt will be made here to retrace in any detail material that has been covered well elsewhere. *See, e.g.* 4 ABA Real Property Probate & Trust Journal 437 (1969) *Ground Leases and Their Financing;* Anderson, *The Mortgagee Looks at the Ground Lease,* 10 U. of Fla. L.Rev. 1 (1957). Thomas, *The Mortgaging of Long-Term Leases,* 39 Dicta 363 (1962); Hyde, *Leasehold Mortgages,* 12 Assn. of Life Ins. Counsel 659 (1955); Friedman, *Lease Provisions Relating to Leasehold Mortgages,* PLI Commercial Leases (4th ed.) 317, which last PLI publication also contains reprints of many of the other articles.

§ **668. Steps prior to signing lease—contract for lease.** In some instances the parties will draw a contract for lease, just as a contract of sale precedes the giving of a deed and the closing of a real estate sale. After all, the parties may want to close the lease deal in escrow and a valid escrow must rest on a prior valid contract to lease. Also *T* will not want to sign the lease until he knows *L's* title is good. Therefore the contract will call for a preliminary search of the title and the issuance of a commitment by the title company to issue its leasehold title policy. If *T's* lawyer is sophisticated, he will insist on a marketable title policy with extended coverage. The marketable policy insures marketability. The extended coverage insures against unrecorded easements, survey problems, rights of parties in possession, etc., found in the standard owner's policy. Because of the *gap period* between the date the title commitment issues and the day the lease is recorded, the contract may well call for the lease transaction to be closed in escrow. If the title commitment reveals any title defects, they are carefully analyzed.

EXAMPLE: The commitment reveals a recorded building restriction. If it limits the use that may be made of the property, the deal will probably have to be killed.

EXAMPLE: The commitment reveals an easement for ingress that runs through the middle of the property. The deal must be killed.

The contract will also call for the seller to furnish a survey within a specified period of time in form satisfactory to the lessee. This is analyzed as is done in the case of real estate.

EXAMPLE: The survey reveals a sewer running through the property. Whether it's here legally or not, it spells trouble. The deal will have to be killed.

This, of course, means that the contract will have to indicate that the presence of sewers, drains, utilities, encroachments of adjoining buildings, etc., gives *T* the right to rescind. The contract is important in all these regards, because discovery of these defects after a work crew has started construction may spell disaster. *See* Chapters 7 and 10.

If there is lack of contiguity between the several parcels to be demised, the deal stops there. And, after the lease is signed, as in the case of any large scale transaction, all the requirements applicable to construction lenders are applicable, and should appear in the lease, including the provisions for architect's certificates, mechanic's lien waivers, monthly date-down of the survey to see if the building is violating zoning ordinance or building restriction lines, or worse yet, is encroaching on neighboring land, where, for example, ornamental projections, such as balconies, intrude over street lines, or where the building is not plumb. *See* Chapter 22.

See also Chapters 7 and 10 to 14 inclusive.

A contract for ground lease may be contingent on rezoning as is often done in sales of the fee title.

§ 669. Steps prior to signing lease—inspection of the premises. The intending purchaser of a fee title makes an inspection to determine the rights of parties in possession, possible unrecorded easements, etc. This is also done by an intending ground lessee. This inspection indicates consideration of a number of non-legal considerations, such as possible interference by the building with streams or drainage, existing power lines, etc. *T* may want *L* to furnish opinion of counsel as to *T's* right to make use of rail transportation via existing spur tracks, sidings, team tracks, etc. *T* will have to make his own check as to adequacy of parking space, public transportation and highways for truck service, though he may ask for *L's* opinion of counsel as to access to highways, *e.g.*, that they are not limited access highways.

§ 670. **Steps prior to signing lease—financial statements.** Before negotiations as to the structure of the lease take place, *L* usually asks for financial statements of *T's* financial stability. If *T* is a subsidiary, it should be ascertained that a guarantee can be provided from the parent and this requirement, including the form of guarantee, previously approved by the parent, goes into the contract for lease.

§ 671. **Steps prior to signing lease—additional adjoining property needed for contemplated improvement—easements and covenants.** If *T* owns adjoining land that will be occupied by the building on the leased land, obviously an elaborate system of easements and covenants will be necessary. *See* Chapter 39. It should be provided for in the contract of lease, delivered in escrow, and recorded with the lease. Alternatively, the land can be sold to the ground lessor and included in the ground lease.

§ 672. **Steps prior to signing lease—environmental problems—energy crisis.** As in the case of land sales, environmental and energy crisis problems are fully explored before any contract or lease is signed.

§ 673. **Steps prior to construction of building—demolition of improvements.** If *T* is to have the right to demolish existing buildings, this right is spelled out in the lease. Usually these buildings are of little value, and consent is readily provided. If there is an existing mortgage, the mortgagee's consent must also be obtained.

§ 674. **Lessor and lessee requirements as to lessor and lessee are described elsewhere.** *See* Chapters 5 and 6.

§ 675. **Description.** Informal descriptions are common in store leases. In a ground lease, nothing less than a full legal description will suffice. It should be checked against the title policy. *See* Chapters 8 and 9.

For a mortgagee's protection the leased premises must not go beyond the mortgaged premises. Otherwise, foreclosure of the mortgage creates a situation where there are two landlords and one tenant. One landlord cannot control the other. One might default in his obligations, declare an improvident forfeiture, etc.

§ 676. **Subject clause.** In every substantial lease, the landlord should feel concern about the implied warranties of title the courts might read into the lease. 3 Thompson, *Real Property* (1959) § 1129. Hence, a subject clause will be included in the lease along the lines of the subject clause in a contract of sale or warranty deed. *See* Chapter 10. One such subject clause follows:

Subject, however, to:

(1) The terms and conditions of the agreement dated June 12, 1872, between Addison Ballard, Potter Palmer and Walter S. Williams, recorded in the Recorder's Office for said County in Book 242, Page 300 as Document No. 110060, establishing an open court or area way for light and ventilation to the buildings situated on Lots number (1) and four (4) in Block number three (3) in Fractional Section number Fifteen (15) Addition aforesaid;

(2) The terms and conditions of the party wall agreement, dated June 12, 1872, between Addison Ballard and Walter S. Williams, recorded in the Recorder's Office for said County in Book 734, page 179 as Document No. 141565, and recorded as Document No. 821395, relating to the wall on the line between said Lots number one (1) and two (2) in the Assessor's Division aforesaid;

(3) Possible right or easement to maintain telephone wires, pipes, conduits and other facilities, used by the City of Chicago or for public utilities, which enter or cross the Demised Premises;

(4) Covenants, conditions, easements and restrictions affecting the title to the Demised Premises at the time of the acquisition of such title by the Lessor.

(5) Terms, covenants and conditions contained in the deed of even date herewith by which the Demised Premises are conveyed to the Lessor by Hilton Hotels Corporation;

(6) The state of facts disclosed by the plat of survey prepared by Chicago Guarantee Survey Company, dated December 7, 1962, and identified as its order number 6211021;

(7) Present and future zoning and building laws, ordinances, resolutions and regulations of the City of Chicago and all present and future ordinances, laws, regulations and orders of all boards, bureaus, commissions and bodies of any municipal, county, state or federal sovereigns now or hereafter having or acquiring jurisdiction of the Demised Premises and the use and improvement thereof;

(8) Revocable nature of the right, if any, to maintain vaults, vault spaces, basement and subbasement spaces, areas, structures, marquees or signs, beyond the building lines;

(9) The rights of tenants and occupants presently in, or under agreement for, possession of portions of the Building and enjoying, or hereafter to enjoy, the use thereof; and all unperformed obligations of any former owner of the Demised Premises with respect thereto;

(10) The effect of all present and future municipal, state and federal laws, orders and regulations, if any, relating to tenants or occupants of the Building, their rights and rentals to be charged for the use of the Building or any portion or portions thereof;

(12) Violations of law, ordinances, orders or requirements that might be disclosed by an examination and inspection or search of the Demised Premises or the Building by any federal, state or municipal departments or authority having jurisdiction, as the same may exist on the date of the commencement of the term of this Lease, and which the Lessee covenants and agrees to remove promptly as is hereinafter provided in Article 8 of this Lease;

(12) The condition of the Demised Premises as the same may be on the date of the commencement of the term of this Lease;

(13) All taxes, assessments, water meter and water charges, accrued or unaccrued, fixed or not fixed;

(14) Any defects of title, or any encumbrances affecting the Demised Premises or encroachments, existing at the date of the commencement of the term of this Lease;

(15) The matters hereinbefore expressly excepted from the Demised Premises and such legal implications as may arise therefrom.

See also Chapter 10.

§ 677. Use provisions. Use provisions in *commercial leases* tend to be rather strict. If the landlord in a shopping center wants a Walgreen Drug Store at a particular location, he does not want the space converted into sales of men's wear. In a *ground lease,* the situation is different. The very length of the lease insures that circumstances will change. Hence, the tenant will want a clause permitting *any lawful use*. This also makes it easier or the leasehold mortgagee to dispose of the leasehold if he acquires it by foreclosure.

§ 678. Rental. The ground lease is a net lease. Hence the provisions regarding rent parallel those of the net lease. The amount of rent is a matter of negotiation by the parties. If the lessee will mortgage the leasehold, he must remember that the mortgagee is vitally interested in the rent he will have to pay if he forecloses. Rent escalation clauses, for example, arouse anxiety on the part of prospective lenders, for obvious reasons.

Where the lease requires *T* to construct a building, the lease may call for payment of rent to begin when the estimated construction period has expired, with a stated time limit for completion.

Step-up rentals of stated amounts taking place at stated intervals can be evaluated by the prospective lender, whereas rent tied to a Consumer Price Index obviously cannot.

While the ground lease is a net lease, there have developed in recent years certain variations in the structuring of rent so as to insure L of some equality of purchasing power that might otherwise be eroded in consequence of the impact of continuing inflation. For example:

(a) Some 99-year leases call for a participation by L in the cash flow after payment of all expenses including rent and mortgage debt service.

(b) Some ground leases will provide for reappraisals of the land every 20 years, and an adjustment of the rent based upon a stated or agreed upon percentage factor to be used as the multiplier.

(c) Some leases provide for escalations every 5, 10, or 15 years, predicated on an increase in the Consumer Price Index.

§ 679. **Rent abatement.** The ground lease is a net lease and, like other net leases, calls for payment of rent without abatement or offset for any cause whatever except as specifically provided therein.

§ 680. **Term of lease.** The term of the lease is a matter for negotiation. However, state law limiting the duration of leases must be checked into. Requirements of state law for length of mortgageable leases must also be checked, for all institutional lenders are prohibited from lending on leaseholds unless the lease is of a duration specified by statute. In any case, the term of the lease must be long enough so that if the leasehold mortgagee forecloses, he will be able to operate the property long enough to recoup his losses on the foreclosure and obtain a return of his principal and interest. Often the lease runs for a stated term, with an option or options to renew. The freedom of choice these options give may be lost, since leasehold mortgage lenders sometimes insist on their exercise when the mortgage is given.

§ 681. **Construction and reconstruction of building—hazard insurance.** The typical ground lease calls for T to construct a building. Obviously, the lease and accompanying documents will describe the building in detail and will spell out when and how the stages of construction will progress. This should tie into the leasehold mortgage, because the lender will wish to control the time and manner in which his construction disbursements are made. The construction contract should track with these two documents. The safeguards common in construction loans on the fee are present. There may be provisions for architect's certificates on each disbursement, with the architect certifying that the balance of loan funds are sufficient to complete the building. There may be requirements for title company examination of lien waivers on each draw. Each draw will be policed to see that there is no substantial deviation from the construction provisions that might operate to release the surety company that has given construction bonds, and so on.

The lease requires T to reconstruct a destroyed or damaged building. The provisions again are similar to those in other net leases. T will argue for some flexibility as to the nature of a reconstructed building, since times and neighborhoods change. The lease requirements as to insurance are much like those in a net lease. Builder's risk insurance is required where a building is to be constructed or reconstructed. The lease may call for the insurance proceeds to be paid over to the leasehold mortgagee (if it is an institutional lender) to apply in reconstruction of the building. A like provision may be found in the eminent domain clause, where there is a partial taking, and the portion not taken is susceptible of reconstruction. Or the proceeds may be payable to a bank or trust company, to disburse on architect's certificates, lien waivers, etc. The problem of reconstruction during the final years of the term is similar to that encountered in net leases. It may be folly for *T* to reconstruct an economically outmoded building he cannot efficiently operate. Hence, the lease may provide for simply restoring the land to the vacant condition that existed before the lease began, if the leasehold mortgagee consents, with some appropriate division of the insurance proceeds after mortgage debt has been retired. The same considerations are applicable where substantial demolition takes place as a result of exercise of the power of eminent domain.

The "rebuilding clause" may provide that the new building shall be of comparable physical and economic value as the building destroyed, and that such new improvements are to be consistent with the highest and best physical and economic use of the demised land.

Where the building is destroyed or materially damaged near the close of the lease, if *L* will not agree to a clause terminating the lease in such event, so that *T* remains bound to rebuild, *L* should at least agree to an extension of the lease for a stated period of time in such case to give *T* the benefit of the new building.

A common provision in leases calls for insurance proceeds to be paid to a bank or trust company, which will disburse same to rebuild the building. The clause must give the trust company much discretion and protection. Many persons have found that no bank or trust company will take on this headache. Alternatives should be provided.

T should be permitted to make minor alterations without *L's* consent. Major alterations, *e.g.*, converting a hotel into an office building, should require *L's* written consent, also the written consent of the mortgagee. This consent will be conditioned on providing the same protection demanded when new construction is taking place.

A short form of construction clause follows:

Construction of Building. On or before _____, _____, Lessee shall commence, and shall thereafter diligently pursue to completion, the construction upon or over the demised area, or the major part thereof, at the sole cost and expense of Lessee, a modern multi-story fireproof building or buildings, the major portion of which shall be used for office purposes and which will reasonably exploit the demised area. Such building or buildings shall hereafter, for convenience, be referred to as the 'building.' Lessee shall diligently go forward with and complete construction of the building.

The building and appurtenant structures, shall be constructed in accordance with detailed plans, drawings and specifications and a schedule of work, which shall be submitted prior to commencement of construction to Lessor with a written request for his approval, which approval shall not be unreasonably withheld, in order to determine whether they are in accordance with the standards prescribed above, and the other requirements and provisions of this Lease.

If, after construction has begun, Lessee desires to make material changes in, or additions to, plans, drawings and specifications, Lessee shall furnish them to Lessor with a written request for his approval, which approval shall not be unreasonably withheld, in order to determine whether they are in accordance with the standards prescribed above and the other requirements and provisions of this Lease.

During such construction Lessor, and any architect, engineer or other representative Lessor may select to act for it, may inspect (but shall have no duty or obligation to inspect) the work being performed upon the demised area and the materials being used in, or to be used in, performance of such work. If during construction of the building or other improvements, Lessor, its architect, engineer or other representative shall determine that any materials do not substantially conform to the approved specifications or that the building or improvements are not being constructed in accordance with approved plans, specifications or drawings, prompt notice thereof may be given by Lessor to Lessee specifying the nature of the deficiency or defect or omission. Upon the receipt of any such notice, Lessee shall promptly take such steps as may be necessary to correct such defect, deficiency or omission.

Lessee, upon the completion of the building, at its sole cost, shall furnish and equip the building as a modern high-grade, first-class, commercial office building of the City of Chicago with all the furnishings, facilities and equipment required for that purpose and of a standard and quality at least equal to other modern commercial office buildings within the downtown area of the City of Chicago and during the continuance of this Lease shall make such renewals and additions to such furnishings, facilities and equipment as may be necessary to operate a high-grade commercial office building of the City of Chicago.[1]

§ 682. Steps prior to completion of building—zoning changes. In our times, new developments are sometimes unwelcome. Neighbors may seek a zoning change to bar the planned building. *T* would like to see a clause that if such a change takes place before his building achieves non-conforming use status, he will have the right to terminate the lease. The leasehold mortgagee ought not object because non-conforming use status can be achieved without expenditure of mortgage funds.

§ 683. Dedications. The project may depend upon the dedication of streets or strips for street widening. Obviously, the lease must contain clauses requiring *L*, as fee owner, to join in such dedications.

§ 684. Easements for utilities. The project may require the grant of easements to utility companies. The utility companies want this to come from *L* as well as *T*, and this should be provided for in the lease.

§ 685. Eminent Domain. The matter of partial taking has already been mentioned. Where there is a total taking, the lease provides that upon such taking the lease terminates. The division of the award is a matter that usually winds up in spirited negotiation. The same problem crops up in other net leases. *See* Chapter 28. However, in the ground lease, *T* has usually constructed a building and argues that, after the leasehold mortgagee has been paid off, *L's* share of the award should be limited to land value when the lease was made. *L*, obviously, will argue that this ignores the appreciation in land value that normally takes place. There is no universally accepted formula. The problem of reconstruction with condemnation proceeds in the last years of the term has already been discussed.

Some lessors contend that as the lease matures, their right to the eventual ownership of the improvements becomes more valuable.

EXAMPLE: In a 50-year lease providing that the improvements constructed by *T* become the property of *L* at the lease termination, this right becomes more tangible and valuable to *L* as each year of the lease expires. Acting on this premise, some lessors, therefore, insist upon a clause in their long-term leases where their participation in condemnation proceeds increases, ratably, as each year of the term is consumed.

---

[1] © Copyright Ill. Continuing Legal Ed. *Commercial Real Property Transactions* § 2.34 (1972).

§ **685a. Bankruptcy.** To some unknown extent, some of *T's* rights under a lease can be extinguished by rejection of the lease by *L's* trustee in bankruptcy. 26 Bus. Law. 1391; Kratovil, *Mortgages*, § 349. Where *T* erects improvements under the lease and the lease expressly provides that *T* shall not be compelled to surrender the premises until payment for the improvements has been made or rendered, this creates a right or lien good against the trustee in bankruptcy. *In re New York Investors Mutual Group*, 153 F.Supp. 772, aff'd 258 F2d 14. Obviously, this clause can be a big help to *T*. Some writers believe that the trustee in bankruptcy is bound by covenants running with the land. 31 U. of Chicago L.Rev. 467, 491. Hence *T* will seek the protection of such covenants. An option to purchase is a covenant running with the land, 51 CJS *Landlord & Tenant* § 81 (2) p. 235, 38 ALR 1163. A covenant to extend or renew can be a present demise 51 CJS *Landlord & Tenant* § 54, p. 164. Or it can be a covenant running with the land. 1 Tiffany Real Property (3d ed. 1939) § 126, p. 208, 38 ALR 1163. In either case an argument can be made that the trustee is bound. Couching these interests in terms of covenants running with the land offers some prospect of defeating the trustee in bankruptcy. Admittedly, some case law runs to the contrary.

§ **686. Assignments and subleases.** Some older ground leases permit assignment of the ground lease but require the assignment to be recorded with an assumption of personal liability therein. Modern ground leases often omit the assumption provision, the theory being that if the leasehold mortgagee is forced to foreclose, he will be able to dispose more freely of the leasehold if the assumption is not present. To put this into better focus, remember that by virtue of privity of estate, each assignee of the leasehold estate will be liable to the landlord for defaults or breaches of running covenants occurring during his ownership of the leasehold estate, but if there is an assumption, the liability becomes contractual and continues beyond his disposition of the leasehold to others whom he cannot control. Both the leasehold mortgagee and each subsequent assignee will want to be liable only so long as they own the leasehold estate.

Since *L* is making the lease on the security of the improvements to be constructed, there is some justice in *L's* contention that, except for assignment by way of leasehold mortgage or foreclosure thereof, no assignment or sublease of the entire premises shall be made until the building has been completed. Often the lease requires *T* to furnish surety bonds for completion of the building. It is not easy to relate these to performance by an assignee or sublessee. Default by the party assured in the bond (the original tenant) might very well give the surety a bond defense. Perhaps a solution might be to forbid assignment unless the surety company is willing to substitute the assignee of the lease as the party assured in the bond.

Other than as indicated herein, the lease must not contain any restriction on *T's* right to make assignments or subleases. It is of the essence of a ground lease that *T* has unfettered power to operate, and this means free selection of subtenants, and to mortgage or sell the leasehold, and to have his mortgagee, when he forecloses, similarly unfettered.

However, some ground leases provide that assignment is permitted as long as *T* is not then in default under the lease.

At times it is provided that on the making of an assignment (except one forbidden by the lease) the liability of the assignor for future defaults and breaches of covenant is terminated. Leasehold mortgagees insist on this. A leasehold mortgagee who has foreclosed wants no liability after he has sold his interest to a third party. This may be coupled with a requirement that each assignee sign an assumption of personal liability during the period of his ownership of the leasehold estate. There is also a clause stating that no leasehold mortgagee shall have personal liability for rent or breach of covenant under the lease until and unless he acquires the leasehold estate by foreclosure or assignment in lieu of foreclosure.

§ **687. Leasehold mortgage protection.** In addition to the negative precaution of seeing to it that the ground lease contains no restriction on assignment (except during the construction phase) the ground lease will affirmatively consent to the making of a leasehold mortgage and foreclosure thereof, or to the giving of assignment thereof in lieu of foreclosure.

Where provisions regarding the leasehold mortgage are built into the ground lease, some provision is needed to the effect that any takeout or refinancing lender succeeds to the position of the original leasehold mortgagee. Some lawyers like this clause to extend to any mortgage given to finance permitted alterations.

Among the other clauses found in a ground lease for the protection of the leasehold mortgagee against termination of the lease are the following: (1) T is to furnish L an executed counterpart of the mortgage. (2) No surrender, merger, cancellation, or other termination of the lease or any modification of the lease between L and T shall be effective as to E without E's prior written consent. (3) Any notice, or demand, other document of any kind whatever served by L upon T included but not limited to notice of default under the lease shall also be served on E, but L shall not be required to serve an assignee of the mortgage unless and until a copy of the assignment is lodged with L, and whenever ownership of the mortgage passes into the hands of more than one party, all such owners must furnish L a written designation of the party to be served on behalf of all such owners. (4) E shall have the right to cure T's defaults and perform all his covenants. (5) As to any default or breach of covenant that can be cured by E without taking possession of the premises. E shall have _____ days to cure defaults or breaches after L has given E notice of intention to terminate the lease or disposses T. (6) As to any default or breach that can only be cured by taking possession, E may furnish L a guarantee of its performance under the lease of all T's obligations, including the cure of all defaults and breaches, and that E will proceed with reasonable diligence to take possession of the premises and either foreclose the mortgage or acquire the leasehold by assignment in lieu of foreclosure. (7) Any acquisition of the leasehold by E may be taken in the name of a nominee. (8) L will not terminate the lease as long as E performs promptly all its covenants in the guarantee. (9) L may require reasonable security to accompany the guarantee if E is other than an institutional lender.

In lieu of, or in addition to, provisions like the foregoing for preservation of the lease against termination, it may be covenanted and agreed that in case of termination of the lease for default or breach of covenant by T, (1) E may serve notice on L of its desire to enter into a new lease for the balance of the term at the same rentals and with the same covenants contained in the lease, said notice to be served on L _____ days, prior to the termination by L, which notice shall be accompanied by a payment of all arrears of rent *and* a reasonable sum to compensate *L* for his expenses, including reasonable attorneys fees, in establishing the new relationship and a guarantee satisfactory to *L* that *E* will cure all *T's* defaults and breaches other than arrears of rent. (2) The new lease commences as of the termination of the old one, but shall be prior and superior to all rights, liens and encumbrances that would have been extinguished by foreclosure of the leasehold mortgage, though the validity of this clause is not clear. (3) Each subtenant is obliged to attorn to *E* if *E* so demands.

Such a clause, since it is basically a contract to make a lease, may be subject to dissaffirmance by *L's* trustee in bankruptcy. And as to *E*, since it seems to be an option to receive a lease, it probably should contain the usual perpetuities escape clause that it will expire 20 years after the death of the last living descendant of X.

It is best for the leasehold mortgagee to join in the lease under a clause stating that he joins for the sole purpose of evidencing his acceptance of the provisions of the lease relating to leasehold mortgages, thus making him a third-party beneficiary.

The survival clause in a lease is well understood. It was originally contrived in order to enable *L* to oust a defaulting *T*, but to do so in such a way that the lease *survived* so that *T* remained liable for rent accruing after the ouster. There seems no legal reason why this clause cannot be assigned a new function. Draft the clause so that it explicitly gives the leasehold mortgagee the right to demand possession and gives *L* the right to place in possession of the premises after *T's* ouster any leasehold mortgagee, expressly naming the current leasehold mortgagee if possible, and that this in no wise causes a surrender, merger, or other impairment of the lease or leasehold mortgage, but shall be deemed a continuation of the lease as though same had been assigned by *T* to the leasehold mortgagee, with the latter having an irrevocable power of attorney to sign the occupancy agreement. This offers some solution to the problem where foreclosure of the leasehold mortgage is likely to take time and *T* has breached covenants, like the covenant to repair that requires the presence on the land of some responsible party attending to the needed repairs, so that subtenants can be persuaded to remain. At the same time, foreclosure of the leasehold mortgage proceeds concurrently to eliminate junior liens. If this clause passes muster with the courts, it might ward off attacks by others having claims or liens against *T*. Whether it would be effective against *L's* trustee in bankruptcy is another matter. At all events if this clause is simply added to the arsenal of protective clauses in the lease, it can do the leasehold mortgagee no harm and might do a great deal of good. It is not a complete novelty. In the sublease-attornment clause somewhat similar language is found, at times. *See* Chapter 36.

§ **688. Leasehold mortgage protection—the default clause.** Obviously, a leasehold mortgagee cannot accept a lease in which the default clause contains provisions calling for automatic termination of the lease in case of bankruptcy, receivership, or even default or breach of covenant. Such clauses are helpful in occupancy leases, because they make it possible to oust the tenant by simple forcible detainer proceedings and keep the tenant out of bankruptcy proceedings. But the leasehold mortgagee will insist on a default clause that he can live with. The automatic termination clause is simply unacceptable.

§ **689. Division and apportionment of leasehold.** The lease may contemplate the construction of two independent buildings, each to be financed separately. In such case, the lease will provide for separate leasehold mortgages, with a detailed provision for separating the lease into parts, with an elaborate provision for cross-easements needed when separation of the leasehold estates takes place. It is best to spell out that these easements survive foreclosure of any of the leasehold mortgages. There must be no cross-default provision, for that would be objectionable to the separate leasehold mortgagees.

Many problems arise in the area of apportionment.

EXAMPLE: *L* dies intestate, leaving several heirs, or *L* conveys to co-tenants. Here the reversion is divided into undivided interests. The right to rent may therefore be divided. The question of the rights of the cotenants to enforce covenants and conditions arises. Covenants are probably apportioned. 21 C.J.S. *Covenants* § 82. Whether conditions can be apportioned is another matter. 1 Tiffany, *Real Property* § 210; 37 Yale L. J. 179; 50 ALR2d 1365.

EXAMPLE: *L* conveys the north half of the leased land to *A,* and the south half to *B.* Again the same problems arise.

EXAMPLE: The leasehold is divided into undivided interests or into geographic parts. Again problems arise. 1 Am. Law Ppty. 300; 99 ALR 220; 49 Am.Jur.2d 413.

To the greatest extent permitted by local law the parties should draft around the problems.

EXAMPLE: If geographic division of the leasehold is contemplated, that should be provided for, and breaches of covenant or condition as to one part should not affect the other part.

§ 690. **Improvements by tenant.** Whether *T* is to have the right to remove improvements erected by him is a matter that the lease should cover in detail. Even a skyscraper erected by *T* may be *removable* if the lease so provides. Of course, there is little likelihood that the building will be removed. But *T* can threaten to do so, brick by brick if necessary, and his rights give him bargaining power. Thus the lease will provide, at a minimum, that *T* has the option of purchasing *L's* fee at a price fixed by a three-man appraisal, or that *L* has the option of buying the building at a price fixed by a three-man appraisal, or that *L* has the option to purchase the building or granting *T* a specified renewal option, and so on. If *T* fails to exercise any of his options, the lease will provide that his right of removal ends and the improvements become *L's* property when the lease ends. Notice, here, that in a long-term lease there is a shifting of title to the building at a period far beyond that fixed by the rule against perpetuities, but all courts have assumed that the arrangement is valid. Whether the building is erected by *T* or a subtenant makes no difference so far as *L* is concerned.

§ 691. **Renewal options.** There is a technical distinction between an option to renew and an option to extend. The option to renew is more common, for it requires only unilateral action and may be exercised, under the usual lease clause, by the simple giving of notice.

Obviously, no renewal clause is valid if it takes the lease over the maximum duration specified by stated law.

§ 692. **Warranties.** An intending purchaser of valuable property obtains many warranties from the seller, *e.g.,* that the seller has no knowledge of impending condemnation or litigation with neighbors. The ground lessee wants the same warranties, and they are described in the contract for lease.

35

Leasehold Mortgages

§ 693. In general. Many general observations and suggestions concerning the validity, law, and structure of leasehold mortgages will be found elsewhere. Thomas, *Mortgaging of Long Term Leases.* 39 Dicta 363, 2 Powell, *Real Property* § 245; Goldberg, *Sales of Real Property* 299 (Pennsylvania law); McDonald, *Leasehold Mortgages,* 1957 Proceedings California Land Title Association 63; California Land Security and Development, § 1.22; Kratovil, *Mortgages,* Chapter 30. As is evident much of the material must deal with provisions in the lease necessary for the mortgagee's protection.

§ 694. Steps prior to signing mortgage—analysis of ground lease. Before *E* commits to make a leasehold mortgage, the lease is carefully analyzed to make sure the rent and all other provisions of the lease are satisfactory to *E. See* Chapter 34.

§ 695. Steps prior to signing mortgage—leasehold—mortgagee's protection—checking existing leases. If the building has been completed before the leasehold mortgage transaction takes place, and there are existing occupancy subleases, these will be checked by any prospective leasehold mortgagee to see if they contain satisfactory rent provisions, covenants, attornment and subordination clauses etc. For the mortgagee's further protection, he may want the ground lease to require the lender's approval on future subleases.

§ 696. Steps prior to signing mortgage—title searches—title insurance on leasehold mortgage. Obviously the well-informed leasehold mortgagee insists on marketable title and title insurance on the leasehold mortgage. The leasehold mortgagee as a rule, wants no fee mortgage or other lien ahead of his ground lease. This is why some ground lessees want a contract for ground lease coupled with a provision for title search and title insurance on the leasehold, with a provision for later date title search to cover recording of the lease, this portion of the transaction to be closed in escrow. This title search will also reveal non-lien items, such as restriction reverter clauses that might endanger the ground lease or that might make the investment an unlawful one where an institutional lender is involved. Even if the original mortgagee is an unregulated lender, he may wish later to assign the mortgage to an institutional lender. *See* Chapters 10 to 14 inclusive.

§ 697. Mortgagor and mortgagee requirements as to mortgagor and mortgagee are discussed elsewhere. *See* Chapters 5 and 6.

§ 698. Property mortgagee—in general. The granting clause of a leasehold mortgage may take the following form:

The mortgagor hereby grants, mortgages, charges, assigns, transfers and sets over to the Mortgagee:

(i) The leasehold estate created by the certain lease ("the Lease") of the lands described in Schedule A hereto made by and between _____ as lessor and the Mortgagor as lessee, dated _____, and recorded in _____ which leasehold estate includes but is not limited to all improvements and fixtures now or hereafter erected thereon ("the Leasehold Estate"); and

(ii) All rights and benefits of whatsoever nature derived or to be derived by the Mortgagor under or by virtue of the Lease, including without limitation the right to exercise options, to give consents, and to receive monies payable to the lessee thereunder; and

(iii) All subleases of the Leasehold Estate or any part thereof now or hereafter entered into by the Mortgagor, the subreversions thereunder and all rights and benefits to be derived by the Mortgagor therefrom; and

(iv) All rents, income, issues and profits of the Leasehold Estate; and

(v) All right, title and interest of the Mortgagor in and to all and singular tenements, hereditaments, easements, rights, privileges and appurtenances of the Leasehold Estate at any time belonging or in any wise appertaining thereto, and all right, title and interest of the Mortgagor in and to any streets, ways, alleys, gores or strips of land adjoining the said lands or any part thereof, the same being hereinafter collectively called "the Mortgaged Property".

TO HAVE AND TO HOLD the same unto the Mortgagee its successors and assigns for and during the balance of the unexpired term of the Lease.

§ 699. Property mortgaged—alternative clause.

Together with:

1. All rights and interest of whatever character of the mortgagor, in and to the buildings and improvements now or hereafter on the above described premises.

2. All right, title and interest that mortgagor may hereafter acquire in and to said premises.

3. All rights of mortgagor under said Ground Lease or any extension, renewal, or modification thereof, including Mortgagor's rights in security deposits, advance payments of rent, and without limitation, all other rights of the Mortgagor under said documents or any of them, or in or to said premises.

4. The subreversions in all subleases now or hereafter existing as to all or any part of said premises, and all rents and other moneys due or to become due thereunder, and all rights of the Mortgagor thereunder, including Mortgagor's right to cancel or modify said subleases or any of them.

5. Except as otherwise provided herein, all rights of the Mortgagor under any condemnation award made in connection with said premises (whether for taking or damaging, full or partial taking, inverse condemnation, temporary taking, taking of a limited interest or otherwise) or in the proceeds of any and all insurance policies written in connection with said premises or the improvements thereon.

6. [Here add rights in streets, vaults, etc. *See* Chapter 9.]

7. [Here add rights in machinery, appliances. *See* Chapter 8.]

8. All options to renew or purchase contained in said lease.

All the foregoing are hereafter referred to as the "Mortgaged Property."

§ 700. Rent—escalation. Where the lease provides for rent escalations keyed to some cost-of-living index this creates obvious problems for E. Rent increases can wipe out T's equity. There is no satisfactory solution. L wants the escalation. Some compromises have been tried. E may argue, for example, that L should agree with E on a long-term moratorium on rent escalations. Or he may ask for a provision that in the event he acquires the leasehold by foreclosure or assignment in lieu of foreclosure, rent reverts to the pre-escalation status. Obviously this requires a clause or modification agreement of the lease. An escalation based on increase of revenue from subtenants is less objectionable.

§ **701. Joinder of fee owner in leasehold mortgage—rent escalation.** The joinder of the fee owner in the leasehold mortgage ends controversies as to rent escalations. Foreclosure of the mortgage can extinguish the lease or leave the mortgagee in position to revise the lease terms as to rent. *See* Chapter 34.

§ **702. Construction leasehold mortgage.** The earliest mortgage on the leasehold of a ground lease is almost always a construction mortgage. All the protections any construction lender demands are applicable. However, the lender should be especially strict in his requirements concerning use of the funds for items other than bricks and mortar, *e.g.*, broker's fee. It is the building erected by *R* that gives *E* his security.

§ **703. Refinancing provisions.** Whenever the leasehold mortgage also covers the fee, the lease must look to the future. There will be refinancings, extensions, mortgage consolidations, modifications of the lease or mortgage, subsequent mortgages by the landlord, etc. The lease should cover the agreements of the parties on this score.

§ **704. Covenants and warranties.** In a leasehold mortgage the mortgagor represents, covenants and warrants as follows:

(1) That the said ground lease is in full force and effect and unmodified.

(2) That all rents (including additional rents and other charges) reserved in the said ground lease have been paid to the extent they were payable prior to the date hereof.

(3) The quiet and peaceful possession of the Mortgagee and Mortgagor further agrees to defend the leasehold estate created under said ground lease for the entire remainder of the term set forth therein, against each and every person or persons lawfully claiming, or who may claim the same or any part thereof, subject only to the payment of the rents in said ground lease reserved and to the performance and observance of all of the terms, covenants, conditions and warranties thereof.

(4) That there is no existing default under the provisions of the said ground lease or in the performance of any of the terms, covenants, conditions or warranties thereof on the part of the lessee to be observed and performed.

That the Mortgagor will pay or cause to be paid all rents, additional rents, taxes, assessments, water rates, sewer rents, and other charges mentioned in and made payable by said ground lease, for which provision has not been made hereinbefore, when and as often as the same shall become due and payable, and will cause the lessor of said premises to pay any portion of said taxes, assessments, rates, charges and impositions to be borne by the lessor that might become liens on the said premises or its leasehold estate within sixty (60) days of the date when due, and the Mortgagor will in every case take, or cause to be taken, a proper receipt for any such item so paid and will within ten (10) days after the time when such payment shall be due and payable deliver, or cause to be delivered to the Mortgagee, the original receipts for any such payments.[1]

And further covenants:

That the Mortgagor will at all times promptly and faithfully keep and perform, or cause to be kept and performed, all the covenants and conditions contained in the ground lease by the lessee therein to be kept and performed and in all respects conform to and comply with the terms and conditions of the ground lease and the Mortgagor further covenants that it will not do or permit anything to be done, the doing of which, or refrain from doing anything, the omission of which will impair or tend to impair the

---

[1] © Copyright Illinois Institute for Continuing Legal Education, *Mortgages and Foreclosures* 1973 § 1.64. Reprinted by permission.

security of this Mortgage or will be grounds for declaring a forfeiture of the ground lease, and upon any such failure aforesaid, Mortgagor shall be subject to all of the rights and remedies of Mortgagee in this Mortgage contained.

That the Mortgagor also covenants that it will not modify, extend or in any way alter the terms of said ground lease or cancel or surrender said ground lease, or waive, execute, condone or in any way release or discharge the lessor thereunder of or from the obligations, covenants, conditions and agreements by said lessor to be done and performed; and said Mortgagor does by these presents expressly release, relinquish and surrender unto the Mortgagee all its right, power and authority to cancel, surrender, amend, modify or alter in any way the terms and provisions of said ground lease and any attempt on the part of the Mortgagor to exercise any such right without the written authority and consent of the Mortgagee thereto being first had and obtained shall constitute a default under the terms hereof and the entire indebtedness secured hereby shall, at the option of the Mortgagee, become due and payable forthwith and without notice.

§ 705. Default provisions. A suggested default provision is as follows:

That the entire indebtedness shall immediately become due and payable at the option of the Mortgagee, if the Mortgagor fails to give the Mortgagee immediate notice of any default under the ground lease or of the receipt by it of any notice of default from the lessor thereunder or if the Mortgagor fails to furnish to the Mortgagee immediately any and all information which it may request concerning the performance by the Mortgagor of the covenants of the ground lease, or if the Mortgagor fails to permit forthwith the Mortgagee or its representative at all reasonable times to make investigation or examination concerning the performance by the Mortgagor of the covenants of the ground lease, or if the Mortgagor fails to permit forthwith the Mortgagee or its representative at all reasonable times to make investigation or examination concerning such performance. The Mortgagor further covenants and agrees that it will promptly deposit with the Mortgagee an original executed copy of said ground lease and any and all documentary evidence received by it showing compliance by the Mortgagor with the provisions of the ground lease and will also deposit with the Mortgagee an exact copy of any notice, communication, plan, specification or other instrument or document received or given by it in any way relating to or affecting the ground lease of said premises which may concern or affect the estate of the lessor or the lessee in or under the ground lease or in the real estate thereby demised, and upon the Mortgagor's failure so to do, the Mortgagee may, at its option, declare the whole of said principal sum due and payable at once.

That in the event of any failure by Mortgagor to perform any covenant on the part of lessee to be observed and performed under the said ground lease, the performance by Mortgagee in behalf of Mortgagor of the said ground lease covenant shall not remove or waive, as between Mortgagor and Mortgagee, the corresponding default under the terms hereof and any amount so advanced by Mortgagee or any costs incurred in connection therewith, with interest thereon at the post maturity rate, shall be repayable by Mortgagor without demand and secured hereby.

That to the extent permitted by law, the price payable by the Mortgagor, or by any other party, so entitled, in the exercise of the right of redemption, if any, from sale under order or decree of foreclosure of this Mortgage shall include all rents paid and other sums advanced by Mortgagee, in behalf of Mortgagor, as lessee under the said ground lease.[2]

This would be in addition to the usual clause giving the right to take possession on default, collect rents, manage the operation, make repairs, cancel or modify subleases etc:

In any case in which under the provisions of this Mortgage the Mortgagee has a right to institute foreclosure proceedings, whether before or after the whole principal sum secured hereby is declared

---

[2] © Copyright Illinois Institute for Continuing Legal Education, *Mortgages and Foreclosures* © 1973 § 1.65. Reprinted by permission.

to be immediately due as aforesaid, or whether before or after the institution of legal proceedings to foreclosure the lien hereof or before or after sale thereunder, forthwith, upon demand of Mortgagee, Mortgagor shall surrender to Mortgagee and Mortgagee shall be entitled to take actual possession of the premises or any part thereof personally, or by its agent or attorneys, as for condition broken, and Mortgagee in its discretion may, with or without force and with or without process of law, enter upon and take and maintain possession of all or any part of said premises, together with all documents, books, records, papers and accounts of the Mortgagor or the then owner of the premises relating thereto, and may exclude the Mortgagor, its agents or servants, wholly therefrom and may as attorney in fact or agent of the Mortgagor, or in its own name as Mortgagee and under the powers herein granted, hold, operate, manage and control the premises and conduct the business, if any, thereof, either personally or by its agents, and with full power to use such measures, legal or equitable, as in its discretion or in the discretion of its successors or assigns may be deemed proper or necessary to enforce the payment or security of the avails, rents, issues, and profits of the premises, including actions for the recovery of rent, actions in forcible detainer and actions in distress for rent, hereby granting full power and authority to exercise each and every of the rights, privileges, and powers herein granted at any and all times hereafter, without notice to the Mortgagor, and with full power to cancel or terminate any lease or sublease for any cause or on any ground which would entitle Mortgagor to cancel the same, to elect to disaffirm any lease or sublease made subsequent to this Mortgage or subordinated to the lien hereof, to make all necessary or proper repairs, decorating, renewals, replacements, alterations, additions, betterments and improvements to the premises as to it may seem judicious, to insure and reinsure the premises and all risks incidental to Mortgagee's possession, operation and management thereof and to receive all of such avails, rents, issues and profits.

Upon or at any time after the filing of any bill to foreclose this Mortgage, the Court may, upon application, appoint a receiver of said premises. Such appointment may be made either before or after sale without notice, and without regard to the solvency or insolvency, at the time of application for such receiver, of the person or persons, if any, liable for the payment of the indebtedness secured hereby and without regard to the then value of the premises or whether the same shall be then occupied as a homestead or not, and without bond being required of the applicant. Such receiver shall have the power to take possession, control and care of said premises and to collect the rents, issues and profits of said premises during the pendency of such foreclosure suit and, in case of a sale and a deficiency, during the full statutory period of redemption, whether there be redemption or not, as well as during any further times when the Mortgagor, its heirs, administrators, executors, successors or assigns, except for the intervention of such receiver, would be entitled to collect such rents, issues and profits, and all other powers which may be necessary or are useful in such cases for the protection, possession, control, management and operation of the premises, during the whole of said period. The Court from time to time may authorize the receiver to apply the net income in his hands in payment in whole or in part of: (i) the indebtedness secured hereby or by any decree foreclosing this Mortgage, or any tax, special assessment, or other lien which may be, or become superior to the lien hereof, or of such decree, provided such application is made prior to foreclosure sale; (ii) the deficiency in case of sale and deficiency. Any such proceedings shall in no manner prevent or retard the collection of said debt by foreclosure otherwise.

The proceeds of any foreclosure sale of the premises shall be distributed and applied in the following order of priority: First, on account of all costs and expenses incident to the foreclosure proceedings, including all such items as are mentioned in the paragraph 33(b) hereof; second, all other items which under the terms hereof constitute secured indebtedness additional to that evidenced by the Note, with interest thereon as herein provided at the Post Maturity Rate; third, all principal and interest remaining unpaid on the Note; fourth, any overplus to Mortgagor, its successors or assigns, as their rights may appear.

That the failure of the Mortgagee to exercise the option for acceleration of maturity and/or foreclosure following any default as aforesid or to exercise any other option granted to the Mortgagee hereunder in any one or more instances, or the acceptance by Mortgagee of partial payments hereunder shall not constitute a waiver of any such default, except as may be provided by law, nor extend or affect the grace period, if any, but such option shall remain continuously in force. Acceleration of maturity, once claimed hereunder by Mortgagee, may, at the option of Mortgagee, be rescinded by written acknowledgement to that effect by the Mortgagee, but the tender and acceptance of partial payments alone shall not in any way affect or rescind such acceleration of maturity except as may be provided by law nor extend or affect the grace period, if any.[3]

§ **706. Curing default clause.** A clause along the following lines is often encountered:

> Mortgagor covenants and agrees that he will at all times fully perform and comply with all agreements, covenants, terms and conditions imposed upon or assumed by him as tenant under the aforesaid lease, and that if Mortgagor shall fail so to do Mortgagee may (but shall not be obligated to) take any action Mortgagee deems necessary or desirable to prevent or to cure any default by Mortgagor in the performance of or compliance with any of Mortgagor's covenants or obligations under said lease. Upon receipt by Mortgagee from the landlord under said lease of any written notice of default by the tenant thereunder, Mortgagee may rely thereon and take any action as aforesaid to cure such default even though the existence of such default or the nature thereof be questioned or denied by Mortgagor or by any party on behalf of Mortgagor. Mortgagor hereby expressly grants to Mortgagee, and agrees that Mortgagee shall have, the absolute and immediate right to enter in and upon the mortgaged premises or any part thereof to such extent and as often as Mortgagee, in its sole discretion, deems necessary or desirable in order to prevent or to cure any such default by Mortgagor. Mortgagee may pay and expend such sums of money as Mortgagee in its sole discretion deems necessary for any such purpose, and Mortgagor hereby agrees to pay to Mortgagee, immediately and without demand, all such sums so paid and expended by Mortgagee, together with interest thereon, from the date of each such payment at the rate of _____ percent per annum. All sums so paid and expended by Mortgagee, and the interest thereon, shall be added to and be secured by the lien of this Mortgage.

§ **707. Covenants—miscellaneous covenants.** Among other covenants common in a leasehold mortgage are those (1) forbidding modifications or surrender of any subleases without lender's consent; (2) requiring that R will notify E promptly in writing after learning of any condition that with or without the passage of time or the giving of any notice might result in a default under or the termination of the lease; (3) That R will preserve its title to and interest in the Mortgaged Property and does hereby and will forever warrant and defend the same to E against the claims of all persons and parties whomsoever, and; (4) that R will at its cost, without expense to E do, execute, acknowledge and deliver all and every further acts, deeds, conveyances, mortgages, assignments, transfers and assurances in the law as E requires assuring, granting, mortgaging, charging, assigning, transferring, setting over and confirming unto E the Mortgaged Property, including property which the Mortgagor may be or may hereafter become entitled.

However, the provisions in the leasehold mortgage designed to preserve the lease from termination or modification and for the preservation of subleases must be supplemented by provisions in the ground lease itself, preferably with joinder therein by the leasehold mortgagee. *See* Chapter 34.

If the ground lease is one previously existing, that is, one not executed concurrently with the making of the leasehold mortgage, it will often be necessary to have L and T and preferably E also, join in a modification of the lease that will introduce the protections needed for the leasehold mortgagee. At times, this is done by a side

---

[3] © Copyright Ill. Continuing Legal Ed. *Mortgages & Foreclosures* § 1.71 (1973). Reprinted by permission.

agreement between L and E, but this is somewhat unsatisfactory in that it is not clear that this can be made to enure to the benefit of a takeout lender, whereas a modification of the lease itself clearly accomplishes that result.

Leasehold mortgage clauses commonly include: (1) No liability on E until he acquires ownership of leasehold by foreclosure or assignment in lieu of foreclosure, otherwise, in title states, he may be liable from execution of mortgage; (2) As to each assignee, beginning with leasehold mortgagee who has foreclosed or acquired leasehold in lieu of foreclosure, no lease provision burdening assignment (requiring assumption, for example) is applicable, and each such assignee is liable for rent and breach of covenant only during time he owns leasehold; (3) leasehold mortgage lien covers options to renew or purchase, security deposits, condemnation award, insurance proceeds, etc.

In addition to the covenants contained in large-scale mortgages an important covenant is the mortgagor's covenant to pay all rentals and other charges required to be paid by the lease and to keep and perform all of the covenants of the lease. Also the mortgagor should covenant, represent, and warrant that (1) the ground lease is valid and subsisting; (2) the ground lease has not been modified; (3) all rentals and other charges required by the ground lease have been paid; (4) all covenants on the tenant's part have been observed; (5) all the covenants on the landlord's part have been observed.

In those instances where the lender chooses to require the monthly payments of principal and interest to include payments on taxes, insurance, etc., provision should be included for monthly payments on the ground rent.

If the mortgage is to be on an existing lease, it must be analyzed for objectionable covenants on T's part. The leasehold mortgagee, if he forecloses, will become the tenant and will be obligated to perform the tenant's covenants in the lease. A separate agreement can be made with the fee owner that such covenants are not to be enforced against the leasehold mortgage.

Of course, the usual clauses found in a mortgage in large scale transactions also find their way into the leasehold mortgage. *See* Chapter 25.

§ 708. Assignment restrictions—restrictions on transfer of ground lease. Just as a lessor in a commercial lease restrains assignment so that he can control the identity of his tenant, and requires assumption of personal liability by the assignee where he consents to the assignment, so does the leasehold mortgage require E's consent to any disposition of the ground lease by R and makes the assignee's assumption of personal liability a pre-condition to his consent, but without release of R's personal liability.

§ 709. Lease deposit clause—modifications by mortgagee forbidden. At times, a clause is found stating that mortgagor deposits or will deposit with the mortgagee T's original of the lease and all existing and future modifications of the lease, but mortgagee will not terminate or modify the lease as long as mortgagor is not in default.

§ 710. Subleases. Because E regards subleases as valuable assets should he be forced to foreclose, the mortgage will prohibit any assignment, mortgage, or other disposition whatever by R of his rights or interest under any sublease. Other restrictions on R with respect to subleases are: (1) No sublease of all of the property without E's consent. (2) No cancellation modification, surrender, etc., of sublease without E's consent. (3) No payment of rent in advance by subtenant. (4) R will perform all covenants under every sublease. (5) *R* will notify *E* of any litigation, notices, or other matters whatever that might extinguish any sublease or reduce *R's* rights thereunder.

As has been pointed out elsewhere, some mortgagees obtain an assignment of *R's* interest in all present and future subleases and record this with the mortgage.

§ 711. **Subleases—attornment by subtenants.** The provision for attornment by subtenant may take the following form:

> The Mortgagor covenants that it will cause each sublease or license granted in respect of the Mortgaged Property to contain a clause whereby the sublessee or licensee thereunder agrees that upon an Event of Default occurring hereunder and upon demand by the Mortgagee it will attorn to or become the tenant or licensee of the Mortgagee, or of any purchaser from the Mortgagee in the event of the sale of the Mortgaged Property pursuant to foreclosure proceedings, for the then unexpired balance of the term of, and upon all the terms and conditions of, such sublease or license.

§ 712. **Anti-merger clause after acquired titles.** You will often find a clause stating that the leasehold shall not merge in the fee even though both become vested in the lessor, lessee or some third party. This is included because the mortgagee will want to sell the leasehold *as a leasehold* if he forecloses. This clause is usually accompanied by a clause conveying to the mortgagee any title or interest *T* may later acquire in the premises. It may be accompanied by a provision that *T,* on demand, will execute a supplemental mortgage in recordable form covering such after-acquired property. This is done because an after-acquired property clause does not bring the mortgage into the chain of title. Kratovil, *Mortgages* § 267.

§ 713. **Anti-marshalling clause.** Where the tenant under the ground lease and the fee owner join in the fee mortgage, a foreclosure ought to give the purchaser at the foreclosure sale good title to the fee free and clear of the lease. There is, however, a marshalling of assets problem, discussed elsewhere. Kratovil, *Mortgages*, §§ 377, 388. Hence, an anti-marshalling of assets clause is routinely included. *Ibid.*

> Anti-marshalling clause. The doctrine of marshalling of assets is expressly made inapplicable to this transaction. In any foreclosure, separate sale of the fee and leasehold estate is not required. No release of portions of the mortgaged property or of the personal liability of any person or any modification, extension or agreement with third parties relating to said premises, including arrangements with sublessees or other lienors in any wise affects the lien of this mortgage or the rights of the mortgagee hereunder.

§ 714. **Assignment of leases and rents.** There is every reason for the leasehold mortgagee to insist on a separate assignment of leases and rents, that will operate on the sub-reversions and rents of the subleases. Kratovil, *Mortgages*, § 303. It will contain many of the provisions routinely found in such an assignment, including a prohibition of modification or cancellation of subleases without the mortgagee's consent or prepayment of rent thereunder. *Ibid.* In some states there are decisions that such an assignment is not recordable. Kratovil, *Real Estate Law* § 411. Hence the lease should refer to the assignment, incorporate it by reference, and attach a copy as a schedule. In such states, a financing statement should also be filed as a UCC filing.

§ 715. **Options to renew.** If the leasehold mortgagee counts on the period of a renewal option as part of his security, he may require the option to be exercised before the loan is disbursed. This is done to get around the problem created by a trustee in bankruptcy's possible right to reject or dissafirm at renewal option.

If renewal options were not exercised prior to the making of the leasehold mortgage, *R* covenants to exercise them prior to their expiration. Alternatively, *R* must give *E* seasonable notice and give *E* the right to exercise the renewal option. Because of doubt as to right to separate a renewal option from the leasehold, *E* must be given the right to exercise the option in *R's* name.

§ 716. Junior mortgages. As in the case of large-scale mortgages, *E* may wish to prohibit the placing of any junior mortgage on the leasehold. Where *E* consents to the placing of a junior mortgage: (1) It must be expressly subject to *E's* mortgage. (2) The junior mortgagee must be forbidden to extinguish subleases junior to his junior mortgage to the extent local law permits it. *E* wants these subleases. (3) Foreclosure of the junior mortgage must be a judicial foreclosure, so that the subtenants can be omitted as parties. Power of sale foreclosure cannot be controlled as to the junior interests sought to be preserved. Also a receiver can be appointed to collect rents from the sublessees for the benefit of the junior mortgagee. (4) Funds collected by the receiver are funneled to payments on the ground lease and first mortgage before the junior mortgagee receives anything.

§ 717. Books and records. *E* normally requires *R* to keep books and records and make them available to *E*. *E* also wants access to all subleases. As in the case of large mortgages generally, periodic financial statements are required.

§ 718. Mortgages on the fee. *T* would like to see a clause in the lease forbidding any mortgage of the fee as long as the leasehold mortgage exists and as long as a leasehold mortgage exists that arises out of foreclosure of the leasehold mortgage (or assignment in lieu of foreclosure) and the giving of a leasehold mortgage in connection with a sale of the leasehold. Institutional mortgages are confined to leasehold mortgages where no prior encumbrance exists. A mortgage on the fee, though subordinate to the original leasehold mortgage, could complicate subsequent leasehold refinancing.

§ 719. Leasehold mortgage of key tenant. If a key tenant mortgages his leasehold, foreclosure of the mortgage will result in his removal from the shopping center. The effect on other tenants must be considered, especially if their leases permit termination when the key tenant moves out.

§ 720. FHLMC requirements. FHLMC requirements as to leasehold mortgages are as follows:

a. Home Mortgages:

(1) The use of such leasehold or ground rent estates for residential properties is a customary practice in the area in which the mortgaged property is located; residential properties in the area consisting of such leasehold or ground rent estates are readily marketable; mortgages covering such residential properties are acceptable to private institutional investors generally; and the provisions of the leasehold or conveyance reserving ground rents are those customarily acceptable to private institutional lenders in the area.

(2) The lease must be recorded.

(3) The leasehold must be in full force and effect and be subject to no prior lien or encumbrance by which it can be terminated or subjected to any charge or penalty.

(4) The original term of the lease, together with any renewals enforceable by the mortgagee, shall terminate not earlier than 10 years after the maturity date of the mortgage.

(5) The lease must be in a standard form generally acceptable to institutional mortgagees for leasehold mortgage purposes, providing that the lessee may mortgage leasehold estate, and containing no conditions under which the leasehold may be terminated for lessee's default without the mortgagee having a right to receive from lessor notice of such default and to cure such default.

b. **Multifamily Mortgages:**

(1) The lease (including all amendments thereto) must be recorded in full and the original recorded copy (or, with FHLMC's consent, a recorder's certified copy) be submitted with the mortgage documents.

(2) The leasehold shall be subject to no encumbrances or liens not permitted pursuant to Section 2.1(b) of the Master Selling Agreement Conventional, and shall contain no terms requiring or permitting subordination to such liens or encumbrances without lessee's consent.

(3) The original term or exercised renewal of the lease, together with any renewals enforceable by the mortgagee, shall terminate not earlier than 10 years after the maturity date of the mortgage, and the mortgage shall provide for payments on the principal thereof in amounts which would be sufficient to amortize completely the loan were the payment period to terminate within the term of the lease as required above (i.e. not later than 10 years prior to the expiration of the original term of the lease). For example, in the event the lease term were 30 years, and the mortgage secured a 15 year loan, the periodic payments could be scheduled for a 20 year amortization, with a "balloon" at maturity after 15 years.

(4) The lease shall contain provisions satisfactory to FHLMC with respect to the following (see Appendix page 5):

(i) permit mortgaging of the leasehold estate;

(ii) permit assignments without lessor's consent;

(iii) provide for release of an assigning lessee;

(iv) permit leasehold mortgagee to be an insured under hazard insurance policies;

(v) provide for payment of hazard insurance proceeds to leasehold mortgagee or insurance trustee;

(vi) provide for notice of default by lessor to leasehold mortgagee as a condition of validity of such notice of default;

(vii) provide for right of leasehold mortgagee to cure default for account of lessee within time permitted to lessee for such cure plus reasonable additional time;

(viii) provide for new lease of same priority to be given to leasehold mortgagee if lease terminates because of default not curable by leasehold mortgagee, or in the alternative, for no termination for noncurable default so long as no default in rent exists;

(ix) provide for payment to leasehold mortgagee (or trustee for restoration in the case of partial awards) of condemnation award to which lessee is entitled, which award must be not less than the total award minus the value of the land considered as unimproved;

(x) provide that in case of partial taking, lessee will restore regardless of sufficiency of award;

(xi) provide for leasehold mortgagee's right to acquire lease in its own name or in the name of the nominee upon foreclosure or assignment in lieu of foreclosure;

(xii) provide for leasehold mortgagee's right to exercise renewal options; and

(xiii) contain no provisions for termination in the event of damage or destruction so long as leasehold mortgage is in existence.

References: Practicing Loan Institute, *Construction Lending* Real Estate Law & Practice Course Handbook Series #77 containing, among other things:

1. Commitment letter.
2. Construction loan agreement (three forms).
3. Leasehold mortgage—construction of building.
4. Guaranty of completion of building.
5. Construction clauses for mortgage.
6. Construction mortgage.
7. Buy—sell agreement.
8. Consent of prime contractor to construction loan agreement.

36

Priorities Between Mortgages and Leases—Subordinations, Non-Disturbance and Attornment Agreements—Bringing Fee Under Leasehold Mortgage

§ 721. **In general.** In today's complex transactions, keeping track of priorities as between leases, subleases, and mortgages is perhaps the draftsman's most important task. The possibilities are quite numerous.

1. **EXAMPLE:** L gives T a ground lease in 1973 and L gives E a mortgage in 1974. The lease is prior to the mortgage. Foreclosure of the mortgage simply transfers the reversion to E if he is the successful bidder at the foreclosure sale.

2. **EXAMPLE:** L gives E a fee mortgage in 1973 and gives T a lease in 1974. The mortgage is superior to the lease, and foreclosure will extinguish the lease.

3. **EXAMPLE:** In Example 2, assume that E and T enter an attornment and non-disturbance agreement under which foreclosure of the mortgage will extinguish all interests except that of T. Foreclosure of the mortgage then leaves E as landlord and T as tenant. The mortgage and all interests deriving from L (except the lease) are extinguished. A careful attorney would want the title search brought down to cover the recording of the attornment agreement on the ground that rights created by L prior to that time might not be extinguished. They argue that the attornment agreement is little more than a contract to give a lease in the future, and title might relate back to the date of the recording of the contract to cut off interests arising thereafter, but interests arising prior to the contract are another matter. Again, since the contract is a personal one between T and E, the rights of sublessee are left in doubt. This can be covered by a clause in the attornment agreement giving sublessees the benefit thereof and by a clause in the sublease giving the sublessee the benefit of any subsequent attornment agreement.

4. **EXAMPLE:** The facts are as in Example 2, but, in addition, the prime tenant T gives E-2 a mortgage on his leasehold. Both leasehold and leasehold mortgage are subject to E's fee mortgage. Foreclosure thereof wipes out the leasehold and leasehold mortgage.

5. **EXAMPLE:** L gives E a fee mortgage in 1973 and gives T a lease in 1974. T gives E a sublease

in 1975. In 1976 *T* gives *E-2* a mortgage on the leasehold. The sublease being prior in time, primes the leasehold mortgage. Therefore the leasehold mortgagee must insist on a security assignment to him of the prime tenant's subreversion and all rights under the sublease, so that on the foreclosure he will be able to collect rent from the subtenant. Alternatively the leasehold mortgagee could request a subordination of the sublease coupled with an attornment and non-disturbance agreement. Better yet, provision should have been made for the problem when the sublease was executed. The sublease should have contained a clause subordinating it to the future leasehold mortgage and for joinder of the subtenant in the leasehold mortgage provided it runs to an institutional lender, does not exceed specified amounts, and contains a non-disturbance clause. As to short subleases, you can probably rely on a clause in the lease stating that all subleases hereafter executed for periods less than _____ years shall be subordinate to any institutional mortgage on the leasehold.

6. **EXAMPLE:** *L* gives *E* a fee mortgage. Thereafter, *L* gives *T* a lease. Thereafter, the fee mortgage comes due and *L* needs to refinance. Release of the old mortgage will elevate the lease to the first priority unless you rely on conventional subrogation to give the new mortgage the same priority as the old one. Therefore, the lease should contain a clause keeping it subordinate to any refinancing of the existing first mortgage.

7. **EXAMPLE:** *L* gives a fee mortgage to *E*. Thereafter, he gives a lease to *T*. *T* gives a sublease to *S* and *S* mortgages his subleasehold to *E-2*. If *E* forecloses, all these later interests are extinguished.

8. **EXAMPLE:** *L* gives *T* a long lease. *T* places a mortgage on the leasehold. *L* "subordinates" his fee to the leasehold mortgage. Kratovil, *Mortgages* § 246. Foreclosure of the mortgage extinguishes the lease.

The problems are numerous. Kratovil, *Mortgages,* Chapter 21.

§ 722. **Bringing the fee under the leasehold mortgage.** Where the transaction contemplates construction loan financing by *T*, and the mortgage is being arranged for currently and *L* is willing to subject his fee title to the mortgage, the lease clauses will describe the construction mortgage in detail, and may provide for *L's* joinder in the mortgage, with a clause specifically exonerating him from liability on any express or implied covenants in the lease on *T's* part. The construction lender may insist on the mortgage simply describing the real estate, as the property mortgaged, without reference to the separate estates of the landlord and tenant. Legally this is unobjectionable because *L's* reversion plus *T's* leasehold estate comprise the entire fee title. The mortgage will contain an anti-marshalling of assets clause, so that at the foreclosure sale the lender will not be required to offer the fee and leasehold for sale separately. If *L* is willing to subject his fee to a future mortgage on the leasehold, then he should covenant to join in the mortgage or to give a supplemental mortgage, for many title companies are unwilling to insure a "subordination" of the fee to a leasehold mortgage. Future subordinations are legally vulnerable. The clause for future subordination must contain a wealth of detail describing the kind of mortgage the landlord is willing to sign. In practice, of course, some landlords will not covenant to join in the mortgage. Despite exculpatory language landlords fear some sort of liability attaches from joinder in the mortgage. Alternatives are, as suggested, a clause "subordinating" the fee to a subsequent leasehold mortgage or a clause giving *T* the right to subject *L's* fee to the leasehold mortgage. Some lenders and some title companies are dubious about these alternatives. The courts have not been kind to future subordinations. Kratovil, *Mortgages,* Chapter 21. And there is virtually an absence of case law on the other alternative.

A problem with the future subordination occurs if the fee owner is an individual who dies leaving minor heirs. Bankruptcy is another problem, because an agreement to subordinate might be considered an executory contract, which the landlord's trustee in bankruptcy might disaffirm. Federal liens and other liens may attach against the landlord before the mortgage is signed, and title companies probably would be unwilling to insure the mortgage in such event. Even if the period of time between the making of the lease and the making of the mortgage is a brief one, problems can arise.

To recapitulate, most title companies balk at relying on a so-called subordination of the fee to a leasehold mortgage. They want such a subordination bolstered by a supplemental mortgage, executed by the fee owner, at the time the leasehold mortgage is recorded, conveying the fee to the leasehold mortgage as security for payment of the leasehold mortgage debt, but without liability of the fee owner for payment of the debt or for breach of covenant. The fee owner's agreement to sign this document can be placed in the lease. *L* should agree to sign or consent to all supporting documents, such as assignment of leases and rents, fixture and chattel liens, etc. Alternatively, the fee owner can join in the leasehold mortgage and supporting documents.

At times, you will encounter a lease that gives *T* the power to sign *L's* name on the leasehold mortgage. This concept is virtually untested in the courts. There is some authority for the subordination of the fee to the leasehold mortgage. In the order of preference: (1) The specific supplemental mortgage signed by the fee owner at the time the leasehold mortgage is signed is gilt-edge legally, as is joinder by the fee owner in the leasehold mortgage. (2) The specific subordination signed by the fee owner at the time the leasehold mortgage is signed will probably stand up in most states, though it presents problems when a power of sale foreclosure is contemplated. (3) The automatic subordination provision in the lease that subordinates the fee to leasehold mortgages to be executed in the future presents all the problems inherent in automatic subordinations. (4) The lease clause giving *T* the power to sign *L's* name to a future leasehold mortgage is just as weak as the automatic subordination. *See* Kratovil, *Mortgages,* Chapter 21. This clause must not be confused with the lease clause giving *T* the right to mortgage the fee *and requiring L to join.*

For forms, see 4 ABA Real Prop. Prob. & Tr. 437, 466 *et seq* (1969); PLI *Land Acquisition and Development,* Real Estate Law and Practice Course Handbook Series No. 87 (1973).

§ 723. Subordination of fee to leasehold mortgage. Among the contract provisions where a fee is to be brought under the lien of leasehold mortgage are (1) *T* must not be in default in rent payments or in breach of the lease covenants at the time of the mortgage. (2) The purpose for which the loan proceeds are to be disbursed is set forth in detail, *e.g.,* bricks and mortar in construction only; land cost; title charges, loan commissions, etc. (3) Spell out whether mortgagee is obligated to police disbursement to see that loan proceeds are used only for authorized purposes and consequence of his failure to do so. (4) Set forth terms of mortgage, including maximum principal, maximum interest, term of mortgage, whether it will be only to an institutional lender (describing institutional lender, including real estate investment trust, if desired). (5) State if title search is to be brought down to recording of mortgage and what are permitted objections to title. (6) State whether mortgagor is to be personally liable, etc.

§ 724. Subordinations—automatic. Automatic subordinations that subordinate to a future mortgage usually require that the mortgage be to a regulated institutional lender, such as a bank, insurance company, savings and loan association, also pension and welfare foundations, real estate investment funds, and charitable foundations.

The problems involved in the so-called automatic subordination have been recounted elsewhere. Kratovil, *Mortgages,* Chapter 21. One of the problems, of course, is the fact that where a purchase money mortgage is subordinated to later construction loans, the construction loan money may be diverted to non-construction expenditures, and thereby the construction loan's priority is lost. Title companies are reluctant to insure these automatic subordinations.

§ 725. Subordinations—participations. A landlord who subordinates or agrees to subordinate his fee to a mortgage usually specifies that the lender is to be an institutional lender, for such lenders make conservative loans and are less likely to foreclose. To get maximum protection, it should be provided that participations in the mortgages will be sold only to an institutional lender. Friedman, *Leases* § 8.3.

§ 726. Subordination of purchase money mortgage to construction financing. The legal problems involved in subordinations are formidable. If a purchase money mortgage is to be subordinated to a future construction loan, it is, of course, necessary to describe the construction loan in some detail, including the type of lender, principal amount, interest rate, terms of loan, including time and manner of repayment, maximum maturity, etc. It should provide that R subordinates his mortgage to such construction loan and that the construction lender is under no duty to police his disbursements so as to protect R. It should contain a covenant calling on R to sign a specific subordination as soon as the construction loan mortgage has been executed. It should call for a legend on the purchase money mortgage and note indicating its subordination to the construction mortgage. This is especially important as a protection against assignment of the purchase money mortgage to an innocent purchaser having no knowledge of the subordination. Kratovil, *Mortgages,* Chapter 21.

§ 727. Subordinations—future mortgages—premises to be mortgaged. If T is to subordinate his lease to a future mortgage, he must determine whether he is willing to subordinate to a mortgage that covers property additional to that under lease. This should be specifically covered.

§ 728. Subordination of contract of sale. Where a contract of sale is signed, and the buyer applies for financing, he is invariably asked to supply the lender a copy of the contract. This is part of the appraisal process. The contract antedates the mortgage and is superior to it. The buyer has a lien for refunding of his earnest money if the seller defaults. This lien ought to be subordinated to the mortgage by provision in the contract or by a separate instrument.

§ 729. Sublease—attornment agreement. On a big sublease, it is not uncommon for the fee owner and sublessee to enter into an agreement under which, if the ground lease is terminated for a cause other than descruction of, or material damage to, the building or a taking by condemnation, the relationship of landlord and tenant will spring up between the fee owner and sublessee as though the fee owner had entered into the sublease as lessor, subject to such reasonable changes as the situation at that time might dictate, but free and clear of any modifications in the sublease made after the date of the attornment agreement. *Aultman v. Seabora Oil Co.*, 129 Fla. 1, 175 So. 901. Usually the agreement calls for an attornment agreement to be signed by both parties, recognizing that each party has all the rights and duties specified in the sublease, except that (1) no advance payment of rent made by the sublessee to his sublessor shall be good against the fee owner; (2) any offsets or defenses the sublessee might have against the sublessor are not good against the fee owner; (3) the fee owner does not succeed to any existing liabilities of the sublessor to the sublessee. There have been such agreements wherein the document concluded by the fee owner demising the premises to the subtenant, on the terms aforesaid, subject only to the conditions precedent set forth in the attornment agreement. The probable reason for this precaution lies in the area of bankruptcy law. A fee owner's trustee can reject his contracts, but his right of rejection of leases is more restricted. Kratovil, *Mortgages,* Chapter 34.

Where the sublease is of the entire building, the fee owner may want the attornment agreement to require the sublessee to cure all the ground lessee's defaults. This is a matter for negotiation.

To assure the fee owner that he will be able to step in as the sublessee's landlord, the agreement will call on the subtenant to refrain from any surrender or other termination of the sublease. And, especially in a net lease of a building, the fee owner may want a covenant that the sublessee will observe and perform all the covenants of the ground lease, for if he does this there will be no occasion to terminate the ground lease.

Where the prime lease is subject to a prior fee mortgage, there may be at the time of the lease or thereafter an attornment agreement protecting the lease against extinguishment if the mortgage is foreclosed. At all events, the sublessee wants a clause in his sublease giving him the benefit of any attornment agreement entered into between the fee mortgagee and prime lessee.

And the prime landlord and the leasehold mortgagee will want the sublessee to be obligated to pay rent to them.

CLAUSE: In case of a termination of the Prime Lease, Tenant will, at the election of the Prime Landlord, attorn and pay the rent hereunder to the Prime Landlord; and in case of a proceeding to foreclose a mortgage on the Prime Lease, Tenant will, at the election of the holder of such mortgage, attorn and pay the rent to such holder.

§ 730. Sublease subordinations and attornments.

Largely for the protection of the leasehold mortgagee, an occupancy commercial lease may contain a clause subordinating it to the present and future ground leases and to present or future fee or leasehold mortgages. However, a lender who forecloses may want to keep some or all of the tenants as tenants, even though the effect of the foreclosure is technically an extinguishment of such leases. Thus, the lease may give any foreclosing lender the right to have the tenant "attorn" to the lender. The lender thus lives in the best of all possible worlds. But the Triple A tenant who occupies a good deal of space in the building does not want the lender to have the right to oust him. He may, therefore, insist on a clause whereby the lender who has foreclosed will recognize the continued tenancy of the tenant. Thus we have a combination subordination, attornment, and non-disturbance clause. In a stronger form, the sublease clause provides that in case of termination of the ground lease, the sublease continues as a direct lease between the tenant and the fee owner. There is little or no case law on the legal nature of agreements such as these. For example, it is unclear what sublease covenants survive. The Triple A tenant may want the documents to spell out his protection as to items he considers important, such as his rights under the sublease to participate in a condemnation award or to have hazard insurance applied to rebuilding. If the sublease is consented to in writing by the fee owner and leasehold mortgagee, obviously this strengthens the sublessee's position against them and lays a foundation for arguing the ''relation back'' doctrine so far as intervening lienors are concerned.

§ 731. Sublease attornment and non-disturbance provisions compared.

Where an attornment agreement is utilized to protect a sublease against destruction of the prime lease by reason of the prime tenant's default or breach of covenant, it is logical to conclude that this is the limit of the sublessee's protection. For example, if there is substantial destruction of the premises by fire or a substantial taking by condemnation, one can conclude that the attornment agreement was not intended to operate, and, indeed, it should so provide. It was not intended to cover such a situation. A similar problem arises where a mortgagee enters into a non-disturbance agreement with a tenant. Here again, the prime objective is to protect T against the consequences of a default by R that results in extinguishment of $R's$ interest by foreclosure. Again, T needs protection against this result. But destruction by fire or taking by condemnation present a different problem. If T is to have any rights in these proceeds, this must be spelled out explicitly. The normal answer one would anticipate is that T has no such rights unless they are contracted for.

References: See Friedman, *Leases,* for excellent discussion and forms.

37

Building Restrictions

§ 732. **History.** Early restrictions on land use were often capricious or whimsical. For example, a landowner might attach to a gift of land to a church a requirement that the minister wear a black gown in the pulpit. Scott, *Control of Property by the Dead,* 65 U. of Penna. L.Rev. 527, 535 to 537. Enforcement of restrictions in equity began with *Tulk v. Moxhay,* 2 Phillips 774 (Ct. of Chancery 1848). This made possible the general plan type of restriction, which became a favorite of American land developers. Thus it has been said:

"American courts developed the doctrine of equitable servitudes, whereby agreements by the owner of land not to use it for particular purposes or in a specified manner are enforced in equity against subsequent purchasers of the land with notice, from the famous English case of Tulk v. Moxhay, 2 Phil. 774, 41 Eng, Rep, 1143 (Ch. 1848). See 2 American Law of Property § 9.24 (Casner ed. 1952). The doctrine of Tulk v. Moxhay met the need growing in the nineteenth century for a legal device which would serve to preserve urban and suburban residential neighborhoods from encroachment by business and other undesirable uses. *Ibid.* Enforcement of building and development plans have constituted a large part of the cases under this head of equity jurisdiction. *See* 5 Powell, Real Property § 679 (Boyer ed. 1962). *See* generally Paulus. *The Use of Equitable Servitudes in Land Planning,* 2 Williamette L. J. 399 (1963)." (1965 Law Forum 228, 232-233).

This is not surprising, since zoning did not come into its own until its validity was sustained by the Supreme Court. *Village of Euclid v. Ambler Realty Co.,* 272 U.S. 365 (1926). Thus from roughly 1850 to 1926 any effective land use control rested upon private building restrictions and the concept of the general plan. The outstanding virtue of the general plan lies in the fact that each lot owner in the subdivision can enforce it against all the other lot owners. 26 C.J.S. *Deeds* § 167 (2). In the early days of the general plan, developers created the restriction by clauses in deeds. This was simply an application to building restrictions of drafting practices employed in creating covenants enforceable at law. However, the practice created difficulties. For example, if substantially identical restrictions did not appear in substantially all of the deeds by the subdivider, the courts held no general plan existed. *Clark v. McGee,* 159 Ill. 518, 42 NE 865 (1896). This, in turn, led to the later practice of incorporating building restrictions in the subdivision plat, since no doubt could exist as to the general plan nature of such restrictions. 2 American Law of Property § 9.25 (1952). In more recent times, building restrictions have grown so complex that incorporation in a plat became unwieldy. Thus,

319

there was developed the declaration of restrictions, usually prepared and signed by the developer simultaneously with the plat of subdivision and referred to in the plat of subdivision. In this fashion the declaration, being incorporated by reference in a recordable instrument, namely the subdivision plat, imparted constructive notice. *Spencer v. Poole*, 207 Ga. 155, 60 SE2d 371. Later decisions held that the declaration, of itself, was a recordable instrument and served to impart constructive notice. *Davis v. Huguenor*, 408 Ill. 468, 97 NE2d 295. This is where we are at present.

Other problems and devices exist, of course, and some of these will be discussed herein.

§ 733. **The home association.** The home owners association was developed as an instrument for the enforcement of general plan building restrictions in the old-fashioned subdivision of single-family dwellings.

EXAMPLE: *R* plats a subdivision of 100 lots and in the accompanying declaration of restrictions creates a restriction that only single-family dwellings shall be erected and a fifteen-foot front building line shall be observed. The declaration also provides that *XYZ Corporation,* a nonprofit corporation, whose members are the lot owners in the subdivision, shall be empowered to enforce the restrictions and shall collect an annual assessment from each lot owner. Ultimately *R* sells out all the lots. He now has lost interest in protecting the lot owners. *E,* a lot owner, begins construction of a store that will come all the way to the street line. Any one homeowner might be disinclined to hire a lawyer and engage in litigation. However, *XYZ Corporation* warns *E* to discontinue construction and to remove the foundations he has constructed. *E* knows this is no empty threat. He complies.

§ 734. **Legal form of association.** The *home association* has been called a *private government*. 11 Washburn L. J. 230. It is an incorporated, nonprofit corporation formed under the declaration of restrictions. *Merrionette Manor Homes v. Heda*, 11 Ill. App. 2d 186, 136 NE2d 556; *Garden Dist. Prop. Owners Assn. v. New Orleans*, 98 So2d 922; *Neponsit Property Owners' Ass'n. v. Emigrant Industrial Savings Bank*, 278 N.Y. 248, 15 NE2d 793; *Rodruck v. Sand Point Maintenance Comm.* 40 Wash. 2d 565, 295 P2d 714. Unincorporated associations must be avoided, for these have very little in the way of legal existence. *Moffat Tunnel League v. U. S.* 289 U.S. 113, 40 Ind. L. J. 420. Moreover, in any unincorporated association the members have the risk of unlimited liabilities, for example, for personal injuries. Likewise, an unincorporated association cannot hold ownership of land. *Delaware L. and Dev. Co. v. First Church*, 147 A 165 (Del); 55 Mich. L.Rev. 67, 235. Therefore a non-profit corporation should be formed. Since it has no profit motive, there is no need to form a business corporation, which must pay taxes, etc. 49 Los Angeles Bar Bull. 509.

Thus, there is something of a misnomer here. We constantly talk of the *home association*. But in truth there is no true legal association. The body selected to act as the home association is a non-profit corporation. For convenience we shall refer to the body as the *home association*.

The association is formed in accordance with the declaration. There are a corporate charter and bylaws. In the beginning the developer and his associates are the members of the corporation. A non-profit corporation, be it noted, has no shareholders. It has members. As homes are sold, each homeowner automatically becomes a member of the corporation.

§ 735. **Association as a vehicle for endorsing restrictions, liens, and covenants.**

In any land development where both a home association and a declaration exist, the right of enforcement of restrictions, liens, and covenants is transferred by the declaration to the home association. *Merrionette Manor Homes v. Heda*, 11 Ill. App. 2d 186, 136 NE2d 556; *Garden Dist. Prop. Owners Assn. v. New Orleans*, 98 So2d 922; *Neponsit Property Owners' Assn. v. Emigrant Industrial Savings Bank*, 278 N.Y. 248, 15 NE2d 793; *Rodruck v. Sand Point Maintenance Comm.* 40 Wash. 2d 565, 295 P2d 714. At times it is suggested that the association is acting as agent of the property owners. *Neponsit Ppty. Owners Assn. v. Emigrant Ind. Sav. Bank*, 278 N.Y. 248, 15 NE2d 793. At other times it is suggested that it is acting as a third-party beneficiary of the covenants in the declaration. 2 Powell, *Real Property*, § 81; 40 Ind. L. J. 430. Or it is said that the association is the assignees of the developer. *Ibid.* Occasionally it is simply said the association is a "convenient instrument by which the property owners may advance their common interests." *Neponsit Property Owners Assn. Inc. v. Emigrant Ind. Sav. Bank*, 278 N.Y. 248, 15 NE2d (1938), 24 Cornell L. Q. 133; In re *Public Beach, Borough of Queens*, 269 N.Y. 64, 199 NE 5 (1935). It does no harm to lump all these thoughts into the declaration.

FORM: *XYZ Home Association,* as agent for the property owners under an irrevocable agency coupled with an interest, as beneficiary of all the covenants, restrictions, liens and provisions herein contained and as assignee of declarant, is vested with the right in its own behalf and in behalf of all owners and parties interested in the land described in this declaration to enforce all the covenants, liens, restrictions and provisions herein contained.

§ **736. The declaration.** Since all that is needed to create enforceable building restrictions is a recorded document that gives public notice of such easements, a recorded declaration will again suffice for this purpose, when followed by deeds referring thereto. *Davis v. Huguenor*, 408 Ill. 468, 97 NE2d 295; *Kosel v. Stone*, 146 Mont. 218, 404 P2d 894; *Lawrence v. Brockelman*, 155 N.Y.S. 2d 604.

For obvious reasons, the *developer* must not retain the right to modify the restrictions. This may destroy the general plan and render the restrictions unenforceable. 19 ALR2d 1282. Also the declaration must be recorded before any deed or mortgage is recorded, for any deed recorded before the declaration will not be subject to the restrictions, easements, or other rights created by the declaration. All deeds are expressly made subject to the declaration.

§ **737. Deed clauses to implement the declaration.** To fully implement the declaration it is necessary to insert a clause in the deed to the home buyer or apartment buyer. Such a clause might be as follows:

SUGGESTED FORM: Subject to Declaration of Easements, Restrictions, Liens, and Covenants dated _____ and recorded in the Office of the Recorder of Deeds of _____ County, as Document No. _____ which is incorporated herein by reference thereto. Grantor grants to the Grantee, his heirs and assigns, as easements appurtenant to the premises hereby conveyed, the easements created by said Declaration for the benefit of the owners of the parcel of realty herein described. Grantor reserves to himself, his heirs and assigns, as easements appurtenant to the remaining parcels described in said Declaration, the easements thereby created for the benefit of said remaining parcels described in said Declaration, and this conveyance is subject to said easements and the right of the Grantor to grant said easements in the conveyances of said remaining parcels or any of them, and the parties hereto, for themselves, their heirs, personal representatives, and assigns, covenant to be bound by the covenants, restrictions and agreements in said document set forth. Said covenants and restrictions are covenants running with the land both as to burden and benefit, and this conveyance is subject to all said covenants and restrictions as though set forth in full herein. The land hereby conveyed is also subject to the liens created by said Declaration, and same are binding on the grantees, their heirs, personal representatives, and assigns. All of the provisions of said Declaration are hereby incorporated herein as though set forth in full herein.

In one decision it was held that the filing of the declaration would suffice to create restrictions even though they were not mentioned in the subdivider's deeds. *Kosel v. Stone,* 146 Mont. 218, 404 P2d 894. But in California precisely the opposite has been held. There the declaration is totally ineffective unless the deeds refer to it. *Smith v. Rasqui,* 1 Cal. Reptr 478. However, it suffices to state in the deeds that the land is "subject to covenants, conditions, restrictions and easements of record." *Davis v. Huguenor,* 408 Ill. 468, 97 NE2d 295; *Seaton v. Clifford,* 100 Cal. Reptr 779. Obviously this is a poor practice. 84 ALR2d 780. The full suggested form should be used in the deeds by the subdivider.

After the restrictions have been properly created by means of the declaration and a deed by the developer containing the full clause, later warranty deeds may contain a brief subject clause to relieve the grantor of liability on his warranty covenants.

Where the owner of a condominium apartment, PUD unit, or townhouse is placing a mortgage on his property, a clause is inserted in the mortgage along the following lines:

CLAUSE: Subject to Declaration of Easements, Restrictions, Liens and Covenants dated _____ and recorded in the Office of the Recorder of Deeds of _____ County in Book _____ page _____ as Document No. _____, which is incorporated herein by reference thereto. Mortgagor grants to the mortgagee, its successors and assigns all rights of every description created by said declaration for the benefit of the mortgaged premises, same to run with the mortgaged land. The provisions of said Declaration regarding liens of assessments are also incorporated herein by reference thereto.

§ 738. Creation of general plan restrictions by deed. Some subdividers continue to use deeds in the creation of general plan restrictions. This system faces legal obstacles. For example, the decisions make it difficult to establish an intention to create a general plan.

EXAMPLE: A subdivider conveys out by deeds which vary in the restrictions they impose. No general plan exists. For a general plan to be created by deeds there must be substantially identical restrictions inserted in substantially all of the deeds by the subdivider. 4 ALR2d 1364.

EXAMPLE: All lots are conveyed out by the subdivider by printed form deeds containing identical restrictions. Suppose, however, the restriction is so worded that it does not reveal any intention to create a general plan but seems to restrict only the lot described in the deed, as where it provides: *"The lot hereby conveyed* shall be used for residence purposes." However, all deeds contain an identical provision. In most states, this is sufficient to create a general plan. *Clark v. McGee,* 159 Ill. 518, 52 NE 865 (1896); *Snow v. Van Dam,* 291 Mass. 477, 197 NE 224. But in a few states a general plan is not created. *Werner v. Graham,* 181 Cal. 174, 183 Pac. 945; 3 Tiffany, *Real Property,* (3d ed. 1939) § 865.

Of course, these difficulties can be obviated by use by the subdivider of deeds containing identical restrictions, each restriction being preceded by the phrase *"all lots in this subdivision* are subject to the following restrictions." *Brite v. Gray,* 377 SW2d

223 (Tex. 1964). This shows that a general plan is intended, but it creates a constructive notice problem, to be discussed later.

Again a subdivider who has platted a subdivision of 100 lots may convey 50 scattered lots each containing identical restrictions preceded by the phrase "The lot hereby conveyed is subject to the following restrictions." Then he loses interest in the development and sells the remaining lots by a deed containing no restrictions to a purchaser who makes deeds containing no restrictions. Here no general plan exists. Unless the deed shows on its face an intention to create a general plan ("all lots in this subdivision are subject to the following restrictions"), there is no general plan unless substantially all deeds by the subdivider convey substantially all lots in the subdivision by deeds containing substantially identical restrictions.

Finally even if the subdivider deeds out substantially all lots by deeds containing identical restrictions or by deeds revealing an intention to create a general plan ("all lots in this subdivision are subject to the following restrictions") a question of constructive notice remains.

EXAMPLE: *R*, a subdivider in a subdivision of 500 lots, conveys Lot 100 to *E-1* by a deed stating that "all lots in this subdivision are subject to the following restrictions." Later he conveys Lot 500 to *E-2* by a deed containing no restrictions. The question is whether *E-2* is charged with notice of *R's* intention to create a general plan as revealed in *R's* deed of lot 100. The problem is a formidable one. Checking the records on 500 lots for a deed that reveals an intention to create a general plan for the whole subdivision is no mean task. The authorities are divided. The weight of authority is to the effect that if a deed or a contract for the conveyance of one parcel of land, with a covenant or easement affecting another parcel of land owned by the same grantor, is duly recorded, the record is constructive notice to a subsequent purchaser of the latter parcel. The rule is based generally upon the principle that a grantee is chargeable with notice of everything affecting his title which could be discovered by an examination of the records of the deeds or other muniments of title of his grantor. 16 ALR 1013. There is authority, however, for the view that the record of a deed is not constructive notice of a covenant or restrictions therein, to a subsequent purchaser from the same grantor of another parcel of land which is affected by the covenants or restrictions. 16 ALR 1013, 1015.

§ 739. General plan. Obviously the restrictions should set forth an intention to create a general plan, for example:

CLAUSE: All of the foregoing restrictions are intended to constitute a general plan for the benefit of and enforceable by all present and future owners of or parties interested in any of the lots in the subdivision aforesaid or any part thereof and their heirs and assigns as well as by the Home Association aforesaid.

The language about "parties interested" is merely declaratory of the existing law, for example, that mortgagees can also enforce general plan restrictions. *See, e.g., Storey v. Brush*, 256 Mass. 101, 152 NE 225. The reference to owners of a part of a lot is declaratory of existing law. *Anderson v. Henslee*, 11 SW2d 154. The statement that lot owners may enforce despite the existence of a home association also having that right is also declaratory of the existing law. *Schick v. Perry*, 12 Utah 2d 173, 364 P2d 116. Nevertheless the existence of litigation on all these points suggests the advisability of spelling them out.

§ 740. Covenants running with the land. It is not necessary that the restrictions be created as covenants running with the land. The entire concept of covenants running with the land is a concept peculiar to law courts where the plaintiff is seeking to obtain damages for breach of covenant. General plan restrictions, by contrast, are creatures of equity enforced typically by resort to an injunction suit. There is no harm in adding language in the *declaration* to the effect that the covenants run with the land.

CLAUSE: All of the foregoing are also covenants running with the land at law as well as in equity and are binding upon and inure to the benefit of the successors and assigns of the declarant and all present and future persons owning or having an interest in any of said lots or a part thereof.

It will also be noticed that the *deed clause* refers to the liens and easements created by the declaration. Of course, the condominium and planned unit development create liens and easements. This provision is included for the sake of completeness. No further discussion of the special problems peculiar to covenants, liens or easements is contained herein.

§ **741. Necessity of restricting the use of the land.** The courts are divided on the question of whether a restriction that restricts only the type or use of a *building* inferentially restricts the use of the *land*. For example, where the restriction provided that no building erected on the land should be used for any purpose other than as a private dwelling place, the landowner was enjoined from using the vacant land as a parking lot. *Hoover v. Waggoman*, 52 N.M. 371, 199 P2d 991 (1948). And where a restriction permitted only one single dwelling house to be erected, but said no more than that, the court nevertheless blocked the operation of a miniature golf course. *Bohm v. Rogoff*, 256 Mich. 199, 239 N.W. 320 (1931); *see* Annot., 155 ALR 528 (1945), also 32 Mo. L.Rev. 299. But other courts are less helpful. Thus, in *Granger v. Boulls*, 21 Wash. 2d 597, 152 P2d 325 (1944), a restrictive covenant against erection of a building to be used for purposes other than a private residence or dwelling did not prevent the keeping of chickens, cattle and livestock on the vacant land. The moral is that the well-drawn restriction must also restrict the use that can be made of *vacant land*.

§ **742. Necessity of restricting use of building as well as type of building.** Occasionally a restriction restricts the *type of building* to be erected, but does not restrict the *use* that can be made of the building. Here again the authorities are divided. For example, a deed restriction provided that "only one new residence building costing not less than \$4,000.00" shall be erected on the lot conveyed. Such a structure was erected, but a purchaser attempted to hold religious services therein. The court enjoined such use, saying:

"In the instant case, the wording of the restriction goes to the construction of the building to be placed on the lot. It would be unreasonable to say that it does not also cover its use. If, after a residence has been constructed on a lot with a restrictive covenant in the deed, the owner could thereafter use the building for a millinery store, restaurant, beauty shop, antique shop, or numerous other uses to which, but for the prohibitions in a zoning ordinance, it would be suitable and available, the covenant would be of little value and the general plan of restriction, which would otherwise inure to the benefit of all purchasers, would be circumvented." *Strauss v. Ginzberg*, 218 Minn. 57, 15 N.W.2d 130, 155 ALR 1000 (1944) and annotation following.

But a minority of the courts refuse to embark on such a rescue expedition. For example, where a restriction provided that only a private dwelling could be erected the court refused to enjoin use of the dwelling for a convalescent home. *Jones v. Park Lane*

Home for Convalescents, 384 Pa. 268, 120 A. 2d 535 (1956). The moral, of course, is that the well-drawn restriction must restrict the *use* of the structure as well as the *type* of structure to be erected.

To cope with the problems pointed out in this and the preceding paragraph, the following form is suggested:

SUGGESTED FORM: Except as herein provided, only one detached single-family dwelling and attached private garage appertaining thereto shall be erected on said premises. No use shall be made of said premises except such as is incidental to the occupation thereof for residence purposes by one private family residing in a detached, single-family dwelling.

§ 743. Permitted non-residential uses.

At times subdivision restrictions have been recorded locking the entire subdivision into single-family dwellings and serious problems have arisen when the residents sought to erect a chuch or school. 13 ALR2d 1239. Hence it is necessary that the subdivider determine in advance of recording what areas are to be permitted use for church, school or other purposes, and an appropriate clause inserted, for example:

CLAUSE: Notwithstanding the provisions of paragraph _____ limiting construction and use of lots in this subdivision to single-family dwellings, lots _____ may be used for church, church school, church athletic house and field and parish house, and residential and car parking accommodations for church and church school personnel.

If it is desired to broaden this clause to permit parking for parishioners or to permit use of the lots for general school purposes, obviously broader language will be needed.

§ 744. Outbuildings.

In subdivisions where the buildings are to be substantial, provision may be included permitting the erection of a guest house and servants' quarters. In appropriate areas the restrictions might grant permission for the erection of stables for riding horses used by occupants of the dwelling on the premises and their guests.

§ 745. Building lines.

The volume of case law on the subject of building lines is monumental. See, for example, 36 ALR2d 861 dealing with the question of what type of structure or erection is deemed a violation of a building line; 30 ALR2d 559 dealing with "fronting" type restrictions where a corner lot is involved; 55 ALR 332 and 172 ALR 1324 dealing with encroachments over the building line by awnings, balconies, bay windows, cellar doors, area ways, gates, ornamental projections, porches, porticos, port-cocheres, bay windows, show windows, steps, and walls; 18 ALR3d 850 defining "building" within the meaning of building restrictions, touching on matters such as signs, billboards, roads, embankments, tracks, structures with roof and walls, and structures with roof and no walls; also 23 ALR2d 937 discussing fences, walls and hedges as violations of building restrictions. The topic is also discussed in 26 CJS *Deeds* § 164 (2). If the developer is serious about keeping front, side and rear yards in their natural state, he can include a strict clause along the following lines:

CLAUSE: No structure, erection or construction of any kind or size whatever or any part thereof shall be permitted in the front, side, and rear yards established by the front, side, and rear building lines depicted on the said plat of subdivision, whether at ground level or above or below the same, but water and utility lines and drainage facilities shall not be deemed a violation of this restriction, nor shall hedges, vegetation, ornamental trees, or open patio areas. However, all such permitted items, except those installed by Declarant must first be submitted to the Architectural Control Committee provided for herein.

If the topography of the subdivision requires retaining walls, this clause should be modified to permit them to the extent desired.

Corner lots and irregular lots may also require special treatment.

§ 746. **Side yards.** Side yards on which no structure of any kind is to be erected may be specified either as a fixed number of feet in width or as a percentage of the width of the lot. Some draftsmen, in fixing side yards, prefer to omit the side yards from the plat altogether and to refer in the declaration to the "side property line of the plot built upon," rather than to the "side lot line." This is done because, for example, a home owner who buys an extra twenty feet or so may site his house so that it straddles a "side lot line" but is a comfortable distance away from the "side property line." When this is contemplated, some draftsmen add a provision to the effect that "in this context 'plot' denotes the ownership of the area built upon."

§ 747. **Minimum lot size and frontage.** Perhaps as a precaution against lot splitting, which it is feared cannot be prohibited because of the rule against restraints on alienation, some draftsmen include a minimum plot size and frontage restriction. Because lots tend to be irregular and vary in size in today's developments, some draftsmen use a rather flexible provision:

CLAUSE: Any dwelling erected on part of any lot in this subdivision shall be erected on a plot having a minimum lot size and frontage equal to or greater than that of the largest lot occupied by any part of said dwelling, and in this context the word "plot" denotes the ownership of the area built upon.

§ 748. **Minimum building size.** It is not easy to draft a minimum building size restriction when one recalls that a ranch house (single-story), split level, or two or more story house could be erected. Perhaps phrasing the restriction in terms of square feet or cubic feet would help solve the problem.

SUGGESTED FORM: No single-family dwelling shall be erected on said premises unless it contains a total living area of _____ square feet or more, excluding from living area the areas of utility rooms and attics.

§ 749. **Maximum height.** Some draftsmen limit the height of any structure in the subdivision. This is done to avoid interference with view and to exclude exotic structures. Limiting the height in terms of "stories" is open to the objection that an exotic structure may contain stories of exotic height.

§ 750. **Incidental use of residence for business or professional purposes.** There is a wealth of litigation concerning the propriety of using part of the buildings restricted to residence purpose for business or professional use, such as dressmaking, beauty shop, doctor's office, insurance business, real estate business, etc. 21 ALR3d 641. This problem is affected by the presence of a negative restriction forbidding use of the premises for a business or trade. Occasional use of a residence as a doctor's office in these circumstances is permitted by some decisions. If it is desired to cover this situation, a clause is necessary.

CLAUSE: No more than one room in any residence erected in this subdivision may be used by the owner for professional purposes incidental to his practice of his profession elsewhere, but this does not sanction the use of any room for trade or business of any kind.

§ 751. Negative restrictions.

As has been stated, it is best to draft restrictions affirmatively, stating what type of structure and use is permitted. However there will always be a need for some negative restrictions, such as those forbidding pets and signs.

§ 752. Pets.

A common provision is to the effect that no animals or poultry shall be kept on said premises other than no more than two domesticated housepets not kept for commercial or breeding purposes. If you want to permit riding horses, this provision will have to be revamped.

§ 753. Racial restrictions.

Restrictions relating to race, color, or creed are now invalid. *Steuer v. Glevis,* 243 So.2d 453 (Fla. 1971). An inclusion of a racial restriction may make the whole document not recordable. *Mayers v. Ridley,* 465 F2d 630. Obviously all such restrictions *must* be omitted from your draft.

§ 754. Model homes.

In a remarkable decision it was held that construction of a model home is a business use that violates residential restrictions. *Shields v. Welshire Develop. Co.,* 144 A2d 759. This decision is probably erroneous. *City of New York v. Jack Porter,* 161 NYS2d 731. Obviously one should draft around this by a provision like:

Construction of model homes is expressly permitted as long as they conform to the restrictions hereby created.

§ 755. Approval of plans—architectural control.

Many declarations contain a provision for approval of plans by an architectural committee or by the developer before construction begins. Such provisions are valid. 40 ALR3d 864. There is no magic in this device, however. For example, where the developer refused to approve plans calling for a structure having a modern design set in a subdivision of traditional architecture, the court held the refusal to approval was unreasonable. 40 ALR3d 888. This and other decisions teach the doctrine that if restrictions are to exist as to type of residence, size of structure, cost, type of garage, etc., the restrictions should be set forth separately and reliance on plans approval provisions should be minimal.

A form relating to architectural control is as follows:

No building, fence, wall or other structure of landscaping shall be commenced, erected or maintained upon the properties, nor shall any exterior addition to or change or alteration therein or change in the exterior appearance and specifications showing the nature, kind, shape, height thereof or change in landscaping be made until the plans, materials and location of the same shall have been submitted to and approved in writing as to harmony of external design and location and relation to surrounding structures and topography by the Board or by an Architectural Control Committee composed of three (3) or more representatives (who are not required to be members of the Association) appointed as provided in the By-Laws of the Association. The Association may, in its sole discretion, require a reasonable fee for review of said plans and specifications.

Plans and specifications for final approval shall include the following:

A. Complete plans and specifications sufficient to secure a building permit in the City of _____, including a plot plan showing a lot and block and placing of residences, garage, outbuildings and walls or fences.

B. Front elevations and both side elevations, or front elevation and one side elevation and rear elevation of building, plus elevations of walls and fences.

C. A perspective drawing if deemed necessary by the Committee to interpret adequately the exterior design.

D. Data as to materials, color and texture of all exteriors including roof coverings, fences and walls.

E. One set of blueprints shall be left with the Architect or Architectural Committee until construction is completed.

F. No hedge, fence, walls, railing or other structure over 36 inches in height shall be permitted in front of any front setback line unless approved by the Architectural Committee and same shall be placed at least three (3) feet back of the front property line.

Should the Committee fail to approve or disapprove such plans and specifications and location within thirty (30) days after submission of the plans to them, then such approval will not be required, but all other conditions and restrictions herein contained shall remain in force.

The committee's approval or disapproval as required in these covenants shall be in writing. In the event the committee, or its designated representative, fails to approve or disapprove within 30 days after plans and specifications have been submitted to it, or in any event, if no suit to enjoin the construction has been commenced prior to the completion thereof, approval will not be required and the related covenants shall be deemed to have been fully complied with.

An extremely important provision should be included:

CLAUSE: If at any time the Committee has ceased to exist as such, and has failed to designate a representative to act for it, the need for Committee approval is dispensed with.

§ 756. Duration of restrictions modification, extension and release of restrictions.
The duration of general plan restrictions is a matter of intention as expressed in the instrument creating the restrictions. 2 *Am. Law of Ppty* § 9.22. Restrictions may be created though unlimited in point of time. *State v. Reece*, 374 SW2d 686; *Loeb v. Watkins*, 240 A2d 513 (Pa. 1968). Perpetual restrictions do not offend against the rule against perpetuities. *Harris v. Pease*, 135 Conn. 535, 66 A2d 590; *Mc Kinnon v. Neugents*, 167 SE2d 593. Nor do they constitute illegal restraints on alienation. 10 ALR2d 824. But doubts will be resolved against perpetual duration. 20 Am. Jur. 2d *Covenants and Conditions* § 180. A reasonable duration will be deemed to be intended even if the restriction uses words like "forever," "perpetual" or "never." *Metrop. Inv. Co. v. Sine*, 376 P2d 940; *Robb v. Atlantic Coast Line RR*, 154 So2d 871 (citing U.S. Supreme Court); *Duncan v. Academy*, 350 SW2d 815, *Edney v. Powers*, 224 N.C. 441, 31 SE2d 372; *Gulf Oil Corp. v. Levy*, 181 Md. 488, 30 A2d 740. Pound, *Progress of the Law-Equity*, 35 Harv. L.Rev. 813, 821 (1920). *But see Morton v. Sayles*, 304 SW2d 759 and *Barnes v. Anchor Temple Assn.* 369 SW2d 893.

Obviously man is incapable of drafting restrictions that will serve a useful purpose forever. Hence machinery must be included in the restrictions for modifying or terminating them.

In the absence of such a provision, courts may come to the rescue, for example, by a construction that a limited duration was intended. Or, analogously, the courts may hold where a restriction has been observed for a substantial period of time it has served its purpose and ceases to exist. *Barnett v. County of Washoe*, 86 Nev. 730, 476 P2d 8 (1970). This is analogous to the cases declaring conditions subsequent at an end after they have been substantially observed over a long period of time. *Jordan v. Hendricks*, 173 NE 288, 6 *Ind. L. J.* 452; 31 *Columb.L.Rev.* 509; *Amerc. Steel Foundries v. Melinik*, 74 Ind. App. 617; *Gray v. Railroad*, 189 Ill 400, 59 NE 950; *Savanna School*

Dist v. McLeod, 290 P2d 593; *Miller v. Atchison Rwy Co.*, 325 F. Supp. 604 (1971); *McArdle v. School District*, 136 NW2d 422. So far as the initial duration of the restrictions is concerned, if a date is to be stated in the restrictions, one theory is that the restrictions should last through the lifetime of the original mortgages made by the first homeowners, which is a period of roughly twenty-five years. 1959 *Wisc. L.Rev.* 451, 459; 15 *Kan. L.Rev.* 582, 586. The method suggested by the Federal Housing Administration is automatic extension of the covenants for ten-year periods following a fixed period of thirty years, unless a majority of the lot owners at the end of one of these periods agree to a change. The automatic renewal clause has the advantage of projecting the intended scheme into the distant future but permits later change at the discretion of the property owners themselves, who are best situated to balance the conflicting interests.

A variation of the renewal clause following a fixed term of years is a clause providing for termination unless affirmative action is taken by a majority of the owners to renew the restrictions for another term, usually shorter than the original one. With this type clause the benefits of useful covenants may be lost by the oversight of the residents. As the existence of covenants rarely occurs to the typical owner until his property is threatened by some violation, the burden of remembering and re-recording the covenants after thirty years would seem to be unwarranted. The automatic renewal clause is preferable. 15 *Kan. L.Rev.* 582, 586. Care must be exercised in expressing the percentage vote. A ''majority of the lot owners'' is not the same as a vote of ''the owners of a majority of the lots.'' For example, a lot owner may die leaving fifteen heirs, and a question will arise whether they are entitled to one vote or fifteen votes. Probably one vote per homesite or per apartment is a workable rule, such vote to be cast only if a majority of the owners of that lot or apartment agree on their vote. The same observations are applicable to an amendment of the declaration in any other respect.

A somewhat controversial clause is as follows:

CLAUSE: In no event shall these restrictions continue in force more than fifty years from the date of recording of this declaration.

Here the thinking is that after fifty years the Home Association and Architectual Control Committee will have ceased to exist, the subdivision will have been fully developed, changes may have occurred in the area, the local Marketable Title Act may have called the continued existence of the restriction in question, zoning will suffice to protect those who remain, and part of the restrictions will be obsolete, such as the minimum building area restriction, yet going through the mechanics of modification, or release may be almost impossible. The few remaining vacant lots may become unsightly dumping grounds and remain virtually unsaleable because of the restrictions. On the other hand some lot buyers planning expensive homes unrealistically long for protection ''forever.''

The question also comes up as to the voting rights of persons other than the fee owners, for example, mortgagees. There are no decisions squarely in point, but in a number of cases involving such restrictions the courts have decided the question without mention of the mortgagees. *Sharp v. Quinn*, 214 Cal. 194, 4 P2d 942 (1931); *Morgan v.*

Sigal, 114 Conn. 39, 157 Atl. 412 (1931); *Strauss v. J. C. Nichols Land Co.* 327 Mo. 205, 37 S.W.2d 505 (1931).

Probably it is best to cover this point, for example:

CLAUSE: Only owners of the fee title shall be permitted to vote on modification, extension, or termination of these building restrictions.

Mortgagees can protect themselves by mortgage covenants requiring the mortgagee's written consent to any such vote, but this practice makes the restrictions virtually "unamendable."

The right to "modify" does not include the right to "nullify" the restrictions. *Kempner v. Simon,* 119 Misc. 60, 195 N.Y.S. 333. And an attempted release will be set aside if it operates to the prejudice of the homeowners. *Berger v. Van Sweringen Co.* 6 Ohio St.2d 100, 106, 216 NE2d 54, 52 Cornell L. Q. 611. The cases that provoke most litigation are those where a right to modify or release was reserved in the developer. 4 ALR3d 570. Obviously such a right should never be included.

Where the right is reserved in some percentage of the homeowners, even there a release or modification must not operate on one lot only. It ought to benefit, it has been argued, all the restricted lots and any modifications or release voted by the required majority must be general in its nature. *Steve Vogle & Co. v. Lane,* 405 SW2d 885.

EXAMPLE: A majority of the landowners voted to take one lot out of the restrictions so that a filling station could be erected on it. This was invalid. *Riley v. Boyle,* 434 P2d 525.

However an amendment as to four lots has been sustained. *Failla v. Meaux,* 237 So2d 688.

It might be best to include a clause fettering the right.

CLAUSE: The right to modify or release part or all of these restrictions shall be exercised reasonably.

For the rest, requiring a percentage of say 75% or more of the homeowners would seem to help assure reasonable exercise of the right.

A matter concerning which there appears to be little or no law involves the necessity of recording consents to modification, extension or abrogation of restrictions. For example, suppose that the proper percentage of lot owners have signed consents, but the consents have not been recorded. One of the consenting lots is sold to a purchaser who does not want the restrictions modified or abrogated. Is he bound by the unrecorded consent? Perhaps it might be best to provide that "any consent given by a lot owner pursuant to this paragraph shall not be binding upon an innocent purchaser of said lot for value prior to the recording thereof." This would compel the recording of consents and would compel consents to be prepared in recordable form, with acknowledgments, etc. Perhaps an additional provision along the following lines would also help:

CLAUSE: When the required number of consents has been obtained, the Home Association shall record an appropriate instrument reflecting the modification, extension, or release of restrictions consented to.

In recent restriction plans, subdividers have often included a clause giving themselves the right to waive or dispense with the restrictions as to some or all of the lots. This is dangerous. A number of courts have held that such a provision destroys the uniformity necessary to a general plan, and therefore the restrictions cannot be enforced by one lot owner against another. 19 ALR2d 1282.

And where the right to modify or release restrictions is reserved in the subdivider, only he can exercise the right, and when he conveys out all the lots, the right ends. *Pulver v. Mascolo*, 237 A2d 97; *Richmond v. Pennscott Builders, Inc.*, 251 NYS2d 845.

§ **757. Marketable Title Acts.** In many states Marketable Title Acts have been enacted. 71 ALR2d 846; 13 U of Miami L.Rev. 51; 53 Cornell L.Rev. 45; 2 Drake L.Rev. 79; 44 Ia. L.Rev. 77; 47 Ia. L.Rev. 413; 47 Ky. L. J. 605; 1957 Law Forum 491; 44 N. C. L.Rev. 99; 51 Minn. L.Rev. 356; 29 N. Dak. L.Rev. 265; Basye, Clearing Land Titles (2d ed.) 366. Some of these specifically apply to covenants affecting land. Others may be construed to include such covenants. Since the main policy of such acts is to facilitate title searching rather than to impose substantive limits on the duration of interests [*see* Note, 40 Ind. L. J. 21] (1964), it would seem that covenants can be perpetual under a Marketable Title Act if recorded periodically. However, the Home Association must keep an adequate check on this to make sure that timely recording or re-recording takes place.

§ **758. Limitations period.** In the absence of a limitations provision in the declaration, delay in enforcing the restrictions will bar relief only under the nebulous rules regarding laches and estoppel. 12 ALR2d 394. This creates a problem, since the presence of building restrictions violations makes title unmarketable, *Herb v. Severson*, 32 Wash. 2d 159, 201 P2d 156; *Lohmeyer v. Bower*, 170 Kan. 442, 227 P2d 102. Hence the declaration should contain some limitations provision:

CLAUSE: Any action brought to enforce these restrictions must be brought within _____ months after the violation of restrictions first occurred.

§ **759. Revival of expired restrictions.** Where restrictions have expired by their terms they are probably not revived by inclusion of a "subject clause" in a deed. *Korn v. Campbell*, 119 App. Div. 401, 104 NYS2d 462, aff'd 192 NY 490; *Smith v. Second Church of Christ, Scientist*, 87 Ariz. 400, 351 P2d 1104, 84 ALR2d 766. The practice of including such a clause after expiration of the restrictions is a poor one.

§ **760. First building rule.** There are few cases holding that building restrictions, depending on their language, can be construed as applying only to the first building constructed. *Kakas Bros. Co. v. Kaplan*, 118 NE2d 877 (Mass. 1954); *De Sanno v. Earle*, 273 Pa. 265, 117 Atl 200, *Rouss v. Bardwill*, 7 NYS2d 527; *Glenmore Distilleries Co. v. Fiorella*, 272 Ky. 549, 117 SW2d 173, 26 CJS *Deeds* § 170. To obviate such a construction you can use a clause like:

CLAUSE: All of these restrictions apply not only to the first building erected on each lot, but also to any building thereafter erected as long as these restrictions remain in force and effect.

§ **761. Type of building material.** A common restriction states that all buildings shall be of stone or masonry construction. Under such a restriction, a brick veneer structure satisfies the requirements of the restriction. *Luciano v. Paratore*, 88 NYS2d 715. Aluminum siding and stucco siding would be violations. 41 ALR3d 1297-1298. It is probably a good idea to add a phrase that use of concrete blocks or cinder blocks in the exterior walls is forbidden, since "masonry construction" has not been judicially defined in many states.

§ 762. Vehicles. Some restrictions provide that all vehicles (including automobiles, snowmobiles, campers and trailers) must be kept in enclosed garages, and no vehicle other than for private passenger use shall be stored in any garage. Some restrictions provide that no trailer, camper, structure of temporary character, tent, garage or other building shall be used in this subdivision at any time as a residence either temporarily or permanently.

§ 763. Garbage and refuse disposal. A common provision as to garbage and refuse disposal is as follows:

GARBAGE AND REFUSE DISPOSAL. No lot shall be used or maintained as a dumping ground for rubbish. Trash, garbage or other waste shall not be kept except in sanitary containers. All incinerators or other equipment for the storage or disposal of such material shall be kept in a clean and sanitary condition.

§ 764. Oil and mining operations. A common provision as to oil and mining operations is as follows:

OIL AND MINING OPERATIONS. No oil drilling, oil development operations, oil refining, quarrying or mining operations of any kind shall be permitted upon or in any lot, nor shall oil wells, tanks, tunnels, mineral excavations or shafts be permitted upon any lot. No derrick or other structure designed for use in boring for oil or natural gas shall be erected, maintained or permitted upon any lot.

§ 765. Signs. A common provision relating to signs is as follows:

SIGNS. No sign of any kind shall be displayed to the public view on any lot except one professional sign of not more than one square foot, one sign of not more than five square feet advertising the property for sale or rent, or signs used by a builder to advertise the property during the construction and sales period.

§ 766. Maintenance. A form for this is as follows:

The land and all improvements shall be maintained by the owner in good condition and repair.

§ 767. Height of trees and shrubs. A form to cover this is as follows:

Only those trees and shrubs which are indigenous may exceed a height of 8 feet.

§ 768 Fences. A form is as follows:

All fences, screens, and similar exterior structures shall be constructed solely of wood, except for nails, bolts, and other hardware. Retaining walls, animal enclosures, and tennis court fencing may be of other materials, as approved by the Architectural Control Committee.

§ 769. Enforcement by subdivider who has conveyed all the lots. Most decisions hold that after the subdivider has conveyed out all the lots in the subdivision, he lacks a pecuniary interest that equity will protect and can no longer seek equitable relief against violations of general plan restrictions. 3 Tiffany, *Real Property* (3rd ed. 1939) § 864. However there is also authority to the contrary, holding that the subdivider may enforce the restrictions in these circumstances. *Van Sant v. Rose,* 260 Ill. 401, 103 NE 194, criticized 9 Ill. L.Rev. 58, 27 Harv. L.Rev. 493, 16 Mich L.Rev. 97. If the subdivider can bring himself to do so, he could include a provision that:

CLAUSE: No previous landowner (including the declarant) shall have the power to enforce these restrictions after he has disposed of all his land in the subdivision.

After all the Home Association was created to police the restrictions. Let it assume that role.

§ **770. Enforcement of restrictions—phased developments.** The current practice of developers in developing piecemeal or in stages the entire area set aside for development creates some restrictions problems. Normally, restrictions from one platted subdivision ought not to pour over into another adjoining platted subdivision by the developer, either as to benefit or burden unless the plan in some way reveals an intention that this shall take place. The decisions are discussed in 52 Cornell L. Q. pp 611-612. Other decisions are *Reid v. Standard Oil Co.* 107 Ga. App. 497 (1963), *Carey v. Shellburne,* 43 Del. Ch. 292, 224 A2d 400 (1966), and *Gammons v. Kenneth Park Development Corp.,* 61 A2d 391 (Del. 1948). Perhaps the most disturbing of the recent decisions is *Finucan v. Coronet Homes,* 191 SE2d 5 (S.C. 1972). In that case, under peculiar facts, the court held that restrictions poured over from one plat to another despite the statement in the first declaration that the restrictions should not affect other land of the developer. The moral to be drawn from this decision is that each plat must be given a different *name* and the statement of intent must be explicit, for example:

CLAUSE: The restrictions created by this declaration benefit and burden only the land described in this declaration. Notwithstanding the sharing of present or future facilities by other land, whether developed by the declarant or others, the general plan created by the restrictions hereby created extends only to the land described in this declaration, and there is no intention to benfit any persons other than those having an interest in the land described herein. The existence of easement rights or convenant benefits by persons owning land or having an interest in land outside the land described in this declaration does not confer upon them any right whatever to enforce the restrictions hereby created.

This clause is also helpful in eliminating enforcement by landowners outside the subdivision on the theory that they are third party beneficiaries. 2 Tiffany, *Real Property* (3rd ed. 1939) § 866.

§ **771. Reverter clauses.** The use of reverter clauses in general plan restrictions is bad practice. Numerous decisions hold that a condition can only be enforced by the grantor or his heirs. General plan conditions pose formidable problems. Kratovil, *Real Estate Law* § 511. Conditions also complicate financing, because some institutional lenders, notably life companies, cannot lend on the security of land burdened with conditions. Other lenders not similarly fettered simply refuse to make such loans. Obviously reverter clauses must be avoided.

§ 772. General form for declaration and home association charter and by laws. A reasonably satisfactory form of declaration, home association charter and by laws can be procured from FHA. It is FHA Form 1400.[1]

---

[1] © Copyright Robert Kratovil, *Building Restrictions Draftsmanship Lawyer Supplement*, published by Chicago Title Insurance Co. (1973). Reprinted by permission.

38

Easement Draftsmanship

§ **773. General observations on easement drafting.** Upwards of 90% of the litigation involving easement grants results from skimpy draftsmanship. You can probably draft a valid easement grant in very few words.

EXAMPLE: *R* grants to *E* an easement of ingress and egress over the East 10 feet of Blackacre.

Suppose that *E* owns Whiteacre, improved with a residence, immediately adjoining the easement. No doubt that tract is dominant. He also owns a vacant lot east of Whiteacre. Was that also intended to be part of the dominant tenement? Or suppose that east of Whiteacre is a street and *E's* vacant lot lies east of and adjoining the street. Is it dominant? Or suppose that at the time of the easement grant *E* owns only Whiteacre, but later acquires a vacant lot east and adjoining. This is the problem of non-dominant land. Or suppose Whiteacre is a tract large enough to be divided and sold into fifty different ownerships. Does each have the right to use the easement? As can be seen, all of the problems could have been anticipated and covered in a well-drawn grant. Such grants, it must be stated, are rare indeed. Hence a model easement grant is included here. (The notes appearing in this part refer to notes included at the end of this chapter.)

§ **774. Contract for easement.** If the grantee is paying a substantial price for the easement, he may wish to enter into a contract along these lines (Form No. 20):

CONTRACT FOR EASEMENT

John Smith, seller, and _____ his wife, contract to grant to Henry Brown, (the grantee) for the sum of $_____ the following:

A perpetual easement for ingress and egress over, under and across the easement premises described as follows:

(here describe easement premises)
which easement shall be appurtenant to:
(here describe dominant tenement).

The easement grant shall warrant the seller's title to the easement premises subject only to the following permitted objections:
(here list permitted objections)

Within ____ days from this date seller shall deliver to the grantee a commitment of a title insurance company satisfactory to the grantee to insure the title of seller to the easement premises in the sum of $____ subject only to the permitted objections, and if within ____ days from receipt of commitment by the grantee the seller is unable to clear said title of all but the permitted objections, this contract shall, at the option of the grantee, become null and void.

A copy of the easement grant to be executed is attached hereto and made a part hereof.

§ 775. Model easement grant. (Form No. 21):

This EASEMENT GRANT is made between ____ (hereinafter referred to as "the grantor") and ____ (hereinafter referred to as "the grantee").

The following recitals of fact are a material part of this instrument:

A. The grantor is the owner of a tract of land described as follows and hereafter referred to as "Parcel 1":

(Here insert legal description)

B. The grantee is the owner of a tract of land described as follows and hereafter referred to as "Parcel 2":[1]

(Here insert legal description)

C. The grantor wishes to grant and the grantee wishes to receive an easement over, under and across what part of Parcel 1 described as follows and hereafter referred to as "The easement premises:"[2]

(Here describe the land to be subject to easement)

D. Parcel 1 is presently improved with a building used for ____ and Parcel 2 is improved with a building used for ____.

Now, therefore, in consideration of ____ and other valuable consideration, the receipt and sufficiency of which are hereby acknowledged,[3] the following grants, agreements, and covenants and restrictions are made:

1. GRANT OF EASEMENT. The grantor hereby grants[4] to the grantee, his heirs and assigns,[5] as an easement appurtenant to Parcel 2,[6] a perpetual[7] easement for ingress and egress[8] over, under and across the easement premises.

2. USE OF EASEMENT PREMISES. Use of the easement premises is not confined to present uses of Parcel 2, the present buildings thereon, or present means of transportation.[9] The installation or maintenance by the grantee of pipes, conduits, or wires, under, upon or over the easement premises is forbidden.[10] Exclusive use of the easement premises is not hereby granted.[11] The right to use the easement premises, likewise for ingress or egress, is expressly reserved by the grantor. In addition, the grantor reserves the right to make the following uses of the easement premises:

a. The right to erect a building over the easement premises, provided all of such structure shall be located at a height of not less than ____ feet above the surface of the easement premises, but construction of the improvement shall be so conducted as not to unreasonably interfere with grantee's use of the easement premises during construction.[12]

b. Any subsurface use that does not unreasonably interfere with grantee's use of the easement premises.[13]

3. USE OF PARCELS 1 AND 2. As long as this easement grant remains in effect Parcel 2 shall not be used for other than commercial or residential purposes and no building other than one suited only for commercial or residence purposes shall be constructed thereon.[14]

4. ADDITIONS TO DOMINANT TENEMENT. Said easement is also appurtenant to any land that may hereafter come into common ownership with Parcel 2 aforesaid and that is contiguous to Parcel 2.[15] An area physically separated from Parcel 2 but having access thereto by means of public ways or private easements, rights or licenses is deemed to be contiguous to Parcel 2.

5. DIVISION OF DOMINANT TENEMENT. If Parcel 2 is hereafter divided into two parts by separation of ownership or by lease, both parts shall enjoy the benefit of the easement hereby created.[16] Division of the dominant tenement into more than two parts shall be deemed an unlawful increase of burden and use of the easement may be enjoined.

6. PARKING. Both parties covenant that vehicles shall not be parked on the easement premises except so long as may be reasonably necessary to load and unload.[17]

7. PAVING OF EASEMENT. Grantee covenants to promptly improve the easement premises with a concrete surface at least _____ feet in width suitable for use by delivery trucks and[18] will at all times maintain same in good repair.[19]

8. WARRANTIES OF TITLE. Grantor warrants that he has good and indefeasible fee simple title to the easement premises, subject only to the following permitted title objections:[20]

(here list encumbrances)

9. TITLE INSURANCE AND ESCROW. Should grantee so desire, he may apply forthwith for a title insurance policy insuring the easement hereby granted and grantor will make available for inspection by the title company any evidence of title in his possession.[21]

10. RELOCATION OF EASEMENT. Grantor reserves the right to relocate the easement premises as follows.[22]

1. He shall first notify the grantee of the proposed relocation by mailing notice to the grantee at his last address furnished pursuant hereto showing the proposed relocation, probable commencement and completion dates, all by mailing same, postage prepaid, at least 30 days prior to commencement of relocation.

2. The easement premises shall be moved not more than _____ feet from their present location.

3. Grantor shall improve the new easement premises with a concrete driveway similar to the one replaced, to be suitable for use by delivery trucks, with connections at the termini of the driveway to be replaced, and reasonably convenient for the uses then existing on Parcel 2.

4. At the completion of the work, grantor shall record an easement grant in recordable form granting the new easement to the grantee, shall cause the same to be delivered to the grantee, and shall furnish the grantee evidence of title satisfactory to the grantee showing an unemcumbered easement in such grantee, whereupon the change in location of the easement premises shall become effective, and appropriate releases of the prior location shall be executed in recordable form and exchanged between the parties hereto, their successors or assigns.

11. RUNNING OF BENEFITS AND BURDENS. All provisions of this instrument, including the benefits and burdens, run with the land and are binding upon and enure to the heirs, assigns, successors, tenants and personal representatives of the parties hereto.[23]

12. TERMINATION OF COVENANT LIABILITY. Whenever a transfer of ownership of either parcel takes place, liability of the transferor for breach of covenant occurring thereafter automatically terminates, except that the grantor herein remains liable for breaches of covenants of title set forth in Paragraph 8.[24]

13. ATTORNEY'S FEES. Either party may enforce this instrument by appropriate action and should he prevail in such litigation, he shall recover as part of his costs a reasonable attorney's fee.[25]

14. CONSTRUCTION. The rule of strict construction does not apply to this grant. This grant shall be given a reasonable construction so that the intention of the parties to confer a commercially usable right of enjoyment on the grantee is carried out.

15. NOTICE. Grantor's address is _____ and grantee's address is _____. Either party may lodge written notice of change of address with the other. All notices shall be sent by U.S. mail to the addresses provided for in this paragraph and shall be deemed given when placed in the mail. The affidavit of the person depositing the notice in the U.S. Post Office receptacle shall be evidence of such mailing.

16. RELEASE OF EASEMENT. The grantee herein may terminate this instrument by recording a release in recordable form with directions for delivery of same to grantor at his last address given pursuant hereto whereupon all rights, duties, and liabilities hereby created shall terminate. For convenience such instrument may run to "the owner or owners and parties interested" in Parcel 1.[26]

17. JOINDER OF SPOUSE. _____ spouse of grantor joins herein for the purpose of releasing dower, homestead and all other marital rights, all of which are waived with respect to this easement.[27]

In witness whereof the grantor, his spouse and the grantee[28] have hereunto set their hands and seals this _____ day of _____A.D. 19_____.

_____(Seal)

_____(Seal)

_____(Seal)

NOTES FOR MODEL EASEMENT GRANT

1. It is not necessary to describe the dominant tenement in the easement grant. The area intended to be served can be gathered from the attendant circumstances. However, as appears from the General Observations, questions often arise. Hence it is good draftsmanship to describe the dominant tenement.

2. Often enough R, owning Blackacre, grants to E an easement of ingress and egress over "Blackacre." Obviously it was never the intention of the parties that E would roam over all of Blackacre. The courts have devised a means of pinning down the easement area. 110 ALR 174. But to fail to pinpoint the easement premises is wretched draftsmanship.

3. Since easements existed long before the doctrine of consideration was invented, no recital of consideration is necessary. Occasional decisions nevertheless mention the presence of consideration. It seems best to recite consideration.

4. Words of grant are necessary according to a few decisions. This corresponds to the requirement of words of conveyance in a deed. The numerous decisions holding that easements can be created by contract are obvious proof that the requirement is less formal in easement drafting.

5. There are many statutes to the effect that words of heirship are not necessary to create a fee simple by deed. Easements are rarely mentioned, but by analogy the word "heirs" is not needed to create a permanent easement. But there are some court decisions saying that an easement endures only for the life of the grantor unless words of heirship are included. *Elwell v. Miner*, 174 NE2d 43.

6. An easement appurtenant need not be so characterized. Normally the courts will strain to find the easement is appurtenant rather than in gross. Good draftsmanship requires that the proper label be affixed.

7. The same estates exist in easements as exist in corporeal hereditaments. Thus, you can have an easement in fee simple, for life, for years, etc. *Texas Co. v. O'Meara*, 377 Ill. 144, 36 NE2nd 256; 154 ALR5. It is not the practice to use the estates terminology. Instead of talking of an easement *in fee simple*, we talk of a *perpetual easement*.

8. There is no such thing as a plain "easement." It must be for ingress and egress, for light and air, or for some other specific purpose.

9. The opening sentence of paragraph 2 is a statement of existing law. 3 ALR3d 1287. However, it forces the parties to think about changes that will take place in the future. If the dominant owner tears down his store and erects an industrial plant, will the servient owner be unhappy with this turn of events? If he will be, he must provide against this.

10. This is also a statement of existing law. 3 ALR3d 1278. Again the existence of litigation indicates the need for covering this point.

11. An easement that excludes the servient owner from use of the easement premises is extremely rare. *Etz v. Morrow*, 72 Ariz. 228, 233 P2d 442. An exception is the railroad easement, which is exclusive by its very nature. But dominant owners always seem surprised when they hear the rule stated. Hence it belongs in the grant.

12. This is also a statement of existing law. *Sakansky v. Wein*, 86 N.H. 337, 169A 1; *Minneapolis Athletic Club v. Cohler*, 177 NW2d 786 (Minn. 1970). The presence of litigation indicates it is not generally understood. Of course, there are easements one cannot build over, such as a pipeline easement. *Tide Water Pipe Co. v. Blair Holding Co.*, 42 N.J. 591, 202 A2d 405; 28 ALR2d 626. This would block the dominant owner's efforts to repair a break. For similar reasons the servient owner cannot put a lake over a pipeline easement. *Sumrall v. United Gas Pipeline Co.*, 97 So2d 914.

13. Also a statement of existing law. *E.M. & S. W. R.R. v. Sims*, 228 Ill. 9, 81 NE 782.

14. The dominant owner can change the nature of the use unless the easement grant restricts this right.

15. The dominant tenement is determined at the time the easement is created. Land acquired by the dominant owner thereafter is non-dominant land. It cannot use the easement. *Weathers v. Icoa Life Ins. Co.*, 460 P2d 361 (Ore. 1969). This is the most common error in easement drafting and the most costly. Of course, one can easily draft around the problem. You can make the additions to the *dominant tenement clause* much broader, if you wish. For example:

"Said easement is appurtenant to any land in the Northwest quarter of Section 34 that may subsequently come into common ownership with said dominant tenement."

In passing, attention is drawn to the fact that by the modern rule contiguity of the dominant tenement to the easement premises is not required. *Allendorf v. Daly*, 6 Ill. 2d 577, 129 NE2d 673.

16. The easement runs in favor of all parts where the dominant tenement is later divided. 10 ALR3d 960. There are some limits, however, which the courts have not clearly defined. 10 ALR3d 968. This grant sharply limits the right to divide.

17. This again is a statement of existing law. 37 ALR2d 944. Litigation over parking suggests the need to spell this out.

18. In the absence of such a clause there is no duty on the dominant owner to pave the way.

19. The dominant owner has the right, though not the duty, to repair. Kratovil, *Real Estate Law* § 43. *But see Lynch v. Keck,* 263 NE2d 176 (Ind. 1970).

20. Warranties of title exist only as expressly included in the grant.

21. Where beneficial use of his land by the dominant owner depends on dependable access via the easement, he needs title insurance on the easement as much as he needs title insurance on the land.

22. The servient owner has no right to relocate the easement unless the easement grant confers this right. An awkwardly located easement can virtually destroy the value of industrial or commercial property.

23. Covenants running with the land can be included in the easement grant. An easement grant creates the requisite privity of estate.

24. The original covenantor remains liable even after he has disposed of his land. This clause reverses the rule.

25. A litigant pays his own attorney unless the contract provides otherwise.

26. The dominant owner may wish to get rid of his covenant liability by terminating the easement when other means of ingress have been acquired. This form of clause eliminates the need for a title search of the servient tenement to get the names of the parties to whom the release is to run.

27. The authorities are divided as to the need for a spouse to join. *See, e.g. Arkansas State Highway Comm. v. Marlar,* 447 SW2d 329 (Ark. 1969).

28. Since covenants by the grantee are included it is appropriate for all parties to sign and acknowledge this document. Of course, it should also be recorded.*

References: Kratovil, *Easement Draftsmanship and Conveyancing,* 38 Calif.L.Rev. 426 (1950).

---

* Copyright New York Law Journal (1973). Reprinted by permission.

39

Declaration of Restrictions, Easements, Liens, and Covenants

§ 776. In general. The legal and practical aspects of the Declaration of Restrictions, Easements, Liens and Covenants have been described elsewhere. Kratovil, *Real Estate Law*, Chapter 34. Documents, including the declaration, that are useful in setting up a planned unit development will be found elsewhere. *See* Chapter 39.

§ 777. Lien of assessments—subordination to mortgage. An important clause in the declaration is one subordinating the lien of the assessments to the mortgage on the home unit. Such a clause is as follows:

SUGGESTED FORM: The lien of the assessment provided for herein shall be subordinate to the lien of any mortgage or mortgages now or hereafter placed upon the properties subject to assessments and running to a bank, savings and loan association, insurance company or other institutional lender; provided, however, such subordination shall apply only to the assessments which have become due and payable prior to a foreclosure sale or transfer of such property in lieu of foreclosure. Such sale or transfer shall not relieve such property from liability for any assessments thereafter becoming due nor from the lien of any such subsequent assessment.

§ 778. Deed clause. A clause is necessary in the deed of the home unit incorporating the terms of the declaration. Kratovil, *Real Estate Law* § 603.

40

Planned Unit Developments
and Town Houses

§ 779. Definition and description. Planned Unit Development (PUD) is a means of residential land development which sets aside traditional pre-set land use controls in favor of more administrative discretion to local authorities. It permits a mixture of land uses (*i.e.*, residential, commercial, and industrial), creativity in design (including both the clustering and mixing of dwelling types), and finally the provision of open space to be used by and maintained for the residents of the proposed development. The tract of land is developed as a whole according to a plan with one or more of its nonresidential elements potentially able to serve regional as well as local needs. 1 Environmental Affairs 694 (1973).

§ 780. Planning aspect. Planned development in this case refers to physical development via mid-range (4-8 years) programming. The time span embraced here is sufficiently large to make it worthwhile for a community to attempt to control its tempo and sequence of development, yet sufficiently small to make the developer's cash flow requirements and management capabilities realistic.

For PUD, the program plan keys on balance: a balance in the use of land in terms of residential and non-residential requirements; balances among public open space, commons to be used and maintained by groups and associations, and private lands; variation in location and grouping of buildings to create a choice of physical environments; and walkways, roads and highways of different types to ensure safe and convenient movement of people and vehicles.

§ 781. FNMA approval. FNMA has prepared an extensive manual outlining its requirements for loans it is requested to purchase. It has an extremely valuable and detailed section on its requirements with respect to PUD and condo loans. All persons dealing with PUD and condo loans should be familiar with this work. Moreover, it is supplemented from time to time so that the latest thinking is incorporated. FNMA and FHLMC so completely dominate the residential mortgage market at present that it is incumbent on all practitioners to be familiar with their requirements. In their field, their requirements will become the standard.

§ 782. Documents for the PUD. The United States Department of Housing and

341

Urban Development has prepared *Suggested Legal Documents for Planned-Unit Developments*. The forms (FHA form 1400, VA Form 26-8200) include:

1. Instructions for Use of Legal Documents for Planned-Unit Developments.

2. Forms of special clauses for the Declarations.

3. Form of deed clause.

4. Form of Declaration (FHA Form 1401, VA Form 26-8201).

5. Form of Articles of incorporation of Home Association (FHA form 1402, VA form 26-8202).

6. Form of by-laws of Home Association (FHA form 1403, VA form 26-8203).

These forms represent adequate legal draftsmanship.

§ **783. Town house in general.** At least in parts of the country, town houses are erected on a modest scale. For example, a common town house development in the Chicago area places two parallel five-unit structures at right angles to the street, with a common walk between the two structures affording access, with a row of ten-unit parking lots along the alley to the rear.

§ **784. Declaration of easements.** The declaration of easements, covenants, and restrictions for a development of this character tends to be rather simple, like that appearing at the end of this chapter (Form No. 22). The customary detailed deed and mortgage clauses contain appropriate references to the declaration (Forms No. 23 and No. 24).

PUD References: 9 San Diego L.Rev. 28; 1 Real Estate L.J. 5; 2 *id.* 523; 35 Mo.L.Rev. 27; 7 ABA Real Property Probate & Trust Journal 61.

Form No. 22

DECLARATION OF EASEMENTS

WHEREAS, CHICAGO TITLE AND TRUST COMPANY, a corporation of Illinois, as Trustee under the provisions of a Trust Agreement dated the 7th day of March, 1961 and known as Trust No. 20052, is the holder of the legal title to all of the parcels of real estate hereafter described, located in Cook County, Illinois; and

WHEREAS, certain of the said parcels of real estate as hereinafter more particularly described are intended as dwelling sites, said parcels so intended being hereinafter referred to as "dwelling parcels" upon which it is intended to erect so-called "town houses", each town house being a single family private residence erected on a separate dwelling parcel. Said town houses are to be constructed in groups, such that each group constitutes a more or less continuous structure with party walls straddling the boundaries between the dwelling parcels, all as depicted on plat attached hereto and made a part hereof and identified as Exhibit "1" hereof; and

WHEREAS, certain of said parcels of real estate herein included as more particularly described hereafter are intended as parking sites, said parcels so intended being hereafter sometimes referred to as "parking parcels" opening on the public alley at the rear of all of the real estate described herein, said parking parcels having one stall each with dividing lines or boundaries dividing one from the other, but each of said parking parcels, however, to belong to and be related to one of the dwelling parcels hereinafter mentioned, all as hereinafter described; and

WHEREAS, each of the parcels of real estate hereinafter described solely for convenience and identification thereof in the present instrument are, at the times herein referred to, identified or designated as follows:

Each dwelling parcel by a letter of the alphabet;
Each parking parcel by the letter of the dwelling parcel to which it belongs or is related, followed by the letter "P",
and that all of the said parcels are legally described more particularly as follows:

DWELLING PARCELS

A. The South 36.17 feet.
B. The North 21.33 feet of the South 57.50 feet.
C. The North 21.33 feet of the South 78.83 feet.
D. The North 26.57 feet of the South 105.40 feet.
All being of the following described tract and measured along the east and west lines of the said tract:

Lot 491 (except the west 10 feet thereof), the west 5 feet of Lot 489, and all of Lot 490 in Sheffield's Addition to Chicago in the Northwest Quarter of Section 12, Township 40 North, Range 13, East of the Third Principal Meridian, in Cook County, Illinois, according to the plat recorded as Document Number 9141070.

PARKING PARCELS

AP. The West 5 feet of Lot 489 and the East 10 feet of Lot 490 (except the South 105.40 feet of each lot).

BP. The West 10 feet of the East 20 feet of Lot 490 (except the South 105.40 feet thereof).

CP. Lot 490 (except the South 105.40 feet thereof and except the East 20 feet thereof).

DP. Lot 491 (except the West 10 feet thereof and except the South 105.40 feet).

All being in Sheffield's Addition to Chicago aforesaid.

and

WHEREAS, the said CHICAGO TITLE AND TRUST COMPANY, as Trustee under the above mentioned Trust Agreement, intends to sell and will sell, convey and mortgage some or all of the parcels so improved, and desires and intends that the several purchasers, owners, mortgagees thereof, and all persons acquiring any interest therein now or hereafter shall at all times enjoy the benefits of and shall hold their said individual parcels subject to the rights, easements, burdens, uses and privileges hereinafter set forth.

NOW, THEREFORE, the said CHICAGO TITLE AND TRUST COMPANY, as Trustee aforesaid, does hereby declare that the following rights, easements, covenants, burdens, uses and privileges shall and do exist at all times hereafter among the several owners, purchasers or mortgagees of the said parcels of real estate in this instrument described in the manner and to the extent herein set forth, and that the declarations contained herein shall be binding upon and inure to the benefit of each and every such parcel in this instrument described:

(1) All dividing walls which straddle the boundary line between dwelling parcels and all walls which serve two or more town houses shall at all times be considered party walls. The cost of maintenance, repair or replacement of said party walls shall be borne equally by the owners of the town houses served thereby.

(2) The owner or owners of each town house shall be responsible for the maintenance, repair or replacement of that portion of the common roof and gutter system as is located or installed upon or attached to such town house.

(3) Easements for ingress and egress and for the installation, use, maintenance, repair and replacement of public utilities including sewer, gas, electricity, telephone and water lines for the use of the dwelling parcels hereinafter designated and described are hereby created over, under and across the following described real estate:

   (a) The west 5 feet of Lot 489.
   (b) The east 10 feet of Lot 491.

All being in Sheffield's Addition to Chicago aforesaid. All in accordance with plat hereto attached and made a part hereof as Exhibit "1". Said easements shall be used in common by the present and future owners, occupants and mortgagees of, and all persons now or hereafter acquiring any interest in the respective parcels hereinbefore described.

(4) Any and all other facilities of any kind presently existing or hereafter installed, designed for the common use of any two or more dwelling parcels, shall be perpetually used in common by such dwelling parcel owners or occupants.

(5) Other than the structures contemplated and intended to be erected or constructed upon the said several dwelling or parking parcels herein described and designated, or identical structures erected in replacement thereof, no exterior structures, entrances or additions or additional buildings shall be built upon any portion of the hereinabove described parcels.

All outside painting and decorating of said several dwelling parcels shall conform in color and quality to the outside painting and decorating of all other dwelling parcels.

(6) All easements herein described are easements appurtenant, running with the land; they shall at all times inure to the benefit of and be binding on the undersigned, all its grantees and their respective heirs, successors, personal representatives or assigns, perpetually in full force and effect.

(7) Reference in the respective deeds of conveyance, or in any mortgage or trust deeds or other evidence of obligation, to the easements and covenants herein described shall be sufficient to create and reserve such easements and covenants to the respective grantees, mortgagees or trustees of said parcels as fully and completely as though said easements and covenants were fully recited and set forth in their entirety in such documents.

This Declaration of Easement is executed by the CHICAGO TITLE AND TRUST COMPANY, as Trustee as aforesaid, in the exercise of the power and authority conferred upon and vested in it as such Trustee (and said CHICAGO TITLE AND TRUST COMPANY hereby warrants that it possesses full power and authority to execute this instrument), and it is expressly understood and agreed that nothing herein shall be construed as creating any liability on said CHICAGO TITLE AND TRUST COMPANY.

IN WITNESS WHEREOF, CHICAGO TITLE AND TRUST COMPANY, as Trustee as aforesaid, has caused these presents to be signed by its Assistant Vice President and its corporate seal to be hereunto affixed and attested by its Assistant Secretary, this _____ day of July, A.D. 1961.

                                        CHICAGO TITLE AND TRUST COMPANY,
                                        as Trustee aforesaid,

                              By _____
                                        Assistant Vice President

ATTEST:

_____
     Assistant Secretary

(acknowledgment as in deed)

Form No. 23

<u>COVENANT TO BE INSERTED IN DEEDS</u>

Subject to Declaration of Easements and covenants by grantor dated the _____ day of ____ _____, A. D., 1956, and recorded in the Office of the Recorder of Deeds, Cook County, Illinois, as Document No. _____, which is incorporated herein by reference thereto. Grantor grants to the grantees, their heirs and assigns, as easements appurtenant to the premises hereby conveyed the easements created by said Declaration for the benefit of the owners of the parcels of realty herein described. Grantor reserves to itself, its successors and assigns, as easements appurtenant to the remaining parcels described in said Declaration, the easements thereby created for the benefit of said remaining parcels described in said Declaration and this conveyance is subject to the said easements and the right of the Grantor to grant said easements in the conveyances and mortgages of said remaining parcels or any of them, and the parties hereto, for themselves, their heirs, successors and assigns, covenant to be bound by the covenants and agreements in said document set forth as covenants running with the land.

Form No. 24

<u>CONVENANT TO BE INSERTED IN MORTGAGES</u>

Grantors also hereby grant to the mortgagee, its successors or assigns as easements appurtentant to the above described real estate, the easements set forth in the Declaration of Easements and Covenants recorded in the Recorder's Office of Cook County, Illinois as Document Number _____ and grantors make this conveyance subject to the easements and agreements reserved for the benefit of adjoining parcels in said Declaration, which is incorporated herein by reference thereto for the benefit of the real estate above described and adjoining parcels.

41

Condominiums

§ 785. **In general.** Some legal and practical aspects of condominium ownership have been described elsewhere. Kratovil, *Real Estate Law*, Chapter 31.

§ 786. **Description of condominium's legal aspects.** In a condominium apartment, the purchaser of an apartment receives a deed that gives him absolute ownership of the apartment that he has purchased and ownership of an undivided interest or share in the common elements hereinafter described.

§ 787. **The declaration.** The declaration is the most important document in the condominium package. It combines several things. First, it contains provisions required or permitted under the local condominium statute. Second, its structure is that of the declaration of restrictions, easements, liens, and covenants. *See* Chapter 39. Third, it contains provisions deemed appropriate or beneficial to the developer, mortgage lenders, or condominium purchasers in the project in question. Fourth, if it is a condominium on a leasehold, it contains complex provisions made necessary by that fact alone. Fifth, if it is an "add on" condominium, it will also contain complex provisions. Sixth, if it is a "time-split" resort type condominium, it will also contain complex provisions dealing with this situation.

§ 788. **The declaration.** Before any of the apartments are conveyed, the owner-developer makes, signs and records a declaration that contains certain basic items. Variations in state law make this a state-by-state problem.

The declaration should be executed by the landowner, acknowledged and witnessed in accordance with the local requirements for recording, and should be recorded in the recorder's office.

§ 789. **Land descriptions in the declaration.** The declaration should describe the following elements: (1) the land comprising the entire project area, for which a traditional legal description can be used, but which should be given a distinctive designation, for example, *the project parcel;* (2) each apartment by whatever method is employed, giving it in addition a distinctive number, as Apartment Parcel 1; (3) the land and space that are to be owned in common by the apartment owners, for which one shortcut would be a description such as "the project parcel excepting Apartment Parcels 1 to 100, both inclusive, all hereinabove described."

§ 790. **TV provisions.** If the developer means to generate additional profit by operating and renting a central TV antenna or a CATV system, the declaration will restrict installation of such things by the unit owners, making this a section that cannot be amended. Then the declaration reserves exclusive easements to the developer's corporation for these purposes.

§ **791. Declaration—repairs, maintenance, and the like.** There will be little argument about interpretation of the declaration as to repair and maintenance of elevators, corridors, etc. But disputes may arise as to repairs and maintenance of balconies, doors, windows, etc. The duty to repair and maintain such items should be spelled out, and need not follow ownership. Since uniform appearance is desirable, there ought to be some restriction to the effect that no change will be made in the exterior appearance of the building.

§ **792. Recreational condominiums—right of first refusal.** The right of first refusal is usually omitted in recreational condominiums. These people are not too concerned about their neighbors.

§ **793. Restrictions in the declaration.** Much the same problems arise as are confronted in building restrictions generally. Thus, you encounter the problem of restrictions on pets, or, in retirement condominiums, restrictions on children. Where you have restrictions against children, they stand up better if they are in the form of restrictions against *occupancy* by young children. Restrictions against sale to persons having young children may run afoul of the rules forbidding restraints on alienation.

§ **794. Amendment—mortgagee's rights.** Some lenders require a covenant in the condo mortgage that the condo owner will not vote for an amendment of the condo declaration or by-laws without the written consent of the mortgagee. This poses a problem, since you don't know, without looking at 100 mortgages, what consents are required for a valid amendment. If you put this in the declaration, you can add a clause that each unit vote shall be accompanied by a written consent of the mortgagee, certified by the unit owner that this is the only mortgage on the unit, this certificate to be conclusive for vote counting purposes. The fear of acceleration will keep the unit owners honest.

§ **795. Common areas—other means of enforcing payment of assessments.** When an owner does not pay, the association may resort to non-legal pressures such as keeping other owners informed of the delinquency through association circulations or denying the delinquent owner use of recreational facilities during delinquency. The latter remedy must be provided for in the declaration as it restricts a property right, namely, the respective owner's non-exclusive right to use the common area. 9 San Diego L.Rev. 28, 60.

§ **796. Other documents.** Among the other documents that figure in a condo are: (1) Tentative declaration. The final declaration, under many state laws can be recorded only after the building has been completed. Meanwhile, contracts of sale are entered into on the basis of a tentative declaration, which is recorded, for convenience, and referred to in the contracts of sale. (2) Contracts of sale of condo units. (3) Deeds by developer of condo units. (4) Corporate charter of condo corporation. (5) Bylaws of condo corporation. (6) Initial rules and regulations, governing the use of the apartments by the unit owners. (7) Initial management agreement between the condo corporation and the first building manager. (8) Surety bond assuring completion of building free of mechanic's liens. (9) Construction mortgage and the usual applications, commitment, and other mortgage documents. (10) Individual mortgages on the condo units. These are placed of record as a sale is closed, and the construction mortgage is released as to the unit sold.

§ **797. Description—tracking with declaration.** The plat or survey should track with the declaration. If, for example, the declaration gives the apartment boundary as the planes of the inner surface of the apartment walls, as extended, excluding wall and floor coverings, you may be excluding windows and doors from the apartment ownership. The plat or survey should show this set of facts. Whatever items become part of the condominium's common elements, the duty of repair and maintenance of such items rests on the condominium association. The sales plat ought to track with the declaration and the official plat or survey.

§ **798. Retention of public areas by developer.** In some condominiums, the developer retains ownership of some public areas such as parking areas, swimming pools, etc., and makes a charge for the use of the same. Legislation eliminating this feature seems likely. At all events, where this feature is valid, the area in question must be plainly marked on the condo map as "Not included in this project—ownership retained by developer." The developer may then lease the tract to the condo corporation, on a net lease, which forbids assignment or sublease without lessor's written consent. There may be a clause subordinating the lease to future mortgages. This is done before any condo units have been sold, so that at that time the condo promoters are dealing among themselves and have no duties to protect others. *Wechsler v. Goldman*, 214 So.2d 741, 24 U. of Miami L.Rev. 578, 602-604.

§ **799. Purchase contracts.** Many purchase contracts will be issued before the construction loan commitment is given, or the commitment will be contingent on the procuring of a percentage of purchase contracts. Hence, the construction mortgagee's rights are subject to the rights of the contract purchasers. *State Savings & Loan Assn. v. Kauaian Develop. Co., Inc.*, 50 Haw. 540, 455 P2d 109 (1968). Accordingly, subordinations of these contracts to the construction mortgage must take place. Probably the subordination will have to be definite and detailed to be valid, 26 ALR3d 855. All early purchase contracts are contingent on developer's signing up firm contracts for the purchase of, say 80 percent of the units. The construction lender's commitment is also contingent on this.

Many of the contract of sale provisions will be like those in other contracts of sale, *e.g.*, contract contingent on obtaining financing. Other provisions will be peculiar to the condo situation, *e.g.*, provision for partial release of blanket mortgage at closing. Also, if the purchaser is to receive a lease until the deal is firmed up by sale of condo units, the provision for lease, consequences of default, switch from sale to lease should be covered.

Where a deed to a condo unit to be given before the building has been completed, some provision is needed in the contract or deed that the contract of sale provisions providing for construction of a building are not merged in the deed.

The developer usually insists on a clause on the first sale that the contract will terminate if the developer is unable to complete construction within _____ years owing to events beyond his control, such as flood, material shortages, etc.

§ **800. Real estate commission.** In some states, the project must be approved by some regulatory body. In these states, earnest money deposits are held in escrow until final approval is obtained. Construction financing is contingent on final approval or is not given at all until final approval is obtained.

§ **801. Disclosure statutes.** All disclosure statutes should be complied with. Even in the absence of such a statute it is a good practice to furnish any unit purchaser a complete package of the legal documents and have him receipt for the same.

§ **802. Mechanic's liens.** It is some protection to the contract's purchasers to know that there is a 100 percent performance and payment bond. Ideally, the contract of sale should be contingent on showing of such a bond.

§ **803. Reservations.** Some developers, as a means of testing the market, have a prospective purchaser who is not willing to sign a firm contract of sale make a deposit that "reserves" a unit for later purchase. The deposit the prospective purchaser makes is refundable on demand and is placed with a bank or trust company.

§ **804. Mortgage loan pre-conditions.** A particular lender may choose to make his loan commitment conditional on obtaining loan commitments on a stated percentage of the units in the building. He does not want to be involved unless he has a major "piece of the action."

§ **805. Lease of unit pending sale.** It is common for a developer to lease an unsold unit with a clause providing for cancellation on 60 days notice if the unit is sold.

§ **806. FHLMC requirements.** The FHLMC requirements as to condominium mortgages are illuminating:

With respect to each home mortgage covering a condominium unit, Seller shall deliver with the mortgage a written designation of those warranties regarding condominium regimes, set forth below, which Seller is unable to make, if any. See Section 6.01(h). If such designation is submitted, it shall serve as Seller's request for approval of such exceptions. In such case, if FHLMC so requires, Seller shall submit the declaration of condominium or master deed, the by-laws and regulations of the condominium project, and such other documents pertaining to the regime and operation of the condominium as FHLMC shall require, for approval by counsel to FHLMC at Seller's expense; or FHLMC may require Seller to obtain and submit opinions of counsel provided by counsel acceptable to FHLMC, which opinions shall be obtained at Seller's expense.

In addition, whether or not such designation is submitted by Seller, FHLMC may require Seller to submit condominium documents for approval by counsel to FHLMC at Seller's expense.

Seller makes the following warranties with respect to the condominium regime related to each home mortgage covering a condominium unit (except to the extent that Seller designates, as provided above):

Seller warrants that by virtue of (i) the declaration of condominium or master deed and the by-laws and regulations of the condominium project and other constituent documents (hereafter "condominium documents"), (ii) a written agreement in favor of all mortgagees of units in the project with the association of owners of the condominium, (iii) state law, or (iv) a combination thereof:

a. The holder of the mortgage is entitled to written notification from the association of owners of the condominium of any default by the mortgagor of such unit in the performance of such mortgagor's obligations under the condominium documents which is not cured within thirty days.

b. Any holder of the mortgage which comes into possession of the unit pursuant to the remedies provided in the mortgage, or foreclosure of the mortgage, or deed (or assignment) in lieu of foreclosure, shall be exempt from any "right of first refusal."

c. Any holder of the mortgage which comes into possession of the unit pursuant to the remedies provided in the mortgage, foreclosure of the mortgage, or deed (or assignment) in lieu of foreclosure, shall take the property free of any claims for unpaid assessments or charges against the mortgaged unit which accrue prior to the time such holder comes into possession of the unit (except for claims for a pro rata share of such assessments or charges resulting from a pro rata reallocation of such assessments or charges to all units including the mortgaged unit).

d. Unless all holders of first mortgage liens on individual units have given their prior written approval, the association of owners of the condominium, except to the extent permitted in 3.03(i) below, shall not:

    (1) change the pro rata interest or obligations of any unit for purposes of levying assessments and charges and determining shares of the common elements and proceeds of the project;

    (2) partition or subdivide any unit or the common elements of the project; nor

    (3) by act or omission seek to abandon the condominium status of the project except as provided by statute in case of substantial loss to the units and common elements of the condominium project.

    e. All taxes, assessments and charges which may become liens prior to the mortgage under local law shall relate only to the condominium unit and not to the project as a whole.

    f. All amenities to which the appraisal relates (such as parking, recreation and service areas) are a part of the condominium regime and are covered by the mortgage to the same extent as are all other common elements.

    g. The condominium regime has been created and is existing in full compliance with requirements of the condominium enabling statute of the jurisdiction in which the condominium project is located and all other applicable federal or state laws.

    h. Any proposal or plan pursuant to which the condominium regime is subject to additions or expansion (e.g. so-called "phase projects" or "add-ons") complies with the following limitations:

    (1) unit owners shall have a minimum percentage undivided interest in the common elements, and a maximum interest subject to diminution to no less than such minimum, each such percentage interest to be stated in the Declaration;

    (2) the conditions on which any change in such percentage of undivided interest in common elements may take place are fully described in the Declaration, together with a description of the real property which may become a part of the condominium regime;

    (3) no change in the percentage of undivided interest may be effected more than seven years after the date the Declaration becomes effective.

§ 807. **FNMA.** Both as to the Condo and the PUD, FNMA is introducing an innovation. It will require the mortgage banker who originates the loan to furnish opinion of counsel. The opinion will include a representation that the attorney has reviewed the condo documents and that they conform to the local condo statute and other state laws, including even local securities laws and environmental regulations. Other factors to be covered will include disposition of insurance proceeds and condemnation awards. The opinion must cover precautions for the buyer's protection, such as deposit in escrow of the buyer's purchase money and that the developer's control of swimming pools and other amenities is restricted. *See also* § 781.

§ 808. **Destruction of building.** A clause relating to destruction of the building is as follows:

    This Declaration does hereby make mandatory the irrevocable appointment of an attorney-in-fact to deal with the property upon its destruction or damage, for its repair, reconstruction or obsolescence and to maintain, repair, replace and improve the condominium units, buildings, and common elements, or any portion thereof. Title to any condominium unit is declared and expressly made subject to the terms and conditions hereof, and acceptance by any grantee of a deed or other instrument of conveyance from the Declarant or from any owner or grantor shall constitute appointment of the attorney-in-fact herein provided. All of the owners irrevocably constitute and appoint the SILVER QUEEN WEST AT WILDERNESS Condominium Association as their true and lawful attorney in their name, place and stead for the purpose of dealing with the property upon its damage or destruction or obsolescence as is hereinafter provided. As attorney-in-fact, the Association, by its President and Secretary or Assistant-Secretary or its other duly authorized officers and agents, shall have full and complete authorization, right and power to make, execute and deliver any contract, deed or other instrument with respect to the interest of a condominium unit owner which are necessary and appropriate to exercise the powers herein granted. In the event that the Association is dissolved or becomes defunct, a meeting of all of the condominium unit owners shall be held within forty-five (45) days of either such event. At such meeting a new attorney-in-fact, to deal with the property upon its destruction, damage or obsolescence, shall be appointed. Said appointment must be approved by the owners representing an aggregate ownership interest of seventy-five percent (75%), or more, of the common elements. Repair and reconstruction of the improvements as used in the succeeding subparagraphs means restoring the improvement(s) to substantially the same condition in which they existed prior to the damage, with each unit and the general and limited common elements having substantially the same vertical and horizontal boundaries as before. The proceeds of any insurance collected shall be available to the Association for the purpose of repair, restoration, reconstruction or replacement unless all of the owners and all first mortgagees agree not to rebuild in accordance with the provisions hereinafter set forth.

(a) In the event of damage or destruction due to fire or other disaster, the insurance proceeds, if sufficient to reconstruct the improvement(s), shall be applied by the Association, as attorney-in-fact, to such reconstruction, and the improvement(s) shall be promptly repaired and reconstructed. The Association shall have full authority, right and power as attorney-in-fact, to cause the repair and restoration of the improvement(s). Assessments for common expenses shall not be abated during the period of insurance adjustments and repair and reconstruction.

(b) If the insurance proceeds are insufficient to repair and reconstruct the improvement(s), and if such damage is not more than sixty percent (60%) of the total replacement cost of all of the condominium units in this project, not including land, such damage or destruction shall be promptly repaired and reconstructed by the Association, as attorney-in-fact, using the proceeds of insurance and the proceeds of a special assessment to be made against all of the owners and their condominium units. Such deficiency assessment shall be a common expense and made pro rata according to each owner's interest in the common elements and shall be due and payable within thirty (30) days after written notice thereof. The Association shall have full authority, right and power, as attorney-in-fact, to cause the repair, replacement or restoration of the improvement(s) using all of the insurance proceeds for such purpose, notwithstanding the failure of an owner to pay the assessment. The assessment provided for herein shall be a debt of each owner and a lien on his condominium unit and may be enforced and collected as is provided in paragraph 23. In addition thereto, the Association, as attorney-in-fact, shall have the absolute right and power to sell the condominium unit of any owner refusing or failing to pay such deficiency assessment within the time provided, and if not so paid, the Association shall cause to be recorded a notice that the condominium unit of the delinquent owner shall be sold by the Association, as attorney-in-fact, pursuant to the provisions of this paragraph. Assessments for common expenses shall not be abated during the period of insurance adjustment and repair and reconstruction. The delinquent owner shall be required to pay to the Association the costs and expenses for filing the notice, interest at a rate which is periodically promulgated by the Board of Directors or its agents, on the amount of the assessment and all reasonable attorney's fees. The proceeds derived from the sale of such condominium unit shall be used and disbursed by the Association, as attorney-in-fact, in the following order:

(1) For payment of taxes and special assessments liens in favor of any assessing entity and the customary expenses of sale;

(2) For payment of the balance of the lien of any first mortgage;

(3) For payment of unpaid common expenses and all costs, expenses and fees incurred by the Association;

(4) For payment of junior liens and encumbrances in the order of and to the extent of their priority; and

(5) The balance remaining, if any, shall be paid to the condominium unit owner.

(c) If the insurance proceeds are insufficient to repair and reconstruct the damaged improvement(s), and if such damage is more than sixty percent (60%) of the total replacement cost of all of the condominium units in this project, not including land, and if the owners representing an aggregate ownership interest of seventy-five percent (75%), or more, of the common elements do not voluntarily, within sixty (60) days thereafter, make provisions for repair, replacement and reconstruction, which plan must have the approval or consent of all of the first mortgagees of record, then the Association shall forthwith record a notice setting forth such fact or facts, and upon the recording of such notice by the Association's President and Secretary or Assistant Secretary, the entire remaining premises shall be sold by the Association pursuant to the provisions of this paragraph, as attorney-in-fact for all of the owners, free and clear of the provisions contained in this Declaration, the Map, Articles of Incorporation and the By-Laws. Assessments for common expenses shall not be abated during the period prior to sale. The insurance settlement proceeds shall be collected by the Association, and such proceeds shall be divided by the Association according to each owner's interest in the common elements, and such divided proceeds shall be paid into separate accounts, each such account representing one of the condominium units. Each such account shall be in the name of the Association, and shall be further identified by the condominium unit designation and the name of the owner. From each separate account the Association, as attorney-in-fact, shall forthwith use and disburse the total amount (of each) of such accounts, without contribution from one account to another, toward the partial or full payment of the lien of any first mortgagee against the condominium unit represented by such separate account. Thereafter, each such account shall be supplemented by the apportioned amount of the proceeds obtained from the sale of the entire property. Such apportionment shall be based upon each condominium unit owner's interest in the common elements. The total funds of each account shall be used and disbursed, without contribution from one account to another, by the Association, as attorney-in-fact, for the same purposes and in the same order as is provided in subparagraph (b)(1) and (5) of this paragraph.

(d) In the event of such damage or destruction under subparagraph (c) of this paragraph, and if a plan for repair, replacement and reconstruction is adopted as therein provided, then all of the owners shall be bound by the terms and other provisions of such plan. Any assessment made in connection with such plan shall be a common expense and made pro rata according to each owner's interest in the common elements and shall be due and payable as provided by the terms of such plan, but not sooner than thirty (30) days after written notice thereof. The Association shall have full authority, right and power, as attorney-in-fact, to cause the repair, replacement or restoration of improvements using all of the insurance proceeds for such purpose, notwithstanding the failure of an owner to pay the assessment. Assessments for common expenses shall not be abated during the period of insurance adjustment and repair and reconstruction. The assessment provided for herein shall be a debt of each owner and a lien on his condominium unit and may be enforced and collected as is provided in paragraph 23. In addition thereto, the Association, as attorney-in-fact, shall have the absolute right and power to sell the condominium unit of any other refusing or failing to pay such assessment within the time provided, and if not so paid, the Association shall cause to be recorded a notice that the condominium unit of the delinquent owner shall be sold by the Association. The delinquent owner shall be required to pay to the Association the costs and expenses for filing the notices, interest at the rate as periodically promulgated by the Board of Directors or its agents of the amount of the assessment, and all reasonable attorney's fees. The proceeds derived from the sale of the condominium unit shall be used and disbursed by the Association, as attorney-in-fact, for the same purposes and in the same order as is provided in subparagraph (b)(1) through (5) of this paragraph.

(e) The owners representing an aggregate ownership interest of eighty-five percent (85%), or more, of the common elements in this project may agree that the common elements are obsolete and adopt a plan for the renewal and reconstruction, which plan has the approval of one hundred percent (100%) of the first mortgagees of record at the time of the adoption of such plan. If a plan for the renewal or reconstruction is adopted, notice of such plan shall be recorded, and the expense of renewal and reconstruction shall be payable by all of the owners as a common expense, whether or not they have previously consented to the plan of renewal and construction. The Association, as attorney-in-fact, shall have the absolute right and power to sell the condominium unit of any owner refusing or failing to pay such assessment within the time provided, and if not so paid, the Association shall cause to be recorded a notice that the condominium unit of the delinquent owner shall be sold by the Association. The delinquent owner shall be required to pay to the Association the costs and expenses for filing the notices, interest at the rate which shall be periodically promulgated by the Board of Directors or its agents on the amount of the assessment, and all reasonable attorney's fees. The proceeds derived from the sale of such condominium unit shall be used and disbursed by the Association, as attorney-in-fact, for the same purposes and in the same order as is provided in subparagraph (b)(1) through (5) of this paragraph.

(f) The owners representing an aggregate ownership interest of eighty-five percent (85%), or more, of the common elements may agree that the condominium units are obsolete and that the same should be sold. Such plan or agreement must have the unanimous approval of every first mortgagee. In such instance, the Association shall forthwith record a notice setting forth such fact or facts, and upon the recording of such notice by the Association's President and Secretary or Assistant Secretary the entire premises shall be sold by the Association, as attorney-in-fact, for all of the owners, free and clear of the provisions contained in this Declaration, the Map, the Articles of Incorporation and the By-Laws. The sale proceeds shall be apportioned among the owners on the basis of each owner's interest in the common elements, and such apportioned proceeds shall be paid into separate accounts, each such account representing one condominium unit. Each such account shall be in the name of the Association and shall be further identified by the condominium unit designation and the name of the owners. From each separate account, the Association, as attorney-in-fact, shall use and disburse the total amount (of each) of such accounts, without contribution from one account to another, for the same purposes and in the same order as is provided in subparagraph (b)(1) through (5) of this paragraph.[1]

§ 809. The add-on—in general.
The "add-on" on "expandable" condominiums presents some rather novel legal problems.

EXAMPLE: *D,* a developer, plans a high-rise condominium on Parcel A. If it is successful, he will build a similar high-rise on Parcel B adjoining. Both buildings will use walks and roads that traverse both parcels, a parking area located partly on each parcel, and a swimming pool located on a third parcel, Parcel C, adjoining both parcels. At the outset, the purchasers of units in the building on Parcel A will each have a 4 percent interest in the common elements including the roads, walks and parking area on Parcel A and the swimming pool adjoining. If *D* decides to build on Parcel B, several things must take place.

1. The Owners of units on Parcel A must automatically have their share of the common elements that will also be used by Parcel B unit owners reduced to 2 percent.

2. *D* must be in a position to convey to unit owners of Parcel B the 2 percent that was subtracted from the share of Parcel A unit owners.

3. The mortgages on Parcel A units must suffer a similar subtraction.

4. The common elements located entirely in each of the two buildings (corridors, stairways, elevators, etc.) should become limited common elements, since the unit owners in the other building have no genuine occasion to utilize them.

5. And if *D* plans additional buildings, provisions must be included for additional additions and subtractions.

As can be seen, this notion was not envisioned when the first condominum statutes were drafted and it makes rather heavy demands upon the traditional common law real property concepts. Nevertheless, it is believed that proper documentation will make the whole thing workable.

§ 810. The add-on-declaration—the general clause.
To set the stage for the transaction, a clause is included in the Declaration of Condominium that spells out the intention to create an "add-on" condominium:

The area comprised within the present development is herein denominated the "Condominium Area." The developer reserves the right to annex to the Condominium Area all or a portion of the land described as follows:

(which area is denominated herein the "Development Area.")

No rights of any character whatever of any unit owner in annexations within the Development Area attach until an amended declaration is filed of record annexing part or all of the Development Area to the condominium hereby created. Upon the recording of such amended declaration the land therein described shall be deemed to be governed in all respects by the provisions of this Declaration of Condominium. The right is reserved to add land to the "Development Area" by a declaration stating such intention and describing the land so added.

---

[1] Reprinted by permission of Fairfield and Woods, of Denver.

This clause accomplishes several purposes: (1) The unit purchasers in Parcel A are given notice that the project can expand and are given notice of the perimeters of the expanded area: (2) All persons are notified that on expansion, the tract, as expanded, is one condominium: (3) Unit purchasers in Parcel A and Parcel B are told to look to a coming Amended Declaration for a definition of their rights in the annexed areas.

§ 811. **The add-on-partial invalidity clause.** As will be seen, the techniques employed are of the "suspenders and belt" variety. Several devices are employed, and it should be made clear that they are supplementary to each other, for example:

> Various provisions of this declaration and deeds and mortgages of the units and common elements contain clauses designed to accomplish a shifting of the common elements. None of said provisions shall invalidate the other, but each shall be deemed supplementary to the other toward the end that a valid shifting of the common elements can be accomplished.

§ 812. **The add-on-power of appointment.** The Declaration states that the deed is deemed to reserve to the developer a power of appointment in favor of unit owners in Parcel B. There appears to be no legal objection to the use of such device. Unit owners in Parcel A take with constructive notice of this power, the consequence of which is to subtract part of their ownership in the common elements. Such a clause is as follows:

> Each deed of a unit shall be deemed to reserve to the developer the power to appoint to unit owners, from time to time, the percentages in the common elements set forth in amended declarations.

§ 813. **The add-on-clause creating a power coupled with an interest.** The developer will retain some fee ownership in both Parcels A and B when the annexation of Parcel B into the condominium takes place. This, it is argued is a sufficient "interest" to qualify under the "power coupled with an interest" rule. The clause giving the developer such a power to shift percentages in the common elements is as follows:

> A power coupled with an interest is hereby granted to _____ as attorney in fact to shift percentages of the common elements in accordance with amended declarations recorded pursuant hereto and each deed of a unit and common elements in the Development (as herein defined) shall be deemed a grant of such power to said attorney in fact.

§ 814. **The add-on-clause estopping the unit owner from contending that the condominium is not a statutory condominium.** The objections to a "common law" condominium are well-known and will not be restated here. Since a great number of people will change position in the belief that a statutory condominium was created, the unit owners and persons claiming under them should be estopped by a clause in the Declaration as follows:

> Each Unit Owner by acceptance of the deed conveying his Unit agrees for himself and all those claiming under him, including mortgagees, and this Declaration is in accordance with the Condominium Property Act.

§ 815. **The add-on-safety-valve easement clause.** Whether or not the condominium is a statutory one, all the unit owners can be guaranteed common law easements for the enjoyment of the common elements by a clause as follows:

Each Unit Owner shall also be entitled to a perpetual easement, appurtenant to said Unit, for the use of the Common Elements in the Condominium Declarations herein mentioned and for the purposes in said Declarations set forth.

§ 816. The add-on-deed provision. The deed provision must be drawn with meticulous care. One suggested clause is as follows:

Together with a percentage of the common elements as set forth in Declaration recorded as Document _____ which percentage shall automatically change in accordance with amended declarations as same are filed of record pursuant to said Condominium Declaration recorded as Document _____ and together with additional common elements as such amended Declarations are filed of record, in the percentages set forth in such amended Declarations, which percentages are hereby conveyed effective on the recording of amended Declarations as though conveyed hereby.

This deed is given on conditional limitation toward the end that the percentage interest of the grantees in the common elements shall be divested *pro tanto* and vest in grantees of other units in accordance with the terms of said Declaration recorded as Document _____ and amended declarations recorded pursuant thereto, and a right of revocation is also reserved to the grantor to accomplish this result.

The acceptance of this conveyance by the grantees shall be deemed an agreement within the contemplation of the Condominium Property Act to a shifting of the common elements pursuant to the Condominium Declaration recorded as Document _____ and to all the other terms of said Declaration, which is incorporated herein by reference thereto, and to all the terms of the amended Declaration recorded pursuant thereto.

Several comments are offered: (1) The deed does not set forth a specific percentage of the common elements, but refers to the original Declaration and amended Declarations for such percentage. The deeds and declarations will be read together, and this should satisfy the statute. The Declaration as to Parcel A sets forth the 4 percent percentage. This is clear as crystal. The amended Declaration when Parcel B comes in states a new percentage, 2 percent, and this again is crystal clear. (2) The deed conveys an after-acquired title in the Parcel B common elements to the unit owners in Parcel A. This is perfectly commonplace. Enurement of title by warranty deeds, by deeds of bargain and sale, by deeds expressing such intention, and by estoppel presents no novelty to the real property owners. (3) The deed creates a conditional limitation. It is quite clear that a deed can state a condition which, if it occurs, can shift title from the grantee to a third person. 28 Am. Jur. 2d *Estates*, § 335. Here the condition that triggers partial divestiture of a percentage of the common elements is the filing of an Amended Declaration bringing in Parcel B. (4) The deed contains a right of revocation. Such a clause is valid. 28 Am. Jur. 2d *Estates*, § 154. Again, we have here another device that enables the developer to reduce the percentages of the common elements in Parcel A when Parcel B is added. The percentage thus revoked back into the developer can be conveyed to the unit owners in Parcel B. (5) Shifting of title under the Statute of Uses is also an additional legal concept utilized here. (6) The shifting is set forth both in the deed and Declaration, so that no unit owner can pretend ignorance of the device. (7) The last paragraph of the deed clause is an effort to utilize the language of some statutes that a changing of the unit percentages can be effected by agreement of the unit owners.

§ 817. The add-on-mortgage clauses. Each mortgage on a unit will need a mortgage clause, somewhat along the following lines:

The lien of this mortgage on the common elements shall be automatically released as to percentages of the common elements set forth in amended declarations filed of record in accordance with the Condominium Declaration recorded as Document _____ and the lien of this mortgage shall automatically attach to additional common elements as such amended declarations are filed of record, in the percentages set forth in such amended declarations, which percentages are hereby conveyed effective on the recording of such amended declarations as though conveyed hereby.

§ 818. The add-on-preservation of lien for common expenses. Once a lien for expenses is assessed to unit owners in Parcel A, it ought not be reduced by addition of Parcel B to the project. Hence, the following clause in the Declaration:

The recording of a Supplemental Condominium Declaration or Consolidated Master Condominium Declaration shall not alter the amount of the lien for expenses assessed to the Unit prior to such recording.

§ 819. The add-on-time limit. The declaration must contain a time limit, because shifting executory interests are subject to the rule against perpetuities. It is best to keep the period short.

§ 820. The add-on—limited common areas. Where the statute permits this, the Declaration and Amended Declaration can provide that when an annexation is made, the facilities physically peculiar to building A shall be limited common elements for the unit owners in that building, and the same for Unit B. In such case, the unit owners would have a greater percentage in the limited common elements than they would have in the general common elements.

§ 821. The add-on "Chinese Menu" approach. A more conservative approach to the problem is the "Chinese Menu" approach. Here the original Declaration lists a percentage of the common elements if no annexation is made. A separate and smaller percentage is set forth in a separate column if Parcel B is added. A third column lists a still smaller percentage if Parcel C is added and the declaration stops there. Each buyer in Unit A knows the smallest percentage to which his percentage in the common elements can be reduced. It has the advantage of certainty but lacks the advantage of flexibility.

References on the add-on: 9 San Diego L.Rev. 28, 41; 9 Law Notes 19; 1970 Law Forum 160; 1 Valp. U. L.Rev. 85; 14 Hastings L. J. 320 (plat approval laws).

§ 822. FHA forms. Some rather basic forms of condo documents are available from HUD: (1) FHA Form 3276-A Enabling Declaration. (2) FHA Form 3281 Management Agreement. (3) FHA Form 3277 By-laws.

§ 823. Condo mortgage forms present difficult problems. A sample form (Form No. 25) follows (reprinted by permission of Equitable Life Assurance Society of the United States):

§ 824. Contract of sale. An Illinois form of contract of sale of a unit in a completed building follows (Form No. 26):

Form No. 25

661-RM701
72-7

CONDOMINIUM DEED OF TRUST

WITH ASSIGNMENT OF RENTS

𝕿𝖍𝖎𝖘 𝕯𝖊𝖊𝖉 𝖔𝖋 𝕿𝖗𝖚𝖘𝖙, made this .... day of ....
19........, between ....
....
hereinafter referred to as, the Trustor, ...
....
hereinafter referred to as, the Trustee, and THE EQUITABLE LIFE ASSURANCE SOCIETY OF THE UNITED STATES, a corporation duly organized and existing under the laws of the State of New York, having its principal office at 1285 Avenue of the Americas, New York, N. Y. 10019, hereinafter referred to as, the Beneficiary,

WITNESSETH: That the Trustor grants, transfers and assigns to the Trustee in trust, with power of sale, that real property in City of .... County of .... and State of .... (said State being hereinafter referred to as, the "State") described as follows:

which described real property does not exceed 3 acres.

AND ALSO, all the estate and interest, homestead or other claim, as well in law as in equity, which the Trustor now has or may hereafter acquire in and to the real property, including but not by way of limitation, the percentage of common elements constituting a part thereof, together with all easements and rights of way used in connection therewith or as a means of access thereto; and all and singular the tenements, hereditaments and appurtenances thereof, including all fixtures and articles of personal property now or at any time hereafter attached to or used in any way in connection with the use, operation and occupation of the real property, and any and all buildings and improvements now or hereafter erected thereon, all of which collectively hereinafter shall be referred to as, the premises. The fixtures and articles of personal property shall include but without being limited to, all window shades, inlaid floor coverings, wall beds, washing machines, dryers, dishwashers, disposals, stoves, ranges, ovens, refrigerators, radiators, and all heating, lighting, plumbing, gas, electric, ventilating, refrigerating, air-conditioning and incinerating fixtures and equipment of whatsoever kind and nature, except household furniture not specifically enumerated herein, and are hereby declared and shall be deemed to be fixtures and accessory to the freehold and a part of the premises as between the parties hereto, their heirs, legatees, devisees, executors, administrators, successors and assigns, and all persons claiming by, through or under them.

AND ALSO, all of the rents, issues and profits of the premises, SUBJECT, HOWEVER, to the right, power and authority hereinafter given to and conferred upon the Beneficiary to collect and apply such rents, issues, and profits.

FOR THE PURPOSE OF SECURING:

ONE: The payment of an indebtedness in the principal sum of ....
.... Dollars ($...........................) with interest thereon according to the terms of a certain Note of even date hereinafter referred to as, the Note, which by reference is hereby made a part hereof, executed by the Trustor, delivered to the Beneficiary and payable to its order, and any and all extensions or renewals thereof.

TWO: The payment of all other sums with interest thereon becoming due or payable under the provisions hereof to either the Trustee or the Beneficiary.

THREE: The performance and discharge of each and every obligation, covenant and agreement of the Trustor herein contained.

To HAVE AND TO HOLD the premises upon the following express trusts, to wit:

A. TO PROTECT THE SECURITY OF THIS DEED OF TRUST THE TRUSTOR AGREES:

1. To keep the premises in good condition and repair; not to remove or demolish any building or improvement erected thereon; to complete or restore promptly and in good and workmanlike manner any building or improvement which may be constructed, damaged or destroyed thereon, and to pay when due all claims for labor performed and materials furnished therefor; not to suffer any lien of mechanics or material men to attach to the premises; to comply with all laws affecting the premises or requiring any alterations or improvements to be made thereon; not to commit, suffer or permit waste thereof, or any act upon the premises in violation of law or of any covenants, conditions or restrictions affecting the premises; to cultivate, irrigate, fertilize, fumigate, prune and do all other acts which from the character or use of the premises may be reasonably necessary, the specific enumerations herein not excluding the general.

2. To promptly, upon receipt thereof, deliver to the Beneficiary a true copy of every notice of default received by the Trustor with regard to any obligation of the Trustor under the provisions of the Condominium Act of the State, (the "Condominium Act"); the Declaration of Condominium (the "Declaration"); the Rules and Regulations (the "Rules and Regulations"); or the By-Laws (the "By-Laws") adopted by any organization or corporation created to facilitate the administration and operation of the Condominium of which the premises form a part (the "Association").

3. To keep and perform all covenants, agreements and provisions in the Declaration, By-Laws and Rules and Regulations on the part of the Trustor to be kept and performed, and failure of the Trustor so to do within a period of thirty (30) days after notice from the Association or from the Trustee or Beneficiary, or in the case of such default which cannot with due diligence be cured or remedied within such thirty (30) day period, if Trustor fails to proceed promptly after such notice to cure and remedy the same with due diligence, such failure shall constitute a default hereunder.

4. That if any action or proceeding be commenced either at law or in equity purporting to affect the security hereof (except an action to foreclose this Deed of Trust or to collect the debt secured thereby), to which action or proceeding the Beneficiary of this Deed of Trust is made a party, or in which it becomes necessary to defend or uphold the lien of this Deed of Trust, or in which it may be necessary or proper to prove the amount of the indebtedness, the Beneficiary may appear in or defend any such action or proceeding; and in any such event, the Beneficiary may be allowed and paid; and the Trustor hereby agrees to pay all costs, charges, disbursements and fees, including the cost of evidence of title, as well as reasonable attorneys' fees, incurred in any such action or proceeding in which the Beneficiary may appear; and all such sums and the interest thereon, at the highest rate permitted by applicable law, shall be a lien on the premises, prior to any right or title to, interest in or claim upon the premises, attaching or accruing subsequent to the lien of this Deed of Trust, and shall be deemed to be secured by this Deed of Trust and by the Note which it secures. In any action or proceeding to foreclose this Deed of Trust, or to recover or collect the debt secured thereby, the provisions of law respecting the recovery of costs, disbursements and allowances shall prevail unaffected by this covenant.

5. To pay as the same become due and payable: All taxes and assessments affecting the premises, including assessments on appurtenant water stock; all taxes upon the debt secured hereby; all incumbrances, charges and liens, with interest, on the premises or any part thereof, which appear to be prior or superior hereto, and all costs, fees and expenses of this Trust, and to deposit with the Beneficiary, all receipts or other satisfactory evidence of the payment of taxes, assessments, charges, claims and liens of every nature affecting or which may affect the premises or any part thereof; also for any statement regarding the indebtedness secured hereby, any amount demanded by the Beneficiary not to exceed the maximum allowed by law at the time such request is made.

6. That should the Trustor fail to make any payment or to do any act as herein, or in the Declaration or By-Laws, provided, then the Beneficiary or the Trustee, but without obligation to do so and without notice to or demand upon the Trustor and without releasing the Trustor from any obligation hereof, may: Make or do the same in such manner and to such extent as either may deem necessary to protect the security hereof, including specifically, without limiting their general powers, the right to pay any and all rents, taxes and assessments affecting the premises, including, but not by way of limitation, all payments to the maintenance and reserve funds and all assessments as required by the Declaration or By-Laws or any resolution adopted by the Association pursuant to either thereof and including assessments on appurtenant water stock and taxes upon the debt secured hereby, as the same become due and payable, and, also, the right to make additions, alterations, repairs and improvements to the premises which they or either of them may consider necessary or proper to keep the premises in good condition and repair, the Beneficiary or the Trustee being authorized to enter the premises for such purposes; pay, purchase, contest or compromise any encumbrance, charge or lien which in the judgment of either appears to be prior or superior hereto; and, in exercising any such powers, pay, necessary expenses, employ counsel and pay his reasonable fees.

7. The Trustor shall not, except with the prior written consent of the Beneficiary: (a) institute any action or proceeding for partition of the property of which the premises are a part; (b) vote for or consent to any modification of, amendment to or relaxation in the enforcement of any provision of the Declaration or By-Laws; and (c) in the event of damage to or destruction of the property of which the premises are a part, vote in opposition to a motion to repair, restore or rebuild.

8. To pay immediately and without demand all sums so expended by the Beneficiary or the Trustee, pursuant to Clause A.6. above, with interest from date of expenditure at the highest rate permitted by applicable law.

B. IT IS MUTUALLY AGREED THAT:

1. The Association will at all times, while any of the indebtedness secured hereby remains unpaid, keep or cause to be kept insured the units (including the premises) and the common elements, now or hereafter constituting the condominium project, of which the premises form a part, against such hazards and in such amounts, in such form or forms of policies and with such endorsements thereon, all as specified in the Declaration and By-Laws, and in companies selected by the Association, authorized to do business in the State, and will pay or cause to be paid the premiums thereon at the time and place the same are payable, and, at the option of the Beneficiary, will deposit true copies of such policies and renewals thereof with the Beneficiary. In the event the Association or the Trustor fails or refuses to provide the said insurance coverage, and the evidence thereof, as above required, the Beneficiary or the Trustee, but without obligation to do so, and at the expense of the Trustor, may take out fire insurance with extended coverage, vandalism and malicious mischief endorsements, covering the premises for its benefit as Beneficiary, and may add the premium therefor to the unpaid balance of the indebtedness secured hereby. All casualty insurance policies shall have a Standard Mortgagee Clause attached, modified to provide that the insurance proceeds shall be payable to the Association or to an Insurance

Trustee, as provided by the Declaration, and such insurance policies shall provide that they shall not be cancelled without at least 10 days prior written notice to the Beneficiary. In the event of loss or damage to the units or the common elements or any part thereof, the Trustor will give immediate written notice to the Beneficiary, who may make proof of loss if not made promptly by the Association. The proceeds of any such insurance shall be applied, subject to and in pursuance of the provisions of the Declaration and By-Laws, on account of the cost of rebuilding or repairing the units and common elements damaged or destroyed, provided the proceeds of insurance collectible by the Association or the Insurance Trustee are sufficient to pay for such rebuilding or repairing, or, if insufficient, the deficiency is furnished by the unit owners, otherwise, or in the event the unit owners elect not to restore the damaged property, such insurance proceeds, to the extent payable to the Beneficiary and the Trustor, shall be applied to the indebtedness secured hereby. If the Trustor shall procure any other insurance of the kind herein described, the same, even though not required hereunder to be carried by the Trustor, shall be made payable to and claimable only by the Beneficiary and, whether so made payable or not, may be recovered by the Beneficiary in any appropriate proceedings and shall be similarly applied. In the event of foreclosure of this Trust Deed or other transfer of title to the premises in extinguishment of the debt secured hereby, all right, title and interest of the Trustor in and to any insurance policies then in force shall pass to the purchaser or assignee. The Trustor or the Association is free to procure the required insurance from any insurance company authorized to do business in the State.

2.   Any award for damages now or hereafter made in connection with any condemnation of the units (including the premises) or the common elements or any part thereof now or hereafter constituting the Condominium project, of which the premises form a part, for public use and any award or damages arising from any cause of action for injury or damages to the said units or the common elements, whether or not the Trustor shall be in default hereunder, is hereby assigned and shall be paid to the Beneficiary and applied by the Beneficiary upon any indebtedness secured hereby in such order as Beneficiary may determine, subject, however, to the prior right of the Association or the Insurance Trustee to receive and use such award for the restoration of the said units or the common elements pursuant to the Declaration and By-Laws. The Trustor agrees to execute such further assignments of any such awards or damages as the Beneficiary may require.

3.   By accepting payment of any sums secured hereby after its due date, the Beneficiary does not waive its right either to require prompt payment, when due, of all other sums so secured or to declare default for failure so to pay.

4.   Without affecting the liability of any person, including the Trustor, for the payment of any indebtedness secured hereby or the lien of this Deed of Trust upon the premises for the full amount of the indebtedness then remaining unpaid (other than any person or property specifically released by the Beneficiary), the Beneficiary may, at any time, or from time to time and without notice do any one or more of the following: Release any person now or hereafter liable for payment of such indebtedness or any part thereof; extend the time or otherwise alter the terms of payment of any indebtedness; accept additional security therefor of any kind; or substitute or release any property securing such indebtedness.

5.   At any time or from time to time, without liability therefor and without notice, upon written request of the Beneficiary and presentation of this Deed of Trust and the Note for endorsement, and without affecting the personal liability of any person for payment of the indebtedness secured hereby, the Trustee may: Reconvey any part of the premises; consent to the making of any map or plat thereof; join in granting any easement thereon; or join in any extension agreement or any agreement subordinating the lien or charge hereof.

6.   Upon written request of the Beneficiary stating that all sums secured hereby have been paid, and upon surrender of this Deed of Trust and the Note to the Trustee for cancellation and retention and upon payment of its fees, the Trustee shall reconvey, without warranty, the premises then held hereunder. The recitals in such reconveyance of any matters or facts shall be conclusive proof of the truthfulness thereof. The grantee in such reconveyance may be described as "the person or persons legally entitled thereto."

7.   As additional security for the indebtedness secured hereby and for the performance of all other obligations of the Trustor hereunder, the Trustor hereby gives to and confers upon the Beneficiary the right, power and authority, during the continuance of these Trusts, to collect the rents, issues and profits of and otherwise deal with the premises, as hereinafter in this paragraph provided, reserving to the Trustor the right, prior to any default by the Trustor in the payment of any indebtedness secured hereby or in the performance of any agreement hereunder, to collect and retain such rents, issues and profits as they become due and payable. Upon or at any time after any default, the Beneficiary, at its option, without notice, and irrespective of whether Declaration of Default has been delivered to the Trustee and without regard to the adequacy of security for the indebtedness hereby secured, either in person or by agent with or without bringing any action or proceeding, or by a receiver to be appointed by a court, may enter upon, take possession of, manage and operate the premises, or any part thereof; make, cancel, enforce or modify leases; obtain and evict tenants, and fix or modify rents and do any acts which the Beneficiary deems proper to protect the security hereof, and either with or without taking possession of the premises, in its own name, sue for or otherwise collect and receive such rents, issues and profits, including those past due and unpaid, and apply the same, less costs and expenses of operations and collection, including reasonable attorneys' fees, upon any indebtedness secured hereby, and in such order as the Beneficiary may determine. The entering upon and taking possession of the premises, the collection of such rents, issues and profits and the application thereof as aforesaid, shall not cure or waive any default or notice of default hereunder or invalidate any act done pursuant to such notice.

8.   In the event of the passage, after the date of this Deed of Trust, of any law of the State, deducting from the value of the premises for the purpose of taxation any lien or charge thereon, or changing in any way the laws for the taxation of deeds of trust, or debts secured by deeds of trust, for state or local purposes, or the manner of the collection of any such taxes, so as to affect this Deed of Trust, the Beneficiary at its option may, at any time after the expiration of 30 days from and after the effective date of any such law, declare all sums secured hereby immediately due and payable by the execution and delivery to the Trustee of a written declaration of default and demand for sale, whereupon all sums secured hereby shall become and be immediately due and payable.

9.   Upon default by the Trustor in the payment of any indebtedness secured hereby or in the performance of any agreement hereunder, or upon failure of the Association to maintain fire and extended coverage insurance as above required, or upon failure of the Association to keep the common elements in good condition and repair, the Beneficiary may declare all sums secured hereby immediately due and payable by delivery to the Trustee of a written declaration of default and demand for sale, and the Trustee or the Beneficiary shall thereafter file or

cause to be filed for record a notice of such default and of election to cause the premises to be sold. The Beneficiary also shall deposit with the Trustee this Deed of Trust, the Note and all documents evidencing expenditure secured hereby.

Notice of sale having been given as then required by law and 3 months having elapsed after recordation of such notice of default, the Trustee, without demand on the Trustor, shall sell the premises at the time and place of sale fixed by it in the notice of sale, either as a whole or in separate parcels and in such order as it may determine, at public auction to the highest bidder for cash in lawful money of the United States, payable at the time of sale. The Trustee may postpone the sale of the premises by public announcement at such time and place of sale, and from time to time thereafter may postpone such sale by public announcement at the time fixed by the preceding postponement. The Trustee shall deliver to such purchaser its Deed conveying the premises so sold, but without any covenant or warranty, express or implied. The recitals in such Deed of any matters or facts shall be conclusive proof of the truthfulness thereof. Any person, including the Trustor, the Trustee or the Beneficiary as hereinafter defined, may purchase the premises at such sale.

After deducting all costs, fees and expenses of the Trustee and of this Deed of Trust, including the cost of evidence of title in connection with the sale, the Trustee shall apply the proceeds of the sale to the payment of: All sums expended under the terms hereof, not then repaid, with accrued interest at the highest rate permitted by applicable law; all other sums then secured hereby, and the remainder, if any, to the person or persons legally entitled thereto.

10. In the event of any default hereunder, the provisions contained in the foregoing subparagraph B.7. and B.9. shall not be construed to preclude the Trustee or the Beneficiary from enforcing any appropriate remedy against the Trustor, or from proceeding by suit to foreclose, or by suits at law or in equity to enforce payment of all sums secured hereby as the Trustee may elect or as the Trustee may be advised.

11. The Beneficiary may at any time or from time to time substitute in such manner as may be provided by law a successor or successors to any Trustee named herein or acting hereunder, which successor-Trustee shall thereupon succeed, without conveyance from the Trustee-predecessor, to all of its powers, duties, authority and title; or in the event of the absence of any such law providing for the substitution of trustees in deeds of trust, the Beneficiary may, with like effect, make such substitution from time to time by instrument in writing executed and acknowledged by the Beneficiary and recorded in the office of the Recorder of the county or counties in which the premises are situated. Said instrument shall contain the date of the execution of this Deed of Trust, the name of the original Trustor, the Trustee and the Beneficiary, the book and page where this Deed of Trust is recorded, and the name of the new Trustee.

12. Except insofar as now or hereafter prohibited by law the right to plead, use, or assert any statute of limitations as a plea or defense or bar of any kind, or for any purpose, to any debt, demand, or obligation secured or to be secured hereby, or to any complaint or other pleading or proceeding filed, instituted, or maintained for the purpose of enforcing this Deed of Trust, or any rights thereunder, is hereby waived.

13. The invalidity of any one or more covenants, phrases, clauses, sentences or paragraphs of this Deed of Trust shall not affect the remaining portions or any part thereof, and this Deed of Trust shall be construed as if such invalid covenants, phrases, clauses, sentences or paragraphs, if any, had not been inserted herein.

14. The trusts hereby created shall be irrevocable by the Trustor.

15. This Deed of Trust applies to, inures to the benefit of, and binds all parties hereto, their heirs, legatees, devisees, executors, administrators, successors and assigns. The term, Beneficiary, means the original Beneficiary hereunder or any future owner and holder, including pledgees, of the Note secured hereby. In this Deed of Trust, whenever the context so requires, the masculine gender includes the feminine and/or neuter, and the singular number includes the plural. All obligations of each Trustor hereunder are joint and several.

16. If the State is a "community property" state and if this Deed of Trust and the Note are executed by a married woman, and if such Deed of Trust describes any community property of such married woman and her husband, and if all sums secured by this Deed of Trust are not paid in full out of the proceeds of the Trustee's sale, or otherwise, such undersigned married woman hereby assents to the liability of her separate property for any unpaid balance of all sums secured by this Deed of Trust, subject, however, to any limitation or restriction now provided by law upon the recovery of a deficiency judgment following a sale under a purchase money deed of trust, and upon the further express condition that such assent shall not be deemed to create a present or any lien, charge, or obligation upon such separate property, and that such property can be resorted to in satisfaction of such unpaid balance only by attachment, execution or other legal process.

17. The Trustee accepts this Deed of Trust, duly executed and acknowledged, when it is made a public record as provided by law. The Trustee is not obligated to notify any party hereto of pending sale under any other deed of trust or of any action or proceeding in which the Trustor, the Beneficiary or the Trustee shall be a party unless brought by the Trustee.

18. The Beneficiary may release for such consideration, or none, as it may require, any portion of the premises without, as to the remainder of the security, in anywise impairing or affecting the lien and priorities herein provided for the Beneficiary or improving the position of any subordinate lienholder.

19. Provided, however, that upon the payment of the indebtedness secured hereby and the performance of all the covenants and conditions contained herein and in the Note, the Beneficiary will execute and deliver to the Trustor a request to the Trustee to reconvey the premises to the Trustor. It is understood, however, that all recording and other expenses incurred in effecting such reconveyance shall be borne by the Trustor.

C. THE INSERTION BY THE TRUSTOR of his mailing address opposite his signature hereto shall be deemed to be a request by the Trustor that a copy of any notice of default and of any notice of sale hereunder be mailed to him at such address as provided by law.

MAILING ADDRESS FOR NOTICES			SIGNATURE OF TRUSTOR
Street and Number	City	State	
....	....	....	....
....	....	....	....
....	....	....	....

Form No. 26
Real Estate Sale Contract

1. _____

agrees to purchase at a price of $_____ (Purchaser)
described in Exhibit A attached hereto in _____ County, Illinois. on the terms set forth herein, the real estate
(If legal description is not included herein at time of execution, _____ *is*
authorized to insert it thereafter.)
commonly known as unit _____ at _____ together with its undivided interest in the common elements, and
with approximate unit dimensions of _____ x _____, together with the following personal property presently located thereon:
(strike items not applicable) (a) strom and screen doors and windows; (b) wall-to-wall, hallway and stair carpeting; (c) window shades and draperies and
supporting fixtures; (d) venetian blinds; (e) electric, plumbing and other attached fixtures as installed; (f) water softener; (g) refrigerator(s); (h)_____
_____ range(s); and also

2. _____
_____ (Seller)
(Insert names of all owners and their respective spouses)
agrees to sell the real estate and the property, if any, described above at the price and terms set forth herein, and to convey or cause to be conveyed to
Purchaser or nominee title thereto (in joint tenancy) by a recordable _____ deed, with release of dower and homestead rights, and
a proper bill of sale, subject only to: (a) covenants, conditions and restrictions of record, terms, provisions, covenants, and conditions, of the Declaration
of Condominium and all amendments, if any, thereto; (b) private, public and utility easements including any easements established by or implied from the
Declaration of Condominium or amendments thereto, if any, and roads and highways, if any; (c) encroachments, if any; (d) party wall rights and agreements, if any; (e) existing leases and tenancies; (f) limitations and conditions imposed by the Condominium Property Act; (g) special taxes or assessments
for improvements not yet completed; (h) installments not due at the date hereof or any special tax or assessment for improvements heretofore completed;
(i) mortgage or trust deed specified below, if any; (j) general taxes for the year_____ and subsequent years including taxes which may accrue by
reason of new or additional improvements during the years (s) _____ . (k) installments due after the date of closing of assessments established
pursuant to the Declaration of Condominium; and to_____
3. Purchaser has paid $_____ (and will pay within _____ days the additional sum of $_____) as earnest money to be
applied on the purchase price, and agrees to pay or satisfy the balance of the purchase price, plus or minus prorations, at the time of closing as follows:
(strike subparagraph not applicable)

(a) The payment of $_____
(b) The acceptance of the title to the real estate by Purchaser subject to a mortgage (trust deed) of record securing a principal indebtedness (which the
    Purchaser [does] [does not] agree to assume aggregating $_____ bearing interest at the rate of_____ % a year, and the
    payment of a sum which represents the difference between the amount due on the indebtedness at the time of closing and the balance of the pur-
    chase price.

4. This contract is subject to the condition that Purchaser be able to procure within _____ days a firm commitment for a loan to be secured by a
mortgage or trust deed on the real estate in the amount of $_____ . or such lesser sum as Purchaser accepts, with interest not to exceed
_____ % a year to be amortized over_____ years, the commission and service charges for such loan not to exceed_____ %. If, after making
every reasonable effort, Purchaser is unable to procure such commitment within the time specified herein and so notified Seller thereof within that time,
this contract shall become null and void and all earnest money shall be returned to Purchaser, provided that if Seller, at his option, within a like period of
time following Purchaser's notice, procures for Purchaser such a commitment or notifies Purchaser that Seller will accept a purchase money mortgage
upon the same terms, this contract shall remain in full force and effect. *(Strike paragraph if inapplicable.)*
5. This contract is subject to the condition that Seller be able to procure release or waiver of any option of first refusal or other preemptive rights of
purchase created by the Declaration of Condominium within the time established by said Declaration. If, after making every reasonable effort, Seller
cannot procure such release or waiver within the time provided and so notifies the Purchaser thereof within that time, this contract shall become null and
void and all earnest money shall be returned to Purchaser; provided that if said option or pre-emptive right is not exercised within the time established
by the Declaration of Condominium, this contract shall remain in force and effect for that period of time which the Declaration of Condominium provides for completion of the sale should the option or pre-emptive right not be exercised. If the Declaration of Condominium contains no such option pro-
pre-emptive right, this clause shall be null and void and no part of this contract.
6. The time of closing shall be on_____ . or 20 days after notice that financing has been procured if the above paragraph 4 is
operative, or on the date, if any, to which such time is extended by reason of paragraph 2 of the Conditions and Stipulations hereafter becoming operative
(whichever date is later) or if paragraph 5 above becomes operative, as mutually agreed, unless subsequently mutually agreed otherwise, at the office of
_____ or of the mortgage lender, if any, provided title is shown to be good or is accepted by Purchaser.
7. Seller shall deliver possession to Purchaser on or before_____days after the sale has been closed. Seller agrees to pay Purchaser the sum of
$_____for each day Seller remains in possession between the time of closing and the time possession is delivered.
8. If and when purchase price is received by Seller from Purchaser or through exercise of pre-emptive option, Seller agrees to pay a broker's commission
to_____
in the amount set forth in the broker's listing contract or as follows: _____
9. The earnest money shall be held by _____
for the mutual benefit of the parties.
10. Seller agrees to deliver possession of the real estate in the same condition as it is at the date of this contract, ordinary wear and tear excepted.
11. A duplicate original of this contract, duly executed by the Seller and his spouse, if any, shall be delivered to the Purchasers within_____days
from the date below, otherwise, at the Purchaser's option, this contract shall become null and void and the earnest money shall be refunded to the
Purchaser.

This contract is subject to the Conditions and Stipulations set forth on the back page hereof, which Conditions and Stipulations are made a part of this
contract.

Dated _____

Purchaser _____ (Address) _____

Purchaser _____ (Address) _____

Seller_____ (Address) _____

Seller_____ (Address) _____
*Form normally used for sale of residential condominium unit other than unit in a building under construction or conversion.

CONDITIONS AND STIPULATIONS

1. Seller shall deliver or cause to be delivered to Purchaser or Purchaser's agent, not less than 5 days prior to the time of closing, a title commitment for an owner's title insurance policy issued by the Chicago Title Insurance Company in the amount of the purchase price, covering title to the real estate on or after the date hereof, showing title in the intended grantor subject only to (a) the general exceptions contained in the policy, (b) the title exceptions set forth above, and (c) title exceptions pertaining to liens or encumbrances of a definite or ascertainable amount which may be removed by the payment of money at the time of closing and which the Seller may so remove at that time by using the funds to be paid upon the delivery of the deed (all of which are herein referred to as the permitted exceptions). The title commitment shall be conclusive evidence of good title as therein shown as to all matters insured by the policy, subject only to the exceptions as therein stated. Seller also shall furnish Purchaser a statement from the Board of Managers, treasurer, or managing agent of the condominium certifying payment of assessments for condominium common expenses; and if applicable, proof of waiver or termination of any right of first refusal or similar options contained in the Declaration of Condominium together with any other documents required by the Declaration of Condominium or by-laws thereof as a pre-condition to the transfer of ownership, and an affidavit of title in customary form covering the date of closing and showing title in Seller subject only to the permitted exceptions in foregoing items (b) and (c) and unpermitted exceptions, if any, as to which the title insurer commits to extend insurance in the manner specified in paragraph 2 below.

2. If the title commitment discloses unpermitted exceptions, Seller shall have 30 days from the date of delivery thereof to have the exceptions removed from the commitment or to have the title insurer commit to insure against loss or damage that may be occasioned by such exceptions, and, in such event, the time of closing shall be 35 days after delivery of the commitment or the time specified in paragraph 6 on the front page hereof, whichever is later. If Seller fails to have the exceptions removed, or in the alternative, to obtain the commitment for title insurance specified above as to such exceptions within the specified time, Purchaser may terminate this contract or may elect, upon notice to Seller within 10 days after the expiration of the 30-day period, to take title as it then is with the right to deduct from the purchase price liens or encumbrances of a definite or ascertainable amount. If Purchaser does not so elect, this contract shall become null and void without further actions of the parties.

3. Rents, water and other utility charges, fuels, prepaid service contracts, general taxes, accrued interest on mortgage indebtedness, if any, and other similar items shall be adjusted ratably as of the time of closing. If the amount of the current general taxes is not then ascertainable, the adjustment thereof except for that amount which may accrue by reason of new or additional improvements shall be on the basis of the amount of the most recent ascertainable taxes. The amount of any general taxes which may accrue by reason of new or additional improvements shall be adjusted on the basis of_____.

All prorations are final unless provided otherwise herein. Existing leases, if any, shall then be assigned to Purchaser. Seller shall pay the amount of any stamp tax imposed by law on the transfer of title, and shall furnish a completed Real Estate Transfer Declaration signed by the Seller or the Seller's agent in the form required pursuant to the Real Estate Transfer Tax Act of the State of Illinois, and shall fulfill the requirements of any local ordinance with regard to a transfer or transaction tax.

4. The provisions of the Uniform Vendor and Purchaser Risk Act of the State of Illinois shall be applicable to this contract.

5. If this contract is terminated without Purchaser's fault, the earnest money shall be returned to the Purchaser, but if the termination is caused by the Purchaser's fault, then at the option of the Seller and upon notice to the Purchaser, the earnest money shall be forfeited to the Seller and applied first to the payment of Seller's expenses and then to payment of broker's commission; the balance, if any, to be retained by the Seller as liquidated damages.

6. At the election of Seller or Purchaser upon notice to the other party not less than 5 days prior to the time of closing, this sale shall be closed through an escrow with Chicago Title and Trust Company, in accordance with the general provisions of the usual form of Deed and Money Escrow Agreement then in use by Chicago Title and Trust Company, with such special provisions inserted in the escrow agreement as may be required to conform with this contract. Upon the creation of such an escrow, anything herein to the contrary notwithstanding, payment of purchase price and delivery of deed shall be made through the escrow and this contract and the earnest money shall be deposited in the escrow. The cost of the escrow shall be divided equally between Seller and Purchaser. *(Strike paragraphs if inapplicable.)*

7. Time is of the essence of this contract.

8. All notices herein required shall be in writing and shall be served on the parties at the addresses following their signatures. The mailing of a notice by registered or certified mail, return receipt requested, shall be sufficient service.

References on condominiums: 7 ABA Real Prop. Prob. & Tr. J. 7; 1965 ABA Real Prop. J. 19; 34 Ala. Law 28, 45; 17 Ala. L.Rev. 375; 31 Albany L.Rev. 32; 15 Am. U. L.Rev. 255 (D.C.); 19 Bus. Law 233; 44 B.U. L.Rev. 137; 42 Conn. B. J. 144; 63 Columb. L.Rev. 987; 2 Conn. L.Rev. 1; 4 Conn. L.Rev. 669; 11 De Paul L.Rev. 319; 13 *id.* 117; 40 Ind. L. J. 57; 13 Kan. L.Rev. 543; 51 Ky. L. J. 46; 14 Hastings L. J. 263, 309; 21 Hastings L. J. 243; 1 Houston L.Rev. 226; 14 Hastings L. J. 189; 10 La. B. J. 215; 23 Mercer L.Rev. 405; 51 Mich. S.B.J. 371; 43 Mich. S.B.J. 13; 51 Mich. S.B.J. 371 (representing the purchaser); 44 Miss. L. J. 261; 29 Mo. L.Rev. 238; 44 Neb. L.Rev. 658; 44 N. D. L.Rev. 345; 39 Okla. B. J. 939; 11 Prac. Law 35; 38 St. John's L.Rev. 1; 17 S. C. L.Rev. 335; 36 So. Calif. L.Rev. 351; 15 S. D. L.Rev. 423; 17 Stan. L.Rev. 842; 29 Tex. B. J. 731; 41 Title News 2, 28; 47 Title News 83; 37 Tul. L.Rev. 482; 1 Tulsa L. J. 73; 33 U. Cin. L.Rev. 463; 36 U. Colo. L.Rev. 451; 17 U. Fla. L.Rev. 1; 1970 U. Ill. L. F. 157; 1 Val. U. L.Rev. 77; 5 L Va. L.Rev. 961; 7 Wake Forest L.Rev. 355; 46 Wash. L.Rev. 147; 15 Western Rev. L.Rev. 597; 2 Williamette L. J. 434.

Texts: Clurman and Hebard, *Condominiums and Cooperatives* (1970); Lippman, *Condominium Development* (2d ed. 1972 PLI); Goldstein, *Cooperatives & Condominiums* (PLI 1969); Rohan and Reskin, *Condominium Law and Practice.*

Development and Finance of Condominiums (PLI Real Estate Law and Practice Course Handbook Series No. 88).

Commercial and industrial Condominiums (PLI Real Estate Law and Practice Course Handbook Series No. 76).

Structuring an Incremental Residential Condominium, The Practical Lawyer, Oct. 1974, page 11.

42

Representations and Warranties

§ **825. In general.** In the large-scale transaction, numerous representations and warranties are exacted of *R*. Some are legal in nature, such as those to the effect that as a foreign corporation it is in good standing in the state of its incorporation. Others are factual, such as the representation that *R* knows of no threatened litigation with neighbors or others or of plans to condemn the property. As to legal representations these might run along the following lines.

The company represents and warrants as follows:

Corporate Organization and Power. The Company (a) is a corporation duly organized, validly existing and in good standing under the laws of Delaware; (b) is duly qualified at the time of the Closing as a foreign corporation to do business in each state in which a Property is located; (c) has the corporate power to acquire, own, lease and give a lien and security interest on and in the property constituting the Mortgaged Property as defined in the Mortgage, and to engage in the transactions contemplated by this Agreement; and (d) has the full power, authority and legal right to execute and deliver this Agreement, the Notes, the Mortgage, the Leases and the Assignment and to perform and observe the terms and provisions of such instruments.

Capital Stock and Liabilities. The Company has no liabilities except as contemplated by this Agreement. The Company's assets are not less than its liabilities, both determined in accordance with generally accepted accounting principles, and the Company is solvent.

Litigation-Taxes. There are no actions, suits or proceedings pending or, to the knowledge of the Company, threatened against or affecting the Company at law or in equity before any court or administrative officer or agency which might result in any material adverse change in the business or financial condition of the Company. The Company is not in default (a) in the payment of any taxes levied or assessed against it or any of its assets or (b) under an applicable statute, rule, order, decree, writ, injunction or regulation of any governmental body (including any court).

Compliance with Other Instruments. The Company is not a party to any contract or agreement or subject to any charter or corporate restriction or to any order, rule, regulation, writ, injunction or decree of any court or governmental authority or to any statute which materially and adversely affects its business, property, assets, or financial condition. Neither the execution, delivery or performance of this Agreement, the Notes, the Mortgage, the Leases or the Assignment, nor compliance with the terms and provisions hereof and thereof, conflicts or will conflict with or results or will result in a breach of any of the terms, conditions or provisions of the charter documents or by-laws of the Company, or of any law, or of any order, writ, injunction or decree of any court or governmental authority, or of any agreement or instrument to which the Company is a party or by which it is bound, or constitute a default thereunder, or result in the creation or imposition of any lien, charge or encumbrance upon any of its property pursuant to the terms of any such agreement or instrument, except the lien and security interest created, and as permitted, by the Mortgage.

Governmental Authorization. No authorization, consent, or approval of any governmental authority is required for the execution and delivery of this Agreement, the Notes, the Mortgage, the Leases or the Assignment. If, on the Closing Date, any such authorization, consent or approval shall be required, the same shall have been obtained or made on or prior to the Closing Date.

Events of Default. No event has occurred and is continuing which would constitute an Event of Default under, and as defined in, the Mortgage or would constitute such an Event of Default but for the requirement that notice be given or that a period of time elapse, or both.

Obligations to the Lessee. The Company has no unsatisfied obligations of the Lessee or any other person except those arising out of or incurred in connection with the acquisition by the Company of any Property.

Appraised Value of Properties. The Appraised Value of each Property is as specified in Schedule B to the Lease covering such Property.

§ 826. Seller's representations and warranties. A clause relating to seller's representations and warranties is as follows:

Seller represents and warrants to and covenants with the Buyer as follows:

(a) The zoning classification of the premises is _____ and the present buildings, structures, improvemements and uses are in compliance with all zoning laws, other laws and ordinances, rules and regulations applicable thereto.

(b) All required certificates of occupancy, underwriters certificates relating to electrical work and zoning, building, housing, safety, fire and health approvals and all other permits necessary to operate the premises have been issued and will be assigned, where appropriate, to Buyer at settlement.

(c) The first mortgage held by _____ is not, and will not be at settlement hereunder, in default in any respect, and there are, and there will be no notice of breach of covenant requests or correspondence from the mortgagee which are uncomplied with. Amounts of payment and the time for such payments under said mortgage shall not be modified, altered, changed, or in any way amended prior to the date of settlement hereunder. All installments of principal and interest payable prior to the date of settlement, pursuant to the provisions of the mortgage and mortgage note, will have been paid strictly in accordance with said provision through midnight of the day prior to the date of settlement or allowance made therefore at the time of settlement. The present balance as of the date of this Agreement on said mortgage is $_____. The copy of said mortgage which is attached hereto as Exhibit _____, is a true and correct copy of said mortgage and there are no other agreements, amendments or modifications affecting the terms thereof.

(d) Seller agrees to assign, without additional cost to Buyer, Seller's interest in all guarantees and warranties from any contractors, subcontractors or suppliers covering any items of personal property or portions of the improvements placed in or on the premises where he is unable to transfer the document containing said guarantees and warranties.

(e) No assessments for unpaid public improvements have been made against the premises. Seller covenants that if any work for public improvements, including but not limited to, streets, curbing, sidewalks, sewer, water, electric, gas lines was begun before the date hereof, Seller shall be responsible for the total assessments and charges that will be made against the premises for the said work when completed. Seller knows of no public improvements which have been ordered to be made and which have not heretofore been completed, assessed and paid for.

(f) All covenants contained in all leases to be performed by Seller or lessor by the date of settlement hereunder will be fully performed and paid for and at the time of settlement no tenant will have any right of set-off or counterclaim. Except as set forth in Exhibit _____ all leases shall be in full force and effect at the time of settlement. Exhibit _____ also contains a full and complete list of all tenancies in existence at the execution of this Agreement, as well as a complete list of all notices received by the Seller as of the date of this Agreement from tenants now in possession indicating their desire to terminate their leases. There are no rights of use or occupancy for any portions of the premises now in effect or hereafter to come into effect except for the tenancies under the leases listed in Exhibit _____. The information set forth in Exhibit _____ as to names of the tenants, the space leases, the terms and rentals, is true and correct. Except to the extent set forth in Exhibit _____, no lease has been extended or amended, no lessee has any right to renew or extend the term of its lease and there are no sums to be credited to any lessee by reason of alterations, rental allowances, reductions in rent or for free rental periods. No modifications, changes or amendments will be made to any leases after the date of this Agreement. No brokers or other intermediaries are entitled to receive leasing brokerage or other compensation out of or with respect to rents accruing under the leases listed in Exhibit _____ and no future leases will make provisions therefore. No tenant is in arrears, and all rental payments are current, except as set forth in Exhibit _____. All decorating and alteration work which the Seller under any lease affecting any part of the Premises may be contractually obligated to perform for any tenant has been performed or will be performed prior to the date of settlement at the cost of Seller. All items of personalty included in this sale are listed on Exhibit _____ and are owned by the Seller free and clear of any conditional bills of sale, chattel mortgages, financing statements, security agreements, or other security instruments of any kind. All leases affecting the premises have been exhibited to Buyer together with any modifications or amendments thereto and same shall be made available to Buyer upon Buyer's request between the date of execution of this Agreement and the date of settlement.

(g) Attached hereto as Exhibit _____ is a Statement of Profit and Loss prepared by _____ in accordance with generally accepted accounting principles consistently maintained, through the years 19___, and 19___, showing all income and expenses relating to the operation of the premises for that period, which statements are true and correct in all respects and present fairly the results of operation of the premises for the period covered.

(h) All public utilities required for the operation of the premises either enter the premises through adjoining public streets and/or highways, or if they pass through adjoining private land do so in accordance with valid public easements or private easements which will inure to the benefit of the Buyer at settlement.

(i) There is no litigation or proceeding pending or, to Seller's knowledge threatened against or relating to the premises or any part thereof, nor does Seller know or have reason to know any basis for any such action other than possible claims adequately covered by insurance and routine action by the landlord against the tenant.

(j) Seller has no knowledge of any pending or threatened condemnation or eminent domain proceedings which would affect the premises or any part thereof.

(k) The roads designated on the plot plan attached hereto as Exhibit _____ have all been dedicated and accepted by the appropriate public authorities and the maintenance of said roads is not an obligation of the Seller nor will the same become an obligation of the Buyer after settlement.

CLAUSE: Seller represents and warrants that he has no knowledge of any fact that would interfere with the development of the property for single-family dwellings. Specifically, he represents and warrants that, to his knowledge; (1) no acquisition of all or part of the property for public purposes has been proposed; (2) no other by any public body is planned that would interfere with such development; (3) that no claims of adjoining owners adverse to seller or to the development have been made; (4) that no physical conditions exist that would interfere with home construction; and (5) that seller's right of access to adjoining public ways has not been questioned.

§ 827. Representation by landlord.

It is appropriate for *L* to represent and warrant that *T* can legally use the demised premises for the use specified in the lease. After all, *L* knows the zoning and has a title policy showing building restrictions, if any.

§ 828. Fiscal representations.

E will want a representation as to financial statements.

CLAUSE: *R* warrants and represents that the statements of ineome and loss by _____ Certified Public Accountants, attached hereto are true and correct and were prepared according to generally accepted accounting principles. The data furnished said accountants was true and correct and no data was withheld which would have adversely affected such statements.

§ 829. Representations and warranties—individual joinder. Especially where *R* is a corporation that will be dissolved immediately after closing, it is best for *E* to insist that *X*, as President, and *Y* as secretary, of the corporation join in all representations and warranties. They can be sued individually or sent to jail after *R* has been dissolved.

43

Legal Opinions

§ **830. In general.** In a large-scale transaction, the parties often call for formal legal opinions of counsel, and the closing of the transaction is conditioned upon the receipt of a favorable legal opinion. However, the law firm giving the legal opinion needs protection against negligence liability. Hence, the provisions regarding legal opinions tend to be rather complex. Thus, a loan agreement may state that as a condition of closing, and with respect to the key documents in the transaction ("Operative Documents") the lender shall have received from _____ a favorable opinion addressed to the lender as to:

(a) the due authorization, execution and delivery by the Borrower of this Agreement and the legality, validity, binding effect and enforceability against the Borrower of this Agreement; (b) the due authorization, execution and delivery by the parties thereto of the Operative Documents and the legality, validity, binding effect and enforceability against said parties of the Operative Documents in accordance with their respective terms; (c) the due authorization, execution and delivery by the Borrower of the Note, the legality, validity, binding effect and enforceability against the Company of such Note, and such Note being entitled to the benefits of the security of the Mortgage and the Assignment; (d) the due recording, registration and filing of the Mortgage (including any financing statements or similar instruments with respect thereto), the Leases (or memoranda thereof) and the Assignment; (e) the Mortgage being a valid, first lien on and prior security interest with respect to each Property for the benefit of such Notes, subject only to Permitted Encumbrances (other than the Assignment), as defined in the Mortgage, existing on the date of the execution and delivery of the Mortgage; and (f) such other matters incident to the transactions herein contemplated as you may reasonably request.

But lender's special counsel may not wish to make an independent study of the local law. Hence the requirement may go on to say:

Lender's special counsel may base such opinion, as to questions of law of the state in which any Property is located, upon an opinion of local counsel referred to in Section _____ and shall not be required to make an independent examination of such law.

This does not mean that lender's counsel is a rubber stamp. In their vast experience, lender's counsel may well differ with local counsel on some points and an accommodation between the two firms may require research by both.

As to the validity of documents executed by a lessee and his guarantor, and the existence of all corporate acts necessary to the validity of such documents, the requirement may state:

As to matters of the authorization, execution and delivery of the Leases and the Assignment by the Lessee, and the Assignment and the Guaranty by the Guarantor, such counsel may (except insofar as the charter documents, by-laws and authorizing resolutions of the Lessee and the Guarantor are concerned) base such opinion upon the opinion of counsel for the Lessee and the Guarantor referred to in Section _____.

As to the title to the property and recording of key documents the requirement may state:

With respect to the Company's title to the Properties and the validity and priority of the lien and the security interest created by the Mortgage, such counsel may base their opinion upon the policies of mortgage title insurance (or commitments therefore) referred to in Section _____. As to the recording, registration or filing of the Mortgage (including any financing statements or similar instruments with respect thereof), the Leases (or memoranda thereof) and the Assignment such counsel may rely upon advice of such recording, registration or filing given by the title company or companies issuing such policies or commitments.

Some requirements may go on to state:

However, opinion of counsel shall set forth all title problems not insured against by the policy and how these have been disposed of.

This means, for example, that opinion of counsel might state that:

The title policy does not insure against questions of usury, but opinion of local counsel states that no such questions exist inasmuch as corporate borrowers are exempted from the usury laws and that the present transaction does not constitute an illegal attempt to evade the usury laws.

Or the opinion might state:

The title policy does not insure against violations of the doing business laws by you (the lender) but in our opinion the transaction has been so structured that it is legally unnecessary for the lender to comply with such laws at this time, because the loan has been duly insulated from such laws. Kratovil, *Mortgages*, § 77.

It is important, in other words, to avoid rubber stamp opinions by lender's special counsel. The contract must insure that counsel make a bona fide in-depth analysis of all of the legal problems.

Factual matters pose a problem. For example, if counsel is giving an opinion that the building is a valid non-conforming use, he is stating that the building was erected before enactment of the ordinance that made the building a non-conforming use.

Hence the requirement for opinion may state as follows:

As to any factual matters involved in the opinion of such counsel, they may rely, to the extent that they deem such reliance proper, upon one or more certificates setting forth such matters which have been signed by an official, officer, authorized representative or general partner of the particular governmental authority, corporation, firm or other person or entity concerned.

Here counsel will be calling for some building department official to certify the date of completion of the building backed up by an affidavit of an officer of the borrower corporation.

The contract may make closing contingent on favorable opinions from counsel for others, such as the lessee and his guarantor, for example:

Closing is contingent on receipt by lender and his special counsel from _____, counsel for the Lessee and the Guarantor of favorable opinion addressed to you, dated the Closing Date and satisfactory in form and substance to you and your special counsel, as to (a) the due organization, existence and good standing of the Lessee and the Guarantor under the laws of the State of Delaware; (b) the due qualification of the Lessee and the Guarantor as foreign corporations to do business and their good standing in each state in which a Property is located or the non-necessity of such qualification under the laws of any such state; (c) the power, authority and legal right of the Lessee to enter into, execute and deliver the Leases and the Assignment and of the Guarantor to enter into, execute and deliver the Assignment and the Guaranty; (d) the due authorization, execution and delivery by the Lessee of the Leases and the Assignment and by the Guarantor of the Assignment and the Guaranty, and the legality, validity, binding effect and enforceability against the Lessee and the Guarantor of such respective instruments; (e) the absence of any conflict with or breach of any terms, conditions or provisions of, or default under, the charter documents or by-laws of the Lessee or the Guarantor or to the best of the knowledge of such counsel or any law, order, writ, injunction or decree of any court or governmental authority or any agreement or instrument under which obligations of the Lessee or the Guarantor for borrowed money have been or may be issued, or any other agreement or instrument to which the Lessee or the Guarantor is a party or by which it is bound which would result from the execution and delivery by the Lessee of the Leases or the Assignment or by the Guarantor of the Assignment or the Guaranty or the consummation of the transactions therein contemplated or compliance with the provisions thereof; and such other matters incident to the transactions contemplated hereby as you or your special counsel may request.

In turn, the counsel specified will want the contract to give them the right to rely, to some extent on others, for example:

Such counsel may base such opinion as to questions of law of the states in which the Properties are located upon the opinions of counsel referred to in Section _____ and as to any questions of law of the State of _____, upon the opinion of counsel referred to in Section _____ and shall not be required to make an independent examination of such law. As to any factual matters involved in the opinion of such counsel, they may rely, to the extent that they deem such reliance proper, upon one or more certificates setting forth such matters which have been signed by an official, officer, authorized representative or general partner of the particular governmental authority, corporation, firm or other person or entity concerned.

The contract may, at times, require a rather serious commitment by local counsel:

Opinion of counsel should state whether under present local statutory and decisional law any rules exist which, given the structure of this transaction, could materially interfere with practical realization of the lender's rights thereunder.

This probes for some esoteric knowledge for example, a transaction may be so framed that in *formation* of the contract, insulation may have been achieved, and compliance with local doing business laws would not be necessary. However, in the *performance* of the contract, the lender might, for example, be compelled to take over completion of the building. At that moment he is hiring contractors, buying materials, and supervising construction. If local law considers this "doing business," he might not, be able to bring actions, for example, against a contractor whose performance is faulty, or even against the local surety on a performance bond.

§ 831. **Opinions as to risk exposure.** A sophisticated party may request an attorney to furnish an opinion as to areas of exposure not mentioned in the title documents.

EXAMPLE: *R* records a construction mortgage to *E* in a state where prior recording gives *E* priority over mechanic's liens. *E* forecloses the mortgage because the contractor and owner have become insolvent and work has stopped. Now *E,* as the new owner, must enter into a new general contract. As a mortgagee covered by an ALTA Loan Policy, his protection against mechanic's liens does not extend to the new situation. The mechanic's liens arising out of work done under the new general contract are *E's* problem. The attorney may advise *E* of the risk and counsel procurement of a *completion bond* rather than the usual *performance* and *payment bonds.*

There has been some criticism of legal opinions. Lawyers for corporations do not hesitate to give opinions as to regularity of corporation action, for they have attended to all these matters and know they have followed the rules. But if the transaction skirts the edges of danger, the opinion at times is silent. It is dangerous to stick one's neck out. Representing the adversary in the deal, the lawyer for the adversary is entitled to a clear-cut admission in the other lawyer's opinion that the dangerous area is not covered. He can then go to his client and point out the danger, recommending a full-fledged brief of points and authorities. This costs money, of course, but the lawyer is derelict in his duty if he fails to point this out. After the authorities have been briefed, the risks may remain evident, more conspicuously so if conflicting decisions highlight the danger. Many recent illustrations come to mind, many in the securities field, some in the bootstrap acquisition cases, some in extraterritorial jurisdiction of federal courts, many in the law of usury, many in the area of "doing business" laws. Here the client must be asked to take the risk, to request guarantees, indemnities, surety bonds, or special coverage by title companies. It simply is unthinkable for a responsible attorney to sweep risks under the rug.

References: 1973 Duke L. J. 371; 28 Bus. Law. 915.

44

Air Rights

§ 832. In general. The literature on the subject of air rights is comprehensive:

Wright, *The Law of Airspace* (1968); Reeve, *Influence of the Metropolis on Property*, 182-85 (1954); *Conveyance & Taxation of Air Rights*, 64 Columb. L.Rev. 338 (1964); Fagg, *Airspace Ownership*, 3 J. of Air Law 400 (1932); Bell, *Air Rights*, 23 Ill. L.Rev. 250 (1928); Becker, *Subdividing the Air*, Chicago Kent Rev. (1927); Mickelson, *Space Law and Air Rights*, 49 Ill. B.J. 812 (1961); Crawford, *Some Legal Aspects of Air Rights*, 25 Fed. B. J. 167; Ball, *Division into Horizontal Strata of the Landspace above the Surface*, 36 Yale L. J. 616 (1930); *Airspace*, 1960 Ill. L. Forum 303; Davis, *Air Rights Developments*, 2 Land Use Controls 1 (1968) (very valuable); *Airspace Utilization*, 5 Suffolk L.Rev. 1009 (1971); *Proprietary Interests* and *Proprietary Estates in Space*, 42 Ind. L. J. 225; Haverfield and Dalton, *Allocation of Property Interests in Air Space*, 20 U. Fla. L.Rev. 237; *Property Rights in Airspace*, 20 U. of Pittsburgh L.Rev. 603; Morris, *Air rights are Fertile Soil*, 1 Urban Law 247 (1969); Carnhan, *Relative Rights and Remedies of Users and Surface Proprietors in Air Space*, 1966 Ins. L. J. 406; Hodgman, *Air Rights and Public Finance*, 42 So. Calif. L.Rev. 628 (1969); 58 Dick. L.Rev. 144; 29 N.Y.U. L.Rev. 169; 12 U. Fla. L.Rev 1; 24 Kan. City L.Rev. 196; 28 U. Pitt. L.Rev. 661; 24 Tenn. L.Rev. 643; 31 Minn. L.Rev. 384; 57 Dick L.Rev. 188; 58; *id*. 141.

The questions discussed in *Griggs v. County of Allegheny*, and related questions, have been the subject of a number of articles in recent legal periodicals:

See 50 A.B.A.J. 345 (1964); 42 P. U. L.Rev. 565; 35 U. Colo. L.Rev. 259 (1963); 30 Fordham L.Rev. 803 (1962); 66 Dick L.Rev. 107 (1961); 30 Fordham L.Rev. 803 (1962); 48 Ky. L. J. 273 (1960); 13 Hastings L. J. 397 (1962); 1962 Law Forum 274; 23 Md. L.Rev. 96 (1963); 47 Minn. L.Rev. 889 (1963); 57 N. W. U. L.Rev. 346 (1962); 24 U. Pitt. L.Rev. 603 (1963); 14:2 W. Res. L.Rev. 376 (1963); 16 S.W.L.J. 346 (1962).

§ 833. Methods used. Various methods have been adopted in the development of rights in space in Chicago and are as follows:

1. The leasing of space (the "air lot") lying above a certain horizontal or inclined plane at an elevation a designated number of feet above Chicago City Datum together with an easement in the subjacent space for the construction of supporting columns and foundations. As an alternative to the easement, the lease of the air lot can also include a lease of areas beneath the air lot needed for columns, caissons, foundations, etc.

2. The conveyance of the fee simple title to all of the space lying above a certain horizontal or inclined plane at an elevation a designated number of feet above Chicago City Datum together with an easement in the subjacent area for the construction of supporting columns and foundations.

3. The subdividing by plat of all the land, property and space at, above and below the surface of the earth into lots lying in different horizontal or inclined planes and designating said lots as air lots, prism or column lots, cylinder or caisson lots, girder lots, bracket lots, etc. This is the method described in the article entitled "Subdividing the Air."

4. The conveyance of the fee simple title to the entire parcel of land, but reserving to the grantor a permanent and perpetual easement of all the land, property and space extending downward from and below a certain plane a designated number of feet above Chicago City Datum, for example, where a railroad is conveying, an easement for the movement of trains in this area, and granting to the grantee of the fee an easement within such reserved space for the construction of supporting columns and foundations.

5. The condemnation of the fee simple title to the entire parcel of land by a public body with provision in the condemnation judgment and confirmatory deed reserving an easement in favor of the owners for the continued occupation by the existing building in the space above a certain plane a designated number of feet above Chicago City Datum.

§ 834. Subdividing the air. The method described as "Subdividing the Air" is described in Kratovil, *Real Estate Law*, § 6 as follows:

In the case of the Merchandise Mart in Chicago, which was erected over the tracks of the Chicago and Northwestern Railroad, a plat or map was made and recorded, showing a subdivision in three dimensions, as follows:

1. An air lot. This consists of the space lying above a plane 23 feet above the earth's surface.

2. Quadrangular prism or column lots (for steel columns to support the building). These extend from the surface of the earth up to the air lot and occupy portions of the surface not occupied by railroad tracks.

3. Cylindrical or caisson lots. These extend from the surface of the earth down to the center of the earth. The bottom of each column lot rests within a caisson lot.

The column lots, which share the level through which the trains move, were made narrower than the caisson lots to eliminate interference with the movement of trains. The railroad thereupon sold the air lot, the column lots, and the caisson lots to the Merchandise Mart, but retained ownership of the remainder of the tract.

The "air lot" was described as follows:

All the land, property and space at and above a horizontal plane 23 feet above Chicago City Datum bounded, etc., (here the horizontal boundaries of the lot are given).

The caisson lots were described as follows:

All the land, property and space at and below horizontal plane zero Chicago City Datum in 600 complete cylinders formed by projecting vertically downward from said plane, the circles forming the boundaries of said lots as represented on the plat.

The prism lots were described as follows:

All the land, property and space in 600 quadrangular prisms of the horizontal dimensions shown on the plat, extending vertically between horizontal planes respectively at zero and 23 feet above Chicago City Datum.

Figure 44-1 describes the end result:

§ 835. Advantages of each method. Subdividing the air is cumbersome. You have a lot of legal descriptions. Any change in the columns made necessary by engineering considerations would require an amended plat and new deeds, which might be difficult to procure. If the columns are not located by the contractor at the place indicated on the plat,

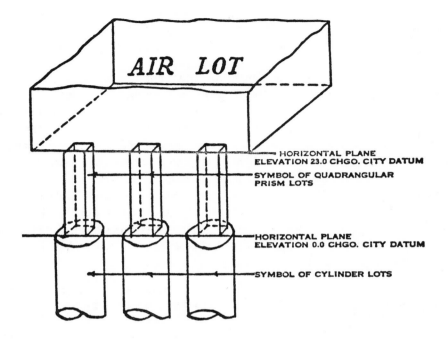

Figure 44-1

that also requires an amended plat and new deeds. On the other hand, in actual practice the procedure works. No insurmountable problems exist. If you want to cover possible settling of the building, you include easements to maintain the encroachments thus caused, as is done routinely in condominiums. And once the grantee owns the fee to his areas, no one can take it away. Moreover, separate taxation of the two fee interests is assured. Conveying the fee to the air lot with easements for support beneath the air lot has the virtue of flexibility. Easement descriptions need not be as precise as deed descriptions. Indeed grants of unlocated easements are common. And "roving easements" are perfectly valid.

Reference: 9 ABA Real Property Probate & Trust J. 183 (1974).

INDEX